second edition

PRODUCTION MANAGEMENT

SYSTEMS AND SYNTHESIS

MARTIN K. STARR

Columbia University

PRODUCTION MANAGEMENT
systems and synthesis   Second Edition

MARTIN K. STARR

to JUDITH and BILL who have implemented three important futures: REED, DICK, and GRANT.

ISBN: 0-13-724401-0

Library of Congress Catalog Card Number: 73-170037
Printed in the United States of America

10 9 8 7 6 5 4 3 2 1

PRENTICE-HALL INTERNATIONAL, INC., London
PRENTICE-HALL OF AUSTRALIA, PTY. LTD., Sydney
PRENTICE-HALL OF CANADA, LTD., Toronto
PRENTICE-HALL OF INDIA PRIVATE LIMITED, New Delhi
PRENTICE-HALL OF JAPAN, INC., Tokyo

preface

The first edition of this book appeared in 1964. Much has happened since that time and these happenings can be grouped into two major classes. First, there are technical advances; second, the growth of system's understanding. Strange as it may seem, management appears to be more aware of technical improvements, available through mathematical modeling and computer abilities, than of increased systems' abilities (to plan for and control large, complex systems).

The first edition of this book took an uncertain stand, attempting to straddle the mathematical and the systems-oriented approaches to production management. This *second edition* avoids such hedging. This is a *systems book*. It is designed for the student of management, whether he is technically trained or not. The book addresses the problems of the manager who can call upon technical experts for specialized problems, but who knows he must rely upon himself for managerial functions.

To understand the spirit of this book, it is essential to recognize the relationship of systems analysis to systems synthesis. The distinction between analysis and synthesis is neither esoteric nor academic. Analytic behavior follows what might be called *principles of disassembly*. It exists in terms of operations that involve division, dissection, classification, separation, partitioning and segmentation. Using analysis we take the production system apart. We study the pieces and attempt to improve them. Then we reassemble, hoping for a better system. But, because of interactions and dependencies among the parts, often the reassembled production function will not be improved. It may even be impaired.

Knowledge of the principles of synthesis is required to put things together in a measurably *satisfactory* way. To achieve this objective, it can be necessary to modify analytic results. Synthesizing behavior should be viewed as a set of *conditions for reassembly* involving operations of summation, integration, unification, combination, amalgamation; i.e., in general, the *gestalt* point of view. (Gestalt occurs with the recognition of organized totalities, such as "man," rather than the cataloging of distinct parts, such as cells, muscles, heart and brain.)

Analysis requires patience and *perseverance with detail*. Lists of relevant factors are developed as well as measures of relations. In contrast, synthesis accomplishments are associated with sudden insights as with the Eureka (I've got it) phenomenon. Synthesis involves various aptitudes associated with architecture; whereas analysis and construction engineering share a common foundation. Synthesis thrives on creative overview abilities that take advantage of penetrating insights to prepare broad new principles for operating systems.

Management is a synthesizing function. Therefore, mathematical analysis is used, not produced by the manager. He employs analysis for descriptive purposes so that he may better diagnose and prescribe for the system's performance. As a life-style, the analytical orientation may be antithetical to the manager's necessary capacity to generalize. In any case, specialization is not essential for generalizing ability, although specialists who can also generalize, are known to have assumed leading managerial roles in their organizations.

It is important to note that analysis is commonplace in the production management field whereas synthesis is not. Accordingly, few production managers have risen to high managerial (leadership) roles in their companies. There is evidence that new forces are now at work. Although generalists in production management are still "rare birds," when they exist, they appear to move rapidly into high-level management positions. This combination of abilities is likely to become a most important "leverage" factor in the technological systems of the next several decades.

This book has been revised with the intention of providing an up-to-date, systems-oriented view of the production management field. Our focus is on the management of the system. The executive is expected to understand in logical (not mathematical) terms what analytic tools are available and how he can relate them to the performance of the total system with which he must deal. Such comprehension is expedited by the identification of a reasonable, but simple, analog of the production function and its management. The task of constructing a useful analog has been accomplished by means of a generalized input-(process)-output model of systems.

Production management has been defined in the most general terms so that it encompasses all transformation procedures that fit the input-output construct. Problems are viewed as questions that often cross functional organizational lines; and that concern how to interconnect sets of input-output subsystems so that the large system can perform in a satisfactory manner. Often the participating subsystems will be required to turn in suboptimal performances. And the larger the system, the more likely it is that subsystems *must* be designed to operate in a fashion that runs counter to intuition. The approach taken by this book allows such counter-intuitive solutions to be found.

The nature of problems is highly general. Manufacture provides only one set of problem types. Industries engaged in transportation, communication, extractive processes or providing services also can be included, as can hospitals, libraries, military and public administration systems. Total systems are composed of many different processes that are the results of different operations which are then, in turn, composed of some set of fundamental elements —common to all operations. Elements of (physical) work are entirely familiar to production managers who have special knowledge about such small operations. The same cannot be said about production management's knowledge of decision elements. Yet without an understanding of decision-making, it is unwise to hope for even a modicum of success in achieving synthesis. Consequently, the decision-theory framework (new to the production management field) is explained and maintained throughout the book.

The structure of the text would still be incomplete without paying attention to behavioral elements and the interrelations of men, machines, and facilities. It is essential to recognize the physiological, psychological, psychiatric, and sociological factors that help to explain the roles of people in the system. These people include consumers, stockholders, competitors, suppliers, and managers, in addition to the expected concern for workers.

Synthesis requires that the production manager cooperate with other managers. He must appreciate the interacting roles of finance, marketing, and production. To convey appropriate perspectives, this book presents two chapters written by specialists in finance and marketing. They constitute strongly systems oriented materials.

Synthesis also necessitates recognition of the interactions of internal systems with the external world. These include the effects of competition on the production management function as well as legal, institutional, and governmental restraints; economic effects—both national and international; vendor relations; community and union attitudes; and social system factors in general.

Synthesis develops when adequate differentiation is drawn between:

(a) PLANNING the production system with respect to products, processes and facilities
(b) IMPLEMENTING the production system design. (PERT is an integral part of the book's structure.)

(c) CONTROLLING operations at various levels of systems involvement with computers, automation, and the concept of management by exception.

Synthesis is exemplified by establishing coherent interactions between methodology and technology. We learn a great deal from the history of these "ologies" and the way in which production management has responded to change. In fact, it is reasonable to consider reading Chapter 13, which presents some history of the production management function, before doing anything else. It is advantageous to assign Chapters 14 and 15 (on finance and marketing interactions with production) as supplementary reading to be accomplished concurrently with the first few chapters of the book. In this way, the student can perceive the challenge of synthesis while studying the essentials of the production management field. Because of cultural constraints, students of production management often tend to resist the *notion* that their success is dependent upon their breadth of view; a *notion* with which top-managers will agree unanimously.

Although this book is an introductory text, its demands are great. True, mathematical finesse is not required; only a minimum ability with algebra is needed; and prior knowledge of the field is not assumed. On the other hand, the scope of the coverage is broad. The text is challenging since it assumes that the student wishes to become a manager who can resolve complex problems. This is an intensely demanding objective.

I acknowledge with appreciation the many sources (indicated throughout the book) which supplied materials for figures, tables, and in some cases, text. Particularly, I want to thank Gerald P. Brady, Professor of Business Law at the Graduate School of Business, Columbia University, for his counsel on sections dealing with the patent laws; and Professsor Murray Mohl of the Graduate School of Business, Rutgers University, for his helpful review.

With gratitude I acknowledge the *vital* contributions made by Professor Rein Peterson of the Faculty of Administrative Studies, York University, Toronto, and Mr. William T. Moran, Marketing Research Director, Lever Brothers Company. Their work relates production management with finance and marketing in important ways that have never been accomplished before. The success of cross-discipline communication to achieve the goal of synthesis is brightly illuminated by their coordinated efforts.

Judith L. Dumas helped me manage the logistics of this revision for which I thank her. Jerrold Katz contributed significantly to the preparation of a detailed teacher's manual.

Polly Starr helped me in so many ways that only Elizabeth Barrett Browning could tell me how to count them.

MARTIN K. STARR

contents

part **INPUT-**
two **OUTPUT**
MANAGEMENT

chapter six
information management

chapter seven
product management

chapter eleven
facilities management

chapter twelve
manpower management

PRODUCTION MANAGEMENT

What might have been is an abstraction
Remaining a perpetual possibility
Only in a world of speculation.
What might have been and what has been
Point to one end, which is always present.
Footfalls echo in the memory
Down the passage which we did not take
Towards the door we never opened. . .

T. S. Eliot, BURNT NORTON
Reprinted by permission of T. S. Eliot.

part one PRODUCTION-SYSTEMS MODELS

The objective of this book
is to present the study of production management
in unified terms. Developments in planning methods,
decision theory,
and systems analysis
have made this possible.

chapter
one
**the
systems
concept**

Production management encompasses a wide array of problems, many of which
are *unique* to the production area. A production manager must be able to deal
with all problems that are relevant to his area—unique or otherwise. This responsibility of management takes various forms, for example, the *decision,
planning, design,* or *policy-making function.* The choice of terms depends partly
upon common usage, but mostly upon the specific nature of the problem.

In addition to designing, planning, making policy, and reaching decisions,
production managers must *implement* their decisions. Thus, theory is translated
into practice, plans are realized, and designs are converted into physical realities.
A lot of time may be spent in deciding, but the decision itself occurs at a given
moment. Implementation, on the other hand, is seldom instantaneous. Frequently it is a function requiring continuing guidance and *control,* another major
production management activity. It is necessary to *evaluate* the extent to which
an implemented decision accomplishes an objective. Control necessitates such
3 evaluation. It may be, for example, that the wrong decision was chosen and

must be changed. On the other hand, the decision might be satisfactory but the manner of implementation can be at fault.

Production management responsibilities, as discussed above, center on two major areas. These are: (1) *design of the production system* which includes product, process, plant, equipment, and so on, and, (2) *development of the control systems* to manage inventories, product quality, production schedules, and productivity. For both areas, new approaches are required when competitive, economic, and technological changes occur.

THE PRODUCTION-MANAGEMENT CYCLE

Design of the production process is fundamentally different from the design of systems which control the performance of the process. This distinction accounts for the difficulty in perceiving a unified production management field. Consider, for example, the difference between (1) designing a road system and (2) developing the placement and timing of traffic lights to use that road system in the best possible way. Plant and facilities are the means. Operations are the ends. To illustrate, the hospital is the plant; staff and equipment are the facilities; X-rays, blood tests, bed care and operations are the ends.

Consider the production-management cycle shown in Figure 1.1. Operations are at the center of the diagram because they are the dynamic "doing" elements of the production process. Yet, it is clear that we cannot dismiss *any* of the other elements of the figure. Operations cannot exist without them. The process

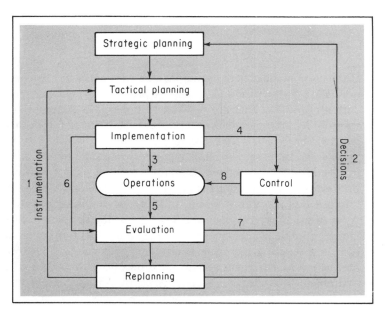

FIGURE 1-1
The production-management cycle.

is a time-stream of operations which is kept under control, just as a car being steered along a winding highway must be controlled.

As Figure 1.1 demonstrates, planning never ceases in the production area. Of course, once the plant has been chosen and equipped, the layout finalized, and the operations begun, the company is committed to a number of major strategic decisions. Only in the event of the most dire emergencies would it be likely that *substantial* modifications would be made. But as the facilities age, the commitment to them is reduced and greater flexibility returns.

If major investments in system design are at the core of our considerations, we say that a *strategic* decision is warranted. On the other hand, if implementation patterns are central to the manager's problems, then we say that a *tactical* decision is called for. This distinction is useful. Tactics are applied to the methods and instruments of implementation; strategies refer to the design decisions. Thousands of tactical decisions are being made all the time in *real* situations by the production manager, and other managers as well. Few strategic decisions can be made by managers. When they are made, it is usually high up in the organizational hierarchy.

Minor design modifications characterize the tactical level. For example, individual jobs can be redesigned, machines replaced, and materials altered. Such changes are represented by loop 1 which has a greater volume of usage than planning loop 2 which operates when "start up" of a new process is required. Following the various connections of the figure, we observe that *operations* is engaged in a central way through a series of connections 3, 4, 5, 6, 7, and 8 to implementation, control, and evaluation. And this control subset is essential to the organization's planning system. From this we realize how closely interconnected are the strategic and tactical areas of the manager's job.

Also, this diagram reflects the great variety of production-management responsibilities. It includes the facilities and abilities for the detailed consideration of such factors as:

1. Product design
2. Job and process design
3. Equipment selection and replacement
4. Labor skills and training programs
5. Input materials selection including raw materials and subcontracting
6. Plant selection and layout
7. Scheduling steps of the plan
8. Implementing and controlling the schedule
9. Operating the production system

The above are concerned with the design of the production process. In addition, the diagram includes consideration of control systems, thus:

1. Inventory-control policies
2. Quality-control policies

3. Production-schedule control policies
4. Productivity- and cost-control policies
5. Constructing control systems
6. Implementing and operating control systems
7. Modifying policies and designs

When we start detailing them, these two areas are seen to be different from one another. Yet they must be harmoniously related if the production management function is to achieve its objectives. Figure 1.1 only barely suggests the nature of the required relations. Let us, therefore, take a closer look at the total system before we attempt to examine each part.

OPTIMALITY AND MULTIPLE OBJECTIVES

Optimal means the "best possible." It does not connote an unobtainable perfection. In other words, it is an operational objective to seek an optimal solution. The *measures of effectiveness* for the design of a total production system would include, at least, the following:

1. Costs of running the system
2. Quality of the output
3. Production rate and productive capacity
4. Flexibility to adjust to changing circumstances
5. Social value of the system

We see that the results obtained for any one of these dimensions of effectiveness will interact with the results that can be obtained for the others. For example, lowered costs can frequently be achieved by downgrading quality. (Either a net social gain or loss—with lower prices vs. lower quality.) Large capacity and high production rates may also lower costs but decrease flexibility to adapt to change. (Sometimes the net result will be a gain and sometimes a loss.)

Then what do we mean by optimal?

The answer is that a *balance* must be found between the *opposing relations* (or objectives) in a system. The decision to be rendered must maximize the over-all utility of the system that is to be constructed and operated.

Figure 1.2 illustrates some of the opposing forces that are involved in the major strategic planning area concerned with "how much diversification for the company?"

As the company becomes more specialized its production rate can increase and, as a result, it is able to reduce delivery times. Because of intensive involvement with only a few items, product quality can usually be increased and operating costs can be reduced. All these effects are beneficial for the company.

FIGURE 1-2
Opposing factors
for the diversifica-
tion problem. (A
problem of con-
flicting multiple
objectives.)

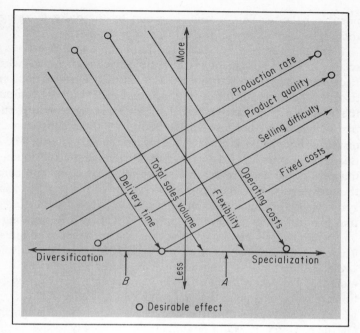

On the other hand, increasing specialization implies the need to increase brand share in the specialized market. Advertising and sales promotion dollars must work harder because of competition and saturation effects.[1] Consequently, selling efficiency can be expected to decrease. Fixed costs will rise because of investments in specialized higher volume equipment. The company's adaptability in the face of change will drop off, and the total sales volume for a fixed promotion budget will fall because marketing variety has been reduced. These latter effects are not desirable for the company. Of course, the statement of this problem is simplified, but this does not mask the essence of the problem. At what level of specialization should the company operate? Is point "A" better than point "B"? There is at least one point that is the "best possible" or optimal point. It is that point which achieves the optimal balance between penalties and rewards.

THE TOTAL SYSTEM

The same kind of reasoning concerning penalties and rewards (as outlined above) applies also to the design of the *total* system. The production process *factors* and the control system *factors* interrelate. The design criterion for the total system is that the opposing forces of reward and penalty are in the best

[1] William Moran, "Marketing-Production Interaction." See pp. 474-79.

possible balance. This is what is meant by the optimal configuration for the total system. But how is the total system defined?

Start with *purpose*. The manager outlines a set of objectives. *Everything* that relates to his achievement of those objectives *must be included* in the system. Because such systems (considered as a list of relevant variables) pose problems that are too large for intuitive grasp, and exceed (even) computer capabilities, the manager (reluctantly) *partitions* his large system into subsystems. Only partial effects on purpose are embodied in these subsystems. The results of decisions bounce back and forth between the subsystems. The manager knows this, but for practical reasons, agrees to examine the subsystems as if they were independent of each other. In his own mind, he counts on being able to relate the subsystems when the chips are down, in such a way as to improve the total system's performance. The manager views himself as an integrating medium that can ultimately achieve his purposes. This is a demanding role.

The manager's analysts know that the manager sees himself in this role. Therefore they recognize that, when possible, subsystem decisions should be avoided. The big system should be considered. All relevant objectives must be included. The relationship of reward and penalty for various design configurations must be examined with respect to all objectives. This does not mean that wholly inclusive, quantitative studies are required to design the total system.[2] On the contrary, it would be unrealistic and costly to use this approach. Good judgment is frequently the best recourse available. *But,* such judgment should be supplied in terms of the total system and in the light of complete understanding of the nature of optimality. The manager is therefore the key to *the systems concept.* To explain this more formally, a system is, by definition, a group of activities, functions, or components having managerial purposes that can be bounded. The parts of the system must all relate to the manager's purposes. The rule for bounding these activities, functions, or components is: *all relevant interdependencies, interactions, and relationships must be enclosed within the boundaries of the system.*

Because it is very hard to think about large and complex systems, it is particularly helpful to determine the conditions under which it would be legitimate to consider separate parts of the system. We could think first about the production process, then, having chosen a design for it, we could turn our attention to the design of the control system. Similarly, parts of each system could be tackled separately. This would greatly reduce the complexity of the job to be done.

EFFECTIVENESS VS. EFFICIENCY

We have already distinguished between strategies and tactics by assuming that the latter is an alternative related to the means of carrying out the former.

---

[2] As we shall see subsequently, operations research studies are far more likely to be employed for control-system design than for that of the production process.

Basically, we are differentiating between decision alternatives where effectiveness is involved (strategies), and decision alternatives where efficiency is involved (tactics). Thus, decisions can be designed to alter the behavior of subsystems and thereby affect the system's performance, or can change the system in its broadest sense, causing all subsystems to adjust to the new, major policy revisions that apply at the total systems level. We call the latter a strategic change; the former, a tactical one.

A strategic problem can be divorced from tactical considerations when the worst tactical result for the best strategic possibility is better than the best tactical result of any other strategic possibility. Figure 1.3 demonstrates this case in terms of one dimension. There are three strategies A, B, and C. The best tactic for each strategy is identified by the subscript B, the worst by the subscript W.

FIGURE 1-3
Estimated range
measures of sys-
tem's performance.

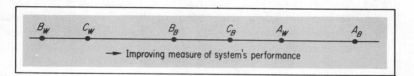

The manager in this example would be correct to choose strategy A without considering interactions of strategies and tactical possibilities. But how would he know this? If the distance between each strategy's best and worst tactic (i.e., sensitivity to tactics) was small, and if the distance between strategies, in terms of expected average performance, were large, then it would not be essential to worry, for example, about *how* to make something at the same time as worrying about *what* to make. Thus, the figure illustrates that even if tactic A_W must be used, with strategy A the performance is still better than any obtainable with other strategies.

If we limit our considerations to strategies B and C we find that C_B is superior to *all* of B's tactical possibilities but C_W is not better than B_B. With such overlaps of strategic ranges, the correctness of evaluating strategies independent of tactics must be seriously questioned.

The design of the production system can be equated with the issue of effectiveness. The design of the control system is more closely related to the efficiency concept. In many cases, the real industrial situation is similar in nature to the case of strategy A where it is permissible to reach production design decisions before considering the problems of control. However, the production manager must be alert to spot those situations in which a serious *suboptimization* will occur as a result of indifference to efficiency considerations.

The character of *suboptimization* requires detailed definition. In essence, it is the result of strictly subsystem decisions only designed to optimize the performance of subsystems. When, because of dependencies, the total system's performance is rendered less good by these decisions, then suboptimization rather than optimization has occurred.

To exemplify this situation, we may note it has been characteristic of the production field that stress is placed on efficiency problems instead of effectiveness problems. In other words, a minimal number of strategies (with respect to optimization) would be examined. Then a decision would be reached. This would be followed by intensive and diligent effort to render the strategic choice as efficient as possible by considering tactical alternatives. Suboptimization potentials receive the major share of attention in such cases.

These suboptimization characteristics are rapidly disappearing from the production management scene. There is more leverage for achieving outstanding performance by concentrating on strategies, and more danger, as well, of ignoring critical tactical *interactions*. The problem of achieving optimization has been recognized, and efforts have been shifted to obtain a proper balance between tactical and strategic considerations. Tactics are seen to interact with strategies rather than being independent of them. Major psychological revisions in the production manager's style of working are involved, so these changes have not come easily.

OBJECTIVES AND CONSTRAINTS

Frequently when several objectives coexist, it is possible to single out the most important one so that an optimal solution can be obtained with respect to it. Because of the nature of conflicting objectives, it is almost always true that the other objectives cannot be optimized at the same time. Necessarily, therefore, only the most important objective can be optimized subject to constraints and limitations that are imposed by the other objectives.

Many examples of this situation suggest themselves. We can *maximize* the quality of a product under the condition that we will not spend more than *a given number* of dollars on equipment, materials, and other production factors. Similarly, we can *minimize* the cost of manufacturing a particular item subject to *given quality conditions* or other production constraints. In general, constraints may take several forms:

1. The constrained objective is to achieve a given intermediate value (not a maximum or minimum value).
2. It is to be equal to or greater than a given value.
3. It is to be equal to or less than a given value.
4. It is to lie within a specified range.

When the achievement of a specific objective is to be maximized (or minimized), it follows, then, that the side conditions for such maximization must be specified in one or more of the above forms for the problem to be completely stated. This is a responsibility frequently encountered by the production manager. He must recognize that it is almost never possible to maximize the achievement of all relevant and important objectives in a system simultaneously. Situations in which this can be done pose trivial problems.

Therefore, the interesting cases are those in which both objectives and constraints must be determined and specified. This applies to the design of a "best possible" production process; and also to the design of "best possible" control systems. It is apparent that even if we can achieve true optimization for our major objective we can do no better than an overall suboptimization because the other objectives have to be treated as constraints. It is essential that production managers realize that this state of affairs exists whether a formal method or an intuitional approach is used. It is the only legitimate way to treat problems posed by multiple, conflicting objectives. It is far more desirable that its use be conscious than unaware.

TEMPORAL SUBOPTIMIZATION

Another way in which the phenomenon of suboptimization appears is in terms of the planning horizon[3] that is used. It is never enough to specify that our objective is to maximize profit; it is necessary to state how long a period of time is being considered. As illustrated in Figure 1.4, a strategic alternative that will maximize profits for the company over a one-year span may not succeed in doing the same thing over a two-year period. We see that a planning horizon which looks ahead for one year would conclude that the second strategy was superior. However, if a planning horizon of two years is employed, the first

FIGURE 1-4
Temporal suboptimization as function of the planning horizon.

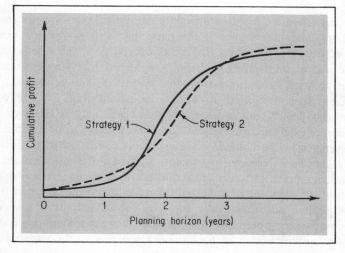

[3] That is, the proposed length of a planning period.

strategy becomes the preferred alternative. In our illustration, the situation reverses again after approximately three years.

Production managers are well aware of the fact that temporal suboptimization can occur. Why then do they not choose a very long planning horizon? Several answers can be given. First, the further the planning horizon is extended the more uncertain the results of the plans become. The believability of prediction is diminished as we move into the future. Therefore, the production manager may prefer to take his chances with a one-year forecast—and to act on this basis—than to accept a greater risk by choosing a strategy that is supposedly optimal after three, five, or ten years. Fundamental conditions upon which forecasts and predictions are based frequently change after a number of years.

Second, the company may need a given amount of profit in the immediate present and cannot wait patiently for the long-term prospects to mature. Thus, the amount of working capital required to survive is a logical constraint on the profit objective that can produce suboptimization.

Third, there is the belief that switches in profit, of the kind shown in Figure 1.4, do not frequently occur. Although it appears legitimate, in many cases, to accept this point of view it is certain that situations do arise in which serious temporal suboptimization will occur as a result of a too-short planning horizon.

With respect to the design of the production process, this warning must be taken quite seriously. In the design area, long-term decision problems arise. Commitments must be made today, the rewards and penalties of which will first come to light many years in the future. On the other hand, the design of a control system is less vulnerable to temporal suboptimization.

SUBOPTIMIZATION BY CONFLICTION

Objectives are formal statements that reflect the value systems of companies, groups, and individuals. If the participants in a situation possess conflicting objectives, it is necessary that either one party or the other come out on top or else that a compromise solution be achieved. The very essence of compromise is negotiated suboptimization. In the marketplace, economic and social forces achieve their own kind of competitive equilibrium. But, the production management department in its day-to-day operations is relatively immune to the effects of external competition. The marketing department shoulders this burden. Nevertheless, the company's efficiency as compared to competitive efficiencies is a significant competitive factor. It is in this sense that the relationship of product quality with respect to competitive qualities is clearly relevant. However, it is in the planning of the production facilities—the design of the process—that competitive positions really must be considered. Such competitive decisions encompass long planning horizons and they are difficult to change. Thus, when designing a new product, developing a new process, or planning a manufacturing operation (including plant, equipment, and so on), competitive behaviors must be taken directly into consideration by management. Here, we are dealing with

FIGURE 1-5
Suboptimization by
confliction.

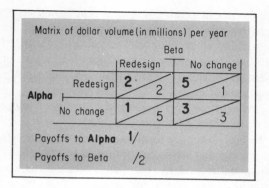

Matrix of dollar volume (in millions) per year

		Beta	
		Redesign	No change
Alpha	Redesign	2 2	5 1
	No change	1 5	3 3

Payoffs to **Alpha**   1/

Payoffs to Beta   /2

questions of effectiveness. Both production and marketing management must be fully cognizant of the possible impacts of competitive behaviors.

To illustrate the nature of a relatively simple, competitive situation, let us examine Figure 1.5. Two companies, Alpha and Beta, are competing for the same market. Each of these companies is considered to have only two available strategies, namely, redesign the product or do not change the product design. We see from the payoff matrix that if Alpha redesigns its product but Beta makes no change, then Alpha will make $5 million and Beta will make only $1 million. On the other hand, if Beta redesigns its product and Alpha makes no change, then Beta obtains $5 million and Alpha only $1 million. If both companies make no change they will each continue to net $3 million. On the other hand, if both proceed to redesign their products, their respective profits will be reduced to $2 million because of tooling costs and other investments.

What is each participant likely to do in this case? If Alpha and Beta compromise (at the possible expense of the consumer) they can each make $3 million. On the other hand, either Alpha or Beta or both may decide to take the chance that the other company will do nothing. Thinking that they can get the jump on the other; that they can increase their profits to $5 million, they will secretly prepare to introduce a new design. (Even if a compromise agreement is reached, can Alpha trust Beta and vice versa?)

It is primarily in the effectiveness area that issues of this kind arise. Significant investments in research, plant, and equipment are at stake. The fact that the operations area of production management is not directly related to the market and to competition, does not alter the fact that the design of the production process is intensively involved with these factors. Poorly chosen suboptimizations can play havoc with the long-term results of the company.

SUBOPTIMIZATION AND OPPORTUNITY COSTS

We must keep clearly in mind that *opportunity costs* play a major role in developing a reasonable set of production management constraints. These costs represent the difference between the reward that would be obtained if the "best possible" alternative was chosen (i.e., the optimal value) and the reward that is obtained as a result of the (suboptimal) alternative that is actually chosen. Constraints produce opportunity costs. Therefore, constraints that arise as a result of unessential or irrelevant production management policies can lead to unnecessary opportunity costs.

Opportunity costs should be considered in terms of unnecessary constraints that are imposed. Alternatively, opportunity costs can be viewed as penalties for not obtaining the best suboptimal solution when nothing better can be done. If the production manager's thinking is not tuned to opportunity costs, he is likely to incur sizable penalties for his company without his knowing it—and for that matter without anyone else knowing it or ever learning about it.

A product design that is selected from among a number of feasible alternatives will have zero opportunity cost if it is the optimal design. But how is anyone to tell that an untried design would have been better? While it is not always possible to know when an opportunity cost has been incurred, it is critical to know that this weakness in system's evaluation exists. Opportunity costs are extremely important in new product development and in the design of the production process. They are also important with respect to the design of adequate control systems, but in quite a different way. As will be discussed, the penalties incurred for suboptimization in control systems tend to be cumulative and remediable.

To exemplify the calculation of an opportunity cost, assume that five strategies, called $S_1, S_2, \ldots, S_5$ are being considered and that each is expected to produce gross revenue at a given cost, yielding net profit as shown below.

	COST	REVENUE	PROFIT
S_1	60	100	40
S_2	40	90	50
S_3	30	50	20
S_4	70	80	10
S_5	90	120	30

Recasting these in terms of opportunity costs, we subtract the lowest (best) cost from all other costs in its column; we subtract all revenues from the largest (best) revenue in that column; we subtract all profits from the largest (best) profit, thus:

	COST	REVENUE	PROFIT
S_1	30	20	10
S_2	10	30	0
S_3	0	70	30
S_4	40	40	40
S_5	60	0	20

Since zero opportunity cost is the best cost value we can get, it becomes immediately apparent that a cost minimization study, or a revenue maximization study can provide contradictory results—and that neither will necessarily produce optimal profits. Since profit is a larger systems dimension than cost or revenue, both of which it includes, the opportunity costs for profits is the best systems measure that is available. In social systems, some comparable measure of *benefit* is desirable but seldom easy to find.

THE PRODUCTION SYSTEM

A process is composed of a set of operations. The traditional production management notion stated that if each operation was made as efficient as possible, then: (1) the set of operations known as the process would be most efficient, and (2) if the process was most efficient, then, its economic value would be maximized.[4] Modern production management recognizes that both of the above points *may* be wrong. The field of production management has changed. It no longer concentrates attention on individual operations. The effect is that production management can no longer be viewed in the same way as it used to be. Getting work done is still the core issue, but the manner of getting work done that is most compatible with the company's objectives has been subjected to new criteria. *Measures of effectiveness* that are process-oriented and systemic in nature are now being used in addition to *measures of efficiency* that are operations-oriented.

Production management is applicable to all forms of organized work. Work is not limited to manufacture. Consequently, production management is not restricted to manufacturing processes. The system of operations required for the production of both goods and services are considered to be part of present-day production management. This means that office operations, hospital and library services, power production, government and military systems, and transportation and communication systems are amenable to production management analysis and synthesis.

In general, however, production management is not a term applied to the activities of an individual or a small group. Frank Gilbreth[5] is reputed to have learned to have shaved simultaneously with two razors—one in each hand. He looked upon all his daily activities as operations which were susceptible to production management. Most individuals attempt to schedule their appointments intelligently; to maintain reasonable inventories of groceries, toothpaste, and aspirin; to invest in labor saving devices, and to find convenient and economic living quarters. Even if they were to study these problems in an explicit fashion using *scheduling techniques, inventory theory, equipment, and plant selection techniques*—we would not be inclined to think of them as production

[4] Because cost was assumed to be minimized.
[5] See pp. 395, 429.

managers. The same is true, but to a lesser extent, of small retail store owners. But when a retail store grows to be a department store, there is nothing eccentric about calling this production management. When the volume of (repetitive and nonrepetitive) operations becomes great enough, a production system, requiring competent management, comes into being. Even though only one Mars rocket is to be built, the size of the project easily qualifies this system—although it lacks many repetitive[6] operations—as being a major production management undertaking. In concluding this discussion we must emphasize the fact that a semantic difficulty afflicts any management that hangs on to the notion that production is simply fabrication. The image that persists, erroneously, is that the study of production relates to an understanding of lathes and milling machines. The production manager knows that this type of system is only one subsystem of the many with which he is prepared to deal.

ORGANIZATIONAL RELATIONS

Like an apple, the total organization can be sliced in many different ways. The analogy with the apple is not a bad one because having sliced the apple in one manner we obtain a different image than if we had sliced it in another way. Furthermore, any one plane of dissection prohibits the simultaneous achievement of others. This point can be illustrated in another way. When we look at a statue, a building, or a product from the front, we do not simultaneously see it from the back. Looking at it from the top negates the possibility of viewing it from the bottom. Each is a unique point of view of the same structure. In this sense, the interpretation of production is dependent upon the viewpoint and perspective that is used. The modern production management point of view cuts across departmental and divisional lines. It recognizes the existence of other viewpoints, such as those of marketing and financial management. In addition, it is cognizant of the fact that these other points of view cut across many of the elements that are fundamentally in the domain of production. Such concepts sharply diverge from the notion of a production management entity that can be isolated on an organization chart, shown in Figure 1.6.

It is easy to see how this difference can create problems. Many industrial organizations interpret the organization chart in a literal sense. They accept the concept of fixed organizational boundaries and the idea, bluntly stated, that each division should mind its own business. In this framework production people are expected to deal with technology, engineering, materials, equipment, and plant. Problems concerning product acceptance in the marketplace, price, distribution, promotion, and advertising are out of bounds. The reverse is also true. The production department rejects "interference" from other divisions. This tradition is at odds with modern production management philosophy.

Management today is aware that divisional decisions must include a realistic

---

[6] Repetitive operations bring to mind the concept of mass production. It is erroneous to assume that mass production is synonymous with production management.

FIGURE 1-6
The static concept
of organizational
management.

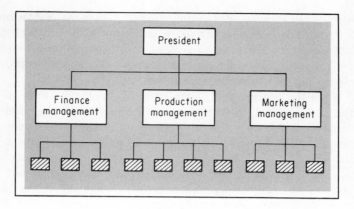

appraisal of factors that fall outside their nominal organizational boundaries. Furthermore, decisions and policies in one area affect the utility of decisions and policies in other areas. From this fact emerges the requirement that *boundaries must be redefined* according to the nature of the decision problem. (Figure 1.7 is an attempt to illustrate this requirement.) Arbitrary, traditional boundaries can inflict large penalties on the company. Faced with increasing competitive pressures, many organizations have recognized the need to realign divisional viewpoints, to achieve integration and synthesis; a blend, a coming together. In other words, they have accepted the systems philosophy to replace the older notion that sanctifies divisional boundaries.[7]

The systems concept, as previously noted, operates on the premise that decisions must include all factors that are relevant to the problem, no matter how

FIGURE 1-7
The boundary of a
problem transcends
traditional lines of
division.

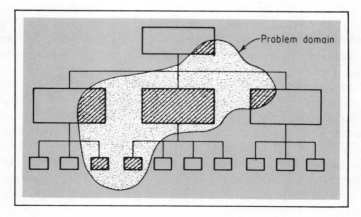

[7] Divisional boundaries are useful when they represent areas of special knowledge and the assignment of responsibility for particular functions.

17

many organizational entities are involved.[8] Then, each division contributes in its own area of specialization to the resolution of the problem. Decisions of this kind are not made in an arbitrarily defined vacuum. Problems which are improperly bounded violate the systems concept. This myopic approach to problem solving can produce severe penalties.

When the systems philosophy prevails, divisional points of view are reconciled and coordinated with the overall objectives of the company. Why then should there ever be a unique production management viewpoint in a company that accepts the systems philosophy? It would appear that a single point of view would exist, namely, the company's point of view. Because each problem includes all relevant factors—no matter where they exist organizationally—then the company's objectives should prevail. Theoretically, this is true. Realistically, at least two difficulties interpose themselves.

The objectives of individuals and small groups within the organization can be at variance with each other and with the organization's objectives. (Previously this was referred to as the problem of confliction.)

Let us consider an example of how this occurs. The Gamma Company determines that it can achieve savings by subcontracting its die-cast work. The die-casting department is to be closed down. The head of the die-casting department cannot be expected to view this decision in the same way that other company executives will see it. (How can he identify with company objectives when his services are about to be terminated?) The manager of the production department may also resist this decision. His budget will be cut; his importance in the organizational hierarchy will be diminished. In many ways, less startling than in this case, personal objectives can conflict with company objectives. *Management is seldom, if ever, certain that the correct decision is being made.*

The Gamma problem would have no serious relevance were it not for this fact that even while closing down an entire department, managers know that they may have done the wrong thing. They are prepared for arguments. The manager of the production department states that the company's objectives cannot be attained by discontinuing the die-casting operations. He points out that the calculated cost savings are being interpreted as though they were equivalent to profit increases. He might also argue that *even if* short-term profits were improved, long-term profits would suffer. He can fault the allocation of overhead charges which represent an allocation of fixed costs that are general to the company and of which each department is assigned some (arbitrary) percentage. Or, he might state that profits are means to an end and not ends in themselves. Additional arguments can be developed. These include the (intangible) costs of laying off workers or requiring that they be absorbed in other jobs, the loss of goodwill in the community, and the loss of prestige in the industry. Who is to say with certainty what these intangible costs would be? The production department may suffer a loss of morale. Attracting skilled workers could become more difficult. Other departments of the company might fear that the same

---

[8] The factors that are relevant to a great number of problems fall primarily within the jurisdiction of one particular organizational division. Production management has many such problems. Therefore, the divisional arrangement coincides, in these cases, with the systems boundaries.

thing will happen to them. Increased turnover is a possibility. Can new difficulties in dealing with the union be anticipated?

At the same time a rash of arguments can be advanced that the study was improperly conducted; the estimates that were used were bad; the quotes from vendors are vague, misleading, and incomplete; the subcontracting vendors will raise their prices as soon as the die-cast department is shut down; the quality of the subcontracted work will not compare with present quality; the process of changing over will cost money that should be subtracted from the estimated savings; the loss of the die-cast department will limit new product opportunities and adversely affect company know-how; and that delivery lead times will be more erratic.

Because decision problems are complex, it is impossible for any study to evaluate with precision all the relevant factors. The gap is filled by judgment, intuition, and the application of whatever is meant by common sense. As long as this gap exists, unique divisional viewpoints will continue to exist. The production management viewpoint will be fashioned by the obvious human objectives of individuals within the production departments and by the traditional divisional responsibility to get work done.

CONCLUSIONS

We have examined some systems aspects of the production management field. It has been pointed out that an important dichotomy exists, namely, that the design of the production process is interrelated but quite different from the design of control systems that are necessary for operating the production process. Still, it is vital that the interrelation between the two not be ignored, which is a fundamental systems concept.

Fortunately, with reasonable frequency, these areas are separable to some extent. The design of the production system tends to involve long-term considerations. These decisions are nonrepetitive commitments of major importance; the situations are unique and without prior history to serve as a guide; and the decisions tend to be irreversible.

The issues germaine to the design of the control system, on the other hand, are repetitive-type decisions. Encountered repeatedly, they rapidly provide a backlog of useful historical data. They are generally reversible and can be modified, usually, at low cost and in a minimum period of time.

The production management cycle is designed to provide for change. Such change may be required because external factors are altered. Change is also part of the improvement concept wherein the system hunts for more successful forms and better means of coping with events. Thus, it is reasonable to say that although optimal systems are the objectives of production managers (because true optimization is almost impossible to obtain), the operational objective is for a good suboptimal system that can undergo gradual and continued improvement. Similarly, the control system may not produce true optimal results.

Instead, satisfactory performance is the designer's goal. Approximating methods will frequently be utilized instead of optimal-seeking methods. The former methods, for example, will be found being applied to inventory systems, production scheduling, and line balancing.[9]

The production system with its many complex aspects achieves unification and is capable of being viewed as an integrated entity because of the common, major objectives which all the elements of the system share. It is legitimate to study and treat the system in part rather than in its entirety, only when such parts independently affect the level of achievement of the objectives and do not, in any way, affect the contributions of all other parts in the system. The objectives, which are the core of all production management activities, will determine the approach to problems and the attitudes and behaviors of production managers.

We have introduced the fundamental notion of effectiveness versus efficiency based upon the differentiation between strategies and tactics. In our terms, the design of the production system raises questions of effectiveness. The design of the control system introduces questions of how to insure the achievement of operating efficiencies. And, it has been pointed out that we cannot expect to obtain the "best possible" design for the production system because suboptimal situations occur for a number of different reasons. When suboptimization occurs an opportunity cost arises. The production manager must be able to distinguish between the kinds of opportunity costs that characterize issues of effectiveness and those which arise with respect to efficiency.

PROBLEMS

1   The production management cycle shown in Figure 1.1 applies uniquely to the production function. Why is this so?

2   *a*. Explain why, and in what way, the following constitute examples of production operations:

1. The use of a test market to compare consumer responses to different promotional campaigns
2. The Census
3. The Stock Exchange
4. Launching a weather satellite
5. Cooking a meal
6. Shaving
7. Playing a game of golf
8. Hospital care
9. A card game, for example, bridge
10. Manufacturing fountain pens
11. Growing corn

---

[9] The line balancing problem refers to the way in which machines and human components of a production line are matched with respect to their characteristic production rates. See pp. 225-26. for a discussion of this subject.

12. Raising chickens
13. Petroleum blending
14. Mining titanium
15. Library systems

b. Give some other examples.

c. Discuss how issues of "effectiveness vs. efficency" apply in each of these examples.

3 Why is it useful, wherever possible, to divide decision problems into those which involve strategies and those which deal with tactics?

4 Identify some of the multiple objectives that underlie decisions of the following types:

a. Should product X be redesigned?

b. Should a lock be put on the tool bin?

c. Should the factory be painted?

5 In what sense is driving a car a production operation? Now, extend the question to a fleet of buses.

6 How does the systems concept involve suboptimization as an intrinsic characteristic?

7 *a.* A process is composed of a set of operations. If each operation is made as efficient as possible, then the set of operations would be most efficient. Why might this not be true?

b. If the process is most efficient, then why might not economic value be maximized?

8 What justification is there for stating that production management is not limited to manufacturing?

9 Why must production, marketing, and finance cooperate with each other for the benefit of the organization?

references

BAUMOL, WILLIAM J., *Economic Theory and Operations Analysis* (2nd ed.). Englewood Cliffs, N. J.: Prentice-Hall, Inc., 1965.

BECKETT, JOHN A., *Management Dynamics: The New Synthesis.* New York: McGraw-Hill Inc., 1971.

DOOLEY, A. et al., *Basic Problems, Concepts, and Techniques,* Casebooks in Production Management. New York: John Wiley & Sons, Inc., 1968.

ECKMAN, D. P. (ed.), *Systems Research and Design.* New York: John Wiley & Sons, Inc., 1961.

ELLIS, D. O., and F. J. LUDWIG, *Systems Philosophy: An Introduction.* Englewood Cliffs, N. J.: Prentice-Hall, Inc., 1962.

GARRETT, LEONARD, and MILTON SILVER, *Production Management Analysis.* New York: Harcourt Brace Jovanovich, Inc., 1966.

HALL, ARTHUR D., *A Methodology for Systems Engineering.* Princeton, N. J.: D. Van Nostrand Co., Inc., 1962.

HARE, Jr., VAN COURT, *Systems Analysis: A Diagnostic Approach.* New York: Harcourt, Brace Jovanovich, Inc., 1967.

MCKEAN, R. N., *Efficiency in Government through Systems Analysis.* New York: John Wiley & Sons, Inc., 1958.

MCMILLAN, JR., CLAUDE and RICHARD F. GONZALEZ, *Systems Analysis: A Computer Approach to Decision Models* (revised edition), Homewood, Illinois: Richard D. Irwin, Inc., 1968.

OPTNER, S. L., *Systems Analysis for Business Mangement* (2nd ed.). Englewood Cliffs, N. J.: Prentice-Hall, Inc., 1968.

POSTLEY, JOHN A., *Computers and People.* New York: McGraw-Hill, Inc., 1960.

SCHODERBEK, PETER P. (ed.), *Management Systems.* New York: John Wiley & Sons, Inc., 1967.

STARR, MARTIN K., *Systems Management of Operations.* Englewood Cliffs, N. J.: Prentice-Hall, Inc., 1971.

chapter
two
models
of
the
system

A model is a representation of reality. It is constructed in such a way as to explain the behavior of some but not all aspects of that reality. The reason that a model is employed is that it is always *less complex* than the actual situation. It is a convenient way of studying the interacting complexities of the real world. That is why planes are flown in wind tunnels or small ships towed through tanks filled with mercury (which fairly well simulates how water would act with the big ship.) Flight simulators allow pilots to be trained to handle dangerous situations which in reality could be deadly. In all cases, the model must be a good representation of those dimensions that are related to the systems objectives; otherwise, it will not be useful and, therefore, will not be used.

Without question, the recognition that we can employ models has increased their use and the use of models has completely altered the nature of production management. Many successful models have been developed in the production management field. Undoubtedly, the production function is represented by the most complete set of problem-solving and decision-making models that exist in any organizational division of industry. In our approach to production management models we will consider in this chapter two of the most basic models of the production system, namely, the input-output model and then the breakeven model. Chapter 3 examines the structure of decision models and the factors required to reach a decision. Then, in Chapter 4 planning models are discussed. They provide the means for achieving optimal or near-optimal plans for projects such as the design of the production process. Finally, in Chapter 5, the fundamentals of control models including the notions of cost and profit control, feedback loops, statistical quality control, and performance variance are treated.

Models can be concrete (such as architectural models of buildings, designer's prototypes of autos, maps, charts and blueprints) or abstract (such as organization charts and systems of mathematical equations). The total unification of the production management field would be achieved if we could write out the entire system of equations to describe the effect of all relevant factors on the systems objectives. (Such equations would certainly have to contain probability or risk statements, but this in no way affects the fact that they are a theoretical possiblity.) All the relevant variables would interact with each other in such an equation much as they would in the real world. Given such equations, it would be theoretically possible to solve them and, thereby, to determine the optimal course of action for the organization.

At this time it is virtually impossible to write, let alone solve, such a total system of equations. But, at least in theory, a production department equation, a total enterprise equation, a national equation, or a world equation might be written. The theoretical possibilities are not challenged or altered by the scope of the undertaking even though the practical limitations become formidable at a level far below that of the production department's system. Because we are unable to produce or solve such equations, it is essential that we structure our thinking in such a way as to parallel the underlying meaning that is implicit in the total system. Fortunately, we are able to do this to some extent.

INPUT-OUTPUT MODELS

One of the most fundamental models of the production system is the input-output model, pictured in Figure 2.1.

FIGURE 2-1

Input (I) ⟶ | Transform (T) | ⟶ Output (O)

Production is *any process* or procedure designed to *transform* a set of *input* elements into a specified set of *output* elements. The *system* is the set of all such interconnected input-output elements.

A production system can be broken down into the three component parts of inputs, outputs, and process. The diagram shown in Figure 2.2 illustrates the way in which various ingredients are brought together and transformed so as to accomplish the *objectives* for which the system was designed.

The process can be complicated; many kinds of inputs can be required; a variety of outputs can emerge. But the idea of *transforming* a set of inputs so that they yield a set of outputs is not complex. Computer operations epitomize

FIGURE 2-2
The input-output pro-
cess model.

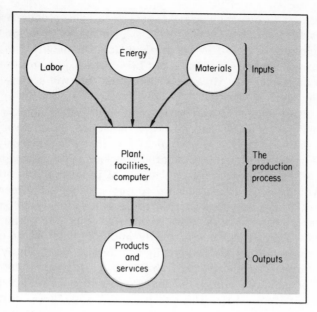

this sequence. Programming structures the transformation process; information inputs are transformed in accordance with the program instructions, and printed output is made available to the manager for action or for his further analysis. The design of an actual input-output process for manufacturing, computer processing, transportation, etc. is another matter. It can be expensive and difficult.

OUTPUTS AND REVENUE

Specification of the desired output or outputs is usually the starting point for production management systems planning.[1] Outputs are moved to the marketplace where they generate revenue. Financial considerations may dictate that a search be made for some activity that will produce a satisfactory return on the invested capital.[2] The possession of extra capital is frequently the prime motivation for a search to discover desirable outputs.

Juxtaposed to this is the case where a potentially valuable output is known but sufficient capital is not at hand and must be raised by the financial guardians of the company. The qualifications that earn the title of "valuable output" are that some group of individual consumers, companies, or institutions would be interested in acquiring one or more units of this output under conditions that can be profitable (or somehow beneficial) for the producer.

For example, the sales manager learns that a competitor has introduced a new product or service which is receiving strong consumer acceptance. He then

---

[1] William Moran, see pp. 479-86.

25 [2] ROI = return on investment; a common abbreviation.

suggests that his own management consider this new product or service possibility. New ideas can also come to the sales manager from sources operating in the marketing field and in the marketplace. Frequently a market survey will uncover a consumer need that is not being satisfied. A creative employee in the organization may just "dream up" an output that will achieve an economically satisfying level of demand.

The starting point can also be traced to input factors and to process factors. If a new material or a new energy source is developed, the discovery may suggest an output that was either overlooked or one that was previously technologically or economically unfeasible. Similarly, a technological discovery can lead to the design of a new process that is capable of producing an entirely new output which could satisfy an unquenched consumer demand. Numerous cases are on record of where a byproduct of a process is suddenly recognized as having marketable characteristics. Here, the existence of one output creates the possibility for another. Because of the dynamic character of the marketplace, new output opportunities are continually developing. A previously unwanted product or service can unexpectedly shift into a situation where it is under substantial demand. Of course, the converse is also true. An accepted product can begin to lose popularity. This can be traced, sometimes, to the activities of a competitor, but it can also be explained as a shift in consumer wants.

THE PROCESS AND FIXED COSTS

The output is expected to have *greater value* than the combined values of the inputs and the investment in the process, when the latter is properly amortized.[3] This is different from the engineering expectations for physical systems where, at a theoretical best, the output can equal the input. Because of friction and heat losses the usable output in the physical world is less than the sum of the input energies. Thus, the efficiency of a process (η) in engineering terms is:

$$\eta = \frac{\text{Useful Output}}{\text{Input}} \leqq 1$$

Such efficiency would produce bankruptcy in the economic world. The efficiency of a production process, from the viewpoint of the physical system, is measurable in the above terms, but production management is beholden to economic criteria. In economic systems, the efficiency, (η), must be greater than one, indicating that a profit can be made. Furthermore, it is only partly true that as the engineering efficiency increases so does economic efficiency. Production managers understand and integrate both the engineering and the economic points of view, in their daily activities.

A process consists of production elements that represent primarily *fixed costs*. These are costs that do not vary as a function of the output rates. What kind of costs are invariant to the operating level of the company? Although

[3] See pp. 371-74.

there is a convention that applies here, nevertheless, a good deal of interpretation is possible in the assignment of costs to this fixed charge category. For example, depreciation allowances that result from age characteristics are invariant to the amount of use that the equipment receives. Consequently, it would seem appropriate to include such expenses as part of the fixed cost category. (On the other hand depreciation that results from use would appear to violate this concept.) Another fixed cost might be municipal taxes that are independent of the company's revenue. Fixed power and light charges and basic insurance charges also belong in this cost category. For the most part, fixed costs arising as a result of investments in plant and facilities are depreciated as a function of time and not as a function of production volume.

INPUTS AND VARIABLE COSTS

Inputs are *variable* cost production elements. Such costs are paid out on a per-unit (of volume) basis. Direct labor and direct material costs are typical. They can be charged directly to each unit of production. Variable costs, as a system of input classification, also create certain anomalies of classification. There are, for example, indirect labor charges that are associated with office work. Such costs are difficult to attribute to a particular unit of output or on a cost-per-piece basis. Therefore, normally they are assigned to the accounting category of overhead costs. Similarly, salaries paid to supervisory personnel fall outside the definition of variable costs. In fact, irregularities are generally treated as fixed costs.

Basically, materials, labor, and energy constitute the input. Plant and facilities make up the process. It is relatively apparent that by means of the inputs to the production process management exercises most of its *day-to-day* control over the outputs. Alterations of the process are more usually too costly.

FIXED- AND VARIABLE-COST SYSTEMS

Management exercises *operating control* over the production system in two different ways:

1. By controlling the inputs with respect to input rates, cost, quality, and so on, it controls the *variable costs.*
2. By altering the process (or procedure), that is, by rearranging the process elements, it controls the *fixed systemic costs.*

Managers have found it convenient to divide the field of production management into three parts.

1. Variable-cost systems—considered to be the major production management responsibility.

2. Fixed-cost systems—considered to be partly a production management responsibility but fundamentally a major responsibility of financial management.[4]

3. Revenue—considered to be a major marketing responsibility, falling outside the production management domain.[5]

Variable-cost systems have generally been touted as being the major concern of production managers. Over the years, it has become increasingly apparent that fixed-cost systems are also fundamental to production management, requiring real cooperation between the financial managers and the production managers.[6] Revenue considerations have not been as well blessed. Although it is no revelation that quality, cost and, therefore, price, product availablity, and variety are completely related to both marketing and production,[7] nevertheless, the divisions seldom achieve the level of cooperation that these situations appear to require.

THE BREAK-EVEN CHART[8]

To illustrate the concern of production management with these three factors we need only consider the rapid acceptance and application of the break-even chart by the field. This schematic device is illustrated in Figure 2.3.

FIGURE 2-3
The break-even chart.

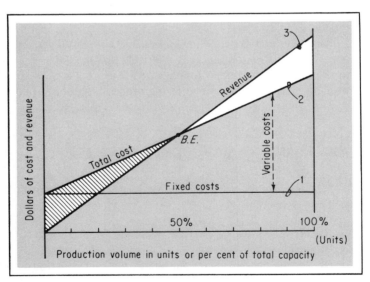

---

[4] Rein Peterson, "The Financial Context of Production Management Decisions," pp. 436-62.
[5] William Moran, pp. 474-77.
[6] Rein Peterson, pp. 442-47.
[7] William Moran, pp. 481-92.
[8] See pp. 431 concerning the development of break-even analysis.

The chart consists of an ordinate, (y axis), and an abscissa, (x axis), so it can be represented by conventional Cartesian coordinates. The ordinate presents a scale of dollars against which fixed costs, variable costs, and dollars of revenue can be measured. The abscissa can be dimensioned in terms of the production volume, that is, the number of units that are made by the company in a given period of time. It isn't difficult to translate this as a percent of the total capacity that the company has available. All the aforementioned dimensions will be found on Figure 2.3.

In addition, we observe that three lines have been marked on the chart. We shall consider each of these in turn. Line number 1 is a fixed-cost function. Recalling the fact that the break-even chart applies to a specified period of time, we observe that the fixed charges behave in the expected manner, that is, they do not change as a function of increased volume or increased utilization of capacity. We had previously defined fixed costs by this special characteristic.

Line number 2 on the chart is an increasing linear, monotonic[9] function that increases with increasing volume. In the real world such linearity is neither expected nor obtained. Nevertheless, for our first examination of the break-even chart the assumption of linearity is not a major concession because linear relationships do adequately describe many situations. In any event, the production field has, in the past, accepted this assumption for a great number of cases. The second line reflects the variable cost components which by definition increase with additional volume. On our chart, these variable costs do not begin at the zero level. They are instead added to the fixed costs which would exist in any case at a zero production level. Consequently, this second line is a total cost line which results from the summation of fixed and variable costs. The triangular area lying between the fixed costs and total costs would then be the variable costs that are assigned to the production system.

Thus, for example, for each unit of a particular item that we make, a certain fixed amount of labor is required and the necessary materials must be assembled and utilized to produce that unit. If materials that are used for one unit cost $0.10, then the total material charges for one hundred units would be $10.00 and the total material charges for one thousand units would be $100.00. That is why this second function increases as we move to greater utilization of capacity. Harking back to our original fixed-cost elements, we now observe that only depreciation which is applicable to machine utilization would be included in the variable-cost section. Taxes that are levied on the basis of units produced or revenue obtained would also be appropriately included in the variable-cost class. Some power and light charges, heating charges, storage charges, and insurance charges are characterized by the definition of variable costs.

We have now defined the total costs that are applicable to a company's operations. The categorization of fixed and variable-cost charges is completely relevant to the analysis of the production function. It fits conveniently with the useful assumption of an input-output system. The schematic form which we are explaining can be translated into mathematical terms. But for purposes

---

[9] Generally increasing, never decreasing—and in this case at a constant rate because of the assumption of linearity. Decreasing monotonic functions can be explained in the same way, but in the reverse direction.

of communication with production people the break-even chart in its graphical form is an extremely useful device. It is accepted and understood by practicing production managers. As such, it constitutes an important bridge between modern and progressive production practice and the old-time traditional way of viewing decision making in this field.

The third line shown in Figure 2.3 is our revenue line. It is also a monotonic function that increases with greater production volume. Here, too, we have a situation in which we are utilizing the assumption of linearity. But how long can this go on? At some point we know that total revenue will not increase at the same rate, as the company manufactures greater and greater quantities of an item. The market for the item becomes saturated. It is necessary for the company to lower its price in order to obtain a greater share of the total market that is available.[10] Traditionally, a linear relationship is utilized to describe revenue. This implies that our company is operating at a relatively low level in the total market, such that free competition could adequately describe its situation.

The cross-hatched area between the total cost line and the revenue line represents loss to the company, that is, the area to the left of the break-even point. The white area between these same lines represents profit to company and lies to the right of this point. Therein lies the definition of the break-even point—*no profit, no loss.* The break-even point occurs for a given volume of production or a given utilization of plant capacity. Figure 2.4 shows the relationship of profit to production volume. The y axis measures amount of profit. Here we observe all the debilities of the linear system because profit begins as negative profit or loss and increases linearly throughout the range of values. As we stated, this could only be applicable to a company that met the very

FIGURE 2-4
Profit vs. production
volume.

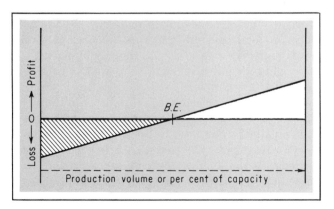

[10] Pricing problems are a mysterious and ill-defined area. Although we have generalized the effect of saturation as being correlated with price, this is not always the case. There are well-known instances where a company achieves a major market or at least increased revenue as a result of raising their price. Here we are dealing with the psychology of the consumer and the fact that a market may not exist for a low-price product because it does not carry sufficient prestige value to the consumer.

specific conditions which we previously enumerated. But it is still good enough for a first approximation, in many cases.

Two factors would have to be considered in reaching conclusions about any specific break-even situation. The first would be the position of the break-even point. The second would be the amount of profit on a marginal basis that is obtained for each additional unit of capacity that can be utilized. This is the slope of the line in Figure 2.4. In other words, if the profit line shown in Figure 2.4 was rotated so that it fell almost on top of the x axis, then very little profit would be obtained as a result of increased utilization of plant capacity. If the slope of this line was increased, (in terms of the figure this means mechanically rotating it about the break-even point), then greater returns could be obtained *once* demand exceeded the break-even point. At the same time it should be noted that, because of the assumption of linearity the losses or penalties for operating under the break-even point also become proportionately greater as we move farther away from the break-even point. This is true more or less in most practical situations.

Our second concern has to do with the translation of the break-even point itself. If it is moved to the right, then the company must operate at a higher level of capacity before it is worthwhile for it to engage in business. Conversely, by reducing the value of the break-even point (moving it to the left) the pressure of this demand upon the company is decreased. But decisions can be complex with respect to these two criteria. Notice that in Figure 2.5 we have drawn two profit lines. Each is presumably descriptive of a result obtained from different production configurations. Alternative A has a lower break-even point than alternative B. This makes A more desirable than B with respect to this criterion. But the profit function B has greater marginal returns once the break-even point has been reached. B is preferred, therefore, with respect to this criterion. If the company is able to operate at point a, then both alternatives yield equal profit.

FIGURE 2-5
Profit vs. production volume for alternative production configurations.

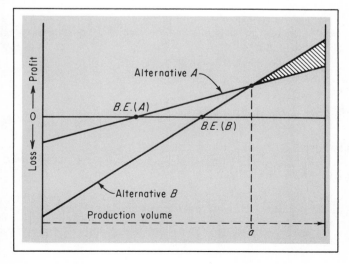

If we can operate at a volume in excess of point *a*, then alternative *B* is preferred. If we cannot, then our choice must be for alternative *A*.

The interrelationships of costs, sales, revenues, and profits give rise to situations as that depicted in Figure 2.5. Thus, one plan may require a smaller investment than another but produce a product of poorer quality, resulting in lower sales volume. Of course, we could decrease the selling price to achieve increased sales volume; but this might not compensate as far as revenue is concerned; and often, the lower investment process must operate with higher variable costs. These effects must be felt or else *no decision problem exists.* Only in "Wonderland" could a particular plan improve quality, lower investment, decrease variable costs, and permit higher prices with increased sales volume. Specifically, we invest in facility improvement to achieve lower variable costs, improve quality, and derive the associated market benefits. Each alternative has its own patterns of interconnected expenditures, costs and benefits. The whole system is an integrated one. Much of the necessary perspective (but not all) has been available through diligent analysis of the break-even chart. Missing factors will appear when we consider decision theory and decision models.

MATHEMATICAL FORM

It is quite straightforward to translate the graphical break-even chart into its algebraic equivalent. Some individuals prefer the visual form whereas others prefer the mathematical statement. The choice ultimately depends upon the use that is to be made of such analyses. When communication with production personnel is required, the visual approach is generally more effective.

To begin, let us assign symbol equivalents to the relevant factors.

REV = Gross revenue-per-time-period T.
$PRICE$ = Price per unit with the assumption that the market will absorb everything that can be made at the same price.
VOL = Number of units made in time period T and, therefore, sales volume in time period T.
FC = Fixed costs-per-period T.
VC = Variable costs-per-unit of production.
TC = Total costs-per-period T.
$PROFIT$ = Total profit-per-period T.

The revenue line for period T is given by:

$$REV = PRICE \times VOL$$

The total cost line for period T is equal to:

$$TC = [FC + (VC)\,VOL]$$

Total profit for the interval T is (*in terms of volume*) then:

$$PROFIT = (REV - TC) = [PRICE \times VOL - FC - (VC) VOL]$$
$$= [(PRICE - VC) VOL - FC]$$

EXAMPLE 1.

$T = 1$ year

	ALTERNATIVE 1	ALTERNATIVE 2
	NO CONVEYER	INSTALL CONVEYER
VOL	18,000 units per year	18,000 units per year
FC	$10,000 per year	$12,000 per year
VC	$0.50 per unit	$0.45 per unit
PRICE	$2.00 per unit	$2.00 per unit

for Alternative 1:

$$PROFIT = (2 - 0.50)(18,000) - 10,000 = \$17,000 \text{ per year}$$

for Alternative 2:

$$PROFIT = (2 - 0.45)(18,000) - 12,000 = \$15,900 \text{ per year}$$

The break-even point is easily calculated by setting $PROFIT = 0$, then[11]

$$\text{Break-even Point } (VOL) = \frac{FC}{PRICE - VC}$$

For Alternative 1:

$$\text{Break-even (Point } (VOL) = 10,000/(1.5) = 6,667 \text{ units}$$

For Alternative 2:

$$\text{Break-even Point } (VOL) = 12,000/(1.55) = 7,742 \text{ units}$$

It is a simple matter to convert from units of volume to percent or fraction of capacity. For example, the break-even point as a fraction of total capacity for Alternative 1 is: $6667/18,000 = 0.37$ and for Alternative 2, it is: $7,742/18,000 = 0.43$. We note that the profit at full capacity utilization for Alternative 1

[11] This relationship is valid only when $PRICE - VC \geq 0$, i.e., when $PRICE \geq VC$. Ordinarily, it is assumed that pricing follows an analysis of costs and therefore, no competent manager would accept a price that doesn't cover the variable costs *with room to spare*. Consider, however, the plight of regulated industries, e.g., airlines, where operating costs could grow faster than changes in rate structure. The worst possible break-even value would be infinite. Negative break-even volumes have no meaning.

promises $1,100 more profit than Alternative 2. Also, in terms of the break-even point we prefer Alternative 1 because it has a lower value. In this example, there is no doubt that we should select Alternative 1.

EXAMPLE 2.

$T = 3$ months or 1 quarter

	ALTERNATIVE 1	ALTERNATIVE 2
	MACHINE *A*	MACHINE *B*
VOL	5,000 units per quarter	5,000 units per quarter
FC	$2500.00 per quarter	$3500.00 per quarter
VC	$0.50 per unit	$0.10 per unit
PRICE	$2.00 per unit	$2.00 per unit

First, let us test the profit for each alternative at an estimated 3,000 units per quarter which is 60 percent utilization of capacity.

For Alternative 1:

$PROFIT = (2 - 0.50)(3000) - 2500 = \$2,000$ per quarter

and for Alternative 2:

$PROFIT = (2 - 0.10)(3000) - 3500 = \$2,200$ per quarter

Next, for full capacity utilization, for Alternative 1:

$PROFIT = (2 - 0.50)(5000) - 2500 = \$5,000$ per quarter

and for Alternative 2:

$PROFIT = (2 - 0.10)(5000) - 3500 = \$6,000$ per quarter

Thus, Alternative 2 is preferred both at the point of estimated plant utilization and at full utilization, but, the break-even points are:
for Alternative 1:

Break-even point $(VOL) = 2500/(1.5) = 1667$ units or $1667/5000 = 0.333$

for Alternative 2:

Break-even point $(VOL) = 3500/(1.9) = 1842$ units or $1842/5000 = 0.370$

Here, we see that Alternative 1 has a superior break-even point. It is clear that something else must be added to our analysis if it is to make sense. That something extra will be risk estimates associated with varying levels of utilized capacity.[12] First, however, let us consider the effect of our assumption of linearity.

THE NONLINEAR BREAK-EVEN CHART

It is readily apparent that the anticipated volume of operations is a critical factor in the determination of a production system's design. If the market is such that at a certain price unlimited demand exists, then for these linear systems we would always operate as far to the right as our plant capacity permits.

FIGURE 2-6
Break-even chart with
the assumption of a
decelerating revenue
as product price is
lowered to achieve
full plant utilization.

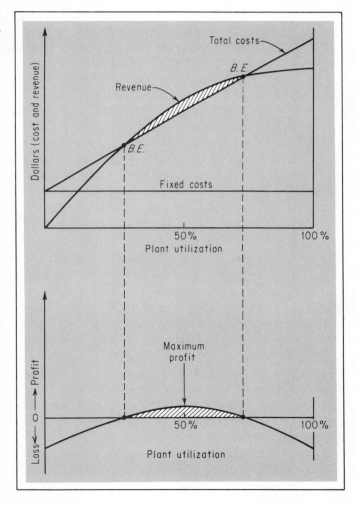

[12] See pp. 62–66.

Of course, in reality at some point linearity ceases to be a reasonable description of the market's responses. Increased volume can only be obtained by a decrease in price or an increase in promotional and selling costs. These two situations are shown in Figures 2.6 and 2.7. The combination of these effects is illustrated in Figure 2.8.

Each of these diagrams is accompanied by a graph of the profit that can be obtained at different percentages of productive capacity. We may note there is a "best possible" point, that is, a point at which the total profit is maximized. To achieve this level of production requires cooperative effort on the part of all the major management divisions. Financial management must provide enough funds so that adequate capital exists to create the facilities necessary for the specified volume of production. The marketing department must be able to deliver the estimated number of customers and their sales at the price that is incorporated in the revenue line. And, of course, production must be able to deliver the goods in the required volume at the expected cost and quality.

We see that production management must help to determine a *configuration of production elements* that will yield a maximum profit—if that is the company's

FIGURE 2-7
Break-even chart with the assumption of accelerating promotional costs required to achieve full plant utilization.

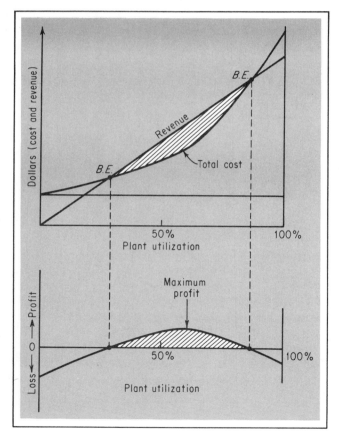

FIGURE 2-8
Break-even chart with
both   assumptions,
that is, decelerating
revenue and acceler-
ating costs.

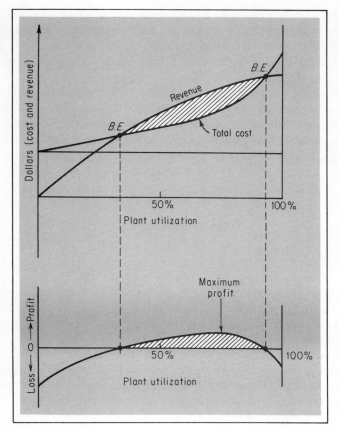

objective. However, the problem of succeeding in doing this is complicated far
beyond anything that a break-even chart can show. A danger of abstractions is
that all kinds of difficulties are represented in a simple fashion that belies the
truth of the situation. Accordingly, one must be very careful in applying such
tools as the break-even chart.

Let us examine this warning with respect to the break-even model. First of all
the break-even chart, even when couched in nonlinear form, represents only
one product. For most companies, decisions must include the fact that a product-mix is involved. The line consists of a number of different items or services.
These must share resources including capital and management time. The break-
even chart is difficult to utilize when such additional complications are encountered. In addition, a specific period of time is embodied in each break-even chart.
If we assume that the company can sell five million units over a five-year period,
but only ten thousand in the first year, then the result of a five year analysis may
be quite appealing; whereas on the basis of a one-year analysis, the product
would be rejected. But cost estimates applied to a five-year period might not

37

be sufficiently believable to allow management to act on them. Further, unexpected costs can arise. For example, if the company overproduces, then overstock units could only be sold by reducing the price. If the unsold units are held in inventory, they will create additional costs such as storage, insurance, and carrying costs.

For each situation some maximum profit (optimal) situation exists. Whether it can be found or not is another matter. But only with the nonlinear break-even chart does this fundamental optimization objective of production management appear. The traditional break-even approach overlooks this particular aspect of the problem.

CONCLUSIONS

Of all the attitudes that are common to the production management field, the desire for efficiency and cost control is the most entrenched. In the production management cycle the areas of implementation, operations, and control are especially susceptible to stringent cost analysis. Throughout its history, production management has been cost oriented; just as marketing management has always been sales oriented. These traditional points of view can be difficult to reconcile and coordinate. They seldom jibe with the systems philosophy. This limited production management viewpoint which fosters divisional isolation is changing. From the recognition of the interdependencies reflected by break-even analysis, modern production management has begun to alter its views, moving rapidly beyond the constraining frontiers of exclusive attention to cost reduction. Other organizational divisions also are modifying and discarding those points of view that erroneously foster uncoordinated planning and isolated divisional decision making.

The production management viewpoint is no longer static. It is merging with other divisional management viewpoints, and they are all coming closer together in the ultimate sense of framing a single, over-all company viewpoint. But total unification—if it will ever be realized—is still a long way off.

The elements of the production management problem are quite readily discernible. There is an input-output system which is the core of the production system. The foundations of this system are the relationships that specify the behaviors of fixed and variable costs, revenue, sales volume, and profit. A variety of decision problems occur with respect to the design of the input-output system. These relate to the total response of the system. By adjusting fixed costs, changes can be brought about in variable costs, in revenue, and in profit. Thus, *the design and operation of the total system can only be unified by recognizing the fundamental requirement that all parts of the system must operate together in some well-balanced fashion. All decisions made in the system and all actions that are taken must be related to major common objectives.*

PROBLEMS

1 Production management is said to be cost conscious. In what way can this attitude lead to serious suboptimizations?

2 Name several input-output systems. Discuss their components and describe their transformation characteristics.

3 Detail some situations in which nonlinear analysis might be required for the breakeven chart.

4 The Gamma Company has engaged a management consultant to analyze and improve its operations. His major recommendation is to totally conveyorize the production floor. This would, of course, represent a sizeable investment to the Gamma Company. In order to determine whether or not the idea is feasible, a break-even analysis will be utilized. The situation is as follows: the cost of the conveyor will be $200,000 to be depreciated on a straight-line basis over a ten-year period, that is, $20,000 per year. The reduction in operating cost is estimated at $0.25 per unit. Each unit sells for $2.00. The sales manager estimates that based on previous years the Gamma Company can expect to obtain a sales volume of 100,000 units—this represents 100 percent of their capacity. Present yearly contribution to fixed costs is $100,000. Present variable cost rate is $0.50. Should the company install this conveyor?

5 The Omega Corporation is considering the advantages of automating a part of their production line. The company's financial statement is shown below:

OMEGA CORPORATION		
TOTAL SALES		$40,000,000
Direct Labor	$12,000,000	
Indirect Labor	2,000,000	
Direct Materials	8,000,000	
Depreciation	1,000,000	
Taxes	500,000	
Insurance	400,000	
Sales Costs	1,500,000	
Total Expenses		$25,400,000
Net Profit		$14,600,000

The above report is based on the production and sale of 100,000 units. The production manager believes that with an additional investment of $5,000,000 he can reduce variable costs by 30 percent. The same production volume would be maintained. Using a five-year, straight-line depreciation (that is, $1,000,000 per year), construct a break-even chart. If the company insists on a 20 percent return on its investment, should they automate? (Discuss briefly your treatment of all costs.)

6 In psychology, stimulus-response experiments are frequently utilized. What kind of a system is this? Why is it used? Does it have any implications with respect to the utilization of men and machines in a production system?

7 *a.* List as many variable costs as you can.
b. List as many fixed costs as you can.
c. To what extent is accounting data available in various organizations with respect to such items?

8 What is overhead cost or burden? How should it be treated in a break-even analysis?

references

ACKOFF, R. (ed.), *Progress in Operations Research,* Vol. I. New York: John Wiley & Sons, Inc., 1961.

ARONOFSKY, J. (ed.), Progress in Operations Research—Vol. III. New York: John Wiley & Sons, Inc., 1968

CARZO, R. Jr. and J. N. YANOUZAS, *Formal Organization: A Systems Approach.* Homewood, Ill.: Richard D. Irwin, Inc., 1967.

CHURCHMAN, C. W., R. A. ACKOFF, and E. L. ARNOFF, *Introduction to Operations Research.* New York: John Wiley & Sons, Inc., 1957.

DEAN, JOEL, *Managerial Economics.* Englewood Cliffs, N. J.: Prentice-Hall, Inc., 1951.

FORRESTER, J. W., *Industrial Dynamics.* New York: John Wiley & Sons, Inc., 1961.

GREENLAW, P. S., L. W. HERRON, and R. H. RAWDON, *Business Simulation in Industrial and University Education.* Englewood Cliffs, N. J.: Prentice-Hall, Inc., 1962.

HERTZ, D. B. and R. T. EDDISON (eds.), *Progress in Operations Research—Vol. II.* New York: John Wiley & Sons, Inc., 1964.

KASNER, EDWARD, and JAMES NEWMAN, *Mathematics and the Imagination.* New York: Simon and Schuster, Inc., 1963.

MILLER, D. W. and M. K. STARR, *Executive Decisions and Operations Research,* (2nd ed.), Englewood Cliffs, N. J., Prentice-Hall, Inc., 1969.

M. I. T. Notes on Operations Research, 1959. Cambridge, Mass.: M.I.T. Press, 1959.

SASIENI, M., A. YASPAN, and L. FRIEDMAN, *Operations Research, Methods, and Problems.* New York: John Wiley & Sons, Inc., 1959.

SPENCER, M. H. and L. SPIEGELMAN, *Managerial Economics.* Homewood, Ill.: Richard D. Irwin, Inc., 1959.

WAGNER, H. M., *Principles of Management Science,* Englewood Cliffs, N. J.: Prentice-Hall, Inc., 1970.

chapter
three
decision
models

Decision models are at the crux of both planning and control. Many of the terms connected with the development and application of decision models have been introduced in the preceding material. We now must examine them in detail.

DECISION THEORY

Abstract decisions can be formulated in comprehensive terms. Thus, a decision situation is composed of five basic elements. These are:

1. *Strategies or plans constructed of controllable variables;*[1]

2. *States of nature* composed of noncontrollable variables;

3. *Outcomes* which are observations of results that occur when a specific strategy is employed and a particular state of nature exists;

4. *Forecasts* of the likelihood that each state of nature will occur; and

5. *The decision criterion* which dictates the way in which the information above will be used to select a single plan to follow.

[1] Variables are *factors* which can appear in a problem with different values. Some variables have only two states as, for example, a switch which is either on or off. This is called a binary variable. Other variables exist within a closed range, such as time of day which runs froms 00 : 01 to 24 : 00. Some variables cannot take on negative values, for example, age or hardness. Profit and loss, where loss is treated as negative profit can, at least in theory, assume large minus values. Finally, certain variables are limited to discrete scales (only integer values can occur) for example, the number of students in a class. Others, such as temperature and weight are continuous.

Decision theory applies to all types of decision situations, but we are concerned only with production and operations management decisions. Because we want a unified approach, we must discuss all the elements of the decision process *as they particularly relate to the production function*. It has been recognized by those conversant with the field of production management education, that the traditional treatment of this area tended to overlook some of the vital aspects of the problem.[2] Further, having lacked a comprehensive framework for the consolidation and organization of information, the tendency was to pile fact upon fact, logical analysis upon logical analysis, and method upon method. The result was fragmentation (analysis) and not integration (synthesis). Present-day practitioners, however, have recognized the role that decision theory can play in relating the parts to each other. Production management education need no longer be treated in terms of an amorphous collection of facts, principles, and methods. This advance is attributable in large part to decision theory.

ANALYSIS AND SYNTHESIS

The key word is *synthesis*. It is the essence of production management endeavors when the system's philosophy prevails. Production management is not a container inside of which can be found tools, techniques, a body of past experience, and a conglomerate mixture of numbers, names and symbols. These fragments have been examined over the course of many years. The multitude of decision problems that comprise production management have been identified and their special characteristics have been analyzed. Analysis is the process of breaking down a system into parts that can be more easily examined. Synthesis is the reverse procedure—where the parts are integrated to form the whole. Both are essential if understanding is to be reflected by implementation.

Great stress has always been placed on analysis in the production management field. Synthesis has not been similarly favored because so little has been known about it except that it can be accomplished (without an idea of how well) by the intuition and judgment of executives. There is a basis for objective and rational synthesis. Process systems of partial or full automation must be formally synthesized; there is no other way.

To achieve synthesis we must be able to identify a structure (a framework) that will permit the simultaneous consideration of all production factors. For example, we cannot determine the best production process for unit x and for unit y independently and then put the two together; there may be a different best process for units x and y when considered together. Similarly, the decision problem concerning what materials handling equipment to use interacts with problems running the gamut from plant selection and product line composition to how many ashtrays the company will keep in stock for its employees. A

2 See the following reports concerning methods of business education: Robert A. Gordon and James E. Howell, *Higher Education for Business* (New York: Columbia University Press, 1959); Frank C. Pierson, *The Education of American Businessmen* (New York: McGraw-Hill Book Company, Inc., 1959), pp. 475–503.

limited supply of investment funds and restrictions of other resources creates a situation which requires over-all treatment of factors. Separate analytic results that indicate a number of best subsystem strategies will seldom sum together to yield an over-all best strategy. *The decision framework is a great advance in achieving synthesis.*

THE NATURE OF ALTERNATIVES

Given two plans. *A* and *B*, the decision problem consists in selecting one of them. If that type of choice must be made regularly, it is most typically a short-term control-type situation. Infrequent comparisons that involve large investments are most likely to be long-term planning-type situations. Long-term decisions are characteristically saddled with multiple objectives and instabilities, so that guesses as to what will eventually happen will seldom possess the same degree of belief that can be obtained for short-term, repetitive, systems. Decision theory is compatible with the requirements of both types of situations. though a lot more can be done with the short term cases.

Plans (strategic or tactical) are proposed courses of action. They can be quite general or highly detailed There would be no need to plan if only one course of action could be taken. Planning is needed because choice exists. Simply stated, when there are no alternative ways available for achieving an objective, there is no decision problem.[3]

Part of the production manager's job is to foster and encourage the development of alternative means for accomplishing an end. In this way decision problems are created that must then be resolved. By introducing more alternatives the production manager can make it more difficult and costly to find the best choice. However, a best choice from many alternatives is *likely* to be better than the best choice from only a few alternatives. But sometimes the decision problem becomes easier to resolve when many alternatives are created. This is so when an alternative that is clearly superior to all the others appears. In either case, the purpose served by creating alternatives is to permit closer attainment of the company's objectives.

We can summarize this as follows: There is a cost for creating alternatives and a cost for choosing among alternatives. The reward comes from the extent to which the chosen alternative succeeds in achieving the objectives. There is no known relationship between the ability to create *and* the knowledge of how to choose the "best possible" alternative, but there can be no doubt that they are related.

---

[3] A variant of this situation is called Hobson's choice.

"A choice without an alternative ; the thing offered or nothing ;—so called in allusion to the practice of Thomas Hobson (d. 1631), at Cambridge, England, who let horses, and required every customer to take the horse which stood nearest the door." (Webster's *New International Dictionary,* Second Edition, Unabridged.)

This presupposes that the choice of "do nothing" is not a legitimate alternative—a point of view with which we do not agree.

STRATEGIC DECISION LEVELS

Decision making is the process by which the selection of an alternative is made. It is not the process by means of which the plans are formulated. One or more measures of the effectiveness of each plan is required. The number of such measures is related to the number of objectives. Measures of effectiveness are the only formal means of comparing alternative plans. It is the job of production management to choose a plan, implement it, and monitor the results to make certain that they are consistent with expectations.

Methodology has very little to do with the *creation* of alternatives. The development of alternatives is partly in the technological domain and partly in the managerial domain. The nature of a specific problem determines the extent to which each domain participates. If the situation is primarily devoted to a technical problem, such as the construction of a blanking die[4] or the design of a new polymerization[5] procedure, then technological knowledge will predominate. On the other hand, if a new plant site must be selected or a guarantee policy developed, then management's ability to perceive and structure possiblities will dominate the enumeration of feasible alternatives. Decision level will also play an important part in determining the character of the alternatives.

In general, we use the term strategy to distinguish an alternative. We do not mean, however, the military definition, namely: strategy is "the science and art of employing the armed strength of a belligerent to secure the objectives of war. More restricted, the science and art of military command, exercised to meet the enemy in combat under advantageous conditions. Also a kind or instance of it."[6] The word strategy was, at one time, exclusively a military term. It has, however, been widely accepted by present day management for several reasons. First, because it connotes the fact that competitors exist whose respective plans can affect each other. In the early days of American industry competition was more an academic matter than a reality. The development of many small companies in the same industry approximated conditions of free competion. Monopolies, although the reverse of free competition, similarly had no reason for including competitors' behaviors in their plans.[7] But, as we know, things changed. The government took an active interest in combating monopolistic practices[8] and, at the same time, the expanding distribution networks of growing companies brought them into direct competition with each other.

Industry has become increasingly aware of the fact that competion exists on many levels. Each company competes not only with organizations that produce goods in their own product class, but also with any product or service that siphons off funds that could have been spent on the company's product. Even

---

4 Blanking is the process of punching a piece of material from flat stock which will then undergo further operations.
5 The chemical reaction whereby a number of molecules of the same or different kinds form a complex molecule of high molecular weight, called a high polymer, which has different physical properties from the original molecules.
6 *Webster's New International Dictionary*, Second Edition, Unabridged.
7 Monopolies were not necessarily large. Patents fostered monopoly situations. See pp. 180-86.
8 The Sherman Anti-Trust Act (1890), for example.

in a totally theoretical, planned economy, competitive factors operate. If the consumer spends his money for clothing and shelter, he thereby reduces his ability to buy food, hard goods, entertainment, and luxury items. It will be recognized that such factors as government taxation and insurance are part of both national and international competition for the consumers' dollars.

Production management planning requires awareness of the competitor. The use of the word strategy helps to keep this need in focus. The design of a product, the composition of a product line, the selection of equipment, the specification of quality standards, the kinds of materials that will be used, the design of the process, including plans for achieving automation—all these considerations and others cannot be measured for effectiveness unless the behavior of competitors is taken into account. The production manager thinks in terms of "our strategies" and "their strategies." *Game theory*[9] provides some strong conceptual insights but in practical terms, it is a weak tool. *Simulation* methods[10] allow another approach to the problem of estimating competitor effects. But no matter what methodology is employed, the production manager is *not only* responsible for creating plans for his own company *but is also* responsible for helping to predict the range and effect of plans that competing companies might use. This vital management function is easily overlooked. The production manager is under pressure to "keep things rolling." Preoccupation with his own company's strategies is so intense that he is likely to find little time to dwell on competitors' strategies. This has been characteristic of the production function. It explains in part why a massive effort has been expended on automating day-to-day chores, that is, the short-cycle systems. It is a clear-cut *management* responsibility to free itself of routine efforts in order to provide enough time so that the nonroutine requirements can be fulfilled.

TACTICAL DECISION LEVELS

Where strategy goes, tactics must follow. The dictionary definition of this word is also primarily intended for military situations. "The science and art of disposing and maneuvering troops or ships in action or in the presence of the enemy, so as to use in action the resulting dispositions. Hence, any system or method of procedure; especially adroit devices or expedients for accomplishing an end."[11] We see that tactics refers to more *concrete* procedures than does strategy. In fact, we can say that a tactic is a means of carrying out a strategy.[12]

---

[9] *Game theory*, developed by John Von Neumann and Oskar Morgenstern, is a mathematical theory for determining which strategies should be chosen by a group of competing players. See pp. 12-13.

[10] *Simulation* methods are based on the construction of a detailed network of connected operations. Rules are supplied which govern the occurrence of events in this network. Runs of events are then made through the network, and measures of effectiveness are applied so that different network arrangements and different rules can be compared. See pp. 95-97, 390-92.

[11] *Webster's New International Dictionary*, Second Edition, Unabridged.

[12] We should note that a strategem is "an artifice or trick in war for deceiving and outwitting the enemy; hence, in general, artifice; deceptive device." (*Webster's New International Dictionary*, Second Edition, Unabridged.) thereby, a tricky tactic. The word is not interchangeable with strategy.

An important part of every tactical choice is the instrumentation that it implies as the means of converting a general plan into a specific course of action. These instruments for the production management field are the men, materials, and facilities that can be utilized to bring a strategy to fruition. For example, we can specify that one possible design strategy is a V-type engine block. A second strategy might be the utilization of the conventional vertical, in-line arrangement of pistons and cylinders. A third strategy might be a horizontally opposed piston arrangement. Here, then, are three strategies. As soon as we begin to consider the way in which we shall manufacture each of these engine types we require specification of equipment, etc., as indicated in the matrix below.

	STRATEGY	TACTICS	ESTIMATED COSTS*
S_1:	V-type engine	Facilities and Skills and Methods and Materials	xxx
S_2:	Vertical, in-line pistons		xxx
S_3:	Horizontally opposed pistons		xxx

* cannot be obtained without considering at least one feasible tactical alternative for each strategy.

Concerning tactics:

1. We have noted the connection between tactical considerations and short-term planning; and between strategies and long-term plans. Production management has been traditionally oriented toward tactics. Of all organizational areas it is the one that is most involved with tactical instruments. It is impossible to study the production management area without paying due regard to the tactical or operations problems.

2. A number of tactical possibilities follow from a single strategy. Thus, detail is multipled as we move down this ladder. Seldom will there be only one configuration of instruments that can be used to achieve a specified strategy. The job-machine scheduling problem is a typical example.[13] In the usual case there are many thousands, if not millions or billions, of ways of sequencing specific jobs through the plant. Each possible schedule is a tactical variant. Because of the *multiplier effect,* that is, one strategy giving rise to millions of possible plans on the tactical level, it is easy to understand why a production manager might get bogged down. Because of special involvement with tactics, production management is particularly susceptible to this condition. Consequently, there would be less time available to think about strategies. At most, only a few production management strategies would be considered. Creativity in the strategic

[13] See pp. 230-58.

area would be minimized at the expense of exploring detail at the tactical level. Finding a best schedule is a different form of creativity than determining a best design. (We should note that a chess game is very much like a job-machine scheduling problem. The number of possible playing patterns is very great but totally defined by the rules of the game. Yet chess masters are remembered for their brilliant games, and their achievements must be classed as a type of creative effort.)

3. Strategic evaluation implies that a tactical choice has been made. We have already discussed this point on pp. 5–6. We could not compare the three engine designs previously mentioned with respect to cost unless a method for fabricating each of them had been proposed. Because many different ways for manufacturing each design exist, it is implicit that some kind of evaluation of many tactical alternatives for each strategy has been obtained. The work required to evaluate each alternative however, is overwhelming. Therefore, some method of bypassing all this work must be used. But, what is this method? Herbert Simon has pointed out that all men are constrained by bounded rationality.[14] By this he means that an intuitive selection of a few reasonably appealing alternatives, in effect discards all other alternatives. The reduction in the number of alternatives allows the time to study the few remaining ones. The procedure is not an optimizing one, and it is to be expected that substantial opportunity costs (see pp. 13–15) arise when making selections in this way.

    Another approach is to choose a strategy and then spend all your energy trying to find its best possible tactical arrangment. This is the efficiency position held by production managers for many years. Then, with recent awareness of scientific method, management began to state that questions of effectiveness should be dealt with before questions of efficiency. Thus, we do not start improving the manufacturing process for V-shaped engines before we elect to make V-shaped engines instead of vertical or horizontal ones. The systems concept requires this approach. It is the production manager's job to understand the nature of the efficiency-effectiveness problem. He should recognize those situations that call for efficiency studies; those that can be analyzed exclusively for effectiveness; those which must be treated as a totality; and those for which methodological analysis is too costly to be fruitful.

4. Tactical consideration produces yet another issue. This is the degree of *control* that can be exercised over the instruments. We do not have to overelaborate to bring the point across. Some instruments are very accurate and some are not. A good marksman with

FIGURE 3-1
Differing degrees of control over instruments will produce variation in the results obtained from tactics.

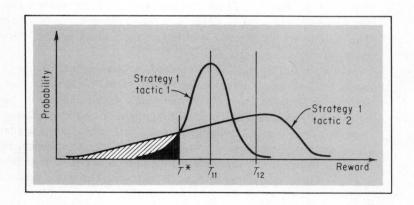

[14] Herbert A. Simon, *Models of Man*. (New York: John Wiley & Sons, Inc., 1957), p. 199.

a fine rifle may be able to hit bull's-eyes 99 per cent of the time. Lower the quality of either instrument[15] and the score falls off. Figure 3.1 illustrates this situation for two different tactics that are designed to achieve a given strategy. The first tactic employs more accurate instruments than does the second tactic. This greater control is exhibited by a narrower distribution. The second tactic has a higher average reward, $T_{12} > T_{11}$. But a comparison of the areas to the left of T^* (assume it is the minimum acceptable reward) shows a significantly greater likelihood of unacceptable rewards occurring if the second tactic is used.

GLOBAL STRATEGIES

Strategies are to tactics as the branches of a tree are to the twigs that emanate from them. Moving in the other direction, from a single trunk the branches emerge. The trunk of the production management world can be called the global strategy. It is strategy on a metalevel. For our example, the company had a problem which logically preceded the choice of an engine design. This was a product class and investment area decision. Should the company make airplanes, automobiles, motor scooters, aircars, or hydrofoil ships? Perhaps it should produce kites; or maybe a service business would be best? There is always the alternative of just investing available funds in stocks, bonds, and savings banks. The pattern of decision is clear enough. Having commited the company to an investment plan at the most global level, we proceed down the ladder of strategic possiblilties until eventually the issues of specific, tactical instrumentation prevail. But, using the conclusions reached in the previous section, we know that the global decision could not have been rendered without an estimate of strategic alternatives. These, in turn, required estimates of tactical alternatives. A change in instrumentation can be reflected at the apex of the *pyramid*. Thus, a technological change that affects instrumentation can create a new strategic possibility and can shift decisions made at the global levels. We see this interconnected system operating with increasing frequency as companies leave their traditional fields in the search for diversification. Diversification is a part of global strategy. There are also examples of companies that drop entirely their traditional line of business in order to move into a new field of endeavor. The production manager is involved at the highest level of management with such questions.

Although not as quickly recognized, *methodological change* can produce the same kind of result as a *technological breakthrough*. Because of inventory theory, for example, the costs of operating a particular line of business may be substantially altered. Profit comparison might bring about a change in strategy— even in global strategy. Judging from the past, global strategies tend to be more insensitive to methodological advances than to technological ones. This may turn out to be illusory and inspired by a preconceived notion that only techno logical changes are of paramount importance. The development of high-speed

[15] Both man and machine.

electronic computers (a technological advance) plus the creation of ingenious methods that are only feasible with computers is a good example of how closely related both kinds of change can be.

Decision theorists have made little use of the notion of tactics or of global strategies as compared to local strategies. This is due to the fact that a real decision system can contain more or less detail, but *the theory is unchanged by detail. The level of a decision is important in practice and not significant to theory. It has been our purpose to emphasize the practical consideration of decision systems before explaining the theoretical basis for choosing among plans.* Above all, the production manager must never lose sight of the fact that he is dealing with a total problem. When he speaks of short-term plans he is working at the tactical level. He knows that these decisions are predicated on the fact that the right local and global strategies are being used. When the production manager is involved with long-term planning he must be aware of the possible sensitivity of his evaluations to tactical alternatives. He knows that in global issues the production department is merely one of a number of specialties which must pool their information and their viewpoints with those of the rest of the organization. Although he may treat long-and short-term problems as being essentially separate, he will merge them as required, following one of the major requirements of the systems concept.

STRATEGIC INNOVATION

The decision theorist calls an alternative action at any level of complexity and organizational involvement, a strategy. In this sense, strategic alternatives must be developed before a decision can be made. How does this get done? Specifically, knowledge of technology and methodology fuses with principles of managing, and data about the company, vendors, and competitors. Rarely will several individuals create an identical strategy even though they are all trying to achieve the same goal. Undoubtedly, this is due in part to their respective experiences which differ. But other factors also operate; one person alone can produce many alternative plans. Until we are able to understand the nature of thinking and the characteristics of creativity we shall not be in a suitable position to explain the *innovation* of strategies. The use of strategies by *imitation*, on the other hand, is not difficult to explain. In particular, for short-term repetitive situations a company desires to imitate some of its previous behaviors. The frequent alteration of strategies can be costly. When one deals with longer-term situations, it is reasonable to include strategies that are based on industry and company experience. So a degree of copying is neither unexpected nor undesirable. At the same time, opportunities for innovation always exist. If our company does not innovate perhaps our competitors will. By luck, by serendipity,[16] and by an unusual combination of circumstances, every now and

---

[16] Serendipity: The gift of finding valuable or agreeable things not sought for; a word coined by Walpole in allusion to a tale, "The Three Princes of Serendip," who in their travels were always discovering by chance or by sagacity, things they did not seek. (*Webster's New International Dictionary*, Second Edition, Unabridged.)
Note that while serendipity includes luck, which is sheer chance, it also permits sagacity to operate.

then a brilliant strategy appears. It is imperative that our decision system should be able to recognize the fact that transistors, jumbo jets, and lasers, under proper circumstances, provide feasible results and innovative advantage of being "there" first. At the same time, our decision system must be able to sort through a set of possibilities that are quite conventional and pick out the best of that lot. Perhaps the careful consideration of various strategic alternatives feeds inspiration and ultimately leads to a better set of strategic possibilities. This may be the only way in which decision theory supports the creative process.

STATES OF NATURE

The concept of strategies is not difficult to relate to the job of production management. On the other hand, the specification of states of nature is less likely to be recognized as part of the historical goal of production management. *States of nature* describe those factors in a situation that affect the expected results of a plan of action but which are fundamentally not under the manager's control. Weather, political events, and the state of the economy are three examples.[17] Appropriate to the production area are such states of nature as failure rates of equipment, price changes by vendors, invention of new materials, process technology innovations, consumer demand levels, labor turnover rates, and absenteeism. Under some circumstances, a degree of control can be exercised over such states of nature. For example, by selecting different kinds of equipment, or by utilizing preventive maintenance—both of which are strategic functions—some control over failure rates is available. Similarly, salary level—a strategic variable—can alter turnover and absenteeism, but the control is both indirect and incomplete.

A probability distribution is the only possible basis for attempting to forecast which state of nature will prevail. In other words there is an observed or estimated *likelihood* that each state should occur, say x times in one hundred trials, That likelihood is measured as the probability of occurence of the state of nature. There is a 0.50 probability that the state of nature "heads" will occur with each toss of a true coin. (We can represent this p [heads] $= 0.50$.) The meteorologist just announced a thirty percent probability of percipitation tomorrow, i.e., p (rain) $= 0.30$. Figure 3.2 illustrates a 5-state probability distribution where the state of nature, A, has only one chance in a hundred trials of appearing, i.e., $p_A = 0.01$ whereas state of nature C has the highest probability $p_C = 0.40$. The sums of these probabilities will be 1.00, indicating that one of these states of nature must occur, thus: $p_A + p_B + p_C + p_D + p_E = 1$.

We shall return to consider the importance of the decision forecast, but first, let us explore the character of states of nature such as A, B, C, D and E. How do they happen to get *noticed*? And why is it so important that they should be? To answer the second question, first: the Tacoma bridge fell because of an unrecognized state of resonance; and thousands of children were born as

---

[17] An old German proverb states: "Time, women and luck change with the blink of an eye."

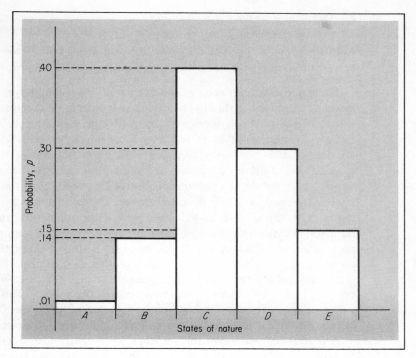

cripples because a tranquillizing drug had not been tested adequately with pregnant women.

Until recently the *tendency* in the production management field was to look the other way when noncontrollable or partially controllable variable components of states of nature appeared on the scene. This is particularly true with respect to short-term planning and in many past cases it has been justified. We should note, however, that the manager often decides how far ahead and with what detail *he should look* for reasons that may not benefit the organization. By considering it unnecessary to look far ahead, or in detail, the manager uncomplicates his immediate problems. But the question of how planning periods that are shortened for managerial convenience affect organizational performance (in the long run) remains unanswered. From the large systems point of view, it is clearly important to know when you can and when you can't ignore future states of nature.

Experience and current practice yield categories of problems that fit various classes of decision situations. *Each specific case must be judged on its own merits.* When we are able to ignore states of nature we call this class of decision problem "decision making under certainty," (abbreviate this as DMUC). Some typical examples of production systems models that are based on the assumption of certainty are:

1.   Machine loading models, that is, assigning various jobs to different machine centers; sequencing these jobs through specific facilities;

2. Determining an optimal product mix;

3. Optimal assignment of men to jobs;

4. Deriving an optimal traffic plan for shipping goods from factories to warehouses;

5. Determining optimal production runs; that is, how many units to produce at one time.

Exceptions exist for each of the five situations listed above, but the majority of cases are solved without considering uncontrollable variables, and therefore, states of nature. Even though many problems seem to fall into the DMUC category, the assumption of certainty must never be taken for granted. There are many cases in both long and short-term situations, when production management must be prepared to enumerate explicitly the relevant states of nature. Such cataloguing of the uncontrollable features of the problem may be vital to the success of the decision maker. For problems where risk or uncertainty exist, the planner must surely have some states of nature in mind. Too frequently, these are only the most probable states of nature—or what the particular individual thinks in the sense of bounded rationality are the most probable states. Unless some kind of objective, formal procedure is used, there is no opportunity for group participation in this endeavor. Oversights cannot be remedied. Differences of opinion among the members of the production management team cannot be discussed and removed. The decision function cannot be logical until *relevant* states of nature are recognized.

A partial explanation of the tendency on the part of production management to avoid consideration of noncontrollable elements arises from the fact that the recognition of states of nature can require delving into economics, politics, psychology, sociology, and anthropology. The manager with broad experience in life is more likely to be an effective enumerator of states of nature than an individual who has preferred a limited existence. That being the case, it is understandable that a mechanistic process-oriented production manager might shy away from this aspect of the decision problem. Only a well-rounded individual has the breadth of perception and the inclination to search in depth that is demanded. Yet this is not enough. *Recognizing that certain states of nature exist can be a special kind of creative act.* It is hardly desirable to wait until after a plan has been chosen to discover that something unexpected could occur and invalidate the wisdom of that plan. The special kind of creative people, who with a type of Sherlock Holmes perception, deduce the existence of important states of nature, must be found and consulted. The requisite talents of these people are large memory banks easily accessible to their deductive and inductive reasoning abilities.

States of nature are intended to describe everything that might happen *within a specific time period* that can affect the relative value of the decision that we make. Thus, depending upon the type of problem, varying amounts of rain, the phases of the moon and their effect on the tides, floods, earthquakes, and other catastrophes, war and peace, inflation, deflation, prosperity, depressions, recessions, strikes, delivery lead times, material discount schedules, government taxation, and consumer demand can play significant roles in the evaluation of a set of plans. It should be noted that as the problem moves into the realm of *tactical* decisions the diversity of states of nature tends to *decrease*. The states become more predictable than those which apply to local or global strategies.

SETTING UP THE OUTCOME MATRIX

Let us symbolically represent strategies (whether global, local, or tactical) by S_i, where i can take on any value 1 through n. Thus, if $n = 2$, we have only two strategies; if $n = 5$, we have five strategies; as long as n is given an integer value we have a finite set of strategies. There are times when an infinite set of strategic possibilities exists, that is, $n = \infty$.

We shall represent states of nature as N_j, where j can take on any values 1 through m. When $m = 1$, then each company strategy produces a unique result, i.e., DMUC. It is equivalent to saying that no matter what happens in the environment the same outcome will result. When the noncontrollable variables can combine to produce an infinite number of combinations, then $m = \infty$. Decision models apply to both finite and infinite cases for strategies and states of nature.

A particular strategy and a specific state of nature produce a unique set of results called an outcome, O_{ij}. This is the outcome for the ith strategy and the jth state of nature. We observe, measure, and record only those results that are of interest. The production management objectives determine what is of interest. For example, a product design (S_1) operating under a given set of environmental conditions (N_1) will fail after a stated number of hours; or it may require a certain amount of maintenance; it can provide a measurable level of performance satisfaction. In addition, it produces a specific volume of sales; some number of returns will be experienced; a calculable portion of plant capacity will be used up; a given amount of materials, labor, and energy will be consumed; a certain contribution to profit will be made. These typify outcomes of different kinds.

The table below presents an example of an *outcome matrix* where four designs are being evaluated under five different environmental or use conditions.

The generality of the matrix is apparent. In the symbolic form that it is written, the strategies might equally-well describe such diverse situations as the best way to lay out the plant; the choice of an optimal numbering system for a catalogue; or where to go on a vacation. Accordingly, the states of nature would describe relevant noncontrollable factors applicable to each case. For each intersection an outcome measure must be obtained that would adequately describe the objectives of the planning operation. If multiple objectives exist, multiple outcome entries would appear at each intersection.

	N_1	N_2	N_3	N_4	N_5
S_1	3	5	4	2	8
S_2	5	3	2	4	6
S_3	4	4	4	4	4
S_4	4	5	4	2	8

For this example, let us presume that the objective is to choose that design which promises the longest expected lifetime of use. The (4 × 5) matrix produces

20 cells or intersections. At each intersection an entry can be made that describes the average lifetime of the particular design, operating under the specific conditions.

Outcomes are obtained in at least three basically different ways:

1. By means of estimates and guesses;
2. By observation, laboratory experimentation, engineering data, etc.
3. By a knowledge of relationships that have previously been hypothesized (a theory).

All three of these methods are commonly used. In many cases combinations can be employed. It is worthwhile to point out that we are not discussing the means by which a choice is to be made between strategies. Outcomes relate only to what will happen when a particular strategy is used and a specific state of nature has occurred.

As might be supposed, the use of estimates and guesses is prevalent in long-range situations. Although estimates are employed in short-term planning and control systems, the other methods for obtaining outcomes are used more often. There is unknown room for error when estimates are supplied to describe outcomes. Mental operations are required which defy description simply because they are totally internalized and part of the process of cerebral behavior—about which science knows almost nothing. It would appear that a mental image is constructed from prior experiences which is as close a representation of the situation that is being analyzed as can be developed. Then, somehow, the estimator must be able to modify the complex parallel that he has built in his mind to obtain a good fit with the situation that concerns him. That is why the range of experience of an estimator is important. Unless his library of experience is great, he cannot be expected to call up from memory sufficiently good analogs.

A particular characteristic of long-range decisions is that the situations that must be examined are likely to be quite unique. Therefore, the ability to find a basic pattern begins with the assumption that one exists. Clearly, the use of decision theory is not a mechanistic endeavor It is an exercise requiring great imagination and full use of knowledge and experience. Consider the following situations for which outcome measures would have to be supplied by estimates.

EXAMPLE 1

S_i The design of a vertical takeoff (VTO) aircraft is on the drawing board. The design can develop in a number of different ways. Only some of the major characteristics have been totally fixed at this point in the process.

N_j There are competitors' plans which are in the same stage of development. None of the designs are sufficiently specified to permit a model to be built.

O_{ij} We desire to estimate the *superiority or inferiority* of each of our company's possible designs as compared to each of the possible competitive designs— in terms of maneuverability, economy of operation, economy of maintenance, cost of development, and so forth.

EXAMPLE 2

S_i We are concerned with plans to locate and develop a new plant in a foreign country. Our strategies represent the spectrum of possible locations.

N_j We have essentially no control over the political and economic conditions that exist in each country. These states of nature might be described in terms of social stability, form of government, state of the economy, and education level of workers.

O_{ij} In this example we might estimate a single outcome for each intersection, namely, profitability of the plan. (We should note, however, that multiple outcomes would result if we require outcome measures related to profitability after one year, five years and ten years.)

EXAMPLE 3

S_i Our strategic alternatives represent several possible variations of a new antibiotic. None of these have been produced—even in test quantities. This is because each variant requires substantial investments before even limited quantities can be made available.

N_j Various types of users of the drug constitute the set of states of nature. Thus, we include diabetics, children with measles, elderly people with high blood pressure, and pregnant women.

O_{ij} Multiple outcomes must be estimated for the main effects and the side effects of each drug.

EXAMPLE 4

S_i Several designs have been suggested for the control equipment required by the guidance system of a space probe.

N_j States of nature must include estimates of the conditions of outer space, including gravity level, temperature range, and so on. A proper description of each state of nature requires the specification of a particular combination of the various noncontrollable variables that would adequately describe outer space conditions.

O_{ij} The primary estimate concerns reliability. Cost in this case can be treated as a negligible factor.

EXAMPLE 5

S_i A number of different machines can be used to perform a particular task. None of the machines has ever been built. When the decision is made, the selected machine must be custom built. The construction of any one machine is costly.

N_j The company can draw upon a labor group that possesses different levels of skill. This distribution might be specified in terms of the various skill levels presently available for the company operations.

O_{ij} Outcome estimates would be multiple—and would include productivity, production rate, number of rejects, and various costs that are associated with set-up times, maintenance, and initial investment.

Each of the above decision problems is a unique system. Totally different technological backgrounds are required to provide meaningful estimates. The managerial responsibilities differ markedly as well. But with respect to the basic pattern of the decision system we find a high degree of homogeneity. Now, let us consider that an initial investment is required to bypass the estimation stage and obtain experimental evidence. Although this investment may be quite small in comparison to the eventual requirements of the plan, nevertheless, the decision to study the problem on an experimental level represents a commitment of funds. For some of the examples previously listed, estimates may be exceedingly difficult to obtain. When the test conditions are very costly, the production manager may be compelled to reach a decision on the basis of estimates. Often, he can only afford to obtain a sample of experimental outcomes for each decision alternative.

Experimental methods are more easily associated with short-term than with long-term systems. Even in a long-term situation, the decision maker can frequently find a way to hold back in the extent to which he commits himself. Thus, a pilot plant instead of a full scale plant, may be set up to test a new process. Pilot plants often cost several millions of dollars. If the full scale investment had been made, the risk might have been multiplied many times.

Similarly, a company will be forced to choose among many alternative plans for new products without having any experimental evidence available. Then, having reduced the size of the problem by use of estimates, it might be feasible to move a few selected product plans to test market before making the single big commitment. Once a prototype, or model, has been constructed for each of several strategic possibilities, it is feasible to use the laboratory for tests of physical properties such as toxicity, strength of materials, and reliability. Behavioral outcomes can be obtained by experiments where a chosen sample of individuals are involved. Such experiments can be used to evaluate consumer responses, worker attitudes and abilities, vendor relationships, and community reactions.

Quite atypical of the long-term planning situation, but reasonably familiar to control-system design is the use of theory and hypothesis. This is the third way in which outcomes can be derived, i.e., *by analytic means* such as a mathematical equation or a set of logical postulates. The existence of a theory implies that a pattern has been found which can explain the situation. Because this kind of outcome derivation applies to a large segment of production management problems, let us take a closer look at what is involved. We have to understand the nature of the relationships between strategies and states of nature.

The controllable variables of a strategy may be representable in numerical terms. The same applies to the noncontrollable variables. A mathematical function is used to relate these two kinds of variables and to derive the outcomes that they will produce. In mathematical terminology, outcomes are called *dependent variables*. The controllable and noncontrollable variables are called *independent variables*. As before, the outcomes are represented by O_{ij}, where i is the particular strategy used and j is one of the states of nature that can occur. Let us write this symbolically.

$$O_{ij} = f(S_i, N_j)$$

We read this as follows: The dependent variable O_{ij} is a function of the independent variables S_i and N_j. Now, of course, the critical question concerns the nature of the actual function. We require a specific model. For example, a hypothetical relationship might be:

$$O_{ij} = S_i N_j$$

(If S_i were a variable length and N_j a variable width, then O_{ij} is quickly recognized as a measure of area.)

Alternative product or service plans do not lend themselves easily to such kind of expression. Neither do plant location plans, process design plans, or most of the other long-term production management problems. Engineering problems, inventory problems, and scheduling problems on the other hand, do fit this pattern. That is why, as we move from the strategic to the tactical level, a great number of situations can be resolved within a mathematical framework.

DETERMINING OUTCOME RELATIONS

An important relationship found in a number of classes of production management problems is of the form:

$$O_{ij} = \frac{aN_j}{S_i} + bS_i + c \tag{1}$$

We do not have to explain what these letter symbols mean in concrete terms. We know that each unique combination of a strategy and a state of nature produces an outcome described by equation 1. a, b, and c are specified constants[18] of the system. The methodologist has developed a mathematical model to describe a particular system. He is told that the company's objective is to find a minimum (or, in some cases, a maximum) value for the O_{ij}'s. He learns that no fractional values can occur for S_i and N_j. They must take on only integer values.[19] Assume that by means of observation and experimentation, values

[18] A constant is a system factor—under no one's control—which plays a part in determining the outcome. But it is fixed and invariant for all relevant situations.
[19] Such a condition would apply to cases where S_i might be the number of secretaries to be used in a workpool and N_j the number of reports to be typed by them in a week. Fractions of secreataries would be even more distasteful than fractions of reports.

for $a, b,$ and c were determined as follows: $a = 20, b = 5$ and $c = 0$. This means that:

$$O_{ij} = \frac{20N_j}{S_i} + 5S_i \tag{2}$$

With no need for further data, the outcome matrix can be constructed, simply by substituting different values of S_i and N_j in Equation 2.

		STATES OF NATURE, N_j				
		1	2	3	4	....
	1	25	45	65	85	....
	2	20	30	40	50	....
Strategies	3	21.7	28.3	35	41.7	....
S_i	4	25	30	35	40	....
	5	29	33	37	41	....

For example, when $S_i = 4$ and $N_j = 3$:

$O_{43} = 20(3)/(4) + 5(4) + 0 = 35.$

Each value of S_i in combination with each value of N_j produces a single outcome. Real equations are often more complex, but the nature of the method used is unchanged. The table we have constructed shows only integer values specified for the strategies and states of nature. If this restriction did not hold, then the matrix would be enormously expanded because fractional values would exist for both types of independent variables.

We should note that for each column of this particular outcome matrix, a minimum value of O_{ij} occurs when a specific strategy is used. It isn't necessarily the same strategy that yields a minimum for each state of nature. Thus, the minimum value of the outcomes can occur with different levels of the strategic variable. (In the case of the third column there is a tie, so either the third or fourth strategies can be used to produce a minimum.) To underscore the real value of the approach we are discussing, it is worth noting, at this point, that Equation 1 is typically associated with inventory problems where:

S_i is the ordering policy, specifying the number of units that would be purchased with each order or made with each production run;
N_j is the demand for this item which is seldom controllable although to some extent advertising and promotion can affect it.

Three kinds of costs, $a, b,$ and c apply to this system.

Contractual arrangements permit complete knowledge of demand and, therefore, assure control over the states of nature. In this contract case (demand being fixed and known) the problem is one of DMUC. The manager, after studying the outcome matrix can pick that combination of S_i and N_j that he finds most favorable. However, as a general rule, the manager cannot control the selection of the state of nature N_j. Instead, there is a probability distribution of p_j's which describes the relative likelihoods that each demand state of nature will appear.

USING THE DECISION MATRIX

The production manager must determine how likely it is that each state of nature will occur before he can select an optimal strategy. To begin, he must be able to identify *all* of the relevant states of nature. Then, he attempts to *forecast* the likelihood of occurrence for each of the states of nature. The existence of a forecast *converts* the outcome matrix into a decision matrix.

For example, assume that the production manager is concerned with the costs of four possible production schedules (strategies 1, 2, 3, and 4). The costs relate to how a number of different items are sequenced through machine centers and how the size of the production runs that are used affect the efficiency of these operations. States of nature, N_1 through N_5) are five different patterns of demand for the various items that include all demand patterns that could possibly arise. The forecast $\{p_j\}$ for each demand pattern has also been supplied. The decision matrix might be:

Decision Matrix of Weekly Costs (In Thousands of Dollars) for Alternative Scheduling Strategies

STATE OF NATURE: N_j	N_1	N_2	N_3	N_4	N_5
FORECAST: p_j	0.1	0.2	0.1	0.4	0.2
Strategy 1	10	12	14	12	8
Strategy 2	8	12	16	14	10
Strategy 3	16	14	12	14	15
Strategy 4	14	14	14	14	14

It appears that a complex relationship describes the way in which the controllable variables interact with the noncontrollable variables to produce outcomes. In fact, this would be true; costs of overstock, carrying stock, understock, setting up equipment, and of idle facilities would be interacting with each other in a variety of ways.

Twenty different computations (or simulations) were required to produce this matrix. In addition, the forecast for the five states of nature had to be derived. The first forecasting step would be to identify the states of nature by specifying the range of demand levels that might occur for each item. In order to deal with a reasonable number of states of nature, the demand levels would be grouped into reasonable *classes*. For example, say there are three items. Demand could be equal for requiring the use of one, two, or three of them, i.e., 1/3, 1/3 and 1/3; on the other hand, unequal demands such as 1/6, 2/3, 1/6, could exist where it is most likely that two units will be needed.

Then, several questions must be answered: What is the probability of each pattern? Reference is usually made to what has happened in the past. Even so, should observations be taken over the total year, a particular season, or a particular month? Having answered such questions, and based upon forecasting skills (see pp. 122-35) a preferred set of observations would be made and grouped into a frequency distribution. Assume that fifty weeks of observations are available.[20] When sorted into their appropriate classes it might have been found that:

DEMAND PATTERN	OBSERVED FREQUENCY	PROBABILITY
N_1	5	0.1
N_2	10	0.2
N_3	5	0.1
N_4	20	0.4
N_5	10	0.2
	50	1.0

How believable are these probabilities? We can have a high degree of confidence in our forecast if we know that the system that *underlies* the appearance of the states of nature is unchanging, and that our sample provides a good description of the relative frequencies with which the states of nature occur. Both of these conditions are required. We could have a very accurate description of what happened in the past, but the past may not be indicative of the future. Assuming that the fundamental conditions from whence the states of nature are derived remain unchanged, then we say that the system is stable. Stability is a vital concept for all management activities but particularly so for production management. The relevance of stability for short-term planning is critical. It is a basic assumption. Stability is much more likely to exist for a short rather than long time interval. Statistical quality control, (pp.119-20, 317) is one of the most powerful tools that the production manager possesses because, when properly used, it can inform him of the fact that a once stable system is no longer so.

Let us now review what we know about states of nature and their associated predictions. The vital considerations are:

1. How many states of nature are relevant?
2. Are we able to identify all the relevant states of nature?
3. Can we determine the "true" frequencies of occurrence of these states of nature?
4. Are these frequencies fixed, that is, is the state of nature (causal) system stable?

---

[20] The question of what constitutes an adequate sample is more a technical issue than one which can be determined by intuition. Here, the production manager must turn to methodology. This is *not* an area for judgment to operate.

We have gathered enough information to proceed to the final step of the decision process. Strategies, states of nature, outcomes, and predictions are assembled in a decision matrix. Now what do we do?

(DMUR) DECISION MAKING UNDER RISK

If two or more states of nature are relevant; if all the relevant states of nature can be identified; and if a high degree of believability can be placed on the forecast with respect to the probability of occurrence of these states of nature, then decision making under risk (DMUR) exists. Let us say that each state N_j has a probability p_j of occurring. Then the sum of all p_j's, taking into account every possible value for j, must be one. Mathematically we write:

$$p_1 + p_2 + p_3 + p_4 + p_5 \ldots + p_j \ldots + p_m = 1.00$$

If there are five relevant states of nature, then $n = 5$.

We know that when a problem conforms to the specifications of DMUR it must be resolved by using *averages or expected values*. This satisfies the fact that over a period of time the ups and downs of the system will average out to produce the result given by the expected value. Short-term systems with repetitive behaviors readily lend themselves to this form of analysis. In fact, the *expected value criterion* is applicable for any single decision when the estimated probabilities have a high degree of believability.[21] Let us now use the information presented in the decision matrix on p. 59 to reach a decision. We proceed to obtain the expected value EV_i for each strategy, i. Because the probabilities sum to one, the expected value will be given by the formula:

$$EV_i = p_1 O_{i1} + p_2 O_{i2} + \ldots + p_j O_{ij} + \ldots p_m O_{mn}.$$

For example, $p_1 O_{11} + p_2 O_{12} + p_3 O_{13} + p_4 O_{14} + p_5 O_{15} =$ the expected value for the first strategy. Thus, we are saying that the average value of the ith strategy will be equal to the sum of the products of each row entry multiplied by its appropriate p_j. In this way we derive:

$$EV_1 = 1.0 + 2.4 + 1.4 + 4.8 + 1.6 = 11.2$$
$$EV_2 = 0.8 + 2.4 + 1.6 + 5.6 + 2.0 = 12.4$$
$$EV_3 = 1.6 + 2.8 + 1.2 + 5.6 + 3.0 = 14.2$$
$$EV_4 = 1.4 + 2.8 + 1.4 + 5.6 + 2.8 = 14.0$$

The scheduling strategy S_4 is invariant (insensitive) to demand patterns.[22] By studying the abstract decision matrix, we do not find out why this is so. We

[21] This statement may not be intuitively appealing, nevertheless, it is statistically correct for stable systems. In any case, it is seldom a matter for discussion because in situations where a decision is to be rendered only once, it is unlikely that the forecast probabilities, if they can be obtained, possess the same degree of believability that applies to repetitive decision systems.

[22] There is the same outcome for all the states of nature.

need an explanation of what constitutes S_4. Perhaps it is as simple as letting the foreman and his dispatchers determine schedule—subject to a budget limit of $14,000. Assuming that our objective is to utilize that plan which affords the lowest total weekly cost, then S_1 is the indicated choice.

It may be useful to reiterate the conditions under which the first plan can be chosen with equanimity by the production manager. First, the outcome values must be measured with relative accuracy; second, the predictions must be believable; third, the outcome measures must represent the objectives. Many short-term and some long-term production problems can be tackled within the framework of DMUR. Long-term predictions are of dubious validity, and risk methods when used in this area must be taken with a grain of salt. They can still be guides, however. Both behavioral and physical types of problems are amenable to the methods of risk analysis. In general the investigation of indeterminate physical systems produces a relatively high degree of accuracy whereas the same type of risk study represents a rather crude approach to the behavioral phenomena.

Some examples of problems that properly belong to systems of DMUR would be: machine breakdowns and process failures; frequency of rejects; distribution of delivery intervals (lead times); measures of worker productivity; and the analysis of relatively stable consumer demand systems. These same methods are not likely to be useful when an attempt is made to forecast events that will occur in a vaguely-seen future such as; long-term consumer demand for a new service; new product consumer demand (where the new product represents a substantial innovation and there is nothing comparable to utilize as a guide); speculative real estate ventures; developments in architectural style and available building materials; technological changes; stock market indices; wage rate demands and union attitudes; and the state of the economy.

DECISION MATRIX AND THE BREAK-EVEN CHART

Let us consider an example of break-even analysis where the volume of demand is not known with certainty. Although we shall use a service industry for this illustration, viz., airlines, this is a legitimate production management problem. It deals with actions required to move individuals from one place to another, in keeping with the expectations and needs of these individuals. Various alternative strategies exsist for the airlines. Suppose that Alpha Airlines would like to determine whether they should convert *from* Mach 1 jets to Mach 2 jets. The company could draw up break-even charts for the alternatives they are considering. Assume that they determine that Figure 3.3 holds for Mach 1 planes and that with the conversion to Mach 2 jet aircraft Figure 3.4 applies.

Figure 3.3 depicts the fact that the company has a lower investment in aircraft, but its variable costs of operating are relatively high. By converting to a Mach 2 jet fleet, it substantially increases the fixed costs, but succeed in lowering the variable costs. Assuming that there are no surcharges for Mach 2 jets, and that the same revenue line can be used for each situation, we then have a case where the present Mach 1 fleet achieves a lower break-even point than the proposed Mach 2 equipment. This means that the "load factor" must be higher if the conversion is approved; a result that would have great significance for the industry.

But, at the same time we note that as compensation for this poorer break-even point, the Mach 2 aircraft produce higher marginal returns on profit. This

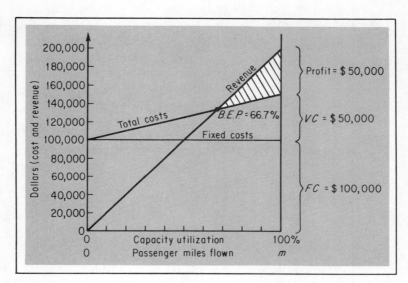

FIGURE 3-3
Break-even chart for Mach 1 jets.

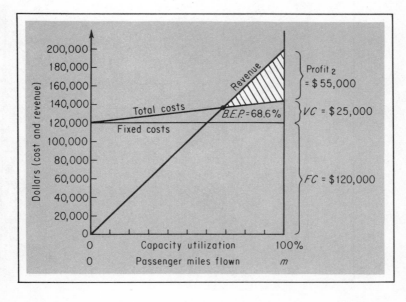

FIGURE 3-4
Break-even chart for Mach 2 jets.

means that if Alpha Airlines is able to operate at higher passenger (and cargo) loads than the break-even point—then a substantially greater profit can be obtained by converting the fleet.

Something, however, is missing from this analysis. Namely, a forecast for the various levels of consumer demand for seats and for aircraft miles to

FIGURE 3-5
Risk analysis of the break-even chart for Mach 2 aircraft.

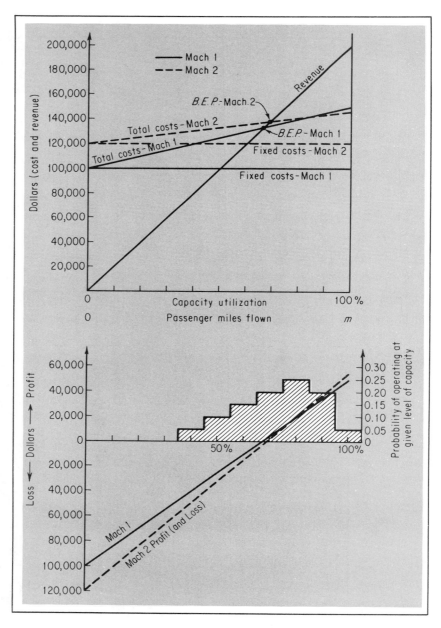

be flown is required.[23] A different amount of profit is associated with each level of consumer demand. Therefore, we can apply our probability distribution to describe the relative likelihood that different amounts of profit will be obtained.

Let us assume that a probability distribution has been determined to describe the relative likelihoods that different profit levels will be achieved. Figure 3.5 combines the two break-even charts depicted by Figures 3.3 and 3.4, and shows these accompanied by a probability distribution. It should be noted that the assumption is made that demand probabilities are independent of the type of plane that is flown—an assumption that may not stand up to reality.

As in all probability distributions, the sum of the probabilities equals one (see pp. 124–30). We calculate the expected value of this irregular distribution to be equal to a load factor of about 73 per cent, i.e., $0.05(40\%) + 0.10(50\%) + 0.15(60\%) + 0.20(70\%) + 0.25(80\%) + 0.20(90\%) + 0.05(100\%) = 73\%$. A distribution such as this can be derived when necessary strictly by executive judgment.

Having this information on hand we can now multiply each of the profit levels (including negative profit) by the probability that it will occur. We do this for both alternatives. Thereby, we derive an average or *expected profit* for both cases that we are investigating. We assume that the outcomes and probablities in the matrix below have been determined in such a way as to endow them with a relatively high degree of believability.

In this and the following matrix, let:

p_K = Probability of $K\%$ utilization
N_K = Percent of capacity utilized
S_1 = Mach 1 planes in the air fleet
S_2 = Mach 2 planes in the air fleet

Outcomes (Measured in Thousands of Dollars)

p_K	0	0	0	0	.05	.10	.15	.20	.25	.20	.05	
N_K	N_0	$N_{.10}$	$N_{.20}$	$N_{.30}$	$N_{.40}$	$N_{.50}$	$N_{.60}$	$N_{.70}$	$N_{.80}$	$N_{.90}$	$N_{1.00}$	EV_i
S_1	−100	− 85.0	−70	−55	−40	−25	−10	+5	+20	+35	+50	+9.50
S_2	−120	−102.5	−85	−67.5	−50	−32.5	−15	+2.5	+20	+37.5	+55	+7.75

Obtaining the expected value, we discover that Mach 1 aircraft will produce a higher level of profitability than Mach 2 aircraft. The method of DMUR obviates the need for any discussion or consideration of the break-even point or the marginal returns of profit. This is the most meaningful solution to our problem.

To further illustrate the nature of this method and the way in which the decision model overrides the limited sense of the break-even chart when used

[23] Equivalent to an estimate of sales volume and, thereby, related to production capacity.

in its conventional form, let us examine the effect of using a different probability distribution where all other values remain the same. The appropriate matrix is:

Outcomes (Measured in Thousands of Dollars)

p_K	0	0	0	0	0	0	0	.20	.25	.20	.35	
N_K	N_0	$N_{.10}$	$N_{.20}$	$N_{.30}$	$N_{.40}$	$N_{.50}$	$N_{.60}$	$N_{.70}$	$N_{.80}$	$N_{.90}$	$N_{1.00}$	EV_i
S_1	−100	− 85	−70	−55	−40	−25	−10	+ 5	+20	+35	+50	+30.50
S_2	−120	−102.5	−85	−67.5	−50	−32.5	−15	+2.5	+20	+37.5	+55	+32.25

	N_j
S_1	O_1
S_2	O_2
S_3	O_3
S_4	O_4
S_5	O_5
S_6	O_6
S_7	O_7
S_8	O_8
S_9	O_9
S_{10}	O_{10}
S_{11}	O_{11}
S_{12}	O_{12}
S_{13}	O_{13}
S_{14}	O_{14}
S_{15}	O_{15}
S_{16}	O_{16}
S_{17}	O_{17}
S_{18}	O_{18}
S_{19}	O_{19}
S_{20}	O_{20}
S_{21}	O_{21}
S_{22}	O_{22}
S_{23}	O_{23}
S_{24}	O_{24}
S_{25}	O_{25}
S_{26}	O_{26}
S_{27}	O_{27}

Our result has shifted. Preference now goes to Mach 2 aircraft. This is true in spite of the fact that the break-even points associated with both types of planes remain unchanged. We recognize that the increased marginal return rate of the Mach 2 planes has overwhelmed the break-even point advantage to be gained from the Mach 1 type aircraft. The reason for this is that the second probability distribution is more skewed to the right than the first one.

By following this procedure; that is, by using a probability distribution—we have removed the need for a break-even point analysis. This is true because fundamental to the entire concept of the break-even point is the fact that all decision makers have in mind an estimate of the likelihood that the company will operate below or above that point. Without this estimate in mind, the break-even point is meaningless. By using a statistical approach we have succeeded in relating the two factors that previously were treated as separate components; namely, the position of the break-even point and the marginal rates of return. Our method has merged them into a single over-all decision matrix.

(DMUC) DECISION MAKING UNDER CERTAINTY

If only *one state of nature* is relevant, then we have DMUC. The matrix running along the side of this page is a typical, albeit limited, example. When such a column contains millions or billions of entries, it is easy to see why methodology would be required to seek and find a particular kind of value. We search through such enormous columns of outcomes for many production management problems. Depending upon our objective, we locate that outcome or those outcomes which most closely fit the bill. The objective might be to maximize profit, then the plan *i*, producing the largest value of O_i will be chosen. If the objective was to minimize cost, then the reverse kind of search would be used. It is also quite possible that some specified intermediate value is wanted. The strategy coming closest to satisfying this requirement will be chosen. The only reason that DMUC can present a problem is the size of the search required. Then, searching time and the expense of deriving all the necessary outcomes by brute force can be prohibitive.

Now, let us consider several points that have been left unanswered from prior discussion. It will be recalled that production management, in particular, deals with tactical problems. Furthermore, as we move from strategies to tactics, the number of variants increases rapidly. *Consequently, whoever must deal with problems at the tactical level must be prepared to handle a great number of variants.* These are typically short-term decisions. They tend to be repeated many times over. Losses sustained by not getting the best possible plan are minor for any one decision. But when repeated over and over again, such losses can mount up to very sizeable sums of money. Therefore, it is reasonable for such cases that substantial refinement be utilized in the enumeration of possible plans. That is why production management decisions, more than those of any other area, must deal with thousands of variants, and why the character of the *search process* is so important to production managers.

The number of ways that jobs can be scheduled through a large plant are usually of the same order of magnitude as the number of electrons in the universe. Yet this kind of decision must be made daily or weekly. A reasonably good plan could be found by a Gantt layout chart[24] which is a trial and error type method. Linear programming (LP)[25] provides an analytical model for efficient search under certain circumstances. When employed in conjunction with a computer, the LP model can be expected to quickly locate the theoretically *optimal* plan for the conditions that are stated. In practice, the actual choice may differ somewhat from the theoretically optimal plan simply because not all the relevant constraints are satisfactorily stated, or because the assumptions inherent in the model may not be perfectly fulfilled by reality.

In this book we shall encounter a number of methodological techniques that are useful for resolving problems of DMUC. But of great importance is the warning: We can only use linear programming or any other search technique that assumes the single state when the single state is a fair assumption.[26] When probability distributions exist but are ignored, then expected values often are used as if they were the outcome values for DMUC. This can lead to incorrect assumptions about the system. If the single-state assumption is arrived at by cutting corners and ignoring or overlooking essential states of nature, then the manager's degree of belief in the solution will be quite low, . . . often to the point of "why bother with the study?"

(DMUU) DECISION MAKING UNDER UNCERTAINTY

The third major class of decision problems concerns situations that cannot be categorized as DMUC or DMUR. With decision making under uncertainty, we can only expect to enumerate a finite number of states of nature. The char-

---

[24] See pp. 161, 231.
[25] We discuss LP in some detail on pp. 187–194.
[26] DMUC can be viewed as a special case of DMUR, where the probabilities of all the states of nature, except one, would be zero.

acter of uncertainty is associated with the fact that we then acknowledge a total inability to estimate the likelihood of occurrence for each of these states of nature. In other words, we have no way of assigning the p_j values. (This is entirely different from not being able to name the relevant states of nature.)

Many methods (quite philosophical) exist for treating problems of uncertainty. A great deal of decision theory is in fact concerned with this one particular aspect of decision making. Practically speaking, however, it is rare (if ever) that a manager will accept the idea that he is completely uncertain. As a result, it is more reasonable to treat all problems having more than one state of nature as belonging to the class of DMUR problems. But, we must recognize that they occur with varying levels of believability, according to the manager's faith in his own estimates for the values of the p_j.[27]

PROBLEMS

1   Why is it particularly useful for production management to differentiate between decision making under certainty, risk and uncertainty?

2   What is the significance of a global strategy as compared to a local strategy?

3   It has been suggested that a methodological discovery can have as marked an effect on the system as a technological breakthrough. Discuss this idea from the point of view of determining whether there is any precedent for the statement.

4   Why is it important to differentiate between analysis and synthesis?

5   Solve the decision problem posed on p. 53 (where the objective is to choose that design which promises to maximize the expected life of the product), under the following probability conditions:

Values of p_j

	N_1	N_2	N_3	N_4	N_5
Condition 1	0	1.00	0	0	0
Condition 2	0.20	0.30	0.50	0	0
Condition 3	0	0	0.30	0.30	0.40
Condition 4	0.20	0.20	0.20	0.20	0.20

Comment on the character of these various conditions and their effects on the results.

6   Develop the appropriate decision matrix for each of the problems below. This requires describing specific strategies and relevant states of nature. Load the cells of the matrix with reasonable estimates for the outcomes. Assign appropriate probabilities. Solve the problem that you have designed. The generality of the decision matrix approach for resolving problems should be evident from the ubiquitousness of these situations.

I   Strategies: A number of different equipment selection plans
States of nature: Equipment failure rates
        Outcomes: Measures of downtime
        Objective: Minimize downtime

[27] One of the most appealing approaches to DMUU is based on the principle of insufficient reason. It states that since there is no reason to believe that one state is more likely to occur than any other, they should all be treated as having equal p_j's. Thus, if there are five states of nature, we would have $p_1 = p_2 = p_3 = p_4 = p_5 = 1/5$.

II	Strategies:	Various plant layout arrangements
	States of nature:	Varying demand levels for different items in the company's product mix
	Outcomes:	Measures of bottlenecks and delay
	Objective:	Minimize delay

III Strategies: Different production materials, for example, various metals versus various plastics
States of nature: Varying costs for these materials and different levels of consumer demand
Outcomes: Profit measures
Objective: Maximize profit

IV Strategies: Varying number of repairmen
States of nature: Probabilities of machine breakdowns
Outcomes: Measures of the cost of downtime
Objective: Minimize cost

V Strategies: Different computer systems
States of nature: Varying data loads on the department
Outcomes: Measures of the age of information
Objective: Minimize age of information in the system

VI Strategies: Different numbers of toll booths
States of nature: Varying numbers of arrivals
Outcomes: Measures of customer waiting time
Objective: Minimize customer waiting time

VII Strategies: Various arrangements of supermarket checkout counters
States of nature: Number of customers with small and large orders that come into the store
Outcomes: Measures of idle time of checkout clerks and customer waiting time
Objective: Minimize total cost of checkout clerks idle time and waiting time of customers

VIII Strategies: Different catalogue numbering systems
States of nature: Various users of the catalogue
Outcomes: Measure of errors in ordering
Objective: Minimize ordering errors

7 Explain the statement: the problem of achieving synthesis is too complex to permit the exclusive use of judgment. It is too large for a purely methodological treatment. Properly used, the combination of objective and subjective treatments can be synergistic. (Synergistic means that the total effect of the system is greater than the sum of the individual effects of the parts of the system operating independently.)

references

CHURCHMAN, C. WEST, *Prediction and Optimal Decision.* Englewood Cliffs, N. J.: Prentice-Hall, Inc., 1961.

——, *Theory of Experimental Inference.* New York: The Macmillan Company, 1948.

HOUGH, LOUIS, *Modern Research for Administrative Decisions.* Englewood Cliffs, N.J.: Prentice-Hall, Inc., 1970.

HOWELL, JAMES E., and DANIEL TEICHROEW, *Mathematical Analysis for Business Decisions,* 2nd ed. Homewood, Ill.: Richard D. Irwin, Inc., 1971.

KAUFMANN, A., *The Science of Decision-Making.* New York: McGraw-Hill Book Company, 1968.

LUCE, R. DUNCAN, and HOWARD RAIFFA, *Games and Decision.* New York: John Wiley & Sons, Inc., 1958.

MILLER, D. W. and MARTIN K. STARR, *Executive Decisions and Operations Research,* 2nd ed. Englewood Cliffs, N.J.: Prentice-Hall, Inc., 1969.

SCHLAIFER, R. ROBERT, *Analysis of Decisions Under Uncertainty.* New York: McGraw-Hill Book Company, 1967.

SHULL, F. A., Jr., A. L. DELBECQ and L. L. CUMMINGS, *Organizational Decision Making.* New York: McGraw-Hill Book Company, 1967.

SIMON, H. A., *The New Science of Management Decision.* New York: Harper & Row, Publishers, 1960.

STARR, MARTIN K., *Product Design and Decision Theory.* Englewood Cliffs, N.J.: Prentice-Hall, Inc., 1963.

WALD, A., *Statistical Decision Functions.* New York: John Wiley & Sons, Inc., 1950.

WASSERMAN, PAUL, with FRED S. SILANDER, *Decision-Making, An Annotated Bibliography.* Ithaca, New York: Cornell University Graduate School of Business and Public Administration, 1958.

project-
planning
models

Formerly, we distinguished between the design of the production system and
its operation. Project planning which includes designing and implementation of
that design usually requires a good deal of time. In contrast, short-interval
control models apply to operations.

PROJECT PLANNING

Methodology is one of the means to manage technological systems. The
other means are judgment, intuition, and know-how. There is a blend; each
organizational area having its own characteristic mixture, depending upon the
stage of development of its methodology. Obviously, at every methodological
level some human participation is required. The amount of judgmental participation is highest in the case of long-planning intervals.

As the planning interval decreases, the precision of predictions improves
markedly. Figure 4.1 illustrates the way in which the believability of a prediction deteriorates as the planning interval increases. Decision-making methods
can be used for long-term situations, *but* the degree of belief in the results is

often poor. When decision-making methodology is employed for long-term planning, it means something different to management than when it is being used to resolve short-term problems.

Long-term planning is required to start any new enterprise. It must also treat diversification. An existing enterprise will continually assess its productive position with respect to organization, facilities, process, product line, distribution system, technology, and methodology. Whether starting out from scratch or encouraging the growth and the diversification of an existent organization,

FIGURE 4-1
A prediction regarding the value of x after an interval of time Δt is to be made. If the degree of belief in the prediction is to remain constant, then the limits between which x might lie will expand at an accelerating rate.

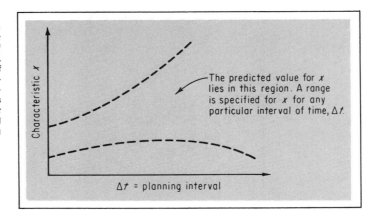

it is only through systems planning that an acceptable long-range synthesis can be achieved. The following basic steps are involved:

1. A planning group is formed.
2. Objectives are stated.
3. Enumerate *every activity* that must be followed to achieve the objectives.
4. Sequence the activities listed above.
5. Allocate such resources as materials, equipment, and manpower to each of the activities on a first-pass basis, subject to later revision.
6. Estimate the time and cost required to accomplish each activity and to achieve the objectives.
7. Revise the plan until an acceptable total plan is evolved.
8. Develop an organization that can implement, monitor, and control the plan.[1]

Note that Step 3 requires that the plan be stated in sufficient detail to capture all of the essentials. For example, it may be necessary to consider the research and development (R&D) phase for new product and service development, questions of patentability, design of the environment, and plant selection, layout, and design. A *project* consists of strategies and tactics specified in such a way that all critical considerations can be scrutinized objectively.

---

[1] It should be noted that this is a different kind of control operation than is required for repetitive situations, such as inventory, quality, and schedule control.

DEGREE OF REPETITION

Project decisions result in actions that are almost never repeated under similar circumstances. Thus, the decision to move a plant to a new geographic area is a major commitment that is best described as a *project*. As each step is accomplished or a stage completed, it is unlikely to be repeated ever again in the same form. Thus, developing the first spaceship bound for Alpha Centauri is a project, long-term and nonrepetitive. Contrast this with the decision to place an order for materials that are used to make a high-volume production item. Such ordering decisions are made repeatedly. Similarly, scheduling jobs on various machines is a daily or weekly proposition for many companies.

DEGREE OF REVERSIBILITY

By the very nature of long-term problems, large investments are required. This means that a mistake can be serious. A company can be competitively crippled or rendered bankrupt. There exist *ruin thresholds* in long-term planning situations where a single decision can push the company across a threshold from which there is no return. Short-cycle decisions, if repeated over and over again, can also result in ruin when the decision repeatedly imposes even a small penalty on the company. But generally, *corrective action* can be taken so that a new and better decision is substituted for the old one. If it is noticed that rejects, customer returns, back orders, machine-idle time, set-up costs, or absenteeism are increasing, steps can be taken to correct these weaknesses long before any one-way doors are passed. Nonreversibility characterizes long-term planning distinguishing it from short-term cases.

We can see why the type of methodology employed for projects as compared to repetitive operations would be different. Complex methodology lends itself to repetitive decision situations. This is true because repetition in a reasonably stable system provides historical evidence that can be used for forecasting future events. Also, gradual changes can be introduced because penalties accumulate over a period of time. Experience and judgment are more likely to be effective than formal methodologies in the long-term situation where problems tend to be unique and lacking in specific precedence. Nevertheless, because it is so important, useful methodology has been developed to assist in project management. What can such methodology do?

1. It can categorize and summarize a mass of information so that it is as useful as possible to the project manager.
2. It can organize problem areas, making all relevant variables explicit so that administrators can communicate with each other about the project.
3. It can produce long-term predictions, and estimates of their applicability.
4. It can structure projects, so that details will not be forgotten; so that actions will be taken in appropriate sequence; intelligent allocations of resources will be made, and; control over the development of the project will be insured.

5. Alternative strategies can be *tested* by various methods to determine how sensitive a particular strategy is to the things that competitors might do as well as to the relative accuracy of predictions and estimates.

Project decisions are frequently founded upon nothing more than opinion. If differences of opinion exist, the *reasons* for the differences are vital. The reasons may be expressible only in qualitative terms. This in no way permits an executive group to dismiss differences of opinion. Reasons for disagreements about complex project decisions are exceedingly difficult to uncover. Almost without exception, systematic explication is an absolute necessity. Belief in predictions will tend to be of a low order. Nevertheless, they can be useful as a guide. Two considerations, especially applicable to long-term planning situations can be derived when the degree of belief in predictions is low.

First: there should be a preference for decisions which promise greater flexibility. That is, other things being equal, decisions that permit corrective actions to be taken at a future date are preferred to decisions that cannot be changed once they are made. A strategy that can produce a catastrophic outcome—although with very small likelihood—will be avoided, even though it has a higher profit expectation. This is because the penalty for irreversibility is likely to outweigh simple profit considerations. Second: there is a preference for decisions that promise a reasonably good expected outcome, across a broad spectrum of "likely" states of nature; as compared to decisions that produce exceptionally good expected outcomes with states of nature that are unlikely to occur.

SENSITIVITY ANALYSIS

At this point let us momentarily pause to consider the nature of sensitivity analysis. It is particularly important in situations where forecasts are applied to project planning. To illustrate what is involved, let us examine the various outcomes estimated for Project A. (See Figure 4.2, also pp. 128–30.)

PROJECT A PAYOFFS	PROBABILITY
−2	0.1
−1	0.1
0	0.1
+1	0.2
+2	0.2
+3	0.3
sum =	1.0

The expected payoff in this case is: $-0.2\ -0.1\ +0\ +0.2\ +0.4\ +0.9 = +1.2$. Assume that the forecast carries sufficient believability to permit the utilization of the methods of DMUR, even though the interval of time for which these estimates apply may be five years or more in the future. In reality, the degree of belief in such estimates may be quite low.

Then, as an alternative procedure, the manager could supply *ranges* for the estimates. It is certainly easier to state that a forecasted likelihood might fall between two values than to specify that it is exactly some given number. Using these ranges, we can begin to utilize a procedure that is identifiable as a form of sensitivity testing. A number of *"what if . . . "* questions can be asked. For example, what if the probability of an outcome of -2 is really 0.15? One answer can be given immediately, namely, some other probability (or probabilities) must be decreased. Try for example, the contention that the probability of a zero payoff is only 0.05. The expected reward would change to $+1.1$. That is the answer to the "what if" question that was asked. Proceeding in this manner, by using range estimates for the probabilities, many variations can be developed on the basic theme. Ordinarily, there would be a great number of configurations. However, if the range estimates are very narrow, this would act as a damper on the proliferation of possibly significant distributional forms.

The *key* to sensitivity analysis is that some changes in the distribution will not affect the final decision whereas others will. If the indicated choice shifts when only minor changes are made in the probability distribution, then we can say that the system is sensitive. On the other hand, if the decision is not altered as a result of distributional changes—and particularly when extreme values of the ranges are used—then we can say that the system is insensitive or invariant to errors of estimation. It will be remembered that the solution shifted in Chapter 3 when the demand probability distribution was altered, from Mach 1 to Mach 2 aircraft. How often would such shifts be expected to occur for a reasonable range of probability values?

If the production manager cannot supply narrow probability ranges (and this will frequently be the case for project planning) then he must utilize other methods for resolving his problem.[2] Only in a system where one particular strategy is superior to all other strategies with respect to every possible state of nature, does the question of sensitivity cease to be a problem.

Sensitivity estimates can be applied not only to forecasts, but to outcomes, as well. When properly used, sensitivity analysis represents an important planning technique. However, the manager must thoroughly understand the nature of sensitivity testing before he can call upon it for assistance. The goodness or believability of numbers that are used to study and resolve a problem will always constitute a primary consideration. A methodologist may not be conscious of the fact that believability is of paramount importance to the manager; or granted that he is, it is unlikely that he will be able to assess the critical areas for sensitivity analysis without clear guidance. Unless sensitivity considerations are consciously included in the system study, management may not be willing to accept the results obtained for a given problem, even though diligent and rigorous work was involved in deriving them.

It is always important to evaluate estimates, observations, and theoretically

---

[2] As the ranges spread, the problem approaches the case of decision making under uncertainty (see pp. 67–68).

derived quantities. We use sensitivity testing whenever believability is a major concern. Ultimately, it is the production manager's responsibility to objectively assess the believability of all the elements entering into a problem's solution and, thereby, he can determine intuitively the value or worth of that solution.

UTILITY TRANSFORMS

Still another factor must be considered before we are able to understand planning models. Figure 4.2 shows the payoffs that can be obtained from the two projects, A and B. The payoff scale is linear. That is, an equal interval separates each million dollars of reward or penalty. Stated another way, a four million dollar loss is considered to be exactly twice as much of a penalty as a two million dollar loss. Is this realistic? If not, what is wrong?

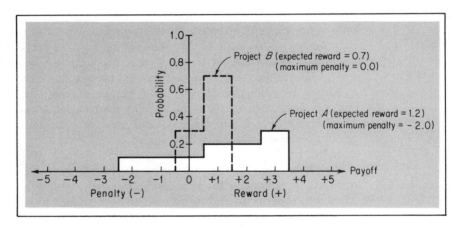

FIGURE 4-2
Two projects compared on a linear scale. Project A is preferred to Project B on the basis of expected reward. B is preferred to A on the basis of avoiding maximum penalty.

At least two different things are awry. Let us take the penalty side of the payoff scale first. Suppose that project A is chosen. Then a loss of up to two million dollars can occur. But what if the company will be bankrupt if it experiences a loss greater than one million dollars? The importance of the penalty changes at the threshold level of one million dollars. A moment of thought tells us that the undesirability of negative reward increases at an accelerating rate as the ruin threshold is approached. Major losses in one area can curtail other profitable activities and destroy reserves that permit flexibility. The company becomes vulnerable to the capriciousness and whims of nature's chance-cause systems. Using a linear scale and the expected value criterion, the loss of four million dollars would be totally offset by a gain of four million dollars if their respective probabilities were held to be equal. The exact same result would occur if the off-setting losses and gains were only fifty dollars. This is not sensible.

Now let us consider the direction of positive reward on the scale. First, compare a one million dollar gain with a two million dollar gain; then compare a fifty million dollar gain with a fifty-one million dollar gain. In both cases the superior reward is greater by one million dollars. But how about percentage improvement? We have:

$$\frac{2-1}{1}(100) = 100\% \tag{1}$$

$$\frac{51-50}{50}(100) = 2\% \tag{2}$$

Similarly, if the numbers were 100 and 101, the change would represent only a one percent improvement. The difference between one billion dollars plus one million dollars and one billion straight is almost negligible. In estimating the value of rewards there is a decelerating effect for a fixed increment of reward as it is added to increasing levels of reward.

One of the implications of what we are saying is that *companies of different sizes must necessarily evaluate payoffs in uniquely different ways.* A company with assets of five million will perceive a reward of one million dollars as being a substantial gain, viz., (100) (6 — 5)/5 = 20.0 percent. But a company capitalized at five hundred million might consider such a reward to be relatively insignificant, viz., (100) (501 — 500)/500 = 0.20 percent.[3]
It should be emphasized that the transformation of outcomes to utilities is a critical management function. *What is good for a large company might spell ruin for a small one.* This vital consideration is frequently overlooked. Responsibility for providing appropriate utilities is, to a great extent, in the project manager's hands because his decisions affect a substantial portion of the organization's assets.

Presume that the manager's utilities for the various payoffs in Figure 4.2 are for Project A:

(I)	(II)	(III)	
PAYOFF	UTILITY TRANSFORM OF PAYOFF	PROBABILITY	(II) × (III)
+3	0.63	0.30	0.189
+2	0.47	0.20	0.094
+1	0.26	0.20	0.052
0	0.00	0.10	0.000
−1	−0.37	0.10	−0.037
−2	−1.20	0.10	−0.120
		1.00	+0.178 = Expected Utility

[3] These effects were noted by Daniel Bernouilli, a Swiss mathematician in 1730.

and for Project B:

(I)	(II)	(III)	
PAYOFF	UTILITY TRANSFORM OF PAYOFF	PROBABILITY	(II) × (III)
+1	0.26	0.70	0.182
0	0.00	0.30	0.000
		1.00	+0.182 = Expected Utility

The utility transform (of I to II) is the project manager's unique assessment of how he values each payoff level. We should note that his expected utility for Project A is smaller than for Project B. Therefore, Project B will be chosen. However, without the utility transform, the expected reward of Project A (+1.2) is greater than that of Project B (+0.7), so Project A would be selected. This decision is sensitive to the manager's utility transformation. It would not be sensitive to many other kinds of transforms.

THE GANTT PROJECT PLANNING CHART

Project planning is a critical function. Serious errors can lead to the destruction of the enterprise. It is, therefore, not surprising that a great deal of both theoretical and practical effort has been expended to define and develop methods that can adequately deal with the kinds of problem involved in these potential ruin situations.

In the early 1900's, an objective method for project planning was developed known as Gantt Project Planning.[4] The problems which Gantt and production people of his time were faced with had considerably less complexity than the problems which we presently encounter. For his time and situation, the Gantt method was sufficient. In our present-day world, Gantt's trial and error method provides a means of organizing our thinking, but it does not satisfy the need for approaching optimality in complex situations where serious suboptimization can produce crises. Furthermore, Gantt's method requires great amounts of computational time to handle problems of even an average level of complexity. Except for relatively small operations, the Gantt project planning approach is passé. But, it has not been forgotten because the methods which Gantt developed form the fundamental basis for far more elaborate computer-driven planning programs. A great number of computerized, project planning models have become available in recent years. Although they are embryonic in terms of their potential development, nevertheless, they are far superior to the older methods

[4] See Henry L. Gantt, pp. 429-30.

FIGURE 4-3
A Gantt project plan-
ning chart.

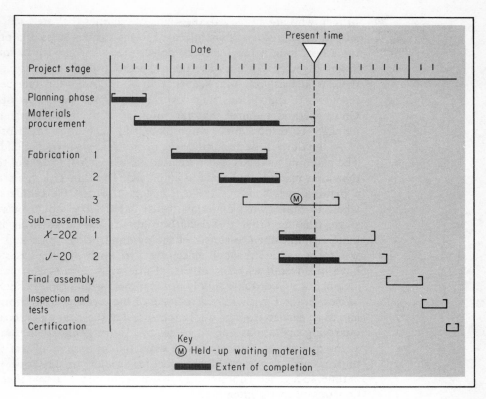

which can no longer satisfy our needs. The fundamentals of these new project planning models will be discussed in the next section. First, however, let
us examine the Gantt approach to project planning.

Figure 4.3 pictures a Gantt Project Planning Chart.[5] The intentions of the
project planner are two-fold. First, to set down—a priori—the steps, stages,
or phases of work that must be followed in order to bring to fruition a non-
repeating project system. Second, to monitor the way in which the steps of
the plan are being carried through, that is, to *track the status* of the project over
a period of time. These two purposes permeate all planning. They can be
translated as: (1) making of the plan; and (2) carrying the plan to completion.

Implicit, however, is a third intention or purpose. In all projects there are
technological sequences which constrain the arrangement of steps with which
a project shall be accomplished. Sometimes (rarely) there is no constraint whatever on the arrangement to be used. Usually, the sequence of steps to be taken
will be determined at the discretion of the project planner who takes into account
the technological restrictions. From the set of all possible arrangements we
would like to find the best arrangement. Furthermore, it is quite apparent that
certain steps can be accomplished faster or slower, depending upon the number

[5] Also, see Figure 4.8.

of men who are employed, the kinds of facilities that are used, and so on. The way in which resources are allocated to the various steps of a project will determine how long it takes to accomplish each phase and how much it will cost. Taken together, both of these points spell out the fact that for any given project there is at least one best sequence to be followed and one best allocation of resources to the various stages with respect to a specific set of objectives. The Gantt method requires that the intuition and good judgment of the project manager be responsible for approximating such an optimal project plan.

At the time of the building of the *pyramids* some foresight had to be exercised. The planning methods that were used have been lost to us, but there is no doubt that some planning method was employed. To begin with, the project of building a pyramid was conceived. Then, in logical order, the builders had to specify where to build, what materials to use, what labor would be required at each stage, (that is, labor to select the site, to clear it, to bring in the necessary materials, and then to construct the pyramid.) If the plan that was determined was to be carried through efficiently, then each of the phases would properly have to dovetail with the others. If not, at various stages materials might be lacking, or an adequate supply of manpower would be missing. From the point of view of the Egyptians, the logistics of the problem were enormous. Materials had to be carried from great distances, and at these far away locations individual quarrying operations had to be set up. Work gangs, therefore, were required at the quarries to transport these giant blocks and, finally, at the building site to construct the pyramid. It is evident that many of these operations co-existed in time, so a general administration was required to see to it that the total operation was properly integrated.

Now the steps to build a pyramid represent a good example of the kind of elements that are involved in present-day projects. But the design, construction and carrythrough of an Apollo moon shot, or the development of a large manufacturing system require coordination and dovetailing to a much greater degree. In the first place, many more factors are involved and secondly, time losses are now of extreme importance. It is true that if the construction teams on the site of the pyramids were not supplied with sufficient building materials, a penalty was suffered. Enormous quantities of food had to be transported to these locations in order to keep the indentured slaves alive. This effort taxed the resources of the Egyptian kingdoms. However, there was no competition, no legal contracts with penalties to be paid if a job was not completed at a stated time, and no best time to get into orbit.

The Gantt Project Planning Chart might have been able to help the pyramid builders, but it cannot succeed in our present complex, project-planning efforts. Because of competitive factors, we recognize that the ability to reach the marketplace as quickly as possible with a new product or service can be a major influence on its success or failure. Excessive planning periods pose the threat of producing an obsolete product if project development takes too long. In the aircraft industry and in the computer field, delay in carrying out a major plan can produce catastrophic results.

We see from Figure 4.3 that the project manager begins by listing the required stages or jobs that are the component building blocks of the project.

These must be sequenced in some sensible order if the project is to be completed. The first of these stages is generally a mental planning process which we have called the planning phase. Therefore, the construction of the chart itself represents a preplan. In the actual planning phase, adjustments are made to the basic set of steps; the order in which they are to be used; the allocation of resources to each step; and the estimated times for completing each job. As a general rule, we require materials, plant, facilities, labor, power, and so forth. This is the big plan. It is *the* long-range plan. Once these steps have been completed, the planning process moves on to the detailed level of utilizing resources and facilities in order to produce the chosen end result. Elapsed time to complete all the steps is usually considered to be of major consequence.

That is where the second purpose of the Gantt Chart appears. Running along the top of the chart is a *time scale*. This time scale can be general, in the sense that it represents a sequence of days, or weeks, or months. On the other hand, calendar dates can be associated with the time scale so that it represents particular points in time. The former approach is useful when estimates of total time involved are required and when the starting point in real time is unknown. For example, assume that capital has to be raised to finance the project, but no one can estimate when the necessary monetary assets will be acquired. All plans will be launched at the completion of this stage, but because the completion date of that stage cannot be set, only an abstract time plan can be constructed.

Usually, estimates are supplied for all steps in the process. Such estimates are based upon some form of commitment to a particular pattern for the allocation of resources. When a starting date is specified, calendar time can be utilized for the time scale. When actual or real time is used, then it is very convenient to use the project plan as a check or control over what is happening so that revisions in the basic plans can be developed as required. There are penalties for delays occurring as a result of poor integration of the planning elements. We cannot afford to have a press shop staffed and waiting with all the necessary tools and dies at their disposal while the research laboratory is still determining the proper materials to be used. Opportunity costs, such as these exemplify, can occur in many different ways in the project planning cycle. The project manager can do a lot to reduce such opportunity costs.

The left-hand column listing all the stages is, in fact, the *operational routine* that is required for the design of our system.[6] It is the system's plan. If we make a mistake here we may cost ourselves out of business. It is also essential to bear in mind that a competitor may have a system plan very similar to ours —or destructive to ours. If his is without error; or if he meets his objectives on time and we do not; or if he is able to achieve the completion of various steps in less time than it takes us; or if he is a better project planner than we are and finds ways to run various steps in parallel while we sequence them, it is quite likely that we will suffer many penalties as a result of our inadequacies. Figure 4.3 indicates that a number of the steps can be operating simultaneously.

---

[6] This may be the construction of a building, the development of a new product, or the publication of a book, magazine, or catalogue.

To recognize this fact, observe the number of project steps that are intersected simultaneously by any given time line. Sometimes a fraction of a job must be completed before the next step can begin. Often, stages can begin simultaneously. The constraints are generally technological, so it would not be strange if, in a particular case, two-thirds of one prior stage and one-eighth of another prior stage must be completed before a third stage can be started.

This is all in the plan, but what about the *actuality*? The darkened portion of each planning box represents the per cent completion of each phase at a particular point in time designated by the time arrow. With succeeding days, the dark portion is lengthened until at completion the box is filled. Thus, we have a running record of accomplishments. But the true course of projects never runs perfectly smoothly. Unexpected situations arise and difficulties may delay certain phases of the project. Typically, while some things lag, others spurt and so some phases are ahead of schedule; others are behind. Specifying the stages of a project and the estimated times is an a priori operation. But it is also an on-going operation. Constant refinement with new data is called for. Regular review is needed in order to adjust and update the running record of accomplishment. In rare instances an entirely new project sequence must be developed because of difficulties that arise.

It will be noted that in Figure 4.3 the arrow appears on the second day of fourth week. Probably, that arrow is moved along on a daily basis. In effect saying, this is today. We look down at each of the stages and see that the dark bars indicate how much of the job has been completed. Some stages lag; others are ahead of schedule. One has not even begun (Fabrication 3) although according to plan it should have.

We have now reviewed all the elements of project-planning in terms of the Gantt Chart. It is an effective way of keeping track of what has happened in terms of what we thought should have happened. It is also a suitable control and accounting device. But what is lacking is that there is no suitable way of using the Gantt Chart to determine how resources might have been allocated in a superior fashion. For example, if manpower had been shifted from stage x to stage y, it might have been possible to accomplish stage x in a shorter period of time. Correspondingly, stage y would have taken longer. Is this better? Another possibility would be to plan certain delays in the system in order to minimize the overall delay. Also, we have not succeeded in associating costs with the various phases nor with the overall project. And as previously stated, problems amenable to Gantt Chart methods cannot possess the complexities familiar in present-day production management situations. Let us, therefore, consider a modern project planning approach, commonly termed, the critical path methods.

CRITICAL PATH METHODS

The weaknesses of the Gantt Project Planning Chart provided the focus for significant developments in the planning of complex projects. A method was required that would permit optimal or near-optimal sequencing and utilization

FIGURE 4-4 Datomatic Reader—PERT/COST Network for Datomatic Reader. [From *Cases in Operations Management*, James L. McKenny and Richard S. Rosenbloom (New York: John Wiley & Sons, Inc., 1969), p. 245.]

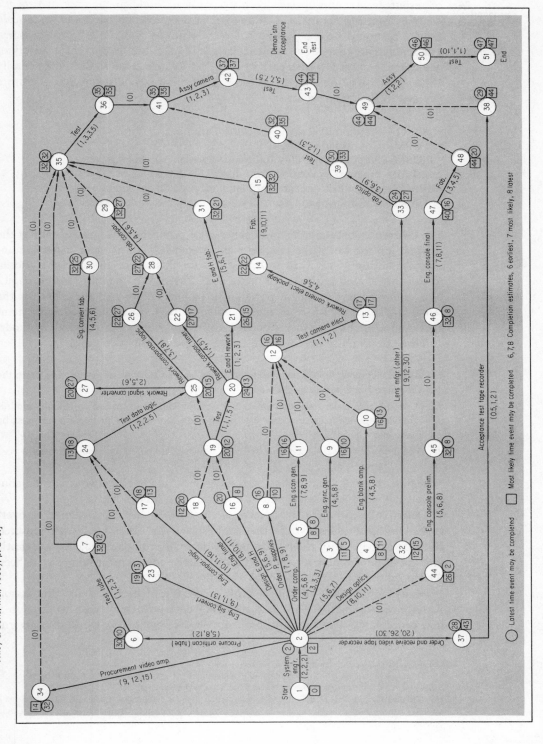

of resources. An appropriate methodology was found in the area of *network analysis*. Starting about 1957, a number of different approaches to large-scale project planning were begun at different locations and for different reasons. The reassurring thing about these efforts is the fact that in spite of a variety of names that emerged to label each system, they all turned out to be fundamentally alike. A rash of acronyms such as those that follow, began to appear in literature devoted to the planning area.

> PERT—Program Evaluation Research Task[7]
> CPM—Critical Path Method
> PRISM—Program Reliability Information System for Management
> PEP—Program Evaluation Procedure
> IMPACT—Integrated Management Planning and Control Technique
> SCANS—Scheduling and Control by Automated Network Systems

The differences between the approaches arise primarily as a consequence of the original job for which the method was developed.[8] All of them share in common the notion of a critical path, and it is for this reason that we have chosen to call this section critical path methods (CPM's). It is the only sensible choice of a name if the descriptive power of a name is of consequence. As for the remaining labels, PERT is the most familiar of all the above to production managers and we shall, therefore, discuss the PERT variant of critical path methods.

Three steps are required to utilize these network analytic tools.

1. All the elements, jobs, steps, tasks, activities, and so on that are required to bring the project to fruition must be detailed.

2. A sequencing order must be determined which is based on technological and administrative dependencies. In other words, all necessary sequential constraints must be made explicit.

3. The time (and cost) to perform each task, activity, and so on must be estimated.

When all this information has been assembled, a PERT network can be constructed. Figure 4.4 presents an example of such a network.

Detail is essential for the success of the CPM's. Activities cannot be overlooked without adversely affecting the results. Various estimates are required for each activity, with the result that for normally complex projects, a gigantic amount of information is generated. Fortunately, computer programs have been developed for most of the network systems.

Many applications of critical path methods can be found for production management projects. Thus, an operating enterprise may wish to develop a new process, build a new plant (for example, see Figure 4.5), work on a govern-

---

[7] Also called, Program Evaluation and Review Technique.

[8] PERT was developed by the U.S. Navy Special Projects Office in conjunction with Booz, Allen and Hamilton. It was one of the first of the network methods, and was used for the Polaris project.

    CPM was developed by E.I. duPont de Nemours and Company and Remington Rand at about the same time as PERT, and was used to plan the construction of a plant. These are the two approaches on which our discussion centers.

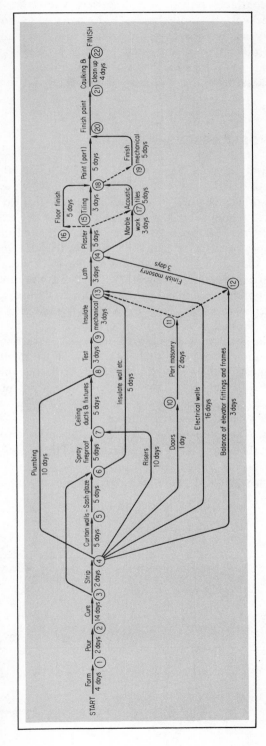

FIGURE 4-5 CPM diagram for a construction of a typical floor in a multistory building. [Redrawn from *Engineering News-Record* (McGraw-Hill Book Company, Inc., January 26, 1961).]

ment contract,[9] provide a new service, or diversify into an entirely new area of endeavor. With all these, CPM's are useful. For our stated purpose, we wish to use the network approach as a means of unifying the totality of activities, problems, decisions, and operations that constitute the project management field. In addition, we intend to provide a planning tool that is operational from the very inception of enterprise activity.

NETWORK REPRESENTATION

Project planning begins with a list of all essential activities; then, it is necessary to describe precedence relations, i.e., which activities *must* go before or follow other activities. A network of arrows (called a directed graph) can be drawn to represent each of the activities of the project and the relations between the activities. Such a network can be constructed in two different ways: *first*, (the more usual) place activities on arcs (we can abbreviate this approach as AOA), then *completion events* and *starting events* are the network nodes; *second*, put activities on nodes (called AON). The variants are shown in Figure 4.6 Each approach has its advantages. With AON it is easier to represent network precedence relations. Dummy activities (described below) are not required. If AOA is used, the sense of time is easily related to the length of the activity arc. Further, the AOA network emphasizes starting or completion events as nodes, and this approach has an advantage for managerial control. AOA also is the most familiar network form, having been employed by the developers of both PERT and CPM. Most network algorithms programmed for computers are developed on the basis of AOA. But AOA networks are more difficult to construct and do require dummies.

If two or more nodes have the same input arrows and the same output arrows, then using AOA procedures, it will be impossible to distinguish between the nodes. See Figure 4.7.
A dummy activity, which takes zero time to accomplish resolves this problem. See Figure 4.8.

FIGURE 4-6
Two activities, *a* and *b*, where *a* is directly followed by *b*. The start of *a* is 1; the completing of *b* is 3.

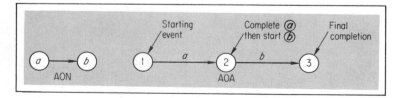

9 Government agencies have found critical path methods so useful that they frequently require this approach from companies working on government contracts. This is particularly true when an integrated effort on the part of several companies is needed.

FIGURE 4-7
Nodes *b* and *c* have the common predecessor *a* and the common successor *d*.

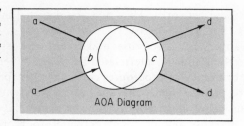

AOA Diagram

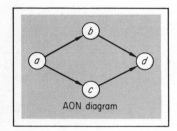

AON diagram

FIGURE 4-8
Nodes *b* and *c* are now placed on arrows. Because of the dummy activity (requiring zero time for completion) arrow *a* precedes arrows *b* and *c*, and arrow *d* follows both of them.

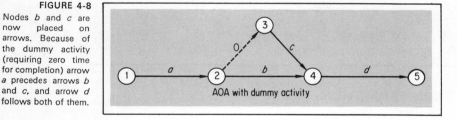

AOA with dummy activity

Further, when two or more activities have some, but not all of their inputs in common, the use of a dummy resolves the problem of representation. See Figure 4.9. For the discussion that follows, we will use AOA representation.

In planning a long-term project, some activities go through a cycle of steps and then repeat themselves many times at increasing levels of detail. Cycles of activities would also be characteristic of control system functions. But cycles

FIGURE 4-9
Nodes *b* and *c* have (*a*) but not (*a'*) as inputs in common. The problem is resolved by the dummy activity 2, 3.

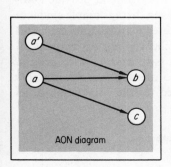

AON diagram

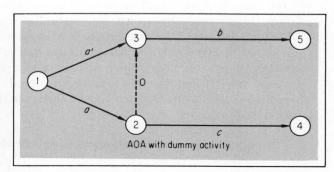

AOA with dummy activity

are not permitted in these networks. They must be depicted in extensive form as shown in Figure 4.10.

Many different arrangements of activities and events are possible. Projects of realistic size can have thousands of interrelated activities. Whenever materials, parts, subassemblies, or particular procedures come together for a new activity, an event circle must be used to signify that the previous activity has been completed. Still, the definition of an activity is subjective. Depending on his style, the project manager may use few or many activities to represent the same project elements.

FIGURE 4-10
PERT networks must be developed in extensive form.

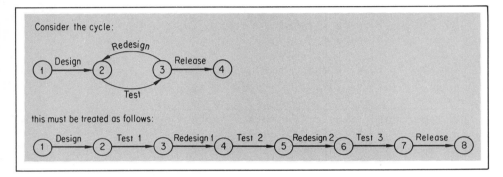

TIME ESTIMATION

The PERT system requires that three estimates be made for each activity. These are estimates of the time that will be required to complete the activity. The planner is asked to supply: (1) an optimistic estimate—called a; (2) a pessimistic estimate—called b; and (3) an estimate of what is most likely—called m. These three estimates are then combined to give *an expected elapsed time*—called t_e. The formula for achieving the combination is:

$$t_e = 1/6(a + b) + 2/3(m)$$

This formula uses more information than a single estimate for activity time.[10] The range, or spread between shortest and longest times should provide additional insight into activity time, but practically speaking there is ample evidence both pro and con. A possible distribution for these three elapsed time estimates is shown in Figure 4.11. Because estimates can be checked against actuality it should be possible to determine what is best for a particular kind of project. In any case, at the heart of the issue is the need to develop some reasonably good estimate for the expected elapsed time required for the completion of an activity.[11]

[10] These values are associated with the estimate of the mean of a Beta distribution.
[11] See the discussion regarding estimates on pp. 54-61, 74-76.

FIGURE 4-11
A *possible* distribution for the elapsed time estimates. (There is no assurance that the three estimates *a*, *m*, and *b*, falling at these positions on the time scale of the distribution will provide a better estimate of the mean than a simple, direct estimate of t_e.)

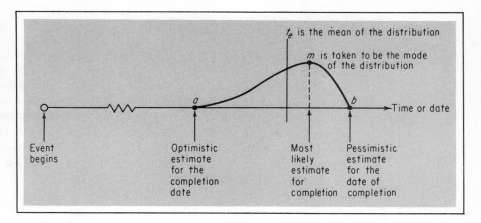

t_e is the mean of the distribution

m is taken to be the mode of the distribution

Time or date

| Event begins | Optimistic estimate for the completion date | Most likely estimate for completion | Pessimistic estimate for the date of completion |

In addition, an estimate of the variances associated with the expected value of elapsed time is also frequently supplied for the PERT system. Variance (represented by σ^2) is a measure of the spread of a distribution. A tall and thin distribution has an almost zero variance; whereas, a flat and shallow distribution has a large variance. The square root of variance, called the standard deviation (and represented by σ) often is used to represent the spread of a probability distribution. An important statistical rule supports the fact that the sum of the variances of a number of consecutive estimates of sequenced *independent* activities measures the variance of the total sequence. The independence referred to is in respect to activity times, i.e., how long it should take to accomplish each operation; not with respect to starting and finishing times by the clock and the calendar. For example, if three estimates, t_{e_1}, t_{e_2}, and t_{e_3} are made, each of them having a particular variance measure σ_1^2, σ_2^2, σ_3^2, then the variance of the sum of these estimates is given by $\sigma_1^2 + \sigma_2^2 + \sigma_3^2$. This relationship is depicted in Figure 4.12. The formula for the variance of our distribution[12] (shown in Figure 4.11) is given by $\sigma^2 = [1/6(b - a)]^2$.

FIGURE 4-12
The variance, σ^2, of combined estimates is equal to the sum of the variances of the individual estimates of *independent* activities.

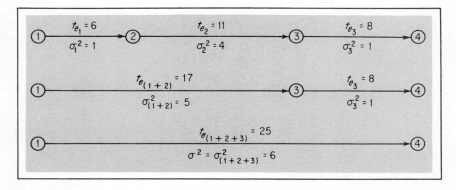

$t_{e_1} = 6$ $\quad t_{e_2} = 11$ $\quad t_{e_3} = 8$
$\sigma_1^2 = 1$ $\quad \sigma_2^2 = 4$ $\quad \sigma_3^2 = 1$

$t_{e_{(1+2)}} = 17$ $\quad t_{e_3} = 8$
$\sigma_{(1+2)}^2 = 5$ $\quad \sigma_3^2 = 1$

$t_{e_{(1+2+3)}} = 25$
$\sigma^2 = \sigma_{(1+2+3)}^2 = 6$

[12] Associated with the estimate of the variance of a Beta distribution.

CRITICAL PATH COMPUTATIONS

Let us take an abstract PERT network (see Figure 4.13) and work with the estimates which are shown there. Each arrow is labeled with an expected elapsed time. In addition, the variance is shown for each activity as a number within the parenthesis. We obtain a *cumulative* total time for each branch, moving along the particular branch from the beginning of the project to the end, and call these values T_E. Each cumulative total gives the earliest expected clock time that each event can begin. The event circles, or nodes, enclose these numbers. It will be noted that as we sum along different branches until we arrive at a junction node, that the joining branches can carry a different cumulative number to that node. Whenever this condition arises at a junction node, *we accept the largest value of T_E.* All further accumulation proceeds with this larger number which is the earliest possible clock time for that event node. The last node in the network represents *project completion.* It bears a value which is the

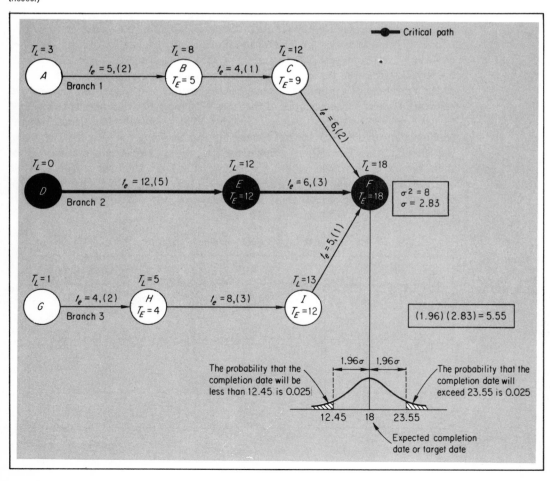

measure of the maximum cumulative time; that is, the time required to perform the longest time sequence of activities in the network. Examination of Figure 4.13 will show that the middle branch dominates the cumulative total that has been carried forward. This branch requires the longest elapsed time for completion and is called the *critical path* of the system.

Now let us see how we make use of the critical path that has been determined. Starting with the largest cumulative total, $T_E = 18$, which resulted from the middle branch, and which is the estimated time for *job completion*, we now move backwards through the network. Then, successively we subtract from each previously accepted T_E value all expected elapsed activity times, t_e, that immediately precede it in the network. The values derived by subtraction, called T_L, are assigned to the event nodes that precede their respective activities. In some cases, when moving backwards, two or more branches converge on a node such that the values of T_L produced by subtraction are not equal. Then, *we accept the smallest value of T_L*. The values of T_L are measures of the latest possible clock time at which that activity can be started in order to complete the project according to its critical path time.

MEASURE OF SLACK

The difference, $T_L - T_E$, can now be obtained for each event node. It describes the amount of *slack* that exists at each node. By slack we mean that the specified time estimates can slip by the amount of slack that exists, and the total job can still be completed on time. As expected, at every node of the critical path, which, by definition dominates the system, $T_L - T_E = 0$. In general, a branch has as much slack as the time required to complete the branch requirements is *less* than the time required to complete the project stages that make up the critical path. For our example, the top branch has the most slack and the bottom branch has a small amount. This finding is not trivial because we know now that it would be wasteful to do any expediting[13] on either the top or bottom branches. The critical path, middle branch, cannot be allowed to slip. If it does, it will directly affect the project completion date. Therefore, the major emphasis of project control should be assigned to the critical path. This information was not available from the Gantt chart.

DISTRIBUTION OF COMPLETION TIMES

We can see from these results why this system is called PERT/*TIME*. Time is the only factor under consideration. It is the fundamental dimension of the planners' objectives. With this idea in mind, the variance measure can now be used. We sum the variances, proceeding along the critical path branch. Thus,

[13] This now well-known term was first used by Henry Kaiser in connection with the critical shipbuilding schedules of World War II.

for the final event which signals completion of the job we can obtain not only the expected time for project completion but also an estimate of the variance around this expected value. Figure 4.13 shows a distribution with both tails cut off at the limit of 1.96 standard deviations (plus and minus from the mean value). Each tail contains the probabilities of an event occurring approximately 25 out of 1000 times.[14] The upper tail contains long completion dates. The lower tail contains short completion dates. Thus, moving 1.96 standard deviations (1.96σ) in either direction gives us a range of times for job completion within which there is a 95 percent probability that the actual completion date will fall. Stated another way, we have determined, utilizing a 1.96σ criterion, an earliest and latest project completion date.

The computations to determine the critical path, slacks, completion variance, etc. do not require that an actual network be drawn up; the computer program handles them in an algorithmic fashion that is quite similar to the steps required for completing the table below.

TABLE 4.1 Computations Associated with PERT Network (in the general form utilized for computer systems)

EVENT	T_E	T_L	SLACK $(T_L - T_E)$	CUMULATIVE VARIANCE
F	18	18	0	8
C	9	12	3	3
I	12	13	1	5
E	12	12	0	5
B	5	8	3	2
H	4	5	1	2
G	0	1	1	0
D	0	0	0	0
A	0	3	3	0

SCHEDULE CONTROL

At any stage of the project, the manager can ask for a progress report. Each activity, on a regular basis, reports where it stands. The computer can print out, on command, those activities that are ahead and those that are behind, as well as measures of degree. A shift might occur of the critical path. New slack values appear. Control over schedule is excellent. The network is, of course, continually updated to reflect project progress.

[14] This assumes that a Normal distribution applies which would be the effect of considering many Beta distributions combining to form a single distribution for the project as a whole.

Number of Standard Deviations (σ) ± from the Mean	Probability that the Actual Time Falls Within the Specified Range
1σ	0.680
1.64σ	0.900
1.96σ	0.950
3σ	0.997

TRADING-OFF RESOURCES

The method that we have used can be further interpreted to imply that a better arrangement of resource utilization might be found. Any alteration that reduces the time of the critical path would decrease the amount of slack that has been observed in the other branches of the network. A reasonable approach would be: (1) to obtain and employ new resources toward this end, and (2) to shift resources, wherever possible, from the branches having the largest amount of slack to the critical path.

Considering the second alternative, let us assume that the length of time it takes to complete each activity is linearly related to the number of men employed on the job. Assuming that the skills required are interchangeable between branches, we could then bring the entire network into better balance by shifting manpower resources from slack branches to the critical path. This has been done for the previous example, and the results are shown in Figure 4.14.

FIGURE 4-14
A perfectly balanced PERT network is achieved—for the example, in the text —by trading off re- sources. (Note: We have permitted the resources to be frac- tionated.) *Now, all branches are critical paths—there is no slack in the system. The target date has been improved by $1\frac{1}{4}$ time units.*

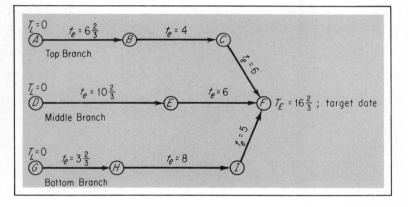

In general, we cannot hope to achieve such perfect balance because men, ma- chines, and other resources cannot be fractionated at will, and because all skills and facilities are not readily interchangeable between branches. But to the ex- tent that changes can be made, we usually do achieve considerable improve- ment in the time performance of the system. The ability to recognize slack paths, and to trade-off resources in the manner that we have described above, makes critical path methods significantly more useful than the older methods associated with the Gantt Project Chart. The paths of greatest slack provide the best opportunities for improving the target date of the project. On the other hand, they also point to places where effort would be wasted in expediting work to meet scheduled deadlines.

Sometimes it is possible to utilize whatever expediting and control facilities exist to improve the variance along the critical path. By doing this, we do not change the target date but instead, we reduce the risk of substantially deviating from the target date.

PERT COSTS

The utilization of the critical path method has been extended in a number of different ways. Of interest to project planners is the desire to run the project on a crash basis, i.e., minimum time. There is also the wish to maximize the quality of the work or the performance characteristics of the system. Another major objective is to minimize cost. The relationships of cost and time have received considerable investigation. Various time-cost systems have been developed and others are being developed to attempt to resolve this problem, which we recognize as one of conflicting multiple objectives.

The PERT/*COST* system starts in the same way as does PERT/*TIME*, that is, we construct the representative network of activities and events. We shall use the network shown in Figure 4.15. However, in this case we have developed two different estimates for each branch. These are: (1) a minimum time estimate and

FIGURE 4-15
A PERT/*COST* network with hypothetical data. For minimum cost, 0–2–3 is the critical path, with $T_E = 22$ and cost = 14. The slack for 0–1–3 is $T_L - T_E = 5$. Assume that T_E must be no greater than 20. The best COST/TIME ratio applying to the critical path is associated with activity 2–3 (see Figure 4.16). Making the required change, we obtain: $t_{23} = 8$; $c_{23} = 4\frac{1}{3}$. This gives 0–2–3 as the critical path with $T_E = 20$ and cost = $15\frac{1}{3}$. The slack for 0–1–3 is $T_L - T_E = 3$.

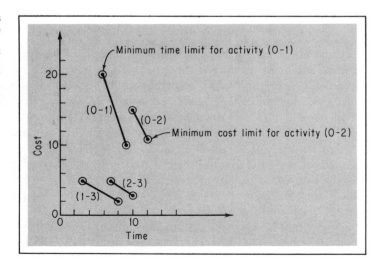

FIGURE 4-16
Some representative COST/TIME relationships where the weak assumption is made that linearity prevails over the specified range. The end points are assumed to be limits.

its cost; and (2) a minimum cost estimate and its time. Figure 4.16 shows the way in which these factors might be related for each of the branches of our network.

The minimum cost estimate (the second of the two listed above) is used for each activity, and the critical path is determined for those data. The result will then be a completion date that is based upon minimum cost requirements for completing the project. This completion date and the length of time required to complete the project under minimum cost conditions may be too great to be tolerated. Accordingly, alternative times, requiring greater costs, can then be substituted for chosen minimum cost activities *along* the critical path. In this way, the critical path can be shortened until such time that: (1) another path becomes critical; or (2) a satisfactory compromise with the original critical path is achieved. As a rule of thumb, we make compromises for those activities along the critical path where the ratio of increasing costs for the activity with respect to decreasing time for the activity is smallest. Thus, we select that *critical path activity* where: $|\Delta \text{ cost}|/|\Delta \text{ time}|$ is *smallest*. Then the next biggest ratio is used, and so on until a satisfactory compromise between time and cost is achieved. If the critical path switches, we make our next alterations along the new path.

The PERT/*COST* method can be modified to meet the particular requirements of a given project. It is not an optimizing technique. Instead, it is a logical attempt to utilize reasonable trade-offs between cost and time, where they count, in order to obtain an approximation to an optimal result. Where quality, cost and time can be formally related, an extension of these trade-off notions is not difficult to construct.

NETWORK SIMULATION

Because variance of activity times exists, it is reasonable to expect that occasions will arise where the activity times actually experienced along the critical path will be substantially less than had been expected and, simultaneously, by chance, the experienced times along a noncritical path will be much greater than had been expected. The result might well be that the path designated as critical would shift to being noncritical, and another path would become critical.

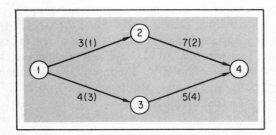

One of the best ways to examine the sensitivity of a network to such shifting patterns is by means of *simulation*. Consider the network illustrated in Figure 4.17

The path 1, 2, 4 is the critical one, based on expected activity times. But, we note that path 1, 3, 4 is very close to being critical and has much higher variances for both its activities than does the top path. We can anticipate that, every now and then, a result such as the following could occur.

ACTIVITY	EXPERIENCED TIMES	PATH TIME
1, 2	2	
2, 4	6	8
1, 3	5	
3, 4	7	12

In other words, the critical path would shift. But, how often might such an interchange arise? To answer this kind of question, let us construct a Monte Carlo simulation model.

First, we set down the probability distribution (p) for the various possible activity times along each arrow of the network. Let us presume that the probabilities are as follows:

ACTIVITY (1, 2) TIME	p	M.C.N.	ACTIVITY (2, 4) TIME	p	M.C.N.	ACTIVITY (1, 3) TIME	p	M.C.N	ACTIVITY (3, 4) TIME	p	M.C.N.
1	0.05	00–04	3	0.02	00–01	1	0.10	00–09	2	0.05	00–04
2	0.15	05–19	4	0.03	02–04	2	0.10	10–19	3	0.10	05–14
3	0.60	20–79	5	0.05	05–09	3	0.10	20–29	4	0.15	15–29
4	0.15	80–94	6	0.20	10–29	4	0.30	30–59	5	0.20	30–49
5	0.05	95–99	7	0.40	30–69	5	0.10	60–69	6	0.15	50–64
			8	0.20	70–89	6	0.10	70–79	7	0.10	65–74
			9	0.05	90–94	7	0.10	80–89	8	0.05	75–79
			10	0.03	95–97	8	0.10	90–99	9	0.10	80–89
			11	0.02	98–99				10	0.10	90–99

Monte Carlo numbers (called M.C.N.) are associated with each probability in such a way that a unique set of numbers, proportional to the probabilities have been assigned in each case. That is, considering activity (2, 4), two out of one hundred times, it is expected that an activity time of 3 will occur. Accordingly, two Monte Carlo numbers (00 and 01) have been assigned to the possibility that the activity time will be 3. Similarly, the probability that the activity time will be 8 is 0.20. And, twenty unique Monte Carlo numbers (70, 71, 72, . . . , 89) have been assigned to that eventuality.

All that remains to be done is to find a way to select *randomly* two-digit numbers, and to use these random numbers to generate a pattern of activity times. The character of random numbers (for which tables exist[15]) is that each random number is as likely to occur as any other. Then, assume that four random numbers are drawn: 68, 93, 05, 14. These numbers are matched against the Monte Carlo numbers. Random number 68 falls in the Monte Carlo range 20–79 for activity (1, 2). It signifies an activity time of 3. Random number 93 matches with an activity time of 9 for activity (2, 4). Random number 05 matches with an activity time of 1 for activity (1, 3). And random number 14 matches with an activity time of 3 for activity 3, 4. For this first simulation run, our results are that the upper branch (1, 2, 4) has a total time of 3 + 9 = 12. The lower branch (1, 3, 4) has a total time of 1 + 3 = 4. In this case, the critical path is more critical than ever.

When repeated many times, a reasonable simulation of what could happen is obtained. A sample of 10 runs is illustrated below.

SIMULATION OF ACTIVITY TIMES

RANDOM NUMBERS										
(1,2)	(2,4)	(1,3)	(3,4)	(1,2)	(2,4)	SUM	(1,3)	(3,4)	SUM	CRITICAL PATH
27	65	51	80	3	7	10	4	9	13	1,3,4
99	45	68	46	5	7	12	5	5	10	1,2,4
26	41	26	72	3	7	10	3	7	10	tie
37	56	83	61	3	7	10	7	6	13	1,3,4
38	03	90	59	3	4	7	8	6	14	1,3,4
71	45	38	26	3	7	10	4	4	8	1,2,4
93	55	71	06	4	7	11	6	3	9	1,2,4
01	94	57	83	1	9	10	4	9	13	1,3,4
45	09	78	65	3	5	8	6	7	13	1,3,4
60	23	46	66	3	6	9	4	7	11	1,3,4

A definite reversal of our concept of the critical path has occurred. The path 1, 2, 4 has turned out to be critical 6 out of 10 times, or 6 out of 9 times if we delete the tie result. The implications of this result, especially for large networks, are that simple definitions of the critical path, based on expected values can be misleading and that the project manager should be aware of the sensitivity of his project network to chance events, isolating for special treatment those activities with high variance that might seriously affect his target date.

CONTINGENCY PLANNING

Planning long-term projects requires that many important decisions will be made *as* the project *evolves*. Thus, inherent in the planning network are decision points and the subsequent alternative paths that choice implies. Network

[15] See David W. Miller and Martin K. Starr, *Executive Decisions and Operations Research* (2nd ed.), (Englewood Cliffs, N.J.: Prentice-Hall, Inc., 1969), pp. 585–588.

methods are being developed for contingency planning which permit alternative paths to be taken into consideration when laying out the plan of the project.[16] These methods can use probability statements to describe the relative likelihoods that alternative branches of the network will be followed. It should be noted that the critical path methods previously discussed never allowed a choice to be made with respect to which of two branches at a junction node might be employed *after* the project plan was drawn up. Yet, in many projects, it makes little sense to hide the fact that decision alternatives will eventually appear, and that it is wise to be prepared for such contingencies.

PLANNING HORIZONS

No discussion of planning systems can be complete without turning our attention to the way in which outcomes are affected by the length of the planning horizon. By this term we connote how far ahead the decision maker is thinking and planning. This is important because usually there will be a difference between decisions that are rendered on a one-year, five-year, ten-year, or twenty-year span of time.

We observe that a given period of time must always be specified in determining costs, revenues and profits. We cannot simply multiply a yearly cost by the number of years that it will be incurred in order to determine the total costs applicable to the planning horizon. To point this up, let us compare two plans. In the first we will build a plant. In the second we will rent it. These two kinds of costs are not the same. Some method is required to compare costs that are incurred immediately or within a short period, such as buying, as compared to those which represent a *stream* of costs over a period of time, such as renting. Similarly, we require a way of comparing the income that will be obtained over a period of time from alternative product designs, where one product has an expected life of five years and another promises a smaller income stream, but taken over a ten-year life. As another example, a process design change or an inventory study will produce different streams of savings over various periods of time.

For most systems, the length of time over which the monetary stream is reckoned will affect the conclusions that can be reached. A method of *discounting* is required to resolve the issue that has been raised. The premise upon which discounting is based is that a sum of money to be received at some future time has less value than the same sum of money owned at the present time. Essentially, this method provides for a comparison between an investment made in the present as compared to a stream of smaller payments made over a period

---

[16] For example, see Howard Eisner, "A Generalized Network Approach to the Planning and Scheduling of a Research Project", *The Journal of the Operations Research Society of America*, Vol. 10, No. 1, January-February 1962, pp. 115–125. Also, Martin K. Starr, "Planning Models," *Management Science*, Vol. 13, No. 14, December 1966, pp. B115–B141.

of time. We can either derive the *present value* (or worth) of the stream of payments and compare it to the investment, or we can determine what stream of payments (perhaps borrowed from the bank) would be equivalent to the investment. In both cases, an interest rate and a planning horizon must be specified.

To illustrate, assume that it is possible to buy a plant for $1,000,000. An alternative is also offered, namely, to rent at $80,000 per year. The question that must be answered is: How do these plans compare? It is frequently necessary to measure stream factors (annuities) in the same terms as investment factors. First, we must obtain an estimate for the value of money. For example, 6 percent per year would be the amount that could be obtained by investing a given sum of money in high grade stocks. The estimate of this interest rate will vary depending upon the size of the company, its growth potential, and capital requirements. We shall employ the 6 percent rate, recognizing that it is an absolute necessity to determine the appropriate rate of interest.

We ask the question: What is the present worth of an $80,000-per-year income stream as a function of the length of the planning horizon that is employed? The formula for present worth (or present value) that we utilize is:

$$PW = N \sum_{n=0}^{n} \left(\frac{1}{1+r}\right)^n - N = N \sum_{n=1}^{n} \left(\frac{1}{1+r}\right)^n$$

where:

PW = present worth
N = $80,000, the yearly rental value
r = interst rate, 6 percent per year
n = the planning horizon of n years.
$\sum_{n=0}^{n} \left(\frac{1}{1+r}\right)^n$ = the sum of terms $\left(\frac{1}{1+r}\right)^0 + \left(\frac{1}{1+r}\right)^1 + \left(\frac{1}{1+r}\right)^2 + \cdots + \left(\frac{1}{1+r}\right)^n$

This equation assumes that the first rental payment is made at the end of the period. Consequently, each dollar paid out costs us less than a full dollar, viz., $0.94. If we had that dollar at the beginning of the period, we could have invested it at 6 percent per year. At the end of the year we would have $1.06, but we would only be required to pay out $1.00. The actual cost would be $1.00 − 0.06 = $0.94. Thus, by deferring payment we decrease the cost of such payments to us.[17]

The following table shows the way in which present worth changes as a function of the planning horizon.[18]

---

[17] If the payment is made at the beginning of the period, we would alter our formulas as follows (for n + 1 payments):

$$PW = N \sum_{n=0}^{n} \left(\frac{1}{1+r}\right)^n = N + N \sum_{n=1}^{n} \left(\frac{1}{1+r}\right)^n$$

[18] Tabled values are available for different interest rates and time periods. See, for example: R. S. Burington, *Handbook of Mathematical Tables and Formulas* (New York: McGraw-Hill Book Company, 1965).

n(years)	$\left(\dfrac{1}{1 + 0.06}\right)^n$	$\displaystyle\sum_{n=1}^{n} \left(\dfrac{1}{1 + 0.06}\right)^n$	$(80{,}000) \displaystyle\sum_{n=1}^{n} \left(\dfrac{1}{1 + 0.06}\right)^n$
1	0.943	0.943	75,440
2	0.890	1.833	146,640
3	0.840	2.673	213,840
4	0.792	3.465	277,200
5	0.747	4.212	336,960
6	0.705	4.917	393,360
7	0.665	5.582	446,560
8	0.627	6.209	496,720
9	0.592	6.801	544,080
10	0.558	7.359	588,720
11	0.527	7.886	630,880
12	0.497	8.383	760,640
13	0.469	8.852	708,160
14	0.442	9.294	743,520
15	0.417	9.711	776,880
16	0.394	10.105	808,400
17	0.371	10.476	838,080
18	0.350	10.826	866,080
19	0.331	11.157	892,560
20	0.312	11.469	917,520
21	0.294	11.763	941,040
22	0.278	12.041	963,280
23	0.262	12.303	984,240
24	0.247	12.550	1,004,000
25	0.233	12.783	1,022,640

We see that in the 24th year the income stream of $80,000 per year is equivalent to the purchase price of $1,000,000. Thus, it takes a planning horizon of about 24 years to balance the investment proposal. It is likely that the decision would be to rent because a planning period of 24 years is quite long, and up to that time it is less expensive to rent the facility. Carrying our thinking one step further, if an infinite planning horizon is utilized, then the series of payments has a convergent property which yields a measure of the value of the payment stream over this infinite time period. This is approximated by:

$$PW = \frac{N}{r} = \frac{\$80{,}000}{0.06} = \$1{,}333{,}333$$

Thus, if an infinite planning horizon is used for the project, then it would be better to take advantage of the investment possibility. Acknowledging that a variety of possibilities exists for choosing the span of the planning horizon, what factors underlie an appropriate choice?

The length of a planning horizon is frequently related to the computation of the payoff period. This is the length of time required before an investment pays for itself, that is, before it begins to produce additional capital for the company. The computation of the payoff period is performed *without discounting.*

$PP =$ Investment/Income per Time Period

where PP equals payoff period.

We see that a straight computation which ignores the discounting effect will indicate a shorter planning horizon than would be obtained if discounting were used. Thus, for example, if the investment required for a new product is $1,000,000 and it is expected to produce an income stream of $80,000 per year, the payoff period (without discounting) would be:

$$1,000,000/80,000 = 12.5 \text{ years.}$$

However, when discounting is taken into consideration, we know that a period of 24 years would be required for the investment to pay for itself. Generally speaking, it is advisable to utilize discounting for such computations. But, it must be pointed out that the planning horizon will be critically affected by the choice of interest rate that is charged. If a four percent rate per year is used, then about 18 years would be required to pay off the investment. If the rate is two percent per year, then the result would be approximately 15 years.

There is a variety of criteria that can be employed for long-term decisions. The choice depends upon the planning horizon that is being used. Thus, for example, we can state:

$$\frac{\text{Annual Income Stream}}{\text{Investment}} \geq r \tag{1}$$

$$\frac{\text{Required Income Stream at Present Worth for } n \text{ Years}}{\text{Investment}} \geq 1 \tag{2}$$

$$\frac{\text{Required Income Stream at Present Worth for Lifetime}}{\text{Investment}} \geq f \tag{3}$$

where $f > 1$.

The first formulation is the inverse of the payoff period computation. It expresses the fact that the annual return on our investment must be equal to or greater than the interest rate that could be obtained by using an alternative investment. The planning horizon, in this case, is just one year.

The second formulation is based upon the selection of a period of time, n, to be the length of the planning horizon. For this planning horizon, we require that the break-even point will occur in the nth year.

The third formulation represents the number of times that we would like the income-stream to pay for a given investment over its lifetime. Here, the planning horizon is infinite. Each criterion can result in different decisions. If nothing else, production management should be aware of the significance of the planning horizon to the resolution of long-term problems. A consistent policy that is generally understood and shared by the participants of the project is a necessary requirement for a successful planning operation.

PROBLEMS

1　Would you say that the airline matrix developed on pp. 65–66 was sensitive? (Test it with relatively small alterations to determine its sensitivity characteristics.)

2 The Delta Company manufactures a full line of cosmetics. A competitor has recently brought out a new form of hair spray that shows every sign of sweeping the market and destroying Delta's position in the market. The sales manager asks the production manager what the shortest possible time would be for Delta to reach the market with a new product packed in a redesigned container. The production manager sets down the following PERT structure:

Activity	Initial Event	Terminal Event	Duration
Design product	1	2	
Design package	1	3	
Test market package	3	5	
Distribute to dealers	5	6	
Order package materials	3	4	
Fabricate package	4	5	
Order matrials for product	2	4	
Test market product	2	7	
Fabricate product	4	7	
Package product	7	5	

   a. Construct the PERT diagram.
   b. Estimate the durations that you think might apply in a reasonable way.
   c. Determine the critical path.
   d. Neither the sales manager nor the production manager are satisfied with the way the project is designed, but the production manager insists that because of the pressure of time the company will be forced to follow this plan. In what ways does this plan violate good practice?
   e. By trading off resources would it be possible to reduce your critical path time?

3 In the example above, it was suggested that a reasonable method be employed for estimating the durations of activities. Now, employ the parameters of the Beta distribution, see pp. 88–89. Discuss the relevancy of this latter approach in terms of the comparison between your first estimates and these new ones.

4 Discuss the difference between long- and short-term production planning as it would relate to:
   a. A government planner
   b. A large corporation with many subsidiaries
   c. A medium size company
   d. A machine tool manufacturer
   e. A manufacturer of soap
   f. A dress manufacturer

5 How does the concept of utility provide differentiation between companies in terms of:
   a. Their relative sizes
   b. The number of years that they have been in business
   c. Their type of industry

6 Draw up an approrpriate PERT diagram for the following projects:
   a. A football play
   b. Moving a piano
   c. Dictating a letter
   d. Having a group of three people solve the following problem as rapidly as possible with full accuracy:

$$\frac{(10.314)^4}{(6.501)^2} + \frac{(3.241)^3}{(1.008)^5}$$

7 Determine the present value of an income stream that is associated with a new product, where anticipated revenue changes as follows:

Years after Release	Revenue (*million $*)
1	0.2
2	0.5
3	1.2
4	1.8
5	2.0
6	1.0
7	0.6
8	0.0

(Use the table on p. 100. This assumes that a discounting factor of 0.06 per year is applicable.)

8 Convert the project planning chart (Figure 4.18) below into an appropriate critical path diagram. Make whatever assumptions you require. Discuss the advantages of each form of representation.

9 Develop a table for $n = 1, \ldots 10$ and $\sum_{n=1}^{n} \left(\frac{1}{1 + 0.10}\right)^n$ similar in structure to the table for 0.06 shown on pp. 100.

FIGURE 4-18
Project planning chart
for new car introduc-
tion. (*Courtesy Chrys-
ler Corporation.*)

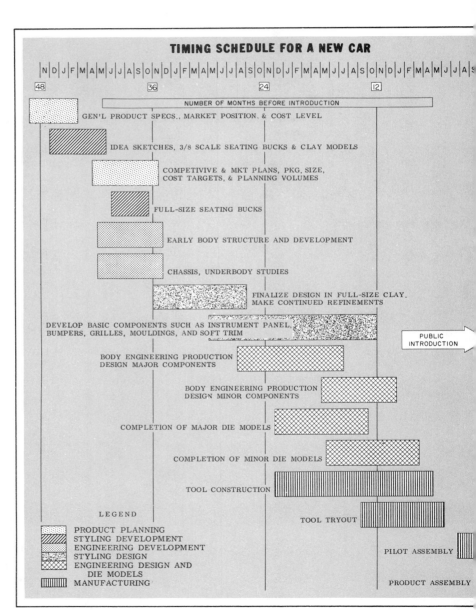

FIGURE 4-18
Project planning chart for new car introduction. (*Courtesy Chrysler Corporation.*)

references

ARCHIBALD, R. D. and R. L. VILLORIA, *Network Based Management Systems (CPM/PERT)*. New York; John Wiley & Sons, 1967.

BATTERSBY, A., *Network Analysis for Planning and Scheduling,* 2nd ed. (New York: St. Martin's Press, Inc., 1967.

EVARTS, H. F., *Introduction to PERT.* Boston: Allyn & Bacon, Inc., 1964.

IANNONE. A., *Management Program Planning and Control.* Englewood Cliffs, N.J.: Prentice-Hall, Inc., 1967.

KELLEY, J. E., JR., "Critical Path Planning and Scheduling: Mathematical Basis," *Operations Research,* IX, No. 3 (May-June, 1961), 296–320.

LEVIN, R. I. and C. A. KIRKPATRICK, *Management Planning and Control with PERT/CPM,* New York: McGraw-Hill Book Co., Inc., 1966.

MILLER, R. W., *Schedule, Cost, and Profit Control with PERT.* McGraw-Hill Book Co., Inc., 1963.

MALCOLM, D. G., and J. H. ROSEBOOM, C. E. CLARK, and W. FAZER, "Application of a Technique for Research and Development Program Evaluation," *Operations Research*, VII, No. 5 (Sept.-Oct., 1959), 646–669.

NASA-PERT B Computer Systems Manual (Catalog No. NAS 1. 18: P94/3). National Aeronautics and Space Administration, Director of Management Reports, Washington 25, D. C., 1963.

RADCLIFFE, B. M. et al, *Critical Path Method.* Chicago: Canners Publishing Co., 1967.

STOCKTON, R. STANSBURY, *Introduction to PERT.* Boston: Allyn and Bacon, Inc., 1964.

WIEST, J. D. and F. K. LEVY, *A Management Guide to PERT/CPM.* Englewood Cliffs, N.J.: Prentice-Hall, Inc., 1969.

chapter
five
control
models:
forecasting
and
feedback

The manager *plans for what can be*; he *controls what is now*. Control models are the rationalized procedures for running or operating existing production systems.

A CLASSIFICATION BASIS

The structure of control models will differ markedly for two different kinds of production systems: namely, the flow shop and the job shop. We shall discuss, in detail, the special character of each type of shop in Chapter 8. But, for the moment, let us say that the flow shop exists when the same set of operations are performed in sequence repetitively; and the job shop exists where the facilities are capable of producing many different jobs in small batches. The flow shop contains special purpose equipment (designed to mass produce). The job shop contains general purpose equipment (capable of doing a variety of jobs).[1] Clearly, mixtures can be found.

[1] We have just completed discussion of project shops. Like flow shops, projects require a sequence of operations, except that the sequence lacks repetition. Therefore, each project operation conforms to a job-shop step. The methodology for controlling the project has already been given in Chapter 4.

107
control
models:
forecasting
and
feedback

What do we mean by control models? There is inventory level to control, sequences of jobs and work schedules to control, quality control, and so forth. All of these control situations have a common theme running through them. It is this common theme that we want to examine; in other words, those general characteristics that are applicable to all control situations. Historically, the production manager controls the process and the flow of materials and energy through the system. His functions are neither duplicated, checked, nor overlapped by any other organizational entity. Such control is a primary responsibility of production management.

Control *systems* are needed because *disturbances* are constantly arising which shift the process off course. Were this not so, then a process could be adjusted to a standard level of performance from which it would never deviate. Disturbances, by definition, lie outside the immediate control of the production manager. If he were omnipotent, the production manager would remove the cause of all disturbances that produced unfavorable results.[2] On the other hand, if the production manager were omniscient, he would know what disturbances were going to arise and when. He would prepare as best he could to deal with these disturbances.

The best the manager can do, however, is a function of his ability to forecast and the extent of his control. When we say control, we mean the capacity to adapt to a disturbance by a readjustment of strategy. By definition, control is exercised over strategies and thereby, to some extent, over outputs. Also, by definition (Chapter 3), control cannot be exercised over states of nature.

ENVIRONMENTAL CONTROL—TYPE 1

To understand control, we have to bend our definitions a bit. We have to allow that all states of nature could be controlled for a given cost and that for some states of nature that cost would be infinite—meaning that practically speaking, they could not be controlled. At least, this view provides us with a cost basis for understanding omnipotence. Just to illustrate, assume that weather is an important state of nature and that if a plastic dome were built to cover the entire city, then weather would no longer be treated as a state of nature. Not only might the cost be out of reach, but the technology could be unachievable, or the time to achieve might destroy the utility of a research project aimed at obtaining such control. At the moment, we can only achieve weather control by going indoors. But, it is likely that even such states of nature will some day permit a degree of control. In production systems, statistical quality control is utilized to hunt down states of nature that are causing disturbances in the quality of output materials. (See pp. 310-27) These states of nature, called assignable causes of variation, are removed when discovered, so that the production quality can be stabilized. The system's analysis approach is used to

---

[2] It is worth noting that some distrubances improve performance even though they were not anticipated. The inability to plan for their occurrence can override any advantages that might have been gained.

discover the disturbing states of nature and to find ways to remove these disturbances or to isolate the system from them. Thus, we see that the word control can be applied to the production manager's ability to regulate the environment and to remove unwanted states of nature.

FORECAST CONTROL—TYPE 2

By means of forecasts and predictions another form of control is exercised, which we shall also consider in this chapter. By prediction, we refer to the selection of a particular state of nature as *the one* that is most likely to happen. By forecast, we describe the relative likelihoods of the various states of nature. See also footnote 12 p. 122. *Perfect* predictive ability is equivalent to omniscience. We can identify two distinct forms of forecast control. *First*, there is strategy choice based on achieving the maximum or minimum expected value. The forecast plays an instrumental part. *Second*, there is strategy choice based on a predictive ability to select the specific state of nature that will occur. For example, consider the following matrix:

	N_1	N_2	N_3	N_4
S_1		O^*		
S_2	O^*			
S_3				O^*
S_4			O^*	

Assume that the system is adjusted to operate with strategy S_1 in order to obtain the outcome denoted by an asterisk, O^*. This presupposes that the state of nature N_2 is the *standard* environment to which the system has been adapted. Now, let a disturbance occur that shifts N_2 to N_1. A forecast control system of the second type recognizing that this shift has taken place (or will occur) would alter the strategy, substituting S_2 for S_1. We observe that with perfect prediction, perfect *adaptation* is always possible (in this example) no matter which state of nature exists. The system has been designed so that all eventualities can be handled, that is, the outcome O^* can always be obtained by adjusting the controllable variables.

Let us contrast the two types of forecast control we have discussed thus far. Consider a specific situation. The matrix is one of profits.

p_j	0.3	0.1	0.2	0.4	
	N_1	N_2	N_3	N_4	EV
S_1	6	8	5	9	7.2
S_2	4	3	10	12	8.3
S_3	11	5	14	3	7.8

109
control
models:
forecasting
and
feedback

The manager scans his alternatives and recognizes that the best profit (with perfect control) is 14. Assume that he decides to invest in obtaining perfect control. This would allow him to adjust the state of nature to N_3 and set his strategy at S_3. But, there is a cost and a time interval required to research the achievement and maintenance of state N_3. Note that the manager would have to *decide* not to reach a decision based on expected values. Otherwise, the manager would have chosen, S_2, with an expected value of 8.3. This approach has an opportunity cost of $14 - 8.3 = 5.7$. A sensible manager would not be willing to spend more than 5.7 to obtain such perfect control. If his control remained imperfect, the *second* type of forecast control, based on prediction, might be achieved. An early warning device is needed which is able to signal the manager that a certain state of nature *will be* appearing. If the signal states N_1, then the manager shifts to S_3 and gets a profit value of 11; if N_2, he uses S_1 and receives 8; if N_3, he uses S_3 and receives 14; if N_4, he uses S_2 and receives 12. Such ability to predict has value. Depending upon the cost to achieve it, a control investment may be warranted. As the manager's ability to predict becomes increasingly imperfect, he withdraws to his forecast and the use of expected values.

How are predictions made? Forecasts are themselves, one basis for making predictions of what will occur. For example, if a particular state of nature has an extremely high probability of occurring, then the manager may decide to act as if the situation were one of DMUC. The assumption of certainty is an approximation to omniscience. If the prediction is good, particularly with respect to successive states of nature, then the manager's ability to anticipate events permits a strong control system to be designed.[3]

After this discussion, we must recognize that the word control covers many different situations. As it is usually used, it tries to do too much. It does not provide clear enough differentiation.

CORRECTIVE CONTROL—TYPE 3

Often the forecast is suspect, prediction through early warning systems too expensive, if possible, and environmental control out of the question. Still, an important form of control is available. It is based on the existence of feedback concerning the system's performance. As an example, consider an airplane flying on its control system (i.e., automatic). The course of the plane is disturbed by winds and shifting air densities that cannot be controlled, cannot be predicted, and for which forecasts would be of little use if they could be obtained. Yet the plane follows its intended path because a control system exists that observes deviations and corrects for them continuously in reasonable increments.

The control system employs a *monitoring function* as shown in Figure 5.1 Monitoring can be handled by the production manager or by a group of employees who are assigned to this function. Sometimes, a mechanism can be designed to assist in carrying out this function. A monitor can do many things. It studies

---

[3] The direct costs of assuming certainty are ordinarily among the cheapest control system options.

demand for the output of a system. It compares these demand levels with the finished goods inventory and the production rate. (But a monitor makes no decisions regarding what action should be taken.) The monitor simply reports what is happening in terms of measurements of deviations from a standard. It is designed according to need, then being capable of perceiving and reporting on a wide range of performance measures. The monitor always transfers its information to the *control function.*

FIGURE 5-1
The input-output sys-
tem with control.

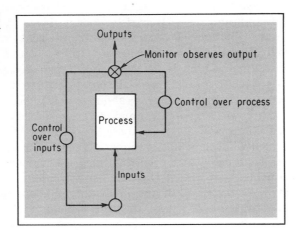

The controller has two options. To achieve correction (1) by operating on the *inputs* to the system, for example, manpower schedules and inventory control; and (2) by altering the *arrangement and productive capacity of the processing units.* The most frequent control is exercised over the inputs. In fact, day-to-day control over inputs is usually required to meet normal fluctuations in demand that occur and to cope with minor disturbances to the system, such as a machine breakdown or an absent employee. The control system is used to keep inputs in balance with expectations for the outputs of the system. Process control is usually more serious than input control. It is used less frequently. When it is employed, it is generally a signal that a significant change has occurred, and that substantial action is required to deal with the situation. Input control is frequently associated with the job shop. Process control is used when a job or flow shop must be redesigned.

TYPE OF FORECASTS

Let us classify the various kinds of system that we can expect to encounter with respect to the kind of forecast that would suffice to describe it.

111
control
models:
forecasting
and
feedback

A. *The Distribution* has only *one state of nature,* that is, DMUC;

B. *A Multistate Stationary Distribution Exists.* The probabilities associated with the states of nature are unchanging, that is, DMUR;

C. *There Is Shewhart-type Stability.*[4] In this case, the probabilities associated with the states of nature can change in some *regular* fashion. At any point in time, however, whatever state of nature exists is independent of all prior states of nature;

D. *There Is Markovian-type Stability.*[5] In this case, the probabilities associated with the states of nature move toward equilibrium values; but whatever state of nature exists at any point in time is *dependent* on the *preceding* state of nature that existed;

E. *There Is Non-Markovian Prior State Stability.* Here, the probabilities associated with the states of nature must change in some *regular* fashion; but whatever state of nature exists at any point in time is *dependent* on some *set* of preceding states of nature that existed;

F. *There Is Instability.* No knowledge exists or can be developed with respect to the behavior of the probabilities of the states of nature, that is, DMUU;

G. *There Is No Knowledge with Respect to the States of Nature.* That is, we cannot enumerate the relevent states.

On the basis of the above classification it should be clear enough why managers often fall short in communicating to each other their problems of control. Much technical knowledge about forecasting and the behavior of systems is required to know what to do when situations A through G are encountered. As we have previously seen, there are various types of control in terms of what can be done about exercising control. By this we mean the distinction between Types 1, 2, and 3 of control. Further discussion of the notion of control includes the extent to which the manager can succeed in implementing a strategy.

CONTROL INSTRUMENTATION

To the extent that we can create powerful strategies that yield promising outcomes under all conceivable, relevant circumstances, control can be exercised through *design*. This is the culmination of technological knowledge and methodological analysis. But we must not overlook the fact that strategies utilize instruments. These instruments are not always totally under control. For example, the driver of an automobile controls his car, but his control is not perfect. The variability of instrument performance is what makes golf an interesting game. Similarly, the control over strategic resources is not always precise. This is characteristic of financial control. It is even more apparent that instruments are variable when we consider human resource control. We say leadership that is an important attribute, but we cannot measure it and we can count upon neither its presence nor its effects. In summary, there is usually an area of tactical uncertainty that is characteristically called a control problem.

---

[4] See Walter A. Shewhart, *Statistical Method from the Viewpoint of Quality Control* (Washington, D.C.: The Department of Agriculture, 1939), and pp. 310-27 for an explanation of the fundamentals that apply to this class.
[5] Named after the Russian mathematician, Markov, whose work has established the fundamental nature of these particular kinds of systems' properties.

CONTROL DYNAMICS

Sometimes, the outcome objectives of the system are changing. For example, in connection with project planning, we speak of keeping the work on schedule. This kind of control requires monitoring the state of progress as a function of both completion times and monetary expenditures. Control is exercised, as possible, by shifting resources to appropriate activities as required. It is not too different to speak about controlling the *landing* of an airplane. As the plane moves to the runway, we require progress reports. Control is exercised in terms of the variables of speed and position. In both cases, control is measured with respect to the position and state of the system along a *dynamic trajectory*.

On the other hand control is the word that is sometimes used to connote the fact that no change has taken place, for example, "the production process is under control." The apparent difference between control over a changing system and a fixed system can be resolved by stating that control refers to controlling deviations from a standard—where the standard can be changing over a period of time—and where deviations are permitted to fall within specified limits. Thus, the situation shown in Figure 5.2 can be said to be under control, even though the objective is changing over a period of time. The same kind of control describes the elements of production scheduling.

FIGURE 5-2
Upper and lower control limits are applied to a trend line. The system is considered to be stable as long as observed results fall between these limits.

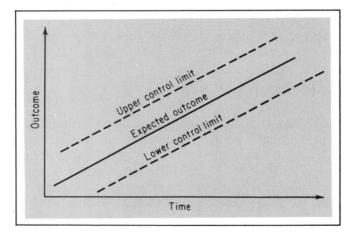

An entirely different kind of control problem occurs when the system is unstable. In this case, we cannot remove disturbances, and we don't know when they will occur. We require corrective control models (Type 3) that are *able* to take care of most eventualities that can arise. It is critical to be able to name what these disturbances might be, but not vital that we associate probabilities with them. If we overlook a relevant state—that may be improbable, but still possible—we can expose ourselves to great risks; for example, an airplane tire might blow out, on an otherwise fully-controlled landing.

113
control
models:
forecasting
and
feedback

Sometimes, it is sufficient to monitor the system, note the occurrence of a particular kind of disturbance, and provide a signal that indicates that an emergency calling for *human intervention* has arisen. This is an interesting case, requiring the design of a proper signal to be communicated across the man-machine interface. At other times, a control mechanism can take care of the disturbances by itself. Thus, if the room temperature drops, the thermostat signals the furnace and turns it on to correct the deviation from standard that has occurred. In the same way, the control system of an airplane handles different kinds of disturbances, such as winds, where no stable pattern for the disturbance exists. In each case, all eventualities must be considered and appropriate strategies built into the control device so that it is capable of treating all of these eventualities. It should be noted that extreme types of disturbances are the most critical and are related to safety margins employed for fail-safe performance.

FEEDBACK CONTROL

Let us consider models that are designed to handle situations where the effects of disturbances that can enter the system are *known* but where the occurrence of these disturbances cannot be predicted and no forecast is avilable, i.e., the pattern of the disturbance is unknown. This must be clearly distinguished from cases where the nature of disturbances or their possible effects are unknown. These latter types of situation range from the difficult to the impossible with respect to control.

The first kind of situation mentioned is readily treated by feedback control. The essence of adaptive automation is embodied in this class of control models. Figure 5.3 depicts the prototype of a generalized feedback-control model. It

FIGURE 5-3
A basic feedback-control model.

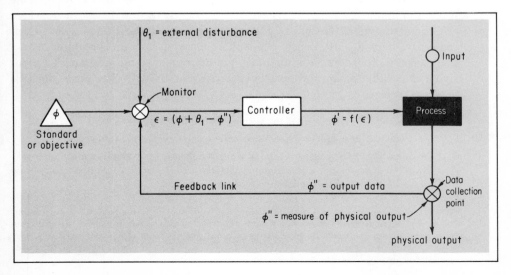

θ_1 = external disturbance

Input

Monitor

Controller

$\epsilon = (\phi + \theta_1 - \phi'')$

$\phi' = f(\epsilon)$

Process

ϕ

Standard
or objective

Feedback link

ϕ'' = output data

Data collection point

ϕ'' = measure of physical output

physical output

is an abstraction of any specific model that the production manager might design to maintain the company's objectives in the face of all reasonable disturbances.[6] The Monitor provides a comparison of the total demands that are made on the system, called $(\phi \pm \theta_1)$, with the actual output of the system called ϕ''. Note that ϕ is the standard or expected demand, and θ_1 is the increase or decrease of demand from the standard. Thus, $\epsilon = \phi + \theta_1 - \phi''$ is the error between what is called for and what is done. For an example, ϕ is the ships heading; θ_1 is the displacement from course caused by current; ϕ'' is the actual heading of the ship. The ship's steering engine follows a corrective policy, $\phi' = f(\epsilon)$.

If the comparison is made from time to time, then the control system is described as a sample-data system. On the other hand, for some systems a continuous monitor is required. Sample-data systems are typified by periodic compilations of orders or stock levels, for example. Thus, each morning the total demand for various items is determined. During afternoons, evenings, weekends, and so on, demand accumulates at unknown rates. Continuous systems would be used to monitor the level of reservoirs, fuel tanks, or the rate of flow through pipe lines. The continuous monitor never sleeps.

Let us reexamine this process now, in some detail. The monitor receives three kinds of information.

1. The system's output (ϕ'') is transmitted to the Monitor by means of a *feedback link*.
2. The system's objective or standard performance (ϕ) can be set either as the production manager's objective or as an expected value for system performance. It is fundamental to the design of the system.
3. The Monitor also perceives and measures θ_1. It is an external disturbance (such as increased demand, $+\theta_1$, or decreased demand, $-\theta_1$.) Thus, it is an *increment* of additional or subtractional demand (above or below the mean demand).

When the output (ϕ'') coincides with the total demand ($\phi \pm \theta_1$), no action is called for. The system must be provided with some means for monitoring (on a continuous or sample-data basis) the quantity $(\phi \pm \theta_1) - \phi'' = \epsilon$, where ϵ is the error signal. Generally, the system is so designed that $\phi = \phi''$. Consequently, when $\theta_1 = 0$, then $\epsilon = 0$, and no corrective action is required. However, when $\theta_1 \neq 0$, the Monitor notes the discrepancy and generates an error signal that calls for an appropriate corrective action (ϕ'). The error signal is produced when:

1. An external disturbance enters the system, that is, $\theta_1 \neq 0$;
2. The production manager changes his objectives and modifies the value of ϕ.
3. The output (ϕ'') decreases because of a process failure, for example, a machine breakdown. The consideration of such internal disturbances (called θ_2) would overcomplicate our model and so we have chosen to ignore them.

---

[6] What is reasonable in one case may not be in another. Thus, with respect to the design of an airplane, it is considered reasonable to design for the odd happening that birds may be drawn into the engines. The probability of this occurrence is very low, but the penalty, if it does occur, is so high that design allowance is made for this state of nature. Such a low probability event, with respect to demand, would seldom be included in designing requisite actions for an inventory control system.

115
control
models:
forecasting
and
feedback

Figure 5.3 includes a Controller in the system—be it man, machine, or a combination. The Controller is the policy-based corrective-action unit. It is designed to transform the error signal into an appropriate control action, $\phi' = f(\epsilon)$. The control action brings about the required change in the process. This controller unit must be designed to accept and interpret the various ϵ signals that might arise. Tracing through the control network, we see that the output of the Controller (ϕ') is designed as a specific function of ϵ. In fact, these functions are the *preplanned* control policies.

The *error signal* is a function of the system's standard (ϕ), the system's output (ϕ''), and the level of external disturbance, θ_1. When θ_1 is zero-valued, the system is performing according to standard specifications. Thus $\phi = \phi''$ and $\epsilon = 0$. When θ_1 takes on nonzero values, we have $\epsilon = (\phi \pm \theta_1 - \phi'') \neq 0$ and $\phi' = f(\epsilon) \neq 0$. The Controller counteracts the disturbance with ϕ'. This produces a new value of ϕ''—and ϵ begins tending toward zero.

CONTROL POLICIES

The model we have been discussing is a generalized version of a *servocontrol* system commonly found in electronic control networks. Automated systems cannot be designed without such models. However not only machine systems are susceptible to this kind of control theory. If a set of control rules, or *policies*, are drawn up to be executed by the *man in the system* when he is fed the appropriate error signal, the result is the same. And, as before, these models can be used effectively whether the likelihood of a disturbance is known *or unknown*. Thus, they are applicable to inventory and production control systems, especially when the demand distribution has not been determined. It is equally useful for anti-aircraft fire control or for an automatic regulator of product quality where the specific states of the noncontrollable variables (evasive action and materials changes, respectively) cannot be accurately predicted.

To illustrate, in decision theory terms, we might have the following matrix of control *instructions* designed to maintain a given outcome.

| | | THE STATE OF NATURE AT t_2 IS: | | | |
		N_1	N_2	N_3	N_4
THE STRATEGY AT t_1 IS:	S_1	go to S_2	stay at S_1	go to S_4	go to S_4
	S_2	go to S_3	stay at S_2	stay at S_2	go to S_3
	S_3	stay at S_3	go to S_2	go to S_2	go to S_1
	S_4	go to S_1	stay at S_4	go to S_2	stay at S_4

Thus, assume that a sequence of disturbances occurs, changing the states of nature in the following way:

$N_2, N_3, N_2, N_3, N_1, N_4, N_3, N_2, N_1, N_4, N_1$

The initial state *of the system* is S_1 and N_2. Then, we have:

t	S_i	N_j	INSTRUCTION
0	S_1	N_2	stay at S_1
1	S_1	N_3	go to S_4
2	S_4	N_2	stay at S_4
3	S_4	N_3	go to S_2
4	S_2	N_1	go to S_3
5	S_3	N_4	go to S_1
6	S_1	N_3	go to S_4
7	S_4	N_2	stay at S_4
8	S_4	N_1	go to S_1
9	S_1	N_4	go to S_4
10	S_4	N_1	go to S_1

FIGURE 5-4
Trajectory of control
strategies.

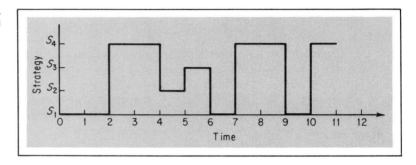

Figure 5.4 shows the trajectory of this control system where the assumption is made that changes in N_j occur instantaneously and at regular intervals. These assumptions can be dropped, with little additional complication.

We have drawn a *kinematic* diagram showing the conditions under which transitions take place between strategies (Figure 5.5). This type of diagram can be useful for exploring the responses and behavior of a control system. We see that whatever strategic state the system is in will remain unchanged if particular disturbances occur and these conditions are different for each strategy. We also observe that every strategic state can be reached from every other one and that no dead ends exist. Many interesting facts characterizing the system can be obtained in this way. Sometimes, the control-instruction matrix will be highly complex, requiring historical information concerning previous strategies and types of disturbances that have been experienced by the system. In spite of this complexity, the essential parts of this description would remain unchanged. The resource of *stored strategies* that can be called upon as needed is usually expensive. The control policy that is adopted must balance the costs of the control system and the cost of technological instruments for achieving *strategic flexibility* against the penalties for not maintaining sufficient control. The design and analysis of control systems can produce very complex

117
control
models:
forecasting
and
feedback

mathematical descriptions of servomechanisms. Simulation methods can frequently be used to test and analyze designs at a lower cost and sometimes with even more accuracy than mathematical methods can produce.

FIGURE 5-5
Kinematic graph of
the control system
transitions under all
possible disturbances.

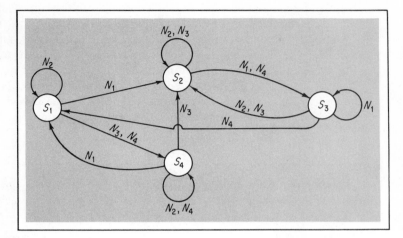

FIGURE 5-5 Kinematic graph of the control system transitions under all possible disturbances.

OPEN AND CLOSED SYSTEMS

The system we have just described was closed. Control theory is able to treat such systems and they are said to be "information tight." This means that the control system receives *all* pertinent information and is able to act directly upon the process to achieve its objectives. Although the information loop is closed, the production system is part of an open input-output process.

We should now contrast closed systems with open systems. The two are illustrated in Figure 5.6. We see that in the case of the open system a disturbance (θ_2) can occur, but the Monitor cannot perceive it except as it affects the output. Also, the control unit can produce some corrective action but it is uncertain how this affects the inputs and/or the process. Such a control unit is not information tight. Many very important systems cannot be treated as closed systems, for example, the economy of a country, the marketplace of consumers, and the behavior of an individual. Only closed systems are amenable to control analysis and design. In open systems, many unknown relations exist; the causes of system changes cannot be discovered; even the fact that a change has taken place may go unnoticed. Open systems appear to have their own internal control system. With respect to the individual, this is usually called an homeostatic mechanism. In Figure 5.6, the very act of measuring has a feedback effect on the process. The internal regulatory mechanisms of open systems tend to maintain the system in a dynamic equilibrium where one kind of change and rate of change is balanced by appropriate counter-rates of change for other components.

Little is known about the internal workings of the process in the case of the open system. Electrical engineers have coined the name "black box" for a process that, for one reason or another, cannot be traced out and explained in detail. Sometimes the process box isn't totally unknowable, just partly so, for example, the human brain or the marketplace. In such cases, it is possible to infer some characteristics of the obscure process by examining the relationships between inputs and outputs. Psychologists refer to this approach to understanding cerebral behavior as stimulus-response analysis.

At best, the open system can be manipulated, adjusted, and modified, but there is little assurance that a specific action will achieve a required result. Fundamentally, the production input-output system is not an open system. It is closed and can be controlled with great effectiveness. Nevertheless, any human in the system is an opening—a breech in the closed system concept. In general, the more automated the system, the greater the degree of closure

FIGURE 5-6
Contrasting open and closed systems.

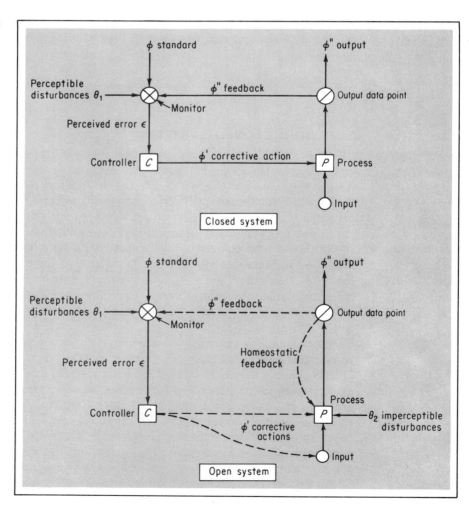

119
control
models:
forecasting
and
feedback

and the higher the degree of control that can be exercised. This is a major reason for the growth of automation. No matter how complete the level of automation, the production system can never achieve complete closure, that is, unless the managerial and consumer functions are automated (a specter we do not wish to contemplate).

THE SHEWHART CONTROL MODEL

Walter Shewhart[7] developed an *extremely important* control model which has found its most fruitful applications in the production management field. Although it is not limited to production applications, it is most naturally suited to the analysis of the machine component of the system. This model which examines output performance, identifies variables as belonging to strategies (controllable) or states of nature (noncontrollable). Then, it specifies whether the instruments of the controllable variables are being used in a controlled way. That is a great deal for one model to do; and, in this respect, the Shewhart model is widely recognized as one of the most important control models ever developed. We shall discuss only briefly the technical aspects of quality control at this time. The subject will be fully covered in Chapter 10 where it is directly applied to the production process. Our present purpose is to examine the implications of the model as a *generalized* production management control method.

A major purpose of using this model is to determine whether or not a stable forecast exists. The goal of the Shewhart model is to *monitor* a process to determine whether or not the system is meeting expectations, delivering the specified outcome, and achieving the production manager's objectives. We must note the particular meanings of the term control when it is used in this context. If instrument disturbances arise that shift the system off its course (they are called *assignable causes of variation*) then something must be done about them. If state of nature factors are responsible (called *chance causes of variation*) then nothing can be done about these, except that their variability must be included in expectations of process performance. The Shewhart control model does not tell what to do about assignable causes, how to do it, when or where to do it. It does not exercise control in this sense.

For the type of systems to which the Shewhart method is applicable, the objectives must be clearly and explicitly stated. For example, part X100 should be cut 3 inches $\pm$ 0.05 inches in length. Assignable causes of variation are disturbances that might occur because of facilities, materials or manpower. The Shewhart control model is designed to recognize that such disturbance has occurred.

The reason this model is of such fundamental importance is that it enables the production manager to separate the two types of causes of variation and not confuse or lump them together. It is true that chance causes of variation are disturbances to the system, but these causes cannot be removed. There are literally millions of such chance causes, including the behavior of particles at subatomic levels. Because of the conglomeration of chance causes, the machine

---

[7] See pp. 119-20.

cannot produce a part that is consistently 3 inches in length. Instead, we obtain a distribution of lengths like the probability distribution shown in Figure 5.7. The Shewhart model establishes a procedure for determining whether the variation that is observed is as small as it can possibly be; that is, whether the variability is the result only of chance cause factors, or whether there is trouble in the system about which something can be done.

FIGURE 5-7
A determinate mecha-
nism produces a dis-
tribution of values
because of *chance
causes.*

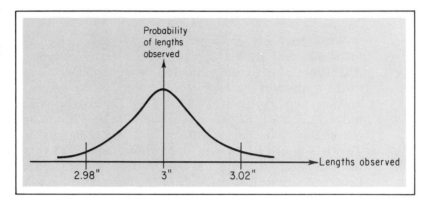

THE CONTROL MATRIX WHEN THE STATES OF NATURE ARE UNKNOWN

The Shewhart control model can be shown to be a variant of the decision matrix. Once this is recognized, we are able to construct a decision matrix where outcomes are substituted for the states of nature. Further, to complete the transformation we measure the new outcomes p_{ij} as the probabilities that the outcome O_j will occur when the strategy S_i is used. Thus, for five outcome levels and three strategies, we have:

		OUTCOMES				
		O_1	O_2	O_3	O_4	O_5
Strategies	S_1	p_{11}	p_{12}	p_{13}	p_{14}	p_{15}
	S_2	p_{21}	p_{22}	p_{23}	p_{24}	p_{25}
	S_3	p_{31}	p_{32}	p_{33}	p_{34}	p_{35}

In so many instances, the states of nature are unknown. This must be the case, by definition, when only chance causes remain to produce variation in the system. We cannot enumerate the relevant states of nature that account for the fact that a milling machine produces a distribution of part sizes rather than an exact duplicate each time.

Because we cannot list all relevant states of nature, this decision matrix is based on the substitution of outcomes for states of nature. In the cells of the matrix we have entered the probability that a specific strategy will produce a

121
control
models:
forecasting
and
feedback

given outcome. If the system is Shewhart-stable, these probabilities remain unchanged over time. Frequently, the probabilities for any given strategy row would describe a Normal distribution. (Note that outcomes can be defined as a function of time, see Figure 5.2.)

Now, let us take a specific case. Assume that a pipe is to be manufactured where the OD (outside diameter) is a critical factor. Further, assume as strategies that any one of three different machines can do this job i.e., S_1, S_2, and S_3. The outcomes are the range of dimensions that each type of machine might produce when the job is properly set up to produce an OD of 5.04.[8] Thus, for example: with S_1, a hand lathe; S_2, a turret lathe; and S_3, an automatic screw machine:

| | | MEASURE OF OUTSIDE DIAMETER (IN INCHES) | | | | | | | |
		5.01	5.02	5.03	5.04	5.05	5.06	5.07	EV
Hand Lathe	S_1	0.03	0.07	0.10	0.60	0.10	0.07	0.03	5.04
Turret Lathe	S_2	0.02	0.05	0.08	0.70	0.08	0.05	0.02	5.04
Automatic screw machine	S_3	0.01	0.03	0.06	0.80	0.06	0.03	0.01	5.04

In this case, all machines produce the same expected value for the OD. But much greater control is available with S_3, and S_2 is better than S_1. The control is greater when the variability is less. (Without any calculations, the probability distributions can be drawn and they immediately reveal the fact that the spread of the S_1 distribution is greater than that of the S_2 distribution which is greater than that of S_3. It should be noted that the expected value of the OD can be obtained for each strategy by multiplying the outcome probability by the outcome value and then summing them. Thus, for example:

$$EV_1 = 0.03(5.01) + 0.07(5.02) + 0.10(5.03) + 0.60(5.04) + 0.10(5.05) + 0.07(5.06) \\ + 0.03(5.07) = 5.04$$

Assuming that these probability distributions are stable and that the probability estimates are believable, then it is required that we use the expected value criterion as discussed on pp. 61–66 and 129–30 where it is explained that the only criterion for reaching decisions under conditions of risk is the expected value. So, strictly on the basis of expected value, the manager will be indifferent. Because of its superior control, he will choose S_3.

Now let us consider a different example for the purpose of illustrating some additional points.

| | (pH) OUTCOMES | | | | | |
	5.8	5.9	6.0	6.1	6.2	EV
S_1	0.0	0.2	0.6	0.2	0.0	6.00
S_2	0.2	0.2	0.2	0.2	0.2	6.00
S_3	0.1	0.3	0.2	0.3	0.1	6.00
S_4	0.1	0.2	0.3	0.2	0.2	6.02

---

[8] Two different kinds of setups, i.e., tools, fixtures, work sequences, etc., would count as two different strategies.

Four different processes are available for producing a soft drink. The pH[9] is to be kept as close to 6.0 as possible. A series of experiments and tests is run, and the results have been organized in a control matrix form.

We observe that strategies 1, 2, and 3 have the same expected values. Again, their distributions are quite dissimilar. Strategy 4 has a higher expected value than is desired. Strategy 3 produces a bimodal distribution.[10] This frequently indicates that at least one assignable cause of variation exists. Such cause enters and leaves the system from time to time, giving rise to two kinds of happenings and bimodality. Generally, the Shewhart criterion would produce evidence of the fact that the S_3 strategy does not conform to a stable system.

In any case, we can observe that the expected value is not a sufficient guide when we do not simply want the largest or smallest outcome. Here, the objective calls for an in-between value. The utility obtained from these outcomes gets progressively worse as we move further away—in either direction—from the objective value of 6.0. Certainly, we will always prefer to choose a process that is capable of producing the required output with minimum variance.

The second strategy would never be used because there are two other strategies that yield the same expected value with less variance. The first strategy it can be shown has the least variance of the first three strategies. Thus, strategies two and three are eliminated. Strategy four is also eliminated; it has a poorer expected value and variance. However, if a new strategy were found that produced the outcome 6.00 with 100 percent certainty, it would be selected.

The production manager must decide for himself what to do[11] when, for example, the objective is 6.00, and two strategies exist such that:

	OUTCOME	VARIANCE MEASURE
S_1	5.03	low
S_2	6.00	high

PREDICTIONS AND FORECASTS

We have come to see that forecast and predictive abilities are of great importance for the achievement of control.[12] The production manager must determine how likely it is that each state of a set of states of nature will occur, before

[9] The symbol pH is commonly used in expressing hydrogen ion concentration. The neutral point is pH 7. Above 7 alkalinity increases; below 7 acidity increases.
[10] Two peaks of maximum probability occur with a valley in between. Most familiar distributions like the Normal or the Poisson are unimodal.
[11] The method described on pp. 343-45 could be helpful in this case.
[12] We distinguish between forecasts and predictions as follows: the weather *forecast* is 0.40 rain and 0.60 fair. We *Predict* it will be fair. You don't need a forecast to predict. When it comes to weather, the ground hog and arthritis are famous predictive mechanisms. And, in horse racing, the odds are the forecast, but the horse you bet on is your prediction.

123
control
models:
forecasting
and
feedback

he can select an optimal strategy. He must evaluate his ability to forecast before he can determine his approach to control.[13]

Chance enters the decision system through the uncontrollable variables that characterize states of nature. Although we have no control or only partial control over these variables, we are not helpless. We may not be able to control the movement of the sun, but we can be precise in predicting its positions. Many actions are predicated on the ability to foretell the future. Because we know what to expect from nature, we can choose an appropriate strategy. In effect, the ability to forecast or predict gives us different kinds of (Type 2) control *over outcomes*, even though we remain helpless with respect to controlling the states of nature (Type-1 control).

Some predictions can be made with relative certainty. The time of sunrise and sunset are good examples. We can also make excellent predictions about the tides; though our ability to predict the weather is nothing to brag about. Generally, natural and physical phenomena can be predicted with greater precision than behavorial phenomena, which can be exceedingly difficult to handle. This generalization begins to map out the area of predictions, but like most sweeping statements it hardly does justice to the true state of affairs. Accordingly, let us attempt a further refinement. Large physical entities, which are assemblages of many small particles, tend to behave in a predictable fashion. Statements about the individual or relatively small groups of particles usually are amenable only to forecast descriptions. Seldom does any one state of nature stand out as being that much more probable than all of the others for the individual.

The development of statistical mechanics in the early 1900's arose in response to new directions of investigation which dealt with problems surrounded by uncertainty. Deterministic analysis was forced to give way to some degree of indeterminism. Thus, even in the physical sciences and in engineering, the existence of states of nature was not recognized until it became a requirement. It was a requirement that upset many philosophers who believed that science would remove all uncertainty and reveal the structure of a perfect universe, i.e., perfect predictive ability.

Where volition and human behavior are involved, the ability to predict usually improves as the number of individuals included in the system increases. The behavior of a single individual is considered, by and large, to be unpredictable; but the behavior of a large group of individuals can be anticipated with some accuracy. If this were not true, sales predictions would be absurd. We can find an analogy between particles and individuals because in both cases, as the number of units grows larger, the predictability tends to improve. But here too, we must be wary. Social and cultural factors tend to reduce the uncertainty of human behavior in certain areas so that an individual becomes almost totally predictable. At the same time, a complex set of group behaviors can interact with each other to produce almost impossible conditions for prediction. The stock market is a good example of this.

The production manager must deal with both behavioral and physical systems. Forecasts are a necessary part of his job. Production management,

[13] That is, type-1 (environmental); type-2a (forecast); type-2b (predictive); or type 3 (feedback) control.

reflecting the scientific attitudes of the 19th Century, began its practice without recognition of this fact. Just as science was forced to give way to indeterminism, so too was production management. The change was gradual. It is not complete and is still taking place. The production function, unlike other organizational functions, is uniquely involved with both determinate and nondeterminate systems. Many technological problems fall into the class of physical phenomena. At this level, precise predictions can be made. On the other hand, production workers tend to complicate life. In fact, for the production manager they have been a prime source of insecurity over the years. The production manager liked to think of men as though they were machines; not because he wished to strip them of their humanity, but because their unpredictable performances (high variance forecasts) introduced the element of uncertainty into the manufacturing process. Other major sources of similar trouble were the consumer and the competitor. As long as demand was greater than supply, and as long as competition was negligible, the consumer and the competitor could be ignored. When this was no longer so, the production manager was delighted to relegate the problems of consumer uncertainty and competitive maneuvers to a specialist in the area, viz., the marketing manager. The employee, however, remained in the production manager's bailiwick.[14] Yet, as we have observed, a forecast has value whether or not it leads to a neat prediction. Further, the majority of predictions are based on the fact that the most likely state of nature in a forecast is a better predictive bet than any other state of nature.

PROBABILITY DISTRIBUTIONS

Based on past observations a frequency distribution is obtained which can be converted to a probability distribution by dividing each category's observed frequency by the total number of observations.

Often, it is useful to compare an observed frequency distribution with the various classes of theoretical distributions in order to be able to classify the type of frequencies that are being observed. Toward this end, it is useful to know that a particular set of frequencies seems reasonably well approximated by a Normal, Poisson, Binomial, Beta, etc., form of distribution. Let us examine a few of these cases from the point of view of forecasting. After all, *a forecast* is simply *a probability distribution* that will apply to a future time.

BINOMIAL DISTRIBUTION[15]

If our interest centers on a situation where only two things can happen— that is, a dichotomy which we call a binary event—then, these two kinds of events can be:

---

[14] Over a period of time this uncertainty is being removed by automation—not by solution of the existing problem. In other words, these problems become less pressing as they become obsolete.

[15] See p. 306 where the Binomial distribution is used to inspect the quality of goods received from a vendor.

125
control
models:
forecasting
and
feedback

1. Equally likely; in colloquial language, 50–50; meaning 50 percent of the time *it is expected* that one thing will happen and 50 percent of the time *it is expected* that the other kind of event will occur. (For example, heads and tails.)

2. On the other hand, one of these events can be *more* likely than the other, for example, the likelihood that it will snow in June (in New Orleans) is smaller than the likelihood that it won't snow. We can say that p is the probability that event A will occur in a given trial (or interval of time) and $q = 1 - p$ is the probability that A will not occur and, therefore, the probability that B will occur in the given trial.

Now, let us run through a series of trials—say n of them. The probability that k of these trials results in an A-type event can be described by the Binomial distribution. Thus:

$$\text{Prob } (k, n, p) = \left[\frac{n!}{k!(n - k)!}\right] p^k q^{n-k}$$

We read this as follows: Prob (k, n, p) is the probability that in n trials there will be k occurrences of the A-type event—if p is the probability that A will occur in any given trial.[16]

For example, let us consider a situation in which for each trial the probability that A will occur is 0.40. If $n = 5$ trials, then:

$$\text{Prob } (0, 5, 0.40) = \left[\frac{(5 \cdot 4 \cdot 3 \cdot 2 \cdot 1)}{0!(5 \cdot 4 \cdot 3 \cdot 2 \cdot 1)}\right] (0.40)^0 (0.60)^5 = 0.07776$$

Similarly,

$$\text{Prob } (1, 5, 0.40) = \left[\frac{(5 \cdot 4 \cdot 3 \cdot 2 \cdot 1)}{1!(4 \cdot 3 \cdot 2 \cdot 1)}\right] (0.40)^1 (0.60)^4 = 0.25920$$

Continuing in this way we obtain the probability distribution that is given below. The resulting distribution is shown in Figure 5.8.

k	PROBABILITY THAT A WILL OCCUR k TIMES
0	0.07776
1	0.25920
2	0.34560
3	0.23040
4	0.07680
5	0.01024
	1.00000

Certain situations are well described by the Binomial distribution, but others

---

[16] We read $n!$ as n factorial. It is equal to the product $n(n - 1)(n - 2) \cdots 1$. Note that $0! = 1! = 1$.

FIGURE 5-8
The Binomial distri-
bution for $p = 0.40$
and $n = 5$.

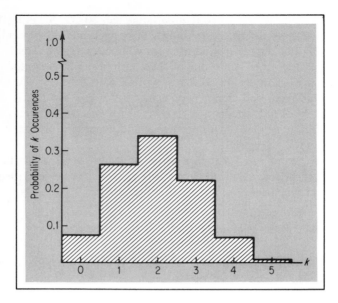

are not. Observed frequency distributions can fit many different patterns—some
of which have no precise theoretical shape that can be derived by formula.
Nevertheless, reasonable approximations often can be made.

NORMAL DISTRIBUTION

Assume that 25 consecutive observations are made of the length of a bar
of stock that is cut to size on a hand lathe. Figure 5.9 illustrates the hypothetical
result and compares it with a theoretical Normal distribution. The empirical
distribution, in this case, appears to be quite close to the Normal. (For an application of the Normal distribution, see pp. 90–92.)

FIGURE 5-9
The comparison of
an observed distri-
bution with a theo-
retical Normal distri-
bution.

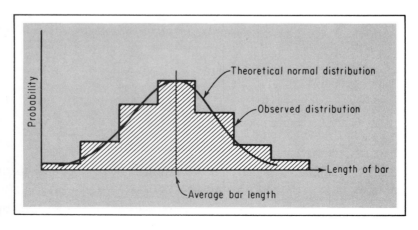

127
control
models:
forecasting
and
feedback

OTHER THEORETICAL DISTRIBUTIONS

Certain theoretical[17] distributions are often found to describe—with surprising accuracy—the relative frequencies and likelihoods of different kinds of events occurring in nature. We have mentioned and shown the Binomial, which is a discrete distribution, and the Normal, which is a continuous distribution. Figure 5.10 displays some examples of the Poisson distribution. It is usually applied to discrete descriptions of relatively rare events. The formula for the Poisson distribution is shown in the caption of Figure 5.10; $P(k)$ is the probability of k occurrences. Note that k can only take on integer values in this formulation, which is why we characterize the Poisson distribution as discrete.

FIGURE 5-10
A family of Poisson distributions with mean of M, that is, $P(k) = \dfrac{M^k e^{-M}}{k!}$.

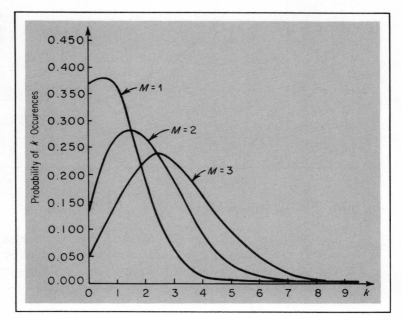

An example of another continuous distribution is shown in Figure 5.11. It is an exponential distribution; a form frequently encountered in production systems. The formula for the exponential distribution is shown in the caption of Figure 5.11. In this case, k can take on integer and fractional values, so the exponential distribution is continuous.

These distributions have significant bearing on our understanding of type-2 controls for production systems. They are easy to use and rapid to apply because so much is known about them in generality. But we must not lose sight of the fact that empirical distributions—obtained by observation and measurement of real systems which do not conform to any well known form, can also play a vital role. Intuitively derived distributions are similarly useful and significant,

[17] For example, Rectangular, Beta, and Hypergeometric distributions, as well as other distributions that are mentioned in the text.

and are certainly better than the attitude that risk factors should not be considered if they are not either based on theory or derived from observation.

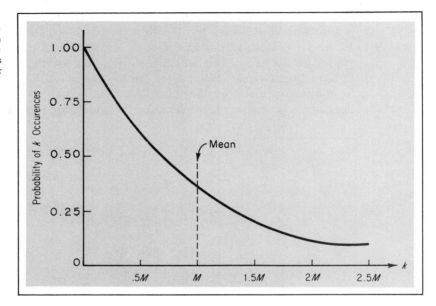

EMPIRICAL DISTRIBUTIONS

Consider our example (pp. 74–78) where the probability distributions were derived from estimates. Figure 5.12 illustrates the same probability distributions as Figure 4.2, but in this case we will assume that frequency measures are available to permit the construction of empirical distributions.

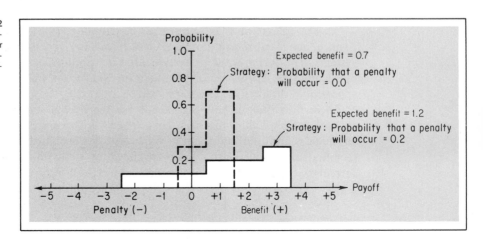

129
control
models:
forecasting
and
feedback

Based on prior experiences (ergo, empiricism) it is projected that strategy A might result in a penalty as great as two. If the very worst happens with alternative B, the company will break even. On the other hand, strategy A could produce as much benefit as three. Strategy B has an upper benefit limit of only one. Each payoff level is associated with an empirically derived probability measure. The *curves* have been drawn as (discrete) step functions. If more information had been available, smaller steps could have been made not only for integer values of payoff, but for fractions of million dollar units as well. As the interval for the measure decreases in size, the discrete distribution begins to approximate a continuous curve. *It should be emphasized that when deriving empirical distributions, the manager is, in effect, weighting his expectations based on observed experiences for the various outcomes. Ultimately, the weights are converted to probabilities so that the sum of the probabilities with respect to any strategy must equal one.*

Six payoff levels are considered for strategy A, thus,

OUTCOME (i)	STRATEGY A PAYOFF LEVEL (x_i)	PROBABILITY (p_i)	$(x_i)(p_i)$ TO CALCULATE EXPECTED VALUE	$p_i(x_i - \bar{x})^2$ TO CALCULATE VARIANCE**
1	-2	0.1	-0.2	$0.1(-2 - 1.2)^2 = 1.024$
2	-1	0.1	-0.1	$0.1(-1 - 1.2)^2 = .484$
3	0	0.1	0.0	$0.1(\ 0 - 1.2)^2 = .144$
4	$+1$	0.2	0.2	$0.2(+1 - 1.2)^2 = .008$
5	$+2$	0.2	0.4	$0.2(+2 - 1.2)^2 = .128$
6	$+3$	0.3	0.9	$0.3(+3 - 1.2)^2 = .972$
		$\sum_i = 1.0*$	$\bar{x} = 1.2$	$\sigma^2 = 2.760$

* Σ is the Greek letter symbol, designated capital sigma. It is used to signify the operation of addition, and is called an operator of summation.
** Variance (σ^2) is measured as $\Sigma_i (x_i - \bar{x})^2 p_i$; therefore, the standard deviation, σ, is determined by: $\sqrt{\Sigma_i (x_i - \bar{x})^2 p_i}$ For this example: $\sigma = \sqrt{2.760} = 1.66$.

Multiplying each payoff level by the probability that it will occur, and totalling these values, produces an average or expected benefit for both strategies.

For strategy A: $[(-)0.2 + (-)0.1 + 0 + 0.2 + 0.4 + 0.9] = 1.2$

For strategy B: $[0 + 0.7] = +0.7$

A has a considerably greater expected benefit than has B. But it also has a two out of ten possibility that some penalty will be experienced, whereas strategy B involves no such danger. (The variance for B is 0.210). Type-1 and type-3 control are out of the question. In terms of type-2 control, what is the sensible course of action?

At least since the time of the Marquis Pierre Simon de Laplace (1749–1827), there has been general agreement that this French astronomer and mathematican correctly stated the solution to problems of this kind. In our terms he would *choose that strategy which produces the most favorable expected value.*[18] But this is the decision formulation of the problem. In control terms, the manager is faced with the following problem of conflicting objectives.

	EXPECTED VALUE	VARIANCE
Strategy *A*	1.2	2.760
Strategy *B*	0.7	0.210
Objective	largest value	smallest value

If he weights the importance of obtaining the largest expected value and the importance of achieving the smallest variance equally, then it is likely that he will choose strategy *B*, since *A* produces *less than* twice as much benefit as *B* but more than 13 times the variance of *B*. Later, (see pp. 343-45) we shall have more to say about this kind of problem.

MARKOVIAN FORECASTS

If an experiment is conducted at an early stage, such as a test market, and there is reason to believe that the system is stable and of the Markovian type, which was previously described, then a model of the following kind can be used.

Assume that the universe is divided into two parts, for example, noncustomers at time t, (NC_t) and customers at time t, (C_t). Over a specified interval we observe that 40 noncustomers become customers; 60 noncustomers remain noncustomers; 70 customers remain customers; and 30 customers become noncustomers. This information based on a market of 200 people is assembled in matrix form. Thus:

		Time 2	
	$\rightarrow$	NC_2	C_2
Time 1	NC_1	60	40
	C_1	30	70

We convert these numbers into transition probabilities such that each row

---

[18] Thus, a maximum value for profit; a minimum value for cost.

131
control
models:
forecasting
and
feedback

sums to unity. Then:

		Time 2	
Time 1	$\overrightarrow{NC_1}$	NC_2 0.6	C_2 0.4
	C_1	0.3	0.7

Now let us suppose that we start at time 1 in a large market with 100,000 potential customers. To begin with, they are all noncustomers. How many customers will we have at time 2? This is easily determined if the assumptions that we have made actually hold. Thus,

$$NC_2 = 0.6(100{,}000) + 0.3(0) = 60{,}000$$
$$C_2 = 0.4(100{,}000) + 0.7(0) = \underline{40{,}000}$$
$$100{,}000$$

To determine the number of customers at time 3, 4, 5, and so on, we use the same relationship, viz.,

$$NC_t = 0.6NC_{t-1} + 0.3C_{t-1}$$
$$C_t = 0.4NC_{t-1} + 0.7C_{t-1}$$

Thus, for $t = 3$, we obtain:

$$NC_3 = 0.6(60{,}000) + 0.3(40{,}000) = 48{,}000$$
$$C_3 = 0.4(60{,}000) + 0.7(40{,}000) = \underline{52{,}000}$$
$$100{,}000$$

And for $t = 4$:

$$NC_4 = 0.6(48{,}000) + 0.3(52{,}000) = 44{,}400$$
$$C_4 = 0.4(48{,}000) + 0.7(52{,}000) = \underline{55{,}600}$$
$$100{,}000$$

We can continue this process until the results *stabilize* and there is only a very minor difference between NC_t and NC_{t-1}; similarly, almost no change between C_t and C_{t-1}. This is called the *steady state* of the system. Figure 5.13 shows the trajectory of the prediction for customers over a period of time. We observe that the steady state result is 57,143 customers. In terms of share, the forecast at steady state is 0.57 for customers and (necessarily) 0.43 for noncustomers.

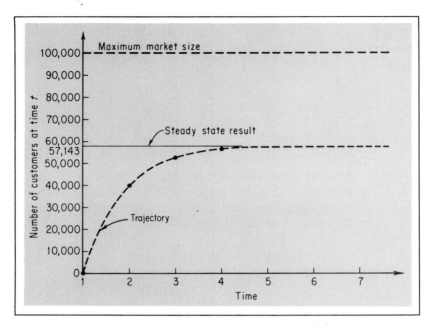

FIGURE 5-13
Forecasts must pro-
ject trajectories as
well as steady states.

HISTORICAL AND SEASONAL PREDICTIONS

When historical information is available, the forecasting and prediction problem takes on some different aspects. The (so called) historical forecast is based on the assumption that what happened last year will happen again. Actually, it is an historical prediction. Thus, for example, if the demand in the previous January was X, then in the coming January it will also be X. This method is effective only if a very stable seasonal pattern exists.

If the mean level appears to be changing over a period of time, but the seasonal pattern remains fixed, then a *base series* modification can be used. For example, assume that in the preceding year the quarterly demands were 40, 20, 30, 10. This gives a yearly demand of 100 units. Now, let us assume that in the current year the yearly demand is expected to increase to 120 units. Then the quarterly predictions would be $(40/100)\,120 = 48$; $(20/100)\,120 = 24$; $(30/100)\,120 = 36$; $(10/100)\,120 = 12$. These quarterly demands total to 120 units.

When the seasonal pattern is not believed to be stable and the system is thought to not change abruptly, but to follow a trend, then a moving average can be used to advantage. Thus, a four-month moving average would be calculated as follows:

$$D_5 = \frac{D_1 + D_2 + D_3 + D_4}{4}$$

where D_t = demand in the tth month. Then,

$$D_6 = \frac{D_2 + D_3 + D_4 + D_5}{4}$$

and

$$D_7 = \frac{D_3 + D_4 + D_5 + D_6}{4}$$

It will be noted that each month's prediction is updated by dropping the first month of the series and adding the latest observation. In this way, trends are taken into account and old information is removed from the system.[19]

LEAST-SQUARES, LAG-LEAD PREDICTION

An important approach for prediction is correlational technique (such as the method of least-squares) when the dependent variables (to be predicted) appear to be related to other factors which *lead* them. Then, it is possible to predict a sequence of outcomes on the basis of observations of the other factor. The least-squares technique is therefore, a method for estimating the value of y in terms of observations of x where y cannot be observed in time, but x can be observed. No causality is implied between y and x because a common causal factor (that is unknown) may account for whatever relationship is found. For example, consider the following data:

i	X_i = NUMBER OF CHILDREN BORN IN YEAR i (IN MILLIONS)	$i + 5$	Y_{i+5} = KINDERGARTEN ATTENDANCE IN YEAR $i + 5$ (IN MILLIONS)
1	3	6	2
2	4	7	3
3	6	8	5
4	4	9	5
5	8	10	6

We assume that the number of children born in a given year *leads* kindergarten attendance by 5 years, and we have, therefore, paired the X_i's with the Y_{i+5}'s

[19] Many control systems utilize *exponential smoothing*. It has proven effective for such diverse applications as tracking aircraft and predicting demand levels for inventory systems. Here, we have:

$D_t = \alpha d_{t-1} + (1 - \alpha)D_{t-1}$

where:
D_{t-1} was the *prediction* for the prior period $t - 1$;
d_{t-1} was the *actual result* observed for the prior period $t - 1$; and
D_t is the *prediction* that is *to be made* for period t.
Generally, α is kept quite small, in the neighborhood of 0.05 to 0.15, in order to decrease the system's response to random fluctuations.

that occurred five years later. Let us fit a least-squares line to these data. We use the *normal equations* (based on the assumption of a *linear* relationship between X_i and Y_{i+5}). The least-squares line is chosen to minimize the variance of the distances of the observed points from that line. The normal equations achieve this objective.

$$\sum_{i=1}^{i=N} Y_{i+5} = aN + b \sum_{i=1}^{i=N} X_i$$

$$\sum_{i=1}^{i=N} X_i Y_{i+5} = a \sum_{i=1}^{i=N} X_i + b \sum_{i=1}^{i=N} X_i^2$$

$N = 5$, which is the total number of pairs of X_i and Y_{i+5}. Then:

i	X_i	Y_{i+5}	$X_i Y_{i+5}$	X_i^2
1	3	2	6	9
2	4	3	12	16
3	6	5	30	36
4	4	5	20	16
5	8	6	48	64
Σ	25	21	116	141

Therefore:

$21 = a(5) + b(25)$

$116 = a(25) + b(141)$

Solving for a and b, we obtain: $a = 61/80$; $b = 11/16$. These values are introduced in the least-squares line:

$$Y_{i+5} = a + bX_i = +\frac{61}{80} + \frac{11}{16} X_i$$

The appropriate line and the actual scatter of values are shown in Figure 5.14. To use this line, let us suppose that when $i = 6$, $X_i = 10$. We see that Y_{i+5} would be predicted to be 7.6375 million. We would use this line for prediction only if the observed data appear to fit it well.

As a general rule, forecasting and prediction procedures are one of the major sources of trouble in developing control models. Different forecasts and predictions for the same phenomena, frequently exist within a single organization. That is, the production manager derives one forecast; the sales manager derives another; branch managers derive still others. It is of critical importance that all parties share the same opinions, and, usually, much stronger control relations can be obtained if the data and experience of all participants are pooled.

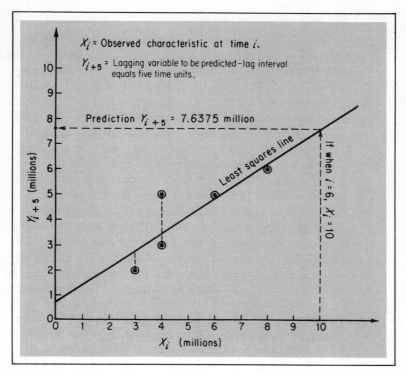

FIGURE 5-14
Least-squares linear
relationship between
a leading indicator
and the variable to be
predicted.

In the figure:

X_i = Observed characteristic at time i.

Y_{i+5} = Lagging variable to be predicted – lag interval equals five time units.

Prediction Y_{i+5} = 7.6375 million

Least squares line

If when $i = 6$, $X_i = 10$

Y_{i+5} (millions)

X_i (millions)

PERSONAL PREDICTIONS

Subjective forecasts and predictions are entirely permissible when no data can be obtained. This would be the case when no historical precedent exists, and this would be true of many new product or new service ventures. A panel of experts might be preferred in some cases to a single estimator. The weaknesses of this method are apparent. Personal bias can distort results, but still worse is the haunting fear that the subjective estimates may be pure gossamer. We can hardly ignore the susceptibility of individuals to illusions and mirages. On the other hand, there is good reason to believe that, frequently, a prediction once made becomes an objective and a goal, because of interaction between the prediction and the will to prove the prediction. This understanding has led to great interest in controlling futures. Since 1970 the subject of "futurology" has blossomed in government, industry and the universities.[20]

 [20] See for example, J. McHale, *The Future of the Future* (New York: Braziller, 1969).

HEURISTIC CONTROL

Heuristic comes from the Greek word, *heuriskein*, meaning to discover. The term has been used by Simon and Newell[21] to describe a particular approach to problem solving, decision making and control. Heuristic models utilize logic, common sense and above all, past experience, to identify (diagnose) an environmental pattern and a prescription for treating it. These models replace the classical mathematical approach when such formal, analytical methods hold forth little promise of being operational. The essence of the heuristic approach resides in the application of selective routines that reduce the complexity of a problem.

Looking at this procedure in another way, the heuristic approach can be used to simulate the decision-making pattern of human beings in the system. The advantages of this approach are consistency, speed, endurance, and the ability to cope with more data and larger systems than is otherwise possible. Of course, heuristics are not limited to control-type situations. They can be applied, for example, to planning. But, they are most easily identified with the feedback systems that characterize control systems. Heuristic models supplement any decision process. They represent a kind of nonfatiguing, all-persevering decision maker that is embodied in a machine to *imitate* the performance of a human being. The concept of heuristic analysis is not particularly applicable to long-range problems. The programming effort required to build the model would not be justified for nonrepetitive decision problems; but it is well-suited to repetitive, complex control situations that refuse to submit to straightforward mathematical analysis. The heuristic approach necessitates capturing the cognitive and inferential skills of the successful Controller.

Heuristics represents a break with tradition. It is a relatively new approach. For many years, the notion that simplicity is a goal for scientific explanations of complex phenomena has been the motivating force in scientific achievement. In this sense, a concise mathematical statement meets the criterion of simplicity. This notion of simplicity can be traced to William of Ockham, who in the 14th century proposed the Principle of Parsimony. Not at all facetiously it has also been called Ockham's razor. The underlying notion of this principle is that conclusions should be accepted which follow from the least number of propositions, assumptions, and steps of reasoning. From this "myth of simplicity," as it has been characterized by Mario Bunge,[22] has sprung reverence for so called "elegant" mathematical solutions which are, in large part, praised for their succinctness. Similarly, astronomical theory has been deeply influenced by the notion of simplicity. Science, today, is still the heir to this tradition.

Whether useful or destructive for the physical sciences, the idea breaks down rapidly when applied to the control of behavioral systems. Thus, one might say that *even if* the principle of parsimony operates effectively for controlling the machine side of the interface, it is hardly applicable on the man side. Heuristic models are not simple in the classic sense. They embody unexplained assump-

[21] H.A. Simon and A. Newell, "Heuristic Problem Solving: The Next Advance in Operations Research," *Operations Research*, Vol. 6, No. 1, January-February, 1958.
[22] M. Bunge, *The Myth of Simplicity* (Englewood Cliffs, N.J.: Prentice-Hall, Inc., 1963).

137
control
models:
forecasting
and
feedback

tions and convoluted reasoning, as required. Only in this way does it seem possible that the most difficult problems regarding the adaptation of men and machines can be resolved. We should recognize the fact that parsimony must be discarded if we are to make significant advances in designing man-machine control systems. The tradition of the principle of parsimony works against us, not for us when we try to control the operations of highly complex systems.

PROBLEMS

1 Give some examples of systems that might be described by the following:
   a. No distribution exists.
   b. A stationary distribution exists.
   c. Shewhart-type stability exists.
   d. There is Markovian-type stability.
   e. There is non-Markovian prior state stability.
   f. Instability exists or, at least, no probabilities can be found to describe the likelihoods of the states of nature.
   g. The states of nature are unknown.

2 A manufacturer of kitchen equipment keeps track of *new housing starts* in his region. He believes that demand for his products follows housing starts by *three* months. Fit a least-square line to the data below which are based on the manager's assumptions.

Month	Sales Volume	Housing Starts
1	$45,000	260
2	60,000	250
3	62,000	320
4	30,000	380
5	40,000	500
6	45,000	480
7	68,000	320
8	75,000	400
9	80,000	350
10	45,000	250
11	30,000	100
12	25,000	150

3 A control matrix is presented on p. 121 to represent the performance of three different machines, viz., a hand lathe, a turret lathe, and an automatic screw machine. All three machines assure the same expected value for the OD of a pipe that is to be made. Use these data to determine variance as a measure of the degree of control that can be obtained with each machine. Comment on your results.

4 Would you prefer a poor prediction or a good forecast for control? Explain your answer.

5 Can control exist without feedback? List some common uses of the word control, such as governmental control, quality control, pressure control, cost control, a pitcher's control, and so on. Do these require feedback? If so, how?

6 A beach umbrella manufacturer had the following monthly sales in the year just completed:

Month	Sales
1	500
2	800
3	1200
4	2000
5	4000
6	8000
7	10000
8	7000
9	6000
10	1000
11	500
12	300

He anticipates a growth in his next year's sales of 40 percent.

a. Prepare a monthly estimate of sales for the coming year.

b. Why is such a monthly breakdown of sales required?

references

ANSOFF, H. I., ed., *Business Strategy.* Middlesex, England: Penguin Books, 1969.

ASHBY, W. R., *An Introduction to Cybernetics.* New York: John Wiley & Sons, Inc., 1956.

BEER, STAFFORD, *Cybernetics and Management.* New York: John Wiley & Sons, Inc., 1959.

———, *Decision and Control.* New York: John Wiley & Sons, Inc., 1967.

BELLMAN, R., *Adaptive Control Processes.* Princeton, N.J.: Princeton University Press, 1961.

———, and R. KALABA, *Mathematical Trends in Control Theory.* New York: Dover Publishing, 1964.

BONINI, C. P., R. J. JAEDICHE and H. M. WAGNER, *Management Controls: New Directions in Basic Research.* New York: McGraw-Hill Book Company, 1964.

BROWN, R. G., *Smoothing, Forecasting and Prediction.* Englewood Cliffs, N. J.: Prentice-Hall, Inc., 1962.

COCHRAN, W. G., and G. M. COX, *Experimental Designs.* New York: John Wiley & Sons, Inc., 1950.

COOMBS, C. A., *Theory of Data.* New York: John Wiley & Sons, Inc., 1964.

CYERT, R. and J. MARCH, *A Behavioral Theory of the Firm.* Englewood Cliffs, N.J.: Prentice-Hall, Inc., 1967.

DE LATIL, P., *Thinking by Machine: A Study of Cybernetics* (Trans. Y. M. Golla). Boston: Houghton Mifflin Company, 1957.

FELLER, W., *Probability Theory and Its Applications,* Vol. I, 2nd ed. John Wiley & Sons, Inc., 1957.

FISHER, R. A., *The Design of Experiments.* Edinburgh: Oliver & Boyd, Ltd., 1947.

FORRESTER, J. W., *Industrial Dynamics.* New York: John Wiley & Sons, Inc., 1961.

FREUND, JOHN E., *Mathematical Statistics*. Englewood Cliffs, N.J.: Prentice-Hall, Inc., 1962.

GOLDBERG. SAMUEL, *Difference Equations*. New York: John Wiley & Sons, Inc., 1961,

GOOD, I. J., *Probability and Weighting of Evidence*. London: Griffin, 1950.

GUILBAUD, G. T., *What Is Cybernetics?* New York: Grove Press, 1960.

HARE, V. C., Jr., *Systems Analysis: A Diagnostic Approach*. New York: Harcourt Brace Jovanovich, 1967.

HERTZ, D. B., *New Power for Management, Computer Systems and Management Science*. New York: McGraw-Hill Book Company, 1969.

IJIRI, Y. *Management Goals and Accounting for Control*. New York: Rand-McNally, 1965,

KAHN, H. and A. J. WIENER, *The Year 2000; A Framework for Speculation on the Next Thirty-Nine Years*. New York: The MacMillan Company, 1967.

KEMPTHORNE, O., *The Design and Analysis of Experiments*. New York: John Wiley & Sons, Inc., 1952.

MANN, H. B., *Analysis and Design of Experiments*. New York: Dover Publications, Inc., 1949.

McDONOUGH, A. M., *Management Systems: Working Concepts and Practices*. Homewood, Ill.: Richard D. Irwin, Inc., 1965.

MESAROVIC, M. D., ed., *Views on General Control Systems Theory*. New York: John Wiley & Sons, Inc., 1964.

MISHKIN, ELI, and LUDWIG BRAUN, JR., *Adaptive Control Systems*. New York: McGraw-Hill, Inc., 1961.

MILLER, DAVID W. and MARTIN K. STARR, *Executive Decisions and Operations Research*, 2nd ed., Englewood Cliffs, N.J.: Prentice-Hall, Inc., 1969.

SEIDENBERG, R., *Post-Historic Man: An Inquiry*. Boston: Beacon Press, 1950.

SIMON, HERBERT A., *Models of Man*. New York: John Wiley & Sons. Inc., 1957.

SINAIKO, H. W., ed., *Selected Papers on Human Factors in the Design and Use of Control Systems*. New York: Dover Publishing Co., 1961.

SINGH, JAGJIT, *Great Ideas In Information Theory, Language and Cybernetics*. New York: Dover Publishing Co., 1966.

STRONG, E. P. and R. D. SMITH, *Management Control Models*. New York: Holt, Rinehart and Winston, 1968.

WIENER, NORBERT, *The Human Use of Human Beings*. Garden City, New York: Doubleday & Company, Inc., 1950.

part **INPUT-**
two **OUTPUT**
MANAGEMENT

chapter
six
information
management

Recently, it has been recognized that all activities are forms of information to be managed. More importantly, that *every* operation has its counterpart in data form and is transformable into data. Plans are information maps; controls are information regulators. Although there is nothing astounding in this realization, because it was always obvious, it has had an important effect—simply because the obvious has now been perceived and used for improved management.

INFORMATION SYSTEMS

Both men and machines require information to accomplish work. Each have characteristic ways of transmitting, receiving, channeling, and storing information. However, the use of mechanical storage systems is needed to augment the limited and fallible human memory system. Libraries, file drawers, microfilm records, and computer memories are important components of the total system, but the machine elements must be viewed in terms of their relationship to the man in the system. This is especially true because information continually flows back and forth across the *man-machine interface*. Men and machines can operate together only when there is adequate communication. Language translation must be taken into account. The syntax and grammar of the machine are far more precise, the vocabulary far smaller, than that of man.

Extensive mechanical storage of information creates serious problems because significant costs must be incurred to maintain it as well as to search through it in order to obtain the required information. The cost of both storage and searching rises as the volume of information that is stored increases. The Dewey Decimal System of categorization developed for information retrieval from library storage has provided a model information storage system. How-

FIGURE 6-1
With an improved information retrieval methods, it is possible to search more effectively, less expensively, and more rapidly. Consequently, the optimum number of units to search increases.

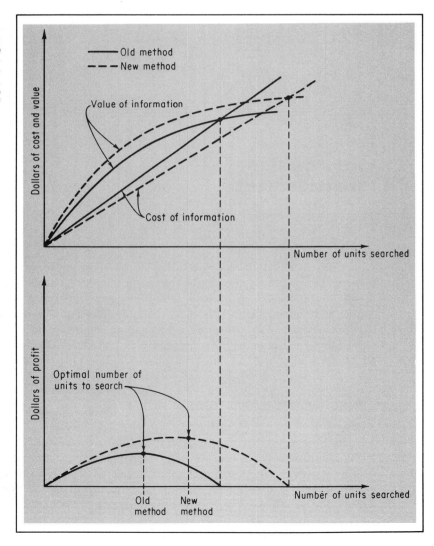

ever, the amount of information available for conducting business has increased at an exponential rate. Far more sophisticated schemes for retrieving information are now required.

It is generally unfortunate that information duplication cannot be reduced to a minimum. The time required to avoid duplicative efforts—by surveying all relevant data files to determine whether or not a result has previously been discovered—may cost a greater amount than would be needed to recalculate or redevelop the same information. That is, for example, when the cost of searching equals or exceeds the cost of research and development, we choose the latter approach. There is only one other potential course of action, that is, reduce the cost of searching. This can be accomplished *if* we can design new systems for information handling and retrieval.

We are in the midst of a technological revolution with respect to information retrieval methods. As in many other circumstances, necessity mothered invention. Much research is being devoted to this subject. Advances in equipment and methods are being realized. As these new data systems are developed, the cost of searching through a given amount of information is being reduced; the value of the recovered information is increasing (in the sense that it is a purer grade of ore); and the probability of locating vital information quickly is being significantly improved. As a result, the optimum number of units of information to search through is being increased. The nature of the change is demonstrated by Figure 6.1.

THE AGE OF INFORMATION

Another aspect of information searching is that it takes a given length of time to recover the information that is needed. The age of information can inflict severe penalties if it becomes excessive. For each situation the definition of what constitutes excessive age will differ. Thus, for example, in the air traffic control situation shown in Figure 6.2, after two minutes the relevant information has aged to the point that it is useless. At speeds of approximately 600 mph, jet aircraft heading on collision courses provide position information which must be acted upon almost instantly. Each situation dictates its own time scale for measuring the age of information. At some age either control is lost, an emergency has developed, or the information has become worthless. Relatively continuous control is an important factor when the system's performance is sensitive to the age of information. If the control system is not continuously fed information, then sample data intervals must be very small.

Another example of the detrimental effect of overly delayed or overaged information is in the inventory area. Here, the critical age of information is a function of various factors such as the demand rate for items, the reserve stock policy (i.e., the extra units carried to meet unexpectedly high demand, see pp. 281, 289–92) and the length of time required to get a replenishment order filled. Let us consider a perpetual inventory system.[1] Assume that the specified

[1] See pp. 289–91.

reorder level is reached for an item and that this information is not sent by the stock clerk to the purchasing department immediately. While the information that will trigger a purchase order is aging, further withdrawals can reduce the stock level and create a serious "out of stock" situation before a new order can even be placed, let alone filled.

Information recovery treats the problem of how to design the information transference characteristics of a system. It is concerned with directing various kinds of information to both men and machines at appropriate points in time. It is a critical determinant of control, safety, and other factors of fundamental importance.

FIGURE 6-2
Information will have aged excessively after spending two minutes at the control center without being acted upon.

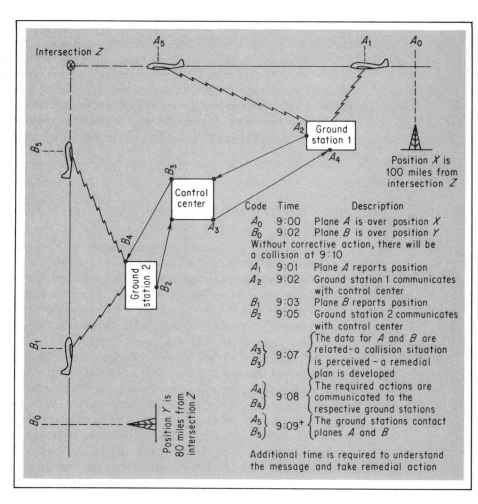

Code	Time	Description
A_0	9:00	Plane A is over position X
B_0	9:02	Plane B is over position Y
		Without corrective action, there will be a collision at 9:10
A_1	9:01	Plane A reports position
A_2	9:02	Ground station 1 communicates with control center
B_1	9:03	Plane B reports position
B_2	9:05	Ground station 2 communicates with control center
A_3 B_3	9:07	The data for A and B are related—a collision situation is perceived—a remedial plan is developed
A_4 B_4	9:08	The required actions are communicated to the respective ground stations
A_5 B_5	9:09+	The ground stations contact planes A and B

Additional time is required to understand the message and take remedial action

THE MEASUREMENT OF INFORMATION

The rate at which information flows in a system is a significant factor. We usually measure the rate of information flow in the unit of *bits-per-period of time*. A *bit*, or *bi*nary digi*t*, is the amount of information that can be developed by a binary device such as a relay or an electric light switch. Two states, *on* and *off*, are characteristic of such binary devices. Frequently, we represent the binary states by 0 and 1.

A single relay ($n = 1$) has two such postions, 0 and 1. Two relays ($n = 2$) can provide four different system states (N) as follows:

STATE	RELAY 1	RELAY 2
1	0	0
2	0	1
3	1	0
4	1	1

FIGURE 6-3
Information is measured in bits and information flow is measured by the number of bits-per-unit of time.

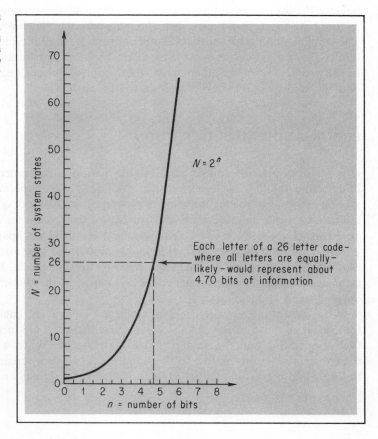

$N = 2^n$

Each letter of a 26 letter code – where all letters are equally-likely – would represent about 4.70 bits of information

N = number of system states

n = number of bits

Three relays ($n = 3$) would provide $N =$ eight states; four relays ($n = 4$) would provide $N =$ sixteen states. We can represent this directly as follows:[2]

$$N = 2^n$$

where:

$n =$ Number of relays (in bits), and $N =$ Number of system states.

We call the number of relays the number of bits. Therefore, for any given number of system states it is possible to determine the number of bits that would be required to furnish such variety. Figure 6.3 furnishes a graph of the function $N = 2^n$.

HUMAN INFORMATION PROCESSING

The average human transmitter or receiver, in any system, is capable of handling about 35 bits-per-second (and about two or three bits at any *instant* of time). Machines can be designed to handle much greater quantities. At the interface, however, where man and machine meet, it is clearly necessary to balance the inputs and outputs. There are the problems of designing communications between men and men; men and machines; and machines and machines. The computer and other mechanical devices cannot be allowed to exceed human limits. This consideration represents a critical factor, particularly with respect to the production management area where control devices, technology, methodology, and human behavior interact continuously.

ERROR AND FAULT DETECTION

A major production control responsibility relates to the information problem of detecting a fault that causes a system's failure. This is a special kind of information retrieval problem. In complex processes, the cause of a failure may be difficult to locate because thousands of causes can create an identical set of *symptoms*. How can the cause of failure be determined as rapidly as possible? *Diagnosis* of faults is often crucial in highly automated systems. When a single element fails the entire system might have to be shut down. It is reasonably estimated that for complex gear, about 50 percent of the system's downtime is devoted solely to locating faults.

When downtime is costly, it is not unusual to provide backup equipment for critical system components. Thus, two identical parts are furnished; the one that is operating and the second that is standing by. When a failure occurs, the entire operation is shifted to the standby unit while a repair crew attempts to locate and correct the failure in the unit that was originally operating. Thus,

[2] Another representation would be $\log_2 N = n$.

duplicating critical components for an airplane, a telephone switching system, a broadcasting station transmitter, or a submarine's air supply unit can be quickly justified on a cost basis.

Investing in duplicate equipment is hardly the sort of action that production managers enjoy taking. The apparent waste and commensurate expense is difficult to accept. Often, the system's components are too expensive to permit any functional duplication to be designed as backup. We observe that the penalty that must be paid for delay in locating a fault will be a function of the type of system. It is also a function of the circumstances under which the failure occurs. Thus, jet engine malfunction on the ground is not in the same league with the equivalent failure aloft. Downtime for a large petroleum refinery at any time can represent substantial costs within a short time. A rapid fault locating (and correction) system would be worth its cost.

FIGURE 6-4
The use of an itemized search procedure to locate a system fault, called X_0. (Search pattern: A-1, 2, 3, . . . 8; B-1, 2, 3, . . . 8; . . . H-1, 2, 3, . . . 8.)

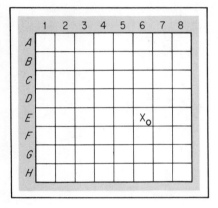

The design of self-repairing equipment is still for most practical purposes quite far in the future. But it is frequently possible to design a system in such a way as to minimize the amount of time required for locating faults. The basic idea behind the method that will be described stems from information theory but we shall have no need to introduce complex mathematics in order to explain this idea. Consider the chess board shown in Figure 6.4. Suppose that the system design is divisible into 64 sections or modules—much like the 64 squares of the chess board. Assume that the system has failed. We know that one of the sections is responsible, but we don't know which one. Accordingly we state that one of the boxes has an "X_O" in it, to represent the module that has failed. How can we locate the source of our troubles?

First, we will illustrate the use of a conventional approach. Section by section (box by box), we test each of the 64 modules in order to find out which one is the malfunctioning unit. On the average, we should locate the faulty module at the 32nd or 33rd test. Assuming that each test requires 5 minutes and that, on the average, one failure occurs each day, we would spend 160 minutes or two hours and 40 minutes trying to locate failures each day. The cost of using this procedure would include searching 160 minutes and repair time and cost which is not stated here plus the down-time cost of a nonoperating unit (for 160 minutes plus repair time).

Now, let us try another approach. The system is divided in two, for example, columns 1 through 4 (called the left hand side) and columns 5 through 8 (called the right hand side). Then, we need a test routine that asks the following ques-

FIGURE 6-5
The use of a binary search procedure to locate a system fault, called X_0. [Search pattern: (1) Left hand or right hand? (2) Upper portion or lower portion? (3) Repeat above steps until fault is located.]

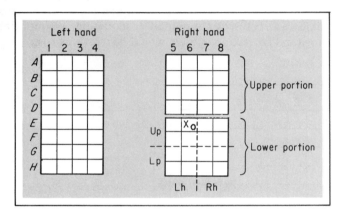

tion: Is the fault in the left or right hand side of the system? (See Figure 6.5.) Since the answer is right hand side, we divide the right hand portion into two sections (as equal in size as possible). Then we ask: Is the fault in the upper or lower part of the right hand portion of the system?

On the basis of the answers to these two questions, the size of the problem has been reduced from 8 × 8 to 4 × 4. We have determined that the fault occurred in the lower, right-hand quadrant of the system. We then repeat the same two questions, this time with respect to the faulty quadrant. Thus, we use a left-right test, followed by an up-down test. The size of the problem is now reduced to a 2 × 2. Repeating the procedure once more, by testing left-right and up-down, we locate the specific module that is faulty.

Six tests had to be used to locate this fault. Assuming the same 5-minute period per question, only 30 minutes or one-half hour would be required to locate the fault. This is less than one-fifth the time that was previously required. It should produce substantial cost savings when the facility is costly or its service critical.

We can tell how many of the up-down, left-right questions must be asked to locate a fault, by noting their relation to the various powers of two. Each question represented a dichotomy—or a binary choice.

$$
\begin{array}{ll}
2^1 = 2 & 2^{11} = 2,048 \\
2^2 = 4 & 2^{12} = 4,096 \\
2^3 = 8 & 2^{13} = 8,192 \\
2^4 = 16 & 2^{14} = 16,384 \\
2^5 = 32 & 2^{15} = 32,768 \\
2^6 = 64 & 2^{16} = 65,536 \\
2^7 = 128 & 2^{17} = 131,072 \\
2^8 = 256 & 2^{18} = 262,144 \\
2^9 = 512 & 2^{19} = 524,288 \\
2^{10} = 1,024 & 2^{20} = 1,048,576
\end{array}
$$

our example $\longrightarrow$ $2^6 = 64$

The exponent is the number of questions asked, and the value of 2 raised to that exponent is the number of the modules. It is interesting to note that the game of 20 questions[3] produces 1,048,576 distinguishably different situations. The key, of course, is to design the right 20 questions, such that the pattern of replies can succeed in identifying the one fault that exists in over one million possibilities.

Thus, assuming that we wish to find a fault that exists in a system composed of 1,048,576 sections and that we search through these sections individually at a rate of one thousand sections per minute, then, we would spend approximately $8\frac{1}{2}$ hours locating the fault. On the other hand, using the binary method that is based on information theory, yet counting at the much slower rate of one question per minute, we can accomplish the same job in 20 minutes. We see that the bigger the system, the more important it is to utilize a rational information method for locating faults.

How can such systems be designed? The system must be able to assess its own operating condition in the binary sense that we have just described, by *searching across different groupings* of the system's sections. We must call upon the ingenuity of the designer to achieve this objective. Many times when a system is being designed it is possible to break it into divisional modules of the type that the operating characteristics of various groupings can be tested by an output measure such as voltage, weight, or pressure. If a failure exists *anywhere* within the grouping it is apparent in terms of a divergence from the expected standard measure. Different measures might have to be used for different groupings. The notion of "left-right" or "up-down" is merely symbolic. It is seldom possible and hardly necessary that each grouping break the total system into exactly equal parts. Technological design constraints will determine what can be done to expedite the search procedure and provide rapid tracking of a system fault.

Before we leave this subject, let us note that faults occur in information systems which also can be costly. It would, for example, be most beneficial if a filing system could be designed along the lines we have discussed so that misplaced items could be quickly located. Such "lost items" are a constant source of irritation and represent a not inconsequential cost for management. Perhaps, searching time is the smallest component of this cost. The lack of vital production

---

[3] The players are allowed to ask twenty questions to try to identify a particular person, event, item, etc., which everyone knows, but the players.

information, inferior decision making, irritation, and lost customer goodwill represent substantial costs that are difficult or impossible to measure.

INPUT-OUTPUT SPECIFICATIONS

For systems development, blueprints and other specifications of inputs, outputs and process factors must be clearly expressed. Every production manager is acutely aware of the information requirements that dominate his decisions and actions. Figure 6.6 presents an example of a production blueprint. Blueprints are one of the production department's most familiar information models. They are used because they can convey pertinent production information, unambiguously in a more efficient manner than any other form of communication. *Blueprints are a detailed description of output.* They explain completely what is to be done. The language of blueprints consists of conventions of spatial configurations and abstract written symbols as well. It is not difficult to learn this language, and it is a practical necessity for production management to understand it. Nonfabricating systems have means of visual expression that are comparable. Consider, for example, architectural blueprints.

FIGURE 6-6
Blueprint of a conveyor take-up unit. [From Warren J. Luzadder, *Basic Graphics*, 5th ed. (Englewood Cliffs, N. J.: Prentice-Hall, Inc., 1970), p. 459.]

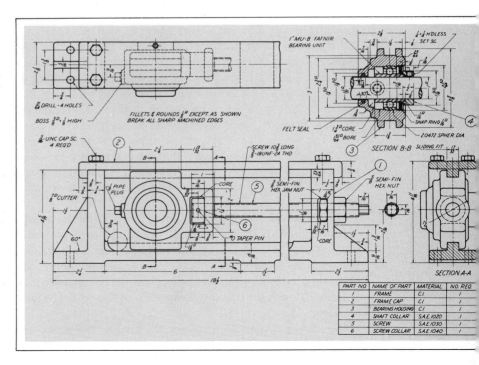

Both product and process blueprints must be drawn in total detail. This is an engineering job requiring highly specialized technological knowledge. The equivalent of the blueprint in service development is a carefully detailed statement of the systems output, that is, the service to be provided under all conditions that are likely to be experienced. A blueprint of output is peculiarly characteristic of physical production, including such products as a building or a ship. On the other hand, the blueprint of process components is as likely to apply to a service process as any fabrication process.

Following blueprints, or their equivalent, *bills of materials*, or their equivalent, must be drawn up. Figure 6.7 illustrates a typical bill of materials. There is nothing sacred about the form that is used. It is the purpose of the form that counts. Materials required to accomplish the job are detailed. Purchased parts are listed. The bill of materials organizes the requirements of the project or job in such a way that further and more detailed accounting by parts can be carried on. In other words, it provides a background for understanding the job, of which the parts are components. According to the particulars of the situation, appropriate forms can be developed.

FIGURE 6-7
Bill of materials.

Item ___Switch Z 33___   Sheet No. _1_ of _2_
Drawings___Z 1–Z 6___   Assembly___5HP MOTOR J___

Part No.	Part name	No./item	Material	Quantity/item	Cost/item	Remarks
CH 20	CASING	1	SF60	0.25 lbs.	$0.15	Cast, trim
SJ 64	DRIVE SPRG.	2	Sprg. St.	-----	$0.08	Purchase
RH 82	1" ROD	3	1045 ST.	4 in.	$0.05	Make
TJ 32	FITTING	1	Ti–6Al–4V	0.10 lbs.	$0.85	Forge, anneal

Next, operations sheets are drawn up and a first pass can be made at specifying the materials handling equipment that will be used. Figure 6.8 depicts an *operations sheet*. This is known by other names as well, including a route sheet and a specifications sheet. At this point, a good deal of information about the structure of the system has been made explicit. The plans are moving toward operational realization. The bill of materials and the operations sheet, or their equivalents, apply to almost any type of production system. Once we reach this stage of development, we are in a position to specify all the materials, components, and subassemblies that must be brought together to realize the base

FIGURE 6-8
Operations sheet.

Part No. __CH 20__   Economic lot size __500__
Part name __CASING__   Process time/pce. __3.5 h__
Blueprint No. _____   Set-up time __2 h__

Use for __Switch Z 33__   Quantity per __1__
         __Switch Z 34__   __1__
         __Sub-contract T 102__   __50. mo.__

Material __SF 60__   Vendor __BQV__
% scrap __10__   Weight __¼ lb. per__   Cost __$0.15 per__

Operation No.	Operation	Machine No.	Tool No.	Department
1	CAST	M235	DX 103	D6
2	TRIM	M81	DX 104	D8
3	DRILL(2)HOLES	M631-5	JigX103	D2
4	BROACH	M631-5	JigX1035	D2
5	TUMBLE	DR3 24	———	DR3

Inspection ____✓____
Authorization ____✓____

FIGURE 6-9
Equipment routing chart. (*Courtesy Trans World Airlines.*)

TRANS WORLD AIRLINES, INC.

BOEING 707-131-B   **ROUTING CHART**

EFFECTIVE JUNE 1, 1970 (EXCEPT AS NOTED)   CHART NO: 4-B   ISSUED: MAY 7, 1970

Assignment of Aircraft at 06:00

	June 1,	June 7,	June 28.
BOS	2	2	2
BDL	1	1	1
JFK	3	3	3
EWR	1	1	1
PHL	3	3	3
BAL	2	2	2
IAD	3	3	3
DAY	1	1	1
IND	1	1	1
CMH	1	1	1
ORD	1	1	1
MKC	1	2	1
ABQ	2	2	2
DEN	1	1	1
TUL	1	1	1
LAX	4	4	4
SFO	4	4	4
ENROUTE Ⓔ	6	6	6
SCHEDULED	38	39	38

Fleet Distribution June 1, 7, 28.

Scheduled	38	39	38
Spares	2	1	1
Maintenance	1	1	1
Overhaul			1
Pilot Training			
Active Fleet	41	41	41

	June 1,	June 7,	June 28
Block Hours Scheduled	431:17	436:33	431:17
Utilization Fleet	11:21	11:12	11:21
Utilization	10:31	10:39	10:31

Legend:
L/M – Line Maintenance
PCK – Pilot Training Check
TCS – Time Control Service
SS – Station Service
Ⓔ – Enroute

TWA FORM 448001   PRINTED IN USA

plan. Again, nothing is sacrosanct about these forms. Sometimes the operations sheets include blueprints of the outputs; at other times they do not. The purpose of the operations sheet is to record and communicate information that is essential for making each part. This is the sole determinant and criterion for the design of the form that will be used. It is intended to achieve a level of specification that can be costed, evaluated, and altered in specific rather than in abstract terms.

When the operations sheets have been accepted and finalized, real implementation of plans can begin. Machines, tools, gauges, fixtures, and jigs required for fabrication can be assembled and inventoried. For nonfabricating operations comparable forms exist. For example, the airline routing chart (Figure 6.9) can be translated into operations, equipment requirements, and other pertinent system specifications.

Recently PERT charts have begun to play an important role in specifying the information "content" of the new product or process. To illustrate, Figure 6.10 traces out many of the steps of information collection that are critical to the successful achievement of new products and processes. Starting with Step 4 in Figure 6.10 and including most of the paths of Figure 6.11, we find that the considerations usually required for feasibility determination appear in the diagram. Then, in Figure 6.12 we see the third phase of our PERT chart, called *"actualization and operations."* These third-phase steps represent the activities required to implement the prior phases. Beginning with Events *D*, *E*, *F*, and *G*, the components of the input-output model are assembled and set up in working order. Thus, the end product of the overall planning sequence is the input-output

FIGURE 6-10
Model PERT network for the design of a production system: Phase I—Product and service development.

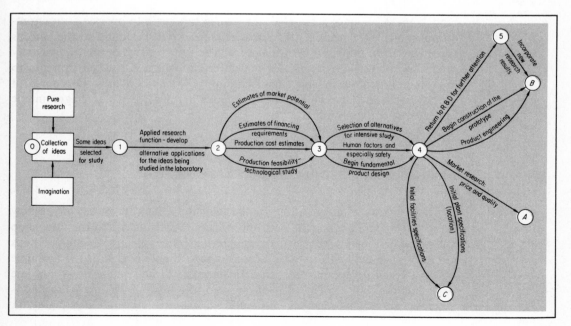

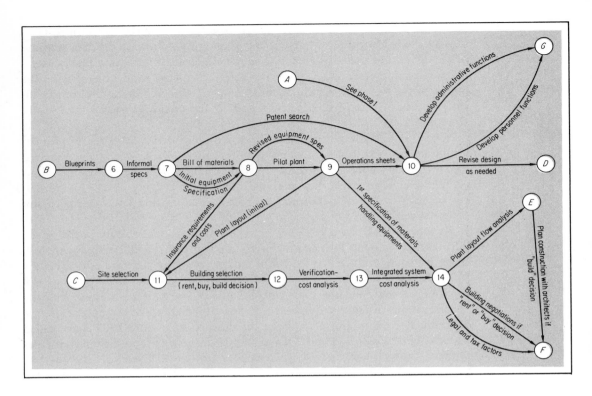

FIGURE 6-11
Model PERT network
for the design of a
production system:
Phase II—Process de-
velopment.

model, 16-23-24. Once assembled, the system can begin to operate as an input-output model. Throughout this book, references will be found to the various activities shown in these PERT diagrams. The PERT chart, or any equivalently direct and objective system is of real informational utility when it comes to providing organization and understanding of many activities. Of course, it should be clear that each situation demands its own particular diagrammatic sequence of activities and events.

ANALYSIS OF INFORMATION SYSTEMS

The structure of information for the job shop differs from that of the flow shop. Both share similarities with the project. Fundamental to the flow shop and projects is the precedence diagram which identifies clearly which operations are to precede and which are to succeed others. Figure 6.13 shows an example of a precedence diagram often used for purposes of illustrating flow-shop line balancing (see pp. 225-26). As will be seen, the function of line balancing is

to group operations together into work stations that have about equal work

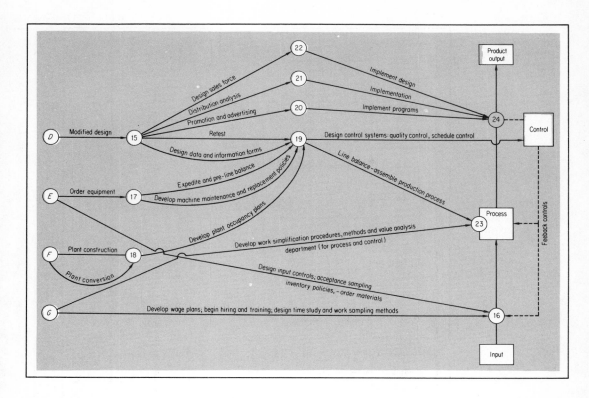

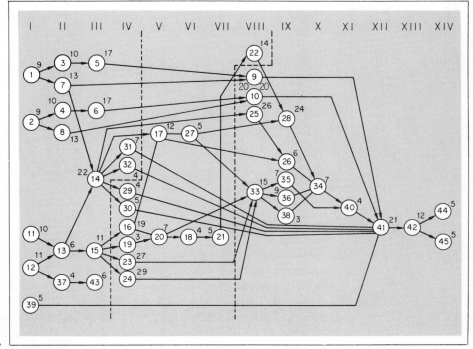

FIGURE 6-14
An assembly se-
quence or a Gozinto
chart.

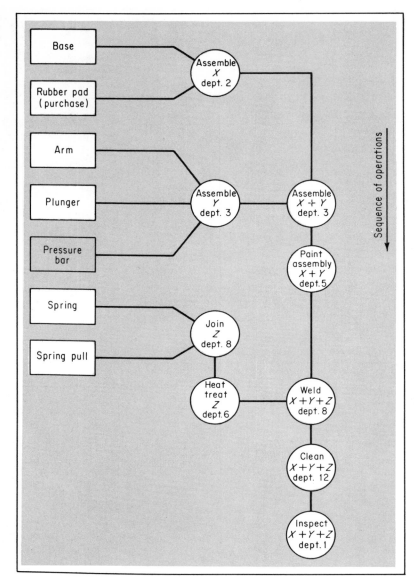

loads (and close to zero idle time). And this is to be done in such a way that
the system's output rate matches the demand rate.

Assembly sequence charts and "Gozinto" (goes into) charts describe the order
of assembly determined by precedence decisions. (See Figure 6.14.) Assembly-
scheduling diagrams schedule the work flow according to calendar time
(see Figure 6.15). Flow diagrams are often used to relate the processing and assembly paths to the facility layout of the plant, and when warranted, layout

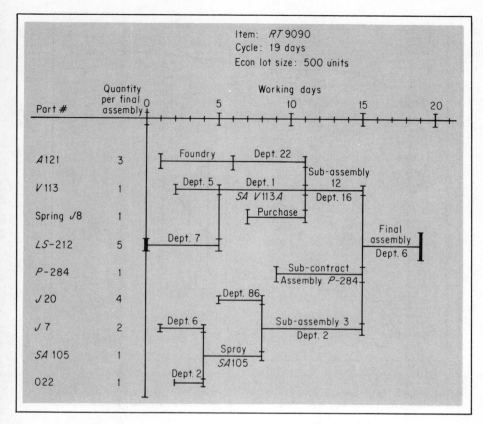

Item: *RT*9090
Cycle: 19 days
Econ lot size: 500 units

FIGURE 6-15
An assembly-scheduling diagram.

decisions are made to achieve improved flow patterns (see Figure 6.16). In the case of projects, the PERT diagrams (see pp. 155-57) represent precedence relations that we have already discussed.

In a job shop, the bills of materials and operations (or routing) sheets hold the key to describing materials requirements, processing steps and operation sequences needed to make each part. Jobs are completed by following specifications for the assembly of parts. Although routing frequently identifies specific facilities at which given operations will be performed, output scheduling is not involved because arrival times at the facilities are not indicated. Further, there is no specification of the work sequence for different parts at a given facility. These forms of information will be treated in Chapter 8 on process management. In Chapter 9 on materials management various inventory questions will be considered. Thus, the information about purchased parts maintained on a stock card includes vendor information, order quantities, price and discount data and expected lead times for deliveries.

In the multi-product job shop, quite often several different jobs share common parts. An *explosion chart* (Figure 6.17) is used to identify the aggregation

159

FIGURE 6-16
Flow process layout
diagram for a system
with multiple product-
mix requirements.

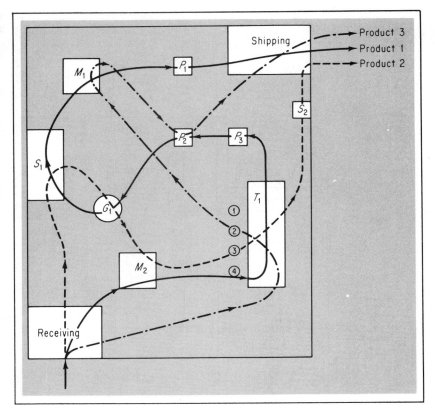

FIGURE 6-17
The explosion chart
is a matrix for explod-
ing end-use demands
for parts based on
expected demands for
jobs.

			JOBS				
PARTS	X 112	PR 5	987	989	TF 5	. . .	MONTHLY REQUIREMENTS
C32	2	–	–	–	–		120
C325	1	1	1	–	–		180
C45	–	–	4	–	–		320
C47	–	–	1	0	1		100
C549	–	–	1	1	1		130
.							.
.							.
.							.
Monthly Demand	60	40	80	30	20	. . .	

of part requirements. This chart which is a compilation of bills of materials for
jobs having common parts, has applicability for both make and buy decisions.
The key is that *total* demands *by parts* must be used as a basis for planning.
Therefore, total job requirements reflecting job-part interdependencies must
be known.

FIGURE 6-18
The Gantt load chart.

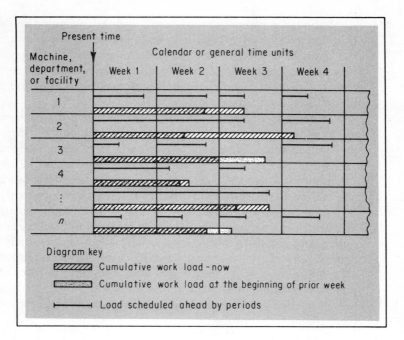

FIGURE 6-19
The Gantt layout chart
(a reserved time plan-
ning system). Status:
(1) job P-284 is
ahead 2 days; (2)
job J20 is ahead 3.0
days; (3) job 0-22 is
ahead 5.5 days; (4)
job M21 is ahead 1.0
day; (5) job R65 is
2 days short of com-
pletion—and 2.5 days
late (M); (6) job
P—285 is 1.5 days
short and 1.5 days
late (set-up time;
will catch up); (7)
job T10—X is 1.5
days short and about
3.5 days late (M) and
(E).

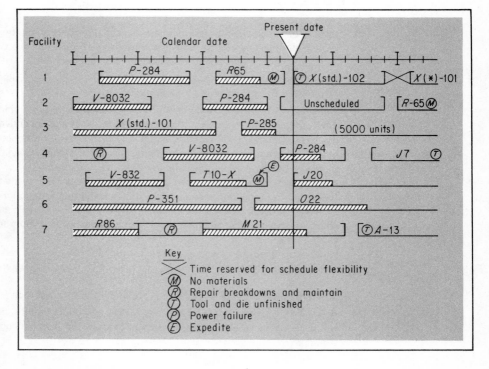

Methods for planning production schedules, assigning and sequencing work have improved greatly. Information requirements have grown commensurately. For example, in Chapter 7 on product management, the concepts of standardization and *modularity* are shown to be clearly related to information management—with great economic advantage to those who recognize the opportunities that information management permits.

Further, for controlling job shop operations a series of *manufacturing orders* are often used. They specify the number of each part to be made, and include their full routing instructions. Among the most critical information functions in the job shop are (1) schedules for production batches, (2) work assignments to specific facilities (called shoploading) and, (3) selected sequences of operations at a facility. In the early 1900's, Henry L. Gantt developed a shoploading chart, (Figure 6.18) as an information format to assist in the assignment function. The chart depicts cumulative workload assigned to machine centers in calendar time. Gantt also developed a layout chart (Figure 6.19) which shows the actual plan of sequencing jobs at each facility. Even now, such charts continue to be used for comparing planned versus actual accomplishments. Various ways of presenting loading and layout information are available which enable control to be exercised over the production system and allow *expediting* to occur when there is schedule slippage.

PROBLEMS

1 Each hour a secretary files four documents in an alphabetic file. If there is a five percent probability that any one document will be misfiled, what are the probabilities that 0, 1, 2, ... 8 documents will be misfiled in a two hour period?

2 In what way does the fact that production is an almost entirely visible function affect its relationship to the rest of the organization?

3 Company X is about to undertake a program to encourage its employees to suggest new products and revisions of present design. A strong incentive is provided. The company employs 5,000 workers, and it is expected that the number of suggestions per year will average one per man. Assuming that the average working year is 250 days, there will be about 20 suggestions per day to be screened.
The suggestions are to be sorted by the sales division. Only marketable ideas will be forwarded to production management. It is decided that production will use an initial screening process in order to eliminate quickly the unworkable suggestions. Those ideas which pass the screening will then be subjected to a more intensive feasibility study.
a. Develop a logical procedure which production management can follow in order to achieve its objectives. Make sure you include all questions required by the decision process.
b. Estimate the number of employees required to administer such a program.

4 Assuming that your company has a long history of bidding for jobs, prepare a study that would be useful in evaluating the results to date and in achieving improvements in bidding.

5 *a.* An important document has been misfiled. There are 131,072 items in the file. The present procedure is to start at A and search through Z until the missing item is found. If we search at the rate of 10 items per minute, how long will it take to find the missing document?

b. Breakdowns in a complex, highly mechanized manufacturing system occur at an average rate of 3 breakdowns per 4 days. There are 32,768 components that could be responsible. The present procedure is to test each component in some specified order until the fault is located.

If the search rate is approximately 200 components per minute, on the average, how long does it take to locate the fault? How much downtime would result per day?

c. For each of these situations, suggest a better approach. Attempt to detail your suggestion and estimate the savings in time and cost that might be made in this way.

6 Draw up an appropriate *bill of materials* for producing the following items:
a. A table knife
b. An office stapler
c. A flashlight

references

ALFORD, L. P. (ed.), *Cost and Production Handbook* (3rd Ed.). New York: The Ronald Press Company, 1955.

BAUMOL, WILLIAM J., *Economic Theory and Operations Analysis.* 2nd ed. Englewood Cliffs, N.J.: Prentice-Hall, Inc., 1965.

BECKETT, J. A., *Management Dynamics, The New Synthesis.* New York: McGraw-Hill BooK Comp., 1971.

BLACK, GUY, *The Application of Systems Analysis to Government Operations.* New York: Frederic A. Praeger, Inc., 1968.

BOWMAN, EDWARD H. and ROBERT B. FETTER, *Analysis for Production and Operations Management* (3rd ed.), Homewood, Ill.: Richard D. Irwin, Inc., 1967.

BROOM, H. N., *Production Management.* Homewood, Ill.: Richard D. Irwin, Inc., 1962.

BUFFA, ELWOOD S., *Modern Production Management* (3rd ed.), New York: John Wiley & Sons, Inc., 1969.

BUFFA, ELWOOD S. (ed.), *Readings in Production and Operations Management,* New York: John Wiley & Sons, Inc., 1969.

CHERRY, COLIN, *On Human Communication.* New York: John Wiley & Sons, Inc., 1957.

COLEMAN, J. S., *Introduction to Mathematical Sociology.* New York: The Free Press, 1964.

DOOLEY, ARCH R., *et al., Casebooks in Production Management, Basic Problems, Concepts, and Techniques.* New York: John Wiley & Sons, Inc., 1964.

EILON, SAMUEL, *Elements of Production Planning and Control,* New York: The Macmillan Co., 1962.

GARRETT, LEONARD J. and MILTON SILVER, *Production Management Analysis,* New York: Harcourt Brace Jovanovich, Inc., 1966.

GAVETT, J. WILLIAM, Production and Operations Management, New York: Harcourt Brace Jovanovich, Inc., 1968.

GEORGE, JR., CLAUDE S., *Management for Business and Industry*, Englewood Cliffs, N.J.: Prentice-Hall, Inc., 1970.

GOETZ, B. E., *Quantitative Methods: A Survey and Guide for Managers.* New York: McGraw-Hill Book Comp., 1965.

HALL, A. D., *A Methodology for Systems Engineering.* Princeton, N.J.: D. Van Nostrand Co., Inc., 1962.

IRESON, W. GRANT, and EUGENE L. GRANT (eds.), *Handbook of Industrial Engineering and Management.* Englewood Cliffs, N.J.: Prentice-Hall, Inc., 1957.

KLIR, J. and M. VALACH, *Cybernetic Modelling.* Princeton, N.J.: D. Van Nostrand Co., 1967.

MCGARRAH, ROBERT E., *Production and Logistics Management.* New York: John Wiley & Sons, Inc., 1963.

MCKEAN, R. N., *Efficiency in Government through Systems Analysis.* New York: John Wiley & Sons, Inc., 1958.

McMILLAN, JR., C. and R. F. GONZALES, *Systems Analysis: A Computer Approach to Decision Models,* 2nd ed. Homewood, Ill.: Richard D. Irwin, Inc., 1968.

MAYER, R. R., *Production Management.* New York: McGraw-Hill, Inc., 1962.

NILAND, POWELL, *Production Planning, Scheduling, and Inventory Control.* New York: Macmillan, Company, 1970.

OPTNER, S. L., *Systems Analysis.* Englewood Cliffs, N.J.: Prentice-Hall, Inc., 1960.

PIERCE, JOHN F., ed., *Operations Research and the Design of Management Information Systems.* New York: Technical Association of the Pulp and Paper Industry, 1967.

ROSCOE, EDWIN SCOTT, *Organization for Production* (3rd Ed.). Homewood, Ill.: Richard D. Irwin, Inc., 1963.

SHUCHMAN, A. M., *Scientific Decision Making in Business.* New York: Holt, Rinehart & Winston, 1963.

SIMON, H. A., *Sciences of the Artificial.* Cambridge, Mass.: The M.I.T. Press, 1969.

STARR, MARTIN K. (ed.), *Management of Production,* Middlesex, England: Penguin Books Ltd., 1970.

STARR, M. K., *Management: A Modern Approach.* New York: Harcourt Brace Jovanovich, 1971.

TIMMS, HOWARD L. and MICHAEL F. POHLEN, *The Production Function in Business: Decision Systems for Production and Operations Management* (3rd ed.), Homewood, Ill.: Richard D. Irwin, Inc., 1970.

chapter
seven
product
management

What production activities should a company pursue? What product mix is most desirable? At one time, such a decision could be made intuitively, supported logically, and remain profitable for many years. But that kind of sales volume stability no longer holds; product life is decreasing. Let us examine all of the relevant product management issues.

PRODUCTS AND SERVICES

A *new* product or service has only limited consumer awareness, so it must build a sufficient market to support continued promotional effort. An *established product* must maintain its market. Even small downturns can affect its profitability, because lacking growth, it is vulnerable to economic changes and competitive actions. A sales volume curve (shown in Figure 7.1) illustrates these situations of growth, maturity and decay. Mature products will be found on the

FIGURE 7-1
The morphology of
products.

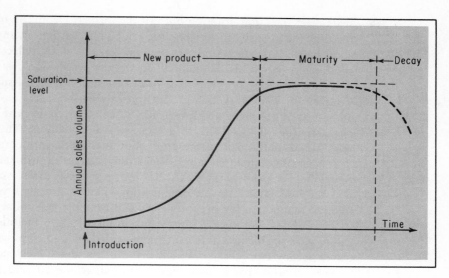

portion of the curve that is close to the saturation level. New products must work their way up. Obsolete products are represented by the dotted portion of the curve which is negative growth or the decay region of the growth curve.

New products have experienced increasingly higher failure rates. Many reasons can be given for this. Competitive actions, for example, may be decisively detrimental. Changes in the economy can produce chaotic conditions. Still, it may be the case that in spite of the high, new product failure rate, the optimal strategy for a company is to introduce many new products. Although each new product has a relatively high likelihood of failure, the one product which is a success is sufficient to pay for the whole program. This approach requires a production management department that can cope with the great number of new products that are constantly being introduced.

Some companies follow this pattern. Others take quite a different view. They utilize careful analysis for the introduction of a single product—or very few products—all of which have relatively high probabilities of success. The question of which approach is better is a problem of synthesis for marketing and production. It may be subject to analysis as a beginning, but a major stumbling block in answering the question lies in the inability to develop good forecasts for marketplace responses. Certainly, the production costs for the alternative configurations can be derived, assuming that believable predictions of production volume are available. Unfortunately, circular reasoning is at work since volume is a function of price, cost is a function of volume and price is a function of cost.

The main difference between products and services seems to be that the ownership of products is possible. They can be purchased, stored away, and consumed in a physical sense. Services, on the other hand, can't be stored; the user does not establish ownership. Hotel rooms and commercial plane and train seats meet the latter criterion but not the former. Definition of services is confused by the diversity of services that can be offered. But, in any case, the differences between products and services that concern us are reflected by the type of production system that is required. Again, the production costs can be derived. It is the marketing problem that throws confusion on the issue of what to do. Chapter 15, The Marketing-Production Interaction, explains how services are embodied in products, and how trade-off considerations exist relating physical characteristics of products with their service potentials. The product-service mix is an essential part of the production manager's considerations.

It is usually stated that fabrication requires larger investments than do service functions. Such differentials exist but they are not as extensive as one might at first suppose. Many service organizations have a greater investment in plant than do manufacturing organizations. For example, telephone utilities, electric power utilities, hotels and restaurants, transportation facilities, and hospitals can require sizable investments. On the other hand, an employment agency or a travel agency can have minimum investments and almost no fixed assets.

Each situation has its own production management ramifications. The realization of this point is relatively new. It stems from the magnificent record of accomplishment compiled by production management researchers beginning with Taylor (pp. 428-29) and carried on by others. With such developments as information theory, decision theory and linear programming—the generality of the production management function was revealed in full scope.

DESIGNING THE SYSTEMS OUTPUT

Every production plan lends itself to three divisions which are useful although somewhat arbitrary (see the PERT diagrams, pp. 155-57).

1. The first can be called product and service development. It includes both research and development (R & D).
2. The second division might be termed the process development stage.
3. The third division is the actualization phase of the plan. It carries the plan to the inception of production operations.

New product or new service development starts with a collection of ideas, and some of these are chosen for further study. Various ways of converting ideas into applications are investigated in the laboratory. Promising alternatives must then be checked for such factors as their production feasibility—in a technological sense—production costs, financing requirements, and possible prices and qualities related to marketability. In addition, the human factors concerned with both product and process are considered from various points of view, including safety. From the alternatives, one or more possibilities are selected for further study because of encouraging evaluations. Product design is begun in earnest and a basic decision is reached concerning the product or service design. Thus begins the developmental phase. Only occasionally do we return to research for help and guidance.

Product development requires product engineering, which includes further cost specification; the beginning of intensive market research, and the inception of plant and facilities specification. At this point we reach a boundary between product and process development. It is not that the product development phase is finished. Rather it is integrated with the further specification of the process.

Service development frequently requires many of the same steps. Office outputs, for example, should be designed and checked in various ways to verify that they are serving the intended purpose—before the office process is installed. A steamship line must design its output, that is, how much cargo, how many passengers, what kind of cargo, and what kind of service to passengers. How else can the process be designed? The facilities must be developed so that they can provide the a priori specified services.

PURE AND APPLIED RESEARCH

Pure research[1] is a generator of ideas. There are many other ways that ideas come into being, but pure research findings are equivalent to *new* knowledge. Thus, they form a base from which creative thinking can be launched. There is no substitute for this foundation. Pure research is the "launching pad" for applied research. The laboratory efforts of applied research are devoted to exploiting pure research results. On the whole, only large companies can afford to engage in substantial amounts of pure research. The investments are large, the risks are significant, and the payoff is usually many years away. At the same time, when the payoff is realized, it is frequently very substantial.

Present pure research allocations by industrial firms in the U. S. A. represent approximately four per cent of the total funds allocated for industrial research and development.[2] The reason that the percentage is so small can be directly attributed to the fact that applied research, with relatively immediate commercial advantages, is the major preoccupation of industry. Although this orientation can provide short-term benefits, in the long run it constitutes economic loss, in the sense of lost opportunities.

RESEARCH AND DEVELOPMENT (R & D)

After pure research comes applied research and then development. As we move in sequence through these phases a greater amount of production management participation is required. Usually, very close coordination is expected during the development phase. We can literally define "development" by this involvement with production management.

[1] The best definition of "pure" research is that it is not "applied"; that is, it has no immediate or obvious utility for increasing man's comfort, or providing physical satisfactions, or increasing his control over the environment. Pure research is, therefore, equatable to the pursuit of knowledge for the sake of knowledge.

[2] National Science Foundation, *Reviews of Data on Science Resources,* No. 12, NSF 68–5 (January, 1968), p. 1.

The R & D function is of critical importance to production management. Each idea forces its own demands in terms of time, money, and talent required to bring it to fruition. Understanding lab work is not a requirement for understanding the relationship of production management and R & D. This is similar to our previous point that knowledge of specific technology was not a requirement for understanding the field of production management. We should also note that R & D is applicable to the service function. Thus, for example, hospital procedures are under constant reevaluation; information retrieval is an area of research that is profoundly affecting library procedures; telephone facilities are constantly being revamped, and the communication industry is one of the largest contributors to the total national research budget.

Some ideas will work and others will not. All R & D work does not succeed. Presumably, if talented people are employed who understand their field, there will be a greater chance of success. But the definition of what constitutes talent is not easy to come by. The use of psychological tests has shown no sign of pinpointing the requisite characteristics for ingenuity and creativity. However, as we proceed along the path from pure research to applied research and then to development, the kind of creativity that is required becomes less difficult to discuss. Also, the ability to forecast the time and effort that will be required to complete a project improves. Accordingly, it is easier to prepare development budgets than pure research budgets. Budget appropriation and control for R & D is one of the most difficult control areas in an organization. Because the outcome of pure research is essentially unknowable beforehand, the question of how much to allocate to which projects is almost unanswerable. The intangibility dissipates as we move toward and through development stages.

But in all R & D, estimates of time and cost are crucial matters. It has been found that schedules of time and cost for applied research and development are subject to a "slippage factor." Figure 7.2 compares predicted and actual

FIGURE 7-2
Typical manpower buildup and phasing-out for project.

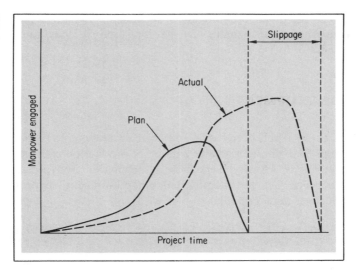

results for the length of time required to complete a project—in terms of manpower allocations that are made. We see that the amount of manpower scheduled increases over a given period of time, then remains constant, and ultimately falls off sharply when the job is near completion. Unfortunately, the actual results seldom conform to the schedule. It takes significantly longer to complete the job than had originally been anticipated. Positive slippage almost always occurs, and characteristically, it is approximately 50 percent. Because of increased manpower requirements, costs are also much greater than had been anticipated.

One would think that knowledge of the characteristic slippage rate would allow product planners to make necessary allowance for both time and cost slippage in their estimates. In this way, they might be able to formulate an exact estimate of the actual date that the product can get to the market. This is a critical time point since so many activities of distribution, promotion and production must be synchronized to it. The question is: Can cost and time estimates be automatically increased by some known percentage to give modified predictions? Experience has shown that such modified predictions will not be met and that the actual results will slip, in any case, by approximately the same percentage as before. But this time, slippage must be applied to the modified predictions. Consequently, self-deception doesn't work. The planner ends up with a worse situation than if he had left well enough alone because the actual time to complete the job is increased.

No one has been able to explain with any assurance why slippage so generally occurs. However, it is reasonable to believe that at the beginning of a project the desire to excel in fulfilling the project's requirements causes people to take many more steps than they would permit at a later point when the pressure of a completion date is upon them. As time grows shorter, the project participants dispense with whatever frills and special investigations they were involved in and they begin to follow the original schedule. Finally, a crash program is undertaken—usually too late. It is certainly remarkable that the average slippage is so consistent, no matter what the prediction that is made. The uniformity of this slippage factor appears to confirm the fact that fundamental behavioral relations are involved.

There is one possibility that suggests itself for dealing with this situation, although under many circumstances it is difficult to achieve. Separate the planning and estimating functions from the research and development teams so that the latter are unaware of the fact that a modified prediction has been made. Under these circumstances it should be possible for the planners to match predictions with actual results. For example, an estimate of two months is made to complete a particular job. Top management accepts this estimate and never indicates that they are in fact planning the project on the basis of a three month period. If habitual slippage of 50 percent operates, then the job should be completed in three months and the "hidden schedule" will be met all along the line.

This procedure has built-in dangers. Should the research and development team guess or sense that top management had a "hidden schedule," then the three month period might slip to a 4.5-month period. If they believe that management had allowed for this, when it had not, then double slippage might occur. We must recognize that slippage is not usually the result of a conscious process. Once research and development teams begin to doubt the intentions and honesty of top management and come to feel that they are victims of a bluff, then confidence in management deteriorates, causing a severe reduction in the team's effectiveness.

Recent work by Norden[3] indicates that the development function gives rise to certain patterns that are independent of the nature of the project. These results make it appear likely that manpower requirements, time, and costs can be forecast with reasonable precision. Norden has found that five basic subcycles underlie most development projects. These are shown in Figure 7.3. This work does not encompass the research part of R & D. Nevertheless, although experimental, it holds forth hope of reducing uncertainty in the important liaison stage between research and actual production operations.

FIGURE 7-3
Typical manpower pattern of an engineering project. [From Peter V. Norden, "Resource Usage and Network Planning Techniques," *Operations Research in Research and Development*, ed. Burton V. Dean (New York: John Wiley & Sons, Inc., 1963), p. 160.]

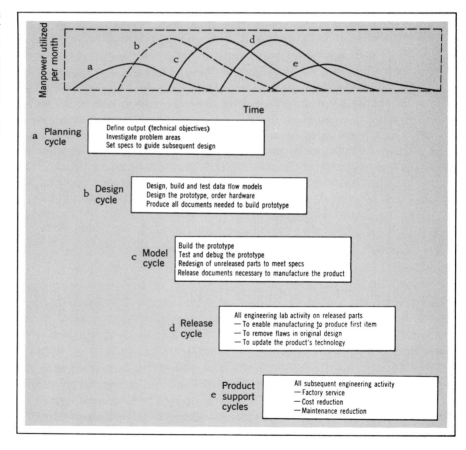

[3] Peter V. Norden, "Resource Usage and Network Planning Techniques," *Operations Research in Research and Development*, Burton V. Dean, ed. (New York: John Wiley & Sons, Inc., 1963), pp. 149–169. See also an updated version of this material in Peter V. Norden, "Useful Tools for Project Management," in *Management of Production*, ed. Martin K. Starr (Middlesex, England: Penguin Books Ltd., 1969), pp. 71–101.

PRODUCTIVITY OF PRODUCT DEVELOPMENT

The productivity of indirect labor including clerical, administrative, and supervisory positions, is difficult to define and measure. And it is even more difficult to measure the productive output of a research and development team. Yet, this is a crucial measurement because of the increasingly large quantities of money that are being spent on R & D. Consequently, even a theoretical analysis of the problem is helpful.

Let us define productivity as some number of units of project accomplishment *per period of time*. We shall assume that environmental and work force conditions remain relatively stable over each particular interval. Thus we shall measure productivity per phase rather than in the aggregate. An average measure of productivity can then be obtained for the total project. Underlying this definition is the belief that research tasks can be divided, at least in theory, into unit phases or accomplishment units. Generally, we would like to maximize the

FIGURE 7-4
Cost and productivity interrelations that underlie the cost/ time analysis of any project phase.

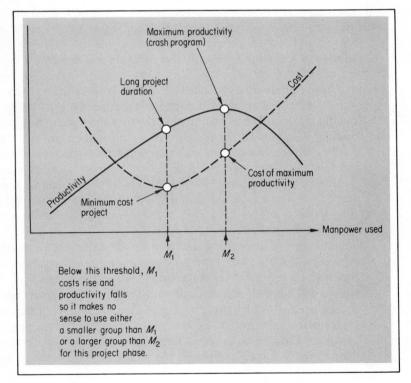

productivity of the research team in each phase so that the total job can be completed in the minimum possible time. A short product development time is often crucial for competitive reasons and because new technology appears so rapidly.

To minimize product development time, it should be recognized that we must employ just the right number of research workers. Yet, another basic objective is to achieve product development at a reasonable, if not a minimum cost. In these terms, it has been observed that the most efficient team size with respect to cost will frequently require a smaller group of research workers than would be needed for maximum group productivity. In other words, group size for minimum cost is smaller than for minimum product development time. Thus the definition of an optimal group size is dependent on the manager's objectives. Put in this way, the existence of these conflicting effects is not at all surprising.[4]

Figure 7.4 illustrates the point that has just been made. The horizontal axis represents the number of workers engaged in any particular phase of product development. For the entire project, consisting of various phases, manpower commitments can be regulated to control project progress and performance. The vertical axis is *measured in two* ways: productivity (the solid line) and cost (the dotted line). As stated, minimum cost occurs before the point of maximum productivity is reached. Cost is determined by the number of workers and the time required to complete the job. Thus, if we have two men earning $12,000 per year and it takes them six months to complete this development phase, then the total cost of this phase of the project is $12,000. On the other hand, if four men are employed, each earning $12,000 per year, and it takes them four months to complete the project phase, then the cost of doing this job is $16,000. Minimum cost in this hypothetical example occurs when two workers are used instead of four.

How is productivity affected? Because the four-man group finishes the project phase in four months it must be higher on the productivity curve than the two-man group. Let us assume that the four-man group produces the maximum number of accomplishments per hour. This is the team size that can finish the job first. More or less than four men will have a somewhat lower over-all team productivity. With this in mind, it is not surprising that two men might have something more than half the productivity of four men. So for our specific example, the four-man team can accomplish the job in the minimum amount of time but at a higher total cost as compared to the two-man team.

Which result do we want? If our objective is to minimize time, then four men are indicated. If our objective is to strike some efficient balance between the cost of doing the job and the time for completion, something less than the maximum productivity group size is indicated. This result is exceedingly important when we are dealing with sizable product development programs consisting of many phases each of which requires substantial team sizes. Frequently, because of marketplace competition, great urgency is attached to the product development program, and the objective is—first and foremost—to obtain maximum productivity and, thereby, minimize the total time to accomplish the job.

OVERSTAFFED PRODUCT DEVELOPMENT

There is a natural tendency to overestimate manpower requirements. The result of this can be quite detrimental. We note that productivity drops off when

---

[4] Reference to pp. 94–95 on PERT/Cost should be illuminating now.

more than an optimal number of individuals are involved on the job. This can be explained in a number of ways, including use of the old adage: "Too many cooks spoil the broth." For those who prefer a logical explanation: productivity falls off above a certain group size because of communication and supervision problems. The number of information links that tie a group together increases as the square of the number of individuals working on the job. Organizational hierarchy and communication channels will reduce this number somewhat. But, in general, if an individual is added to a group of n members, then n

FIGURE 7-5
An information network of n men has complexity of the order of n^2.
$n(n-1)/2 = n^2 - n/2$

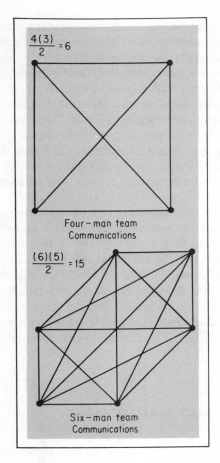

$$\frac{4(3)}{2} = 6$$

Four – man team
Communications

$$\frac{(6)(5)}{2} = 15$$

Six – man team
Communications

new links are added to the information net. Thus, with an n-man team, there are $n(n-1)/2$ information links. For example, with three individuals we have $3(2)/2$, or 3, information links. Now, adding one individual to the group, we have $4(3)/2$ equals 6 information links. The additional individual has increased the number of communication channels by three. Let us take this one step further and add another person to the group of four. We now have $5(4)/2$ equals 10 communication channels—an increase of four. Simple geometric drawings such as those in Figure 7.5 can be used to demonstrate the nature of this formulation.[5]

Overstaffing is a consequence of many basic urges of management. It is only natural to think that a "massive" effort can produce results faster than a minimum cost effort. As we have seen, it is frequently true that minimum cost will not coincide with minimum completion time. But the "massive" effort is likely to overshoot the mark and result in both project delay and additional costs. Our discussion should signal care when preparing research and development budgets. Further, in synchronizing development programs with production—greater forecast accuracy can be obtained if attention is paid to the relationships of time and cost.

What can happen if management overestimates manpower requirements? Assume that a group size is chosen that is somewhat larger than would be required for maximum productivity. As a result of this choice, product development costs will be greater than was expected and the job takes longer than the required time. The result is paradoxical. The manager of development believes that he has underestimated manpower requirements. He attributes the additional cost to the additional time required to complete the project. The next time that a similar job must be undertaken on a tight schedule he employs even more people. This pushes the results further to the right on our curve in Figure 7.4. Productivity is even lower; a longer time is required to accomplish the job; and costs are greater than ever. Instead of correcting his error, the manager is led further astray.

Cost and time estimates are predicated on historical records. Thus, over time, the budgets increase. More and more manpower is allocated to each job. We see that a special form of Parkinson's Law[6] is in operation. Parkinson observed that work expands to fill up time available for its completion, which is another way of saying that people create work which would not otherwise be done. In turn, we require more people to handle the jobs that have been created. The process is self-perpetuating. When we couple this with the productivity paradox that we have just described, we can understand why many organizations have experienced great difficulties in controlling expenditures on new product development.

COORDINATED PRODUCT MANAGEMENT

Research and development is a primary source of production management work. Tight coordination is required. In the later developments stages, production and development merge. Coordination with the marketing function is vital. The following requirements are evident:

[5] It will be noted that we have divided by 2, thus treating all two-way communication channels as though they were one. The factor of 2 is not critical. What is significant is the existence of an n^2 term in the formulation. Thus, the number of communication channels increases as the square of the number of individuals participating in the group.
[6] C. N. Parkinson, *Parkinson's Law* (New York: Houghton Mifflin Company, 1957).

1. The product development objectives must be clearly stated. They should be reduced to the simplest possible terms. Unless this knowledge is shared by all participants, the project will encounter many reverses. Much time will be spent finding out what everyone is trying to do.

2. Expertise is required to outline the steps of the program designed to deliver the specified results. Accurate time and cost estimates are essential. The slippage problem cannot be overlooked.

3. Duplication of steps should, in general, be eliminated. Under some circumstances, however, *parallel path* activities are warranted. Namely:

   (a) If a major conflict of ideas exists and there is urgency to achieve the objectives, then it is sometimes reasonable to allow two or more groups to work independently on the different approaches. Preplanned evaluation procedures should exist so that as soon as it is possible the program can be trimmed back to a single path.

   (b) At the inception of a program—during what might be called the exploratory stage— parallel path research is frequently warranted and can be encouraged. All possible approaches should be considered and evaluated before large commitments of funds have been made.

   (c) When the risk of failure is high, for example, survival is at stake, or when the pay-off incentive is sufficiently great with respect to the costs of achieving it, then parallel path activities can be justified for as long a period of time as is deemed necessary to achieve the objectives.

   (d) Otherwise, duplication should be avoided.

4. Product management should carefully evaluate the steps and phasing of the program. An optimum organization should be set up to handle transitions between phases.

5. One person should be responsible for all major decisions. He must understand the nature of the problem, the technological, marketing and production constraints. Multiple decision makers can produce chaotic conditions.

DECENTRALIZED PRODUCT MANAGEMENT

Product development moves through many phases; different functional areas of interest must be integrated and coordinated. For example, inventory policy can affect delivery delays; national distribution of the product usually requires extensive backup stock; shelf movement will be affected by promotional and advertising timing, etc.

If everyone involved in the product development effort could reach out and communicate their concerns to each other, the network of connections would become unwieldy. For example, with 10 individuals there exist $n(n-1)/2 = 10(9)/2 = 45$ potential two-way communication paths. Assume instead that two groups of 5 individuals each are set to the task at hand, and that one member of each group coordinates activities between the groups. Then, each group has $5(4)/2 = 10$ potential communication paths. With the two groups, there are 20 potential paths for communication plus the additional one required for coordination. Clearly, 21 communication paths is a less complex system to manage properly than is one possessing 45 such paths. The difference between the centralized and the decentralized arrangement accelerates as the total number of participating individuals increases. Thus, with 20 people, the difference is 99 links; with 100 people, it is 2499.

PROTOTYPES

In the last stages of product development the product or service idea has been transformed into a concrete form. The steps involved can be found on the appropriate PERT Chart.[7] Generally, no final decisions have been made concerning the materials and equipment to be used, but a reasonable approximation to final procedures is in the process of being evolved.

FIGURE 7-6
View of an advanced design studio at GM Styling Staff in the General Motors Technical Center, Warren, Mich. In the foreground is a completed fiber glass prototype model of an experimental roadster. The skeleton model in the center of the room is a full-scale seating mockup, which is used to check such things as interior dimensions, seating positions, steering wheel angle, location of controls and ease of entry and exit. Back of that is a full-scale clay model taking shape. On the rear wall (at left) is a full-size color rendering of an experimental car.

An important and exciting phase of the development process occurs when the prototype is made. This is a highly developed model, intended to embody most of the significant characteristics that will be found in the final production line item. Many kinds of prototypes are used. For example, the prototype of an automobile (see Figure 7.6) is frequently made of clay. It is a model of the chassis, intended to reveal the styling and appearance of the automobile so that it can be evaluated on a visual, first-hand basis. A separate hand-tooled model of the engine and other moving parts of the system will also be required before the

[7] See p. 155.

new model goes into production. At a still later stage, a hand-crafted automobile will be developed which represents a total assembly as it will eventually come from the production line. (Note fiber glass prototype in Figure 7.6.)

In the case of a process (for example, a chemical plant) an advanced prototype will take the form of a *pilot plant*. This pilot plant is a scale model of the final plans for the processing unit. It is similar to the final unit in all respects but on a reduced scale. Pilot plants may involve expenditures of millions of dollars. In such cases, they usually represent models of final units that cost *hundreds of millions* of dollars. If the pilot plant produces negative results, then the plans can be reworked or discarded. The purpose of a pilot plant is to spend a *relatively* small sum of money in order to avoid far larger penalties that could occur if such precautions were not taken.

Prototypes must be evaluated with care. It is well known to engineers that a reduction in scale can produce certain observable behaviors that do not accurately describe the performance of the intended, final system. When possible, engineers transform the results obtained from experiments with scale models to overcome the inherent distortions. The same kind of thinking should be applied to all prototypes. Differences in physical size must be properly rationalized as they affect performance. Scaled-down energy inputs and outputs may not behave in *linear* proportion to the full-scale system. Materials aging experiments require a reduction of time, as do most fatigue tests, but the effects of artificially compressing time must be completely understood if the prototype is to be used to predict the performance of the full-scale unit operating in real time. Even for styling and appearance, the scaled-down prototype can mislead design judgment. One does not visualize scale models, whether they are miniatures or of heroic proportions, in the same way as the unit of actual size—although the model is an exact replica in all other respects.

Let us assume that a product design is in the last stages of completion. Alternative colors are being considered. The sales department cannot determine which of these alternatives will be most acceptable. Consequently, the decision is made to test market the alternatives. It is extremely difficult to design a test marketing situation that incorporates all the relevant features existing in the full-scale market. Using sampling theory and a great deal of statistical information, a reasonable approximation can be obtained.[8] A small group of people is chosen in the belief that their behavior will approximate the behavior that will be found when the product is released on a national scale. The *test market*, in this case, might be divided into two parts on a matched sample basis. That is, two microcosms would exist, supposedly identical and each representing the full market. Each microcosm would be given the opportunity to respond to a different alternative. In this way, it would be possible to obtain information concerning which design alternative is likely to be the most acceptable. The products themselves might be prototypes if the production line cannot be set up until a decision is reached. The actual manufacturing process for the product that eventually

[8] See, for example, Frederick F. Stephan and Philip J. McCarthy, *Sampling Opinions—An Analysis of Survey Procedures* (New York: John Wiley & Sons, Inc., 1958); and William G. Cochran, *Sampling Techniques*, 2nd ed. (New York: John Wiley & Sons, Inc., 1963).

will be used can introduce new and special characteristics, not present in the prototypes. These new factors could invalidate the test market results.

There is a great deal that can be said about prototypes and pilot plants. Here is a boundary where research and development, production, and marketing all come together in a crucial test situation. Production managers must be thoroughly familiar with the utilization of prototypes for testing and evaluating and, in general, to reduce uncertainty before major commitments are made by the company. The costs of testing alternative actions which can be figured in terms of direct outlays should always be balanced against the costs of not conducting such tests which can be stated in terms of *opportunity costs*.

PATENTS

At any early stage in the evolution of the new system a careful check should be made of the patent situation. This is not an arbitrary statement nor one which can be ignored because the organization does not intend to obtain patent benefits for a particular design. The patent laws act in two directions: (1) as a *reward* for research efforts; and (2) as a *penalty* for imitating someone else's patented work—albeit, unbeknownst to the imitator.

The intention of the current patent law[9] is to encourage the development of new ideas and the bringing of these ideas to fruition. The patent law is not arbitrary in its definition of fruition, but various court decisions over time have indicated that a high degree of ambiguity exists in the interpretation of what this means. Nevertheless, it has always been intended that an individual or a company should be encouraged to develop new products and processes, and that a degree of protection for a reasonable period of time should be given inventors so that their ideas and their work cannot be imitated by competitors. Without the patent law there would be little incentive to spend large sums of money for the development of entirely new products and services. Usually, large expenditures of time and money are required to research and develop a new product. If a company, having had no expenditure of research funds, could copy someone else's idea and begin to produce it, then, in effect, the first company would be *subsidizing* the second company. This, in a competitive world, would be unlikely to happen to any company more than once. The imitators could put all their funds behind the promotion of their product. The innovator would have spent his money on research. The patent law is intended to protect the innovator. The record substantiates the fact that patents are not an academic issue. More than three million patents have been granted by the U. S. Patent Office—which is under the jurisdiction of the U. S. Department of Commerce. New additions are being made at the rate of approximately 1300 patents granted per week. Almost 2000 patent applications are being received per week but a substantial backlog to be processed has existed for many years.[10]

[9] This law was passed pursuant to the Congress' power under Article 1, Section 8, Clause 8, of the Constitution of the United States of America.
[10] Commissioner of Patents Annual Report Fiscal Year 1969, U.S. Department of Commerce (Washington, D.C.: Patent Office).

Let us assume that two companies are both working on the same kind of product idea. Company A does not intend to investigate or obtain a patent, whereas Company B has taken all necessary steps to obtain patent protection. Company A is unaware of the fact that company B has a *patent pending*[11] that covers the new product developments of Company A. Therefore, Company A proceeds to produce this new item. Let us assume that the product is an instant success. Company A sells one million units in the first year. Meanwhile, Company B receives its patent on the product. Under some circumstances, Company B can sue Company A for *treble* damages. The triple damage claim, if upheld by the courts, can entitle a company which holds a patent that is infringed upon by another company to triple reimbursement on all losses sustained by that company as a result of the patent infringement. This is a *very severe* penalty. It can drastically alter a company's financial solvency. In some cases it can produce bankruptcy. Now, we see why the patent investigation is a must, even though the "inventing" company does not wish to claim the patent benefits.

Patents are granted for the invention of new machines, processes, and products for 17 years from the date that the patent is granted.[12] Design patents which are concerned with the style, ornamentation, and appearance of manufactured articles can be granted for $3\frac{1}{2}$, 7, or 14 years, as requested by the applicant. The patent law was established in 1836 specifically to protect an inventor's return on his research investment.

A number of facts and procedures should be common knowledge to the production manager—particularly when his company does not employ the services of a patent attorney.

1. Patent Search. The Patent Office maintains records of all patents that have been granted, and these are classified in a thorough fashion. The Patent Office publishes the *Manual of Clasification*. It has more than 300 main classes which are broken down into about 60,000 subclasses. (Copies of the Manual can be purchased from the U. S. Government Printing Office.) Further, on a weekly basis, the Patent Office issues the *Official Gazette* (OG). The OG lists new patents that have been granted and permits keeping abreast of recent developments in a particular field, From the point of view of avoiding unnecessary litigation this can be most useful. In addition, "searching" can provide real stimulation for totally new ideas. The patent records, and in particular the more recent patents, represent an incredible compilation of creative case histories. Figure 7.7 illustrates a page of patent announcements as these disclosures are typically made in the *Official Gazette*.

The Patent Office has no responsibility for an unsuccessful search. That is to say, if a party overlooks a proper classification within which he would find an infringing patent, it is simply his hard luck. However, the Patent Office attempts in every way possible to assist the inventor. Searching is not an operation to be undertaken by the layman. A patent attorney trained in Patent Office classification and knowledge of court rulings is in a much better position to

---

[11] *Patent pending* means that the patent has been applied for and that the *Formal Papers* are on file in the Patent Office. The term has no effect in law.

[12] A patent is not renewable except by a Special Act of Congress.

FIGURE 7-7
A typical page from
the *Official Gazette of
the United States
Patent Office.*

wear. In cages having a closed apex, the plastic covering is injection-molded over the cage legs. In cages having an open apex, the plastic covering is molded as a separate sleeve piece which is slipped over the ends of the cage legs.

The device can be used for recreational purposes in a swimming pool, such as propelling a small boat or rubber air-filled mattress, or for directing onto the body of an individual to produce a pleasing sensation, among other uses.

3,509,583
ELECTRO-MECHANICAL HAND HAVING
TACTILE SENSING MEANS
Anthony V. Fraioli, Essex Fells, N.J., assignor to The
Bendix Corporation, a corporation of Delaware
Filed Sept. 9, 1965, Ser. No. 486,069
Int. Cl. A61f 1/06
U.S. Cl. 3—1.1   15 Claims

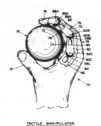

TACTILE MANIPULATOR

An electro-mechanical hand having tactile sensors on links of finger elements of the hand, and motor means supported by inner adjacent links for pivotally driving outer links of the finger elements in response to pressures applied to the tactile sensors on the outer links.

3,509,584
SWIMMING POOL RECREATIONAL DEVICE
Chester A. Sable, 9314 Ethel St., Cypress, Calif. 90630
Filed Sept. 18, 1967, Ser. No. 668,568
Int. Cl. E04h 3/16
U.S. Cl. 4—172   5 Claims

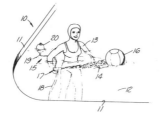

A hand-held nozzle device is connected via a flexible hose to a supply of pressurized water. The nozzle is also connected via a second flexible hose, the other end of which is maintained above the pool water surface by a float. As pressurized water is expelled from the nozzle, it is mixed with air brought via the second flexible hose to form a pressurized stream of water and entrained air.

3,509,585
PORTABLE WEIGHTABLE COVER
Samuel Solomon, 2402 65th St., Brooklyn, N.Y. 10004
Filed Sept. 18, 1967, Ser. No. 668,534
Int. Cl. E04h 3/19
U.S. Cl. 4—172.12   9 Claims

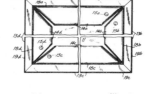

Sleeves of plastic vinyl cover material are affixed to a sheet of plastic vinyl material in the area of the edges thereof. Each of the sleeves comprises a closed envelope adapted to contain ballast and an opening in the envelope for the supply and removal of ballast. Each of the sleeves is movable to a position in juxtaposition with the sheet. A sheet of meshed material on the sheet of cover material is interposed between the sheet of cover material and each of the sleeves at its boundary areas.

3,509,586
SINK STRAINER MOUNTING MEANS
William E. Politz, Delphi, Ind., assignor to Stephen A.
Young, Monticello, Ind.
Filed June 23, 1967, Ser. No. 648,368
Int. Cl. E03c 1/26
U.S. Cl. 4—190   1 Claim

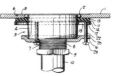

The invention herein is directed to means for mounting a sink strainer which eliminates the necessity to thread a portion of the body of the strainer but at the same time enables rapid mounting and adjustment of the strainer in the drain outlet by the provision of a carrier in which are mounted machine screws which in conjunction with certain pressure members and the flange of the strainer make

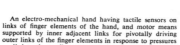

conduct such a search. Large companies usually employ patent attorneys for this purpose. Smaller companies and individuals can easily obtain the services of patent attorneys who, for rather nominal fees, will undertake a thorough search. Should the search reveal a possible infringement of a patent, the patent attorney is usually in a position to advise his client or company on the prospects of continuing with the development of the product.

There is only one place where all U. S. patents are arranged by subject matter. This is the Public Search Room of the Patent Office in Washington, D. C. In addition, over 22 libraries, in various parts of the U. S. A., have numerically arranged sets of U. S. patents in bound books. To use these it is first necessary to locate the patents that might be of interest within the subclasses that are relevant. Over 300 libraries have bound volumes of the OG.

2. Protection of Originality Claim. The right to hold a patent begins with proof of originality. This means that the date of filing for a patent is not significant. It is most important to be able to prove the date when the idea of the invention was first conceived. It is also desirable to be able to prove the dates of written descriptions, blueprints and drawings, working prototypes, and operating tests. Witnesses to these dates are the most effective proof from the point of view of the courts. Thus, even though a patent may not be sought, a company should maintain adequate records of all inventions—properly attested to by witnesses—for its own self-protection.[13]

3. Working Model. At the time that the patent application is issued the Patent Office can insist that a prototype or working model be furnished with the patent application. This requirement is rarely exercised.

4. Patent Application. In addition to the *Formal Papers*, which is primarily a petition for the patent, a description of the invention is required, called the *Specification;* and an explicit definition of the invention called *Claims.* Drawings will be attached if they provide clarification. Skill is required to write the *Specification.* The description is supposed to be sufficiently clear so that an individual who is skilled in the particular area covered by the patent could construct the invention and utilize it.

5. Novelty. The patent courts have over the years interpreted the requirement of novelty in a variety of ways. The definition of novelty has varied from something that is a difference imposed on a basic theme to something that is entirely new. In any case, the claims that are made must distinguish the difference between the invention under consideration from all other efforts in this same area. The claims should be written as broadly as possible. Generally, the less specific the language used, the broader the claim and the greater the scope of the protection obtained. Thus, a claim stating that the invention utilizes a metal box $2 \times 3 \times 5$ is far less effective in affording protection than a claim that merely states a box is used. On the other hand, too broad a claim may not distinguish the necessary difference as described above.

6. Utility. The patent law requires that a patentable invention should have utility. Here again semantic problems lead to interpretations which differ over time. It is difficult to determine what constitutes social utility. For example, one group of economists believes that ornamentation on cars creates real utility for

---

[13] As a service to inventors, the Office instituted the "Disclosure Document Program" under which the Office will accept and preserve documents for two years, which may be used as evidence of the dates of conception of inventions. The documents will be destroyed after two years unless they are referred to in related patent applications within the two-year period. Inventors have used various means to attempt to establish such dates, prior to the submission of their patent applications, for use as evidence in any further controversy. This has included the practice of mailing to themselves or to other persons registered envelopes containing disclosure statements.

the automobile-buying public that likes such things. Another group believes that ornamentation can have no real utility. The issue that must be decided is: how to determine what is useful for the public. Historically, the courts have exercised a great deal of influence in determining what utility is—specifically in terms of patent litigation. We see that the production manager, in this aspect of his job, becomes involved with legal, social, and philosophical questions.

7. Time Limitation. It might be expected that the granting of a patent should obligate the inventor to produce the item in question—in sufficient volume and within a reasonable period of time. After all, only in this way can the fruits of the patent reward be made available to the general public. Surprisingly, the interpretation of the court does not support this point of view.[14] Therefore, if a company obtains a patent on an invention which competes with its present product line, strictly with the intention of keeping it out of production and out of competitors' hands, this does not constitute a violation of the patent laws. The most recent court rulings indicate some disposition to modify this position.[15] Problems such as these are very complex. Because they impinge on vital production management decisions, the availability of expert legal advice is a practical necessity.

When the conditions stated by the patent law are fulfilled, a patent is granted. This guarantees protection in the general case for 17 years. Frequently, companies attempt to extend the period of protection beyond the 17-year period by a procedure that is known as "fencing in." In this case, the basic patent idea is divided into as many components as possible. Each of these components must be present for the successful operation of the invention. If it can be done, patents are obtained, one at a time, on each of the component parts. Thus, at the end of the first 17-year period, a second basic notion is patented. The process continues as long as possible in this fashion. Another form of the same thing is to patent a basic idea and then at a later time to patent improvements of the basic idea. Thus, when the basic idea becomes public property, the first improvement is protected. A company that attempts to produce the basic product without the improvement is operating at a competitive disadvantage which is likely to deter its entering the market.

Only people can obtain patents—not corporations. This means that when a

---

14 Chief Justice Stone, in a Supreme Court case construing the Federal Patent Statutes, indicated that prior Court decisions and the Constitution of the United States support the position that "failure of a patentee to make use of a patented invention does not affect the validity of a patent." (*Special Equipment Co.* vs. *Coe, Commissioner of Patents,* Supreme Court of the United States, 324 U. S. 370, 65 Sup. Ct. 741 [1945]).

    In defining the nature of a patent grant, the Court stated, "the patent grant is not of a right to the patentee to use the invention, for that he already possesses. It is a grant of a right to exclude others from using it."

    Mr. Justice Douglas, in a dissenting opinion, argues that to permit a patentee to suppress the use of one patent to enlarge its monopoly on another is contrary to the limited monopoly control permitted by legislative grace, a block in the development of technology, and irreconcilable with the purpose of the Constitution of the United States, "to promote the Progress of Science and useful Arts." (Art. 1, Sect. 8, Cl. 8.)

15 In 1961, the U. S. Court of Appeals, 5th Circuit speculated as follows: "In a close case the existence of a patent only on paper might tip the scale against holding of infringement." (*Edward Values Inc.* vs. *Cameron Iron Works, Inc.,* 286F. 2nd 939, [5th Cir. 1961].) (Note: This does not refer to the Commissioner of Patents with respect to the issuance of a patent.)

company develops a new idea in its laboratory the idea must be credited to an individual or individuals. The individuals apply for the patent. The company achieves protection by requiring that its employees sign an agreement—as a condition of employment—which states that all patents obtained by the employee as a result of his work with the company are to be assigned by the employee to the company. A good deal of difficulty develops when a comany contends that an individual who is no longer with the company has patented an idea which—it is claimed—he developed during his stay with the company, using their facilities and resources. It is undoubtedly true that many instances

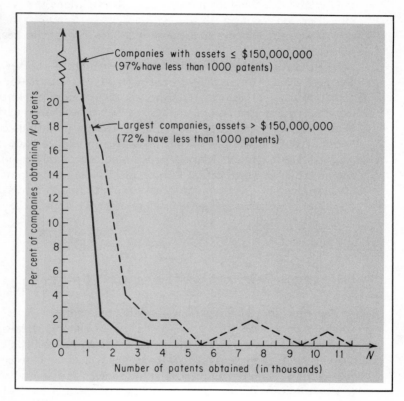

FIGURE 7-8
Distribution of patents
issued to corpora-
tions.

can be cited where an individual has left a company with the intention of setting up his own business based on an idea developed during his former employment. At the same time the seeds of an idea are seldom clear cut. This philosophical, yet practical problem is also of competitive interest. Many production managers have found themselves overly embroiled in issues of this kind.

To conclude this section on patents, let us briefly analyze the way in which company size is correlated with the average number of patents that the company holds. Figure 7.8 shows an approximate curve.[16] The larger companies have a disproportionate share of patents. This trend has continued to increase simply because of the enormous research facilities that are presently required, with our present level of knowledge, in order to come up with patentable inventions.

Of growing interest is the relationship of patent law to inventions developed in connection with government sponsored $R \& D$, because this represents such a large percentage of total research expenditures. Although this is a special subject in its own right, two points set the pattern for decisions in this area. First, the National Inventors Council of the U. S. Department of Commerce was established to assist inventors in bringing their ideas to the attention of appropriate governmental agencies. Second, the Congressional Space Act of 1958 established the government's right to inventions that were discovered by industries contracting with the National Space Administration Agency. Since that time, however, much pressure has been brought to bear to change this policy.

The growth of international trade has highlighted another aspect of patent coverage. There is no fundamental reciprocity between nations with respect to patent protection. However, an expected outgrowth of the European Economic Community is a common patent system. It has been customary for U. S. companies to apply separately for patent protection in various countries. This is normally done when the company engages in export trade with these other nations. The Common Market policy would probably require only a single patent search and application to be made. The relationship of the U. S. patent laws to those of the Common Market countries will have significant bearing on future production management developments, both in the U. S. market and in the export trade.

THE ECONOMIC ADVANTAGES OF VARIETY

The fundamental design question that management must resolve is what products or services to supply. Given that the global, strategic answers have been reached in this regard, then various design possibilities exist and further, there is real opportunity for introducing consumer choice variety into the product line. Variety has marketing advantages and several economic production advantages as well. The first of these is related to the manner in which production capacity is used and the consequent economic evaluation of resources. This is the subject of the next section, where the product-mix problem is treated by means of linear programming. The second production advantage that stems from variety is end-product, assembly modularity. It is the subject of the section that immediately follows product-mix considerations.

[16] Based on material from Distribution of Patents Issued to Corporations (1939–1955). Study of the Subcommittee on Patents, Trademarks, and Copyrights of the Committee on the Judiciary, United States Senate, 84th Congress, Second Session, pursuant to S. Res. 167, Study No. 3, United States Government Printing Office, Washington, D.C., 1957. See in particular, Section 5, pp. 8–9. (No more recent data are available, but the general shapes of the curves would probably hold for some multiple of N.)

LP PRODUCT-MIX MODEL AND THE VARIETY PROBLEM

LP is linear programming. The LP model is capable of maximizing the attainment of one objective subject to a set of constraints being met, which set includes all other objectives. The objective is achieved by employing different activities in various amounts—which requires using up specific limited resources. For example, each possible product design in the product mix is an activity. According to the number of each design that will be made, the limited resources of departmental capacities will be used up. Linear forms express the way in which resources get used up, i. e., the same amount is required for each unit of a particular design that is made. And the same reasoning applies to profit, which is to be maximized. Each unit sold of a particular design contributes an equal amount of profit. It is assumed that all units are sold. Now, let us examine the variety problem as a function of the level at which it is viewed.

At the global level, the variety problem is one of diversification. With respect to diversification, a major issue is the extent to which an organization's assets are convertible. Where there is high resource convertibility, the company's planning can be very flexible. We know that, in general, management ability is highly transferable. Technological knowledge may be the least convertible resource of the production manager, but he himself is generally quite flexible with respect to the kind of technological system that he might manage. Then, at the next level, operating within the accustomed framework of limited resources, a company must determine its optimal product or output mix. In general, the optimal mix is defined as that mix of products and services, using the existing resources and facilities of the company, which will maximize profit. For the determination of optimal mix, the financial, marketing, and production managers must pool their knowledge. The next step down could be called the level of product style, having little to do with alternative uses of resources and facilities. At this third level, the questions asked concern the number of colors, package design alternatives, etc. that should be considered for a *particular item*. Thus, for sales promotion reasons that operate in terms of consumer psychology the question is: How many images, styles, or variations on a theme should be developed? Choice potential seems to interact with the consumer's selection process thereby producing a greater sales volume than could otherwise be obtained. This is due, at least in part, to the fact that a varied offering can appeal to a larger number of specialized segments of consumers. On the other hand, style development costs money. There are more items to stock, more records to keep, more materials to buy (at lesser quantities, e.g., red, yellow, and blue paint, so that discounts will be lower), and so on. There must be an optimal number of styles. The product-mix method of linear programming that we shall discuss shortly can help to determine what this level should be, but fundamentally, the LP method is not genuinely suited for the style problem. And the LP approach is even less suitable for the diversification problem. In both cases, the concept of using up limited resources must be stretched to fit the situation. But, even so, as a first approximation, the LP product-mix model can be used for both diversification and variety problems.

So much for the levels at which the linear programming, product-mix model can be utilized. Within the product-mix problem class we find a number of situations well-suited for this type of analysis. For example, there are blending problems—where the mix can be different petroleum crude stocks to be blended at the refinery; perfume blends, whiskey blends, and cattle and poultry feed mixtures. We also have straightforward product-mix problems representing a blend though of a somewhat different kind.

The explanation of the linear programming technique is facilitated by employing an example. The situation can be kept manageable by considering the possibility of only a *two*-product line. Assume that the company makes only P_1 at the present time. Two departments are required to make the product. *First*, the press shop blanks, draws, and forms the part. Then the item is sent to the *second* department where it is chrome plated. (Specific order is not, however, an essential requirement of the method.) The full capacity of the first department is utilized when ten units are made per day. On the other hand, only $83\frac{1}{3}$ percent of the plating department's capacity is used. Presume that this results from the fact that the minimum plating tank capacity that could be purchased was capable of handling less than ten units per day. The next largest size accommodating 12 units per day was purchased. The departmental *capacities* are the *resource constraints* in this linear programming problem. The item called P_1 returns a profit of $3.00 per unit.

The production manager, wishing to get fuller utilization of his equipment, suggests that the company consider adding another product to the existing line. The new product, called P_2, is developed; a prototype is made and the relevant cost and utilization estimates are made. The marketing department feels that the new product should be sold at a lower price than P_1. On the other hand, P_2 costs less to make. Twenty units could be made in the press shop with full equipment and manpower utilization, but only 12.5 of such units could be processed per day by the plating department if it made only P_2. Thus, for P_2, the capacity of the plating tank is the dominant constraint. In any case, working together, the managers agree that the per-unit profit of P_2 will be only $2.00.

All the above information is summarized in the table below. These questions have to be answered: (1) Should P_2 be added to the line? (2) If so, how many units per day x_2 of P_2 (called x_2) should be made?

		x_1 UNITS/DAY P_1	x_2 UNITS/DAY P_2	RESTRICTION OF FULL UTILIZATION
	Department 1 (press shop)	10%/unit	5%/unit	100%
	Department 2 (plating)	$8\frac{1}{3}$%/unit	8%/unit	100%
Objective:	(Maximize) profit	$3.00/unit	$2.00/unit	

We read the table as follows:

x_1 = The number of units of product-type P_1 that we will make per day.
x_2 = The number of units of product-type P_2 that we will make per day.

Each unit of the P_1 type that is made uses up 10 percent of the daily capacity of department 1 and $8\frac{1}{3}$ percent of the daily capacity of department 2. Each unit of P_2 consumes 5 percent of the daily capacity of department 1 and 8 percent of the daily capacity of department 2. If we make only P_1—as is presently done— we can produce a maximum of ten units (department 1 is the limiting resource). If we make only P_2 we can produce a maximum of 25 units every *two* days (department 2 is the limiting resource).

We should note at this point that if we could only make one or the other, then we would prefer to make P_1 because it promises a daily profit of $30.00, as compared to $25.00 for P_2. Although we can make more of P_2 than of P_1 we cannot make sufficiently more to counterbalance the fact that P_2 has a lower profit per unit. Neither making only P_1 nor only P_2 will provide full utilization of all plant facilities and resources. Therefore, we can consider a mixture which might provide better capacity utilization. Better utilization might, but also *might not*, provide a greater profit. The product mix is subject to the departmental constraints and our objective remains to maximize profit.

Because of the size of this problem it is relatively easy for a production manager to determine what should be done without recourse to linear programming. Various methods can be used to solve this problem. For example, an algebraic approach could be used. Normally, complex problems would be solved by means of the Simplex Algorithm of linear programming which is a matrix method and the basis for many computer programs for solving LP problems. However, to understand what is involved in obtaining a solution, the method that best serves to explain, and which can be used in this case is the geometrical resolution of the problem.

First, let us refer to the previous table so that we can construct the following inequations.[17]

$$10x_1 + 5x_2 \leq 100$$
$$8\tfrac{1}{3}x_1 + 8x_2 \leq 100$$

These inequations fit the format of the linear programming model. They state the way in which each department's capacities will be utilized for different production schedules of P_1 and P_2.

The inequations express the fact that it is impossible to utilize more than 100 percent of any department's capacity. Thus, for example, if $x_1 = 10$, then department 1 is fully utilized. On the other hand, if $x_1 = 5$ and $x_2 = 5$, then only 75 percent of the first department's capacity has been used up. We say that the remaining 25 percent is departmental *slack*.[18]

By substituting different values for x_1 and x_2 we can determine whether either departmental constraint has been violated and also what profit would result from such a plan. The objective is to maximize profit, that is MAXIMIZE

---

[17] The symbol $\leq$ is read *equal to or less than*, expressing the fact that any combination of x_1 and x_2 which does not use up more than 100 percent of each departments capacity can be considered.

[18] When using mathematical methods for solving linear programming problems we would appoint a *slack* variable to represent the departmental slack, for example, x_4. Then the inequation can be converted to an equation in the following way: $10x_1 + 5x_2 + x_4 = 100$.

$[3x_1 + 2x_2]$. Furthermore, we can never produce negative quantities of a product, thus:

$$x_1 \geq 0$$

$$x_2 \geq 0$$

These inequations express the fact that negative amounts of production cannot be allowed.

The table below shows a number of different combinations of x_1 and x_2 values that might be tried. Several of the plans violate the departmental restrictions. For this particular set of trial and error plans, maximum profit is obtained with the fifth plan, which is a feasible product-mix strategy, i.e., it does not violate any of the inequations.

PLAN	x_1	x_2	DEPARTMENT 1 SLACK	DEPARTMENT 2 SLACK	PROFIT
Plan$_1$	5	5	25%	18.3%	25
Plan$_2$	10	5	violation	violation	violation
Plan$_3$	5	10	0%	violation	violation
Plan$_4$	6	5	15%	10%	28
Plan$_5$	7.83	4.35	0%	0%	32.20

FIGURE 7-9
Feasible solution space for the product-mix problem. PL_1 through PL_5 refer to the five plans shown in the table above.

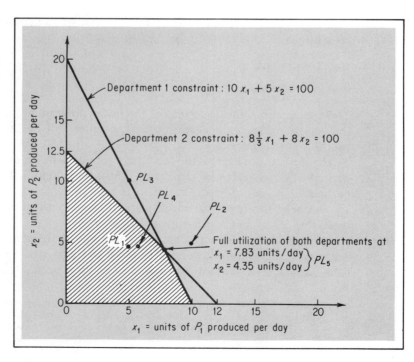

Refer now to Figure 7.9. All of the plans in the table can be found on it.

The two lines that cross each other within the first quadrant represent the two departmental constraints. Each line is appropriately labeled. The area under each of the two lines we have drawn is the equivalent of the mathematical statement of an inequation that has the directional sense of less than ($<$). Thus, all points that fall in the first quadrant and meet the requirements of the constraints must lie within the cross-hatched area or on its perimeter. We call this the *feasible solution space*. The first quadrant is defined by the feasibility constraints, $x_1 \geq 0$, $x_2 \geq 0$. Any combination of x_1 and x_2 that forms an allowable product mix must be part of the cross-hatched space. Also it is simple enough to check and see that any combination of values for x_1 and x_2 that falls on a line produces *100 percent utilization* of whichever department that line describes. Thus, each line stands for the full utilization of the respective department. We should also note that for this case there is only one combination of x_1 and x_2 values that yields full utilization of both departments' capacities. It is the crosspoint. Let us ask a question at this stage but defer the answer until later.

Question: Why does it not automatically follow that any combination of x_1 and x_2 that fully utilizes all production capacity (the crosspoint, in this case) would be the optimal product-mix solution?

Our purpose is to maximize profit. At least one point in the feasible solution space will achieve this result. It is unnecessary to use trial and error methods to determine which point will maximize the profit. We shall superimpose a *family*

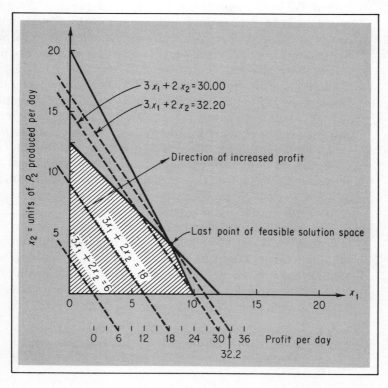

FIGURE 7-10
Family of profit lines superimposed on the feasible solution space.

of profit lines on top of the previous figure. This is shown in Figure 7.10. Each of the dashed parallel lines represents different combinations of x_1 and x_2. All combinations of x_1 and x_2 that belong to any particular profit line produce only one specific level of profit. Thus, consider the line where profit equals 18. If we substitute any one pair of x_1 and x_2 values that falls along this line, that combination (or product mix) will produce a profit of $18.00. Furthermore, all the points that lie on this profit line of $18.00 fall within the feasible solution space.

Will it be possible to obtain an even greater profit? Let us move to the profit line that is labeled $30.00. Again, if we test the profit of each x_1, x_2 pair that falls on this line, we find that they all yield a profit of $30.00 In this case, however, it should be noted that part of this line does not fall within the feasible solution space. We know that those x_1, x_2 combinations that are outside of the feasible space could not be used for the product mix. Nevertheless, because some points do meet the departmental capacity constraints, a profit of $30.00 could be obtained. But this is still not the maximum possible profit.

As the profit lines move upward and toward the right, the profit level increases. *We should, therefore, choose that member of the family of profit lines which is the last one to touch the feasible solution space as the lines move upward.* This is the line of maximum profit. For this example, it occurs at the intersection of the two department constraint lines. The production values for this solution are $x_1 = 7.83$ and $x_2 = 4.35$. With this solution, there is no departmental slack for either department. The profitability is $32.20 per day.[19]

Now, let us answer the question that was previously posed, but left unanswered. We shall do this by raising a different question. What would the optimal product mix be if the relative profitabilities of the different units in the product mix were changed? Let us consider an example where the profitability of the first product has been made equal to $2.00 per unit and the profitability of the second item has been raised to $3.00 per unit. This produces a change in the solution, as is shown in Figure 7.11. This solution leaves unused capacity in Department 1. Even so, because of the orientation of the profit line, profit can only be maximized by ignoring the attraction of full utilization of facilities. The real issue is one of appraising the value of the resources as they contribute to the profit objective. LP methods help a great deal in such evaluation.

A moment of thought will show that: (1) a solution must always occur at a vertex; and (2) as a special case, the solution can occur simultaneously at two adjacent vertices. When this happens, all points on the line that connects the vertices will also be optimal product mix solutions.

The search for a solution is simplified because it must occur at a vertex. This is further illustrated by considering a cost minimization problem. In this case, the solution is obtained by determining the last possible cost line to leave the solution space as we move down and toward the left with our cost lines. This is shown in Figure 7.12. The objective is to minimize the cost function which applies in each case. (Note the caption of Figure 7.12.)

---

[19] The values of x_1 and x_2 in this solution are fractional. If this violates the sense of the solution, then we must utilize the technique of *integer* programming. Frequently, it is quite satisfactory to round off fractional numbers so that a reasonable, discrete solution is obtained which is very close to optimal and which meets the system's constraints.

FIGURE 7-11
The optimal product mix for the profit maximization problem changes when P_1 produces \$2 of profit per unit and P_2 produces \$3 of profit per unit. Thus: maximize $2x_1 + 3x_2$. The solution is: produce 12.5 units of P_2 and no P_1; Total profit = \$37.50 per day.

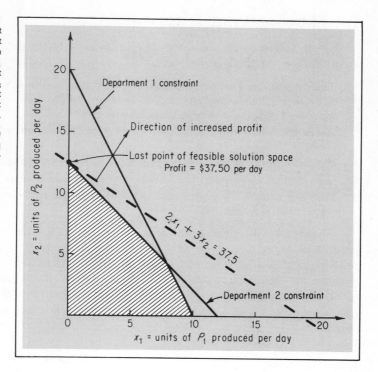

Department 1 constraint

Direction of increased profit

Last point of feasible solution space
Profit = \$37.50 per day

$2x_1 + 3x_2 = 37.5$

Department 2 constraint

x_2 = units of P_2 produced per day

x_1 = units of P_1 produced per day

FIGURE 7-12
For cost minimization, the feasible solution space is $\geq$ the constraints, and the optimum solution is associated with the last possible cost line to leave that space, moving down and left. Assume that P_1 costs \$5 per unit and P_2 costs \$12 per unit; then, Minimize $5x_1 + 12x_2$. The solution is: produce 12 units of P_1 and no P_2; Total cost = \$60 per day.

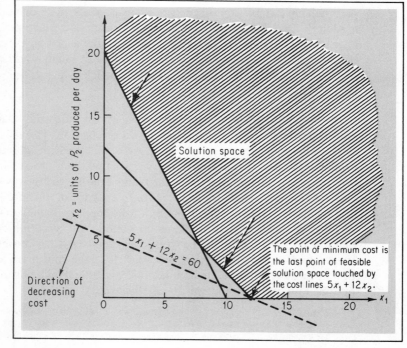

Solution space

$5x_1 + 12x_2 = 60$

Direction of decreasing cost

The point of minimum cost is the last point of feasible solution space touched by the cost lines $5x_1 + 12x_2$.

x_2 = units of P_2 produced per day

x_1

193

THE PROGRAMMING ALGORITHM

We can interpret the mathematical methods of linear programming (such as the Simplex Method) as follows:

1. Begin by selecting a vertex of the polyhedron that is formed when more than two products are involved. (The Cartesian coordinates of the geometric approach no longer apply when more than two types of products are to be mixed.)

2. Test to determine whether an improvement in profit can be made by moving to another vertex.

3. If improvement is possible, attempt to find the best possible change to make.

4. Make the indicated change, i. e., choose the new, improved vertex solution.

5. Steps two through four are repeated until the test, in step two, reveals that no further improvement is possible.

It should be evident that linear programming is not a substitute for ingenious product planning or creative new product development. The character of the product mix is strictly a function of whatever components the production manager has been able to conceive. If the various products that are competing for available capacity are individually excellent, then the product mix will produce a large profit. Otherwise, the best that can be done may not be good enough.

MODULARITY

Another aspect of variety is that of modularity. By this is meant "combinatorial" productive capacities, i.e., the capacities to design and manufacture parts which can be combined in numerous ways. The drive toward product modularity has been forced by external factors and made possible because of internal ones. *Group technology* provides another aspect of these same concepts. It refers to the ordered processing of families of similar parts which are later regrouped into product-line families. The article which follows describes some issues of modularity.[20]

In the course of its normal development, an industrial society begins with an orientation that is focused primarily on production. This is hardly surprising, since technological mastery of a *process* lies at the root of incipient economic progress. Witness, for example, the impact that such process inventions as the printing press, the spinning jenny, the mandrel lathe, and the open-hearth furnace have had on society. During this stage, managers of the production function find themselves actively participating in the topmost managerial affairs.

Then, for evident and fundamental reasons, the situation can change. Production decisions, though recognized as vital, cease to be *critical*. They no longer need to be made at the highest levels of the enterprise. Feasible production alternatives appear much alike, offering little choice. Production decisions become involved with increments of efficiency.

[20] The material on pp. 194 through 209 is a direct quote from Martin K. Starr, "Modular Production—A New Concept," *Harvard Business Review*, Vol. 43, No. 6, November-December 1965, pp. 131–142. With respect to *group* technology, see Manfred Knayer, "Group Technology," *Industrial Engineering* (September 1970), pp. 23–27.

This second stage has more or less characterized the technologies and methodologies of production management for the past 25 years in the West. The production function during this period could be sensibly described as "reliable." Production decisions have become relatively predictable.

It is a tribute to the pioneers of production management that they have been able to remove great variability—and, consequently, risk and uncertainty—from this area of enterprise. On the other hand, by succeeding in this fashion, they have relegated to other areas, such as finance, research, and marketing, the real *leverage* factors in top management decision making.

But now change is occurring once again. Many enterprise managers are aware that something new is creeping into the production sphere. For a while it seemed as if automation were its name. At least the more journalistic spokesmen, sensing a dramatic change, felt obliged to play on this theme. On careful examination, however, it becomes apparent that automation is only a tool of this new force—and even hardly that in its present form.

THE NEW CAPACITY

Many production managers are not prepared to understand what is going on. Some hardly even sense that they are in a truly different era. The reasons for this are clear. There is no precedent to go by, and no means for an individual whose interest centers in one functional area to recognize the existence of the trend.

The change that we are talking about can be briefly described as the consumer's demand for *maximum productive variety* (or maximum choice). To achieve this variety, what I call "modular" or "combinatorial" productive capacities— that is, capacities to design and manufacture parts which can be combined in numerous ways—are required, as well as compatible managerial abilities.

As has been suggested, the drive toward productive variety is being forced by external factors. It is made possible because of internal ones. An overview is needed for the trend to be perceived. We can state that:

1. The force for this change comes from the marketplace.
2. The means for change resides in the production management area, specifically in production's use of—
   ... methodology derived from the management sciences;
   ... technology derived from the physical sciences;
   ... data processing ability obtained from electronic computers.

In other words, the consumer is demanding ever greater variety from which to choose. And new methodologies and technological achievements have developed within the production area which permit the consumer to force this issue (albeit with varying degrees of success).

IRRESISTIBLE FORCES

The speed with which such change will occur is influenced by competitive factors. If there is general management resistance, new forms can be expected to grow at the expense of the reluctant. In any case, various alignments of industrial power will arise according to the ability of each organization to assess and modify its own position in an environment that is undergoing change at an accelerating rate.

The problems that must be faced by the next generation of production managers are numerous. Once again production managers are likely to be assigned top-management positions. All industries will not be similarly affected; their adaptations can be expected to follow different timetables. How to speed up or slow down the rate of change will be a subject of interest; but in the long run the forces for change are irresistible, and the degree of change will be recognized as having been predetermined and not under the manager's control.

Accordingly, I shall undertake . . . to describe modular production and to point out where the effects of the developing combinatorial methods are likely to be felt most strongly. I shall try to focus on the kind of managerial training that will be required in order to provide some assurance of success in meeting new challenges as they are raised. The evolution of equipment, alterations in organizational structure, changes in managerial methods—these are some of the other issues I shall examine.

NATURE OF METAMORPHOSIS

The center of change resides in the production management area, which has long been a stepchild of industrial drama. However, production management cannot swing the change by itself. For those companies that will evolve successfully by maintaining or increasing their total share of a growing market, a new form of effort which will cut across many functional organizational areas is required. We can call this new orientation a "synthesis" to distinguish it from "analysis," the euphemism which epitomizes the traditional production management approach.

Production managers are being called on to find (within their *potential* set of tools and concepts) the operational and economic means for introducing real diversity in production output, using a given configuration of plant and equipment. Real diversity means far more than the illusion of an "adequate" product mix. It signifies the capability to produce a sequence of items (or small batch of items), each of which can differ markedly from preceding and subsequent items (or batches). To achieve differentiation, there will be small batches of units with separate setup charges. And yet, because of the technology and methodology employed, the total charges, including those for setup, can be significantly less than the total revenue obtained in the marketplace.

SPOTLIGHT ON PRODUCTION

It is not difficult to see why production management decisions must be at the core of this activity. Three reasons stand out:

(1) The essence of the depicted capability is technological. The notion of high-volume, low-cost, automated mass production will eventually give way to adaptive automation capable of producing a sequence of unique outputs at no sacrifice of volume and at no significant increase in cost. Already, in fact, this trend is in evidence. Thus:

- In the automobile industry, a large and still increasing number of ordering options for a new car are readily available to the consumer.
- A major petroleum company has designed a gasoline pump that permits the consumer to mix his own blend.
- Self-fitting clothing, such as stretch socks, has a kind of built-in diversity.
- Increases are occurring in the available variety of soap colors, type faces for typewriters, and shades, styles, and scents for lipsticks, nailpolish, perfumes, sun lotions, and other cosmetics.
- There is increased diversity in the size and type of TV sets now available.

In all of these cases, it is growth in technological capability that has permitted such diversity to occur.

(2) The new methodology of production management is capable of providing controls for high output diversity. "Management science," as it is called, has resolved such basic problems as scheduling work, providing adequate inventories, and exercising quality control, thus permitting splendid managerial control over an enormous variety of products in the product mix.

Significantly, management science has been easily and directly assimilated by only one functional area of business—production management. This observation has been made frequently; yet its relevance has been overlooked. Management science and the production function are natural partners. And as management science unfolds, the production function responds.

(3) Because of consumers' attraction to diversity, the ability to produce a real variety offers the kind of high leverage that attracts top management attention. The change represents a fundamental departure from prior conditions in the sense that previously one company's ability to mass-produce identical items could be copied by other firms. But for *modular* production there are no patterns available with which to model and manage the production system. A great deal of innovation and creativity is called for, and with these will be found the inevitable partners, risk and uncertainty, and real vulnerability to astute competitive practices.

CONTROL OF VARIABILITY

Our understanding of the production of real variety can be improved by taking a brief historical excursion. In the early 1900's, students of production management began to learn how to combine many different input elements in a transformation system so as to produce a stream of output units that were sufficiently similar to be interchangeable in every important detail. In effect, to achieve mass production it had been necessary to learn how to remove or control the inherent variabilities of the inputs and the process. This accomplishment can be illustrated as shown in Figure 7.13.

Outputs from such a production system could be mixed together in a bin and withdrawn in any order for assembly with other parts that had been similarly produced. This gigantic step forward in concept revolutionized the production process. In retrospect, the step seems to have been inevitable. For instance, while Eli Whitney was developing the notion of interchangeable parts in the United States, Leblanc was also making the concept operational in France—but neither man was aware of the other's work. (It may be noted as well that the growth of modular production partakes of the same sense of inevitability.)

FIGURE 7-13
Control with mass
production.

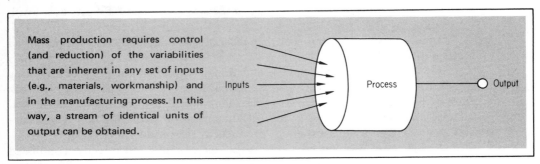

Mass production requires control (and reduction) of the variabilities that are inherent in any set of inputs (e.g., materials, workmanship) and in the manufacturing process. In this way, a stream of identical units of output can be obtained.

Inputs → Process → Output

The effective realization of the relationship shown in Figure 7.13 was the result in no small measure of the efforts of such men as Frederick W. Taylor, Henry L. Gantt, and Frank Gilbreth. Few managers, no matter what their functional area, are unaware of the objectives and achievements of these early pioneers. Somewhat less well known, but totally appropriate to this discussion, is the fact that when it was realized that some variability in the outputs must always exist, Walter Shewhart and his colleagues developed the function of statistical quality control, whereby the level of fundamental or inherent variability could be described and brought under management direction.

As a final step, Henry Ford helped to complete production's conquest over variability by providing an operational instance of coordinated assembly for mass production. The result was that the multiple inputs could be transformed in both space *and time* to afford a controlled stream of output.

With this background in mind, let us turn from developments in the factory to trends in the marketplace.

DEMAND FOR VARIETY

We know that the demand for variety originates at the consumer level. But how much variety does the consumer want? How much is he willing to pay for it?

In the past, operating under a production configuration of the type illustrated in Figure 7.13 marketing management stepped into the breach and accepted the challenge to supply the consumer with apparent variety. Production facilities could not generate as much *real* variety as the market was able to absorb, for the technological capability was lacking, and so was the managerial ability to control the production of diverse outputs. So the marketing function, aimed at diversity, began where mass production (indicated by the single output line in Figure 7.14) left off, and its success is amply illustrated by the important status of marketing in management in recent years.

FIGURE 7-14
Product variety with
mass production.

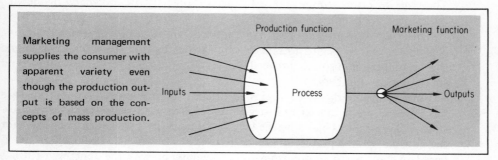

In general, marketing activities directed toward creating variety have represented an increasing proportion of the total costs of an item. The consumer has not been reluctant to accept these services.

INCREASING EXPECTATIONS

Initially, the marketing operation was most effective when the diversity of production was minimal. Each firm established some unique qualities for its brands. The consumer was able to contrast these attributes with those of other brands. Differentiation was based on many subtleties, not the least of which were the name, the package, and the image associations that were created. One basic chemical mixture could be positioned in the marketplace in several totally different ways. Even a single brand might appear to possess quite diverse qualities to different demographic segments of the population if the advertising and promotion could be properly controlled.

But such differentiation was not to be enough. Pressure exerted by the consumer for greater variety began to appear in several different forms. For instance, the consumer began to question the "truth" of apparent variety. As a result, marketing, advertising, and promotion operations have come under the critical surveillance of consumer groups and the government. It appears, however, that disillusionment about brand marketing, to the extent that it exists, has *not* been connected with the purpose of marketing or with the concept of apparent variety, but with the lack of a commensurate measure of *real* variety. The consumer is simply asking for a more significant choice.

Pressure for variety also helps to explain the severe contraction in product life that has been experienced in recent years, and the unusually high failure rate for many new products which require acceptance by a large market segment for economic success, yet are not sufficiently unique to warrant such acceptance. It is also significant that the demand for variety appears to follow a cyclical pattern. The oscillations are correlated with production capabilities and the various phases of technological maturity. The consumer's expectations appear to be entirely in keeping with the state of the art:

As technology advances, the first reaction of the marketplace is to adopt the prototype model of the new technology as widely as possible. Only minimum brand differentiation and almost no variety within a single brand are found. The issue of primary importance to the consumer is the *ownership* of the car, radio, or other product.

Then, as soon as the prototype models are broadly distributed among consumers, a shift begins to take place. Various market segments appear, and the accumulation process proceeds in terms of particular brand names and special model numbers.

Finally, the marketplace begins to discard the notion of "keeping up with the Joneses" and emphasizes instead the uniqueness of the individual's possessions.[21] This trend is based on the fact that the quality of difference has value for the consumer. Acceptable difference is not, of course, a random affair but is based on some personal predisposition. "Keeping up with the Joneses," if it has any meaning, must be interpreted as being acceptably different from the Joneses where the difference can be explained in terms of a purely personal and individual philosophy.

PRODUCTION MEETS THE NEED

Marketing managers have succeeded to *some* extent in presenting the consumer with a choice so that he can exercise his individuality. In part, this has been achieved by stressing nonfunctional factors of quality which can serve to distinguish one product from another. But the consumer's drive for uniqueness appears to be insatiable. For instance, the novelty of European cars led to an unexpected degree of acceptance by U. S. consumers. The capricious affair of the U. S. consumer with compact cars has been of the same type. And the great increase in consumer spending for such services as travel and entertainment can also be accounted for as another way to further one's individuality.

What makes all this so significant is the timing. The drive toward highly personalized possessions comes at a time when the production manager begins to find himself in a position *to deliver this real diversity* without violating reasonable economic bounds. The degree of personalization that is required is more

[21] See Ernest Dichter, "Discovering the 'Inner Jones'" (Thinking Ahead), *Harvard Business Review*, May-June 1965, p. 6.

than that delivered by monogrammed luggage, shirts, ties, and automobiles. It is more than what "key clubs," unique shapes and colors of telephones, or antique household furnishings can provide. It is embodied in the growing success of mail-order variety, in the concept of "do it yourself" (with a great many options to do it "in your own way"), and in other forms which we shall mention presently.

BEGINNINGS OF THE TREND

The kind of timeliness that we observe here is not unusual. There is, if anything, distinct precedent for it—production has responded to market demands before. Only the specifics are different.

FIGURE 7-15
Concept of modular
production.

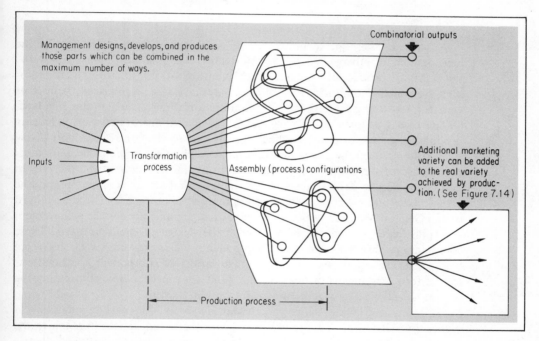

ELEMENTS OF CHANGE

To appreciate the new trend, one can divide the production system into two basic parts:

1. The transformation processes.
2. Assembly operations.

Many different inputs (including materials, skills, information, and power) enter the transformation process. They are combined in various ways to produce a catalog of parts. *It is the essence of the modular concept to design, develop, and produce those parts which can be combined in the maximum number of ways.* Figure 7.15 is intended to present visually some of the aspects of this statement.

This emphasis on maximizing the combinatorial variety of assemblies from a given number of parts is the new element of interest to production managers. It is what is meant by modular capabilities. One accent is on design; a second is on the exercise of adequate managerial controls.

There are numerous examples that can be given of systems which have developed with a *tendency* in this direction—jet engines, originally designed for airplanes, being adapted for use as integral components of power plants; modular office wall panels and furniture permitting a wide diversity of arrangements; and the similar configuration adaptability of prefabricated structures. But none of these examples can suffice to describe what would result from the total planning of a system of this kind; the production manager can now deliver a much greater variety, at a reasonable cost, than his present activities indicate.

RETARDING FACTORS

At present, there are a number of difficulties that stand in the way of the development of advanced modular production:

(1) Many production managers are unaware of the market potential for highly diversified outputs. Accordingly, they have not familiarized themselves with the technological problems of combinatorial design which are involved.

The recent acquisition of new methodological abilities, however, is forcing production men to examine implications for managerial control of richly diversified systems. And the enormous manipulative abilities of electronic computers may reinforce the feeling that some new potential has entered the picture. In particular, recent developments in designing products by computer and the use of visual input-output peripheral equipment aids, such as those employed by the General Motors Corporation, have great significance for the achievement of sophisticated combinatorial variety in the design of modular parts. These computer systems can store design components such as rectangles, circles, force fields, and stress patterns. Indeed, a great variety of component combinations can be tested by means of analytic and simulation procedures, eliminating the need to construct a prototype model for physical testing.

(2) Many marketing managers, though aware of the market potential for highly diversified outputs, are convinced that their traditional approach to the consumer is sound. Without a complete revision in perspective (which inertia prevents), the new potential goals cannot be defined. And one cannot measure how far short he falls from an unspecified goal. As a result, the demands of the marketplace have not been translated into production terms.

(Judging from all indications, research and development managers often suffer from the same difficulty.)

(3) From the viewpoint of society, modular production will bring with it significant costs in the form of obsolescence. Obsolescence occurs not only with respect to the present product line but also with respect to present configurations of plant and facilities. While it can be argued successfully that changeover to modular production need not be total or swift, the fact remains that turning to the modular approach produces a great deal of unplanned obsolescence.

In addition, the design and engineering costs of entering into such production configurations can be exceptionally high.

Management personnel must be trained to cope with both the concepts (for planning) and the realities (for operating). The background essential for this training will be the management sciences. In particular, the combinatorial aspects of mathematical analysis will provide an essential foundation—above and beyond which managerial intuitions can and will continue to be exercised.

In view of the uncertainties, new risks, and difficulties, it is predictable that many otherwise alert executives will tend to look the other way when an issue pertaining to real productive variety is raised. To wait and see, to postpone action until one's hand is forced—these attitudes will tend to be substituted for what is ordinarily called entrepreneurial wisdom.

PRESSURES FOR CHANGE

Meanwhile, however, there will be situations where reluctance to move in the new direction will seem absurd to businessmen involved. The totally new venture, the new or experimental autonomous branch, and industries that traditionally are involved with substantial retooling—these are exemplary situations for the introduction of modular capabilities. In time, such instances may provide the momentum to force still other hands. It seems logical to suggest, as well, that high-volume industries characterized by short product life cycles will react early to the possibilities of modular production, and that industries which characteristically are involved with expensive parts and components will not overlook the potential benefits of modularity.

Only in some ultimate sense can we expect that the *overall* industrial system of the present will evolve to the point where it becomes truly responsive to the selection process of the individual. What we *can* anticipate is the continued fragmentation of the market to ever smaller units that can be serviced with relatively more unique outputs, with *some* enterprising companies capitalizing on the trend.

PLANNING AND CONTROL

At this point I shall depart from discussion of general trends and problems in order to demonstrate in a more precise way what modular production means to management. This demonstration will allow us to draw some important conclusions for those men entrusted with planning and control.

PARTS AND CONFIGURATIONS

A better understanding of the nature of modular capabilities for real productive variety can be obtained by constructing a table of the kind shown in Figure 7.16. We see that, with N different kinds of parts, a total of M different product configurations is derived. Some of these products require several units of a single part; for instance, PR_4 requires two of PA_2, and PR_j requires two of PA_i. The maximum possible variety, i.e., maximum M, that can be obtained with N different parts may be very large. This is especially so when we include both the different possible combinations of the parts and varying numbers of them in combination. Thus:

FIGURE 7.16 Table of Specifications for the Kind and Number of Parts to be Combined for Each of a Given Number of Different End Products

FIGURE 7-16
Table of specifications for the kind and number of parts to be combined for each of a given number of different end products.

VARIETY OF PARTS	VARIETY OF PRODUCTS							
	PR_1	PR_2	PR_3	PR_4	. . .	PR_j	. . .	PR_M
PA_1	1	0	1	1	. . .	0	. . .	0
PA_2	0	1	1	2	. . .	0	. . .	0
PA_3	0	0	0	0	. . .	1	. . .	0
PA_4	0	0	1	0	. . .	0	. . .	0
.	.	.	.	.		.		.
.	.	.	.	.		.		.
.	.	.	.	.		.		.
PA_i	0	0	1	0	. . .	2	. . .	0
.	.	.	.	.		.		.
.	.	.	.	.		.		.
.	.	.	.	.		.		.
PA_N	0	0	0	1	. . .	1	. . .	1

Notes: PA_i denotes the part identified by the stock number i.
PR_j denotes the product variation listed in the finished goods catalog as j. (As shown above, the product j assembly requires one unit of part 3, two units of part i, and one unit of part N. The sequence of assembly is not indicated.)
PA_N denotes the last part listed in our table.
PR_M denotes the last product variation listed in our table; in this case, it is the product using only one unit of part N.

If each part can appear zero, one, or two times (i.e., three options), then the maximum variety that can be derived with N parts will be $3^N - 1$ (one is subtracted because there will be one configuration in which none of the parts appears). Considering only five parts ($N = 5$), the maximum variety (defined in this way) will be 242.

With ten parts, the maximum variety rises to a somewhat astonishing 59,048.

If, in addition, the ways and sequences with which the parts can be combined also add variety, then the number of possibilities rises even faster.

Of course, many of the theoretical possibilities cannot exist and would have no appeal as a product choice for any consumer. But the basic idea of modular design is to have an inventory of parts which can partake in many appealing product configurations. Each order received by the company is translated into a unique assembly configuration. (The same sort of table as shown in Figure 7.16 must have been designed long ago for the first Erector set. It appears that industry is about to take seriously a fundamental principle long embodied in many children's toys.) A useful measure of the effective degree of modular design might be, therefore, the number of products (columns) that can be generated from a given number of parts (rows).

ECONOMIC MODEL

It is now possible to expand the notions that we have been developing into an economic framework. As a convenient approximation, let us begin with the assumption that we can produce fixed but different amounts of each part and that we have N such parts which can be assembled in various ways to yield a variety of M products. If we know the costs of each part, we can combine all of this information by means of a linear programming model to determine an optimal product mix. The objective would be to maximize profits, subject to the constraints imposed by the modular system of parts that has been predesigned and by the productive capacity of the enterprise to produce these parts.

From the fundamental theorem of linear programming we know that the number of parts (as we have defined them) plus the number of any other resource constraints (such as storage space, limited power, or scarce raw materials) will be equal to the maximum number of products that can be included in the ultimate composition of the product mix. But this rule produces the somewhat absurd result that the product mix will be only slightly larger in size than the total number of parts that have been designed by the company. Such a result would defeat the purpose and concept of modular productive capability.

What, then, can account for the fact that many more product configurations than are indicated by the far smaller number of parts would, in fact, be included

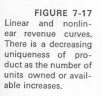

FIGURE 7-17
Linear and nonlinear revenue curves. There is a decreasing uniqueness of product as the number of units owned or available increases.

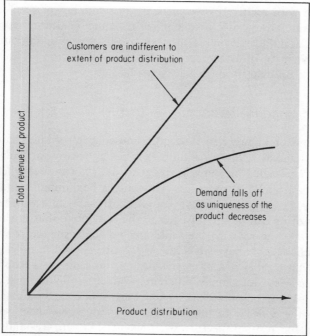

Customers are indifferent to extent of product distribution

Demand falls off as uniqueness of the product decreases

Total revenue for product

Product distribution

in the ultimate composition of the product mix? The answer must lie in the demand of the marketplace for uniqueness. Once we have accepted the fact that the revenue curves for each product configuration are not linear but fall off as the uniqueness of the product class diminishes, we have a satisfactory explanation for expanding the product mix.

Figure 7.17 compares a linear revenue curve with one that decreases as the uniqueness of the product class in the marketplace diminishes. The linear form represents complete consumer indifference to the amount and scope of product distribution. The nonlinear curve of diminishing returns, on the other hand, indicates decreasing consumer responsiveness as the extent of distribution and ownership of a particular product configuration increases. (The decline in responsiveness may be hastened by repeated purchases over time.)

OPTIMAL PRODUCT MIX

The saturation phenomenon is well known in marketing. It is usually based on the notion of an exhaustion of "prime" targets. I am suggesting that the size of the potential market diminishes at a faster rate than can be accounted for by exhaustion alone, or, in other words, that the acquisition of a new customer will remove more than one potential customer from the marketplace. The reason is that every customer added increases the consumer's disenchantment with what he conceives to be boring, commonplace, or ordinary.

When a nonlinear form of the kind shown in Figure 7.17 is encountered, the effect with respect to a linear program is to increase the number of constraints. As a result, the size of the optimal product mix increases. Under such conditions and even with relatively few parts, a great number of product configurations will be required in order to maximize revenue. The more demanding the consumer is for uniqueness in his possessions, the greater the curvature of the revenue lines. And in turn, as the curvature of a revenue line increases, the indicated size of the optimal product mix grows larger.

INTERCHANGEABLE MODULES

In terms of Figure 7.16 the traditional concept of interchangeable parts can be interpreted as follows: All units that belong to any particular parts classification can be treated as being identical. It does not matter whether a given unit of a certain family of parts was made at the beginning or end of a production run. Any member of this family of parts can substitute with equal ease for any member of its own family of parts in the row. Note that this interchangeability exists *within* the rows of the table and not between the rows of the table.

Interchangeable part *modules*, on the other hand, are designed so as to be highly transferable *between columns;* i.e., an interchangeable module enters with equal ease into many different product configurations. In contrast, production as it is conceived today tends to isolate the columns.

Once the concept of interchangeable modules becomes widely accepted, it may well be responsible for developments that are astounding or at least as significant as those which followed from the general adoption of the concept of interchangeable parts.

MEETING THE CHALLENGE

The need and the ability to provide real diversity will certainly vary in many ways. However, management can anticipate some of the important factors that are likely to operate to the advantage or disadvantage of a company, and plan accordingly.

CHANGING OPPORTUNITIES

Some of the more likely factors of differentiation will be discernible in terms of the characteristics of industrial sectors, demographic segmentation, competitive structures, organizational flexibility, executive attitudes, and a variety of exogenous factors which are imposed by the economy and international trade. Since starting ventures will possess advantages over going interests with established production systems, the latter may find themselves being pushed at unexpected times and in unanticipated ways.

Organizations seeking to diversify will encounter new opportunities to branch out. Creating real productive variety—that which comes with modular production—is equivalent to building into the system preplanned potentials for diversification. In a related sense, activities such as long-range planning and master planning necessarily will span new horizons and assume new dimensions.

The marketplace will cease to be treated as a statistical phenomenon that can be described by gas-law models, analogs of random walks, quantum mechanics, or other such models used for deriving average responses and occasionally for obtaining measures of variability. Instead, there will be a growth of interest in the behavior of the *individual*. The marketplace will be most appropriately described as the sum of individual behaviors.

The concept of the highly segmented market will be found to apply quite well to common-market type operations, where consumer diversity occurs because of the structural variants in the environment (e.g., broad cultural differences between consumer segments, and significant production variations caused by price and wage differentials, previously established underwriter codes, and separate systems of national taxation).

INNOVATION IN PRODUCTION

The essential ingredients of change for the production manager are twofold. On the one hand, a veritable revolution in design ability is required in order to move in the direction of interchangeable modules. The roots of such efforts already exist in the well-developed concept of standard parts (e.g., screw threads gauges, and light bulbs) and in standard process operations (e.g., synthetic time standards and computer-controlled equipment). On the other hand, it will be recognized that adaptive automation rather than a fixed-output type is the ideal to be desired. However, the primary significance of adaptive automation will be for assembly operations and only secondarily for the transformation processes.

The use of the computer seems to be the key. It will be a major asset when it comes to coping with the production of real variety. From another point of view, it is also a force for change. When employed in conjunction with appropriate models from the management sciences, such as sequencing models, programming methods, line-balancing and queuing models, and heuristic procedures of many kinds, a new level of managerial control of diversity can be achieved.

Radically different design techniques can also be expected. Modular design is a realistic objective in the light of visual-aid inputs to computers. These peripheral equipments permit almost instantaneous assessment of a designer's work. Complex design constructions and evaluations that formerly required many man-weeks of analysis will be achieved so rapidly that a new sense of creativity will develop.

EFFICIENCY IN DISTRIBUTION

The distribution problem which arises as a result of increased variety is certain to be enormous. Here, too, the role of the computer is likely to be crucial. The rapid communication of individual consumer demands to the production control units, the translation of these demands into specifications appropriate for the transformation and assembly processes, and the distribution of production outputs to the appropriate consumers—all of these steps appear to be feasible because of new insights and abilities *and* the computer.

ORGANIZATIONAL STEPS

It is apparent that we are dealing with a situation that will involve fundamental changes in the enterprise. What is required is the ability to manage a new kind of productivity. An appropriate organizational structure would provide greater responsiveness to the market. In such an organization, production would be in touch with consumers, with the contact mediated by the marketing function. An appropriate organization would also allow the production manager to respond with sensitive perception to developing technologies. To achieve such results, a much higher level of functional integration is called for. It is also quite clear that production management should once again participate in top management decision making.

Simulation methods can be expected to play a crucial role in the development of an appropriate organization. They will provide necessary information, as well as assurance concerning the effect of proposed changes in relationships and procedures. Also, when management simulates the design of modular parts, their assembly into many unique products, the managerial control problems that result, and the distribution problems created by a highly segmented market, it can examine the important characteristics of the total system. Thus, simulation provides a rational means for analyzing an enormously complex system whose diversity promises not less but more satisfaction born of less conformity.

PRODUCT QUALITIES

Cost and quality are critical production management dimensions. The interaction between these dimensions is extremely complex. In general, we can state:

$$\text{Product qualities}[22] = f\,(\text{production costs})$$
$$\text{Price} = f\,(\text{production costs, sales promotion costs})$$
$$\text{Sales volume} = f\,(\text{price, quality})$$
$$\text{Dollar volume} = (\text{price})(\text{sales volume})$$
$$\text{Profit} = \text{dollar volume} - \text{total costs}$$

FIGURE 7-18
There is a level of quality that will maximize profits.

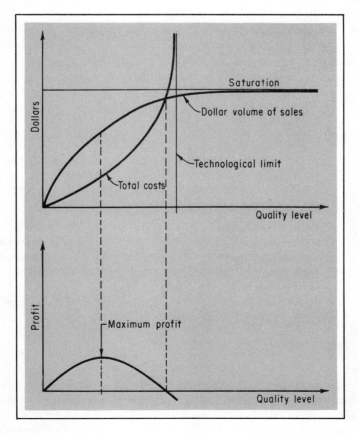

This formulation ignores the competitor, unless we consider our product qualities to be measured relative to competitive qualities. In any case, it is usually a safe bet that both dollar volume and total costs will increase with improved quality. Therefore, there is a level of quality that will maximize profits. The relationship is shown in Figure 7.18. The curve of dollar volume is a decelerating function because of market saturation. No matter how high the quality, there is an upper limit to the level of quality that can be achieved within a given technological framework.

We have been talking about quality in terms that coincide with the consumers' evaluation of quality. To the consumer, quality and "high quality" are the same thing. The production manager has a quandary here. As an individual he wishes to produce an output that possesses "high quality." But he must deliver an output of *specified* quality that is commensurate with the investment in the process and his budget for operating costs. In this latter sense, quality is an agreed upon set of standards and tolerance limits. These specifications are operational terms—not value judgments. But in order to consider quality in operational terms, it is an absolute necessity that dimensions of quality be expressed in measurable terms. The production manager would like to minimize costs and maximize "high quality." These objectives cannot be achieved simultaneously. They are conflicting, multiple objectives. Therefore, it is necessary to specify the quality *constraints*. Then, subject to these, the cost is to be minimized.

Let us examine the attributes of output quality.

I. Functional Qualities
  1. Utility of purpose
  2. Reliability of function
    (a) Accuracy in use over time
    (b) Deterioration of function over time
    (c) Failure characteristics and expected lifetime
    (d) Cost of maintenance and repair
    (e) Guarantees and warranties
  3. Human factors
    (a) Safety
    (b) Comfort
    (c) Convenience

II. Nonfunctional Qualities
  1. Style and appearance
  2. Self-image of user
    (a) Price
    (b) Prestige
  3. Timeliness of design
  4. Style and variety

FUNCTIONAL QUALITIES

In most but not all instances, purpose utility is the most fundamental product quality. It is associated with a specific, functional class of outputs such as toilet soaps, breakfast foods, auto tires, etc. The class is clearly defined by a widely supported social sense of the need for the function. Generally, the product's purpose is relatively clear, but at other times it is intrinsically difficult to state.

In either case, the measurement of how well a product or service performs its intended function is not easy to come by. There are physical evaluations and consumer evaluations. Can we measure how good a food product tastes, how comfortable a chair is, or how convenient a hammer is to use? We can measure the sweetness of the food, the number of springs used in the chair, and the hardness of the steel head. There is always some kind of an assumption about the way in which the measurable, physical factors relate to the consumers' evaluation of the utility of function.

Reliability is an important attribute of the output. It concerns the ability of the output to perform according to *specifications* over a given period of time. This category of attributes raises some interesting problems. Production management is responsible for controlling the quality of the product during its manufacture.[23] Thereafter, each unit of output has a history of its own. Observations, measurements, and specifications of quality must include the variety of possible histories for each unit which is sold.

FIGURE 7-19
Expected perfor-
mance exhibits in-
creasing deviation
from the initial design
standard as a func-
tion of time.

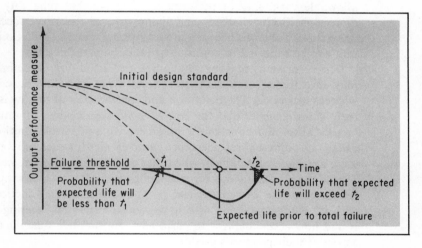

There are a number of different ways that we could go about describing reliability. Thus, when we discuss the reliability of a product, we are referring to the fact that the functional attributes will continue to perform within some set of limits over a given period of time. The width of the limits represents an important aspect of the definition of quality for the design. We expect that parts of the product will become worn with use, whereas other characteristics will age independently of use. Furthermore, chance events can occur that have a significant level of expectation which will affect the performance characteristics. Generally, the expected performance will exhibit increasing deviation from the initial design standard over a period of time, as shown in Figure 7.19.

[23] See Chapter 10, pp. 310-27.

This phenomenon which we call *drift* is characteristic of a great many functional attributes of mechanical, chemical, and electrical products. Consider a simple electric light bulb. When it is first used it will generate some given number of lumens. Then as it ages and as a function of both hours of use and the number of times that it is turned on and off, the output of the bulb will vary. It will produce less and less light. At some point in time the light bulb will fail entirely.

Complete or total failure is easy to define. However, if we can no longer use our light source once its output falls below a certain threshold, then for all functional purposes the light bulb has failed and must be replaced. Our ordinary definition of failure for the light bulb specified a zero output threshold. A *more sophisticated definition* requires the specification of a given level of light below which the unit cannot be said to be performing satisfactorily. Thus, performance specification in terms of *operational limits* is equivalent to failure specification. When talking about quality, the production manager must think in these more complex terms.

A unit can have very erratic performance before it reaches the failure threshold, for example, the light bulb might get alternately brighter and dimmer. This constitutes still another measure of reliability, that is, the specification of allowable variability of performance. We see that reliability is not a simple dimension. Both reliability and failure can be described successfully only by using statistical terms because, at best, we can make a prediction of how long the unit can be expected to continue to function satisfactorily.

There are many reasons why failure and reliability, as definitions of quality, play an extremely important role. Some types of failure do not permit repair, whereas others do. The definition and specification of quality is concerned with *ease of maintenance* and the *cost of replacement parts*. If nothing else, these factors affect the consumer's judgment of quality. A multi-component unit usually has different replacement characteristics for each of its parts. Generally, there are some parts which, when they fail, represent an irremedial breakdown. Should the production manager design a unit in this way, or should he encourage the development of replacement parts and the service function that is tied in with it? He is concerned with how good the sales engineering service function is and how accessible it is to customers. Automobile manufacturers stress this aspect of their product's quality.

The production manager is also concerned with the specification of a *guarantee period*. How long should this period be; what terms are reasonable; how many different components should be covered? Production management is deeply involved in these aspects of quality. The essence of production quality control and quality assurance is embodied in a realistic and complex evaluation of the way in which the product performs over its lifetime. It is only scratching the surface to measure the length of a rod, to observe the number of rpm's of a motor, and so forth, without tying such measurements into the complete evaluation of product quality and performance.

In Chapter 12 we shall discuss the importance of *human factors:* safety, comfort, and convenience, as they apply to manpower management. The human factors area relates equally well to product management. We will avoid duplication by not further developing these specialized topics here. But it is recommended that pp. 413-14 be studied briefly at this time. Thus, in conclusion, functional qualities represent an important category of quality specification. It is essential that production management define these qualities in as unambiguous terms as possible.

NONFUNCTIONAL QUALITIES

Nonfunctional qualities are known to play an important part in the consumer's judgment of quality. They are extremely difficult to measure. Nevertheless, the role of these attributes is quite as important to the production manager and to the company as any that we found in the functional category. Here, we are dealing with questions related to the appearance of the product and the way in which the consumer interprets the intangible qualities of the output. This involves us with the sociological, psychological, and psychiatric implications of quality. To think in such terms requires a temperament and turn of mind that cannot easily be associated with the usual production department. Undoubtedly this is why *industrial designers* have come to play an important role in the development of the styling attributes of a product.

The consumer's image of himself using a specific brand in a specific product class also raises many questions concerning this intangible aspect of quality specification. There has always been a belief in the marketing field that the consumer is motivated, to some extent, by symbolic relationships of the product to his own personal life. One can find references to Freud, Adler, Jung, and related schools of symbol analysis in the literature of the motivational market researcher. In theory, at any rate, the industrial designer is able to communicate with the consumer on the different levels of his needs as a consumer and, thereby, produce a product which receives acceptance both in concept and in form.

For the complete specification of quality, still other attributes play a part. These include the package (which is constrained in form by the design of the unit), the label, and even the instructions given to the consumer for properly using the product. Another element is the variety of choice. We have discussed the product-mix aspect of variety and pointed to the marketing implications of modularity as a means of providing a broad selection base for the consumer.[24]

All these factors taken together establish a frame of reference which is sufficiently psychoanalytic to make the average production man wonder how he can possibly specify quality. Typical of these difficulties are questions concerning the visual appearance and *styling* of a design. Style changes are a function of time. What is in style today can be out of style tomorrow. The way in which one style replaces a previous style should follow some logical pattern—although not necessarily a predictable one with respect to time. In fact, various studies serve to confirm the fact that some form of stability does exist concerning changes in style. Consumer acceptance turns out to be not as erratic as one might suppose

[24] See also pp. 468-71 of William T. Moran.

at first glance. In some cases, style cycles have been found, for example, in the clothing industry, in hair styles, and in millinery styles.[25]

Architects play a primary role in influencing the accepted styles of a particular culture at any point in time. This relationship intrigued many designers and architects.[26] To the extent that *product design follows architecture*, reasonable predictions can be made about the evaluation of nonfunctional design characteristics of products. At the same time, we should not lose sight of the basic principles which, because they underlie all matters of shape and form, relate architecture, engineering, and industrial design.[27]

Each case of product design management demands its own analysis, but certain fundamentals appear to play a part whether we are talking about the ultimate consumer or an industrial consumer.[28]

1. There is an historical basis for the evolution of design forms. Thus, timeliness of a design can be critical. There are well-documented cases of designs that have been rejected because they appeared too soon.
2. There is need for complete specification of quality. It can only be accomplished if a coordinated effort is made by both production and marketing management.
3. There is a technological basis which is predicated on available materials and process know-how.

With respect to the third point, some significant knowledge about technological change is available. It has no specific guidelines to offer product management but it does have important conceptual ones.

TECHNOLOGICAL CHANGE

The fundamental production system constraints are technological. Yet within that framework, ample variations can be developed. We recognize that living in a dynamic and evolving world, the growth of knowledge over time is likely to follow the logistics or growth type of curve. It is generally agreed that we are now at an early stage in our development as shown in Figure 7.20.

In the early 1900's it was believed that good predictions of technological development could be made, based on knowledge of the appropriate growth

[25] See, for example: Agnes Brook Young, *Recurring Cycles of Fashion (1760–1937)* (New York: Harper & Row, Publishers, 1937).
[26] See, for example: Henry Dreyfuss, *Designing for People* (New York: Simon and Schuster, Inc., 1955); Frederick J. Kiesler, "Architecture as a Biotechnique," *Architectural Record* (September, 1939); Le Corbusier, *Toward a New Architecture* (London: Architectural Press, 1948); Raymond Loewy, *Never Leave Well Enough Alone* (New York: Simon and Schuster, Inc., 1951); Eliel Sarrinen, *Search for Form* (New York: Reinhold Publishing Corp., 1948); Walter Dorwin Teague, *Design This Day* (New York: Harcourt, Brace & World, Inc., 1940).
[27] See for example: George D. Birkhoff, *Aesthetic Measure* (Cambridge, Mass.: Harvard University Press, 1933); Samuel Coleman, *Nature's Harmonic Unity* (New York: The Knickerbocker Press, 1912); *Proportional Form* (New York: The Knickerbocker Press, 1920); Ozenfant, *Foundations of Modern Art*, trans. J. Rodker (New York: Dover Publications, Inc., 1952); J. Schillinger, *The Mathematical Basis of the Arts* (New York: Philosophical Library, 1948); D'Arcy W. Thompson, *On Growth and Form*, Vol. I and II, 2nd ed. (Cambridge, England: University Press, 1959 reprint); L. L. Whyte, ed., *Aspects of Form* (Bloomington, Ind.: Indiana University Press, 1961).
[28] It is uncertain to what extent an industrial consumer is concerned with the nonfunctional category of quality specification.

FIGURE 7-20
Estimated growth of
technological knowl-
edge and present
position.

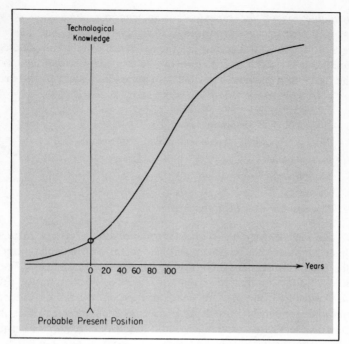

curve.[29] We no longer accept this simple view of life. But that is not to say that prediction of technological development is impossible. Far more complex models of relationships appear to be required than was previously thought to be the case. We have no such models at this time. Yet, the prediction of technolgical change is one of the fundamental responsibilities of the production manager. He is, after all, the only representative of management who is in a position to understand and interpret the scientific developments reported daily in the newspapers and scientific journals.

Before we proceed further, let us consider what technology means. It is one term that is almost exclusively identified with the activities of the production manager. The word *technology* is derived from the Greek *technologia* which means "systematic treatment." In present usage it refers to what is called "Industrial science, the science or systematic knowledge of industrial arts."[30] Here is a strange mixture of terms. It is relatively easy to accept the notion of art in science, but a science of arts is existent only in the form of a systematic knowledge of facts and not laws. As a collection of facts, technology meets one of the requirements of a science, but with respect to theories and laws of technology there is a void, which perhaps interchangeable parts, sequenced assembly, and modular production begin to fill.

The dictionary definition of technology is not particularly useful for our purposes. It overemphasizes systematic treatment and, at best, hints at the notion of reproducibility. A possible alternative definition might be: *The best*

[29] Abbott P. Usher, *A History of Mechanical Inventions* (Boston: Beacon Press, Inc., 1959). See particularly pp. 10–16.

[30] *Websters' New International Dictionary*, 2nd Edition, Unabridged.

available means for repeatedly achieving the production of specified outputs. We say *best* because technology is always evolving and has a history of ante- cedent methods; it also implies the existence of technological change. Whatever definition is used it should convey the fact that technology can be described by the "art" at a particular moment in time. This state of the art should include:

1. A body of factual knowledge;
2. A level of skills and know-how;
3. The "wherewithal," that is, equipment, facilities, and plant;
4. Raw materials;
5. Manpower;
6. Capital;
7. The desire to engage in production.

The last century has witnessed phenomenal changes in technology. Part of this dynamism can be traced to basic scientific discoveries, but the larger factor has been a fundamental change in the production concept. The history of tech- nology indicates that the cause of this revolution was not a unique discovery on the part of one man. Instead, it appears to have developed simultaneously and independently in several places. For example, previously we mentioned that two separate individuals simultaneously came up with the notion of *inter- changeable* parts. Credit for this discovery in the United States is given to Eli Whitney and in France to a man by the name of Leblanc.[31]

There is real precedence for simultaneous discovery in both science and technology. This can be documented in a number of instances. Thus, Taton writes: "The fact that a considerable number of great discoveries were made almost simultaneously by different scientists, working independently, will show that great discoveries often arise when the general level attained by the science of the times renders them almost inevitable."[32] Because of this fact, there is good reason to believe that the course of technology is not totally unpredictable. Rather, the coming together of necessary threshold events—a conjunction of critical factors—produces an environment in which the next forward step can *and will* be taken.

Figure 7.21 provides a graphic demonstration of the type of process that probably exists. Although it is a random process, transitions that can be made from one technological level to another are dependent upon the prior state of the system. This concept is of great importance to the production manager be-

---

[31] The following excerpt from a letter written by Thomas Jefferson to Governor James Monroe of Virginia (in 1801) is of considerable interest.

"Mr. Whitney is at the head of a considerable gun factory in Connecticut, and furnishes the United States with muskets, undoubtedly the best they receive. He has invented moulds and machines for making all the pieces of his locks so exactly equal, that take 100 locks to pieces and mingle their parts and the hundred locks may be put together as well by taking the first pieces which come to hand. This is of importance in repairing, because out of 10 locks, e.g., disabled for the want of different pieces, 9 good locks may be put together without employing a smith. Leblanc, in France, had invented a similar process in 1788 & had extended it to the barrel, mounting, & stock. . . . Mr. Whitney has not yet extended his improvement beyond the lock."

See Jeannette Mirsky and Allan Nevins, *The World of Eli Whitney* (New York: Collier Books, 1962), p. 218.
[32] R. Taton, *Reason and Chance in Scientific Discovery*, trans. A. J. Powerans (New York: Science Editions. Inc., 1962), p. 108.

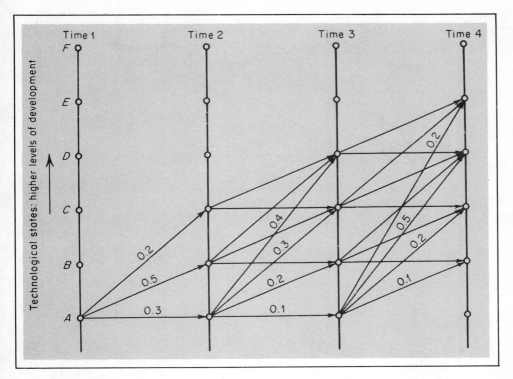

FIGURE 7-21
A pattern for technological change. (Transition probabilities are only shown with respect to the initial technological state A.) The system is in state A at time 1, called A_1. The probability of no change is 0.3. There is 0.7 probability that some change will occur. If a change does occur, there is no probability of returning to state A. By the fourth period, a change must take place. If the change is $A_3 \longrightarrow E_4$, this might be called a technological breakthrough.

cause it is his fundamental obligation to be aware of likely developments that can affect his company's position. There is no other organizational post which bears a similar amount of responsibility in this regard. Our remarks can also be applied to process development. Often, product and process development go hand in hand. Because of sunk costs,[33] process investments are especially vulnerable to the effects of obsolescence produced by technological breakthroughs.

INNOVATION

A major factor in the development of new products and services is the ability to achieve the right level of innovation—to bring forth something that has the "optimal" degree of difference.[34] From a decision theory point of view, innovation is the problem of developing ever better unique strategies. We can begin to understand the nature of this problem by considering trees of strategic alternatives. Figure 7.22 is a design tree for a restaurant. It includes some of the pertinent characteristics of this particular design problem. We see that there are many alternative ways for specifying the design of a process or an output. Thus,

[33] Costs which cannot be recovered.
[34] The conclusion of the previous section stressed the importance of timeliness. That is, an output can be too different too quickly, to receive acceptance. It can also be too much like its predecessors. The value judgment is deeply rooted in the dynamics of the culture.

FIGURE 7-22
A design tree present-
ing some strategic
alternatives for a
restaurant.

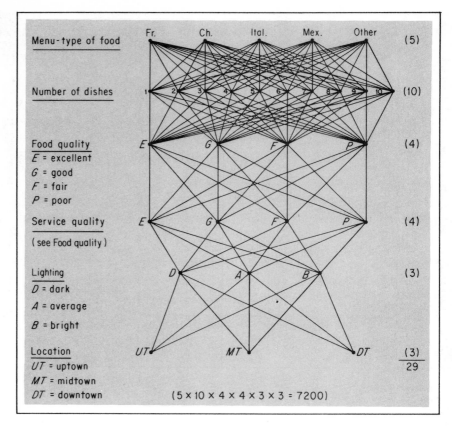

Menu-type of food   Fr.   Ch.   Ital.   Mex.   Other   (5)

Number of dishes   1 2 3 4 5 6 7 8 9 10   (10)

Food quality   E   G   F   P   (4)
E = excellent
G = good
F = fair
P = poor

Service quality   E   G   F   P   (4)
(see Food quality)

Lighting   D   A   B   (3)
D = dark
A = average
B = bright

Location   UT   MT   DT   (3)
UT = uptown   29
MT = midtown
DT = downtown   (5 × 10 × 4 × 4 × 3 × 3 = 7200)

from the point of view of designing a restaurant, the relevant variables include: menu variety (both type of food and variety of offerings), food quality, service quality, atmosphere provided, and many other factors. We see that in this overly simple analysis there are 7200 different kinds of restaurants that emerge as possibilities. If we were to spend just *two minutes* evaluating each possibility, it would take us six weeks to come to a conclusion.

On the other hand, if each variable or characteristic were considered separately, then only 29 factors would have to be analyzed. Spending *two hours* on each factor we would reach our decision in less than a week and a half. The question of whether we should go about designing our facility by the first approach or by the second is a *systems question*. When we know that the characteristics interact with each other (as they surely do in the case of the restaurant), we cannot use the minimum time approach. This would also be true for complex automated systems, for the design of space vehicles, for the selection of a plant site, and for most problems that concern top management. Somewhere in the bundle of tree branches there may lurk a truly great answer to this particular problem and, in general, a superior strategy for a new product or service. How to locate this one (total) branch is the problem of innovation.[35]

[35] For a relevant discussion see Harold Rugg, *Imagination* (New York: Harper & Row, Publishers, 1963).

With no lack of respect for human innovation we should also consider the use of the computer as a means of constructing and exploring complex design trees. At the present time, design by computer is limited to products where well-known engineering relationships are the main factors to consider. The following excerpt describes developments worthy of consideration.[36]

The design of transformers in this range of core-form construction is particularly adaptable to computer techniques, and because of this it has become possible to optimize designs with a degree of sophistication that would have been out of the question as recently as ten years ago.

The early computer programs for power transformers were automated to simulate the trial and error approach of the design engineer, using a flow diagram similar to that shown in

FIGURE 7-23 Early computer programs simulated the trial and error method of the design engineer, following a flow path like the one below. Circles 2 to 10 are the discrete design model. Circles 11 to 14 are performance calculations. The lines within the large circle are iteration paths.

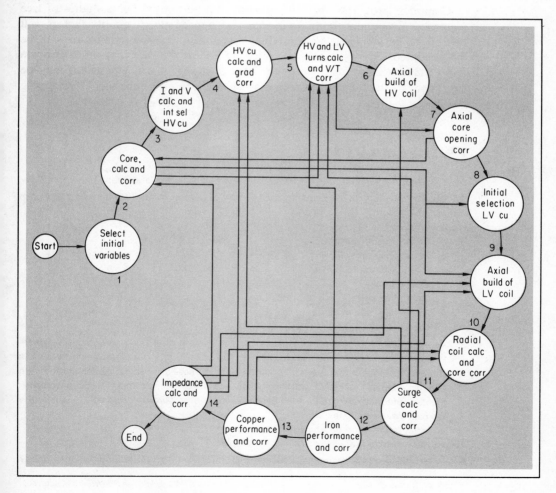

[36] W.T. Duboc, "New Techniques Improve Power Transformers," *Westinghouse ENGINEER*, Volume 27, Number 2, March 1967, pp. 34–40.

Figure 7.23. By iterating through the various sub-programs after starting with certain assumptions based on empirical data from previous designs (Circle 1, Figure 7.23), convergence was obtained. An example of this iterative process would be the case where the surge voltage calculation of the design produced by the initial assumptions (Circle 11) did not meet requirements because of, say, insufficient conductor insulation. Adding insulation, however, affects the radial and axial build dimensions of the coil and other constants so after making this correction, the program must return to Circle 6 and the calculations repeated from there on.

The first programs produced transformer designs comparable to those made by hand, but no attempt was made to optimize them. In recent years, however, through the use of heuristic techniques, ways have been found to approach the problem of optimizing cost logically, including evaluated losses if desired, size or other characteristics, with the result that transformers can be better proportioned and cost and weight improved. It is now possible to optimize almost every commercial order on a routine basis.[37]

Computer programs are being written that permit extensive studies of tree networks. Eventually, both functional and nonfunctional quality factors will be able to be included. New product design and design modification will be differentiated. To stay vital, companies are finding out that they must innovate and update their product line. If the pace of change is too gradual, it may be equivalent to standing still; making no change could be equivalent to stepping backwards.

PROBLEMS

1 *Quality is a production responsibility.* What is meant by this statement?

2 Discuss the concept of reliability as a measure of quality. What does it mean in the case of:
  a. A bar of soap
  b. An automobile battery
  c. Automobile tires
  d. A die-casting machine
  e. Steel girders
  f. A sprinkler system for fire protection
  g. The handle of a suitcase
  h. Aspirin

3 As a manufacturer of automobile batteries you wish to offer the longest possible guarantee period. Your policy is predicated on the belief that a guarantee period which is substantially longer than your competitors' will increase your sales volume and provide a larger share of the market. For this reason, you have specified that the cost of replacements should entirely use up whatever additional profits you receive as a result of the increased sales volume.
  a. What information do you need?
  b. How do you propose to handle this problem?

4 What role does the industrial designer play in the production manager's operations?

[37] From W. T. Duboc, "New Techniques Improve Power Transformers," *Westinghouse ENGINEER*, March 1967, Volume 27, Number 2, p. 37.

5 The optimum size of a development group depends upon your objectives. Discuss why this is so.

6 Estimate the length of time that it should take you to complete Problem 7 below. Then compare the actual result with your estimate. (It can be beneficial to make a practice of estimating the times for completion of various systems studies and then comparing these estimates with the actual results.) Have you observed slippage in many personal situations? How do you account for it?

7 A greeting card manufacturer wishes to diversify his line. His designers have been experimenting with a new plastic material. It is available in thin sheets and lends itself to some unusual effects. The designers have come up with two alternative card designs—both of which appear to be totally acceptable. Because special equipment is required to print and cut this new material, the production manager wants to carefully consider the advantages of either card or the possibility of making both of them. The following data have been made available to him.

	Card A	Card B
Time to print card on one special machine	2.4 minutes	2.4 minutes
Time to cut and fold card on one special machine	4.8 minutes	1.6 minutes
Material required	80 square in.	240 square in.
Estimated profit per card	$0.70	$0.80

The company works a 40 hour week and has 833 square feet of the material on hand and cannot obtain more in the near future. Assume no cutting waste and the requirement that the job be completed within one week. What product mix should the production manager plan to use? Discuss your answer. (See Problem 6, above, before you begin to solve this problem.)

8 *a.* What are the major characteristics of a patentable idea?

    b. Under what circumstances would a company prefer secrecy. Give some examples of where this course of action has been taken by a company.

    c. Why must a patent search be carried out in any case?

    d. What is meant by *fencing-in?*

references

ASIMOW. MORRIS, *Introduction to Design*. Englewood Cliffs, N. J.: Prentice-Hall, Inc., 1962.

DREYFUSS, HENRY, *Designing for People*. New York: Simon & Schuster, 1955.

GERLACH, J. T. and C. A. WAINWRIGHT, *Successful Management of New Products*. New York: Hastings House, Publishers, 1968.

GLEGG, G. L., *The Design of Design*. Cambridge, England: Cambridge University Press, 1969.

GORDON, W. J. J., *Synectics*. New York: Harper & Row, Publishers, 1961.

KAUFMANN, A., M. FUSTIER and A. DREVET, *L'Inventique, Nouvelles Méthodes de Créativité*. Paris: Entreprise Moderne D'Édition, 1970,

MORTON, J. A. *Organizing for Innovation*. New York: McGraw-Hill Book Company, 1971.

NEWTON, NORMAN T., *An Approach to Design*. Cambridge, Mass.: Addison-Wesley Press, Inc., 1951.

SANDKULL, BENGT, *Innovative Behavior of Organizations, The Case of New Products, $S_i AR$*. Lund, Sweden: Student litteratur, 1970.

STARR, MARTIN K., "Product Planning from the Top (Variety and Diversity)", University of Illinois Bulletin, Vol. 65, No. 144, Proceedings, *Systems: Research and Applications for Marketing*, July 26, 1968, pp. 71–77.

STARR, MARTIN K., *Product Design and Decision Theory*. Englewood Cliffs, N. J.: Prentice-Hall, Inc., 1963.

STOCKTON, R. STANSBURY, *Introduction to Linear Programming* (2nd Ed.). Boston: Allyn and Bacon, Inc., 1963.

VASZONYI, A., *Scientific Programming in Business and Industry*. New York: John Wiley & Sons, Inc., 1958.

WILLIAMS, J. D., *The Compleat Strategyst*. New York: McGraw-Hill, Inc., 1954.

chapter
eight
process
management

Production management is uniquely involved with *getting something done*. In what manner do the specific job characteristics affect the management requirements? Production management, after all, is a generic term that is rather loosely applied to a broad spectrum of interrelated parts. No one situation is ever identical to another. The reason that production management can be applied to such a diverse set of operations is that certain principles are easily transferable. They are *independent of the particular job to be done*.

From one point of view, major differences exist between the management of the production function in the chemical industry as compared to the machine tool industry. The same could be stated for comparisons between other industries; between hospital and library management; between different forms of transportation systems; and so on. The differences in physical systems that can be observed can hardly be called trivial. They represent *technological differentiation*. The knowledge of technology is, at best, only partially transferable between industries.

TECHNOLOGICAL DIFFERENTIATION

We can develop technological classification in a variety of ways. For example, the process of transforming input materials into the output product may require manual or machine operations; chemical reactions might be involved; perhaps the process is agricultural; in a rather specialized case, we need the chicken to lay the egg. More detailed breakdowns could specify press shop operations, casting, weaving, or harvesting. We can also categorize technological systems by their characteristic output; for example, clothing, food, appliances, or gasoline.

Sometimes it is useful to separate technologies in terms of the input materials such as coffee beans, crude oil, and iron ore. The difficult classification problem is indicative of the highly specialized nature of each industry, and even of companies within an industry. The appropriate body of knowledge that comprises the technology begins with the broadest physical principles, but rapidly encompasses enormous amounts of detail when engineering and production applications are included.

The study of production management cannot avoid involvement with technology; nor should it attempt to do so. But the utility of treating specific technological systems in detail is of dubious value for understanding production management, in general. There is, however, a distinction in process management that is important. We differentiate between the flow shop, the job shop, and the project.

THE FLOW SHOP AND THE JOB SHOP

Basically, the flow shop consists of a set of facilities through which work flows in serial fashion. The operations are performed repeatedly. The job shop, on the other hand, is not a serially utilized facility. Jobs follow different processing patterns through the facilities in batch fashion. Figure 8.1 provides an illustration of the difference.

Items in the flow shop enter the finished goods inventory one after another, whereas they enter in batches for the job shop. The flow shop is (more or less) what has frequently been referred to as mass production. In some cases, when almost no processing patterns are ever repeated, the job shop is called a custom shop (everything is custom made to order). Mostly, the flow shop is designed to make for stock; the job shop makes to order (or to stock where many different items are stocked in relatively small quantities). The flow shop facilities tend to be *special purpose* equipment, well-designed to deliver the high volume of output needed. Job shop facilities are *general purpose* equipment capable of being outfitted with various tools, dies, and fixtures to do a variety of different jobs at the same basic facility.

Modularity (previously discussed, pp. 194–209) enables the output volume of certain parts to be increased to the point where flow shop processing is

FIGURE 8-1
Serial (flow shop)
versus batch (job
shop) processing.

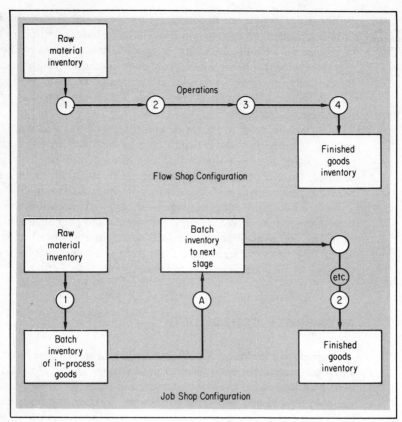

Raw material inventory

Operations

① → ② → ③ → ④

Finished goods inventory

Flow Shop Configuration

Raw material inventory

Batch inventory to next stage

etc.

①

Ⓐ

②

Batch inventory of in-process goods

Finished goods inventory

Job Shop Configuration

feasible. This has benefits: serial production encourages division of labor effi-ciencies in accord with specialization; also, there are economic scale advantages in using special purpose equipment; serial production permits highly coordi-nated promotional, advertising, and marketing activities; and flow-shop inven-tories can be lower than those of job shops where unfinished batches of items must be stored.

LINE BALANCING

The most relevant problem of the flow shop is to achieve a good balance of the capacities and flows of the process. The line-balancing problem arises in the flow shop because jobs must be partitioned into equal work assignments (called stations) to avoid idle time at specialized facilities.[1] Care in planning every detail of the production process is most important for the flow shop.

[1] This is especially characteristic of labor-intensive systems, which explains why much line-balancing work has been focused on assembly-line balancing.

There are degrees of process continuity for the flow shop. They range from fully-automated *paced-flow* systems (usually based on the mass production of items carried by a fixed-speed conveyor) to situations in which the demand for a group of *similar* items is relatively continuous, varying in quantity over time. By similarity of items, we mean that essentially the same production routing and flow is required for each of the items which are run through the system in successive sequences.[2]

Line balancing is a matter of grouping facilities and workers in an efficient pattern. For high-volume production of identical items, costly mathematical studies, using linear or dynamic programming, can be justified to achieve line balance. On the other hand, intermittent flow system are often designed using heuristic procedures, and techniques appropriate for job shop planning.

In discussing job shop management, it is our intention to examine issues of scheduling work, shop-loading departments and sequencing at facilities. Let us consider the over-all or aggregate scheduling problem first. For aggregate scheduling, many different items are treated as though they were of one kind, in terms of their demands on resources.

AGGREGATE SCHEDULING

Aggregate scheduling is achieved by lumping all items together to determine work force requirements, general productivity levels, etc. The schedule that is derived represents an important planning stage for management. It applies to variable flow shops and most job shops. Various methods exist for achieving these schedules. For example, there is a linear programming application.[3] A transportation algorithm allows an even simpler approach.[4] We shall describe the transportation method in a different context at a later point in this chapter, see pp. 239–53.

Aggregate scheduling gains much of its utility from the characteristics of predicting aggregate phenomena. The methodology of aggregate scheduling is entirely dependent on a reasonably good ability to forecast and predict. So the previous pages (122–35) devoted to forecasting should be recalled at this time.

Flow shops and job shops require many different methodological approaches for their planning and control. Aggregate scheduling is, however, a powerful approach applicable to intermittent flow and job shops. Demand and production output are treated in *aggregation* across a variety of different (input) facilities and (output) jobs. The aggregate is treated as one job made by one facility

---

[2] See the discussion of group technology on p. 194.

[3] J.F. Magee and D.M. Boodman, *Production Planning and Inventory Control* (New York: McGraw-Hill Book Co., Inc., 1967), pp. 369–373. See also A. Kaufmann, *Methods and Models of Operations Research* (Englewood Cliffs, N.J.: Prentice-Hall, Inc., 1963), pp. 40–44. For a numerical optimization approach see C.C. Holt, Modigliani, Muth and Simon, *Planning Production Inventories and Work Force* (Englewood Cliffs, N.J.: Prentice-Hall, Inc., 1960).

[4] See E. H. Bowman, "Production Scheduling by the Transportation Method of Linear Programming," *Operations Research*, Vol. 4 No. 1, 1956. Further discussion will be found in E.H. Bowman and R.B. Fetter, *Analysis for Production and Operations Management* (3rd edition) (Homewood, Illinois: 1967), Richard D. Irwin, pp. 134–136.

operating under several different modes, e.g., regular and overtime production. The organization's facilities are used to satisfy varying demand levels over time. Demands for different output are aggregated by considering them all to be demand for the output capacity of the facility.

FIGURE 8-2
Determination of ag-
gregate demand.

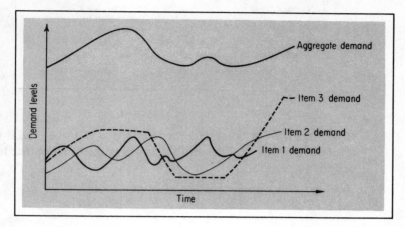

In Figure 8.2 we portray seasonal demand for several different items and transform these into an aggregate demand for our production facilities. The aggregate production schedule over time is called, P_t. The facilities and especially the organization's work force can vary over time. We shall call the work force level at time t, W_t.[5] An additional variable that we usually wish to control over time is the inventory level, I_t. Therefore, given a "good" prediction of aggregate demand S_t over time, the problem to solve is: how should we vary P_t, W_t and I_t so as to optimize the systems performance? Clearly, if the demand predictions are unreliable, then the aggregate method of scheduling is meaningless.

Two strategies suggest themselves. First, vary W_t so that P_t matches the demand S_t as closely as possible. In Figure 8.3 this is pattern B. Second, do not vary the work force, thereby keeping P_t constant over time, i.e., $P_t = P$ for all t. In Figure 8.3 this is pattern A. The latter strategy permits a fixed-paced production output where only routine production sequences need be followed. In a job shop system, there are certain costs that disappear when pattern A is followed but there are other costs that increase.

We expect our solution to represent some combination of changing production rates, changing work force size, varying degrees of overtime utilization and fluctuating inventory levels. Figure 8.4 captures some of the aspects of this system's interrelatedness.

[5] At the period before called $t - 1$, the work force level is W_{t-1}

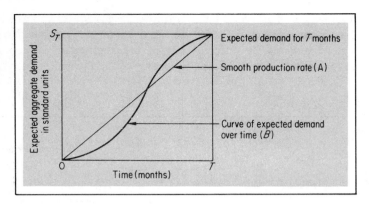

Note, for example, what happens to $(W_{t-1} - W_t)$ when the B-type rule $P_t = S_t$ is followed (where it is assumed that each worker can produce ten units in every period):

t	S_t	P_t	I_t	$\sum_t I_t$	W_t	$W_{t-1} - W_t$
1	420	420	0	0	42	
2	360	360	0	0	36	−6
3	390	390	0	0	39	+3
4	350	350	0	0	35	−4
5	420	420	0	0	42	+7
6	350	350	0	0	35	−7

In this second case (A-type) the work force is maintained at constant level so inventory fluctuates:

t	S_t	P_t	W_t	$W_{t-1} - W_t$	I_t	$\sum_t I_t$
1	420	400	40	0	−20	−20
2	360	400	40	0	+40	+20
3	390	400	40	0	+10	+30
4	350	400	40	0	+50	+80
5	420	400	40	0	−20	+60
6	350	400	40	0	+50	+110

In the usual case, combinations of these effects will be experienced.

Consider the obvious opposing costs in these cases. When the production rate over time, P_t, is smooth, then hiring, training and other work force adjustment costs such as overtime go to zero. When P_t varies with S_t, work force adjustment costs rise. This increase could represent the costs of a constant

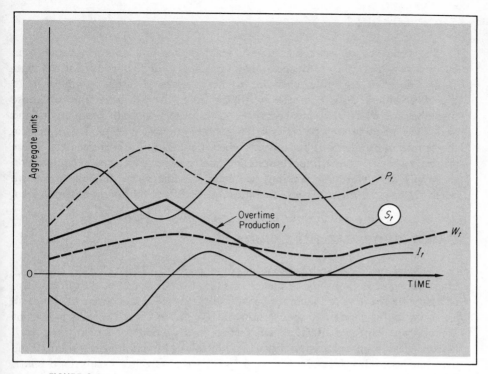

FIGURE 8-4
The aggregate sched-
uling problem re-
quires period by
period solutions that
will optimize the total
system's performance,
recognizing inter-
period dependencies.

size work force engaged in overtime, or a fluctuating work force size, with or
without overtime. Further, when P_t is constant, then demand fluctuations produce inventory costs for both over- and understocks. The extent of these costs
depends on the demand fluctuation. If production rates match demand rates,
then inventory-type costs trend toward zero. Figure 8.5 illustrates these opposing costs.

In such a system there is a total cost, composed of inventory costs and work
force adjustment costs which reaches a minimum value for some particular
production schedule.

FIGURE 8-5
The x-axis represents
the degree to which
production rates (P_t)
match demand rates
(S_t).

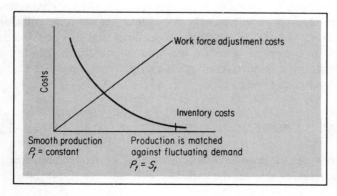

SHOP LOADING

The penalties of poor scheduling, machine loading and sequencing can become very high; they have been under continual study by production management. Given an aggregate schedule, the next step is to assign specific jobs to machine centers. Jobs compete with each other for available time on those machines for which they are best fitted with respect to both productivity and cost. One machine may be superior to another—for a given job—with respect to the rate of production; but inferior when it comes to the cost per part. These anomalies become more important as demand requirements grow in comparison to supply resources. Shoploading problems become more difficult to resolve when the same *general purpose* facilities are preferred for many different jobs.

GANTT SHOPLOADING CHARTS

The first well-known shoploading models were Gantt charts. Henry L. Gantt recognized that only by means of some formal device could the problem of assigning the jobs to machines be suitably attacked. He incorporated no risk elements in his model. If speculation or risk existed, the decision maker or planner was expected to take such factors into account in an informal way. Nevertheless, Gantt charts provided a powerful tool in comparison to anything that had existed before. In Figure 6.18 (p. 161) we see a Gantt load chart. It has a time scale running along the top, whereas the rows are intended to represent machines, departments, or whatever facilities will be required to do the job. The time scale can be labeled in either calender time or in general time. The left hand side of the chart is *now*, whether that be May 21st or merely time zero. Bars and lines, running from left to right, convey various kinds of information—as interpreted by the diagram key.

We can read off the cumulative load that exists with respect to each facility. This backlog of jobs to be accomplished can be shown as it exists at the beginning of the present week and as it existed at the beginning of the prior week. We are interested in this information to find out whether the load and the backlog is increasing, decreasing, or staying about the same. The criterion of what a good load is or what a change for the better might be will depend upon the particular scheduling situation and its unique characteristics. Thus, the Gantt load chart will quickly reveal whether we have sufficient resources and capacity available to handle the work load that has been accumulating. It also helps to determine whether the load is equally distributed among facilities. Perhaps most important of all, it can point out the fact that the character of the load is changing.

GANTT SEQUENCING CHARTS

Now, let us consider the Gantt layout or sequencing chart. In essence, this chart *reserves time* on the various facilities for different jobs. It provides greater

FIGURE 8-6
The Gantt layout
chart is a reserved
time system. Here the
status is: All jobs
are ahead except
RAMCO which is
delayed because of
undelivered materials
and Job 21 whose de-
lay is not explained.
Jobs Tel, P55, and
TRX 12 are not yet
scheduled to begin.
(Shaded areas indi-
cate completion.)

detail than the load chart. Using the Gantt layout chart, shown in Figure 8.6 below, it is possible to schedule production *for some given period of time.* Concurrently, past schedules can be monitored to discover the state of completion of those jobs that have been scheduled to be run in prior time periods. This provides schedule control. (See also Figure 6.19, p. 161.)

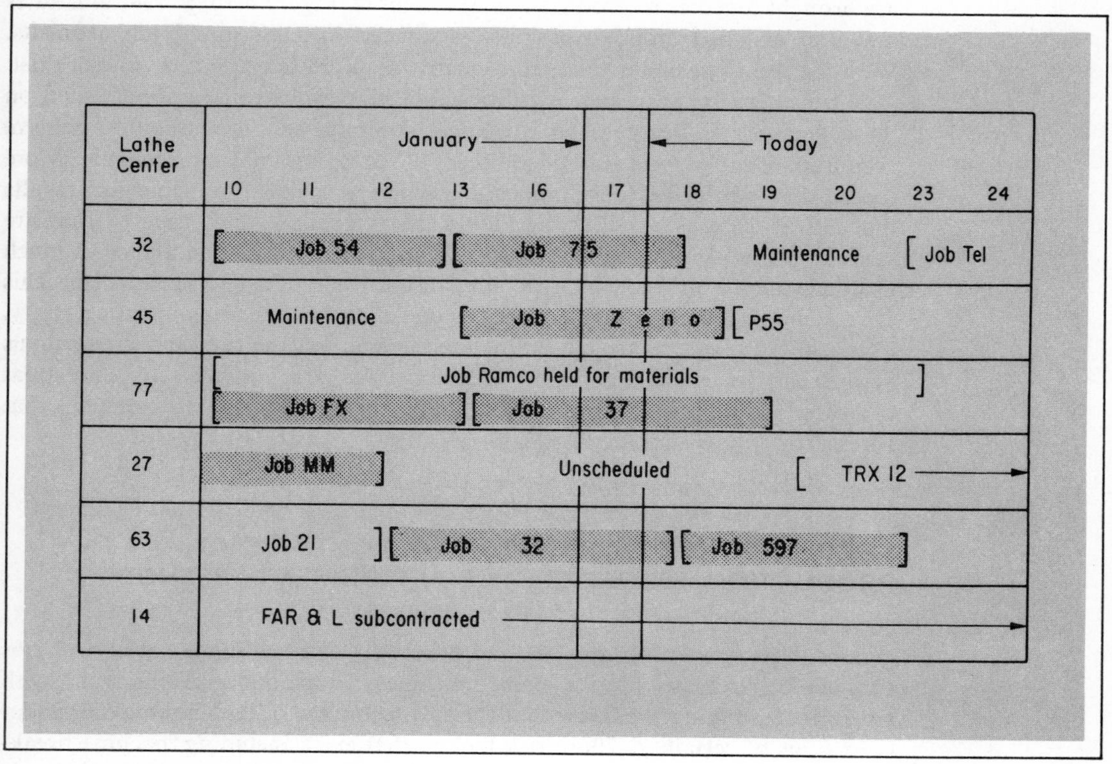

Lathe Center	January →						← Today				
	10	11	12	13	16	17	18	19	20	23	24
32	[Job 54][Job 75]						Maintenance		[Job Tel		
45	Maintenance		[Job Zeno][P55								
77	[Job Ramco held for materials]										
	[Job FX][Job 37]										
27	[Job MM]			Unscheduled			[TRX 12 →				
63	Job 21][Job 32][Job 597]										
14	FAR & L subcontracted										→

For each facility, we observe the job schedule and its state of completion. The present date is indicated by the arrow and its associated vertical lines. Thereby, the chart is divided into time past, present and future. Looking ahead we can observe what the load is but not in the cumulative form of the load chart *which does not specify sequence.* Thus, the difference between loading and sequencing is that the latter specifies the time of assignments. When sequencing, future assignments are time reservations on the facility. They block other assignments from being made. Because sequencing charts may be revised regularly, assigned time can be unblocked if it appears to permit a better schedule. A little time is usually allowed between jobs, to account for machine maintenance,

231

to absorb divergences from estimates and minor variabilities, and to allow for machine setup and takedown. Frequently, additional symbols are attached to these charts to indicate why a job has not been completed and to convey other kinds of useful information by means of a succinct shorthand notation. The Gantt layout or sequencing chart must be continually updated; jobs must be rescheduled, so that it can serve its intended function of providing reasonably good work schedules.

Another chart frequently employed for schedule control is called an *assembly-scheduling diagram*. Here, the appropriate visual schematic is intended to describe the way in which various materials, parts, components, and subassemblies are brought together to produce a final assembly. Figure 6-15, p. 159, illustrates a typical assigned ordering of jobs, sequenced through specific departments. With the use of calendar time, all elements required for schedule control exist.

When there are very many facilities, and many jobs to be accomplished on these facilities, it becomes an extremely complicated proposition to achieve even a reasonably good job schedule, let alone an optimal job schedule. More recent methodological developments provide a means for achieving results that are at least as good as the Gantt charts promise and, usually, that are superior to those supplied. All this is done in much less time and with much less dependence on the health, welfare, and attitude of a few skilled men. This assignment problem is usually treated as one of decision making under certainty. The goal is to search through many alternatives, but the problem is enormous because of the many scheduling variations that are possible. After we treat the shoploading problem, we will examine the sequencing requirements that necessarily *follow* shoploading.

SHOPLOADING FOR (RELATIVELY) CONTINUOUS PRODUCTION FACILITIES—THE ASSIGNMENT METHOD

Linear programming can be used effectively for loading a variety of jobs through departments having many machines. From our previous work with linear programming, we know that this is a technique of decision making under conditions of certainty. Those risk factors that exist, including machine breakdowns, man-machine interactions that produce variability and other disturbances are reserved for later interpretation and action by the production manager. And, this is not different from the Gantt approach. The reason that certainty is assumed is that the kinds of variations that occur are not usually fundamental determinants of process behavior, and process effectiveness is not particularly sensitive to them. When the process is sensitive to one or more risk factors, then linear programming is not the right conceptual approach to accomplish the scheduling job.

In most scheduling situations it is absolutely vital to define the objectives that are to be accomplished. The reason for this need is simple: One does not usually obtain the same job-machine schedule when the objective is to minimize time through the system as one obtains when the objective calls for minimization of cost. Similarly, profit maximization is quite likely to provide a third solution.

First, look at the problem of assigning jobs on a relatively permanent basis to heavy capital equipment. This would epitomize situations where the production facilities tend to be continuously employed on particular jobs.

Assume that four different jobs can be done by four different facilities. We shall postulate that requirements call for almost continuous operation of the facilities. Furthermore, the setup and takedown costs are assumed to be prohibitively high for changeovers.

Let the matrix, below, indicate the operating costs per part for each job on each machine, where the facilities are: A, B, C, and D, and the jobs are: 1, 2, 3, and 4.

	M_A	M_B	M_C	M_D
J_1	3	5	7	4
J_2	6	4	7	2
J_3	2	5	3	5
J_4	8	2	6	1

For Job 1, machine A is preferred. However, Job 3 is also best suited for machine A. We have defined *best suited* to mean that the cost per part is lowest. Thus, *a conflict exists with respect to machine A for Jobs 1 and 3.*

Now let us compare the relative advantages of different machines for a specific job, for example, Job 4. We find that the best machine B assignment is Job 4 and the best machine D assignment is also Job 4. There is a *conflict with respect to the fourth job.* Machines B and D are both best when employed on Job 4. To resolve this problem we derive a set of opportunity costs. First, subtract the lowest cost in each column from all of the costs in that column—doing this for every column in the matrix. For machine A, \$2.00 is the best possible cost. Therefore, if we assign machine A to Job 3, we would have a zero opportunity cost. On the other hand, if we assign Job 1 to machine A, there is a penalty of \$1.00 to be paid (that is, \$3.00 − \$2.00). Similarly, with respect to M_A, Job 2 incurs an opportunity cost of \$4.00, and Job 4 has an opportunity cost of \$6.00. Turning to machine B, we proceed to do the same thing. When machine B is assigned to Job 4 the *best* possible result occurs, that is, a *zero* opportunity cost. The matrix shown below is the *opportunity cost matrix* with respect to jobs for each given machine.

	M_A	M_B	M_C	M_D
J_1	1	3	4	3
J_2	4	2	4	1
J_3	0	3	0	4
J_4	6	0	3	0

If each zero appeared in such a way that the four jobs could be assigned to four different machines—assignments being made to zero cells—the problem would be solved. The result would be a minimum cost assignment. Sometimes alternative assignment patterns exist, all of which have the *same* minimum cost. Any one of them can be chosen. Usually unmeasurable factors provide the basis for decision.

In the present case, we see that conflicts exist. Zero opportunity cost assignments for Job 3 can be obtained in two ways, that is, machines A and C; Job 4 could be placed on machines B and D; and no assignment has been indicated for Jobs 1 and 2. Our next step is to subtract within rows. In this way we obtain job opportunity costs with respect to machines. Thus, the assignment of Job 1 to machine A produces a zero opportunity cost. The assignment of Job 2 to machine D produces a zero opportunity cost. We have developed a matrix of two-way opportunity costs—first, using column then row subtraction[6]—which must, therefore, have a zero in every row and every column. This matrix is shown below.

	M_A	M_B	M_C	M_D
J_1	0	2	3	2
J_2	3	1	3	0
J_3	0	3	0	4
J_4	6	0	3	0

(Because the third and fourth rows obtained their zeros in the previous step, row subtraction produces no further modification.)

We must find out if we have a unique assignment that meets our requirement of a different job on each machine. Let us begin by circling all zeros that are unique in either their rows or their columns. Thus, select the zero representing the assignment of Job 3 to machine C. It is the only zero in column 3. Similarly, circle $J_1 M_A$—unique in its row; circle $J_2 M_D$—unique in its row; circle $J_4 M_B$—unique in its column. Because a different machine is unambiguously assigned to each job, the schedule is completed. The assignments should be made as follows:

ASSIGNMENT

JOB	MACHINE	UNIT COST IN DOLLARS
1	A	3.00
2	D	2.00
3	C	3.00
4	B	2.00

This is the minimum cost schedule. There are no alternatives.

It is interesting to note that initially the number of possible assignments that

[6] The order can be reversed at will.

can be made is n! In this case, n is 4, and, therefore, 24 different assignments are possible. Allowing one minute to evaluate each assignment, the job of determining the optimal schedule would take almost a half hour. By using the assignment algorithm we obtain the optimal solution in one or two minutes. The comparison of computing times—with and without the algorithm—becomes impressive, indeed, as the number of job-machine assignments to be made increases. With 10 machines and 10 jobs there are over three and a half million possible assignments; with $n = 15$, over a trillion unique assignments exist.

Now, let us consider the situation that arises when row and column subtractions do not yield a solution directly. As mentioned in footnote 6, p. 234, the final solution will always be invariant to whether row subtraction or column subtraction is used first. At most, an extra calculation may be required because one is used instead of the other.[7]

We construct the following matrix, using machines P, Q, R, and S with jobs, 1, 2, 3, and 4:

	M_P	M_Q	M_R	M_S
J_1	3	5	9	4
J_2	6	3	7	4
J_3	2	5	8	5
J_4	8	2	6	1

This time, use row subtraction first. The matrix derived is:

	M_P	M_Q	M_R	M_S
J_1	0	2	6	1
J_2	3	0	4	1
J_3	0	3	6	3
J_4	7	1	5	0

We see that no solution is arrived at in this manner. Let us, therefore, proceed to the next step—the use of column subtraction. We obtain:

	M_P	M_Q	M_R	M_S
J_1	0	2	2	1
J_2	3	0	0	1
J_3	0	3	2	3
J_4	7	1	1	0

[7] Row and column subtraction produce opportunity costs (discussed on pp. 13–15). Ultimately, these must be invariant to the order of subtraction. However, interim forms of the opportunity cost matrix do not always appear identical. For example, use column subtraction first, followed by row subtraction for the P, Q, R, S problem and compare your results with those shown in the text.

which does not constitute a solution. To reduce this matrix further we can apply the following steps.

1. Cover all the zeros in the matrix with the *minimum number* of lines possible.[8] We see that three lines will achieve our objective. They can be drawn in several different ways. It is possible to cover with four lines, but this is not the minimum number of lines which we have specified. The matrix below shows one way of covering all zeros with three lines.

	M_P	M_Q	M_R	M_S
J_1	0	2	2	1
J_2	8	0	0	1
J_3	0	3	2	3
J_4	7	1	1	0

2. Choose the smallest uncovered number, which in this case is 1 at $J_1 M_S$.

3. Subtract this number, that is, 1, from every uncovered number in the matrix, including itself. Then add this number to all values that appear at line intersections. This procedure yields:

	M_P	M_Q	M_R	M_S
J_1	0	1	1	0
J_2	4	0	0	1
J_3	0	2	1	2
J_4	8	1	1	0

4. We now test to see whether this result is a solution. In the present case it is not.

5. Therefore, cover all zeros with the minimum number of lines which in this case is three, as before. This is shown below.

	M_P	M_Q	M_R	M_S
J_1	0	1	1	0
J_2	4	0	0	1
J_3	0	2	1	2
J_4	8	1	1	0

[8] When the problem is large, an algorithm for finding the minimum number of lines is desirable. See for example, M. Sasieni, A. Yaspan, and L. Friedman, *Operations Research: Methods and Problems* (New York: John Wiley & Sons, Inc., 1959), pp. 189–190.

6. We repeat steps 2, 3, and 4 described above as many times as required until the final solution is determined.

For this example, at the end of the next cycle of matrix operations we obtain the final solution, viz.:

	M_P	M_Q	M_R	M_S
J_1	0	0	0	0
J_2	5	0	0	2
J_3	0	1	0	2
J_4	8	0	0	0

FIGURE 8-7
Feasible optimal alternatives for machine assignments. (Jobs 1 and 3 can be assigned to Machine P, that is, P_1 and P_3. The same reasoning applies to Q, R, and S.) All five alternatives are optimal solutions.

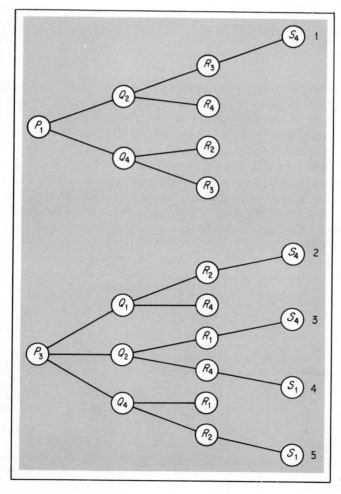

There are five equally desirable alternative schedules indicated by the final matrix. Each of these produces a total cost for one unit of each part of $15.00. Figure 8.7 illustrates the alternate assignments that provide a final solution.

We are now in a position to consider the situation that exists when alternative facilities compete not only for assignments but also for investment funds. That is, assume that the company can afford to buy only four different facilities, but five different models are available. How should the choice be made? Let us compare our four machines P, Q, R, and S with a fifth possibility, called machine T. The following matrix can be written:

	M_P	M_Q	M_R	M_S	M_T
J_1	3	5	9	4	5
J_2	6	3	7	4	3
J_3	2	5	8	5	1
J_4	8	2	6	1	2
J_*	0	0	0	0	0

Note that when a fifth machine is added, there being only four jobs to be assigned and only four machines to be used, a dummy job called J_* can be created. Because this job does not really exist, we utilize *all zero costs* for its row in the matrix. Thus, we express the fact that we are indifferent as to which machine this dummy job, J_*, will be assigned. In this way, the relative qualities of other jobs with respect to machines will force their assignments *before* the dummy assignment is made. Whichever machine the dummy job is assigned to will be dropped from the list of equipment to be selected. Clearly, the machine which is given the dummy job assignment will be the least desirable machine from the point of view of minimizing operating costs. It is the expendable machine.

Going through the steps required by the assignment algorithm, the following solution, will be obtained.

	M_P	M_Q	M_R	M_S	M_T
J_1	⓪	2	6	1	2
J_2	3	⓪	4	1	0
J_3	1	4	7	4	⓪
J_4	7	1	5	⓪	1
J_*	0	0	⓪	0	0

The dummy job is assigned to machine R. Machine T, the alternative that was being considered, *should be obtained* to replace machine R. The same kind of comparisons can be made for other machines that might be specified, such as U, V, X, and so on.

If the problem is couched in terms of profit maximization instead of cost minimization, a very simple transformation is required. We subtract all of the numbers that appear in the profit matrix from the largest number in the matrix. In effect, this converts the profit matrix into a cost matrix. We then follow the same rules as before. If a given job cannot be assigned to a certain machine for technological reasons—or because a contaminating job is already in process on the machine—then we block the assignment by entering a very large cost in the appropriate cell. This will prevent impossible, unwanted, and undesirable assignments from being made.

THE TRANSPORTATION ALGORITHM

Having discussed loading problems for which relatively permanent types of assignments are made, we shall proceed to the situation in which more frequent rearranging of the load is expected. In the case of the relatively permanent assignment, a best facility selected from among a set of alternative facilities could be found for a given job. Because all the jobs were expected to continue for some time, it would have been pointless to break-up or split jobs, assigning portions to different facilities. For the situations we are about to describe, this condition will no longer apply. Consequently, whatever technique we utilize should enable us to place part of a job on one facility and the remainder of it on another. Sometimes it will be reasonable to break the jobs 50–50; at other times 10 per cent might be assigned to each of six facilities, the remainder to a single facility.

The model that we will employ is based upon the transportation algorithm. We shall examine the transportation matrix and its network solution.

Many forms of problems lend themselves to reasonable representation using the transportation model, so it is worthwhile becoming familiar with how the model is set up and how it is solved.

The basic idea of the transportation model is that it allocates a supply of resources to users of those resources, in such a way as to find a pattern of allocation that minimizes costs or maximizes profits. Each source, shipper, or producer can split its allocations between users. And the output of several sources can be assigned to a single user. These relations are reflected in the matrix below where the cost of shipping one unit from a particular producer (P_i) to a specific consumer (C_j) is stated as c_{ij}.

Consumers

	C_1	C_2	C_3	$\cdots$	C_j	$\cdots$	C_m	Supply
P_1	c_{11}	c_{12}	c_{13}		c_{1j}		c_{1m}	s_1
P_2	c_{21}	c_{22}	c_{23}		c_{2j}		c_{2m}	s_2
P_3	c_{31}	c_{32}	c_{33}		c_{3j}		c_{3m}	s_3
$\cdot$ $\cdot$ $\cdot$								$\cdot$ $\cdot$ $\cdot$
P_i	c_{i1}	c_{i2}	c_{i3}		c_{ij}		c_{im}	s_i
$\cdot$ $\cdot$ $\cdot$								$\cdot$ $\cdot$ $\cdot$
P_n	c_{n1}	c_{n2}	c_{n3}		c_{nj}		c_{nm}	s_n
Demand	d_1	d_2	d_3	$\cdots$	d_j	$\cdots$	d_m	

Producers

Constraints on producers' supplies (in a given time period) are indicated by s_i values and consumers' demands are shown by d_j's.[9]

First, let us consider a 2×2 transportation matrix, with the given values for supplies and demands for the period, and unit costs of allocation, as shown.

	C_1	C_2	Supply
P_1	4	6	600
P_2	2	5	400
Demand	300	700	1000

The minimum cost allocations can be determined by (*first*) finding any feasible allocation pattern (i.e., a pattern that properly matches supply and demand totals); (*second*) by examining the effects of making changes in that pattern; (*third*) making changes that assure improvement; and (*fourth*) stopping when no further improvement can be obtained. The similarity to linear programming rules is hardly accidental. Transportation models can always be solved by LP methods.

As an example of a "jumping-off" point solution, assume the following:

[9] The reader's attention is directed to pp. 346-52 in Chapter 11, where the *classic* 'distribution' form of the transportation model is used for plant location decisions.

	C_1	C_2	Supply
P_1	[4] 100	[6] 500	600
P_2	[2] 200	[5] 200	400
Demand	300	700	1000

The *first* requirement is met. For the second condition, we must study four options:

1. If an additional unit is assigned to P_1C_1, thus: $\begin{bmatrix} 101 & 499 \\ 199 & 201 \end{bmatrix}$; the cost changes are $+4 -2 +5 -6 = +1$. Therefore, to make this change would increase costs by one dollar for each extra unit assigned to P_1C_1, so we will not make such changes in the allocation pattern.

2. If an additional unit is assigned to P_2C_2, the same result occurs as we have just described.

3. If an additional unit is assigned to P_2C_1, thus: $\begin{bmatrix} 99 & 501 \\ 201 & 199 \end{bmatrix}$; the cost changes are $+6 -4 +2 -5 = -1$. Therefore, we wish to make this change, assigning as many units as possible to P_2C_2, because each unit so reassigned saves one dollar. How many units can be moved to P_2C_1? We can move 100 units, thus: $\begin{bmatrix} & 600 \\ 300 & 100 \end{bmatrix}$.

4. It will be found that the same reasoning applies to P_1C_2; each unit so reassigned saves one dollar and the maximum number of units that can be assigned to P_1C_2 is 600 ... (actually an identity with point 3 above).

Thus, the optimal assignment for this 2×2 problem has been easily determined. The method we have been employing is called the "stepping stone" procedure.

For larger problems, several obvious questions present themselves, namely: A. How do we quickly derive a jumping-off solution? B. How can the patterns of reassignment be rapidly evaluated?, and C. How do we determine the maximum amount that can be reassigned? Let us consider each of these questions, in turn, using a larger numerical example as a basis for discussion.

	C_1	C_2	C_3	Supply
P_1	[4] 50	[6]	[3]	50
P_2	[2] 50	[5] 110	[8]	160
P_3	[7]	[3] 190	[2] 60	250
P_4	[4]	[5]	[6] 140	140
Demand	100	300	200	600

Starting in the upper left-hand corner, as many units are assigned to P_1C_1 as is *allowed* by whichever constraint dominates, i.e., the row constraint of 50 or the column constraint of 100. In this case, it is the row constraint, so 50 units are entered at P_1C_1, but the C_1 column still has 50 units of unfilled demand. These can be assigned at P_2C_1; however, all of P_2's supply is not yet assigned. In fact, 110 units can be assigned at P_2C_2 which leaves 190 units of C_2's demand to take care of. Continuing in this way, we complete the total matrix of assignments. The procedure we are using is called the *Northwest Corner Method*. It will always satisfy the requirement for an initial, feasible solution, but so would a procedure that starts at any corner. Whatever method is used to obtain an initial, feasible solution, it must produce $M + N - 1$ assignments given a matrix with M rows and N columns.[10] This number does not only apply to initial solutions; it applies to all intermediate solutions, and the final and optimal solution as well.

For question B, the net cost of all assignments that have not been made must be determined. Consider the possibility of assigning units to P_1C_2. The stepping stone configuration is as follows:

PUT IN	UNIT COST	TAKE OUT	UNIT COST
P_1C_2	+6	P_1C_1	−4
P_2C_1	+2	P_2C_2	−5
	+8		−9

The net change is a saving of one dollar. Next, consider assigning one unit to P_1C_3.

PUT IN	UNIT COST	TAKE OUT	UNIT COST
P_1C_3	+3	P_1C_1	−4
P_2C_1	+2	P_2C_2	−5
P_3C_2	+3	P_3C_3	−2
	+8		−11

The net change is a saving of three dollars. This change would be made rather than the previous one which promises a saving of only one dollar. Still, we must evaluate the remaining possibilities for assignments. These are all shown within circles in the matrix below.

[10] There is an exception which results in less than $M + N - 1$ assignments, called the state of degeneracy. This condition is a purely technical problem which can always be resolved by adding a negligible amount to an appropriate row or column total.

1st iteration

	C_1	C_2	C_3	Supply
P_1	[4] 50	[6] ⊖①	[3] ⊖③	50
P_2	[2] 50	[5] 110	[8] ⊕④	160
P_3	[7] ⊖⑦	[3] 190	[2] 60	250
P_4	[4] ⓪	[5] ⊖②	[6] 140	140
Demand	100	300	200	600

Total Cost = 2380

The total cost is $(50 \times 4) + (50 \times 2) + (110 \times 5) + (190 \times 3) + (60 \times 2) + (140 \times 6) = 2380$. The best marginal change is -3 and indicates that assignments should be made to $P_1 C_3$. Before we proceed to question C, however, let us note one more stepping pattern, namely, to evaluate an assignment at $P_4 C_1$, we must assign a unit to $P_4 C_1$, remove a unit from $P_4 C_3$, assign a unit to $P_3 C_3$, remove a unit from $P_3 C_2$, assign a unit to $P_2 C_2$ and remove a unit from $P_2 C_1$. In all cases, the stepping pattern must leave the supplies and demands fully satisfied. The fundamental basis of all stepping patterns is that a horizontal step must allow a vertical step to be taken from it, and then again horizontal and vertical movements can be made until closure is achieved. Thus, for example, two possible patterns are shown in Figure 8.8.

The network on the left details the necessary moves for assigning (in the matrix above) one unit to $P_1 C_3$; the one on the right shows a similar assignment to $P_4 C_1$. Once this network is determined, plus and minus signs can be added to show the increases and decreases in cost caused by such assignment. Starting with the cell to be assigned, alternate plus and minus costs can be entered as

FIGURE 8-8
Two patterns for
network transfers.

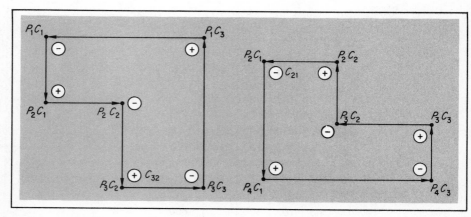

shown in the diagram. In this manner, the marginal costs of an assignment can be determined easily. For example, the marginal cost of assigning one unit to P_1C_3 would be equal to $+c_{13} -c_{11} +c_{21} -c_{21} +c_{32} -c_{33}$.

Referring to question C, how many units can be entered at P_1C_3? The stepping pattern for unit changes must now be examined in terms of how many units are presently assigned to each "take out" position (indicated by negative signs in the network). The smallest such number is the answer. Otherwise, some assignments would become negative which violates the feasibility condition. Thus, for P_1C_2, no more than 50 units (at P_1C_1) can be reassigned; at P_1C_3, 50 units is again the maximum number; at P_3C_1, 50 units, now at P_2C_1 dominate the reassignments; at P_4C_1, 50 units; at P_4C_2, 140 units at P_4C_3 is the minimum number.

We are now ready to make the reassignment to P_1C_3. Then we must go through all of the steps again, reassigning until all evaluations of nonassigned cells indicate that no further improvement is possible. This is done below:

2nd iteration

	C_1	C_2	C_3	Supply
P_1	[4] ⊕3	[6] ⊖2	[3] ⑤⓪	50
P_2	[2] 100	[5] 60	[8] ⊖4	160
P_3	[7] ⊕7	[3] 240	[2] 10	250
P_4	[4] ⓪	[5] ⊖2	[6] 140	140
Demand	100	300	200	600

Total Cost = 2230

The indicated change is to make an assignment of as many units as possible (140) to P_4C_2. Thus:

3rd iteration

	C_1	C_2	C_3	Supply
P_1	[4] ⊖3	[6] ⊖2	[3] 50	50
P_2	[2] 100	[5] 60	[8] ⊖4	160
P_3	[7] ⊕7	[3] 100	[2] 150	250
P_4	[4] ⊖2	[5] 140	[6] ⊖2	140
Demand	100	300	200	600

Total Cost = 1950

This is the final solution; there is none better. Had a zero appeared in the circled evaluations, this would have signified that alternatives existed. It would be up to the operations manager to decide which of the minimum cost alternatives he preferred.

We note that our final solution has six assignments, thus, it meets the condition $M + N - 1 = 4 + 3 - 1 = 6$. Later, see pp. 250–53, we shall show that when supply and demand are not equal, that a dummy slack variable, having *all* zero unit costs can be created to take care of this situation. The dummy, whether it be needed for the rows or columns, is not simply a computational convenience; it has decision-making significance for the manager. Lastly, if we wish to use the transportation model to achieve profit maximization rather than cost minimization, the rule concerning which new assignment is preferred is reversed. The largest possible plus-valued marginal evaluation is chosen to be entered in the network. The procedure stops when all evaluations are negative. The significance of the transportation model is hard to miss. It does not require a square matrix, the solutions are relatively easy to obtain by hand computation. On the other hand it is linear, since unit costs or profits are not able to be changed as a function of volume, and since each matrix applies to a specific period, no allowance is made for interdependencies over time.

SHOPLOADING USING
THE TRANSPORTATION METHOD

Now, let us examine the use of the transportation algorithm for shoploading. We should note that in the situation just described, both the column and the row restrictions have identical dimensions. In other words, producer i can ship *x units of goods* to consumer j, who in turn, requires *x units of goods*. The dimension, units of goods, is the same for all rows and columns. This is not true for the machine loading problem that we are about to discuss. Here the resources of the facilities are measured by the number of productive hours available per week. The matrix shown below lists four machines. The first machine has 40 hours available per week; the second, 60 hours available per week; the third, 80 hours available per week; and the fourth, $41\frac{2}{3}$ hours available per week.

Why this difference between machines? First, there may be two machines of the M_3 type which together give a total of 80 hours in a normal work week. On the other hand, extra shifts may be utilized for M_3. How about M_2? There may be two of these machines, but part of the week is blocked by a previous assignment for one of the two machines. Furthermore, some of the machines may be scheduled for maintenance work and, therefore, would not be available on the production load chart. The connection between the Gantt load chart and the material which we are presently discussing will be readily seen.

There are five jobs to be scheduled for the week. Allowance has been made for those jobs which are already on machines and have been assigned blocked time. In some cases, it is desirable to reschedule the total set of jobs on hand,

MATRIX OF PRODUCTION RATES
(ALL MATRIX ENTRIES IN PIECES PER HOUR)

	M_1	M_2	M_3	M_4	DEMAND (NUMBER OF PIECES)
J_A	3	6	4.8	3.6	300
J_B	3.5	7	5.6	4.2	210
J_C	3	6	4.8	3.6	240
J_D	15	30	24	18	1800
J_E	12.5	25	20	15	400
Available Hours	40	60	80	$41\frac{2}{3}$	
Index Rating	$\frac{1}{2}$	1*	$\frac{4}{5}$	$\frac{3}{5}$	

* The standard machine.

including those with prior assignments. This is particularly apt when set-up costs are low. In fact, throughout our present discussion we shall assume that set-up costs are not significant. If they were large, we would have to take them into account. Frequently, this would prohibit splitting jobs between facilities. The five jobs have specified demands of 300, 210, 240, 1800, and 400 pieces. Therefore, the dimensions of demand are not the same as the dimensions of supply. This creates a problem which must be resolved if the machine loading problem is to be handled by the method we are considering.

The numbers in the matrix represent the production rates that characterize each job and each machine. Productivity is given in terms of pieces per hour. Thus, machine 1 produces three pieces of job A per hour. These matrix entries are comparable to the shipping costs previously utilized for distribution problems.

We shall assume that our objective is to maximize profit. It can be pointed out again that profit maximization is not necessarily the same as cost minimization. Both might be different from the solution for delivery time minimization. The profit objective is global and, consequently, we shall utilize it for this problem. What shall we do about the dimensional problem? We must try to find a *standard machine* against which all the other machines can be compared. Once we obtain a standard unit we can transform all the matrix elements into comparable dimensional terms.

Observe the productivity rates of the various machines. Machine 2 is capable of the greatest production rates for all jobs. Machine 1 has only half of machine 2's productivity. Machine 3 has 0.8 of machine 2's productive capacity, and machine 4 has 0.6 of machine 2's productive capacity. Consequently, we can use index numbers to rate the relative productivities of each machine. The index ratings have been shown in the matrix. We call machine 2 the *standard machine*, denoted by an *, and have assigned it an index of 1.

The key to the concept of the standard machine is that the relative productivities of the facilities are proportional to each other for all jobs. When this is not exactly true, we try to approximate it. Usually, some acceptable approximation is possible. It doesn't matter which machine we call the standard machine. We have arbitrarily chosen the machine that has the greatest productivity rate for the assignment of an index of 1.

Let us now determine the profit rate for each job-machine combination in terms of standard machine hours. First, we observe that each machine requires a different level of operator skill. Each labor skill level has a different wage rate per hour. These data are:

MACHINE	LABOR SKILL	WAGE RATE (DOLLARS PER HOUR)
1	a	6.00
2	c	4.20
3	b	4.80
4	d	3.60

Next, we determine a *labor-cost matrix* in dollars per piece. Job A on machine 1 has a production rate of 3 pieces per hour. If we divide the labor cost per hour by the production rate, we discover that the labor cost is $2.00 per piece for job A on machine 1.[11] Similarly, consider job D on machine 3. This is skill level b—rated at $4.80 per piece. The productivity rate is 24 pieces per hour. We divide 24 into 4.8 and obtain a labor cost of $0.20 per piece. In this way we derive the labor-cost matrix shown below.

LABOR-COST MATRIX—DOLLARS PER PIECE

JOB	M_1	M_2	M_3	M_4
A	2.00	0.70	1.00	1.00
B	1.71	0.60	0.86	0.86
C	2.00	0.70	1.00	1.00
D	0.40	0.14	0.20	0.20
E	0.48	0.17	0.24	0.24

Next, we consider the material cost for each job. The relevant data might be:

JOB	MATERIAL COST (DOLLARS PER PIECE)
A	0.50
B	0.60
C	0.80
D	1.00
E	1.20

[11] Thus: (6) $\dfrac{\$}{hr.}$ ÷ (3) $\dfrac{pieces}{hr.}$ = (2) $\dfrac{\$}{piece}$

Materials for job *A* cost \$0.50 per piece. Materials for job *E* cost \$1.20 per piece. We can now develop a labor + materials—cost matrix in dollars per piece by adding the appropriate materials cost to each row of the labor-cost matrix. The result is:

LABOR + MATERIALS COST MATRIX—DOLLARS PER PIECE

JOB	M_1	M_2	M_3	M_4
A	2.50	1.20	1.50	1.50
B	2.31	1.20	1.46	1.46
C	2.80	1.50	1.80	1.80
D	1.40	1.14	1.20	1.20
E	1.68	1.37	1.44	1.44

The next set of computations will produce the *profit-per-piece matrix*. To obtain this we must know the selling price per piece for each job. Thus:

JOB	SELLING PRICE (DOLLARS PER PIECE)
A	4.00
B	4.00
C	5.00
D	3.00
E	3.00

For each row of the cost matrix, only one selling price applies. From this selling price, row by row, the appropriate labor plus material costs are to be subtracted. For example, job *B* sells at \$4.00 per piece. Each job *B* row entry is subtracted from four; thus, \$4.00 − \$2.31 = \$1.69, \$4.00 − \$1.20 = \$2.80, \$4.00 − \$1.46 = \$2.54, and so forth. By utilizing this approach we have derived the profit-per-piece matrix.

PROFIT-PER-PIECE MATRIX IN DOLLARS

JOB	M_1	M_2	M_3	M_4
A	\$1.50	\$2.80	\$2.50	\$2.50
B	1.69	2.80	2.54	2.54
C	2.20	3.50	3.20	3.20
D	1.60	1.86	1.80	1.80
E	1.32	1.63	1.56	1.56

We must now convert the profit-per-piece matrix into a *profit-per-standard-machine-hour matrix*. To achieve this conversion we utilize the productivity rates of the standard machine. Thus, for example, all elements in the first row of the profit-per-piece matrix are multiplied by 6—the job *A* productivity of the standard machine. All elements in the second row of the profit-per-piece matrix are multiplied by 7—the job *B* productivity of the standard machine. All elements in the fourth row of the profit-per-piece matrix are multiplied by 30, and so forth. The reason that this succeeds in producing a new matrix transformed into terms of profit per standard machine hour is shown by the following relationship.

$$\frac{\text{Profit}}{\text{Piece}} \times \frac{\text{Pieces}}{\text{Standard Hour}} = \frac{\text{Profit}}{\text{Standard Hour}}$$

The profit-per-standard-machine-hour matrix is given herewith

PROFIT PER STANDARD MACHINE HOUR IN DOLLARS

JOB	M_1	M_2	M_3	M_4
A	$ 9.00	$16.80	$15.00	$15.00
B	11.80	19.60	17.80	17.80
C	13.20	21.00	19.20	19.20
D	48.00	55.80	54.00	54.00
E	33.00	40.80	39.00	39.00

We must now convert the machine hours available per week into standard machine hours available per week. These, and all matrix dimensions must be comparable with the profit-per-standard-hour matrix. We do this in the following table.

MACHINE	HOURS PER WEEK AVAILABLE	PER CENT UTILIZATION	EFFECTIVE HOURS AVAILABLE PER WEEK	INDEX	STANDARD MACHINE HOURS AVAILABLE PER WEEK
1	40	0.9	36	0.5	18
2	60	0.9	54	1.0	54
3	80	1.0	80	0.8	64
4	$41\frac{2}{3}$	0.8	$33\frac{1}{3}$	0.6	20
			$203\frac{1}{3}$		156

To begin, we list the number of available hours per week for each machine. Then, for realism, a percent utilization column is also given. This percent utilization, which is derived from operating records, is intended to account for breakdowns, adjustments, and other factors that subtract real time from productive time. By multiplying available hours per week by percent utilization, we determine effective hours available per week. Next, we multiply the effective hours by the appropriate index rating for each machine. For example, the index of M_1 is 0.5; the effective hours are 36; the product is 18 *standard hours* available per week. Effective hours and standard hours are equal for machine 2 because the index of M_2 is 1. The total standard machine hours available per week is 156 hours.

We must complete the conversion to standard terms by developing appropriate numbers for the job restrictions. Job A has a requirement of 300 pieces per week. If we now divide this number by the productivity rate of the standard machine, we will transform the dimension of requirements into standard hours per week. For example:

$$(300)\frac{\text{Pieces}}{\text{Week}} \div (6)\frac{\text{Pieces}}{\text{Standard Machine Hour}} = (50)\frac{\text{Standard Machine Hours}}{\text{Week}}$$

Following through this operation for all jobs, we obtain the following:

JOB	STANDARD ROW RESTRICTIONS
A	300/6 = 50
B	210/7 = 30
C	240/6 = 40
D	1800/30 = 60
E	400/25 = 16
	196 Standard Hours

Now we discover that 196 standard hours are required to do all the jobs, but we have only 156 standard hours available from our machines. Accordingly, we can appoint a *dummy machine* to absorb the overrequirement of 40 standard hours. The complete matrix, entirely in terms of standard machine hours is:

MATRIX OF PROFIT PER STANDARD MACHINE HOUR

	M_1	M_2	M_3	M_4	DUMMY	DEMAND (STANDARD MACHINE HRS.)
J_A	$ 9.00	$16.80	$15.00	$15.00	$0	50
J_B	11.80	19.60	17.80	17.80	0	30
J_C	13.20	21.00	19.20	19.20	0	40
J_D	48.00	55.80	54.00	54.00	0	60
J_E	33.00	40.80	39.00	39.00	0	16
Available Standard Hours	18	54	64	20	40	196

The profits per standard hour assigned to the dummy are all set at zero so that no preference exists with respect to which job will be assigned to the dummy machine. Whichever job is eventually assigned, it will not be done in this week. (We have employed this same reasoning before. See pp. 238–39.)

The transportation algorithm can now be used. The objective, in this case, is to maximize profit. Logically, therefore, all changes in assignments should be made to cells that improve the total profit. The initial assignments can be set down as a Northwest Corner allocation.

NORTHWEST CORNER ALLOCATION OF STANDARD MACHINE HOURS

	M_1	M_2	M_3	M_4	DUMMY	DEMAND
J_A	18	32				50
J_B		22	8			30
J_C			40			40
J_D			16	20	24	60
J_E					16	16
Available Hours	18	54	64	20	40	196

We continue to rearrange these assignments until there is no longer any possibility of improving the profit. The solution to the problem is given in table form below.

TABLE OF JOB-MACHINE ASSIGNMENTS

JOB	MACHINE ASSIGNMENT	NUMBER OF STANDARD MACHINE HOURS	INDEX	NUMBER OF ACTUAL MACHINE HOURS
A	1	10	0.5	20
A	Dummy	40	—	—
B	1	8	0.5	16
B	2	22	1.0	22
C	2	32	1.0	32
C	3	8	0.8	10
D	3	40	0.8	50
D	4	20	0.6	$33\frac{1}{3}$
E	3	16	0.8	20

We observe that job A has been assigned to both M_1 and to the dummy. Job B has been assigned to M_1 and M_2, and so on.

The transportation matrix below will give the number of standard hours for each assignment shown in the above table. Thus:

FINAL SOLUTION IN STANDARD HOUR ASSIGNMENTS

	M_1	M_2	M_3	M_4	DUMMY	DEMAND
J_A	10				40	50
J_B	8	22				30
J_C		32	8			40
J_D			40	20		60
J_E			16			16
Available Hours	18	54	64	20	40	

Now we must reconvert from the standard machine hour system to actual machine hours, which are also shown in the above table. This is straightforward. We divide each standard hour job assignment by its appropriate index number. Thus, all M_1 assignments are divided by 0.5; all M_2 assignments are divided by 1; all M_3 assignments are divided by 0.8, and so on. We ignore the dummy, because the assignment of job A to the dummy is not real. This gives us:

ACTUAL MACHINE HOUR ASSIGNMENTS

	M_1	M_2	M_3	M_4
J_A	20			
J_B	16	22		
J_C		32	10	
J_D			50	$33\frac{1}{3}$
J_E			20	
Actual Machine Hours Available	36	54	80	$33\frac{1}{3}$

To determine the number of pieces that will be obtained for each job, we multiply actual assignment hours by the appropriate, real productivity rates of each machine. Thus, for example, for job D assigned to M_4, the productivity rate is 18 pieces per hour. We multiply $33\frac{1}{3}$ hours by 18 pieces per hour, which yields 600 pieces. The matrix of total pieces is shown below.

MATRIX OF ACTUAL PIECES PRODUCED BY EACH ASSIGNMENT

	M_1	M_2	M_3	M_4	TOTAL UNITS	REQUIREMENTS
J_A	60				60	300
J_B	56	154			210	210
J_C		192	48		240	240
J_D			1200	600	1800	1800
J_E			400		400	400

Job A is the only demand that is not fully supplied. It is short 240 units. This fact does not surprise us because demand exceeded productive capacity.

The model we have just discussed is exceedingly useful when it is possible to approximate the conditions of a standard machine. With ingenuity and good judgment, extraneous factors such as setup costs, variability in production rates, job priorities, and other occurrences that are likely to be encountered in a real production system can be taken into account. Also, it is not unreasonable to compare schedules obtained for maximum profit with those derived for minimizing production time.

SEQUENCING MODELS

Once the shoploading problem is resolved, it is still necessary to determine the exact time sequence for processing jobs on machines. For this purpose, we use a class of algorithms called sequencing models. Many of these sequencing procedures are of only restricted utility because they apply to a limited number of situations. Sequencing models have not been generalized to the extent that other types of production models have been. Nevertheless, it is useful to examine a few variations briefly.

First, consider the problem of sequencing n jobs through two facilities. We shall let these jobs be called $a, b, c, \ldots, n$. The facilities shall be designated as A and B. The two facilities provide service; the n jobs require service in the fixed order A, B.

Thus:

EXAMPLE	A		B
1	Press Shop	→	Assemble
2	Cast	→	Trim
3	Assemble	→	Ship
4	Sandblast	→	Paint

A problem might be set down in matrix form as follows:

	Job			
Facility	a	b	c	d
A	3	5	2	7
B	4	6	8	5

The matrix entries represent the expected hours required to accomplish each operation. There are four jobs and two facilities. Our objective is to minimize the total time required to complete these four jobs. We count from the beginning of the first job to the end of the last job, as they pass through facilities *A* and *B* with the technological sequence fixed. We also impose the additional restriction that *no passing* will be allowed. This means that the job sequence through *B* must be the same as through *A*. Essentially, this is a flow-shop type of configuration.

The method for achieving an optimal schedule, in this case, is quite simple.[12] There are three steps.

STEP 1. Choose the smallest number in the matrix. If that number is in the first row, that is, facility *A*, then place the associated job first in the job sequence. If the smallest number in the matrix is in the second row, that is, facility *B*, then place the associated job last in the job sequence. For our example we place job *c* first in the sequence. Then, cross out the job *c* column and proceed to examine the remaining jobs in the matrix.

STEP 2. Select the smallest number in the remaining matrix. If this smallest number is in the first row, that is, facility *A*, then place this job first *or next to first* if a previous assignment to first place has been made. If this smallest number is in the second row, that is, facility *B*, then place this job last *or next to last* if a previous assignment to last place has been made. For our example, we have already assigned job *c* to first place. The smallest number in the remaining matrix is three, associated with job *a* and facility *A*. Consequently, job *a* is assigned the second place in the sequence. We cross out the job *a* column and turn our attention to the remaining elements of the matrix.

STEP 3. Continue to select the smallest number in the remaining matrix; determine its position, row 1 or row 2, and assign it according to the previous rules. Do this until all jobs have been assigned. Then, in our example, both job *b* and job *d* have the smallest number, that is, five, in the remaining matrix. We can, therefore, either assign job *b* to third place in the sequence or assign job *d* to last place in the sequence. Both actions produce the same result. The final order is *c a b d*. This will result in the shortest period of time for total completion of the four jobs passing through the two facilities. Whenever any kind of tie exists, it doesn't matter which of the tied jobs is given first consideration. However, whichever job is placed in sequence must then be deleted from the matrix and the above rules continue to apply. The method can be used for any number of jobs, but only two machines.

The appropriate Gantt chart can then be drawn to determine the total elapsed time of the sequence and to reveal the amount of idle time experienced by facility *B*. It is instructive to compare the optimal sequence with other sequences chosen at random. We have done this in Figure 8.9 using Gantt layout charts.

There are numerous variations of sequencing models. For example, it is possible to derive an optimal sequence for passing *n* jobs through three facilities,

---

[12] S. M. Johnson, "Optimal Two- and Three-Stage Production Schedules with Setup Times Included," *Naval Research Logistics Quarterly*, Vol. 1, No. 1 (March 1954), pp. 61–68.

but only under certain special circumstances. The model is restrictive, and we shall not consider it here.[13]

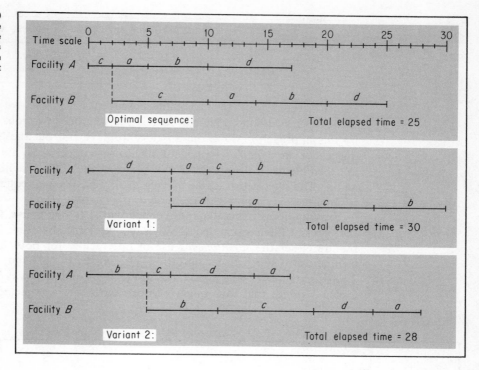

GRAPHICAL SEQUENCING MODELS

Another illustration of sequencing models is based on a graphical method of analysis.[14] In this case, different technological sequences exist *for each job*. Therefore, a job-shop configuration can be expressed in these terms. It will be noted that the method discussed in the previous section imposed the same technological sequence on all jobs. We must limit ourselves to two jobs, viz., J_1 and J_{11}. However, the number of facilities through which these two jobs can be scheduled may be as large as required. Then, let the facilities be called $A, B, \ldots, M$. The objective is to complete both jobs in the shortest possible time. An additional piece of information is needed. Namely, how much time is required for each job at each facility? We shall let these times be denoted by a subscript, for example, A_5 represents five hours spent at facility A.

[13] David W. Miller and Martin K. Starr, *Executive Decisions and Operations Research* (Englewood Cliffs, N.J.: Prentice-Hall, Inc., 1969), 2nd edition, pp. 280–283. See also Martin K. Starr, *Systems Management of Operations,* (Englewood Cliffs, N.J.: Prentice-Hall, Inc., 1971), pp. 294–310.
[14] This method was first presented by S. B. Akers, Jr., "A Graphical Approach to Production Scheduling Problems," *Operations Research,* Vol. 4, (1956), pp. 244–245.

Now, let us turn to a specific example, although the method described is quite general.

JOB	TECHNOLOGICAL SEQUENCE AND TIMES (IN HOURS) AT EACH FACILITY
J_I	Begin $\quad A_5 \rightarrow B_2 \rightarrow C_3 \rightarrow E_5 \rightarrow D_4 \quad$ End
J_{II}	Begin $\quad C_3 \rightarrow D_3 \rightarrow B_3 \rightarrow E_2 \rightarrow A_{10} \quad$ End

Figure 8.10 represents the technological sequences of these two jobs in terms of Cartesian coordinates. (We can readily see why only two jobs can be handled by this approach.) Along the abscissa we have laid out the technological sequence specified for J_I. The same thing has been done for J_{II} along the ordinate. We then block off the area that is common to each of the facilities, A, B, C, D, and E. The intersection space of each facility has an area equal to the product of the time requirements of each job at the facility.

Examination of this diagram reveals that it is impossible to utilize any of the blocked intersection space which has been crosshatched. To do so would require either the *simultaneous* use of one facility for both jobs or replacing an unfinished job with an unstarted job. On the other hand, a point such as 2 represents work being done for J_I at facility A and for J_{II} at facility D. Point 2 also signifies that four hours of work have been completed on J_I and five

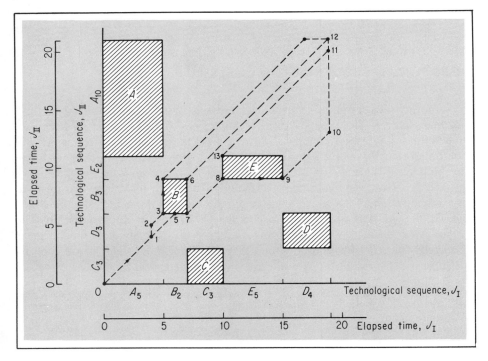

hours of work have been completed on J_{II}. Further, J_{II} has completed its stay at facility C and has only one more hour to go at facility D. Any point in the space can be interpreted in this manner. Point 12 signifies that both J_I and J_{II} are completed.

Any path for completing these jobs must avoid the cross-hatched blocked areas. We start at the origin, point 0, and begin to move upward and to the right, following a diagonal. The diagonal is the most efficient policy because it indicates that we are simultaneously working on both jobs, each at different facilities. As long as we remain on the diagonal we are obtaining full utilization of our productive capacity, however, we cannot always do so. When we reach point 5, we have no alternative but to change direction to the horizontal, because we cannot enter blocked space. A number of different paths have been illustrated in the figure, and all must reach point 12, which represents the completion of both tasks J_I and J_{II}. It requires 19 hours on the x-axis and 21 hours on the y-axis.

There are only three kinds of movements that can be made through this chart. These are: (1) The diagonal movements, representing simultaneous operations, (2) Vertical movements, indicating that J_I is not being worked on, and (3) Horizontal movements that indicate J_{II} is idle. Obviously, we would like to be able to trace a path directly along the diagonal from point 0 to point 12. This cannot be done if blocked intersection space interferes. In our example, facility B stops the diagonal movement. Every situation produces its own unique configuration, and we are stuck with ours. There is a variety of alternate routes which can be taken to avoid going through the space blocked by facility B. We have illustrated some of these. For the purpose of this discussion, we shall only consider four of them:

Path a—0, 1, 2, 3, 4, 12
Path b—0, 1, 5, 7, 8, 9, 10, 11, 12
Path c—0, 1, 5, 7, 6, 12
Path d—0, 1, 5, 7, 8, 13, 11, 12

None of the paths is necessarily optimal. The method we are explaining cannot locate the one path that is optimal for sequencing these jobs through the facilities. Our objective is to discover the path of minimum total elapsed time, but we can only generate a number of alternative paths which are likely to include the optimal sequence. Let us consider, therefore, the four sequencing paths previously described, and determine which one of these provides the best result.

It is simple enough to compute elapsed time. To the total time for J_I operations—this is $(5 + 2 + 3 + 5 + 4) = 19$ hours—add any J_I idle time. The idle time for J_I is represented by the sum of all vertical segments along any given path. Consider the path 0, 1, 5, 7, 8, 9, 10, 11, 12. The vertical segments total eight. Therefore, total elapsed time for both jobs will be $19 + 8 = 27$ hours. To check this result, J_{II} operations require 21 hours. Along the path that we have just followed, the horizontal segments (J_{II}'s idle time) total six. Then, $21 + 6 = 27$ hours, which is identical to our previous result. Proceeding in the same way, we can obtain the following table for paths a, b, c, and d.

We observe that paths c and d provide equal and minimum times. There may be a better sequence than this, but we have not found it.

PATH	TOTAL ELAPSED TIME	JOB I IDLE TIME	JOB II IDLE TIME
a	23	4	2
b	27	8	6
c	22	3	1
d	22	3	1

The graphical sequencing model is certainly useful for rapid computation of reasonably good sequences for production output control. It clearly illustrates that many schedule control difficulties are problems of coping with enormous diversity. When we add more realism through the inclusion of full-scale problems and recognition of risk, our mathematical models are simply whelmed. Consequently, for complex job loading, machine loading, sequencing, and scheduling problems, we frequently prefer or require the use of simulation techniques for determining near-optimal paths through the system. In the last analysis, job simulations are one good way to handle big problems. We will have to be satisfied with doing a very good, even if not a *perfect*, job.

RELEVANT QUESTIONS FOR PROCESS DESIGN

"What's done we partly may compute,
But know not what's resisted."
from Address to the Unco Guild
by Robert Burns

This quotation sums up nicely how things stand when the production manager examines the major commitments associated with the design of the production process. Running a system takes one kind of talent. Designing and building the system calls upon another set of talents. *This is the big challenge.* After all, what can be said to be good practice is based upon past practice. Knowledge acquired by experience is that portion of reality which, "we partly may compute." But every now and then, the chance to do something in a *new* way appears. No history or easily identified precedent exists for it. The inferences required for assurance cannot be justified. Perhaps others have also seen this possibility, "but know not (the result of) what's resisted."

Success in the design phase prohibits fractionation, segmentation, or splintering the system. The unwarranted treatment of problems in false isolation is the main danger that we face.

A number of sample questions relevant to the design phase are raised below. The answer to any one of these should involve the total system. It can only be through such synthesis that a process design of real excellence can emerge.

WITH RESPECT TO THE OUTPUT

1. Are the attributes of the output completely specified? To what extent are they unique?
2. Why has this output been chosen? (Should there be one or more outputs?)

3. Are the estimates that underlie the choice of the specified output accurate and believable? (Is there concensus on this point?)
4. If unique, why has no other company done this before?
5. Why does the opportunity exist? (For how long has it existed?)
6. How will the output be distributed and by whom?
7. How will quality be assessed and assured?
8. How does the production schedule relate to anticipated demands?
9. What mechanisms and policies have been set up for production schedule control?
10. Have proper steps been taken with respect to patent protection?

WITH RESPECT TO THE INPUT

1. What are the manpower requirements?
2. Are there trade-offs to be considered between men and machines?
3. Is the relationship between men and machines likely to change because of technological factors? (Alternatively, when will it change?)
4. What are the expected productivities, and what are the commensurate costs?
5. Have the patterns of work been thoroughly studied?
6. Can the choices of input materials be thoroughly justified?
7. Are these choices likely to change because of technological factors?
8. Have all subcontracting possibilities been considered?
9. Are there alternative sources for the same materials? (Have discounts been considered?)
10. Have adequate inventory management policies been developed?

WITH RESPECT TO THE PROCESS

1. What specific equipment and facilities will be needed? (What is available?)
2. How adequately have sources of equipment supply been investigated?
3. How accurately have machine costs been estimated?
4. What machine capacities and sizes have been estimated for the process?
5. What space requirements have been determined for the total process?
6. Is the plant layout based on short- or long-term assumptions?
7. What kind of maintenance should be used—preventive or remedial?
8. How much maintenance will be required? (Has this been considered with respect to selection equipment?)
9. What are the storage requirements? (Do they fluctuate?)
10. Can the process flow that has been designed be totally justified? How flexible and amenable to change are the lines of flow?
11. Is the basis for materials handling equipment decisions short- or long-term?
12. Have machine setup times been accurately estimated?
13. Has consideration been given to both supply of input materials and demand for output products in locating a plant site?

14. Has the cost of studying the plant location or relocation problem been considered?
15. Have insurance rates and taxes been determined with respect to plant selection?
16. Have the costs, availability, and apparent skills of labor been compared for the various location possibilities? (Has equipment selection been made with this in mind?)
17. What importance have transportation problems and shipping costs played in reaching a location decision? (Can the basis for decision change?)
18. What zoning restrictions and town or state ordinances exist that might affect the location decision? (Do pollution considerations deserve attention?)
19. How available and costly will utility services be such as sewage, water, oil, gas, heat, and electricity? (Will process demands be stable or grow?)
20. Have incorporation fees and procedures been considered?
21. Has the cost of shutting down and moving been taken into account?
22. What consideration has been given to long-run land values? (Is inflation relevant?)
23. Have building costs been properly compared with plant purchase and plant rentals?
24. Should climate have any influence on the location decision?
25. Has there been a thorough evaluation of specific site factors, including drainage, exposure, and so forth? (Has ecological impact been evaluated?)
26. What lot dimensions will be required? Has room for expansion been provided?
27. What internal space divisions have been determined?
28. Is a railroad siding a necessary feature? How many floors should the building have?
29. What colors will be used for walls, ceilings, floors, and machines? Have the illumination needs been properly assessed?
30. What construction materials will be used? Who will control the construction schedule?
31. Has the effect of decisions on competitors been properly surveyed?
32. Have all relevant questions been asked? Have all these questions been answered?
33. Is the chosen course of action the best possible way to proceed?

PROBLEMS

1 The executive offices for five vice presidents of a large bank are on the tenth floor of the bank's new building. The president wants to assign the offices in such a way as to maximize total satisfaction. He therefore asks each vice president to rank his preference for the available offices. The president receives the information in the following form:

OFFICE	VP_1	VP_2	VP_3	VP_4	VP_5
O_1	1	1	2	3	2
O_2	5	3	1	2	3
O_3	4	2	5	1	1
O_4	3	5	4	4	4
O_5	2	4	3	5	5

Rank 1 is the most preferred location.
a. What is the best assignment plan?
b. How does this relate to production schedules?

2   Our company has 4 orders on hand, and each must be processed in the sequential order:

Department A—press shop
Department B—plating and finishing

The table below lists the number of days required by each job in each department. For example, Job IV requires one day in the press shop and one day in the finishing department.

	JOB I	*JOB II*	*JOB III*	*JOB IV*
Department A	8	6	5	1
Department B	8	3	4	1

a. Assume that no other work is being done by the departments. Use a Gantt layout chart to try to find the best work schedule. By best work schedule, we mean minimum time to finish all four jobs.
b. Determine the total time to complete all four jobs when the optimal schedule is used.
c. Compare the results obtained in (a) and (b), and comment on the complexity of such problems when many departments and many jobs are involved.

3   Use the graphical sequencing method for the following problem:

$$J_I \quad A_8 \quad B_6 \quad C_5 \quad D_1$$
$$J_{II} \quad C_8 \quad D_4 \quad A_3 \quad B_1$$

technological $\longrightarrow$ sequence

A, B, C, and D are the facilities, and the notation is equivalent to that used on pp. 255–58.

4   Use the transportation algorithm to solve the aggregate scheduling problem below:

Week

	1	2	3	Closing Inventory	Dummy	Supply
$3O$	7	8	9	10		100
$2O$	6	7	8	9		49
$1O$	5	6	7	8		80
$3R$	4	5	6	7		70
$2R$	3	4	5	6		100
$1R$	2	3	4	5		50
I_0	1	2	3	4		51
Demand	80	120	100	100	100	500

$3O$ = third week overtime

$2O$ = second week overtime

$1O$ = first week overtime

$3R$ = regular shift, week 3

$2R$ = regular shift, week 2

$1R$ = regular shift, week 1

I_0 = initial inventory

5 Use the assignment method to achieve a satisfactory shop loading arrangement for an intermittent flow shop where the per unit profits are given in the matrix below and relatively continuous production (in the quarter) can be expected for each assignment.

MACHINES

JOBS	A	B	C	D	E
1	19	17	15	15	13
2	12	30	18	18	15
3	13	21	29	19	21
4	49	56	53	55	43
5	33	41	39	39	30

6 For the data in Problem 5 a new machine F has become available which can only work on jobs 1, 2 or 3, with unit profits of 14, 11 and 12. Would it be worthwhile to replace one of the present machines with F? After analysis, what information is still lacking?

7 Use the data below to develop a shop loading analysis where splitting of assignments is permitted and assumed to have negligible costs. Assume that the objective is to minimize total job times.

Parts per Hour

JOB	A	B	C	D	DEMAND/WEEK
1	7.5	15	10	20	400
2	4.5	9	6	12	300
3	3	6	4	8	200

Available Hours Per Week	A	B	C	D
	40	40	40	40

references

BELLMAN, R., *Dynamic Programming.* Princeton, N. J.: Princeton University Press, 1958.

BIEGEL, JOHN E., *Production Control.* Englewood Cliffs, N. J.: Prentice-Hall, Inc., 1963.

BOWMAN, E. H. and R. B. FETTER, *Analysis for Production and Operations Management,* 3rd ed. Homewood, Ill.: Richard D. Irwin, Inc., 1967.

BUFFA, E. S., *Modern Production Management*, 3rd ed. New York: John Wiley & Sons, Inc., 1969.

————, ed., *Readings in Production and Operations Management.* New York: John Wiley & Sons, Inc., 1966,

CONWAY, RICHARD W., WILLIAM L. MAXWELL and LOUIS W. MILLER, *Theory of Scheduling.* Reading, Mass.: Addison-Wesley Publishing Company, 1967.

DOOLEY, A. et al, *Basic Problems, Concepts and Techniques, Casebooks in Production Management,* rev. ed. New York: John Wiley & Sons, Inc., 1968.

DORFMAN, ROBERT, PAUL A. SAMUELSON, and ROBERT M. SOLOW, *Linear Programming and Economic Analysis.* New York: McGraw-Hill, Inc., 1958.

EILON, S., *Elements of Production Planning and Control.* New York: The ‚Macmillan Company, 1962.

ELMAGHRABY, S. E., *The Design of Production Systems.* New York: Reinhold Publishing Corp., 1966.

FERGUSON, ROBERT O., and LAUREN F. SARGENT, *Linear Programming: Fundamentals and Applications.* New York: McGraw-Hill, Inc., 1958.

GARRETT, L. J. and M. SILVER, *Production Management Analysis.* New York: Harcourt Brace Jovanovich, 1968.

GAVETT, J. W., *Production and Operations Management.* New York: Harcourt Brace Jovanovich, 1968.

GEORGE, C. S., *Management in Industry,* 2nd ed. Englewood Cliffs, N.J.: Prentice-Hall, Inc., 1964.

GOLD, BELA, *Foundations of Productivity Analysis.* Pittsburgh, Penn.: University of Pittsburgh Press, 1955.

HOPEMAN, R. J., *Systems Analysis and Operations Management.* Columbus, Ohio: Charles E. Merrill Publishing Co., 1969.

HOTTENSTEIN, M. P., *Models and Analysis for Production Management.* Scranton, Pa.: International Textbook Co., 1968.

HOLT, C. C., F. MODIGLIANI, J. F. MUTH, and H. A. SIMON, *Planning Production: Inventories and Work Force.* Englewood Cliffs, N. J.: Prentice-Hall, Inc., 1960.

IRESON, W. G. and E. L. GRANT, eds., *Handbook of Industrial Engineering and Management,* 2nd ed. Englewood Cliffs, N.J.: Prentice-Hall, Inc., 1970.

JOINT ECONOMIC COMMITTEE, CONGRESS OF THE UNITED STATES, "Measures of Productive Capacity," July 24, 1962.

MAGEE, J. F. and D. M. BOODMAN, *Production Planning and Inventory Control,* 2nd ed. New York: McGraw-Hill Book Company, 1967.

MUTH, JOHN F., and GERALD L. THOMPSON (eds.), *Industrial Scheduling.* Englewood Cliffs, N.J.: Prentice-Hall, Inc., 1963.

PROGRESS IN OPERATIONS RESEARCH, Vol. I, Russell L. Ackoff, ed., 1961; Vol. II, David B. Hertz and Robert T. Eddison, eds., 1964; Vol. III, Julius Aronofsky, ed., 1969. New York: John Wiley & Sons, Inc.

SCHEELE, EVAN D., *et al., Principles and Design of Production Control Systems.* Englewood Cliffs, N. J.: Prentice-Hall, Inc., 1960.

STARR, M. K., ed., *Management of Production.* Middlesex, England: Penguin Book, Ltd., 1970.

————, *Systems Management of Operations.* Englewood Cliffs, N.J.: Prentice-Hall, Inc., 1971.

chapter
nine
**materials
management**

Production managers strive to attain organizational goals in varous ways. Input control is one of these. Inputs are relatively simple to control; often they deal with repetitive decision problems. A single decision that deviates from the optimal cannot do much harm. Only the cumulative effects of repeated divergencies from optimal results can impose severe penalties over a period of time. Therefore, control can be used to keep the system on course.

Process inputs produce direct costs. When lumped together these costs constitute a major share of operating costs. Thus, the inputs are associated with the variable-cost line of the break-even chart. This is the area of cost control that is most familiar to production managers. We shall consider two fundamental kinds of inputs, in this chapter materials management, and in Chapter 12 manpower management.

THE MATERIALS SYSTEM

Many companies have been moving toward an organizational integration of materials control functions. In many firms these activities existed as individual operations, each attended by individuals who seldom communicated with each other. Eventually, in the search for greater control, a single, central materials control department appeared in numerous organizations.

Today, many organizations will be found to have a vice president in charge of materials control. The responsibilities vested in a materials control department include at least three subfunctions, namely, procurement or purchasing, inventory control, and acceptance sampling. We shall treat each of these topics, and, in addition, we shall briefly discuss the subject of value analysis which is intimately involved with the optimal selection and specification of materials.

First, however, let us examine Figure 9.1. It is a flow diagram which depicts the various communications that unite the materials control area. We observe that many forms of communication must flow between the organizational units in order to achieve an integrated materials control department. In addition, the materials control department communicates with the production division, with other operating divisions of the company, and in many ways with the external world.

FIGURE 9-1
A detailed block-flow diagram of materials management.

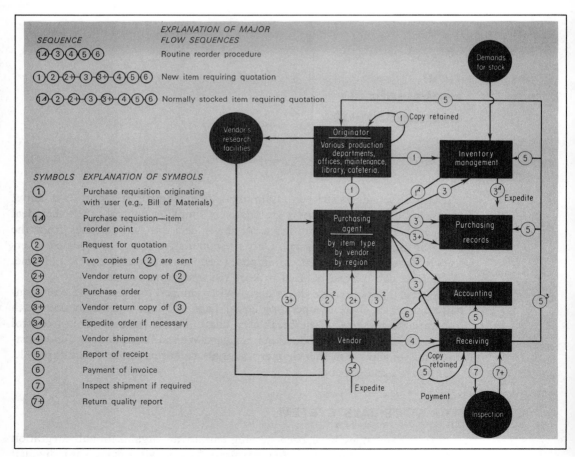

PURCHASING OR PROCUREMENT

The purchasing division occupies a vital and unique position. Through the procurement function the organization operates as a customer. Accordingly, it is susceptible to the marketing strategies of the vendors from whom it obtains the materials that are required for its operations.

Depending upon the extent to which the company requires outside suppliers —and is not self-sufficient—the importance of the buying function increases. For example, a mail order company produces a very small fraction of the materials which it offers for sale. Buyers in such enterprises are responsible, in large measure, for the success of their companies. Commensurate with this responsibility is the remuneration which such buyers receive. At the same time, they must accept the risk of making errors in carrying out their functions. The penalties of errors can be high.

It will be impossible to discuss all the intricate relationships that have been developed by buyers and vendors in order to achieve maximum satisfaction for both parties. One important procedure, however, should be mentioned. It is called *vendor releasing*. In this case, a buyer contracts for a substantial number of units and, thereby, obtains discount prices. The vendor agrees to ship specific quantities of the purchased material at stated intervals. By previous arrangement the approximate shipping quantities for each time period are agreed upon. Generally, the buyer is in a position to change the quantities, from time to time, if he does so with sufficient notice. We can observe how an arrangement, such as vendor releasing, is dependent upon a reasonable forecast of demand and a reasonably accurate specification of the vendor's lead time.[1] It requires a fairly long-term commitment to obtain the benefits of quantity discounts, see pp. 284–86.

Vendor relations depend to a great extent on the nature of a company's operations. Bypassing mail order, wholesale and retail inventories, we can divide purchased inventory into two major groups: (1) materials required for production and (2) materials required for maintenance of plant and equipment. With respect to the first class, some companies purchase manufactured and assembled items; other companies deal primarily with basic raw materials and commodity markets. There is a real difference in the purchasing agent's approach to each of these situations.

Let us consider, for example, the green coffee commodity market from the point of view of a coffee producer. A larger than normal inventory may have to be built up at a particular time, as a result of favorable coffee prices. The cost of holding this inventory must be balanced against the advantage to be gained by overbuying. If the problem is one of underbuying while waiting for a more favorable market, then the cost of running out of stock must be taken into account. Under certain circumstances specialized buying techniques may be involved. These include hedging[2] and speculative purchases, both of which require forward buying.

---

[1] Lead time, or lag time, is the interval that elapses between the placement of an order with the vendor and the receipt of the ordered goods. See pp. 283–84.

[2] Hedging can only be carried on if an organized commodity exchange exists.

THE NATURE OF HEDGING

Hedging involves the buying and selling of commodity futures. Thus, a company fearing that commodity prices will rise, buys a given amount of the material for delivery in a *future month*. The market price is paid plus carrying charges. When the material is actually required for production—before the *future month*—a spot purchase is made for cash and immediate delivery. Simultaneously, a sale is made for delivery in the *future month*. If the price of the commodity has risen, then the selling price of the future contract reflects this as compared to the buying price of the futures. This profit, when applied to the purchase price of the spot transaction, smooths out the rise in price that has occurred. Thus:

1. Our company counts on a raw material cost of $1.00 per pound.
2. Fearing a price rise in this raw material, but having sufficient supply on hand, the purchasing agent buys 1000 pounds for delivery to his company *at some specific future date*—at $1.03 per pound. (This is the present price, the $0.03 reflects carrying costs.)
3. After a period of time, prices have risen. The cost per pound is now $1.50. The company requires and buys 1000 pounds at this price, expecting rapid delivery.
4. But on the same date, the company agrees to sell 1000 pounds for delivery at the *same* future date (as in 2 above) at $1.53 per pound.
5. In this way, the company sells the commodity for future delivery and receives income, on a per pound basis, of $1.53. It has previously purchased material to cover this sale at $1.03. This yields a profit per pound of $0.50.
6. But the company had to pay $1.50 instead of $1.00 per pound to take care of its production requirements—or an increase per pound of $0.50.
7. This results in a *net* change for our company in the price per pound of $0.00. If the price had fallen, similar reasoning applies. The company doesn't benefit from the drop in price, but ends up with zero net change.

The purchase of coffee is only one example of this type of situation. We could, as well, have cited the grain commodity market which affects distilleries and flour mills or the cattle commodity market for both meat and skins. Soft-drink manufacturers must adapt their activities to the sugar market. Textile manufacturers deal with cotton commodities. The confectionery industry buys cocoa. Other commodities include rubber, potatoes, zinc, and cottonseed oil.

COMMODITY BUYING

Although it is exceedingly complicated, commodity buying can be analyzed in terms of a formal model.[3] We shall present a simple example of such a model with the intention of indicating the conceptual basis upon which the problem can be approached and to highlight the kind of information that is required.

[3] William T. Morris, "Some Analyses of Purchasing Policy," *Management Science,* Vol. V (1959), pp. 443–452. With respect to the method used, see also, Richard E. Bellman, *Dynamic Programming* (Princeton, N.J.: Princeton University Press, 1957).

The *objective is to minimize the cost* of a primary raw material input that is characteristically subject to *fluctuating prices.*

STEP 1. We obtain probability estimates that describe the relative likelihood for different commodity prices in each quarter of the year. Such estimates could be obtained by consulting historical records of the particular commodity market. For simplicity, we class the price by whole dollars and use time breaks of three months. In practice these classes can be made as fine as appears to be warranted.

	QUARTER			
COST	1	2	3	4
$4.00	.40	.30	.40	.10
5.00	.40	.30	.30	.40
6.00	.20	.40	.30	.50
Expected Cost	$4.80	$5.10	$4.90	$5.40

STEP 2. Assume that we have to make one purchase in the year. If we defer buying until the fourth quarter, the expected cost will be $5.40. Can we do better than this? We note that if we buy in the third quarter there is a 70 percent chance of doing better, viz., a 30 percent chance of buying at $5.00 and a 40 percent chance of buying at $4.00.[4] Then, Decision Rule A follows:

a. Buy in the 4th quarter if the cost in the 3rd quarter is $6.00.

b. Buy in the 3rd quarter if the cost in the 3rd quarter is $5.00 or less.

The probability that (b) will occur is 0.70. Consequently, the probability that (a) will occur is $1.00 - 0.70 = 0.30$. From this we derive the expected value of Decision Rule A.

Expected Cost (Decision Rule A) = 0.40($4.00) + 0.30($5.00)
$$+ \ 0.30(\$5.40) = \$4.72.$$

STEP 3. If the cost in the 2nd quarter is $4.00, we can do better than this expected cost of $4.72. Decision Rule B is then:

a. Use Decision Rule A if the cost in the 2nd quarter is $5.00 or greater.

b. Buy in the 2nd quarter if the cost in the 2nd quarter is $4.00.

The probability that (b) will occur is 0.30. Hence:

Expected Cost (Decision Rule B) = 0.30($4.00) + 0.70($4.72) = $4.504.

STEP 4. If the cost in the 1st quarter is $4.00, we can do better than this expected cost of $4.504. Decision Rule C follows:

[4] Because of the crude categorization for dollars, we are forced to treat this problem as: ($4.00 and $5.00) < $5.40 < $6.00. With finer price breaks this could be avoided.

a.   Use Decision Rule B if the cost in the 1st quarter is $5.00 or greater.

b.   Buy in the 1st quarter if the cost in the 1st quarter is $4.00.

The probability that (b) will occur is 0.40. Thus:

Expected Cost (Decision Rule C) = 0.40($4.00) + 0.60($4.504) = $4.3024.

We have deduced an optimal policy which has an expected cost of $4.3024. The decision tree in Figure 9.2 recapitulates this policy.

The importance of commodity buying as one form of procurement has induced us to present a commodity buying model. Inventory levels are strongly affected by such buying decisions. It is important that the student of production management be aware of the elements involved in this vital purchasing situation.

FIGURE 9-2
A decision tree for commodity buying policy.

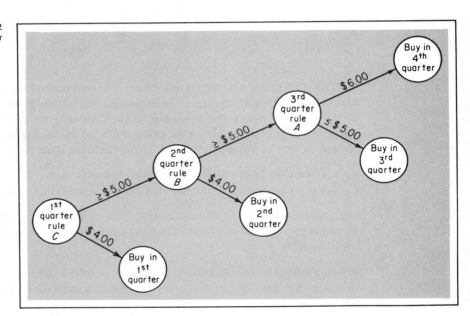

BIDDING

Usually, the purchase of fabricated units and components tends to involve more stable price structures than apply to commodities. An organization will contract with a producer to supply a given number of units of some specific quality. Under some circumstances, the contract may be given on the basis of bids which are offered by potential vendors. The bid system is commonly associated with governmental acquisition of materials. It is also familiar in situations where industrial organizations have no prior vendor arrangements and in which substantial acquisitions are to be made. It is only useful when a competitive market exists for the items to be acquired.

From the bidder's point of view, there is a probability of winning a supply contract which is affected by the *number of bidders* participating in the bidding competition. In general, as the number of bidders increases, the winning bid will be lower. The reason is that different costing systems, capacity and load conditions, skills and facilities, exist for each bidder. As a result, the range of bids will increase. Based on this reasoning, the procurement manager would seemingly want as many bidders as possible. But there is an opposing force at work. As the number of bidders increases, the cost of ordering rises since each bid must be evaluated, not only for costs but for the many intangible factors that must affect the ordering decision. Perhaps, for example, the lowest bidder will promise to meet a delivery schedule which evaluation indicates is unlikely to be fulfilled.

A company does not, of necessity, choose to make its purchases from the organization presenting the lowest bid. Price is seldom the only factor that should be taken into consideration when awarding a contract. Among other things, it is necessary to consider the guarantees of quality, the experience of the vendor, the certainties of delivery, and the kind of long-term supplier-producer relationship that is likely to develop. Transportation costs further complicate the picture. A high bid received from a vendor that is two miles away may be less costly—after transportation—than a lower bid from a potental supplier located 3000 miles away. Thus, it is not enough to compare bids on an FOB point of origin basis.[5]

The purchasing function is immersed in a maelstrom of human relations. There are many mechanical aspects to the achievement of a successful purchasing function, but the human factors cannot be overlooked. Buyers can succeed in achieving special arrangements because of friendly relationships that exist. These are not dishonorable relationships because they include the evaluation of both buyer and vendor of the long-term stability and goodwill of their relationship. Thus, in the business environment of North America, personal friendships are not considered to be a reasonable basis for enterprise decisions. In other business environments, for example, Latin America and The Middle East, personal friendships are considered to be business assets that reduce risk and have monetary value. Part of this cultural difference can be traced to the importance placed upon legal contracts in North America that does not exist everywhere in the world. Because of the enormous growth of international operations, these factors can play a significant role in determining the success of production management in handling the affairs of subsidiaries outside the USA.[6]

MAINTENANCE INVENTORIES

Previously, we mentioned inventories that are primarily maintenance inventories. Consider, for example, an oil refinery: For lack of a few critical parts

---

[5] FOB Detroit. This familiar expression is read "freight on board," Detroit. It means that the price is quoted without shipping charges from Detroit to whatever point of destination is involved.
[6] For a useful discussion of these points, see: Edward T. Hall, "The Silent Language in Overseas Business," *Harvard Business Review*, Vol. 38, No. 3 (May-June, 1960), pp. 87–96.

an entire refinery can be shut down. The cost of lost production may well run into millions of dollars. Should all parts be kept in stock? If so, how many of each kind? How likely is it that a spare part kept in stock for an emergency is, in fact, a reject—a faulty part—that will fail immediately upon use? There are many different kinds of problems that are faced by purchasing agents for maintenance parts. Often, severe *technical* problems are involved in purchasing for the maintenance function of complex technological systems.

Maintenance parts buyers, in particular, must be familiar with production equipment and its requirements. They must also be able to evaluate the quality of the merchandise they acquire. A rational plan should be developed for purchasing and stocking such items. Maintenance inventory policies are a function of the type of maintenance that is used, that is, *preventative* or *remedial* maintenance or a combination of the two, (pp. 369, 408-13). In many systems, the technical basis used for purchasing decisions can be exceedingly critical. When reliability and failure are of major importance, the purchasing function is frequently assigned to a scientifically trained individual. This is particularly necessary when critical specifications are couched in engineering terminology.

A DECISION MODEL FOR MAINTENANCE INVENTORIES

An important class of maintenance inventories is identified with the fact that at the time a major facility is purchased, spare parts can be obtained inexpensively. Later on, however, if it turns out that an insufficient supply of spare parts was acquired, the cost of obtaining additional spares is much higher.

To illustrate, assume that a large punch press has a part which engineering data indicate has a probability of i failures, (p_i) over the lifetime of the machine. There is a cost, c, for each spare part purchased at the time that the press is acquired. When a spare part must be purchased *at a later time*, because not enough were originally purchased, the cost is estimated to be C_u (which includes downtime costs on the press and the larger cost per part charged by the vendor who must treat the spare part request as a special order).

For a simple example of this model,[7] let $i = 1, 2, 3$ meaning that only three failures can occur over the lifetime of the punch press. Also, assume that the probability of 1, 2, or 3 failures is equally likely, i.e., $p_1 = p_2 = p_3 = \frac{1}{3}$. Further, let $c = \$5$ and $C_u = \$40$. The question we wish to answer is: How many spare parts, k, should be ordered at the time of the original purchase? A decision matrix can be constructed to represent this problem. Thus:

---

[7] We could complicate the problem considerably by adding a charge for carrying a part in stock, by treating the probable intervals between failures, by questioning *how many spares* should be reordered at one time, etc. All such issues, and others as well, could be treated in a realistic, but more complicated model.

| | | \multicolumn{3}{c|}{NUMBER OF FAILURES i} | |
| | | 1 | 2 | 3 | EXPECTED COST |
	p_i	$\frac{1}{3}$	$\frac{1}{3}$	$\frac{1}{3}$	
Initial	1	5	5 + 40	5 + 80	45
order size,	2	10	10	10 + 40	$23\frac{1}{3}$
k	3	15	15	15	15

The outcome entries in the matrix are computed by two different relationships. First, when the number of failures equals or is less than the number of parts originally ordered with the press, the cost is simply kc. Second, when the number of failures is greater than the number of parts originally ordered, the cost is $kc + (i - k)C_u$. For example if three failures occur ($i = 3$) and only two parts were originally ordered ($k = 2$), then the cost is $(2 \times 5) + (3 - 2)40 = 50$. After the matrix of total costs is completed, the expected values are obtained in the usual fashion (see pp. 61–62). In our example, the optimal strategy is to order three spare parts with the press. Clearly, the decision matrix lends itself nicely to representing this static[8] form of inventory problem.

CLASSIFICATION OF INVENTORY SYSTEMS

There are many significant distinctions between types of inventories that need to be made. First, let us note, there are items which are functionally critical to operations, no matter how much or how little they cost. For example, the lack of some small spare engine part could ground a 747 aircraft. The need for a cheap pump part might severely slow down a refinery.

Second, there are items that are important because their dollar volume is high. A significant division of all items under materials management is based on the recognition that some few items have high dollar volumes and many others have substantially lower dollar volumes. Figure 9.3 portrays the not unusual case where 25 percent of all items accounts for as much as 75 percent of the company's total dollar volume. This is called the A class of inventory items.

Since *dollar volume* relates directly to inventory costs, *potential savings* available as a result of better inventory policies will be far greater in this A class than in any other. This is particularly apparent when it is pointed out that the *cost of inventory studies* tends to be proportional to the *number of items* under consideration. The B class (another 25 percent of all items) may account for another 15 or 20 percent of dollar volume. The C class often deals with no more than 5 to to 10 percent of the company's total dollar volume although 50 percent of all items inventoried belong in that group. There is no commitment

---

[8] "Static" is defined in the next section.

to provide class breaks at 25 and 50 percent nor a need to abide by three classes. It is essential, however, that the production manager recognize the unequal contributions of different items in his inventory, and the fact that equivalent effort should not be spent on improving the inventory policies of all items.

Another important classification is based on the difference between *static* and *dynamic* situations. In the *static* case, only one inventory decision can be made. The spare parts model is a static case. A well-known problem that is often cited to explain the static situation is the "Christmas tree problem." The man selling Christmas trees can only place a single order for trees. Then, on Christmas day, he finds out whether he estimated exactly right, or guessed over or under. In the case of overestimated demand, salvage value is sometimes available. For example, a department store that overbuys on toys, shipped from abroad in time for the holiday season, can often sell those toys at a discount after the selling season is finished. *Dynamic* situations do not require these same considerations because the demand for such items is continuous. The problem, as we shall see, becomes one of adjusting inventory levels so as to balance the various costs that apply.

FIGURE 9-3
A representative *A-B-C* breakdown. The lion's share of dollar demand is produced by a small percentage of items.

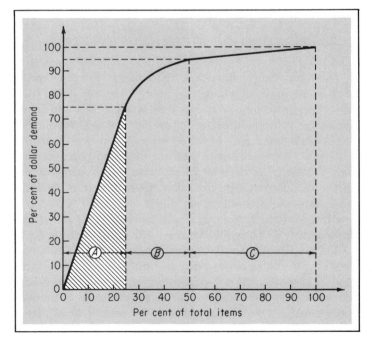

INVENTORY COSTS

The heart of inventory analysis resides in the identification of relevant costs. There are many kinds of cost that apply to the inventory situation. We shall now itemize some of those that are most frequently encountered.

1. *Cost of Ordering.* Each time a purchase requisition is drawn up, both fixed and variable costs are incurred. The fixed costs of ordering are associated with the salaries of the permanent staff of the order department. We also include investments in equipment and properly assigned overhead charges. Fixed costs are not affected by the inventory policies that are followed. The variable cost component consists of the purchase requisition form, the cost of sending this purchase requisition to the vendor; in fact, any costs that increase as the number of purchase requisitions increase. Not to be overlooked are opportunity costs associated with alternative uses of both time and equipment. Thus, the ordering cost for a self-employed shopkeeper must take into account the fact that he could be redecorating his windows, talking longer with a customer, or using his time in some other fruitful manner.

Then, by definition, as the number of orders increases, the fixed costs remain constant; the variable costs increase. For example, a company may be able to process 100 orders per week. If a new inventory policy requires that 150 purchase requisitions—on the average—be processed in a week, then the ordering department must be enlarged. The increase in labor costs and equipment and overhead is considered to be additional variable cost. In this way the ordering cost is determined on top of a base ordering system.

2. *The Cost of Carrying Inventory.* It is well known that manufacturers prefer to maintain minimum inventories. We frequently hear that in times of uncertainty companies begin to cut back on their inventory. Why is this so? The answer is that a company maintains an investment in the form of inventory. Their capital is tied up in materials and goods. If the capital were free, alternative uses might be found for it. For example, the company could take this freed capital and put it in the savings bank, thereby earning interest on the money. On the other hand, somewhat more speculative investments could be made in stocks. The company could purchase additional equipment and expand capacity, or even use this money to diversify. Thus, we see that an opportunity cost exists. By holding inventory the company foregoes investing their capital in alternative ways.

Inventory carrying costs must also include the expense of storing inventory. As was the case for the ordering department, costs should be measured from a fixed base. We must only consider the variable cost component associated with storage—the costs over which the production manager can exercise control in terms of the inventory policies. Thus, if a company has shelf space for 1000 units but can get a discount if they stock a maximum of 2000 units, then to get this discount they must expand their storage capacity, or rent additional space. An appropriate inventory cost analysis must be made to determine whether or not the discount should be taken. The extra costs incurred are a variable cost component associated with holding inventory. It should be noted that the interest charges discussed above are a variable cost which depend upon the number of units stocked, the price per unit, and the interest rate that is determined to be applicable.

Items which are carried in stock are subject to pilferage losses, obsolescence, and deterioration. These costs represent real losses in the value of inventory. Pilferage is particularly characteristic of certain items. Small items, for example, are more likely to disappear than large ones. Tool cribs are provided with attendants and frequently kept locked when the plant is shut down for the night and over the weekend. Tools have general appeal and almost universal utility. They are small enough to filch, ergo, the tool crib concept. Obsolescence can occur quite suddenly because of technological change. Or it can be the kind of loss that is associated with style goods, toys, and Christmas trees. Out of season and out of style, these items lose value and must be sold at a special reduced rate. The problem of determining how much inventory to carry will be affected by the nature of the inventories and the way in which units lose value over time. An additional component of the holding cost includes both taxes and insurance. If insurance rates and taxes are determined on a per unit basis then the amount of inventory that is stocked will determine directly the insurance and tax components of the carrying costs.

As a guide, we can furnish the following table. Hypothetical figures have been entered which are similar to the carrying cost computations of many companies in the USA. Each situation is different, and the production manager must assess those costs that apply to his situation.

A SAMPLE DETERMINATION OF CARRYING COST

Loss due to inability to invest funds in profit-making ventures, including loss of interest	14.00
Obsolescence	3.00
Deterioration	3.00
Transportation, handling, and distribution	2.00
Taxes	0.25
Storage cost	0.25
Insurance	0.25
General supplies	0.25
Pilferage	—
C_c = carrying cost expressed as percent *per year* =	23.00

3. *Cost of Out of Stock.* If a company cannot fill an order there is usually some penalty to be paid. Sometimes, the customer goes elsewhere, and the penalty is the value of the order that is lost. If this customer is annoyed because he had to do without or find a new supplier and he continues to hold a grudge against the company, then the loss of a sale plus the loss of goodwill must be translated into a cost. If the buyer is willing to wait to have his order filled, then the company treats this situation as a back order. Back orders cost money. They can annoy the customer even though he appears to be willing to wait. Many times, a company will attempt to fill the customer's order with a more expensive substitute. The cost factor is not difficult to determine in this case. Whatever the system: Fill or kill,[9] back ordering, material substitutions, and

[9] No back orders allowed.

so on, some costs of being out of stock will occur. The lost goodwill cost is considered to be one of the most significant and one of the most difficult to evaluate.

4. *Other Costs.* The above named costs are the ones that usually are considered most relevant in the determination of inventory policy. Many other costs also play a part in specific cases. Thus, for example, there are systemic costs associated with running the inventory system, costs of delays in processing orders, costs of discounts not realized, setup costs, costs of production interruptions, salvage costs, and expediting costs. In some instances, one or more of these costs will dominate the inventory policy evaluation.

ECONOMIC-ORDER-QUANTITY MODEL

Now let us see how these costs operate in an inventory system and the way in which they can be balanced so that an optimal inventory procedure is followed. We will treat a *dynamic* system under certainty where no stock outages are allowed to occur. By dynamic we mean that inventory does not lose value after a given date, such as Christmas, and that a continuing demand will exist over the long run. Figure 9.4 pictures the relationship of the order quantity x, with variable *ordering costs and carrying costs.* Let $x =$ the number of units purchased per order. We see that as the number of units that are purchased at one time increases, the carrying costs rise. This is line A. On the other hand, as the number of units per order increases the number of orders that must be placed in a year will decrease. This declining ordering cost is line B. Thus, if the demand for a particular item amounts to 500 units per year, we could order all

FIGURE 9-4
Variable ordering costs and carrying costs as a function of the order quantity, x.

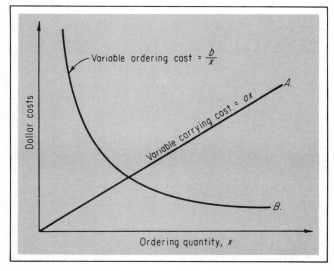

Variable ordering cost $= \dfrac{b}{x}$

Variable carrying cost $= ax$

A.

B.

Dollar costs

Ordering quantity, x

500 units at one time. Only one order would have to be placed per year. The 500 units would gradually decrease from the beginning to the end of the year so that an average of approximately 250 units would be carried in stock for that year. Figure 9.5 portrays the withdrawal pattern. The carrying cost rate must be applied to the average dollar value of the 250 units. Only one order is to be made, so the ordering cost would be incurred only once.

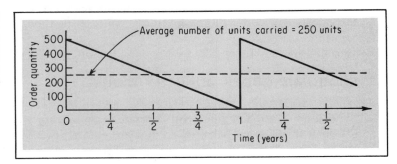

FIGURE 9-5
Continuous withdrawal pattern when x = 500 and only one order is placed per year. The demand is 500 units per year.

Now let us consider the policy of ordering twice a year. There would be 250 units ordered with each of two purchase requisitions. These 250 units get used up gradually[10] until nothing is left. At that point, the next order of 250 units arrives. The stock level shoots back up to a full bin of 250 units. Then the decline begins again until, at the end of the year, nothing is left and another new shipment will be immediately received. We now have half of the 250 units as the measure of the average number of units of inventory, viz., 125 units. The ordering cost is incurred twice but the carrying cost is applied to the smaller average inventory of only 125 units. Figure 9.6 illustrates this, and it also shows

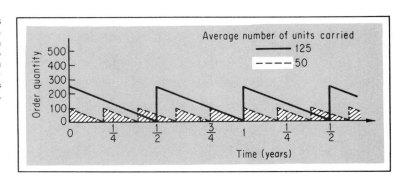

FIGURE 9-6
Continuous withdrawal pattern when x = 250 and two orders are placed each year; also when x = 100 and five orders are placed each year.

---

[10] Meaning at a regular, continuous rate. If this assumption is not met precisely, it is seldom a serious problem so long as total demand in the period is fixed in size.

what would happen with five orders per year. Each purchase requisition consists of a request for 100 units. The average number of units on hand would now be 50, and the variable cost per order is incurred five times.

In each case the total variable cost is the sum of the total variable ordering cost component and the total variable carrying cost component. Thus:

Total Cost = Total Variable Carrying Cost + Total Variable Ordering Cost

The basis of inventory theory is to write an appropriate cost equation including all possible costs, such as obsolescence, pilferage, and so on, if they apply. Then we proceed to minimize this total cost equation. It is quite clear that different costs result from different ordering policies. The smallest possible carrying charges would occur when we placed 500 orders for one unit apiece. On the other hand, a very small ordering cost could be achieved by ordering very infrequently, say once every five years.

FIGURE 9-7
The total cost resulting from different ordering policies, x, is the sum of the carrying costs, line A, and the ordering costs, line B.

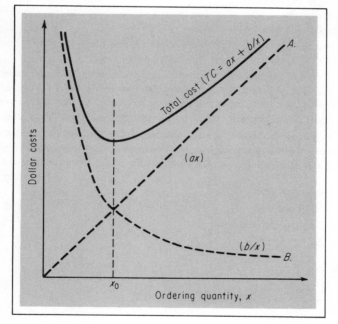

Figure 9.7 shows the plot of the total-cost equation. It is the sum of the two cost factors, ordering cost B and carrying cost A. This equation has a minimum, that is, total cost is minimized when $x = x_0$.

Let us now write an explicit equation for the total cost.

1. The average number of units carried in stock is $x/2$, where x is the number of units purchased per order.

2. The average dollar inventory carried is $cx/2$, where c is the per unit cost of the item.

3. The total carrying cost per year would be $(cx/2)C_c$, where C_c is the carrying cost rate per year (as previously described). This is the first term of the total-cost equation.

4. The number of orders placed per year is z/x, where z is the total demand per year, and x is as has been defined previously.

5. The total ordering cost per year will then be $(z/x)C_r$, where C_r is the variable cost per order. This is the second term of the total-cost equation.

We then describe the total cost (TC) as follows:

$$TC = \left(\frac{cx}{2}\right)C_c + \left(\frac{z}{x}\right)C_r$$

Or more generally: $TC = ax + b/x$. We can minimize this equation in a number of ways:

1. Using calculus, we can take the derivative of total cost with respect to x and set that quantity equal to zero (that is, $dTC/dx = 0$). This determines the point at which zero slope and therefore, Minimum TC occurs. The use of the derivative to determine either maximums or minimums is a general approach. It can be used for complex total-cost equations which have many terms involved.

2. We can use a graphical method. This requires plotting each cost component and then adding them together, as was done in Figure 9.7.

3. We could use trial and error methods, by substituting different values of x into the total cost equation until the minimum total cost was obtained. This approach has general validity for both simple and complex functions. Knowing the shape of the total cost equation helps greatly to define a logical trial and error procedure.

4. In this particular case, another approach can be employed. The minimum total cost will occur, for the specific equational form $ax + b/x$, when the total carrying cost is equal to the total ordering cost. To illustrate this point, let us assume the following values:

$C_c = 0.10$ per year

$c = \$200$ per unit

$z = 10$ units per year

$C_r = \$4$ per order

whence:

$$TC = \left(\frac{200x}{2}\right)0.10 + \left(\frac{10}{x}\right)4 = 10x + 40/x.$$

Setting $10x = 40/x$, we obtain $x^2 = 4$ and $x = 2$. Note the relevant values in the table below:

x	TC	$10x$	$40/x$
1	50	10	40
2	40	20	20
3	$43\frac{1}{3}$	30	$13\frac{1}{3}$
4	50	40	10

The minimum total cost occurs when $x = 2$. Also, for this value of x, the total carrying cost is equal to the total ordering cost, viz., 20.

We wish to stress the fact that this fourth method will only be correct when the equation to be minimized is of the form $y = ax + b/x$. Still, this particular equation provides a good description of production conditions often enough to make this simple approach to obtain a minimum y of considerable value.

More generally, we must observe that when the *rate of change* of the opposing costs is equal, that the minimum value occurs. With an additional increment of x, the carrying cost increases at a faster rate than the ordering cost decreases. When we subtract an increment of x, the ordering cost increases at a faster rate than the carrying cost decreases. Thus, at $x = 2$, the respective rates of change of the two kinds of cost are exactly balanced. This is what is meant by the statement that the marginal costs of the system are balanced. It is the underlying condition for the cost minimization.

Let us treat this approach in general terms in order to derive an equation for the optimal value of x, called x_0, which is the value of x that produces Min (TC). Setting the total carrying cost equal to the total ordering cost, we obtain:

$$\left(\frac{cx}{2}\right)C_c = \left(\frac{z}{x}\right)C_r$$

Then:

$$x^2 = \frac{2zC_r}{cC_c}$$

and

$$x_0 = \sqrt{\frac{2zC_r}{cC_c}}$$

We can illustrate the use of this formula with the same numbers that were previously employed for the example above. We get the same result, of course.

$$x_0 = \sqrt{\frac{2(10)4}{200(0.10)}} = 2$$

This inventory model provides the *economic order quantity*, EOQ. It has great utility. Even when risk does exist in the system, the EOQ model can be employed, and then a *reserve stock level* would be added. Other modifications of this model permit stock outages to occur at some fixed level. Discounts can be examined to see whether it would benefit the company to take advantage of them. When the inventory is self-supplied by the production system, rather than purchased from an external vendor, the model can be converted to indicate the optimal run size. This variant is called the economic lot size model. For all these cases, and many others as well, the appropriate value of x_0 that will produce a minimum cost can be readily determined.

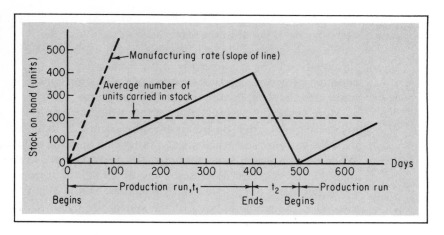

FIGURE 9-8
The economic lot size
model, ELS, is used
to determine the
optimal production
run.

ECONOMIC LOT SIZE MODEL

Having investigated the relationship that describes the optimal order quantity when purchase orders are placed with an outside vendor, let us now consider the comparable problem—identical in all respects except that the company is its own supplier. We call this formulation the economic lot-size model, ELS, because the production run quantity is called a "lot." Figure 9.8 is intended to depict the variations in stock level over time for the self-supplier situation where stock is manufactured by the company. The sharp, saw-tooth form that applied to the EOQ case, where a total shipment of stock was received at one point in time, has been replaced by a gradual stock build-up. The rate of decline would be equivalent in both situations. In this case, x_0 is the optimal run size. The cost of an order is no longer relevant. In its place we substitute C_s, which is the setup cost which is usually much larger than the order cost. Then, all other things being equal, we expect that the optimal run size would be larger than the optimal order size. The setup cost is composed of at least two parts: (1) The cost of labor required to prepare the facility for the new production run and (2) The cost of lost production occasioned by the facility being down while being prepared for the new job. In addition, we shall name two other variables:

p = production rate in units per day

d = demand rate in units per day.

The optimal run size is derived in a manner similar to the derivation of the economic order quantity, with the following result.

$$x_0 = \sqrt{\frac{2zC_s}{cC_c}\left(\frac{p}{p-d}\right)}$$

282 If d is almost equal to p, then x_0 becomes very large, approaching infinity as the difference between d and p approaches zero. This result makes sense. In effect it states: If the demand rate is as great as the production rate, then run the process continuously. On the other hand, if p is very much greater than d, that is, $p >>> d$, then x_0 equals EOQ. This result is also reasonable. The condition that is given approximates the state of being able to receive total replenishment upon request.

As an example of the ELS model, let us use the following numbers:

z = 1000 parts per year = 4 parts per day
C_s = \$200 per setup
c = \$5 per part
C_c = 0.10 per dollar per year
p = 5 parts per day = 1250 parts per year
d = 4 parts per day = 1000 parts per year

The optimal lot size, x_0, would be:

$$x_0 = \sqrt{\frac{2(1000)(200)}{5(0.10)(0.20)}} = 2000 \text{ parts}$$

LEAD TIME

FIGURE 9-9
When Lead Time (LT)
is known, at a spe-
cific level of stock
(RP), a new order
is placed.

For both economic order quantity (EOQ) and the economic lot size (ELS) systems, the lead time required to supply items for inventory must be known. In Figure 9.9, the lead time or replenishment time is called LT.

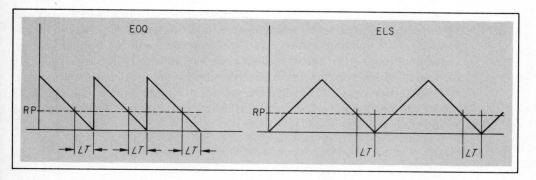

Consider the EOQ case. The obvious components of lead time include the period for recognition of the fact that it is time to reorder; the interval for doing whatever clerical work is needed (vendor releasing has advantages here, see pp. 267); mail or telephone intervals for communicating with the vendor; then,

FIGURE 9-10
Contrasting batch and
serial production
where batch produc-
tion is equivalent to
procurement.

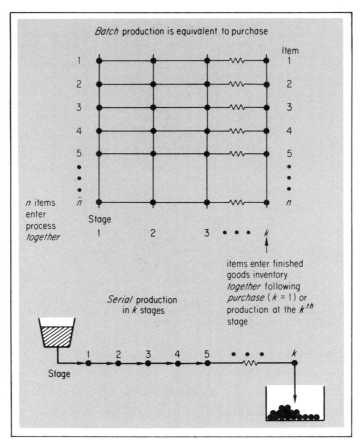

Batch production is equivalent to purchase

n items enter process *together*

Stage

items enter finished goods inventory *together* following *purchase* ($k = 1$) or production at the kth stage

Serial production in *k* stages

Stage

recognition of the order by the vendor who will see whether the requested items are in stock, and if not, will set up to make them. Next, the vendor ships the items, so there is delivery time. The items are delivered but must be processed by the receiving department which may require inspection. Until the items are entered on the warehouse stock cards, the lead time continues. Similar descriptions could be given for the ELS case, where the sometimes illusory advantages of dealing within your own firm, and thereby having greater control, appear.

It should be noted, that when the job shop configuration exists, the EOQ model can be applied to self-supply with batch production. Figure 9.10 helps to illustrate why this is so.

QUANTITY-DISCOUNT MODEL

If a quantity discount is offered, should it be taken? When does the discount potential override the selection of the optimal undiscounted order quantity x_0? By using sets of total-cost equations, it is possible to analyze whether or not a quantity discount that is offered should cancel out the x_0 value associated

with the undiscounted minimum total cost.

The discounting situation is directly reflected by the following schedule:

QUANTITY (x UNITS)	COST PER UNIT	TOTAL COST
$x = 0$ to x_1	c	$TC(c)$
$x = x_1$ and greater	c' (c' less than c)	$TC(c')$

FIGURE 9-11
The discount model involves more than one total-cost equation, but when the discount is specified only one discontinuous curve applies.

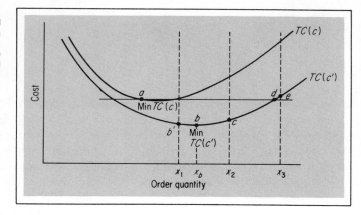

Consulting Figure 9.11, we see that two total cost equations are drawn. Note, each curve includes its own respective dollar volume cost (cz for the first curve and $c'z$ for the second curve) since dollar volume cost is a variable factor of the discount problem.

The top curve $TC(c)$ is based on an undiscounted cost, c. The bottom curve $TC(c')$ is applicable when a discount is available, *but it is only applicable at and above the quantity needed* to obtain the discount. Let x_j be the specified quantity required to obtain the discount. If x_j is x_1 in Figure 9.11, then the discount must be taken. In fact the order quantity should be increased from x_1 to x_b which intersects point b. Point b is the minimum total cost that can be obtained in the discount region. Note, the top curve applies from $x = 0$ to $x < x_1$; the bottom curve applies for $x \geq x_1$. Figure 9.12 illustrates this discontinuity. The cost of point b is lower than that of point b'. Returning to Figure 9.11, when x_j is specified at x_2, then point c provides a lower cost then point a. Point a is the minimum total cost without the discount. Point c is the lowest total cost that is available in the discount region. So x_2 units should be purchased. Again referring to Figure 9.11, if $x_j = x_3$, the intersected cost point is e which is a greater cost than a. Therefore, the order quantity corresponding to point a should be used. The same reasoning can be extended to more than one price break for quantity discounts and a purely mathematical approach can be used as well.[11] If the quantity specified for discount intersected point d,

[11] Martin K. Starr and David W. Miller, *Inventory Control: Theory and Practice* (Englewood Cliffs, N.J.: Prentice-Hall, Inc., 1962), pp. 84–86.

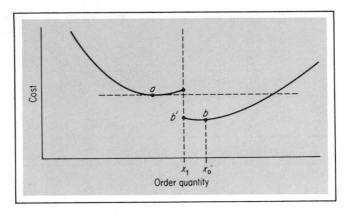

the manager (theoretically) would be indifferent between buying the small amount at point a, or buying the large amount at point d. In fact, the manager would consider a variety of intangibles such as: is the item ordinarily hard to get; is there possibility of a strike; could we corner the supply to our competitive advantage? Is there a speculative advantage? All of these notions could favor point d. On the other hand, does this item spoil easily, does it require a lot of storage space, does it experience a high pilferage rate? These last thoughts are more likely to favor purchasing the smaller quantity associated with point a.

MULTIPLE ITEMS AND AGGREGATE INVENTORIES

Inventories are seldom composed of a single item. Usually, many different items are carried in stock. Even for a single item, it is not unusual to have many associated stockkeeping units (called SKU). For example, in the category "screws," a typical manufacturer's inventory will include various lengths, diameters, number of threads to the inch, wood screws, machine screws, Phillips-head screws, brass screws, steel screws, and so on. In the same way, a department store will carry many different sizes, colors, materials, and styles of socks, and the supermarket stocks a great variety of soups and soaps.

We could, if we had enough information, obtain the optimal order quantity or lot size for each SKU. This would give us the minimum *over-all* total cost system. However, two factors intervene.

1. It costs money to study inventories and to develop policies for each SKU. From the point of view of a break-even chart, the cost of the inventory study increases fixed costs. The savings obtained from the study decrease variable costs. The resultant must represent a sufficient return on the capital invested in the inventory study to make this investment preferable to alternative investments in bonds and stocks, machinery, or additional personnel.

Because this criterion underlies all inventory studies,[12] companies seldom undertake inventory studies of all the items that are needed. Instead, as previously discussed (see pp. 273–74) the items are divided into categories—frequently called *A-B-C*.

2. The company's resources are limited. It is frequently unreasonable to carry the total average dollar inventory that the individual items' optimal policies would require. The capacity of the ordering department may be overtaxed; storage facilities may be filled to capacity; the amount of capital invested in inventory may exceed the amount that the company has available. These limitations, if they exist, require a modification of inventory policy. That is, the theoretical system's optimal is not feasible because it violates other practical system's constraints.

Let us first relax the requirement with respect to unlimited capital resources. We will assume that company policy calls for no more than $2000 to be invested in inventory, on the average. But the sum of the optimal policies for each product requires a total average inventory investment of $2600. What then should be done? The cash limit prevents the use of the individual items' optimal inventory policies. The figures for this example are given below, where $C_c = 0.24$ per year and $C_r = \$48.00$ per order.

ITEM NO. j	c_j	z_j (PER YEAR)	x_0^j	$c_j x_0^j$	$c_j x_0^j / 2 = a_j$
1	$3.50	1400	400	1400	700
2	$2.00	5000	1000	2000	1000
3	$1.00	2500	1000	1000	500
4	$2.00	800	400	800	400

A = Total Average Dollar Inventory = $2600

Let A = Total average dollar inventory, and

$\quad a_j$ = Average dollar inventory of the jth item, which has a per unit cost of c_j, a yearly demand of z_j, and an optimal order quantity of x_0^j.

Then, it can readily be shown that for a *rational* ordering policy:[13]

$$\frac{\text{average dollar inventory of an item } j}{\text{total average dollar inventory of all items}} = \frac{\sqrt{c_j z_j}}{\sum\limits_j \sqrt{c_j z_j}} = \frac{a_j}{A}$$

This important systems oriented equation states that for each item, j, a dollar volume relationship exists with the total dollar volume of all items held in inventory. Defying ordinary intuition, the proportionality is in terms of square roots. That is, the square root of j's dollar volume in ratio with the *sum of the square roots* of all items, including j, specifies the appropriate average dollar investment in j's inventory (called a_j) as a part of the total dollar inventory for all items (called A). We should note that A is not required to be an optimal

[12] And all other improvement studies as well.
[13] Starr and Miller, *Inventory Control: Theory and Practice*, pp. 93–164.

value. It is usually set by (somewhat) arbitrary policy. Managerial intuition can hardly be faulted if it finds square root proportions of parts to the whole difficult to derive. This is especially true after noting that A can be set in an arbitrary fashion. In many companies the value of A (as total company average dollar inventory) is handed down by top management according to its perception of prevailing economic and social conditions and changed without warning from time to time.

Let us derive the necessary values for our example, letting $A = \$2000$, as specified.

ITEM NO. j	$c_j z_j$	$\sqrt{c_j z_j}$	$A\sqrt{c_j z_j}/\sum_j \sqrt{c_j z_j}$	$= \dfrac{c_j x_j}{2}$
1	4,900	70	(2000)(70)/260 =	\$ 538
2	10,000	100	(2000)(100)/260 =	769
3	2,500	50	(2000)(50)/260 =	385
4	1,600	40	(2000)(40)/260 =	308
		$260 = \sum_j \sqrt{c_j z_j}$		$A = \$2000$

We can now recompute the rational order quantities directly.

ITEM NO. j	$c_j x_j/2$	x_j
1	\$538	2(538)/3.50 = 307
2	769	2(769)/2.00 = 769
3	385	2(385)/1.00 = 770
4	308	2(308)/2.00 = 308

This problem is resolved. We should order 307 units of item 1 instead of the optimal order quantity of 400. Similarly, order 769 units of item 2 instead of 1000 units; order 770 units of item 3 instead of 1000 units; and order 308 units of item 4 instead of 400 units.

The same kind of thinking can be applied to the number of orders that are placed assuming that no constraint exists for A. Thus,

$$\frac{n_j}{N} = \frac{\sqrt{c_j z_j}}{\sum_j \sqrt{c_j z_j}}$$

where n_j represents the number of orders to be placed for the jth item, and N stands for the total number of orders that can be made by the order department. This formulation is used when there is an upper limit to the capacity of the ordering department.

The reason that the multiple item inventory policies that we have just described are rational—as compared to other policies that would be irrational—is based on two points.

1. It is not irrational to find oneself unable to achieve the system's over-all optimal state because resource limitations make it impossible to operate at this over-all optimal level.

2. The existence of constraints of one kind or another, if they prohibit the use of the over-all optimal policy, imply the fact that the costs, C_c and C_r, that have been used to determine the over-all optimal policy, cannot both be correct measures of the situation. Therefore, a rational policy is one where an appropriate change in these costs would provide an optimal policy that would meet the constraints. This is what the above formulation succeeds in doing.

PERPETUAL INVENTORY SYSTEMS

The economic lot-size model and the economic order-quantity model are based on the assumption that there will be no variability in demand. In most practical instances this assumption cannot be sustained. As a result, a class of inventory models has been designed to cope with situations where the demand level fluctuates.

Many companies use perpetual inventory systems wherein withdrawal quantities are entered on the item's stock card each and every time that a unit is withdrawn from stock. The withdrawal quantity is subtracted from the previous stock level to determine the present quantity of stock on hand. A minimum level is designated as the reorder level for each item. This reorder point quantity is marked on the respective stock card. When the minimum level has been

FIGURE 9-13
A perpetual inventory system where stock on hand is recomputed with each withdrawal.

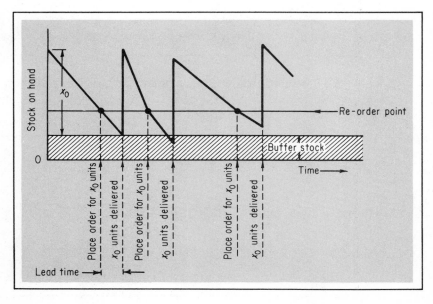

reached, then an order is placed for the economic order quantity, x_0. The level of stock represented by the reorder point is equal to the expected demand in the lead time, plus what is called the reserve stock or buffer stock. This buffer has been designed to absorb a certain percentage of the fluctuations in demand that are likely to occur for each particular item. The reserve stock is geared to provide some chosen level of protection against stock outages. The level that is chosen is based on the balance of out-of-stock costs and carrying costs associated with the reserve stock. We have drawn Figure 9.13 to illustrate the way in which a perpetual inventory system operates.

The calculation of the reorder point is not difficult to accomplish. First, as has been noted, stock must be provided to cover the expected demand *in the lead time period*. Call this *S*. Then additional buffer stock is to be provided which gives some specified level of protection against *going out of stock* in the same lead time interval. Call this additional inventory *B*. Figure 9.14 depicts the situation for a probability distribution of demand in the lead time period.

FIGURE 9-14
Determination of the reorder point. It is *S+B* units where *S* is expected demand in the Lead Time Interval.

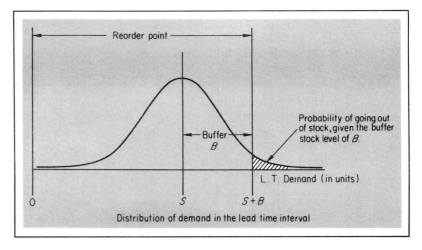

Distribution of demand in the lead time interval

The so-called two-bin system provides a clever way of continuously monitoring the reorder point in a perpetual inventory system. Figure 9.15 is almost self-explanatory in this regard.

FIGURE 9-15
A two-bin perpetual inventory system. When Bin 2 is depleted an order is placed.

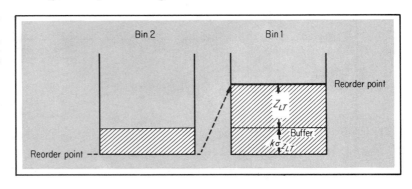

When a replenishment order is received, Bin 1 is filled to the reorder point level. The remainder of the order is placed in Bin 2. Obviously, if Bin 1 is at the reorder point level, all of the incoming items are placed in Bin 2. When Bin 2 is emptied, a new order is placed. The two bin system is not feasible for many kinds of items, but when it is, a great deal of clerical work is eliminated.

PERIODIC INVENTORY SYSTEMS

Periodic systems are based on the determination of a *fixed* and regular review period. Some items may be reviewed once a week, others once a month, semi-annually, or yearly. The optimal period is determined by $x_0/z = t_0$. Usually, certain items have shorter review periods than others. These would be items where, although the demand level is relatively high, the average stock level is kept low, because, for example, the cost per unit is high. At each review, the stock on hand is determined. An order is then placed for a *variable* quantity. This quantity is larger than usual when demand has been greater than expectation. It is smaller than usual when demand has been less than expectation. Thus, in the case of the periodic inventory model, the review period is fixed, but the order quantity is variable. Figure 9.16 illustrates the way in which a periodic ordering system functions.

FIGURE 9-16
A periodic inventory system where stock on hand is computed only at intervals. At that time, an order *x* of variable size is placed.

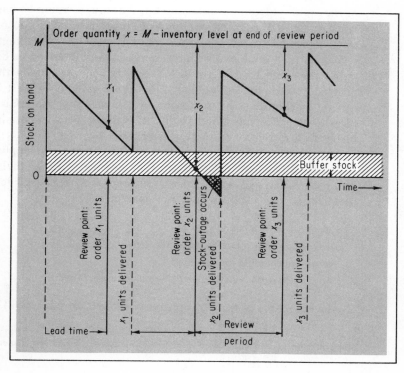

The target level M is determined by calculating the expected demand in a *review period plus one lead time interval*. To this is added buffer stock which offers protection against excessive demand in a review period plus one lead time interval. It may be noted that the same kind of reasoning applies in this case as was used with respect to Figure 9.14. In fact, when the optimal order quantity x_0 is subtracted from the target level M, the stock remaining has an expected value equivalent to the reorder point of the perpetual inventory model (although somewhat greater because the buffer stock for the *periodic model* is larger than it is for the perpetual inventory model). On the other hand, the clerical costs of the perpetual model are higher than those of the periodic model.[14] The clerical cost advantage of the periodic model disappears, however, when on-line, real-time computer systems operate the perpetual model's calculation requirements. As a result, there is a distinct trend toward perpetual systems and away from periodic ones.

VALUE ANALYSIS

Of relatively recent origin, the concept of value analysis has been widely accepted by industry. The fundamental notion of value analysis is that the quality of the production output must be maintained while at the same time the cost of the output should be decreased. Although value analysis is applied to all phases of the production process, in practice, it emphasizes the selection of the input materials. If this were not the case, it would be hard to distinguish value analysis from traditional *methods analysis* which is, according to its own title, dedicated to the study and improvement of production methods. It is inevitable that value and methods analysis must share some common ground; tackle the same kind of problems, and provide essentially the same kind of problem resolution. Undoubtedly, the recent surge of interest in value analysis can be explained, at least in part, by the fact that materials technology has been undergoing rapid and dramatic changes. New materials are constantly being made available through research efforts.

For the most part, the procedures of value analysis are applied to established products rather than to new ones. The essence of value analysis is embodied in the *high degree of organization of the approach*. This is evidenced by a structured set of relevant questions. For example:

1. What is this item intended to do?
2. How much does it cost to make this item?
3. What else could do the same job?
4. How much does the suggested alternative cost?

The taxonomy of quality, previously derived on pp. 209–14, reveals that the

---

[14] The use of the two-bin system, when it is feasible, can reduce the clerical cost of operating a perpetual inventory system because the reorder point signal is automatic. Many items, however, cannot be stored in bins and do not lend themselves to this arrangement.

problems of defining what an item is intended to do are enormously complex and not well understood. Accordingly, the utility of value analysis will be dependent upon the knowledge and creative insight that the individuals who are doing these studies can bring to bear. The value analysis approach has been designed to release such insights by providing a structural framework to encourage the development of alternative strategies. The procedural starting point is the examination of an existing output. The purposes or functions of this output are divided into primary and secondary classes. Significant functions are then related by analogy to other items and then to materials which are thought to provide similar properties.

It is through the *analogic method* that value alternatives are derived. Thus, for example, we might develop comparisons between different joining methods which include adhesion, cohesion, welding, brazing, and mechanical fastenings such as screws, nuts and bolts, lock washers, cotter pins, and nails. Harking back to decision theory, we find that *both methods analysis and value analysis* are primarily intended as a means for *discovering new tactical alternatives.* Any approach that succeeds in improving this aspect of decision making is of real importance when properly used. But we must always guard against investments in efficiency studies before effectiveness issues have been thoroughly considered.[15]

JOB SHOP MATERIALS CONTROL

In the job shop, inventory controls are often based on fulfilling a schedule in line with an outside contract or internal orders placed by other departments. The inventory models previously discussed are less well-suited to this task than are the kinds of controls developed for network models of projects (e.g., PERT).

On the other hand, the extensive complexity of the project networks differs from that of the job shop system where many jobs that are independent of each other must be kept track of simultaneously. The *line of balance* (LOB) technique

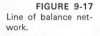

FIGURE 9-17
Line of balance network.

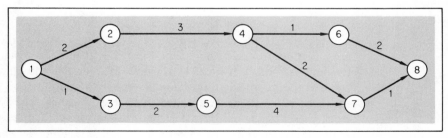

[15] For a more complete description of value analysis procedures, see Lawrence B. Miles, *Techniques of Value Analysis* (New York: McGraw-Hill Book Co., Inc., 1961).

is quite well-suited to this situation.[16] As in the critical path system this approach begins with a network of activities and events. The LOB network uses the *completion* or *delivery* of readily identifiable part components as these events. The activities between the event nodes are processing and assembly operations. Each is associated with specific time estimates as shown in Figure 9.17.

A graph of cumulative production (inventory and shipments) as promised by contract is drawn with respect to calendar time (see Figure 9.18). It should be noted that cumulative production is measured as end-product units. Therefore, if two parts are needed in a unit, that fact is taken into account in the interpretation of the charts. Present time is located on the graph and with it

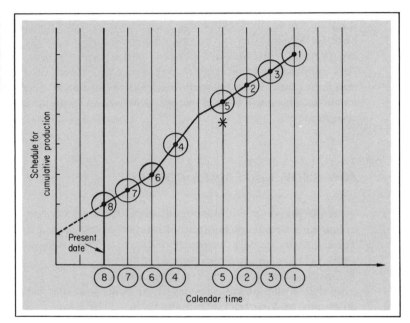

is associated the final event node of the network, 8. All other network nodes are measured from that node, and located at their proper place in time. Where the time line of each event (1 through 8) intersects the cumulative shipment curve is the appropriate inventory level for the part having the specific event number. These points are called the line of balance. The LOB describes the stock level that should have been satisfied for the part in question. Figure 9.19 illustrates these relations in another way for a different network (Shown in

---

[16] In 1941, G. Fouch at the Goodyear Company developed the LOB procedures. They were employed by the U.S. Navy during the second World War and extensively since that time.

the lower right of the Figure). This is the more conventional representation of LOB.

FIGURE 9-19
The conventional
LOB diagram.

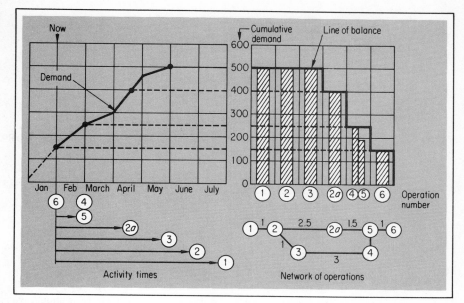

PROBLEMS

1 The C & B Food Company bottles instant coffee which it purchases periodically in quantities of 120,000 lbs. The coffee mixture costs C & B $0.40 per lb. The company ships 1,200,000 one-pound bottles of instant coffee per year to its distributors. The demand is constant and continuous, over time. What carrying cost (in percent per month) is implied by the above policy if an order costs $100 on the average? Discuss your result.

2 Under what circumstances would you prefer a periodic inventory system to a perpetual system?

3 For the spare-part failure model (pp. 272–73) assume that a salvage cost of $2 now exists. Would this alter the solution to the problem?

4 If, in a dynamic inventory problem under certainty the costs are:

c = $10 per item
C_c = 16 percent per year
z = 5000 units per year
C_r = $10 per order

What is the optimal order quantity? Now, assume that you are going to make this same item with equipment that is estimated to produce p = 30 units per day. Also, c then equals $6 per item and C_s = $150 per setup. How has your answer changed? What would you do?

5   A quantity discount schedule has been offered for the situation discussed in Problem 4. It is:

c	x_j
10	up to 300
9	300
8	500

Should either of these discounts be taken?

6   A multiple item inventory problem is based on the following A-type units.

i	z_j	c_j
1	20	6
2	40	10
3	60	15
4	80	9

The costs of carrying and ordering are unknown. How should we proceed?

references

ALFANDRY-ALEXANDER, MARK, *An Inquiry Into Some Models of Inventory Systems.* Pittsburgh, Penn.: University of Pittsburgh Press, 1962.

ALJIAN, GEORGE W. (ed.) *Purchasing Handbook.* New York: McGraw-Hill, Inc., 1958.

AMERICAN MANAGEMENT ASSOCIATION, *Managing the Materials Function.* Report No. 35, Mfg. Division, AMA, N. Y., 1959.

AMMER, DEAN S., *Materials Management.* Homewood, Ill.: Richard D. Irwin, Inc., 1962.

ARROW, K., KARLIN, S., and H. SCARF, *Studies in the Mathematical Theory of Inventory and Production.* Stanford, Calif.: Stanford University Press, 1958.

BROWN, R. G., *Decision Rules for Inventory Management.* New York: John Wiley & Sons, Inc., 1965.

————, *Statistical Forecasting for Inventory Control.* New York: McGraw-Hill, Inc., 1961.

BUCHAN, J., and E. KOENIGSBERG, *Scientific Inventory Management.* Englewood Cliffs, N.J.: Prentice-Hall, Inc., 1962.

BUFFA, E. S., *Operations Management: Problems and Models* (2nd ed.). New York: John Wiley & Sons, Inc., 1968.

CADY, E. L., *Industrial Purchasing.* New York: John Wiley & Sons, Inc., 1945.

ENGLAND, WILBUR B., *Procurement* (4th Ed.). Homewood, Ill.: Richard D. Irwin, Inc., 1962.

FETTER, ROBERT B., and WINSTON C. DALLECK, *Decision Models for Inventory Management.* Homewood, Ill.: Richard D. Irwin, Inc., 1961.

GAVETT, J. W., *Production and Operations Management.* New York: Harcourt Brace Jovanovich, 1968.

HADLEY, G., and T. WHITIN, *Analysis of Inventory Systems.* Englewood Cliffs, N.J.: Prentice-Hall, Inc., 1963.

HANSSMANN, F., *Operations Research in Production and Inventory Control*. New York: John Wiley & Sons, Inc., 1961.

HEINRITZ, S. F., and P. V. FARRELL, *Purchasing: Principles and Applications* (5th Ed.). Englewood Cliffs, N.J.: Prentice-Hall, Inc., 1971.

HILLIER, F. S., and G. J. LIEBERMAN, *Introduction to Operations Research*. San Francisco: Holden-Day, Inc., 1967.

HOLT, C., MODIGLIANI, F., MUTH, J., and H. SIMON, *Planning Production, Inventories and Work Force*. Englewood Cliffs, N.J.: Prentice-Hall, Inc., 1960.

HOTTENSTEIN, M. P., *Models and Analysis for Production Management*. Scranton, Pa.: International Textbook Co., 1968.

MCGARRAH, R. E., *Production and Logistics Management*. New York: John Wiley & Sons, Inc., 1963.

MAGEE, JOHN F. and DAVID M. BOODMAN, *Production Planning and Inventory Control*. New York: McGraw-Hill Book Co., Inc., 1967.

MASSÉ, P., *Les Reserves a la Regulation de l'Avenir* dans la Vie Economique, (2 vols.), Hermann, Paris, 1946.

MILES, L. D., *Techniques of Value Analysis*. New York: McGraw-Hill, Inc., 1961.

MORAN, P. A., *The Theory of Storage*. London: Methuen & Co., Ltd., 1959.

MORSE, P. M., *Queues, Inventories, and Maintenance*. New York: John Wiley & Sons, Inc., 1958.

PRICHARD, J., and R. H. EAGLE, *Modern Inventory Management*. New York: John Wiley & Sons, Inc., 1965.

RICHMOND, S. B., *Operations Research for Management Decisions*. New York: The Ronald Press Co., 1968.

STARR, MARTIN K., and DAVID W. MILLER, *Inventory Control—Theory and Practice*. Englewood Cliffs, N. J.: Prentice-Hall, Inc., 1962.

TEICHROEW, D., *An Introduction to Management Science*. New York: John Wiley & & Sons, Inc., 1964.

WAGNER, H. M., *Statistical Management of Inventory Systems*. New York: John Wiley & Sons, Inc., 1962.

WELSH, W. E., *Tested Scientific Inventory Control*. Greenwich, Conn.: Management Publishing Co., 1961.

WHITIN, THOMSON M., *The Theory of Inventory Management* (2nd ed.). Princeton, N.J.: Princeton University Press, 1953.

chapter
ten
quality
management

Production managers conceive of their field as requiring the *development* and *operation* of a process for *getting work done*. In their opinion, the organization has entrusted them with the responsibility of transforming *input* resources into a desired set of *outputs*. The transformation *process* is to be accomplished in a manner that is most compatible with the company's objectives. The production manager interprets this to mean that the outputs should be of some *assured level of quality* produced at a *minimum cost*.

Quality was discussed at some length in Chapter 7 (see pp. 209-14). The discussion was concerned solely with the consumers' view of value desired and value received. Such a view of quality is *marketing* oriented, requiring the full coordination of production and marketing. The production manager acts as liaison between research and development and the consumer.

But in this chapter we shall be discussing the production manager's *view of quality*. A close approximation to this use of the term quality is *consistency*. A set of standards is defined and all units of production must consistently meet those standards. The consumer may consider such standards to be evidence of low or high quality. The consumer's concern is product service, performance, appearance, etc. The production manager's quality concern, however, is that he meets specifications, *whatever* they may be.

To achieve specified output quality, two basic factors must be treated. The first is that the quality of *input* materials must be maintained at designed levels (i.e., this is quality in the production manager's sense). Second, the *process* must be controlled to deliver the desired output quality.

INPUT QUALITY

First, let us consider that important quality management function of inspecting incoming materials to make certain that they conform to quality specifications. Input standards must be stated explicitly, according to the needs of the process for workable materials and to *insure* that process outputs will satisfy market expectations.

COSTS OF DEFECTIVE INPUTS

Inferior materials create many kinds of costs. For example:

1. *Cost of Unusable Items.*
2. *Cost of Not Having a Part When It is Needed.* The item is thought to be in stock, but in actuality it is not. Only a *"stock phantom"* is on hand which cannot do the required job. This cost can be severe. For example, assume that a generator part, known to fail occasionally, is carried in stock at a quantity level in excess of expected usage. (Specifically, see pp. 271–73 for discussion of the appropriate inventory model.) The high inventory level is geared to the fact that if no spare is on hand, then the generator is shut down. So a large buffer stock is maintained. Then, a failure of this part occurs. The repair team discovers that all the spares are faulty and cannot be used. They should have been inspected when they were received. In the same way, if a company manufactures a product that requires a raw material, or a subcontracted subassembly which is found to be unusable when it is needed, then production is stopped until a new and usable supply can be obtained.
3. *Cost of Disgruntled Customers.* In this case, we assume that the quality of the purchased items does not affect the production process but does affect the final unit. It is the consumer who perceives the difference in quality. It is the producer of the final unit who receives and deserves full blame—with consequent losses—for having passed the inferior material along to the consumer. The vendor of the inferior items enjoys relative anonymity. Inspection of the purchased item could have avoided this cost, but then, in turn, there is an *inspection cost.*

Proper management of the inspection function is based on the need to balance various costs. We spend as much on the inspection process as would be required to offset penalities of the types described above. If it were possible to develop a model that could describe the enterprise as a whole, then materials inspection costs would be part of this model, interacting with many terms. As it is, the best that we can do is to isolate this inspection subsystem and attempt to minimize its characteristic total costs.

ONE HUNDRED PERCENT INSPECTION

Total, or 100 percent inspection, has higher inspection costs than inspecting some portion (a sample) of all items. Such higher costs might be justified if increased accuracy is derived as a result of using 100 percent inspection and the *penalty* for being inaccurate is large. However, total inspection is *seldom the most accurate* method that can be followed. It has been found that 100 percent inspection tends to produce *carelessness* and error due to *fatigue*. The inspector's human debilities become apparent when there are many items to be totally inspected. Furthermore, 100 percent inspection is out of the question where *destructive testing* is required. A manufacturer of fire crackers, bullets, a food product, or soap flakes cannot destroy (eat, taste, make suds, etc.) his total shipment in order to find out if each item comes up to the standards that he has set. In any case, 100 percent inspection, whether it be done by man or machine, is slow, costly, and frequently unreliable—even when it is possible. On the other hand, for a few truly critical items (where performance is a matter of life and death) 200 or 300 percent inspection might be insufficient. Especially, in the project shop (e.g., moon shots), repeated inspection with crosschecks is deemed essential.

SAMPLING INSPECTION TERMINOLOGY

At Western Electric Company in the 1920's, a growing body of statistical theory was used to develop *sampling plans* that could be employed as substitutes for 100 percent inspection. These sampling inspection techniques were applied to purchased and subcontracted parts, raw materials, office supplies, and maintenance parts; and, they could also be used by a producer to conduct sample tests of his own output.[1] The only kinds of sampling procedures that had been used before this were *proportional sampling methods*, which are *completely* wrong in concept (though apparently intuitively appealing to many). Before we can explain why this is so, let us develop the terms and symbols necessary for discussing sampling plans:

1. $N = $ *The lot size.* This is usually the total number of items produced by the vendor within a single shipment. More generally, it can be the total production run of the producer for which the conditions of the system remained essentially unchanged. Thus, it is assumed that the *quality of items within a lot is homogeneous.* This means that the average number of defectives produced by the process does not change from the beginning to the end of the run. The average fraction of defective parts (or average percent) is called the process average and symbolized by $\bar{p}$.

---

[1] At about the same time, the sequential test methods of statistical quality control were being developed. These are more frequently used by a producer to evaluate and control his own output. See pp. 310-27.

2. $n = $ *the sample size*. The items to be inspected should be a representative sample drawn at random from the lot. We don't just inspect material that happens to be at the top of the box. Housewives have always known this when they buy strawberries; managers have not always been so astute.

3. $c = $ *the sample criterion*. This criterion is defined so that when n items are drawn from a lot size of N, and k items are found to be defective, then if $k > c$, we reject the entire lot. If $k \leqslant c$, we accept the lot. Therefore, c is sometimes called the acceptance number of the sampling plan.

PROPORTIONAL SAMPLING

The underlying assumption of proportional sampling is that if we had two lots, A and B, and A was twice as large as B, then we should draw twice as large a sample from A as from B. In effect, the percent of a lot to be inspected was fixed, say at $n/N = K$. If any rejects were found, then the total lot was to be rejected, that is, $c = 0$ was the acceptance number that was used. Operating characteristic curves (called OC curves), a few samples of which are shown in Figure 10.1, clearly demonstrate that the proportional sampling concept is fallacious.

FIGURE 10-1
Operating Characteristic (OC) curves for several proportional sampling plans. In all these cases $c = 0$ and the proportion sampled is 20 percent.

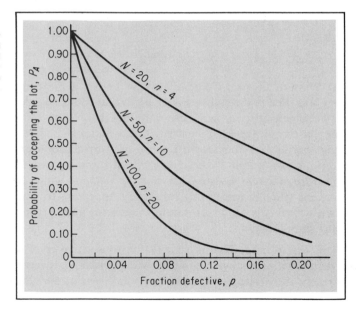

The horizontal axis is the *actual fraction defective* in the lot, called p. The OC curve shows how P_A, the probability of accepting the lot, changes with respect to p for a number of different sampling plans, all of which utilize the same sampling proportion of $n/N = 0.20$ and the same acceptance number,

$c = 0$. Thus, these plans, all of which are based on the *policy* of proportional sampling, produce significantly different results. The probability of accepting a lot of 20 items is much higher than the probability of accepting a lot of 50 items, and more so for 100 items—when proportional sampling is used. This is not an acceptable condition for inspection.

What sampling method should be used then to manage input qualities? The answer is that by choosing appropriate values for n and c, we can develop an *OC* curve that should be acceptable to both the vendor and the buyer. The definition of what is acceptable cannot be the decision of the buyer alone. The situation calls for compromise and *negotiation* between the vendor and the purchaser. Reference to Figure 10.2 shows what is involved.

FIGURE 10-2
Consumer's and pro-
ducer's risks, shown
in this *OC* curve, are
determined by nego-
tiation.

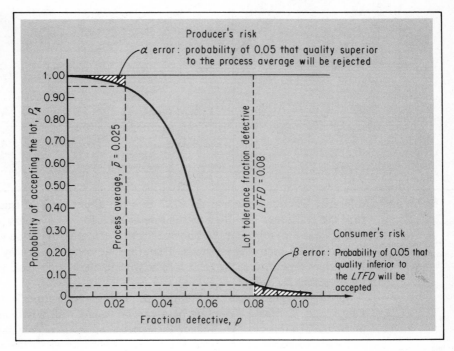

PRODUCER'S AND CONSUMER'S RISKS

The two shaded areas marked α and β are two different kinds of risk. The α area is called the *producer's risk*. It gives the probability that quite acceptable lots will be rejected. Specifically, it gives the probability that lots having a lower fraction of defectives than are normally produced by the process (i.e., the process average, $\bar{p}$) will be rejected by the sampling plan that is shown. On the other hand, the β area represents the probability that unacceptable levels of lot quality will be accepted by the sampling plan. Reasonably enough, this is called the *consumer's risk*. The limiting value, defined by the consumer, is called the lot

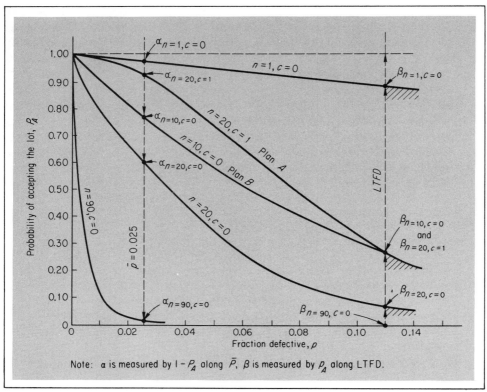

Note: α is measured by $1 - P_A$ along $\bar{P}$, β is measured by P_A along LTFD.

FIGURE 10-3
As the sample size increases, all other factors remaining constant, the plan becomes increasingly discriminating from the point of view of the consumer, that is, β approaches zero, but the cost of inspection increases rapidly as α approaches one. For a given level of β protection there is a sampling plan that minimizes the cost of inspection. Thus, for LTFD = 0.12 and β equals 0.26, Plan A has a lower cost of inspection than Plan B.

tolerance fraction defective, *LTFD*.[2] It is the upper limit of fraction defectives that the consumer is willing to tolerate in each lot. Above this point, he would like to reject all lots. But, he knows that this is impossible if he wishes to utilize inspection by sampling methods. Therefore, he compromises by saying that no more than β percent of the time does he wish to allow such quality to get through his *sampling procedure*.

Given a certain process average, $\bar{p}$, and the consumer's specification of *LTFD* and β, then a sampling plan can be found which *minimizes the cost of inspection*. In this cost, we include the expense of *detailing*, which is the operation of totally inspecting (100 percent) all *rejected lots* to remove the defective pieces. Such a sampling plan imputes a dollar value to the probability of falsely rejecting lots of acceptable quality (i.e., α). If the producer wishes to decrease his α-type risk, he can do so by improving the process average, $\bar{p}$. But, an improvement of this kind may be costly. It is likely that the consumer would be forced to accept part of this increased cost in the form of higher prices. Whether it is the producer or the consumer who bears the cost of inspection—or if they share it—they must agree that the only rational procedure to be followed is to minimize inspection costs and negotiate about the values for *LTFD* and β. Under some circumstances, they might also consider improvements that can be made in $\bar{p}$.

It is important to observe that any sampling plan, of a specific c and n, completely specifies the α and β risks for given levels of $\bar{p}$ and *LTFD*. In turn, the

[2] (If percent defective is used instead of fraction defective the limit is often called *LTPD*.)

sampling plan requires *n* inspections for every lot. If the process average, $\bar{p}$, is the true state of affairs, then α percent of the time the remainder of the lot will be inspected. Thus, the average number of pieces inspected will be: $n + (N - n)\alpha$.

As *n* gets large and approaches *N*, all other factors remaining constant, then the plan becomes increasingly discriminating and α approaches one. The effect is illustrated in Figure 10.3. This results in the average number of pieces to be inspected approximating *N*. On the other hand, we observe that as *n* gets small, approaching one, β increases rapidly and approaches one, while α tends to become zero. In this case, the average number of pieces that will be inspected will be negligible but the consumer's risk will be high. In between these extremes, there exist appropriate values of *c* and *n* that will minimize the average number of pieces to be inspected for some specified level of consumer protection. Thus, in Figure 10.3, Plan *A* requires $[20 + 80(.06)] = 24.8$ pieces to be inspected, on the average; Plan *B* requires $[10 + 90(.21)] = 28.9$ pieces to be inspected. Both Plans provide the same consumer risk.

CONSTRUCTING ACCEPTANCE SAMPLING PLANS

How are the kinds of plans that we have been discussing constructed? One of the most direct approaches is to utilize tables that have been designed for this purpose.[3] On the other hand, *OC* curves can be derived directly from appropriate mathematical statements. The Hypergeometric distribution is used when

FIGURE 10-4
When the lot size, N, is reasonably large, say approximately 1000, the assumption of an infinite lot size does not introduce great inaccuracy into the sampling plan. The Binomial and Poisson methods for deriving *OC* curves assume that $N = \infty$.

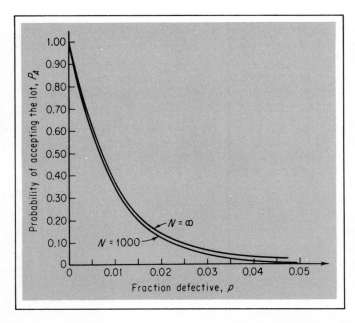

[3] Harold F. Dodge and Harry G. Romig, *Sampling Inspection Tables, Single and Double Sampling* (New York: John Wiley & Sons, Inc., 1951).

the lot size N is small so that the effect of successively sampling N units, $N - 1$ units, $N - 2$ units, etc., can be recognized. When N is sufficiently large, the Binomial distribution or the Poisson distribution can be used. Neither the Binomial nor the Poisson distributions require specification of N, since in both formulations it is assumed to be infinitely large.

Figure 10.4 illustrates the fact that when N equals 1000, the assumption of an infinite N does not introduce great inaccuracy into the sampling plan. In fact, it is frequently quite reasonable to use mathematical methods based upon an infinite lot size when N is equal to much less than 1000.

Consider the following simple Hypergeometric formula for a sampling plan with acceptance number $c = 0$.

$$P_A = \frac{(N - x)! \, (N - n)!}{(N - x - n)! \, N!}$$

where $x =$ the *number* of defectives actually in the lot and x/N is, therefore, the actual fraction defective of the lot.

As we vary x from 0 to N, we determine the different values of P_A that are associated with each level of fraction defectives. Thus, in the case where $N = 4$, $n = 1$ and $c = 0$, the formula for P_A would be:

$$P_A = \frac{(4 - x)! \, 3!}{(3 - x)! \, 4!} = \frac{(4 - x)!}{4(3 - x)!} = \frac{4 - x}{4}.$$

Then, for the different values of x we would get:

x	$x/N = p$	P_A
0	0.00	1.00
1	0.25	0.75
2	0.50	0.50
3	0.75	0.25
4	1.00	0.00

We can illustrate the Binomial computation of the OC curve quite readily. For the situation where $c = 0$, the Binomial formulation becomes:

$$P_A = (1 - p)^n$$

As previously noted, there is no provision for specifying the lot size, N. Then, when $n = 1$, we obtain, $P_A = (1 - p)$. In this case, the results are *identical* with those derivedfor the hypergeometric distribution above. (See pp. 124–26 for further discussion of the Binomial distribution.)

AVERAGE OUTGOING QUALITY LIMIT (AOQL)

In some systems, quality management is assisted by the idea of an average outgoing quality (AOQ). This is a measure of the average or expected percentage of defective items that the producer will ship to the consumer under different conditions of percent defectives.

First, every sampled lot is divided into n units to be inspected, and the remaining $(N - n)$ units. The probable number of defectives in the unsampled portion $(N - n)$ is $\bar{p}(N - n)$. Out of every hundred samples we expect that P_A will be the fraction that is passed without any further examination. These are the only units that cannot be tagged as defectives and replaced (in the sense of detailing). Then, $P_A\bar{p}(N - n)$ is the *expected number of defectives* that will be passed without having been identified *for* every N units processed.

As another approach, the percentage $P_A p(N - n)/N$ is used. This percentage is called the AOQ (average outgoing quality) and it changes value as p does. Note that the value of P_A changes with p in accordance with the specifics of the sampling plan which are based on the values of n and c that are chosen. Thus, AOQ is a function of all of the elements of a sampling plan and can, therefore, be used as a means of evaluating a sampling plan. Specifically, for each value of p an AOQ measure is derived. It is the expected value of the percent defectives that would be passed without detection *if* the process were operating at the value p. The AOQ measure reaches a maximum value for some particular value of p. The maximum value is termed the average outgoing quality limit, (AOQL).

For example, consider the following computations using our previous (Hypergeometric and Binomial) results:

p	P_A	$(N - n)/N$	AOQ
0	1	$\frac{3}{4}$	0
$\frac{1}{4}$	$\frac{3}{4}$	$\frac{3}{4}$	$\frac{9}{64}$
$\frac{1}{2}$	$\frac{1}{2}$	$\frac{3}{4}$	$\frac{12}{64}$ (AOQL)
$\frac{3}{4}$	$\frac{1}{4}$	$\frac{3}{4}$	$\frac{9}{64}$
1	0	$\frac{3}{4}$	0

Perhaps another example, based on a more refined Hypergeometric *OC* curve would help. In this case $N = 50$, $n = 10$ and $c = 0$.

p	P_A	$(N - n)/N$	AOQ
0	1.000	0.8	0.00000
0.04	0.637	0.8	0.02038
0.10	0.311	0.8	0.02488 (AOQL)
0.11	0.242	0.8	0.02130
0.20	0.083	0.8	0.01328
$\vdots$	$\vdots$	$\vdots$	$\vdots$

The maximum value of AOQ has been calculated as 0.02488. It is the **AOQL** also shown on Figure 10.5.

The average outgoing quality limit (AOQL) describes the worst case of percent defectives that can be shipped assuming that the defectives of rejected lots are replaced with acceptable products and that all lots are thoroughly mixed so that shipments have homogeneous quality.

FIGURE 10-5
The average outgoing
quality as a function
of process defective
rate p with the limit
AOQL occurring at
0.02488.

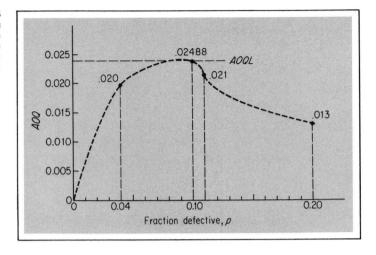

MULTIPLE SAMPLING

Other types of sampling plans are utilized when the amount of inspection required by the single sampling plan appears to be too great. By single-sampling plan, we mean that the acceptance decision must be made on the basis of the first sample drawn. Using double sampling, a second sample can be drawn, if desired. And, in general, with double sampling, inspection costs can be lowered.

The double-sampling plan requires two acceptance numbers, c_1 and c_2 such that $c_2 > c_1$. Then, if the observed number of rejects in the first sample of size n_1 is k_1:

1. We accept the lot if $k_1 \leq c_1$;
2. We reject the lot if $k_1 > c_2$.
3. If $c_1 < k_1 \leq c_2$, then we draw an additional sample of size n_2. The total sample is now of size $n_1 + n_2$. If the observed number of rejects in the total sample is $k_1 + k_2$, then:
4. We accept the lot if $(k_1 + k_2) \leq c_2$;
5. We reject the lot if $(k_1 + k_2) > c_2$.

Figure 10.6 illustrates the way in which double sampling divides the graph space into unique acceptance and rejection regions.

There are also multiple sampling plans and sequential sampling plans. Tables exist[4] which enable a manager to choose an appropriate plan without having to engage in substantially onerous mathematical calculations.

[4] For example, Dodge and Romig, *Sampling Inspection Tables.*

The criterion for choosing a plan has been implicit throughout our discussion. That is, there is some inspection cost per piece which can vary greatly, depending upon the nature of the item and the *definition of a reject*. The definition of a reject is unlikely to be a straightforward matter. Given such a definition, it might require days of testing to determine whether an item is acceptable. For

FIGURE 10-6
Characteristics of a double sampling plan. [*From Eugene L. Grant,* Statistical Quality Control, 3rd ed. (New York: McGraw-Hill Book Co., Inc., 1964), p. 346.]

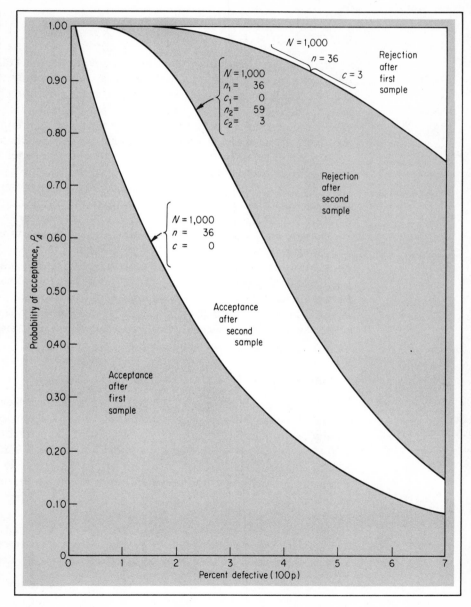

example, a reject might be defined as a unit possessing any three flaws where 100 different kinds of flaws could occur.

It is both instructive and fascinating to see how so many different factors come together in a discussion of this kind. We observe that the process average, the quality expectations, the inspection cost, and the market's acceptance of the output are tightly interwoven and that any approach to production management decision making which bypasses *synthesis* of these issues is bound to be absurd.

OUTPUT QUALITY

Inputs and process are more or less invisible to the market. The impressions of a company that the consumer forms are almost totally dependent on the outputs. Companies do arrange for the consumer to visit their plants or research labs, so that he can be convinced of the efforts taken on his behalf. But on the whole, the consumer's response is not a function of such impressions. Only as the output is a reflection of sound product design, production planning and control does the consumer respond to the company's image. Thus, the willingness of the consumer to pay a given price for an item, his willingness to repurchase the item, and his word of mouth opinions about a particular company's product—all these result from what he perceives in the output.

What is visible in the output? Quality, in its infinite variety, is both difficult to measure and sometimes impossible to define. We must include: functionability, appearance, service offered by the company, the coverage and the period of guarantee, maintenance requirements, and many other factors, (see pp. 209–14). The second consideration concerns how the output volume changes over a period of time and where this output is directed. Included are such *distribution* factors as delivery date, product availability, and the treatment of back orders. Plainly stated, the production manager is responsible for *both* quality control and schedule control.

THE SHEWHART OUTPUT QUALITY MONITOR

As previously mentioned (see pp. 119–20) Walter Shewhart[5] developed a quality control model which completely altered the nature of industrial quality performance. The primary component of this model is a *monitor* which is able to determine whether or not a stable system exists. The Shewhart model *monitors* a process to determine whether or not the system is regularly meeting expectations; delivering the specified outcome within the expected range of variation; and achieving the manager's objectives while maintaining a stable process.

In essence, the monitor distinguishes between the many, small, random factors that perturb but cannot be removed from a system and the relatively large causal factors which are called *assignable causes of variation*. Something

---

[5] W. A. Shewhart, *Statistical Method from the Viewpoint of Quality Control*, W. E. Deming, ed. (Washington, D.C.: Department of Agriculture, 1939).

can and must be done about assignable causes since they are both unwanted and identifiable. The Shewhart monitor, using the methodology of statistical quality control can tell us that something seems to be changing; that the system no longer appears to be following an established (stable) pattern. This is very vital information. Figure 10.7 locates the Shewhart monitor within the flows of the control system.

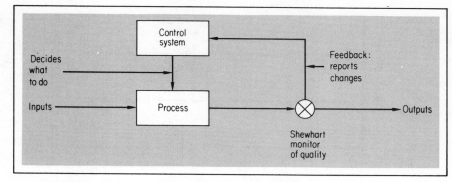

ASSIGNABLE AND CHANCE CAUSES OF VARIATION

Assignable causes of variation are disturbances that can enter the system and remain undetected until large penalties have to be paid for the poor quality of production that has occurred. The Shewhart control monitor is designed to recognize that such assignable disturbances have occurred. Once spotted, assignable causes ordinarily can be removed. At the same time, other causes of variation exist in almost all systems and nothing can be done about them. They are called *chance causes of variation* which can neither be discerned nor removed. Chance causes arise from so many infinitesimal sources that even if a few were found and something done about them, the over-all effect would be negligible. (In prior discussion, pp. 119–20, they were attributed to subatomic phenomena.) It is vital that the manager be able to *separate* the two types of causes of variation and not confuse or lump them together.

The Shewhart model establishes a procedure for determining whether the variation that is observed is as small as it can be. That is, whether the observed variability is the result only of chance cause factors, or whether there is trouble in the system about which something can be done. This control monitor provides differentiation between types of disturbances. It is expected that the output of a determinate machine will produce a stable set of characteristics in the product. But various things can happen. A tool can shift position. The quality of material that is being worked on can change.

Shewhart proposed the notion that by measuring a *sequence* of outputs in terms of a specified characteristic, it would be possible to derive *control limits* that describe the range of process behaviors that *should* be expected *if* the process were stable (see Figure 10.8). Observations are made of the process. As long as the observed values fall within the control limits and do so *without discernible patterns,* no disturbance to the system is believed to have occurred. Thus, as long as the measurements of outputs produced by the system fall between the limits and give evidence of purely random behavior, the process is called stable. When the observed results no longer appear to be random—one test of which is that they fall outside the limits—then the system is termed *out of control* and managerial action is called for.

FIGURE 10-8
Prototype of a con-
trol chart.

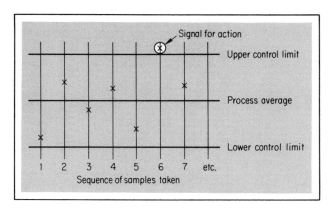

A pertinent aspect of statistical control is the fact that *many* production systems, when they are first translated from design to practice and monitored by the Shewhart control model are revealed to be out of control. By making judicious changes in the *system's design,* the process can be brought gradually under control. Thereafter, it can be monitored for new disturbances that might enter the system.

INSPECTION STANDARDS

There is a *technology* of inspection which is no more appropriate to our present discussion than are the specific technologies of production processes. The production manager is primarily involved with the *concept of specifications,* although in practice this will be translated into a large variety of detailed technical specifications such as hardness, tensile strength, color, and surface finish. To measure these characteristics he must provide his departments with appropriate instruments such as gauges, micrometers, optical comparators, and devices for measuring hardness, tensile strength, and surface finish. These physical outputs are visible and can be measured. It is expected that they will conform to some set of specifications such as are communicated by a blueprint.

In some production areas, however, the specification of output quality is a far more elusive matter than can be dealt with by blueprints. Thus, the problem of providing exact and measurable quality specifications for the tastes of foods, or the odors of perfumes is exceedingly difficult.[6] The derivation of a standard against which quality can be measured is the goal in every case. But, only if standards can be found is it possible to measure quality. Thus, for example, the Food and Drug Administration (FDA) is required to develop and enforce standards that protect the consumer from hazards that he could not otherwise perceive. Setting such standards is not an easy matter, but once they are set, food and drug samples can then be tested to see whether they meet the selected standards. It is not unusual for these standards to be changed as additional laboratory or usage information is acquired. In a somewhat different sense, we have standard yards, standard meters, standard footcandles, and standard colors. Standard intervals between standardized maintenance procedures are specified by government fiat for aircraft.[7]

The realization of standard designs can only exist when quality standards are met. The fact that more than one company subscribes to a set of quality standards accounts for the fact that Company *C* can use a bolt manufactured by Company *A* and a nut manufactured by Company *B*. Standard designs for gauges have been generally accepted and are described as American Gauge Design Standards. Standard bulb sizes, screw threads, radio tubes, flash-light batteries, etc., are related to the interchangability of parts between companies and across industries. The acceptance of such quality standards has had an enormous effect on the growth of industry. Now, we must introduce the question: How should we monitor *and control* our own output to assure consistent achievement of quality standards?

SEQUENCED INSPECTION

We must find out how the Shewhart monitor is used in the areas that statistical quality control is designed to handle. We do not draw samples at random from a homogeneous lot, as we did for acceptance sampling. Instead, it is essential to monitor the *sequence* of the output. For acceptance sampling, the assumption of homogeneity of the vendor's output was assumed. For our own production process, we no longer make this assumption. On the contrary, we ask ourselves: Does our process exhibit homogeneity? If the answer is yes, we then ask: Is our product meeting quality standards? If, again, the answer is yes, then we query: How can we guarantee that it will continue to be homogeneous and of specified quality?

Quality control is an on-going process inspection procedure. It is a *sequential sampling method* which is more powerful in many ways than 100 percent inspection. To insure control, the feedback link shown in Figure 10.7 is required. The inspection operation costs money; and the gain to be derived from this expense at least must offset the costs incurred. Inspection exists of two basically different types. Each has different costs and abilities. Not unexpectedly, the more expensive procedures promise greater responsiveness and control. The

---

[6] For an interesting discussion with respect to these problems of taste and smell, see *Flavor Research and Food Acceptance,* sponsored by Arthur D. Little, Inc. (New York: Rhinehold Publishing Corp., 1958).

[7] Rulings of the Federal Aviation Administration (FAA).

added costs (as usual) occur because greater amounts of more refined information are required.

1. *Classification by Attributes.* This is achieved by sorting the output by type. Thus, for example, we might divide our output into rejects and nonrejects, good and bad, "go" or "no go," or some other binary division. We followed this procedure with acceptance sampling. The definition used to define a defective unit of output may be very complex, nevertheless, the eventual label placed on each unit is *limited* to either accepted or defective.

2. *Classification by Variables.* In this case, *exact* scaled measurements are made of particular variables such as length, hardness, weight, thermal conductivity, thermal expansion, electrical resistivity, dielectrical strength, melting point, modulus of elasticity, impact strength, creep strength, and a variety of other physically measurable quantities for which some standard measure and measuring device are available.

SQC CALCULATIONS

No matter how well-designed a system is, there will always be some variation from a standard level of performance. Consequently, it is only logical to set the standard as a range. That is why, on blueprints, one sees tolerance ranges stated for specific dimensions, for example, 2.41 ± 0.03. It is expected that the actual (and observed) quality of the item will fall within the specified range. Confusion frequently exists regarding the relationship of the engineer's specifications of tolerance and the characteristics of the production process that is used to produce the part. The engineer's *specifications cannot demand more than the process is able to deliver.* To be reasonable, tolerance limits must be adjusted to the abilities of the facility. Every facility has a characteristic output variability that can be translated into a product quality range. Thus, if it is desired to cut a steel bar to a given length, then it is expected that variation evidenced as a distribution of observed values will occur around that specified central point. An engineer can specify tolerances from now until doomsday. Unless there is a machine or facility capable of providing parts that fall within this tolerance range, the objective cannot be achieved. Only by means of a new technological development can such specifications be met.

Statistical quality control, or SQC, is able to differentiate between *chance cause factors*, which are fundamental to all processes and *assignable cause factors*, which can be isolated and removed from the process. Thus, it is possible to determine when a facility is experiencing only the fundamental and inherent variations to which it is always susceptible.

A *control chart* such as the one in Figure 10.8 is the monitor of the control system. The control chart can be used for several purposes. First, to determine the fundamental or inherent variation level of a process. Second, to determine whether the process is stable and continues to be so during the production process. Stability is defined as the condition of a process in which only inherent *chance cause factors* are at work.

Statistical control procedure is based on the fact that the observed variation within each of a set of samples of size *n* can be directly related to the variation between the means of each sample in the set. Thus, for example, consider the set of five samples in Table 10.1. Each sample is composed of four observations.

TABLE 10-1

SUBGROUP SAMPLE NUMBER	OBSERVATION NUMBER				SAMPLE MEAN $\bar{x}$	SAMPLE RANGE R
	1	2	3	4		
1	21	31	39	25	29	18
2	17	44	54	13	32	41
3	36	48	19	41	36	29
4	25	31	38	30	31	13
5	35	21	20	34	27.5	15
					155.5	116

Process Average: $\bar{\bar{x}} = \dfrac{155.5}{5} = 31.1$

Average Range: $\bar{R} = \dfrac{116}{5} = 23.2$

It is to be understood that these samples represent a *sequence* of observations, made over a period of time (see Figure 10.9). Each sample is called a *subgroup;* each subgroup, composed of four observations, is obtained by securing four measures in successive order, without permitting intervening periods to occur. Then an interval of time is allowed to elapse. The next subgroup sample is taken at a later point in time. It is vital that we preserve the order of these samples, though observations can be mixed within samples. Thus, observations taken for Subgroup 2 must not be confused with observations taken for Subgroup 3. The *preservation of order*, in this sense, is crucial to the use of statistical quality control.

FIGURE 10-9
Subgroup size and the intervals between samples are critical determinants of control chart methodology.

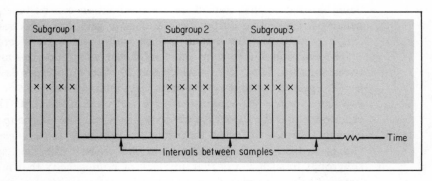

SAMPLE DESIGN

How is the subgroup size chosen? (Why did $n = 4$ in the example above?) How does the interval between samples get set? This much we can say at the start, the interval between samples usually is fixed and unchanging—although methods do exist which decrease the between-sample interval when the value of a subgroup mean approaches one of the control limits. Similarly, if a *run* seems to be developing, the interval would decrease (see p. 319). The point is that in the face of evidence that the system may be running out of control, the subgroup size should increase and the interval between would decrease until 100 percent inspection would be used during the emergency. Cost balance is involved and so are specific system properties. Referring to cost, let us examine Figure 10.10. There is a point x_o at which minimum total cost occurs. In general, as more observations are taken (say in a day) there is an almost linearly increasing

(see p. 319)

FIGURE 10-10
Determining the optimal number of observations to be made in a given interval.

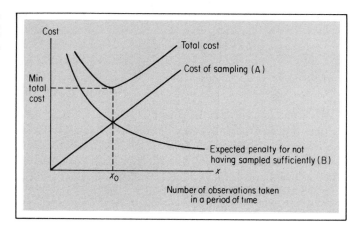

cost, line *A*. As fewer observations are taken, there is a greater chance that the system will go out of control and start producing defective items without it being noticed so that immediate remedial action can be taken. The expected penalty for defective output decreases as *x* gets larger because the expected length of time that the system will be malfunctioning is decreased, curve *B*.

The question still remains, how to choose subgroup sizes and intervals between samples. Thus, if x_o is selected at 20 observations per day should this be $n = 2$ repeated ten times with appropriate intervals between, or $n = 4$ repeated five times, or $n = 10$ once in the A.M. and once in the P.M. The fundamental criterion is that the successive observations within the subgroup should be close enough together to insure that they are relatively *homogeneous* and that no change is likely to have occurred in the process. We then space successive subgroups in such a way that any lack of homogeneity that might occur over time is likely to be picked up. In general practice, subgroup sizes of 4, 5, and 6 can be readily used. The spacing between subgroups will depend on the production rate and the inertial characteristics of the process.

Another important question concerns *how many values are required* before it is possible to set up a control chart. That is, how many subgroups should be collected? In the previous example, we utilized only five subgroup samples. Ordinarily, this is far too few. It is desirable to have at least 25 subgroup observations before attempting to draw up *and interpret* the control chart. But, of course, 25 is simply a rule of thumb.

STATISTICAL QUALITY CONTROL THEORY

It will be noted that for each subgroup, using the associated observations, we have calculated the sample average, or mean value, $\bar{x}$. We can assume equally well that the observations are measurements of the length of a bar, the inside diameter of a pipe, the number of air bubbles in a piece of glass, or the temperature of a water-cooled, moving part. In addition to the *mean value*, we have obtained for each subgroup the difference between the largest observation and the smallest observation. This is the measure of the *range*, called R. Thus, we have obtained the expected value for each subgroup as well as a convenient measure of the variation that appeared in the subgroup.

The variance measure associated with each subgroup's sample size is represented by $\sigma^2_{\bar{x}_n}$, where n is the subgroup size. The standard deviation is simply the square root of this term, that is $\sigma_{\bar{x}_n}$. It is a well-known statistical relationship that:

$$\sigma_{\bar{x}_n} = \frac{\sigma}{\sqrt{n}}$$

where σ is the standard deviation of the basic population from which the sample means are being drawn. The $\sigma_{\bar{x}_n}$'s are called the *standard error of the mean*. These standard deviations are measures of the variability of their respective subgroup distribution. That variability is directly affected by the particular sample size that is represented.

Figure 10.11 illustrates several distributions, each of which is based on a different sample subgroup size, and compares these *distributions of means* to the *population distributions*. The population distribution can be thought of as a distribution of sample means for which the subgroup size is one. In other words,

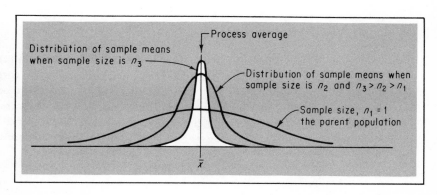

if we set the subgroup size of n equal to 1, we obtain the relationship:

$$\sigma_{\bar{x}_1} = \sigma$$

which is in accord with our definition.

THE RANGE MEASURE

It is frequently more convenient to measure the *range* than to go through the calculation of the standard deviation. Tables have been prepared which give the relationship of the expected range to the population standard deviation for varying sample sizes assumed to be drawn from a Normal universe.[8] This ratio factor is designated as d_2.

$$d_2 = \frac{\bar{R}}{\sigma}$$

Let us introduce this relationship into our previous equation for the standard error of the mean, and thereby derive:

$$\sigma_{\bar{x}_n} = \frac{\bar{R}}{d_2\sqrt{n}}$$

It is usual to position control limits as some specified number of standard deviations away from the expected value of the process. We shall use 3σ control limits, which is the value most commonly selected for industrial systems. Consequently, we can then write:

$$3\sigma_{\bar{x}_n} = \frac{3\bar{R}}{d_2\sqrt{n}} = A_2\bar{R}$$

The A_2 factor is available in table form, (see pp. 000–000) where $A_2 = 3/d_2\sqrt{n}$. The upper-control limit and the lower-control limit, where the process average is $\bar{x}$, would be given by:

Upper-control limit for $\bar{x}$: $UCL_{\bar{x}} = \bar{x} + A_2\bar{R}$
Lower-control limit for $\bar{x}$: $LCL_{\bar{x}} = \bar{x} - A_2\bar{R}$

THE CONTROL CHART

We have gone through this derivation of the control limits to develop understanding of the control chart. Let us, then, proceed to the construction and use of this control chart. Figure 10.12 shows a control chart on which we have marked the upper limit, the lower limit, and the grand process average, which is the mean value of the sample means, called $\bar{x}$. We observe that the distance between the process average and the upper- or lower-control limit is a function

[8] See the tables in E. L. Grant, *Statistical Quality Control* (3rd ed.) (New York: McGraw-Hill Book Co., Inc., 1964), p. 561.

of $\bar{R}$. The value $\bar{R}$, in turn, is the average range obtained for the subgroup samples of size n. Thus, the distance between the process average and the control limits is a function of the average variability associated with subgroups of size n.

On our control chart, in proper sequence, we enter the $\bar{x}$ values which are the subgroup averages. Statistical theory tells us that if the process is stable, then the successive values of the sample means will fall between the control limits 99.7 percent of the time. This is true because 3σ limits were used. If we had utilized limits other than 3σ, we would have obtained different probabilities of exceeding the control limits.

FIGURE 10-12
Control chart for
variables—$\bar{x}$.

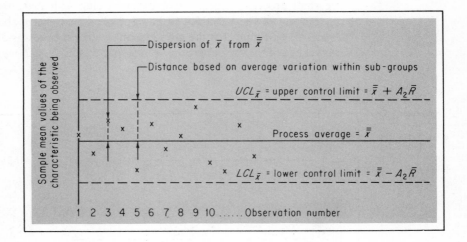

If the character of the parent population changes because assignable causes enter the system, then, this should become apparent when some value of $\bar{x}$ will fall outside the control limits. Another characteristic of an unstable system is that a *run* of values all above or all below the process average may occur. Runs are usually symptomatic that a process is *trending* in a particular direction. For comparison purposes, let us examine the probabilities with which certain control emergency signals will appear when the process is stable. First, the probability of a point falling outside the 3σ limits is approximately 1/380. Second, the probability that nine points in a row will lie on one side of the process average is about 1/256. The probability that ten points in a row will fall on a particular side of the grand mean is about 1/512.

For most manufacturing processes it is assumed that the parent populations of the various output dimensions conform to the Normal distribution. SQC, as described by Shewhart, is based on this assumption. An important question arises then as to what happens when the population is not, in fact, Normally distributed. Ideally, we would like the control system to operate in much the same way. That is, as long as the population remains stable, no matter what shape it has, we would like to be able to use the control criterion to tell us that no change has occurred in the process. It is a delightful gift of nature that distributions of sample means will tend to be Normal even though the population from which the samples are drawn is not Normally distributed. Shewhart had shown that even though samples are drawn from rectangular, triangular, and other types of distributions, the distributions of the sample means tend to be Normal. It is sufficiently true so that, in general, we need not concern ourselves with this problem.

MONITORING VARIABLES

We shall proceed to derive two different charts that are used when scaled measurements of the variables to be controlled have been obtained. In Table 10.1 (p. 315) we found that the grand mean of the process was 31.1 and that the average range of the five subgroups of size four was 23.2. Although five subgroups

FIGURE 10-13
Control chart for
variables, $\bar{x}$, for data
given in Table 10.2.
[A_2 (when $n = 4$) =
0.73.]

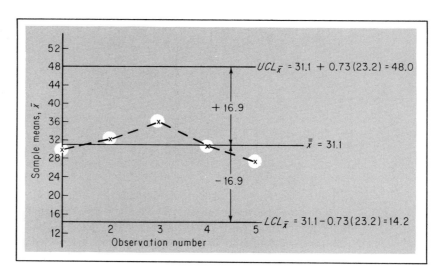

do not constitute a sufficient sample for actual intentions of monitoring a process, nevertheless, it is sufficient for illustrative purposes. Figure 10.13 shows the $\bar{x}$ chart. It has been constructed by means of the formulations previously given for both the upper and lower-control limits of the $\bar{x}$ chart. The A_2 factor is obtained from Table 10.2. A_2 when $n = 4$ is equal to 0.73. This is multiplied by $\bar{R}$ which is equal to 23.2. Then, the product, which is approximately 16.9, is added to $\bar{x}$ for the upper-control limit and subtracted from $\bar{x}$ for the lower-control limit. Our control chart indicates no lack of stability. The same procedures are followed when the number of subgroups is much larger than five.

TABLE 10.2 Factors for Determining from $\bar{R}$ the 3-sigma Control Limits for $\bar{x}$ and R Charts

NUMBER OF OBSERVATIONS IN SUBGROUP	FACTOR FOR x CHART	FACTORS FOR R CHART	
		LOWER CONTROL LIMIT	UPPER CONTROL LIMIT
n	A_2	D_3	D_4
2	1.88	0	3.27
3	1.02	0	2.57
4	0.73	0	2.28
5	0.58	0	2.11
6	0.48	0	2.00
7	0.42	0.08	1.92
8	0.37	0.14	1.86
9	0.34	0.18	1.82
10	0.31	0.22	1.78
11	0.29	0.26	1.74
12	0.27	0.28	1.72
13	0.25	0.31	1.69
14	0.24	0.33	1.67
15	0.22	0.35	1.65
16	0.21	0.36	1.64
17	0.20	0.38	1.62
18	0.19	0.39	1.61
19	0.19	0.40	1.60
20	0.18	0.41	1.59

Upper Control Limit for $\bar{x} = UCL\bar{x} = \bar{\bar{x}} - A_2\bar{R}$
Lower Control Limit for $\bar{x} = LCL\bar{x} = \bar{\bar{x}} - A_2\bar{R}$
Upper Control Limit for $R = UCL_R = D_4\bar{R}$
Lower Control Limit for $R = LCL_R = D_3\bar{R}$
All factors in this Table are based on the Normal distribution.
Source: E. L. Grant, *Statistical Quality Control*, 3rd ed. (New York: McGraw-Hill Book Co., Inc., 1964), p. 562.

The $\bar{x}$ chart is intended to monitor the process average. When measurements of variables are used, it is also possible to construct a chart to monitor the process dispersion. This chart is called an R chart. It is based on the range measures which had to be derived for the $\bar{x}$ chart. We shall not investigate the detailed reasoning involved in the development of the upper- and lower-control limits for the R chart because it closely parallels our previous discussion for the $\bar{x}$ chart. Table 10.2 presents the appropriate equations, as well as the respective D_3 and D_4 values that must be used for the determination of R-chart control limits (just as A_2 was required for the $\bar{x}$ chart). Utilizing the factors D_3 and D_4 obtained from the table, we construct the appropriate R chart for our example. This is shown in Figure 10.14.

SYMPTOMS AND DIAGNOSIS

The construction of the R chart is straightforward, as was the construction of the $\bar{x}$ chart. It is the interpretation of the charts that is of crucial importance. If there is a shift in the population character, then it can be of the following

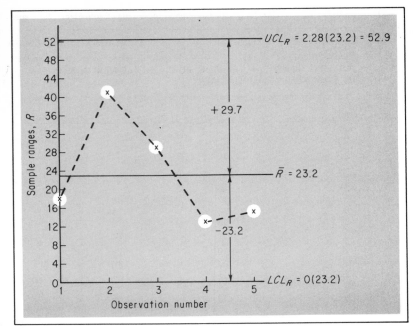

types: (1) The process average may change; (2) The process dispersion may change; or (3) Both of these changes may take place. If only the average changes, this fact will probably be picked up by the $\bar{x}$ chart and not by the R chart. The situation might occur, for example, if the machine setting shifts permanently; that is, the change is of a *sustained* type. In certain cases, the population mean, or process average, will remain unchanged, but the dispersion of the process will shift. For example, an operator may be able to control his output at the mean level, but he does this by working fast at certain times and slow at other times to compensate. Such performance should create a pattern of instability that is likely to be detected on the R chart and not on the $\bar{x}$ chart.

A variety of change combinations can occur when sporadic elements enter and leave the system in some unknown fashion. These assignable causes are more difficult to detect than the sustained types that were discussed above. Other types of changes can also occur. For example, a gradual shift in the mean. Tool wear could account for such *trend* shifts. Worker carelessness can produce the kind of sporadic behavior in which both limits may be repeatedly violated. Runs will appear for a variety of reasons and can usually be associated with trend factors, such as tool or gauge wear. It should be noted that the process is not always the guilty party. The inspectors and/or their tools might account for a signal of instability. To assist management, the entire relevant system must be isolated so that meaningful process conclusions can be drawn.[9]

---

[9] 100 percent inspection does not provide such analytic assistance for the diagnosis of causes of change. The "zero-defects" programs, urged by many companies on their employees should be interpreted, in the light of control theory as being unobtainable goals set for psychological reasons rather than for strictly technological ones.

The use of the $\bar{x}$ and the R chart is one of the most powerful methods available for monitoring the behavior of a process. It is likely that a newly established process *will not be stable at the outset*. It will require attention, refinement, and consideration before it can be brought into control. The process behavior must then be checked against the engineering specifications. The result will influence both the design of the process and the redesign of the output. Figure 10.15 indicates the way in which output tolerance limits and statistical process control limits might be related to each other. We have modified the control limits for Figure 10.15 so that they apply to the parent population. This modification was accomplished by means of the equation for the *standard error of the mean*. The tolerance limits do not require alteration because they already apply to the parent population distribution.

FIGURE 10-15
The relationship of tolerance limits and control limits ($\bar{x}$ values can fall within tolerance limits although x values will fall outside with greater frequency than the specified level of protection).

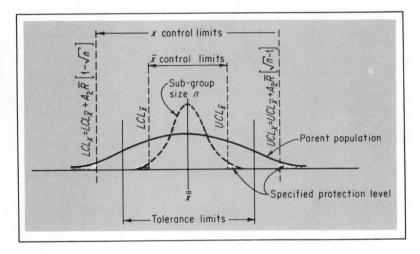

MONITORING ATTRIBUTES

We shall now consider a less elaborate control device, called the p-chart. The p-chart is less expensive to utilize than the $\bar{x}$ and R charts because only a single chart is used, and the required computations are less onerous than those required for the $\bar{x}$ and R charts. The p-chart is called the control chart for *fraction defectives*. It is based on sampling by attributes, which was previously described. The key, as was the case for acceptance sampling, is the ability to define a defective. As might be suspected, because the p-chart is less expensive to use than control charts for variables, it is not as sensitive as the combination of the $\bar{x}$ and the R chart. It is not as good a diagnostic tool because it loses information; even the $\bar{x}$ chart used alone is a more powerful tool. However, the p-chart, with less sensitivity, which can be beneficial (under certain circumstances), will indicate the existence of assignable causes when they occur, and it does this at a lower cost than monitors based on variables.

The data must be collected in the same way as was previously explained for monitoring variables. That is to say, homogeneous subgroups are chosen and a period of time is allowed to elapse between the subgroup observations. The same kind of reasoning applies to the determination of subgroup sizes and between sample intervals as was true for the $\bar{x}$ and R charts. The sequential character of the control chart is as much in evidence as it was before, and the preservation of the order of observation is as crucial. Let us consider an example of a p-chart. Table 10.3 presents data for six consecutive subgroup samples. However, we note that the number of observations made for each subgroup varies in this particular case. It is still possible to construct appropriate control limits, but for the example we have chosen they will vary, as shown in Figure

TABLE 10.3

| SUBGROUP SAMPLE | OBSERVATIONS | | COMPUTATIONS | | | PLOT |
	NUMBER INSPECTED, n	NUMBER DEFECTIVE	σ	UCL $\bar{p} + \sigma$	LCL $\bar{p} - \sigma$	FRACTION DEFECTIVE
1	25	1	0.053	0.128	0.022	0.040
2	25	2	0.053	0.128	0.022	0.080
3	36	3	0.044	0.119	0.031	0.083
4	64	4	0.033	0.108	0.042	0.063
5	25	3	0.053	0.128	0.022	0.120
6	25	2	0.053	0.128	0.022	0.080
	200	15				

$$\bar{p} = \frac{15}{200} = 0.075$$

$$\sigma = \sqrt{\frac{\bar{p}(1 - \bar{p})}{n}} = \sqrt{\frac{(.075)(9.25)}{n}} = 0.263\sqrt{\frac{1}{n}}$$

10.16. The number of observed defectives is recorded for each sub-group. The total number of inspected items is now divided *into* the total number of observed defectives. This gives the process average, $\bar{p}$. For our example, $\bar{p}$, is equal to 0.075. To determine the control limits we utilize the Binomial description of the *standard error of the mean*, that is,

$$\sigma = \sqrt{\frac{\bar{p}(1 - \bar{p})}{n}}$$

This is a function of the subgroup sample size n. Because the upper and lower-control limits are specified in terms of σ, the limits vary as a function of n. For this example we have chosen 1σ limits.

The complete computations are shown in Table 10.3 and are represented in Figure 10.16. When the subgroup size is constant, then the computations are even further simplified. Only one upper and one lower-control limit need be drawn on the p-chart. The advantage of illustrating variable subgroup sizes is that, in practice, it is not always possible to draw samples of constant size.

FIGURE 10-16
Control chart for at-
tributes—p, for data
given in Table 10.3.

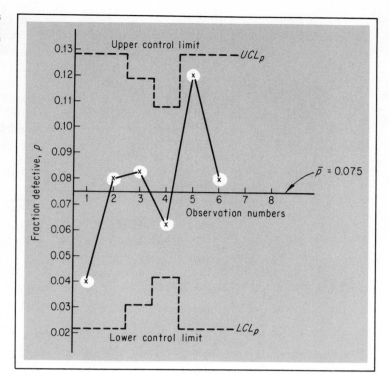

Our sample values fall into the pattern of a stable process. The fifth sub-group value approaches the upper limit but the "alert" is called off when the sixth subgroup values approaches the mean.

DESIGN OF LIMITS

Figure 10.17 illustrates a system in which a lack of control exists. We observe that a point has gone out of control. This usually is taken as a signal that something is awry and that corrective action should be taken. It is always possible, but improbable, that the "out" point occurred by chance. The run lends credence to the notion that a real change might be taking place and provides sufficient supporting evidence to the belief that our observation is not spurious.

For previous examples we chose 3σ and later 1σ limits. *The choice of $k\sigma$ control limits*, as to whether they are 1σ, 2σ, or 3σ, or some value in between, *is a management policy decision.* It is hard to defend a choice of one or another control limit, but the characteristics of the decision are such that if the penalty is high for not recognizing when the process is out of control, then it becomes more desirable to utilize *less than* 3σ limits. The distance between the limits decreases as the size of k decreases. This means that more events are likely to fall outside the control limits.

The choice of k is a matter of balancing costs. Pertinent costs include the expense that occurs when a signal is received upon which action will be taken. The system must be examined in an attempt to track down assignable causes whether or not they exist in reality. An opposing cost is that of inaction when instability actually exists but is not recognized. Such a state of affairs can penalize the process heavily. With this guide in mind, the manager should choose those control-limit values that promise to balance the penalties.

Control-chart values must be regularly reviewed. This includes, $\bar{x}$, $\bar{R}$, and $\bar{p}$ for the fraction defectives chart. Changes detected in averages can, in turn,

FIGURE 10-17
The control chart indicates that the system may be unstable.

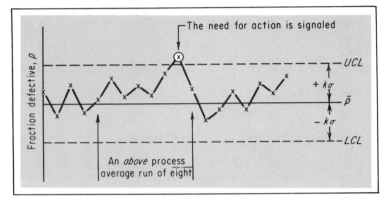

affect the σ value that is computed and utilized. In all control technology it is essential to *review* and *update* the system's parameters so that decisions can be based on "what is" and not on "what was." Particularly, after an assignable cause has been detected and removed from the system, it is necessary to readjust the control limits; sometimes another 25 subgroup observations are required before it is again possible to apply the control criterion.

OTHER APPLICATIONS

Another control chart occasionally used by industry is called the *c*-chart. This control chart can be applied to situations where it is desirable to record the frequency of occurrence of a *number of different types of defects* that are found for a particular item. For example, we can examine telescope lenses for different kinds of defects and flaws. Then, we might list the observed frequency of the different kinds of defects that occur in every inspected unit. When using the *c*-chart, it is most usual to have a subgroup size of 1—although this is not a requirement. It *is* necessary, however, that the defects of different types occur at random with respect to each other. Otherwise the underlying assumptions of the *c*-chart will not be met.

New applications for statistical control systems are being developed all the time. It is even possible to learn something about behavioral systems and worker productivity by means of SQC.[10] It is a requisite that basic processes should be demonstrated analytically to be stable, and if not, made so, before synthesis is undertaken. The parameters of inventory formulations, line-balancing systems, or of sequencing models must be tested for stability before being employed. Otherwise it is quite possible to derive a solution for a system that is shifting, and which no longer exists at the time of implementation.

The subject of statistical control is not one that can be taught in depth, in a matter of minutes. It is essential that *experience* with the process and with the use of the charts be developed. Purely theoretical interpretations gloss over the kind of penetrating insights that an experienced practitioner can obtain from control charts.

SQC has been of enormous significance to the production field, but its full potential has not yet been tapped. Reliability problems become increasingly important as equipment becomes more automated and the production system becomes more complex. Quality assurance for the consumer is the production manager's obligation. The output, the process, and the inputs must be totally interlocked and matched. That is the objective toward which production management constantly strives.

PROBLEMS

1   Omega Electronics is a small company which manufactures a vacuum tube that is highly resistant to vibration and heat. Only destructive testing can be used to check the acceptability of a tube. Each tube is costly. The application of the tube is such that a failure endangers many lives. What inspection procedure would you use?

2   The Yukon Company requires a destructive test to determine the quality of the firecrackers which it manufactures. Assume that five giant firecrackers compose a lot. The company tests one and ships four, if the test is successful. If the test is not successful, the remaining four are sold as seconds.
    a. Specify the characteristics of this single sampling plan and derive the OC curve.
    b. What do you think of this plan?

3   Can quality control exist without feedback? How about quantity control? Explain your answer.

4   A shampoo manufacturer specifies that the contents of a bottle of shampoo should weigh 6 ± 0.10 ounces net. A statistical quality control operation is established and

---

[10] See S. B. Littauer, "Technological Stability in Industrial Operations," *Transactions of the New York Academy of Sciences,* Series II, Vol. 13, No. 2, (Dec. 1950), pp. 67–72. Also, we can readily appreciate why the *p*-chart has been utilized for monitoring observations obtained from work sampling methods, see pp. 392–94.

the following data are obtained:

Sample
Number

1	6.06	6.20	6.04	6.10
2	6.10	5.95	5.98	6.05
3	6.03	5.90	5.95	6.00
4	6.03	6.05	6.10	5.94
5	6.12	6.40	6.20	6.00

a. Construct an $\bar{x}$ chart based on these five samples.
b. Construct an R chart based on these five samples.
c. What points, if any, have gone out of control?
d. Comment on your results and briefly discuss the role of SQC in production management. Include such factors as management's choice of tolerance limits, subgroup size and sample size.

5 A food processor specified that the contents of a jar of jam should weigh 14 ± 0.10 ounces net. A statistical quality control operation is set up and the following data are obtained:

Sample
Number

1	14.02	14.04	14.08	14.06
2	14.10	14.24	14.00	14.90
3	14.80	14.75	14.70	14.51
4	14.59	14.90	14.01	14.02
5	14.96	14.26	14.81	14.17
6	14.40	14.83	14.68	14.93
7	14.86	14.32	14.90	14.04
8	14.56	14.96	14.69	14.63
9	14.85	14.71	14.05	14.91
10	14.75	14.19	14.05	14.09

a. Construct an $\bar{x}$ chart based on these 10 samples.
b. Construct an R chart based on these 10 samples.
c. What points, if any, have gone out of control?
d. What reasons could be given for the appearance of an assignable cause at some time in the future?
e. What can be surmised from the shapes of the curves on these charts?

references

ARMSTRONG, W. H., *Mechanical Inspection.* New York: McGraw-Hill, Inc., 1953.

DODGE, HAROLD F., and HARRY G. ROMIG, *Sampling Inspection Tables* (2nd Ed.). New York: John Wiley & Sons, Inc., 1944.

DUNCAN, A. J., *Quality Control and Industrial Statistics* (3rd ed.) Homewood, Ill.: Richard D. Irwin, Inc., 1965.

FEIGENBAUM, A. V., *Total Quality Control.* New York: McGraw-Hill Book Company, 1961.

FREEMAN, H. O., FRIEDMAN, M., MOSTELLER, F., and W. ALLEN WALLIS (eds.), *Sampling Inspection.* New York: McGraw-Hill Book Company, 1948.

GRANT, E. L., *Statistical Quality Control* (3rd Ed.). New York: McGraw-Hill, Inc., 1964.

HANSEN, B. L., *Quality Control: Theory & Applications.* Englewood Cliffs, N.J.: Prentice-Hall, Inc., 1963.

KIRKPATRICK, ELWOOD G., *Quality Control for Managers and Engineers.* New York: John Wiley & Sons, Inc., 1970.

LANDERS, RICHARD R., *Reliability and Product Assurance.* Englewood Cliffs, N. J.: Prentice-Hall, Inc., 1963.

SHEWHART, WALTER A., *Economic Control of Quality of Manufactured Product.* Princeton, N.J.: D. Van Nostrand Co., Inc., 1931.

TOMPSON, JAMES E., *Inspection, Organization, and Methods.* New York: McGraw-Hill, Inc., 1950.

chapter
eleven
facilities
management

Investment in facilities, plant and equipment is generally so large that it is surprising how little progress has been made in formalizing this decision process. Surprising, that is, until one realizes how complicated and resistant these major decision areas are to normative modeling (i.e., optimization) and quantitative description. Evaluatory approaches that measure return on investment (ROI) are among the most advanced techniques in use (see Chapter 14, pp. 447–60). And, in addition, some structural approaches have been developed. We shall discuss these here. First, let us talk about the plant location problem, then the plant layout problem and finally, the equipment selection problem.

PLANT LOCATION

PLANT CONSTRUCTION FACTORS

What type of shelter is needed to house the production facility? In the next section of this chapter, we shall treat some of the more significant issues involved in making a plant location decision. Sometimes these matters of construction and location are related—often, they are not. Dependency exists when the need to *rent* specialized and *unique* plant configurations is evident to the manager. Building one's own plant removes much of the pressure, as does the requirement for a general plant configuration rather than a highly individualized one.

Each process requires its own kind of protection. An oil refinery can be exposed to the elements. An automobile factory must be enclosed to protect equipment and in-process inventories that would be vulnerable to weather. But, in most flow shop situations there is little ambiguity concerning the shape and form of buildings and basic facilities. Job shops have greater flexibility and more choices available. Therefore, flow shops tend to be located without consideration of the rental opportunities whereas job shop locations may well be determined by such factors.

In general terms, when renting, building, buying, a great many elements must be considered. Expert assistance from architects and building engineers should be obtained to insure the proper evaluation of an existing structure or in order to plan a new structure. Among the elements to be considered are:

1. *Is there enough floor space?*

2. *Is the space open with wide bays so that machines, men, and materials handling equipment can be effectively arranged and utilized?*

3. *How many stories are there?* Early factories were multistoried. With the development of improved transportation, particularly the automobile, plants could be located outside the central city on less expensive land. The one-story building followed from this. It is usually preferred unless sufficient reasons can be found to justify multistory buildings which are more expensive to construct, especially when floor loads are high because heavy equipment must be supported. In certain industries, gravity feed conveyors are used. In such cases, multiple storied buildings are likely to be preferred.

4. *What kind of roof is used?* This was a very important question at one time, not any longer. Roof shapes permit at least a degree of control over illumination, temperature, and ventilation,[1] but technological advances have reduced the significance of roof design with respect to these factors. On the other hand, if the process requires hoists and cranes, then high roofs and ceilings remain a relevant constraint.

5. *What type of construction should be used?* The answer given will in large measure determine the feasibility of converting an old building to conform to a new set of specifications. This answer will be the major determinant of both new construction costs and the speed of construction. In all cases, building codes must be observed. Industrial parks usually require a degree of conformity with respect to construction and appearance. Such factors as foundations, floors, walls, and windows are part of the architectural design of a building. They

[1] For example, the saw-tooth roof construction was extensively used to provide even illumination of work spaces; irrigation of flat roof tops was used for temperature control.

affect layout flexibility and building convertibility. In addition, insurance rates will be dependent upon the type of construction that is used.

6. *What kind of maintenance requirements will there be?* Older buildings usually have greater costs for maintaining the structure. The resale value of a structure may be an important determinant. In general, *special purpose buildings* designed for a unique process make special structural demands and create a lower resale value than *general purpose buildings*. The latter accept process requirements that are not unique but fit a pattern which is satisfactory for many different kinds of processes.

7. *Should we rent, buy, or build?* The answer to this question depends upon what is available. If a suitable building exists, then its cost can be compared with costs that would be incurred if a new building were constructed. Rent or buy alternatives depend upon what is offered. An interesting aspect of this problem is the question: How long should we wait to see what buildings become available? If no suitable structure exists, then an appropriate facility must be constructed. Airline terminals are built for this reason. In the communications field, radio and TV stations are built to specifications. Unused power generating plants are not found in rentable condition. So, clearly, when there is nothing available to meet the need, it must be built. On the other hand, when the process requirements are not unique, many suitable facilities usually can be found. This would apply to office space which is commonly rented. Job-shop manufacturing operations generally can be suitably located in a variety of types of plants that can be rented and/or purchased. The problem of buying, renting, or building should be resolved by means of a comparison of costs based on present worth analysis. To accomplish this we make use of discounting procedures see pp. 98–101 and 451–53.

8. *What conveniences should the building have?* If the building is located at a distance from the city, it might be essential to provide a parking lot as well as cafeteria facilities. Many companies require a medical room or a plant hospital on the premises. There must be adequate rest rooms. In some instances an auditorium is included in the plans. Railroad sidings or ship docking facilities may be of major importance. If this is the case, the construction or rental plan must take such factors into account.

9. *What appearance should the building have?* Different architectural styles appear at different points in time. Attitudes and policies of management will strongly influence these decisions. Some executives consider appearance to be a frill whereas others take it so seriously that they insist on illumination of the building at night and the provision for an impressive view from the air. There is no question that a beautiful building increases employee pride in their company and can influence the consumer's evaluation of the company. On the other hand, how these truisms affect productivity and profit remains an intangible factor.

10. *What should be the location of the building?* The next section considers this question in detail. First, a general location must be found. Then a specific site must be selected. It is frequently necessary to choose between an excellent building in a not-so-good location and a not-so-good building in an excellent location.

PLANT LOCATION FACTORS

The plant selection process, as we have already seen, consists of two different decision problems (construction and location) which can be highly interrelated. We shall now consider the second part of the problem, viz., where should the process be located? A refinery can be located at the oil fields close to its raw material sources. It could also be located adjacent to its market. An automobile factory can be located close to its source of process inputs. The heavy manufacturing operations can be separated from the required assembly operations. Then, the latter can be located close to the markets that desire the process outputs. Multiple facilities pose additional questions concerning the division of functions between several facilities. Although such problems are complex we know that there is some optimal locational arrangement of facilities. The question is: How do we go about determining this optimal arrangement?

Decisions regarding the location of facilities usually require consideration of

FIGURE 11-1
A graphic comparison between purely analytic and purely synthetic production systems.

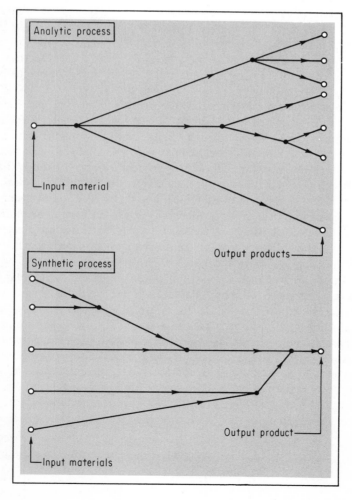

many factors. Sometimes, however, a major factor completely overrides the others. Let us look at this type of analysis.

1. *Location Dependent Upon the Process Inputs.* This is typically the case where bulky or heavy raw materials are essential for the production process. Thus, as a general rule, analytic-type industries are likely to locate near the source of their materials. Figure 11.1 distinguishes between analytic and synthetic production operations. In the case of the analytic system, the basic raw material is broken down, transformed, and decomposed into various products and by-products. In synthetic operations, on the other hand, various materials and parts are fed into the main stream where they are joined together to form a single basic unit. Figure 11.2 (a and b) pictures the flow of materials as exemplified in two typical analytical industries. In one case, the raw material is the cocoa bean, from which four basic products are derived, viz., cocoa butter bars, premium chocolate mix, regular chocolate mix, and cocoa. In the other, crude oil is refined into a number of finished products. Flow charts of this type can be exceedingly helpful for process development of analytic systems. Figure 11.3 (a and b) depicts the beer brewing process and the assembling of an automobile, both typical of *synthetic industries* which are likely to locate near their markets. In the automobile production line each component is brought in at the appropriate point, after which it loses its separate identity. Most processes combine both analytic and synthetic operations. This would even be true for the examples we have used. However, the examples can be distinguished as being *essentially* analytic or synthetic.

In addition to materials that are process inputs, we also have labor inputs, which are discussed in Chapter 12. Labor costs are one of the most important factors in the determination of a suitable plant location for certain labor-intensive industries. Service industries are particularly sensitive to this factor. Companies that employ large labor forces have been known to change their locations to take advantage of a lower wage scale. This motive impelled New England textile firms to close up shop in the North and move South. However, with increasing mechanization, the labor problem has been alleviated to an extent for all industries. There has also been a reduction in differential wage rates by regions of the country. Taken together, these changes have reduced the dependency of the location decision on the cost of labor.[2]

In addition to the advantage of lower wage rates for similar skills, there are more subtle costs of labor. Foremost is the availability of manpower and, in particular, of various skill levels within a particular region. Movement from a high-skill, high-wage rate area to a low-skill, low-wage rate area can only be accomplished when sufficient process mechanization is achieved. The computer has altered the skill requirements and availabilities of white collar functions. Technological progress and computer data processing permit a company to trade off higher machine investments for lower wages and for less manpower and skill. A trade-off potential is created between manpower and machine power which tends to make the location decision less dependent on the expense of both

[2] International wage differentials present something of an illusion. Tariffs, cost of materials, international exchange rates, taxes, and other factors tend to balance out what might otherwise appear to be substantial advantages.

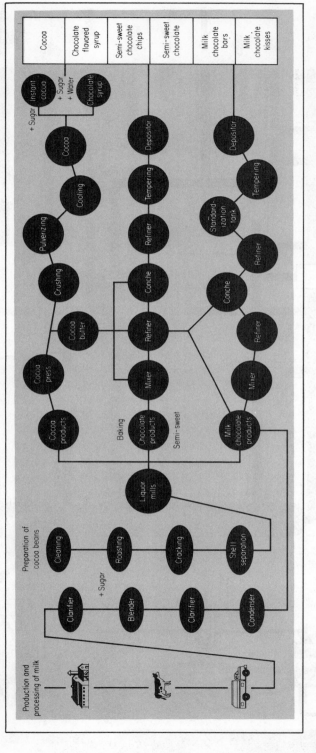

FIGURE 11-2a

Chocolate processing. [© Hershey Foods Corporation, Hershey Chocolate & Confectionery Division, Hershey, Pa., 17033, U.S.A.]

335

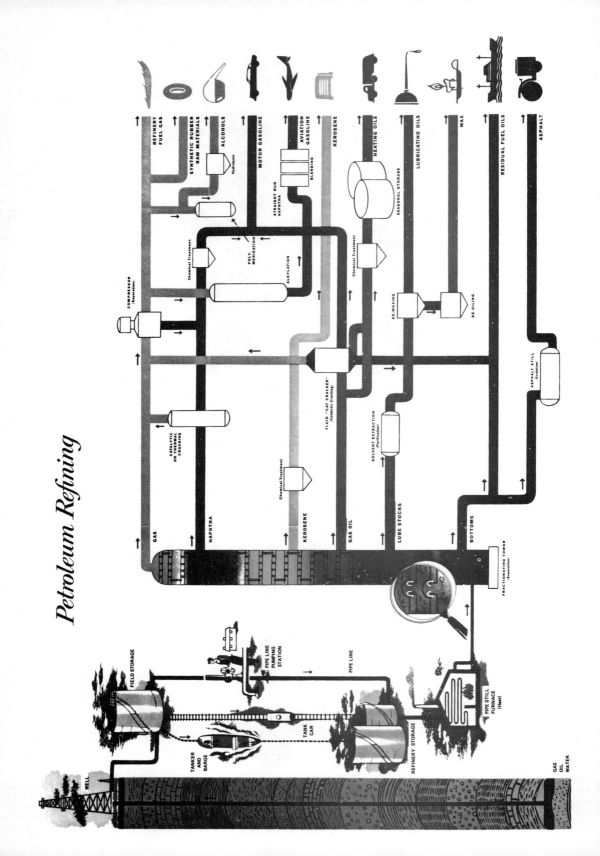

Petroleum Refining

FIGURE 11-2b
Oil refining. [Courtesy
of Refining Depart-
ment of the Humble
Oil & Refining Com-
pany.]

indirect and direct labor. Labor cost evaluation also includes consideration of turnover rates, absenteeism, and employee reliability, as well as costs of hiring and training workers. These considerations were discussed in Chapter 8 where aggregate scheduling was treated.

Different schedules will arise according to the nature of the costs we have just discussed. So we see that the plant location (system's design-type problem) interacts specifically with many other production management problems. The size of a labor market and the attitudes of labor and labor unions can also figure heavily in some plant location decisions. These considerations are likely to affect location decisions with respect to urban labor markets as compared to suburban and rural markets. From various sources, demographic information by areas, such as population size, education, and income can be pooled with industrial data concerning hourly earnings, right to work laws, and so forth. Such a data base, at least allows the manager to be a well-informed decision maker.

2. *Location Dependent Upon the Process Outputs.* The location of the company's markets can be significant under certain circumstances, e.g., characteristic of service industries. Because the facility specializes in service, it is only reasonable

FIGURE 11-3a
Beer Brewing. [Cour-
tesy of Anheuser–
Busch, Inc.]

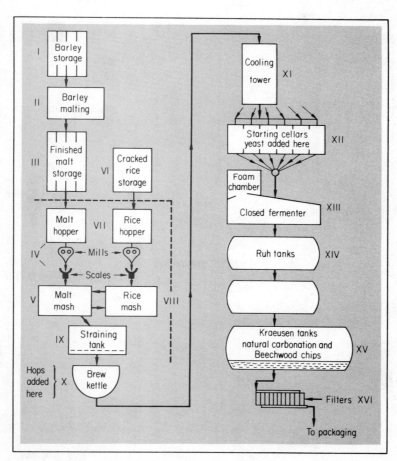

337

HOW AN AUTOMOBILE IS ASSEMBLED

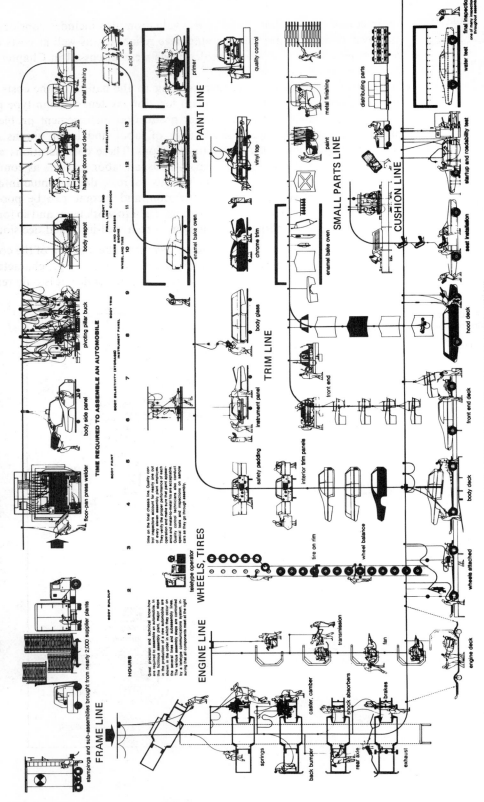

EDUCATIONAL AFFAIRS DEPARTMENT, FORD MOTOR COMPANY, DEARBORN, MICHIGAN

FIGURE 11-3b
How an automobile
is assembled. [Cour-
tesy of Educational
Affairs Department,
Ford Motor Com-
pany, Dearborn,
Michigan.]

◄─────────────

that location should be selected near those individuals who require the service. As previously noted, synthetic industries frequently locate near their markets, because many raw materials must be gathered together from *diverse* locations and assembled into single units.

3. *Location Dependent Upon Process Requirements.* Many processes require special environments. When the technology of the process requires large amounts of water, then only a location where such water resources are available can be considered. If the process contaminates the water system, this can be an overriding factor in the location decision. It is necessary to locate such a plant at a place where the pollution can be controlled. Another common process requirement concerns the need for substantial amounts of power. There are not too many locations that could meet an extremely heavy demand. Accordingly, the size of the location problem is immediately cut down.

Certain processes produce disagreeable odors and in other ways pollute the environment. For such cases, both urban and suburban locations are automatically ruled out. Noise and other community irritants will be treated in a similar fashion. Sometimes, a process is responsive to factors such as temperature, humidity, and weather conditions in general. To a great extent, internal weather conditioning obviates such factors. But this is not always the case. High salinity in the air, arising as a result of a coastal location, must be taken into account when materials and equipment would be adversely affected by such a condition. An additional aspect of the relevancy of weather conditions, which is quite frequently overlooked, can be noted. If a process requires highly skilled individuals to perform certain operations, then absenteeism can be a significant deterimental factor. For such cases, it might be desirable to locate in a region where the common cold would be a less virile destroyer of time. Within some reasonable period for development, space factories will orbit earth providing gravity-free and particle-free environments. Thus, many unique circumstances exist wherein process requirements with respect to environment override all other considerations.

4. *Location Dependent Upon Personal Preferences.* Occasionally the entrepreneurs or chief executives prefer a given location for entirely personal reasons. Not infrequently, having decided to relocate an operating facility, strong monetary incentives must be used to encourage company personnel to relocate with the company. The cost of moving personnel and inducing them to do so must be balanced against the costs of building a new group with the same level of skills and company loyalty in the new location. Frequently, the preferences of the firm's top executives to remain where they are will take precedence over considerations that otherwise might be considered more important.

5. *Location Dependent Upon Tax and Legal Factors.* Because of severe taxes applicable to the corporation, personal income taxes, sales taxes, etc. desirable locations with respect to other variables will be bypassed. In fact, a favorable tax structure provides such basic motivation that many decisions are made to locate a new plant or to relocate a going operation solely for this reason.[3] In addition to tax advantages, communities attempt to attract industries

---

[3] One of the best examples of such location decisions will be found with respect to Puerto Rico, where Operation Bootstrap has been an enormous success because of attractive tax incentives.

by providing industrial parks or properly zoned land at advantageous rates. Although some communities desire any kind of industrial growth, most attempt to attract only certain types of industries. Others have been reluctant and even hostile toward any industrial development. Companies which fail to perceive community attitudes frequently rue this oversight.

6. *Location Dependent Upon Site and Plant Availabilities.* There is a complex "deferred choice" problem that exists. At any point in time a list of available sites can be compiled. Some sites already have a plant built on them which can either be purchased or rented. Other sites require building. Assume that the desirability of each site could be evaluated with a single measure and that a ranked order list of sites has been developed. Figure 11.4 illustrates such a list, and in addition, E_k is shown as a new arrival. The quality of E_k can be measured and it will be placed in its proper rank order in the list.

FIGURE 11-4

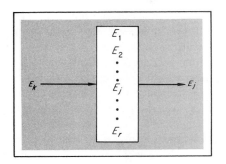

The list also experiences departures, i.e., E_j. Then the question is: When is E_1 good enough so that it can be chosen as a location? If the manager waits, his best choice may disappear; if he doesn't wait, the day after he commits the company to a new location, a preferred one may appear. The problem has striking similarities to the dynamic programming formulation of the commodity buying situation described on pp. 268–70. In this case, the rank order of the evaluation measure is substituted for the commodity price and similar probabilistic information must be collected. The criterion of quality, E_j, is complex and difficult to conceive, let alone measure. The manager must be able to define the type of shelter that is needed to house the production facility and the issues involved in making a plant location decision.

PLANT LOCATION COST DETERMINANTS

We have discussed many variables which affect plant location decisions. It is unreasonable to attempt to consider all such factors that might be relevant in one case or another. However, let us examine the location problem in one other light. A location decision represents an attempt to minimize costs, including *opportunity costs*. For example, there is a cost of staying put and not moving to a new location. The investigation required to choose a new location has a cost all its own which should be considered before undertaking a location analysis.[4]

The plant location problem is of the long-term, nonrepetitive type. The many relevant risk factors are seldom able to be analyzed properly. The plant location decision requires a sizable investment and creates heavy sunk costs.[5] It involves other costs as well. Let us consider two kinds of fundamental cost factors, namely, *tangible* costs and *intangible* costs. The latter are distinguished by the fact that it is almost impossible to *measure* them. They can only be judged intuitively. Although it is difficult to measure many of the tangible costs; nevertheless, to some extent, they can all be measured. Among the tangible costs are:

1. The cost of land;
2. The cost of renting, buying, or building;
3. Transportation costs of raw materials and fuels;
4. Transportation costs of moving finished goods to the market;
5. Power and water costs;
6. The cost of taxes and insurance;
7. Labor costs;
8. The cost of moving, including production stoppage costs incurred during relocation.

In determining an optimal location, it is the significance of intangible costs that places the most severe burden on the production manager. Let us consider a few of these.

1. *Competition for labor* within a restricted labor market introduces a cost that changes over time. It will vary as a function of the attractiveness of a particular region for all industries. The situation is dynamic. When an attractive general location exists, a number of companies begin to move to this area in order to take advantage of its opportunities. Saturation must occur, and at some point competition for the available labor resources can become significant; paradise is transformed to limbo.

2. *Union attitudes* are exceedingly important, but difficult to evaluate. It is seldom possible to do more than intuitively assess such conditions. Militant unions develop reputations that are widely known. But a change of leadership or policy within the union can significantly alter the stereotype. Shifts in the economy and changes in the welfare and fortune of a particular industry will bring about rapid shifts in union attitudes.

3. *Community attitudes* are not measurable. Small enclaves of resistance to industrial developments must not be overlooked particularly when such groups

---

[4] The collection of relevant data is facilitated through the cooperation of regional Chambers of Commerce which are able to provide such information.
[5] See pp. 217, 448–49.

are led by a few individuals who are influential members of the community. It is possible to document specific instances where companies have fully developed plans to move into a new community only to discover that a strong and militant group exists that is prepared to resist the incursion. Because of its investment in the decision that has been made, and because some executives become outraged at being pariahs, some companies will occasionally attempt to fight this battle. Even if the company legally succeeds in installing itself, the enmity that has been aroused will, in all likelihood, prove to be a lasting penalty. The point is important because some major difficulties can arise. For example, the company may discover that bus service has been suspended on routes from the city to the plant location; the community may rezone the plant location so that fire protection is denied. This can produce a dramatic rise in insurance rates until the company is able to develop its own fire protection unit. Other possible sources of difficulty include the municipality's withholding adequate sewage facilities and the passage of new zoning laws that can prevent company expansion, even on its own land.

Problems of this type can also arise when a community becomes disillusioned with the company because of unexpected pollution, noise, or other undesirable process outputs. The various forms that inimical relations can take is limited only by the powers of the city fathers. Community relations should be considered as an integral part of every plant location decision problem. A company that does not make clear to the community the degree to which the environment will be contaminated by operations should not be surprised to find promised favors withdrawn and local groups agitating for its removal.

4. *Local and state ordinances* must be taken into account. There is no direct way to attach a cost to such rulings. Knowledgeable legal assistance is required to interpret the situation so that it can be evaluated. Each location possibility poses its own economic considerations in terms of such costs as workmen's compensation payments, unemployment insurance, waste disposal laws, pollution and smoke control requirements, noise abatement rules, and other nuisance regulations.

5. *The costs of weather* and other natural phenomena should not be overlooked. Such events as hurricanes, earthquakes, and floods can produce heavy penalties. These are acts of nature and cannot always be avoided. At the same time, they are less unexpected in certain areas than in others. Thus, companies in low lying areas near rivers have higher probabilities of being flooded; similarly, well-known earthquake and hurricane zones exist. Normal weather conditions also produce costs that can be associated with specific locations. Companies locating in the North must be prepared to pay for heating equipment and fuel bills. Industries locating in the South may require investments in airconditioning as well as concomitant power expenses. Other costs related to weather concern the maintenance of plant and the deteriorioation of equipment.

How can all these factors be related? Assuming that we could measure all the costs, then we could write an equation of the general form:

Total Costs = f(Tangible, Intangible, and Opportunity Cost Factors) and we would minimize the equation. All matters that might interact with the location decision such as plant layout, output productivity and costs, maintenance and machine replacement costs, market demand, transportation costs, and competitive actions would be included. Because we can't do this, the method outlined in the next section at least offers an approach.

FACILITY SELECTION USING DIMENSIONAL ANALYSIS

Decisions related to intangible cost systems present great difficulties. Several means of resolving these problems can be suggested.

1. Entirely subjective decisions can be made.
2. A quasi-objective approach can be utilized which requires that *preference measures* be stated for various factors that describe different aspects of the system's performance. Weights or index numbers can be used to express preference. These measures are then compared in some objective manner.
3. Methods of decision making under uncertainty can be used (see pp. 67–68).

The major difficulty in evaluating alternative plant and facility designs is the fact that conflicting objectives, having quite different dimensions must be combined, somehow, to provide a reasonable basis for evaluation. Let us develop an example so that we can view this kind of problem in specific terms.

Assume that in searching for a new plant location, two plans have been developed. (The discussion could easily include many more of the factors we have previously discussed without changing, in any way, the significance of what we are about to say.) Let Plan 1 specify building a plant in Boston; while Plan 2 specifies building a plant in Camden. Assume that the proposals have been evaluated as shown in Table 11.1.

TABLE 11.1

	BOSTON	CAMDEN	
OUTCOMES	PLAN 1	PLAN 2	WEIGHT[6]
Building costs and equipment costs—yearly depreciated value	$500,000	$300,000	4
Taxes (per year)	$ 50,000	$ 20,000	4
Power cost (per year)	$ 20,000	$ 30,000	4
Community attitude	1	2	1
Product quality as a function of worker morale and skill	2	3	5
Flexibility to adapt to situations that are likely to occur	1	6	3

[6] The larger the weight the more important the dimension is considered to be, relative to the other dimensions.

Dollars must be added together. Using discounting (pp. 364–66), dollars are made to apply to the same period of time. Furthermore, companies will have different measures for the relative importance of dollars, depending upon their assets. If such factors as community attitude, product quality, and flexibility could be associated with a dollar value, there would not be a dimensional problem to resolve. However, it must be recognized that these latter elements represent *intangible costs*. The attempt to estimate such costs would prove arduous with little conviction that the results are satisfactory. On the other hand, it is possible for the manager to rank the relative merits of the two plans for each intangible factor.

The example utilizes a scale from 1 to 10, where the value of 1 represents the "best possible" result and the value of 10 would be the least desirable. This is because the table is written in terms of costs. (The value 10 would be optimal if the table had been constructed in terms of profit.) Thus, with respect to community attitude, Plan 1 is preferred to Plan 2 although, on the whole, both of them seem to be considered desirable. With respect to flexibility, Plan 2 is apparently quite inferior to Plan 1. Let us turn to the third column in the table—captioned "Weight." These weighting factors (or index numbers) represent the relative importances of the set of outcome-objectives that are being analyzed. According to the weights that have been assigned, product quality is the most important consideration whereas community attitude is least important. Flexibility is rated as being slightly less important than costs. This arrangement of weighting values would undoubtedly change if the company's capitalization were altered; or if the planning objectives were modified. The numbers that we have used represent assignments for a particular set of individuals and circumstances.

Various approaches can be used for obtaining the weights. These include:

1. Using the estimates of that individual who is responsible for this decision.

2. Using an average value, obtained by pooling the opinions of a number of individuals who have different responsibilities with respect to the project;

3. Employing an informal blending of the opinions of a number of individuals to develop a set of estimates and weights that are agreeable to all concerned parties.

A noteworthy characteristic of the third approach is that it creates an opportunity for the project participants to *communicate* with each other about the facility decision. They can do this:

First, with respect to which factors are likely to be critical determinants of the decision.

Second, concerning the estimates for each of the outcomes; a set of which must be supplied for each of the alternative plans.

Third, the weighting factors which indicate the relative importance in each individual's mind for the critical factors required to evaluate the system.

A multiplication method of evaluating alternatives by means of weighting factors is frequently used.[7]

The approach we will employ which is particularly suitable for dealing with intangible factors, requires that preference be expressed as the products of the outcomes raised to powers for each plan. We can then compare the plans in ratio with each other. This is:

$$R = \frac{\text{Preference for Plan 1}}{\text{Preference for Plan 2}} = \left(\frac{O_{11}}{O_{21}}\right)^{w_1} \left(\frac{O_{12}}{O_{22}}\right)^{w_2} (\cdots) \left(\frac{O_{1j}}{O_{2j}}\right)^{w_j} (\cdots) \left(\frac{O_{1n}}{O_{2n}}\right)^{w_n}$$

where estimates are supplied to describe the values of the various outcomes that each plan will produce. For the ith alternative we would have $O_{i1}, O_{i2}, \ldots,$ $O_{ij}, \ldots, O_{in}$. Each outcome objective is then weighted for its relative importance. Let us call the weighting factors $w_1, w_2, \ldots, w_j, \ldots, w_n$. It will be noted that the ratio R is a *pure number* meaning that it has no dimensional involvement.[8] We should note that if all outcomes are measured in the same dimension, e.g., dollars, then this approach would incorrectly treat a single outcome as though it was many outcomes having a variety of dimensional properties.

Let us return to the numerical example stated in Table 11.1. All costs are based on a one-year period, so we add them together yielding $570,000 and $350,000, respectively for Plans 1 and 2. Accordingly, the comparison we are seeking is:

$$R = \frac{\text{Preference for Plan 1}}{\text{Preference for Plan 2}} = \left(\frac{570,000}{350,000}\right)^4 \left(\frac{1}{2}\right)^1 \left(\frac{2}{3}\right)^5 \left(\frac{1}{6}\right)^3 = 0.002$$

Based on this result, we will choose Plan 1 because the ratio is less than 1. That is, the costs in the denominator are greater than the costs in the numerator. Accordingly, we choose the plan in the numerator. The method of evaluation that we have employed is useful for a wide range of project-type decisions. It would be appropriate for product-design decisions, process-design decisions, equipment selection and plant-location plans. On the other hand, when we find that one location factor dominates all others, special methods can be used. The next section considers such a situation. In general, however, plant selection and location involves many variables. Problem resolution is begun by eliminating possibilities that violate fundamental constraints. Hopefully, this will reduce the number of real alternatives to manageable proportions.

---

[7] See for example, the use of this method to evaluate alternative aircraft designs as used by a major aircraft manufacturer, L. Ivan Epstein, "A Proposed Measure for Determining the Value of a Design," *The Journal of the Operations Research Society of America*, Vol. 5, No. 2, April 1957, pp. 297–299. Also, C. Radhakrishna *Rao, Advanced Statistical Methods in Biometric Research*, New York: John Wiley & Sons, Inc., 1952), p. 103; also, see Walter R. Stahl, "Similarity and Dimensional Methods in Biology," *Science*, Vol. 137, 20 July, 1962, pp. 205–212, and P. W. Bridgman, *Dimensional Analysis* (New Haven: Yale University Press, 1922). This is also available in paperbound edition, 1963.

[8] Thus, for example, $\dfrac{(\$)^{w_1}(\text{quality})^{w_2}}{(\$)^{w_1}(\text{quality})^{w_2}}$ = pure number.

When transportation costs dominate the plant location problem (either of raw materials to the plant or of finished goods from the plant to warehouses) then a relatively straightforward model exists for analyzing this situation. There is no real problem if only one market and one raw material source exist. This is illustrated in Figure 11.5.

FIGURE 11-5
Plant location prob-
lem—Factory 1 or
Factory 2? (Where
only one market and
one raw material
source exist.)

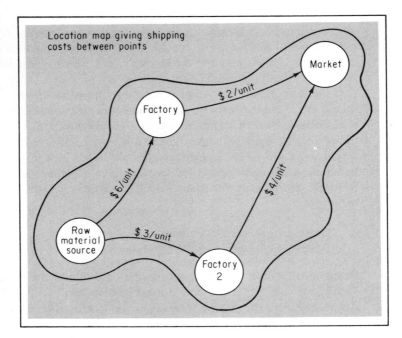

Location map giving shipping costs between points

Market

Factory 1

$2/unit

$6/unit

$4/unit

Raw material source

$3/unit

Factory 2

The raw materials required for one unit would cost $6.00 if shipped to Factory 1, called F_1. The cost is $3.00 if shipped to Factory 2, called F_2. On the other hand, the cost of shipping a finished unit to the market from F_1 is $2.00; from F_2 it is $4.00. Total transportation costs for the factory location F_1 are $8.00 per unit. This is one dollar more than total transport costs for F_2. Therefore, we would choose F_2—if transportation costs are the dominating factor with respect to the choice of location.

Now, let us complicate the problem by creating two markets and by allowing the possibility of multiple facilities. Figure 11.6 illustrates this situation which fits the pattern of a very simple distribution problem. It can be resolved by means of the transportation algorithm which was previously described for the resolution of machine loading problems, see pp. 239–53.

Using the costs specified in Figure 11.6, we can prepare a transportation matrix, where the matrix cell entries are the transportation costs of finished

FIGURE 11-6
Plant location prob-
lem—Factory 1, Fac-
tory 2, or both?
(Where two markets
and one raw mate-
rial source exist.)

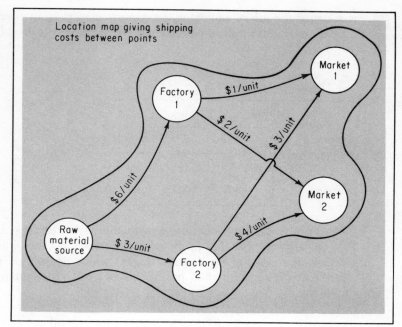

Location map giving shipping costs between points

goods from Factory i to Market j. (Note: Factories are distinguished by rows, $i = 1, 2$; markets are represented by columns, $j = 1, 2$.)

FACTORY (F_i)	RAW MATERIAL TRANSPORT COSTS	MARKET (M_j)		SUPPLY
		M_1	M_2	
F_1	$6/unit	$1/unit	$2/unit	90 units/day
F_2	$3/unit	$3/unit	$4/unit	90 units/day
	Demand	40 units/day	40 units/day	

Also, we have added the description of supply and demand. In other words, each market demands 40 units per day to be shipped from either F_1 or F_2, or a combination. Both factories have been designed so that they can have a maximum productive capacity of 90 units per day. Which *location* should be chosen for our factory? We allow the possibility of choosing both.

In the first place, we must note that total daily supply potential exceeds total daily demand by 100 units, assuming that both factories operate at full capacity. (We shall not permit this to occur.) To correct the theoretical imbalance between supply and demand we create a slack, or *dummy market* (DM) to absorb 100 units per day. The market does not really exist. Therefore, whichever factory is assigned the job of supplying the dummy market is, in effect, eliminated as a location. For example, a possible pattern of shipments would be:

| | MARKET | | | |
FACTORY	M_1	M_2	DM	SUPPLY
F_1			90	90
F_2	40	40	10	90
Demand	40	40	100	180

If this were the optimal solution, we would interpret this matrix as stating that F_2 is the best location; that F_1 should be eliminated because it has been assigned the task of supplying the dummy market which doesn't exist. We also note that the excess capacity of F_2 has been allocated to the dummy, which is as it should be.

Is this result really the best solution? The best solution will result in minimum total transportation costs, so we must test to find out if there is any better arrangement. The matrix of total transportation costs would be:

Total Transport Costs per Unit

| | MARKET | | |
FACTORY	M_1	M_2	DM
F_1	6 + 1 = $7	6 + 2 = $8	$0
F_2	3 + 3 = $6	3 + 4 = $7	$0

The raw material transportation costs have been added to the finished goods transportation costs. Any shipments to the dummy market cost $0 because it doesn't exist. Now, let us raise a number of questions and find the appropriate answers.

1. What is the total cost of the shipping plan described above which eliminated F_1? The cost is calculated directly. There are 40 units shipped from F_2 to M_1 at $6.00 per unit, or $240.00, and an additional 40 units are shipped from F_2 to M_2 at $7.00 per unit, or $280.00. The total cost is $240.00 + $280.00, which equals $520.00 per day.

2. Can we lower this cost by shipping one unit from F_1 to M_1? If we ship one unit from F_1 to M_1, we must rearrange the total shipping schedule, as follows:

| FACTORY | MARKET | | | |
	M_1	M_2	DM	SUPPLY
F_1	1		89	90
F_2	39	40	11	90
Demand	40	40	100	

The cost of this shipping arrangement is: $(\$7 \times 1) + (\$6 \times 39) + (\$7 \times 40)$ = \$521.00 per day. Because one unit shipped from F_1 to M_1 produces a greater cost, more than one unit shipped in this way will be even worse.

3. Can we lower the total cost by shipping one unit from F_1 to M_2? That is:

| FACTORY | MARKET | | | |
	M_1	M_2	DM	SUPPLY
F_1		1	89	90
F_2	40	39	11	90
Demand	40	40	100	

The total cost result is $(\$8 \times 1) + (\$6 \times 40) + (\$7 \times 39)$ = \$521.00 per day. Once again, no decrease in cost has been found. Because no other possibilities exist for alternate shipping routes, we conclude that the original solution was optimal. The location to be chosen is Factory 2.

The procedure that we have been using consists of evaluating the difference in costs that would result from alternative shipping patterns for one unit. If a savings could be made by shifting the pattern, then we would put as many units as possible into the preferred shipment pattern. To illustrate this, let us consider a slightly more elaborate example.

| FACTORY | MARKET | | | |
	M_1	M_2	DM	SUPPLY
F_1	\$7/unit	\$8/unit	\$0/unit	50 units/day
F_2	\$6/unit	\$7/unit	\$0/unit	90 units/day
F_3	\$8/unit	\$10/unit	\$0/unit	90 units/day
Demand	40 units per day	40 units per day	150 units per day	230 units per day

The cost entries in the matrix are *total* transportation costs per unit. The company has an *actual* operating factory, F_1, which has a maximum capacity of 50 units per day. The demand for the product is greater than the supply, viz., 80 units per day. The locations F_2 and F_3 are under serious consideration. Whichever is chosen, it has been decided to install a production capacity of 90 units per day. As before, we assume that transportation costs dominate the plant location decision. Let us make a first allocation, using the Northwest Corner Method. (Again, supply and demand are balanced with a dummy market, DM.)

	MARKET			
FACTORY	M_1	M_2	*DM*	SUPPLY
F_1	40	10		50
F_2		30	60	90
F_3			90	90
Demand	40	40	150	230

We begin in the upper left-hand corner and allocate as many units as possible to F_1—M_1. This is 40 units. More than that would exceed demand. But the supply of F_1 has not been exhausted. Therefore, we move to F_1—M_2 and allocate 10 units. This uses up all of F_1's production capacity. However, M_2's requirements have not been met. Continuing in this manner, we will *always* succeed in deriving an initial allocation.[9]

We must now test to find out whether a cost reduction can be achieved. There are four possible changes that could be made.

1. We could shift 10 units from F_1—M_2 to F_1—DM. Thus:

	MARKET			
FACTORY	M_1	M_2	*DM*	SUPPLY
F_1	40		10	50
F_2		40	50	90
F_3			90	90
Demand	40	40	150	230

If more than 10 units were shifted this would create a negative shipment at the intersection of F_1—M_2, which is a situation that could not be tolerated. Similar restrictions exist with respect to other changes.

---

[9] The number of shipments used should never exceed $M + N - 1$, where·

$$M = \text{the number of markets and } N = \text{the number of factories.}$$

Thus, for the example above, we have: $3 + 3 - 1 = 5$ which is the number of shipments derived by means of the Northwest Corner Rule. We can never obtain a better solution with more than 5 shipments and usually we would obtain a worse one. Although the logic of this point is indisputable, the most convincing demonstrations can be derived by working through a few simple examples, e.g., one factory and many markets; two factories and many markets.

2. We can shift 30 units from F_2—M_2 to F_2—M_1.
3. We can shift 30 units from F_2—M_2 to F_3—M_1.
4. We can shift 30 units from F_2—M_2 to F_3—M_2.

Let us evaluate the marginal change in cost that will result from shipping one unit from F_1 to DM.

1. Ship one unit from F_1 to DM: $+\$0$
2. Ship one less unit from F_1 to M_2: $-\$8$
3. Ship one more unit from F_2 to M_2: $+\$7$
4. Ship one less unit from F_2 to DM $-\$0$
                                      TOTAL $-\$1$

The total cost can be reduced one dollar by making this change. Each of 10 units can be shipped for $1.00 less per unit. This is a total cost reduction of $10.00. Proceeding in the same fashion we find:

1. Shipping 1 unit from F_2 to M_1 produces zero change.
2. Shipping 1 unit from F_3 to M_1 would result in extra expense of $2.00 per unit.
3. Shipping 1 unit from F_3 to M_2 would result in extra expense of $3.00 per unit.

Accordingly, we shift 10 units from F_1—M_2 to F_1—DM. The new transportation matrix appears as follows:

| | MARKET | | | |
FACTORY	M_1	M_2	DM	SUPPLY
F_1	40	⊕1	10	50
F_2	⊖1	40	50	90
F_3	⊕1	⊖3	90	90
Demand	40	40	150	230

We have tested this arrangement to see if any other savings can be made. The marginal cost changes that would result from further modification of the shipping pattern are shown in the circles of the above matrix. Additional improvement is possible. Forty units can be shifted from F_1—M_1 to F_2—M_1. We would then have:

| | MARKET | | | |
FACTORY	M_1	M_2	DM	SUPPLY
F_1	⊕1	⊕1	50	50
F_2	40	40	10	90
F_3	⊖2	⊖3	90	90
Demand	40	40	150	

The marginal cost analysis shows that no further improvements can be obtained. Because Factories 1 and 3 ship only to the dummy, they will be eliminated. The solution also states that Factory 2 will operate at 8/9 of capacity.

The limitations and strengths of the transportation procedure are apparent. In its terms, an optimal plant location can be determined based on relevant cost data. On the other hand, we know that many other factors are usually required to properly evaluate alternative locations. The intangible factors have been totally ignored by this method. When the intangibles are critical, then perhaps a method similar to dimensional analysis should be utilized in conjunction with managerial intuition.

PROGRAMMING APPROACHES TO LOCATION

A variety of mathematical models have been developed to assist in the analysis of location opportunities. For the most part, they represent extensions of the transportation algorithm previously described. As soon as other factors are added, the simple transportation model no longer suffices. Complex mathematical programming considerations hold. Various computer programs have been developed to help search through various combinations of strategic variables in the attempt to locate an approximation to an optimal facility location.[10]

PLANT LAYOUT

Once the process has been specified, and the appropriate types of equipment have been selected, it is then necessary to arrange all the systems' components in an *optimal layout*. In some cases, the plant has been selected; in others, the plant location choice is affected by layout considerations. Generally, for both the job shop and the flow shop, careful thought has been given to the selection of specific machines; and to the number of such machines needed to provide adequate capacity. The possible connections for material flows between the machines has been surveyed and the sensible placement of operators and the number of operators has also been discussed. Usually, however, alternatives exist. The list of alternatives interacts with layout decisions. Facility alternatives constrain layout and layout alternatives constrain facilities. This is not easy to show, because the layout problem even *with fixed equipment selections* is still extremely complex.

BASIC APPROACHES TO LAYOUT

Decisions regarding the arrangement of specific elements are what we refer to as the layout problem. Often, the specific elements are grouped into *machine*

---

[10] See, for example, Robert J. Atkins and Richard H. Shriver, "New Approach to Facilities Location," *Harvard Business Review.* May-June 1968, p. 75.

centers. This helps the production manager by giving him a fewer number of elements to think about. Although physical models of the plant floor and the selected equipment are frequently helpful in guiding arrangement, intuition underlies their use. Models can be two- or three-dimensional. Often, two-dimensional floor plans with cutouts, or templates, representing the various pieces of equipment are used. When conveyors are employed, overhead space requirements may be important and three dimensional models are preferred. These techniques are useful for *approaching* a satisfactory layout, but they do not hold out any promise of finding an optimal layout (as defined below).

Can an optimal layout really be found? At the present time, it is nonoperational to talk about an optimal arrangement. There are too many possible layout variations, and no way to search through them all. As the production process approaches total mechanization and, ultimately, complete automation, then, technological constraints operate. The flow-shop configuration warrants large study investments. The notion of an optimal layout becomes more tenable. For the general case, however, it is desirable to talk about *obtaining* a satisfactory layout.

What is an optimal, or near optimal (i.e., satisfactory) layout? Some of the possible measures of a layout's effectiveness would be:

1. The capacity of the system under different arrangements;

2. The investment and operating costs of various arrangements of the production systems; and

3. The flexibility to change a layout as required.

Clearly, for flow and project shops, it is essential to balance the output rates of consecutive operations. This is the line-balancing problem, see pp. 225–26.

The layout problem is complicated by the question of whether we shall make do with an existing plant or build a new one to our specifications. Frequently, when a plant-rental arrangement is used, basic structural changes either are prohibited or are not economically sensible. When an existing structure has been purchased it may not be economically feasible to knock down walls, add sections, and make other structural changes. Such alterations require investment in plant and such investments must be justified in terms of alternative uses of these funds. The relative permanency desired for any physical arrangement of components is a matter that arises here. If a continuous production line is to be set up, it obviously presents different conditions than would be encountered with a job-shop system.

Given some knowledge of the plant construction, a well-known basic approach to the plant layout problem makes use of schematics, such as flow-process diagrams, flow-process charts, and various forms of dimensional models; all decisions that follow are clearly dominated by intuition. (See Figures 11.7, 11.8, 11.9 and 11.10.) It is reasonable to work with both the flow diagram and the process chart. Thus, for example, an initial layout and system is conceived (e.g., Figures 11.7 and 11.8). Then, various changes are proposed as challengers. Figures 11.9 and 11.10 are representative of proposed improvements.

In general a satisfactory resolution of the plant layout problem is considerably expedited by the use of flow-process layout diagrams, as shown in Figures

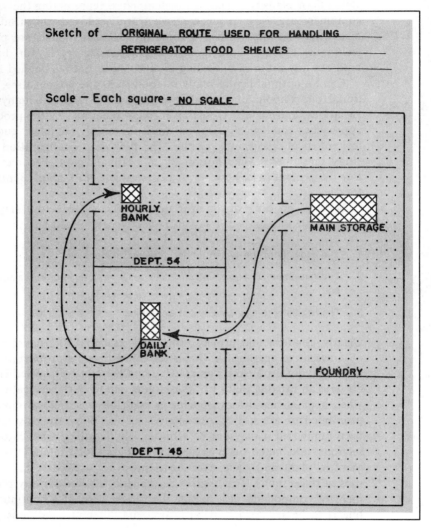

Sketch of ___ORIGINAL ROUTE USED FOR HANDLING___
___REFRIGERATOR FOOD SHELVES___

Scale — Each square = _NO SCALE_

HOURLY BANK.

MAIN STORAGE.

DEPT. 54

DAILY BANK.

FOUNDRY

DEPT. 45

11.7 and 11.9. These diagrams describe the flow of food shelves for a refrigerator manufacturer. The flow path is superimposed on the floor plan. Alternative arrangements of layout produce different flow patterns. Changes in layout are normally made until a satisfactory flow pattern is achieved. In conjunction, appropriate flow-process charts are developed to describe those characteristics of the system's flow that do not lend themselves to visual representation, e.g.,

FIGURE 11-8
Process chart-product analysis for original method of handling refrigerator food shelves from bulk storage to plating department. [From Marvin E. Mundel, *Motion and Time Study*, 4th ed. (Englewood Cliffs, N.J.: Prentice-Hall, Inc., 1970), p. 61.]

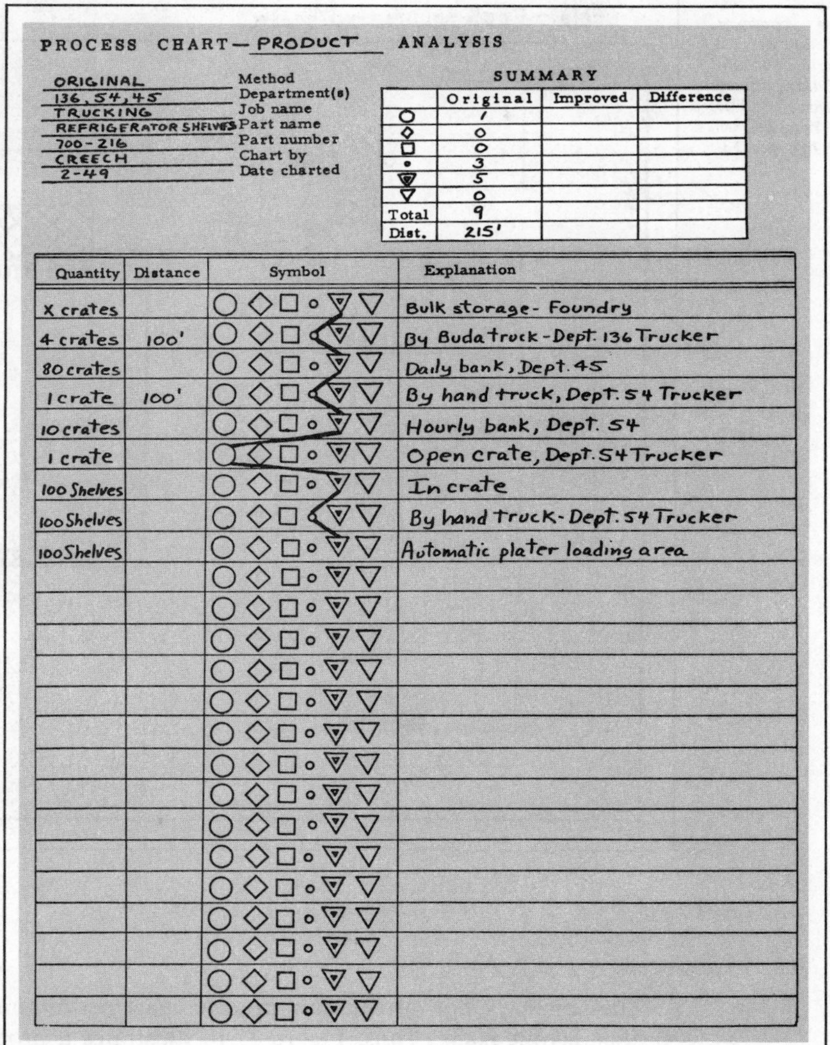

PROCESS CHART — PRODUCT ANALYSIS

	ORIGINAL		
	136, 54, 45	Method Department(s)	
	TRUCKING	Job name	
	REFRIGERATOR SHELVES	Part name	
	700-216	Part number	
	CREECH	Chart by	
	2-49	Date charted	

SUMMARY

	Original	Improved	Difference
○	1		
◇	0		
□	0		
•	3		
▽	5		
▽	0		
Total	9		
Dist.	215'		

Quantity	Distance	Symbol	Explanation
X crates		○ ◇ □ ∘ ▽ ▽	Bulk storage - Foundry
4 crates	100'	○ ◇ □ ∘ ▽ ▽	By Buda truck - Dept. 136 Trucker
80 crates		○ ◇ □ ∘ ▽ ▽	Daily bank, Dept. 45
1 crate	100'	○ ◇ □ ∘ ▽ ▽	By hand truck, Dept. 54 Trucker
10 crates		○ ◇ □ ∘ ▽ ▽	Hourly bank, Dept. 54
1 crate		○ ◇ □ ∘ ▽ ▽	Open crate, Dept. 54 Trucker
100 Shelves		○ ◇ □ ∘ ▽ ▽	In crate
100 Shelves		○ ◇ □ ∘ ▽ ▽	By hand truck - Dept. 54 Trucker
100 Shelves		○ ◇ □ ∘ ▽ ▽	Automatic plater loading area
		○ ◇ □ ∘ ▽ ▽	
		○ ◇ □ ∘ ▽ ▽	
		○ ◇ □ ∘ ▽ ▽	
		○ ◇ □ ∘ ▽ ▽	
		○ ◇ □ ∘ ▽ ▽	
		○ ◇ □ ∘ ▽ ▽	
		○ ◇ □ ∘ ▽ ▽	
		○ ◇ □ ∘ ▽ ▽	
		○ ◇ □ ∘ ▽ ▽	
		○ ◇ □ ∘ ▽ ▽	
		○ ◇ □ ∘ ▽ ▽	
		○ ◇ □ ∘ ▽ ▽	
		○ ◇ □ ∘ ▽ ▽	

Figures 11.8 and 11.10. Note that special symbols are used to indicate different categories of systems behaviors. Figure 11.11 presents the key for interpreting these symbols. There is no totally uniform convention with respect to such symbols, and in practice, many variations will be found.

FIGURE 11-9
Flow diagram for the proposed method of handling refrigerator food shelves. Note that a wall has been broken through to yield direct access to the conveyor. [From Marvin E. Mundel, *Motion and Time Study*, 4th ed. (Englewood Cliffs, N. J.: Prentice-Hall, Inc., 1970), p. 62.]

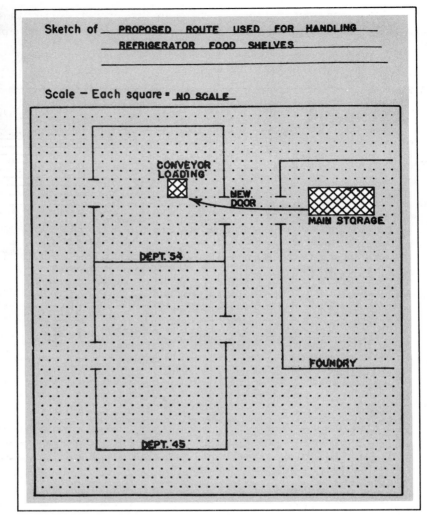

The summary box of the flow process chart permits rapid comparison of various layout plans. Thus, Figure 11.10 illustrates a proposed revision. The summary box of the proposed method reveals that two kinds of improvements will result if the original layout arrangement is changed. These include one less transport and two less uncontrolled storage stages. The travel distance has been decreased by 140 feet. If the first layout is in actual use, then it is necessary to compare the cost of making the change with the reduction in operating costs that can be achieved. The comparison requires the use of an appropriate discounting formulation (see pp. 364–66) so that the stream of savings can be properly evaluated.

FIGURE 11-10
Process chart-product analysis for proposed method of handling refrigerator food shelves from bulk storage to plating department. [From Marvin E. Mundel, *Motion and Time Study,* 4th ed. (Englewood Cliffs, N.J.: Prentice-Hall, Inc., 1970), p. 61.]

PROCESS CHART — PRODUCT ANALYSIS

PROPOSED	Method			
136, 54	Department(s)			
TRUCKING	Job name			
REFRIGERATOR SHELVES	Part name			
700 - 216	Part number			
CREECH	Chart by			
2 - 49	Date charted			

SUMMARY

	Original	Improved	Difference
○	1	1	0
◇	0	0	0
□	0	0	0
○ (transport)	3	2	— 1
▽ (uncontrolled)	5	3	— 2
▽ (controlled)	0	0	0
Total	9	6	— 3
Dist.	215'	75'	—140'

Quantity	Distance	Symbol	Explanation
X crates		○ ◇ □ ○ ▽ ▽	Bulk storage - Foundry
1 crate	15'	○ ◇ □ ○ ▽ ▽	By hand truck - Dept. 54 trucker
1 crate		○ ◇ □ ○ ▽ ▽	Open crate - Dept. 54 trucker
100 Shelves		○ ◇ □ ○ ▽ ▽	In crate
100 Shelves	60'	○ ◇ □ ○ ▽ ▽	By hand truck - Dept. 54 trucker
100 Shelves		○ ◇ □ ○ ▽ ▽	Automatic plater loading area
		○ ◇ □ ○ ▽ ▽	
		○ ◇ □ ○ ▽ ▽	
		○ ◇ □ ○ ▽ ▽	
		○ ◇ □ ○ ▽ ▽	
		○ ◇ □ ○ ▽ ▽	
		○ ◇ □ ○ ▽ ▽	
		○ ◇ □ ○ ▽ ▽	
		○ ◇ □ ○ ▽ ▽	
		○ ◇ □ ○ ▽ ▽	

FIGURE 11-11
Symbol key for flow process chart.

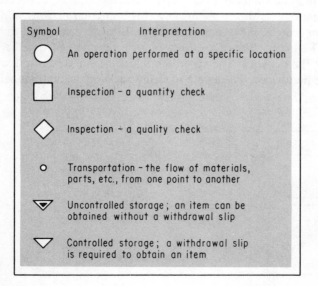

Symbol	Interpretation
○	An operation performed at a specific location
□	Inspection – a quantity check
◇	Inspection – a quality check
○	Transportation – the flow of materials, parts, etc., from one point to another
▽	Uncontrolled storage; an item can be obtained without a withdrawal slip
▽	Controlled storage; a withdrawal slip is required to obtain an item

ASSEMBLY LAYOUT

It is frequently more practical to begin the layout plan in an environment that is totally divorced from the spatial constraints of reality. An assembly diagram, also called a Gozinto (goes-into) Chart, is a flow diagram concerned neither with real time nor real space. Only sequence is presented. Generally, service activities, such as transportation and storage are excluded. An example of a Gozinto Chart is shown in Figure 6.14 (see p. 158). Using this chart, an intelligent arrangement of facilities can be determined based on the essential sequential requirements of the process.

MULTIPLE-ITEM LAYOUT ANALYSIS

The layout problem is much more complicated when a common set of facilities must be shared by multiple products that require different flow paths and sequences through the system. For example, Figure 6.16 (see p. 160) portrays a flow-process layout diagram where alternate routes must be followed by the several products in the company's product mix. To find layout plans that are reasonably close to optimal for such cases requires considerable juggling of the facilities. As a rule, the product that contributes the *greatest percentage to total profit* is given preferential treatment, and the others less so in accordance with their value to the company. At least, this heuristic simplifies the problem. With one major product being processed (flow-shop configuration), it is reasonable to route that product on a *minimum cost path*.

THE STRING-LAYOUT MODEL

Now, let us consider an example of the more abstract (and sometimes quantitative) methods that can be of help in resolving the layout problem. An interesting special case is the *string model*. This approach permits minimum distance, minimum time, or maximum capacity paths to be discovered through a complex maze. The knots, when the pieces of string are joined together, are called the nodes of the network. They represent machines or stations at which operations are to be performed. The length of string between the nodes is called the network

FIGURE 11-12
The use of a string model to determine the minimum network path between any two layout positions. The distance between nodes is the distance (time, cost, capacity, etc.) between stations.

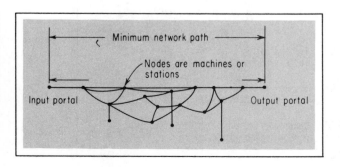

arc. This length is made proportional to the distance between machines that a given layout calls for. The length could also be made proportional to traverse time between stations, to the cost of transporting an item between stations, or to the capacity of each network arc. Such a string model is shown in Figure 11.12.

When the string is stretched taut between any two nodes, we immediately obtain the minimum path between these nodes. Thus, for different input (receiving) and output (shipping) portals, a given layout can be rather quickly compared with alternative designs. The ease with which this model can be applied is its greatest recommendation.

THE LAYOUT PROBLEM

When we consider the layout problem in mathematical terms, we find that it is surprisingly large and complex. This is true, even though we dismiss many of the factors that being intangible are reserved ordinarily for intuition. The layout problem for an average size job shop, strictly in cost terms, is recognized to involve consideration of billions or trillions of alternatives. This explains why the intuitive approach has been so widely used for job-shop layout decisions. It is always possible (even probable) that intuition will overlook some excellent solutions, but one thing is certain, while optimality may be missed by the manager, an illogical and inappropriate solution will not be accepted by him. Let us see why the layout problem for the job shop is so demanding.[11]

FIGURE 11-13
The floor layout of a plant with five location centers or hubs.

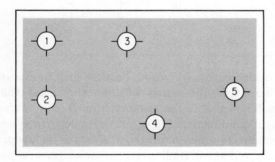

Define the *job shop* as consisting of *n machine centers*, MC_j $(j = 1, 2, \ldots, n)$. Each machine center has a fundamentally different activity. We shall choose, as our objective: *Minimize materials handling costs*.

Given a specific plant, its configuration will constrain the way in which we

---

[11] Clearly, the layout problem of a flow shop or a project shop would be different from a job shop. The layout, in these cases, would actually interact with the line-balance solutions and project tradeoff solutions that we derived in earlier chapters. So, it is most often the job shop layout problem to which we address ourselves.

can assign machine centers to plant areas.[12] Assume that five plant areas are designated, and the question is: How to assign five machine centers to these areas? Figure 11.13 portrays a floor layout with five location hubs. In some sense, these conform to the floor plan of the plant.

The job shop can have many different flow patterns. Its layout problem is complicated because a common set of facilities must be shared by multiple products that require different flow paths and sequences through the system, e.g., Figure 6.16 (see p. 160).

AN ASSIGNMENT-TYPE MODEL

Divide the plant floor into sections. Next, measure either the time or distance required to transport an item from each plant section to all other plant sections. It is then possible to construct a matrix which shows the appropriate cost factor for transporting between any two positions on the plant floor. An example of such a matrix would be:

MATRIX OF TRAVERSE DISTANCES
BETWEEN PLANT SECTIONS
(IN FEET)

		TO POSITION			
		A	B	C	D
	A	·	10	20	32
	B	10	·	16	16
From Position	C	20	16	·	12
	D	32	16	12	·

The diagonal of the matrix is blocked, because such transport has no meaning. Also, as a general rule, the matrix will be symmetrical, that is, the distance from A to B will be equal to the distance from B to A. This is not always the case, especially if unidirectional (e.g., gravity) conveyor systems connect some of the plant sections. In order to determine an optimum layout plan we must discover a closed loop that will result in the minimum traverse path. The first steps to be taken are identical with those used for resolving the assignment problem.[13] The solution will consist of a set of four zeros such that there will be a unique zero in every row and a unique zero in every column. (No diagonal entries are allowed.) In other words, for a matrix of n sections, there will be at least n zeros that meet the requirement stated above.[14]

---

[12] For example, heavy machinery can only be assigned to certain areas. Cranes may require special height clearance, upper floors are needed for gravity conveyors, press shops cannot be located near offices because of noise, receiving and shipping should logically be close to truck docks and rail spurs, etc.

[13] See pp. 232–39.

[14] More than n zeros can exist, as long as the row and column conditions are fulfilled. Additional zeros may permit alternate solutions, but this is not a necessity.

When a solution has been arrived at, it must be checked to see whether or not a complete closed loop has been derived. In the matrix below, we see that the assignment solution produces two closed loops, *A-B-A* and *C-D-C*. Thus, the solution can be read: Move the product from *A* to *B* and from *B* to *A*. Also, move it from *C* to *D* and then back to *C*. This is not satisfactory. There is no instruction for relating *A* and *B* with *C* and *D*.

	TO POSITION			
	A	*B*	*C*	*D*
A	·	0		
B	0	·		
From Position *C*			·	0
D			0	·

A closed-loop solution would look like this.

	TO POSITION				
	A	*B*	*C*	*D*	
A	·		0		
B		·		0	Total Distance = 52
From Position *C*		0	·		
D	0			·	

Another possibility would be as follows.

	TO POSITION				
	A	*B*	*C*	*D*	
A	·	0			
B		·	0		Total Distance = 38
From Position *C*			·	0	
D	0		·		

Assume that *D* represents the packing and shipping department, then, the connection between *D* and *A* can be ignored. With this condition, the total distance in the first closed loop matrix is $20 + 16 + 16 = 52$; in the second case it is $10 + 16 + 12 = 38$. We prefer the latter arrangement. It is reasonable to assume that one of the positions (say *A*) is the receiving point and that another (such as *D*) is the shipping point. Usually, there will be specific input (receiving) and output (shipping) portals. The various network combinations can be explored between these portals.

If the assignment method cannot produce the necessary closed-path sequences, it is possible that judgment may be used to connect two or more closed subloops. Various mathematical techniques have been developed to resolve situations of this type which are called "traveling salesman" problems.[15]

---

[15] The so-called "branch and bound" algorithm can always be used to solve these problems. See, Martin K. Starr, *Systems Management of Operations* (Englewood Cliffs, N.J.: Prentice-Hall, Inc. 1970), pp. 313–23.

The reason that the layout problem is difficult is that machine centers can be *matched* to floor locations in so many different ways. Say that there are n floor locations and n machine centers. Then, each of n different machine centers might be assigned to the first floor location; $n - 1$ different machine centers could be assigned to the second floor location; and so forth. This results in $n!$ possible layout arrangements, which is quite a large number for any value of n greater than 5.[16] Furthermore, the measure of effectiveness for each particular layout configuration has to reflect the distance between floor locations multiplied by the amount of material that will flow between each location as a result of the specific machine centers that are assigned to the floor locations. Such measures of effectiveness have to be recalculated for each configuration. Thus, any method aimed at locating a near-optimal arrangement, must be able to search through a large percent of the $n!$ possibilities.

Heuristic rules for searching have been developed. One of the simplest of these is to minimize the flow of materials between non-adjacent floor locations. In effect, this approach assigns the maximum flows of materials to the minimum distances. But such heuristics are a crude approach to the complex problem that exists for a large job shop.

EQUIPMENT SELECTION

The process can be viewed as equipment selected to provide specific services.[17] Inputs arrive to receive these services; thus, we have providers of service and users of that service. This is the underlying theme of any production process. To understand production, it is essential that we be knowledgeable about the selection of equipment. But we do not expect to get involved with specific technologies. That kind of understanding grows out of having to do a *real* job. On the job, we learn about the specific technology that is being used. Before committing ourselves to any specific technology, there is much that can be learned about the nature of equipment selection in general.

AN ASPECT OF EQUIPMENT SELECTION

Generally, the production process is the heavy investment, fixed-cost portion of the input-output model. The final choice of equipment and facilities to be used is dependent upon: (1) What is available or what can be made; that is, the technological feasibility constraints; and (2) What is economically reasonable. The design of the process, the quality of its outputs, and its operating efficiency will affect the amount of investment capital that can be attracted. If the process lends itself to a *flow shop* system where demand is approximately

---

[16] For example, 10! > 3,600,000.
[17] See pp. 367–71.

balanced by the designed productivity of the facilities, then a great deal of pre-planning and production line-balancing is called for. A less formal and less rigid design is demanded if many different items constitute the output as is characteristic of a *job shop*.

Consider a simple mathematical description of the determining characteristics of each situation. An appropriate formulation can be derived from inventory models. The explanation of this model was developed on pp. 282–84. For our present purposes it will be sufficient to employ the appropriate formulas:

$$(1) \quad TC = \frac{cx}{2}\left(\frac{p-d}{p}\right)C_c + \frac{z}{x}C_s$$

$$x_o = \sqrt{\frac{2zC_s}{cC_c}\left(\frac{p}{p-d}\right)}$$

Substituting the second equation into the first, we find:

$$(3) \quad TC_o = \sqrt{2zC_s cC_c\left(\frac{p-d}{p}\right)}$$

where:

z = Expected demand per year;

x = The number of units made per run;

x_o = The optimal number of units made per run; that is, the run size that will yield minimum total variable costs;

C_s = Cost of setting up the equipment;

C_c = The carrying cost rate per year;

c = The cost of making the part, including labor, materials, and properly assigned overhead costs or burden;

p = The production rate per day;

d = The demand per day;

TC = The total variable cost of using a production run of x units;

TC_o = The optimal total variable cost associated with a run of x_o units.

Thus, TC_o represents the optimal total cost. It is the minimum that can be obtained for a given piece of equipment which has different productivities for different kinds of parts. In other words, TC_o occurs when the best possible arrangement of production runs is used on a given piece of equipment. For a specific facility, if each item that is run on that equipment is produced in the optimum run quantity, then the facility is being optimally utilized.[18] For example, suppose that a machine shop produces two different items on the specified machine. Assume that for optimum run size the first item requires 500 hours on the machine and 400 hours off the machine. If the second item requires 400 hours on the machine and 500 hours between runs, then the machine is both fully and optimally utilized. *This is, in fact, perfect use of equipment.*

Now, however, consider the problem of comparing alternative equipments

---

[18] It can be noted that if $p = d$, then $x_o = \infty$, which is equivalent to continuous production, and $TC_o = 0$ because there would be no inventory carried, no carrying cost, and no setup cost.

for a given item. Differences will exist in setup costs, in the production rate that is possible per day, and in the cost of producing the item. (The variables z, C_c, and d are unaffected by the comparison.) Thus, for example, let us evaluate the two machines A and B, given the following data:

	MACHINE A	MACHINE B
p	64 units/day	81 units/day
C_s	$100	$144
c	$9	$9

Putting these numbers into our formulation we see that machine A has a lower total cost than does machine B for any particular item whose demand does not exceed A's fully utilized production capacity. Although a numerical preference clearly exists for machine A under these conditions, the *total* picture must be evaluated before a final decision is rendered. That is, when a number of items must be processed on a given machine or set of machines it is frequently the case that perfect equipment utilization cannot be achieved. Then, either the machine will be idle a certain percentage of the time, or some of the items cannot be produced under optimal run size conditions. These additional costs must be accounted for before a meaningful comparison of alternative facilities is possible.

This approach is applicable to any type of production system. It is not limited, however, to machines in the customary sense and can be applied to restaurants, libraries, hospitals, and offices as well.

DISCOUNTING ANALYSES FOR EQUIPMENT SELECTION

Quite a different approach is frequently taken to compare alternative facilities when these facilities have different expected service lifetimes and/or when the operating costs change as a function of usage and age. For this situation we make use of discounting functions. As an example, let us compare two different materials handling facilities. These could be different kinds of hand trucks, fork-lift trucks, cranes, or conveyors. We shall assume that an integrated materials handling system has been developed for each alternative.

	MATERIALS HANDLING SYSTEM A	MATERIALS HANDLING SYSTEM B
Estimated service life	3 years	2 years
Investment	$25,000	$20,000
Discount factor	6 percent per year	6 percent per year
Operating cost per year	$2,000	$1,000

It should be evident that operating costs in this table must be related to optimal run sizes for the equipment served by the materials handling facilities. Frequently, the optimal run size requires continuous production, in which case permanent installation of expensive conveyor systems can be employed. Comparisons of this kind are sometimes made without taking into consideration the fact that the operating costs of one of the facilities may have been determined for conditions that are close to optimal whereas the other facility is severely penalized because its costs have not been determined for non-optimal operating conditions. Unfortunately, this transgression occurs more frequently than one would suppose.

Manufacturers of machine tools and other equipment can use the following kind of argument when trying to sell their products. "You have nothing to lose in buying this equipment. If the savings obtained as a result of using the new equipment are not sufficient to pay for it, then we will gladly take it back and make a full refund." A manufacturer's salesman can base this offer on his observation that the operations on the present equipment are inefficient and far from optimal. When the new equipment is installed, a thorough study will be made of how to properly utilize it. This will include efficient work routines and optimal production runs. The advantage of the new machine, at least in part, might be connected with the development of optimal routines rather than being based on fundamental technological advances. If a study of the use of the present equipment were made, savings could also be realized. It is on this basis that an intelligent comparison of alternative facilities can be made—and on no other.

Let us make the required comparison of the alternative materials handling plans, A and B. The calculations are given below. The smallest common period for systems A and B will be six years. During that period of time, system A will turn over twice and system B will turn over three times. Then, using the discounting data (p. 100), for system A (2 cycles), we find:

END OF YEAR	INVESTMENT A	DISCOUNTED OPERATING COSTS	TOTAL DISCOUNTED COST	AVERAGE COST PER YEAR
0	$25,000 × 1.000 = $25,000		$25,000	
1		$2000 × 0.943 = 1886	26,886	$26,886
2		2000 × 0.890 = 1780	28,666	14,333
3	$25,000 × 0.840 = $21,000	2000 × 0.840 = 1680	51,346	17,115
4		2000 × 0.792 = 1584	52,930	13,233
5		2000 × 0.747 = 1494	54,424	10,885
6		2000 × 0.705 = 1410	55,834	9,306

And for system B (3 cycles), we obtain:

END OF YEAR	INVESTMENT B	DISCOUNTED OPERATING COSTS	TOTAL DISCOUNTED COST	AVERAGE COST PER YEAR
0	$20,000 × 1.000 = $20,000		$20,000	
1		$1000 × 0.943 = $943	20,943	$20,943
2	$20,000 × 0.890 = $17,800	1000 × 0.890 = 890	39,633	19,817
3		1000 × 0.840 = 840	40,473	13,491
4	$20,000 × 0.792 = $15,840	1000 × 0.792 = 792	57,035	14,259
5		1000 × 0.747 = 747	57,782	11,556
6		1000 × 0.705 = 705	58,487	9,748

We have discounted both investment sums and operating costs. Year by year these have been added together to give total discounted cost. We could make our comparison with these figures alone. At the end of six years, system A has accumulated total costs of $55,834 which is $2,653 less than system B's total. However, average costs are frequently used as the basis for comparison. These are the total costs divided by the number of years that the cost accumulation represents. Using either the total discounted costs or the average yearly determination of cost, we would select materials handling system A. It should be noted that when the facilities under consideration have different estimated service lives, then we must always use the smallest common cycle of these lifetimes.

The steps that have been followed are quite straightforward. System A requires an initial investment of $25,000. Because it is paid at the beginning of the first year, it is already at present value. At the end of the first year $2000 has been paid out in operating costs. The $2000 is discounted to a value of $1886. In fact, the operating costs are paid out over the period of a year, therefore a more accurate computation might be based on monthly operating charges which are appropriately discounted with the monthly discount factor. We observe that at the conclusion of the first year the average yearly costs for system A are $26,886. This is equal to the total costs for a one-year period of time.

Next, we add the second year's operating costs, properly discounted; and again as though the total was incurred at the end of the second year. These amount to $1780. The second year's operating costs are then added to the previous year's total costs, giving a figure of $28,666. For average yearly costs—over a two-year period—we divide by two. This results in a figure of $14,333. We continue our computations in the same way until the total cycle period is covered. If the equipment has salvage value at the time it is replaced, then the appropriate amount, properly discounted, is subtracted from the total accumulated cost.

Many other techniques can also be used for determining an optimal selection of equipment and facilities. Among such techniques we should include the break-even chart (especially when it is applied in its decision matrix form) and the dimensional analysis approach described on pp. 343–45.

EQUIPMENT QUEUES

Once the technological character of the process has been specified; the procedures to be followed have been generally determined; the relationship of man and machine has been subjected to a critical evaluation; and the appropriate types of equipment have been selected, it is then necessary to arrange all the systems' components into an optimal layout. The general decisions have been made, but consideration must be given also to the selection of specific machines;

Knowledge of the structure of production transformation units is fundamental to understanding the production process. The modular characteristic of the production process is such that many different arrangements are conceivable, but not equally desirable. With this viewpoint in mind, we can add an extra dimension to our thinking. Figure 11.14 contrasts a multiple channel, input-output system (B) with a single channel one (A).

FIGURE 11-14
Service is provided by a single unit in A, and by M units in parallel in B.

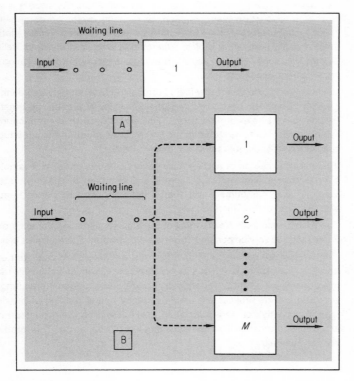

These service models reflect three facts:

1. The single-channel representation for the total production process is an oversimplification useful for conveying the character of the process but of no consequence when

it comes to designing and controlling the real production process. For this purpose a great deal more detail is required.

2. The categorization of facilities as being single or multiple channel is only a beginning. Many other important classes of differentiation exist and have to be considered.

3. To compare alternative process arrangements, it is essential that we develop relevant measures of effectiveness that can be used to evaluate the alternatives. In other words, there must be a sound basis for choosing one arrangement in preference to all others.

Knowledge of the structure of service models is fundamental to understanding the production process, which is composed of queuing modules. The modular characteristic of the production process is such that many different arrangements are conceivable but not equally desirable. The utility of this viewpoint for the production manager will depend on his comprehension of queuing-systems analysis.

Queuing models are concerned with the following generalized situations:

1. The system provides a specific service. By definition, the system is under the jurisdiction of a production manager. Service facilities might be composed of such diverse units as drill presses, milling machines, turret lathes, drop forges, plating tanks, airplane seats, hospital operating tables, supermarket checkout counters, tellers' windows, toll booths, shipping docks, airport runways, restaurant tables, telephone trunk lines, and machine repairmen.

2. Units arrive to receive the service. These can include materials to be machined or plated, travelers, patients, shoppers, customers, ships, airplanes, gourmets, gossipers, and machines that have broken down. The diversity of these applications is incredible—which is why we have stated that a limited conception of the activities that the production function encompasses is no longer feasible.

3. There is an expected or average rate of servicing the units, for example, on the average, 5 units are serviced per day. There is a distribution of servicing rates around a mean value. That is, sometimes more than 5 units are serviced per day—at other times, less than 5 units receive service.

4. There is an expected rate of arrival of the units for servicing, for example, on the average, 3 units require service per day. There is a distribution of arrival rates around a mean value.

5. *Because we are dealing with distributions,* a greater than average number of units can arrive for servicing. It is equally possible that a run of units will require longer than average servicing times. Under such circumstances a queue or waiting line can develop, even though the process has ample capacity and is capable of providing more service than is normally demanded. At other times, less than the expected number of units can arrive or shorter than average servicing times can occur. This produces idle time for service facilities.

MEASURES OF SERVICE EFFECTIVENESS

For the successful operation of any production process, management must decide how much production service capacity is required, what type of facility will provide optimum service, and how to arrange a group of facilities, such as machines in a production line. These problems are particularly characteristic of the production management function. Decisions of this kind represent one of the major controls exercised by production managers. This is especially true when resources can or must be shifted around to meet transient disturbances.

There are also cases where the production manager, instead of providing service, requires it from a subcontractor or vendor. Although there is relatively little control over the services provided by such an outside organization, the production manager can generally choose his source of supply from among several competing offers. Direct facility control offers the greatest opportunity for the application of queuing models. Nevertheless, the role of vendors and subcontractors can be built into the total design of the production system.

Having evaluated the characteristics of a process in terms of these, or other measures of effectiveness, the production management cycle functions to manipulate and regulate whatever controls exist to achieve improvement in the process' performance. Thus, management will control the service function to the extent that it is possible, by:

1. Employing additional servicing facilities.

2. Rearranging existing service facilities. For example, take 3 clerks who perform specialized sequential operations on a purchase requisition and revise the job so that the clerks are specialized by types of purchase orders which are handled entirely by one person. In the same sense, preventive maintenance is a rearrangement of service functions used in place of, or in conjunction with remedial maintenance.

3. Replacing existing service facilities with improved ones. This is partly a function of technological change and partly a function of aging and deterioration of facilities.

4. Establishing a system of priorities, whereby certain units receive attention before others do.

5. Providing special service facilities for units having exceptionally long or short service times.

Equipment control can be achieved by means of policies that regulate the behavior of units waiting for service. Let us briefly examine some of the many possibilities.

1. *Priorities for Service.* If a power failure shuts down a large portion of a refinery, it is to be expected that all other repair work which is going on will be suspended until the cause of the power failure is detected and corrected. This is an example of a *pre-emptive priority.*[19] In this case, even units that are receiving service are returned to the waiting line because of the emergency. Situations also exist where service has to be completed before the priorities take effect.

Sometimes many different levels of priorities exist. Units in the waiting line are arranged in their order of importance; not in the order with which they arrive. It is apparent that a great number of different priority rules can be constructed. The design of these rules will significantly affect the performance of the production process.

---

[19] Repairmen constitute the service facilities; arrivals are equipment failures. If preventive maintenance is used, then arrivals are admitted by appointment and according to a preplanned schedule. Emergencies are assigned pre-emptive priority.

2. *Service Granted on a Random Basis.* As the number of units requiring service increases, and as the number of servers becomes large, a random selection is made from the waiting line. Telephone calls can be handled in this manner, where incoming calls, waiting for service, are selected at random to be given access to the trunk lines. In department stores, for better or worse, customers are awarded service on an "almost" random basis by salesgirls. In some systems it is difficult to know the correct order of arrival. To counteract customer ill will, numbered tickets are made available at the entry portal and service is assigned in this numerical order.

3. *Defection and Deflection.* For various reasons, arrivals may decide to leave the queue after they have joined it. This we call defection. They can return at a later time, or perhaps they will never be seen again. Anyone who has spent hours waiting on lines, searching for parking places, and bucking traffic will appreciate the range of good-will penalties that the inability to defect creates.

Many times, an individual observes the length of the waiting line and decides not to join it. This we call deflection. The individual may not ever return again. Although a penalty occurs, the production manager may not even be aware of it. Observing and measuring defection can be difficult; it is almost impossible to pin down deflection. The design of the process and the environment in which it operates will determine the probabilities of defection and deflection from a waiting line. Where multiple channels exist, as in a bank, one might find himself hopping from service channel to service channel. Such defections to advance one's cause is termed *switching*.

4. *Entrance in Batches.* Some service facilities can render service only after a minimum number of arrivals has appeared.[20] A variant of this rule requires that a fixed number of units receive service at one time. Other rules are based on minimum and maximum waiting times. A great variety of combinations can be found. With such production processes as tumbling or plating, a batch of items are processed together. Elevators provide service in batches, as do Broadway shows and merry-go-rounds. A production process that utilizes batch service will exhibit unique behaviors that no other process design can produce.

5. *First In—First Out.* Of all possible input disciplines, FIFO (First In—First Out) has received the most attention from methodologists. In this case, each unit enters service in the order of arrival. Even when many service facilities exist, a single queue forms, and when a service facility becomes available the first on line enters. Although FIFO rules cover a great percentage of production applications, many others exist that should not be overlooked, for example, LIFO (Last In—First Out), next to last in—first out, and so forth.

SERVICE CONFIGURATIONS

In the area of service arrangements, a variety of possibilities exist. Each situation is circumscribed by its own conditions. The ingenuity of the production manager is called upon to recognize appropriate strategies. It should be

---

[20] This can be coupled with a maximum number which signals that service *must* begin.

371
facilities
management

amply clear why there cannot be any simple approach to the problem of equipment selection. We can single out a number of cases that are more likely to appear than any others and which permit us to generalize the character of these models (see Figure 11.15).

FIGURE 11-15
Alternative arrangements of facilities produce different systems' performances. Thus, three possible arrangements are shown for a system with one *A* facility and four *B* facilities.

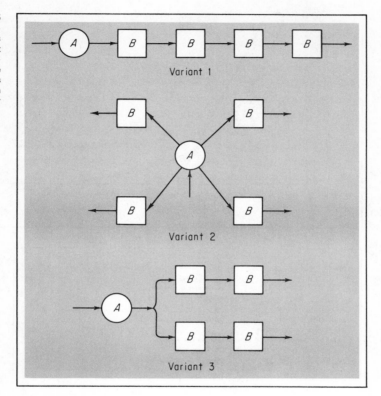

REPLACEMENT OF FACILITIES

The choice and arrangement of facilities can be critical, interacting with plant layout. Over time, a process ages. It must be constantly renewed and updated. Otherwise, there is increasing risk that it will become obsolete. As an expression of this fact, accounting practice attempts to design and apply a depreciation procedure that captures the essence of the way in which the value of a company's facilities changes with *use* and *age* over a period of time.

We must understand the relevance of alternative methods of depreciation with respect to machine replacement. In Figure 11.16 three different methods for calculating depreciation are illustrated. Each of these has its own characteristic advantages and disadvantages.

Straight-line depreciation is applied, for example, to a ten-year period. This

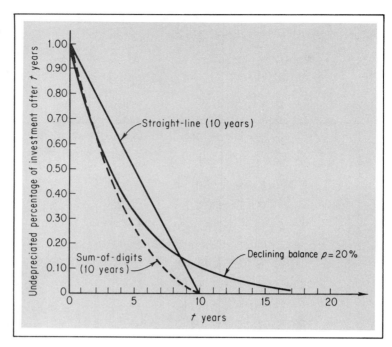

FIGURE 11-16
Three alternative depreciation methods.

FIGURE 11-17a
MAPI summary form. [This form is excerpted from *Business Investment Policy* (Machine and Allied Products Institute, 1958).]

PROJECT NO._____   SHEET I

MAPI SUMMARY FORM
(AVERAGING SHORTCUT)

PROJECT_____Box Machine and Stitcher_____

ALTERNATIVE____Continuing as is_____

COMPARISON PERIOD (YEARS)   (P)_____1_____

ASSUMED OPERATING RATE OF PROJECT (HOURS PER YEAR)   1,200

I. OPERATING ADVANTAGE
(NEXT-YEAR FOR A 1-YEAR COMPARISON PERIOD,* ANNUAL AVERAGES FOR LONGER PERIODS)

A.   EFFECT OF PROJECT ON REVENUE

		INCREASE	DECREASE	
1	FROM CHANGE IN QUALITY OF PRODUCTS	$	$	1
2	FROM CHANGE IN VOLUME OF OUTPUT			2
3	TOTAL	$ X	$ Y	3

B.   EFFECT ON OPERATING COSTS

		INCREASE	DECREASE	
4	DIRECT LABOR	$ 900	$	4
5	INDIRECT LABOR	150		5
6	FRINGE BENEFITS	190		6
7	MAINTENANCE	200		7
8	TOOLING	80		8
9	MATERIALS AND SUPPLIES		16,800	9
10	INSPECTION			10
11	ASSEMBLY			11
12	SCRAP AND REWORK			12
13	DOWN TIME			13
14	POWER	40		14
15	FLOOR SPACE		1,000	15
16	PROPERTY TAXES AND INSURANCE	320		16
17	SUBCONTRACTING			17
18	INVENTORY		1,100	18
19	SAFETY			19
20	FLEXIBILITY			20
21	OTHER			21
22	TOTAL	$ 1,880 Y	$ 18,900 X	22

C.   COMBINED EFFECT

23	NET INCREASE IN REVENUE (3X−3Y)	$	23
24	NET DECREASE IN OPERATING COSTS (22X−22Y)	$ 17,020	24
25	ANNUAL OPERATING ADVANTAGE (23+24)	$ 17,020	25

_____
* Next year means the first year of project operation. For projects with a significant break-in period, use performance after break-in.

Copyright 1967, Machinery and Allied Products Institute.

linear function has the property of decreasing by the same amount each year. That amount is simply N/T, where N is the initial facility cost and T is the facility lifetime over which it will amortized. Thus, at any time t the undepreciated portion will be $N - tN/T$.

The method called *declining balance* involves nonlinear change that is achieved by taking a fixed percentage, p, of the undepreciated balance every year. Thus, at any time t the undepreciated portion will be $N(1 - p)^t$. For example, consider a machine costing \$1,000 with $p = 0.20$. After three years, the undepreciated portion will be \$512. At the end of ten years it will still be approximately \$107. Therefore, the declining-balance method does not fully write off the investment by the end of the ten-year period. Instead, it approaches the full write-off asymptotically, but never reaches it.

The third method is called the *sum-of-digits method*. In this case, for a ten-year period we obtain the sum of $10 + 9 + 8 + 7 + 6 + 5 + 4 + 3 + 2 + 1$ which equals 55. At the end of the first year we depreciate the principal N by an amount $(10/55)N$. For the second year's depreciation we use $(9/55)N$; third-year depreciation equals $(8/55)N$. The total amount depreciated over the ten-year period will be $(10/55)N + (9/55)N + \cdots + (1/55)N$. This is equal to $(55/55)N$—that is, full depreciation. We observe that for each succeeding year the fraction used decreases. In order to determine the denominator value for

FIGURE 11-17b
(cont.)

SHEET 2

II. INVESTMENT AND RETURN

A. INITIAL INVESTMENT

26 INSTALLED COST OF PROJECT	\$ 29,800		
MINUS INITIAL TAX BENEFIT OF	\$ 2,100	(Net Cost) \$ 27,700	26
27 INVESTMENT IN ALTERNATIVE			
CAPITAL ADDITIONS MINUS INITIAL TAX BENEFIT	\$		
PLUS: DISPOSAL VALUE OF ASSETS RETIRED			
BY PROJECT *	\$ 4,000	\$ 4,000	27
28 INITIAL NET INVESTMENT (26—27)		\$ 23,700	28

B. TERMINAL INVESTMENT

29 RETENTION VALUE OF PROJECT AT END OF COMPARISON PERIOD
(ESTIMATE FOR ASSETS, IF ANY, THAT CANNOT BE DEPRECIATED OR EXPENSED. FOR OTHERS, ESTIMATE OR USE MAPI CHARTS.)

Item or Group	Installed Cost, Minus Initial Tax Benefit (Net Cost) A	Service Life (Years) B	Disposal Value, End of Life (Percent of Net Cost) C	MAPI Chart Number D	Chart Percentage E	Retention Value $\left(\frac{A \times E}{100}\right)$ F
Box Machine and Stitcher	\$ 27,700	13	10	1A	89.4	\$ 24,760

ESTIMATED FROM CHARTS (TOTAL OF COL. F)	\$		
PLUS: OTHERWISE ESTIMATED	\$	\$ 24,760	29
30 DISPOSAL VALUE OF ALTERNATIVE AT END OF PERIOD *		\$ 4,000	30
31 TERMINAL NET INVESTMENT (29—30)		\$ 20,760	31

C. RETURN

32 AVERAGE NET CAPITAL CONSUMPTION $\left(\frac{28-31}{P}\right)$	\$ 2,940	32
33 AVERAGE NET INVESTMENT $\left(\frac{28+31}{2}\right)$	\$ 22,230	33
34 BEFORE-TAX RETURN $\left(\frac{25-32}{33} \times 100\right)$	% 63.3	34
35 INCREASE IN DEPRECIATION AND INTEREST DEDUCTIONS	\$ 4,190	35
36 TAXABLE OPERATING ADVANTAGE (25—35)	\$ 12,830	36
37 INCREASE IN INCOME TAX (36×TAX RATE)	\$ 6,415	37
38 AFTER-TAX OPERATING ADVANTAGE (25—37)	\$ 10,605	38
39 AVAILABLE FOR RETURN ON INVESTMENT (38—32)	\$ 7,665	39
40 AFTER-TAX RETURN $\left(\frac{39}{33} \times 100\right)$	% 34.5	40

* After terminal tax adjustments.

the sum-of-digits method for a period of T years, we can utilize the formula, $T(T+1)/2$. Thus, we obtain for $T = 10$ years, $10(11)/2 = 55$.

The straight-line method should be used when the facility is used up in equal amounts over a period of time. This method doesn't penalize any one year in particular. The remaining two methods penalize the initial years more than the latter ones. The declining-balance method leaves some amount of undepreciated value at the time of intended replacement which can be associated with salvage value. Depreciation methods are usually designed to reflect the funding policies of the company for facility replacement, as well as the company's tax situation.

MAPI METHOD

The Machinery and Allied Products Institute of Washington, D.C. has done a great deal to organize the data requirements comprehensively, and to design a method of analysis for the machine replacement problem. The approach called the MAPI system, has been updated and improved with the latest version being described in 1967.[21] The MAPI approach is widely utilized by industry. A critical requirement of this method is that costs should be based on the process and system *performance*. Conversely, costs should not be measured for an individual facility in isolation from the system.

Examining the MAPI Summary Form, Sheet 1, Figure 11.17a, we observe that operating advantage is measured in terms of the effect of the proposed project (where the project can be interpreted as the investment in a new facility) on revenue and on operating costs. Figure 11.17b demonstrates how initial investment and terminal value are used to determine a measure of after-tax return. This measure is, in fact, a kind of urgency rating, being a relative measure of the return on investment (ROI). When the line 40 measure is large, there is justification to go ahead with the proposed project.

Let us go through the required steps with the example illustrated in the figures. We shall introduce the necessary data as we proceed, indicating, where useful, the appropriate lines in the figures.

1. We evaluate the replacement of the present method by a new box machine and stitcher. The installed cost of the new machine is $29,800 less the initial tax benefit ($2,100) determined for this investment. The resulting net cost is $27,700 (Line 26).
2. The disposal value (after tax adjustments) of the present system components is $4,000 (Line 27). No capital additions are required or contemplated if the proposed change is not made. For some cases, extensive repairs might be necessitated if a replacement is not made; but we are not considering ourselves to be faced with such a situation.
3. The initial net investment (Lines 26–27) is $23,700 (Line 28).
4. The comparison period (P) is one year. Note the use of P in line 32.
5. We now calculate the next-year operating advantage to be gained. First, we determine that the project promises no effect on revenue (Lines 1, 2, 3 and 23).

[21] See George Terborgh, *Business Investment Management, A MAPI Study and Manual* (Washington, D.C.: Machinery and Allied Products Institute and Council for Technological Advancement, 1967).

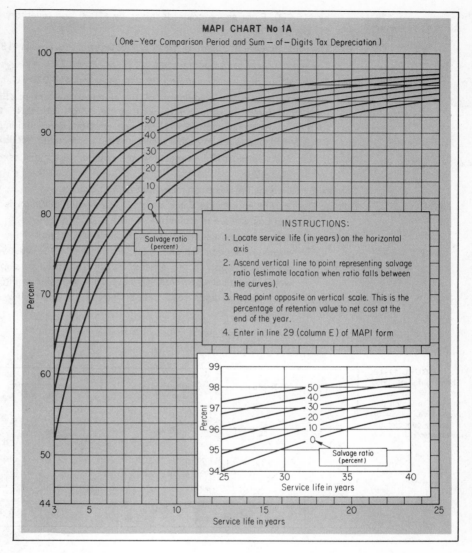

FIGURE 11-18
MAPI Chart No. 1A for determining Retention Value of Project at End of Comparison Period. (In this case, a one-year period where sum-of-digits tax depreciation is used. Charts for other conditions are available.) [This chart is excerpted from *Business Investment Policy* (Machine and Allied Products Institute, 1958).]

MAPI CHART No 1A
(One–Year Comparison Period and Sum – of – Digits Tax Depreciation)

INSTRUCTIONS:

1. Locate service life (in years) on the horizontal axis

2. Ascend vertical line to point representing salvage ratio (estimate location when ratio falls between the curves).

3. Read point opposite on vertical scale. This is the percentage of retention value to net cost at the end of the year.

4. Enter in line 29 (column E) of MAPI form

Salvage ratio (percent)

Service life in years

6. Assuming one shift with 30 operating hours per week, and 40 weeks per year for the new equipment, we obtain 1200 operating hours per year.

7. We now move to the consideration of the facility change on operating costs. These are Lines 4 through 22. For our example, there has been an increase of $900 in direct labor and an increase in indirect labor of $150. Maintenance costs are increased by $200, and downtime is unaffected. We charge ourselves for increased fringe benefits ($190), tooling ($80), power ($40), and property taxes and insurance, *estimating* this increase to be $320. On the other hand, costs for materials and supplies decrease

by $16,800. Floor space costs decrease by $1000 and inventory costs decrease by $1,100.

8. The total increase in operating costs is $1880; total decrease is $18,900.

9. The net decrease in operating costs is $17,020 (Line 24).

10. The resultant next-year operating advantage is also $17,020 (Line 25).

11. Now we look at the calculation of the terminal investment (Figure 11.17b). We refer to Columns A through F as well as the MAPI Chart No 1A (Figure 11.18) for a one-year comparison ($P = 1$) and sum-of-digits depreciation (see Figure 11.16). Other MAPI charts are available for alternative depreciation methods.[22]

Column A : Installed cost of box machine and stitcher, less initial tax benefit is $27,700 (Line 26).

Column B : Service life has been estimated to be 13 years.

Column C : *Estimated* salvage value after 13 years—$2770 which is 10 percent of the net cost shown in Column A.

Column D : We must now use the most appropriate MAPI chart. Three basically different forms of depreciation can apply, see Figure 11.19. What we require is a percentage to apply to the required investment based on depreciation, machine wear,[23] and salvage value. We have only illustrated in Figure 11.18 the one-year, sum-of-digits case, called Chart No. 1A, which we will apply to our example.

FIGURE 11-19
Three different patterns which describe the way in which the productive value of a facility can change over time.

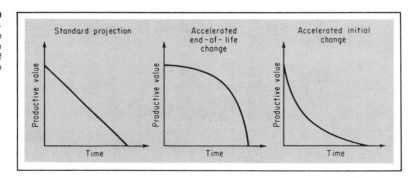

Column E : For our assumptions, we obtain a chart percentage of 89.4 percent, or the decimal fraction 0.894.

Column F : This is ($27,700)(0.894) = $24,760 which is shown on Line 29.

12. The return on investment, after-taxes, is now calculated, (see Line 40 of Figure 11.17b).

[22] Terborgh, *A MAPI Study and Manual.*
[23] This refers to the way in which the facility declines as a profit producer because of technological factors. See Figure 11.19.

13. The after-tax return, as a percentage, is determined to be 34.5. This is a large enough figure to command immediate management attention. The numerical procedures for deriving this number are clearly delineated in Figure 11.17b and will not be repeated here.

14. Based on the figure of 34.5 percent, it is likely that the production manager will replace the present facility with the new box machine and stitcher.

In effect, Line 40 is a measure of investment urgency. Available investment funds can be used in many different ways. There is competition between alternative facilities, dividends to stockholders, increased salaries or wages, improvement studies and so forth. If we can obtain a measure of the relative urgency (or desirability) of alternative investments, then we can determine a reasonable guide for action. The MAPI measure expresses the first year, after-tax funds that are available for return on investment as a percentage of the average net investment (Line 33). By using this measure of effectiveness, or modifications of it, the various process alternatives can be examined in a reasonable manner. Rational policies will dominate the design and control of the process. The major advantage of the MAPI method is that it permits a simple and consistent method to be applied for evaluating all company facilities—and this in terms of an appropriate measure of effectiveness, viz., return on investment (ROI). The fact that taxes are considered is an important strength of the MAPI procedure. Too frequently, taxes are overlooked in the investment decision process.

PROBLEMS

1   The industries listed below tend to form high-density clusters in specific geographic areas. Is there a rational explanation?
    a. Steel
    b. Automobiles
    c. Stock yards
    d. Textiles
    e. Electronics
    f. Aircraft
    g. Rubber
    h. Motion pictures
    i. Books
    j. Cigarettes

2   The Omicron Company has two factories, A and B, located in Wilmington, Delaware and San Francisco, California, respectively. Each has a production capacity of 550 units per week. Omicron's markets are Los Angeles, Chicago, and New York. The demands of these markets are for 150, 350, and 400 units, respectively, in the coming week. A matrix of shipping distances is prepared and the shipping schedule is determined to minimize total shipping distance. Estimate the distances and solve this problem on that basis.

3   Omicron decides to build a third plant. The strongest contenders are Chicago, Illinois and Cleveland, Ohio. The new plant would have a productive capacity of 400 units.

Keeping the market demands unchanged from problem 2 above, what should Omicron do?

4   A small drill press is valued at $1000. It is expected to last 2 years. It costs $4000 per year to operate. A larger drill press can be purchased for $3000. It will last 4 years. It costs $3000 per year to operate. Which drill press should we purchase? (Use a 6 percent discount factor.) Comment on your result.

5   Two jigs are under consideration for a drilling operation to make a particular part. Jig A costs $800 and has operating costs of $0.10 per part. Jig B costs $1200 and has operating costs of $0.08 per part. The forecast for the part (in pieces demanded per year) is:

1st Year	2nd Year	3rd Year	4th Year	5th Year
5000	6000	8000	8000	10,000

The company estimates its return on available funds at 6 percent per year.
a. Approximately at what point in time are the two jigs equivalent in value?
b. What is the average cost per year of each jig at the end of the 5th year?

6   Using the matrix below, determine the best layout for the system.

Locations

		1	2	3	4	5	6
	A	16	25	9	16	7	14
	B	12	22	5	14	9	32
Machine	C	35	41	13	8	14	8
Centers	D	26	14	24	10	31	14
	E	40	15	15	26	16	18
	F	28	11	6	18	19	22

Matrix of costs for each assignment.

7   Compare straight-line depreciation (20 years) with the equivalent sum of digits result. What salvage value would remain after 20 years with a 10 percent rate for the declining balance method? Assume an investment of $10,000.

8   For replacement of facilities, use the example of the MAPI approach given in the text, pages 374–77, but make the following change:
a. Column B—estimated service life—5 years.
   How does this alteration affect the after-tax return? Discuss. Now, go back to the original example and answer the following questions:
b. What tax rate has been used in Line 37?
c. Change the tax rate by cutting it in half. What effect does this have?

9   Use the dimensional method described on pp. 343–45 to resolve the following long-term decision problem.
A choice is to be made between two alternative computer designs, and the following data have been obtained:

	Design 1	Design 2
Cost	$0.5 million	$0.6 million
Speed	2	1
Memory	3	2
Flexibility	4	5
Size	50 square feet	40 square feet

Characteristics are scaled so that large numbers are less desirable than small numbers. Establish your own weighting factors for each of the cases below, and comment on the way that the choice changes as a function of the particular point of view that is employed.

a. The computer manufacturer in terms of the potential market.

b. The mail order company where the unit will control inventory.

c. A weapons-system manufacturer operating under government contract, where the unit will be used for scientific calculations.

references

APPLE, JAMES M., *Plant Layout and Materials Handling,* 2nd ed. New York: Ronald Press, 1963.

DEAN, JOEL, *Managerial Economics.* Englewood Cliffs, N. J.: Prentice-Hall, Inc., 1951.

ISARD, WALTER, *Location and Space-Economy.* New York: John Wiley & Sons, Inc., 1956.

KARASKA, G. J. and D. F. BRAMHALL, *Location Analysis for Manufacturing: A Selection of Readings.* Cambridge, Mass.: M.I.T. Press, 1969.

MAGEE, JOHN F., *Physical Distribution Systems.* New York: McGraw-Hill Book Company, 1967.

MASSÉ, PIERRE, *Optimal Investment Decisions.* Englewood Cliffs, N. J.: Prentice-Hall, Inc., 1962.

MILLER, RICHARD B., *Plant Location Factors United States,* Monograph, Noyes Development Corporation, 118 Mill Road, Park Ridge, N.J. 07656, 1966.

MOORE, JAMES M., *Plant Layout and Design.* New York: The MacMillan Company, 1962.

REED RUDDELL, JR., *Plant Layout.* Homewood, Ill.: Richard D. Irwin, Inc., 1961.

STARR, M. K., *Systems Management of Operations.* Englewood Cliffs, N.J.: Prentice-Hall, Inc., 1970.

chapter
twelve
manpower
management

Undoubtedly the most trying problem that production management has faced over the years has been the question of how to deal with the man in the system. Job evaluation, productivity analysis, and labor cost determination have proven to be elusive, both for definition and for measurement[1], yet, since the contribution of the manpower input to the total cost of the output is usually a sizeable component, the problem of measuring manpower costs has received widespread and continuous attention over many years. In this area there has been a continual improvement of measurement methods, but no sudden illumination or discovery of a panacea. By and large, the problem remains critical for industry. Whenever the man in the system is a significant part of the whole, the difficulty in measuring productivity and in determining wages continues to prove an impediment.

[1] See, for example, A. Abruzzi, "Formulating a Theory of Work Measurement," *Management Science,* Vol. 2, No. 2 (January, 1956), pp. 114–130; also S.B. Littauer and A. Abruzzi, "Experimental Criteria for Evaluating Workers and Operations," *Industrial Labor Relations Review,* Vol. 2, No. 4 (July, 1949), pp. 502–526.

A TWO-PART PROBLEM: FAIR OUTPUT—FAIR WAGE

The problem of determining labor costs has *two* parts. *First:* What is a fair or a reasonable output? That is: How many pieces should be expected per unit of time? The *second* part deals with the question: What is fair wage for fair output? The difficulty of answering these questions is underscored by such further queries as: How can we equate the work done by a secretary and a punch press operator? What is a reasonable salary for the research director as compared to the production manager? If two men work equally hard, but one turns out ten pieces while the second turns out twenty pieces, should we pay them equal salaries? Should a man be paid for time or for physical output?

All these questions seem to hinge on two points that can be studied rationally. First, what value does the company derive from its manpower component? Second, considering the factor of supply and demand for the kind of services that the company requires, how much should it pay?

PRODUCTION COST ESTIMATES FOR LABOR

It is the search for a measure of value that has led to *production standards.* These standards state specifically what the expected productivity is for a particular job. But, the output rate for any one worker is variable. Furthermore, differences exist between workers. How, then, are these standards established? Because manpower is variable, *which individual is the standard man?*

Before we examine the production manager's alternative approaches for the resolution of such problems, let us see why the system he tends requires standards. The answer is that the production manager must be able to compute the real costs of his production efforts. At the highest management levels, this is considered to be one of the most basic responsibilities he has to the company. Let us list some production management activities that require reasonable estimates of labor costs to be made.

1. The break-even chart needs believable estimates. *Direct labor* is part of the variable cost component. *Indirect labor*, administration, and creative endeavors, such as research, are part of the fixed cost component.

2. For the decision matrix, these estimates are required to determine a minimum cost strategy or for the purpose of defining a maximum profit strategy. Even for an informal evaluation procedure, such as the plant selection example on pp. 343–45 we required estimates for labor costs in different areas of the country.

3. For production control, see pp. 226–58 labor costs are a significant dimension for the determination of optimal scheduling strategies.

4. In Chapter 7 the question of an optimal product mix was discussed. To find such a mix we were required to estimate the relative profitabilities of various items that competed for production capacity. For a sensitive system, small errors in estimating labor costs can produce sufficiently different estimates of profit per piece to change the entire aspect of the company's product mix.

5. When evaluating new product alternatives, estimated manpower costs are reflected in proposed price levels, estimated sales volume, and estimated profitability. How can we choose between alternative new products unless it is possible to estimate the labor cost per part and, thereby, the expected profitability?

6. A major decision involves the extent to which a company should automate. This problem boils down to a comparison between manpower costs and machine power costs for approximately the same services. Without reasonably good estimates of the respective costs per part, decisions to automate cannot be based on sound foundations.

7. Many companies traditionally bid for new jobs. With increased government spending, the use of bidding spread. More companies utilize subcontracting than ever before. Bidding systems frequently require estimates that totally predate experience with the production process. If the company hopes to remain solvent, let alone make sufficient profit, it must be able to estimate with a high degree of precision what the labor cost component will be for the job. If it is unable to do this it is usually not advisable to enter a bid.

We have given just a few examples of the way in which manpower costs affect the production manager's performance. Why do we make such a special case for manpower costs? Because they are among the *least certain elements* in the system. We are able to predetermine the costs of purchased materials, power, insurance, and machine and equipment costs. These factors do not introduce the same kind of uncertainty that the the labor cost estimates do. The problem of estimating how much labor will be required to turn out a given volume of output is as complex as the problem of determining consumer demand levels.

With increasing automation the importance of the labor estimation problem is reduced. If for no other reason than to achieve increased levels of certainty, the production manager exhibits a *tendency* to move toward automation. But, as if in compensation, several new problems have arisen. There has been growth in the wage rates of indirect, administrative, sales promotional, and creative personnel. The problem of assigning such costs to the output has not been satisfactorily resolved. In addition, uncertainties in consumer demand exact a greater toll when automated processes are utilized. Mistakes are costly because these facilities demand high investment and are relatively inflexible. In any case, the problem of how to measure the productive capacity and related costs of the manpower component remains a major issue. Let us consider some of the ways in which this problem can be approached.

TIME STUDIES

Jobs differ from one another and so do men. In order to find a common ground for setting standards and for evaluating the efforts and outputs of men, it was necessary to begin the analysis on a very elementary level. Originally, *production studies* were used. These represented situations where the worker

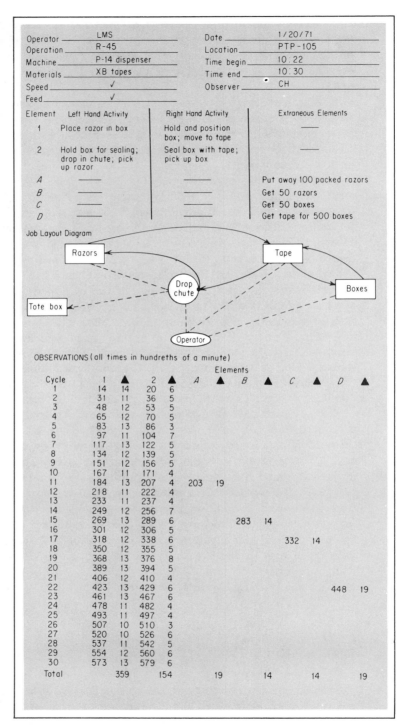

FIGURE 12-1
A time study sheet with 30 cycles. The operation (R-45) is to package razors.

Operator	LMS
Operation	R-45
Machine	P-14 dispenser
Materials	XB tapes
Speed	✓
Feed	✓

Date	1/20/71
Location	PTP-105
Time begin	10:22
Time end	10:30
Observer	CH

Element	Left Hand Activity	Right Hand Activity	Extraneous Elements
1	Place razor in box	Hold and position box; move to tape	—
2	Hold box for sealing; drop in chute; pick up razor	Seal box with tape; pick up box	—
A	—	—	Put away 100 packed razors
B	—	—	Get 50 razors
C	—	—	Get 50 boxes
D	—	—	Get tape for 500 boxes

Job Layout Diagram

OBSERVATIONS (all times in hundreths of a minute)

Elements

Cycle	1	▲	2	▲	A	▲	B	▲	C	▲	D	▲
1	14	14	20	6								
2	31	11	36	5								
3	48	12	53	5								
4	65	12	70	5								
5	83	13	86	3								
6	97	11	104	7								
7	117	13	122	5								
8	134	12	139	5								
9	151	12	156	5								
10	167	11	171	4								
11	184	13	207	4	203	19						
12	218	11	222	4								
13	233	11	237	4								
14	249	12	256	7								
15	269	13	289	6			283	14				
16	301	12	306	5								
17	318	12	338	6					332	14		
18	350	12	355	5								
19	368	13	376	8								
20	389	13	394	5								
21	406	12	410	4								
22	423	13	429	6							448	19
23	461	13	467	6								
24	478	11	482	4								
25	493	11	497	4								
26	507	10	510	3								
27	520	10	526	6								
28	537	11	542	5								
29	554	12	560	6								
30	573	13	579	6								
Total		359		154		19		14		14		19

384

was *constantly* observed over a long period of time. The approach can be compared to 100 percent inspection. Both the job and the worker were studied with patient detail. This method has such shortcomings that it is now almost an historical curiosity. The primary weaknesses are high cost, unreliable results, and belligerent subjects.

The 100 percent sample, as in almost every situation where it has been used by the production management field, eventually gave way to sampling procedures. Present-day time studies are based on sampling methods derived from developments begun in the 1920's. Manpower sampling procedures have a similar history to those previously described for the materials control area. Instead of tracking the worker continuously for long periods of time, so-called time and motion studies evolved. These time study methods, by obtaining a *sufficient sample of observations*, attempted to answer such questions as: How long does it take to do a job, and what is the expected daily output of a worker?

First, the time study man observes the over-all job. Next he breaks the job down into basic elements. These, when added together form the *job cycle*. This cycle should be relatively short and repetitively used. It will constitute the major portion of the worker's job. For long-cycle jobs, time study methods are difficult to apply. The character of a short-cycle, repetitive job will be illustrated in an example, see Figure 12.1.

A *stop watch* is employed to time the cycle elements. A number of different kinds of such watches are available. Each is designed for particular types of applications as well as to satisfy personal preference. We shall only differentiate between the *continuous* and *snap-back* methods for using stop watches. The snap-back approach is used to time each work element directly. When an element is completed, the watch hand is returned to zero to begin timing the next element. Continuous readings are cumulative and require subtraction to determine element times. The snap-back system usually requires a larger sample for the same precision that can be obtained from the continuous method. However, as we shall see shortly, precision is a strange word to apply to the time study area.

Usually, the stop watch is attached to a *time study board* which holds an observation, or time study sheet. Such a time study sheet is shown in Figure 12.1. The illustration presents a completed time sheet that lists the kind of information usually obtained by the time study man. He records as much information as possible about the operation that is being observed. This includes the name of the operator, the machine that is being used, the work elements, the setup being used, the materials, the speed and feed rates, and in general, whatever information characterizes and categorizes the total job. The need for all these data follows from the point that a time study done under one set of conditions may not apply to another set. Thus, if the job is being done on a type *A* facility, it cannot be assumed that a similar production standard will apply to a type *B* facility. Change of materials, locations, and a host of other factors can, and frequently do, interpose themselves. Further, to check on a study by replication, it is necessary to set up the job conditions in as similar a fashion to the initial study conditions as possible.

Let us refer to Figure 12.1. This job has been broken down into two elements. The activities of the *left* and *right hands* are described for each element. Element 1 requires that the left hand should be placing a razor in a box while the right hand holds and positions the box so that the razor can be inserted. Presumably, the right and left hand operations are coordinated. Element 2 finds the left hand holding the box for the right hand which must seal the box with tape. Then the left hand releases the box over a chute which carries the box away. The layout for this job is also pictured on the time sheet. The time study begins:

The observation for Element 1 in the first cycle is entered in the first column; the observation for Element 2 in the first cycle is recorded next. Then, cycle two begins, and so forth. It can be seen that these element values are continuously timed. The sample size is 30 cycles, all of which are listed on our sheet.

After the observations have been made, the time study man goes to his desk and begins to compute. The initial cycle takes 0.20 minutes. Of this, Element 1 consumed 0.14 minutes and Element 2 took the remaining 0.06 minutes.[2] The second cycle ends at 0.36 minutes. This means that the second cycle consumed $0.36 - 0.20 = 0.16$ minutes. For the second cycle, Element 1 required 0.11 minutes and Element 2 used the remaining 0.05 minutes. The rest of the values are obtained in the same way, by subtraction.

In addition to the basic cycle, the time sheet lists *extraneous elements*. These are operations which must be done *every now and then*. For example, the extraneous Element *A* is the requirement that after 100 razors have been packed and dropped into the chute, the tote box they fall into must be taken away. Element *B* concerns the fact that the worker must interrupt his work occasionally to get 500 razors to work on. The other extraneous elements are equally easy to comprehend. We see that the extraneous elements will break into the short-cycle system regularly. Therefore, when we include them, the total job is not really short cycle, but of longer duration. Elements 1 and 2 constitute the *major subcycle* within this system.

The longest cycle is Element *D* which occurs once every 500 boxes. It is, therefore, the shortest, *common-cycle* time for *all* elements in the system. This point is significant; even the shortest cycle, repetitive jobs usually include very long-cycle, extraneous elements. As the time study man observes the way in which the job is being handled he must catch these longer-cycle elements and include them in his study. Thus, we have included observations that are relevant to the extraneous elements in our data. (As shall be seen shortly, *work sampling* is an effective method for coping with the problem of the long-cycle factors.)

PRODUCTIVITY STANDARD

Now, we must obtain a *summary* of what has been observed. A typical summary form is shown in Figure 12.2. All the elements, 1, 2, *A*, *B*, *C*, and *D* are listed. Total times are collected for each element as they appeared in the 30-cycle

---

[2] The stop watch used is a decimal-minute type. It is read directly in hundredths of a minute.

period. Those are the column sums for each element, including the extraneous factors.

The *total time* for Element 1 is 359; for Element 2 it is 154; and it is 19, 14, 14, and 19, respectively, for the extraneous elements *A*, *B*, *C*, and *D*. The number of observations for each element is recorded. There are 30 such observations for Elements 1 and 2. By chance, during this period of time, each extraneous element occurs once. The third row of our summary sheet lists the number of occurrences that can be expected per cycle. We divide the first row by the product of Rows 2 and 3. In this way, an *average time*, or *selected time*, is developed for each of the operations that constitute the job. For example, dividing 359 by (30×1), we obtain 11.97 hundredths of a minute, or 0.1197 minutes for Element 1. For Element 2, 0.0513 minutes, and so forth.

Now we come to one of the most disagreeable jobs in the time study system. This is the choice of an *allowance* or *leveling factor*. Who should the time study man observe? Generally, he chooses an average worker, operating under standard conditions, who presumably uses a routinized method. But if the subject appears to work at something more or less than an average rate, a leveling factor, or allowance, must be applied. For the normal worker the leveling factor is 100 percent. This leaves the resulting system of numbers unchanged. Because of leveling, our efforts to achieve precise measures and our hopes for precision may seem to have been a waste of time. But this is not exactly the case. The leveling estimate introduces a different kind of measurement error than do the time study errors. Clearly, we would prefer neither type of error, but given a choice we would prefer one type rather than both types.

On what basis does the time study man decide whether a worker is performing above, below, or exactly at the normal level? The answer is that time study men, after much practice, can exhibit far more agreement among themselves than would occur by chance, even though the concept of a standard basis for allowances is vague, undefined, and subjective. Training in leveling is accomplished

FIGURE 12.2
Time study summary form.

ELEMENT	1	2	A	B	C	D	
Total time observed	359	154	19	14	14	19	
Number of observations	30	30	1	1	1	1	
Expected cycles	1	1	1/100	1/50	1/50	1/500	
Average time or selected time	11.97	5.13	0.19	0.28	0.28	0.04	
Allowances or leveling factors	0.95	1.00	1.00	1.00	1.00	1.00	
Adjusted time or normal time	11.37	5.13	0.19	0.28	0.28	0.04	
Correction for rest and delay	110%	110%	110%	110%	110%	110%	TOTAL
Standard time	12.51	5.64	0.21	0.31	0.31	0.04	19.02

Productivity Standard: $\frac{60 \text{ minutes}}{\text{hour}} \times \frac{100 \text{ boxes}}{19.02 \text{ minutes}} \cong 316$ boxes per hour in many ways. One of the most successful is by means of motion pictures, where the projector has a variable speed control.

The *allowance* is applied to *average time*, from whence we obtain *adjusted time*, or *normal time*. This is simply the product of the average time and the allowance. Thus, if the leveling factor is 110 percent, meaning that the observed worker is faster than normal, then the adjusted time will be larger than the average time, meaning that the normal (slower) worker can be expected to take a longer than observed time. In the case of the operator who is working at 95 percent of normal, in the judgment of the time study man, multiplication produces a normal time that is smaller than the selected time, meaning that the average worker can go faster.

Even if we could accept leveling with equanimity, we must now add an additional *rough* correction. This is the rest and delay correction factor. Usually, it is assigned values that range from 5 percent to 15 percent, depending upon the character of the job, the degree of personal needs, and so on. The adjusted, or normal time, is multiplied by the rest and delay factor. In this way we derive the *standard time* which is the basis of the production standard. We note that the standard times are listed along the bottom row of the summary box. Each element, including the extraneous elements, has its standard time. The sum of all the elemental standard times is the *standard time of the operation*. In our example this is 0.1902 minutes.

We now can divide 60 minutes per hour by the operation's total standard time. This tells us that approximately 316 boxes per hour is the expected output rate for the job. That is, 60/0.1902 equals a *productivity measure* of 316 boxes per hour. If the wage rate for this class of job is $2.00 per hour, then the labor cost component for the operation would be $2.00/316 = $0.006, or a little more than a half-cent apiece. This would be the *expected cost of the operation*.

Primary weaknesses of time study are: the definition of an average worker, applying the leveling factor, applying the R & D correction, and not recognizing influential extraneous elements. Ingenious answers have been found for some of these problems. Time study is a *skill*. To begin with, the use of the stop watch requires training and practice. The same applies to leveling. Time study practitioners seldom break down elements into less than 0.04 minutes because less than this interval is difficult to observe. The major criticism of time study centers around leveling, but another problem worthy of consideration is the fact that the worker's performance may not be stable in the Shewhart sense (see Chapter 10). Also, the fact that the worker is not necessarily interested in participating in the study and may have no desire to provide an accurate production standard of performance is another criticism. The expert time study man is supposed to sense this and make appropriate changes in the leveling factor. One can question who will win such a contest—the worker or the time study man?

TIME STUDY SAMPLE SIZE

In spite of these objections, some form of time study must be used. Therefore, an issue of importance to the time study field is: How many cycles should be observed? That is, how large a sample should be taken? The formula given below is predicated on the assumption of a degree of accuracy in time studies that is not warranted by the circumstances. Nevertheless, some means must be found for setting a proper sample size. We have:

$$N' = \left[\frac{40\sqrt{N\sum\limits_{i=1}^{i=N} x_i^2 - (\sum\limits_{i=1}^{i=N} x_i)^2}}{\sum\limits_{i=1}^{i=N} x_i}\right]^2$$

where x_i is the ith observation for a particular element, N is the number of cycles observed up to this point, $\sum\limits_{i=1}^{i=N} x_i$ is the sum of all N of the x_i measures, and N' is the number of cycles that *should be* observed. Specifically N' is the required number of cycles to be observed so that we obtain *95* percent confidence that the true element time lies within the range $\bar{x} \pm 0.05\bar{x}$ which is ± 5 percent of the observed average time.

Because the job can comprise many different elements, we must use the element that will dominate the sample size by requiring the largest value of N'. This will be associated with elements exhibiting great measurement variability relative to the average value, $\bar{x} = \sum\limits_{i}^{N} x_i/N$ of the element. In this case element 1 has an average value (12.4) which is larger than that of element 2 (4.8). Yet, because of variability $N'(1)$ is larger than $N'(2)$.

Having completed a partial study, the time study man will check to find out how much further he should go. If he obtains a value for N' that is larger than N, he must continue to take observations. This sample size evaluation procedure is repeated until the largest value of N' is equal to or less than the actual number of observations made, that is, Max $N' \leq N$. Let us examine the following example.

	ELEMENT			
READING i	1 $x_i(1)$	2 $x_i(2)$	1 $x_i^2(1)$	2 $x_i^2(2)$
1	14	6	196	36
2	11	5	121	25
3	12	5	144	25
4	12	5	144	25
5	13	3	169	9
	62	24	774	120
$\bar{x}$:	$\frac{62}{5} = 12.4$	$\frac{24}{5} = 4.8$		

For Element 1: $N'(1) = \left(\dfrac{40\sqrt{5(774) - (62)^2}}{62}\right)^2 = 10.9$

For Element 2: $N'(2) = \left(\dfrac{40\sqrt{5(120) - (24)^2}}{24}\right)^2 = 6.6$

We begin with $N = 5$ observations of the two elements and find that N' for element 1 dominates the sample size. It specifies 10.9 readings. Because we have taken only five readings, we must enlarge the sample size. We might take another five or six readings and then test again. In this way, we keep collecting observations until we find that Max N' is equal to or less than N.

The methods of time study, *in spite of the inherent problems, are widely used by industry*. The need for this kind of information is *fundamental*. At the same time, for many applications, such as long-cycle systems and for pre-estimating jobs that do not yet exist, other methods had to be developed. We shall now consider some of these.

WORK SAMPLING

The ideas fundamental to materials sampling plans were extended to encompass work, i.e., the operations and activitives of the man in the system. In the 1930's, Tippett reported on his experiments with work sampling in English textile factories; and at about the same time, Morrow was utilizing this type of technique in factories in the USA. Just as in the case of materials sampling, the observations to be made represent less than a 100 percent study. Therefore, the observations must be *random* and of sufficient number so that an accurate picture can be constructed of what is going on in the system.

Consider the following. We will divide the day into 450 intervals, each of which is a working minute. On a purely random basis, we will select 54 of these 450 intervals; these will constitute the sample. Thus, if 450 numbered chips were thrown into a bowl—where the chips are numbered consecutively from 1 to 450—then by drawing 54 chips at random from the bowl, we could determine a set of *observation assignments for* each day.

A method simpler to use than the bowl of chips requires *tables of random numbers* (see page 514) and monte carlo number assignments. A random-number table has the important characteristic that there is no pattern whatever to the numbers listed in the table. The numbers are generated by a process that is comparable to withdrawing numbered chips from the bowl. This is true if the procedure of drawing numbers from the bowl is completely unbiased—and every number has an equal chance of being picked at each selection.

The monte carlo assignments could be made as follows. We wish to sample 54 out of 450 minute intervals. This is 0.12 of the total number of daily intervals. Then, let the monte carlo numbers 00-11 stand for: Take an observation; and the monte carlo numbers 12-99 stand for: No observation is to be taken. We now draw 450 pairs of random numbers in succession. As we read successive numbers from the table, we check to find out whether we are supposed to take an observation. Thus, assume the following random numbers:

$$62831 \qquad 04609 \qquad 83826 \qquad 57106 \qquad 38640$$

Reading these off in pairs from left to right,[3] we find:

---

[3] A table of random numbers can be read in any direction consistently, including along table diagonals.

TIME INTERVAL	RANDOM NUMBER	MONTE CARLO INTERPRETATION	WORKING	IDLE
1	62	No observation		
2	83	No observation		
3	10	Observation	x	
4	46	No observation		
5	09	Observation	x	
6	83	No observation		
7	82	No observation		
8	65	No observation		
9	71	No observation		
10	06	Observation		x
.	.	.		
.	.	.		
.	.	.		
etc.	etc.	etc.		

Because all random numbers are equally likely, on the average, 12 out of 100 (or 1.2 out of 10) random numbers will signify that an observation should be made. The sample that we have drawn has delivered three out of ten, but this is in the nature of statistical systems. Sometimes they will be high; sometimes low; in the long run, the results will average out.

The purpose of this elaborate method for drawing a sample is to insure that a good sample is drawn, i.e., one which neither observer nor worker can anticipate. Only in this way can the observations be unexpected and the situation that is observed be known to be unstaged, unpremeditated, and representative. Following the directives of the random numbers, the observer makes his appearance at the work place at the third, fifth, tenth, and so on, intervals. He makes his observations, records them, and departs.

The purpose of the observations, for the above example, has been to determine how much of the time the worker is engaged or idle. If a particular project or operation was the observation base, then categories of what was being done might be used. When a sufficient sample has been taken, ratios can be formed as descriptive measures of what goes on in the system. For example, assume that for a particular day, 45 observations have been made. Forty times, the individual was found to be busy. Then 40/45, or 8/9, of the time the operator can be assumed to have been engaged in a productive task.

The idea of work sampling is not to catch the worker off guard. Rather, it is to map out his activities and to help him utilize his time more fully. A more elaborate study than the one we have just described will help to make this point more apparent. Thus:

	FILING	PHONING	TYPING	OTHER	TOTAL
Number of times observed	60	30	182	28	300
Percent of total	20	10	61	9	100

Many study variations can be made on this basic theme. The sampling study is designed to reveal what many workers and executives cannot tell, viz., how they spend their time. A 100 percent sample might not provide as reliable an answer because the constant presence of the observer would create bias and distortion that occasional sampling is less likely to incur.

WORK SAMPLE SIZE

Designing a study that will reveal *needed* information with measurable reliability that cannot be obtained in a less expensive way is the essence of the work sampling, or operations sampling, technique. But how large a sample is needed? The same question was asked previously with respect to time studies. The answer that we now give is in the same vein. We have:

$$N = \left(\frac{k}{s}\right)^2 p(1 - p)$$

where:

N = The number of observations to be taken to provide a sufficient sample. A sufficient sample is defined by management in terms of k and s.

k = The number of Normal standard deviations required to give a confidence measure of α. When $k = 1$, $\alpha = 68$ percent; when $k = 2$, $\alpha = 95$ percent; when $k = 3$, $\alpha = 99.7$ percent.

α = The likelihood that the true value of p falls within the range $p \pm s$.

s = The accuracy range specified by management such that the true value of p falls within the range $p \pm s$.

p = The fraction of total observations that an activity is observed to occur. When using this formula, we need only compute N for the one activity that dominates the sample size requirements.[4] This will be the activity whose observed p is closest to $\frac{1}{2}$.

An example is the most direct way to reinforce the above explanation. We shall use the office sampling figures that were previously given. The typing activity has a value of p that is closest to $\frac{1}{2}$, viz.; $p = 0.61$. Let $k = 2$ and $s = 0.05$. Then,

$$N = \left(\frac{2}{0.05}\right)^2 (0.61)(0.39) = 381$$

Because only 300 observations were made, it is necessary that an addition be made to the sample. We shall presume that 100 more observations are taken and that $p(\text{typing}) = \frac{240}{400} = 0.60$. Then,

$$N = \left(\frac{2}{0.05}\right)^2 (0.6)(0.4) = 384,$$

---

[4] It should be noted that the sample formula given on p. 389 was based on an interval of the type $p \pm sp$. If we had used that relationship here, our sample size formula would be:

$$N = \left(\frac{k}{s}\right)^2 \left(\frac{1-p}{p}\right)$$

The dominating activity, in this case, will be the one with the smallest p value.

which is smaller than the actual sample, so the sample size is sufficient and we can stop.

Nomographs can be used to reduce computation time. This is desirable when many different samples of varying sizes must be determined. The time and

FIGURE 12-3
A typical nomograph
for calculating sample
size when ($k = 2$). An
example is illustrated
where $s = \pm0.02$, $p =$
0.10, and, therefore,
$N = 900$.

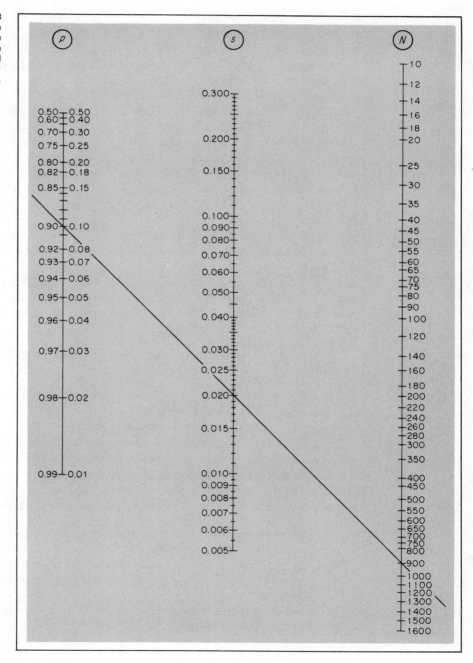

expense that goes into making up nomographs is like an investment designed to achieve sufficient reduction of the variable costs so that the investment is worthwhile. Although the sum of money involved in the nomograph investments is relatively small, nevertheless, the same kind of thinking applies that has run throughout our discussion of the production management field.

A typical nomograph is illustrated in Figure 12.3 where $k = 2$. To use this device, we simply draw a straight line through the specified values and read our result from the single unspecified variable. In this way, we can determine quickly and easily what value of s is *imputed* by given values for N and p. Usually the nomograph is utilized to determine the sample size N. The example that we have previously worked out can be used by the reader as a test case. The scale at the left is labeled p. This would be 0.60 for our example. The middle scale is s, or 0.05. Then, by drawing a straight line through these two points, we read the value for N on the scale at the right.

Nomographs have many applications in addition to work sampling. They are extensively applied in engineering and development work and can be of considerable assistance to management for the design of repetitive decision systems such as are used for inventory evaluation and job scheduling.

Work sampling can be of real value when properly utilized. *Time studies are of little help when noncyclical jobs or long-cycle jobs are involved.* In these cases, it is extremely difficult to measure, or even approximate, productive outputs. For those situations where either work sampling or time studies can be used, work sampling offers attractive advantages, such as the fact that the time study man requires great skill, whereas the work sampling observer can be relatively unskilled. Further, all extraneous elements that can enter the short-cycle job are not always picked up by the time study man. A properly designed *work sampling study will frequently prove to be a more effective way of dealing with special extraneous factors.*

SYNTHETIC TIME STANDARDS

It is difficult to obtain accurate measures of a fair day's output under many circumstances. There is also the problem of preparing estimates for jobs that have not been physically actualized. Both of these motives led to the development of *synthetic*, or *predetermined* time standards. Casting about for some way of categorizing the work measurement field, we can generalize, as follows:

1. Time study is applicable for short-cycle, repetitive operations that are presently being performed and can, therefore, be observed.
2. Work sampling can be used for long-cycle, repetitive operations that are presently being performed so they can be observed. The cycle must be stable or else the sample has no meaning.
3. Predetermined time studies can treat nonrepetitive, noncyclical jobs as well as jobs that are not being performed so they cannot be observed.

The basis of synthetic time standards is the fact that every job is composed of a set of elements that are *common to all jobs*. The unique feature of a particular job is the way in which this common alphabet of elements is used and the way in which the elements are arranged. Frank Gilbreth was one of the first management pioneers to describe such an alphabet of job elements or modules.[5] He called these modules *therbligs* and named 17 of them. For example,[6]

Grasp : Begins when hand or body member touches an object. Consists of gaining control of an object. Ends when control is gained.
Position : Begins when hand or body member causes part to begin to line up or locate. Consists of hand or body member causing part to line up, orient, or change position.
Assemble : Begins when the hand or body member causes parts to begin to go together. Consists of actual assembly of parts. Ends when hand or body member has caused parts to go together.
Hold : Begins when movement of part or object, which hand or body member has under control, ceases. Consists of holding an object in a fixed position and location. Ends with any movement.

From this beginning, A. B. Segur, who had worked with Gilbreth, developed his system of Motion-Time-Analysis (MTA), which was a work measurement procedure utilizing predetermined, standard, work element times. MTA was based upon the fundamental notion that "Within practical limits the times required of all expert workers to perform true fundamental motions are constant."[7]

Once the standard modules. or work elements, were named, then it was possible to study thousands of different operations in which each of these elements appeared. Motion pictures were made of many different kinds of jobs; and these in turn were analyzed to determine the appropriate statistical distribution of element times. Expected standard times were obtained in this way. Tables of such standard times for various work elements are shown in Figure 12.4. This is the system of synthetic standards known as MTM, the methods-time-measurement system.[8]

Another well-known system is that of *Work-Factor*, for which tables of standards are also available.[9] The Work-Factor system recently has been computerized which eliminates a great deal of the work required to establish production standards with predetermined times. The computer operation also has significant advantages in reducing the effort required to revise and update comprehensive standard data. Operations times are computed rapidly, and with great accuracy by replacing the human with a computer. The system also permits a reduction in the effort required for effectively designing motion patterns in the simplification of work (see pp. 399–402).

[5] Frank Gilbreth, see pp. 15, 429.
[6] Marvin E. Mundel, *Motion and Time Study, Principles and Practices*, 4th Ed. (Englewood Cliffs, N.J.: Prentice-Hall, Inc., 1970), pp. 243–248.
[7] J.H. Quick, J. H. Duncan, and J. A. Malcolm, Jr., *Work-Factor Time Standards, Measurement of Manual and Mental Work* (New York: McGraw-Hill Book Co., Inc., 1962), p. 4.
[8] Harold B. Maynard, G. J. Stegemerten and John L. Schwab, *Methods-Time-Measurement* (New York: McGraw-Hill, Inc., 1948).
[9] J. H. Quick, et al, *Work-Factor Time Standards, Measurement of Manual and Mental Work*, pp. 435–446.

TABLE I—Reach—R

DISTANCE MOVED INCHES	TIME TMU				HAND IN MOTION		CASE AND DESCRIPTION
	A	B	C OR D	E	A	B	
3/4 or less	2.0	2.0	2.0	2.0	1.6	1.6	A Reach to object in fixed location, or to object in other hand or on which other hand rests.
1	2.5	2.5	3.6	2.4	2.3	2.3	
2	4.0	4.0	5.9	3.8	3.5	2.7	
3	5.3	5.3	7.3	5.3	4.5	3.6	B Reach to single object in location which may vary slightly from cycle to cycle.
4	61.	6.4	8.4	6.8	4.9	4.3	
5	6.5	7.8	9.4	7.4	5.3	5.0	
6	7.0	8.6	10.1	8.0	5.7	5.7	
7	7.4	9.3	10.8	8.7	6.1	6.5	C Reach to object jumbled with other objects in a group so that search and select occur.
8	7.9	10.1	11.5	9.3	6.5	7.2	
9	8.3	10.8	12.2	9.9	6.9	7.9	
10	8.7	11.5	12.9	10.5	7.3	8.6	
12	9.6	12.9	14.2	11.8	8.1	10.1	
14	10.5	14.4	15.6	13.0	8.9	11.5	D Reach to a very small object or where accurage grasp is required.
16	11.4	15.8	17.0	14.2	9.7	12.9	
18	12.3	17.2	18.4	15.5	10.5	14.4	
20	13.1	18.6	19.8	16.7	11.3	15.8	
22	14.0	20.1	21.2	18.0	12.1	17.3	E Reach to indefinite location to get hand in position for body balance or next motion or out of way.
24	14.9	21.5	22.5	19.2	12.9	18.8	
26	15.8	22.9	23.9	20.4	13.7	20.2	
28	16.7	24.4	25.3	21.7	14.5	21.7	
30	17.5	25.8	26.7	22.9	15.3	23.2	

The time measurement units, *TMU* for MTM are given in terms of 0.00001 hour; for Work-Factor the time unit is 0.0001 minute.

TABLE II—Move—M

DISTANCE MOVED INCHES	TIME TMU				WT. ALLOWANCE			CASE AND DESCRIPTION
	A	B	C	HAND IN MOTION B	WT. (LB.) UP TO	FACTOR	CONSTANT TMU	
3/4 or less	2.0	2.0	2.0	1.7	2.5	0	0	
1	2.5	2.9	3.4	2.3				
2	3.6	4.6	5.2	2.9	7.5	1.06	2.2	A Move object to other hand or against stop.
3	4.9	5.7	6.7	3.6				
4	6.1	6.9	8.0	4.3				
5	7.3	8.0	9.2	5.0	12.5	1.11	3.9	
6	8.1	8.9	10.3	5.7				
7	8.9	9.7	11.1	6.5	17.5	1.17	5.6	
8	9.7	10.6	11.8	7.2				
9	10.5	11.5	12.7	7.9	22.5	1.22	7.4	B Move object to approximate or indefinite location.
10	11.3	12.2	13.5	8.6				
12	12.9	13.4	15.2	10.0	27.5	1.28	9.1	
14	14.4	14.6	16.9	11.4				
16	16.0	15.8	18.7	12.8	32.5	1.33	10.8	
18	17.6	17.0	20.4	14.2				
20	19.2	18.2	22.1	15.6	37.5	1.39	12.5	
22	20.8	19.4	23.8	17.0				
24	22.4	20.6	25.5	18.4	42.5	1.44	14.3	C Move object to exact location.
26	24.0	21.8	27.3	19.8				
28	25.5	23.1	29.0	21.2	47.5	1.50	16.0	
30	27.1	24.3	30.7	22.7				

FIGURE 12-4
(cont.)

TABLE III—Turn and Apply Pressure—T and AP

WEIGHT	TIME TMU FOR DEGREES TURNED										
	30°	45°	60°	75°	90°	105°	120°	135°	150°	165°	180°
Small— 0 to 2 Pounds	2.8	3.5	4.1	4.8	5.4	6.1	6.8	7.4	8.1	8.7	9.4
Medium —2.1 to 10 Pounds	4.4	5.5	6.5	7.5	8.5	9.6	10.6	11.6	12.7	13.7	14.8
Large— 10.1 to 35 Pounds	8.4	10.5	12.3	14.4	16.2	18.3	20.4	22.2	24.3	26.1	28.2

APPLY PRESSURE CASE 1—16.2 TMU.   APPLY PRESSURE CASE 2—10.6 TMU.

TABLE IV—Grasp—G

CASE	TIME TMU	DESCRIPTION
1A	2.0	Pick Up Grasp—Small, medium or large object by itself, easily grasped.
1B	3.5	Very small object or object lying close against a flat surface.
1C1	7.3	Interference with grasp on bottom and one side of nearly cylindrical object. Diameter larger than $\frac{1}{2}$".
1C2	8.7	Interference with grasp on bottom and one side of nearly cylindrical object. Diameter $\frac{1}{4}$" to $\frac{1}{2}$".
1C3	10.8	Interference with grasp on bottom and one side of nearly cylindrical object. Diameter less than $\frac{1}{4}$".
2	5.6	Regrasp.
3	5.6	Transfer Grasp.
4A	7.3	Object jumbled with other objects so search and select occur. Larger than 1" × 1" × 1".
4B	9.1	Object jumbled with other objects so search and select occur. $\frac{1}{4}$" × $\frac{1}{4}$" × $\frac{1}{8}$" to 1" × 1" × 1".
4C	12.9	Object jumbled with other objects so search and select occur. Smaller than $\frac{1}{4}$" × $\frac{1}{4}$" × $\frac{1}{8}$".
5	0	Contact, sliding or hook grasp.

TABLE V—Position*—P

CLASS OF FIT		SYMMETRY	EASY TO HANDLE	DIFFICULT TO HANDLE
1—Loose	No pressure required	S	5.6	11.2
		SS	9.1	14.7
		NS	10.4	16.0
2—Close	Light pressure required	S	16.2	21.8
		SS	19.7	25.3
		NS	21.0	26.6
3—Exact	Heavy pressure required.	S	43.0	48.6
		SS	46.5	52.1
		NS	47.8	53.4

* Distance moved to engage—1" or less.

TABLE VI—Release—RL

CASE	TIME TMU	DESCRIPTION
1	2.0	Normal release performed by opening fingers as independent motion.
2	0	Contact Release.

TABLE VII—Disengage—D

CLASS OF FIT	EASY TO HANDLE	DIFFICULT TO HANDLE
1—Loose—Very slight effort, blends with subsequent move.	4.0	5.7
2—Close—Normal effort, slight recoil.	7.5	11.8
3—Tight—Considerable effort, hand recoils markedly.	22.9	34.7

FIGURE 12-4
(cont.)

TABLE VIII—Eye Travel Time and Eye Focus—ET and EF

Eye Travel Time = $15.2 \times \dfrac{T}{D}$ TMU, with a maximum value of 20 TMU.

where T = the distance between points from and to which the eye travels.
D = the perpendicular distance from the eye to the line of travel T.

Eye Focus Time = 7.3 TMU.

An example of how synthetic times are used to determine production standards, to develop estimates, and to compare alternatives is shown in Figure 12.5.

Using predetermined standards, it is possible to derive a standard time for a job.

1. Describe the job completely and isolate the work elements; this is *analysis.*

2. Determine the appropriate times for each element as specified by the system that is being used.

3. Add the times together; this is *synthesis* requiring that the isolated work elements be independent of each other or that any existing interactions be taken into account so that the sum truly reflects the total time for the job.

FIGURE 12-5

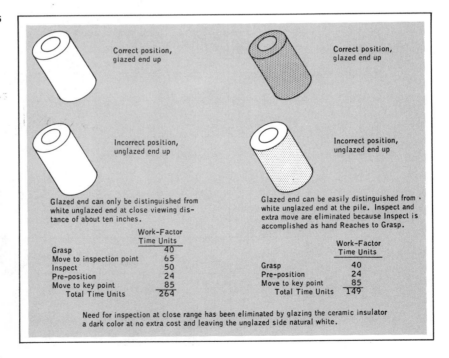

Correct position, glazed end up

Correct position, glazed end up

Incorrect position, unglazed end up

Incorrect position, unglazed end up

Glazed end can only be distinguished from white unglazed end at close viewing distance of about ten inches.

Glazed end can be easily distinguished from white unglazed end at the pile. Inspect and extra move are eliminated because Inspect is accomplished as hand Reaches to Grasp.

	Work-Factor Time Units
Grasp	40
Move to inspection point	65
Inspect	50
Pre-position	24
Move to key point	85
Total Time Units	264

	Work-Factor Time Units
Grasp	40
Pre-position	24
Move to key point	85
Total Time Units	149

Need for inspection at close range has been eliminated by glazing the ceramic insulator a dark color at no extra cost and leaving the unglazed side natural white.

Some advantages of synthetic time standards, when they can be appropriately applied, are:

1. The leveling factor problem is bypassed. It is already included in the synthetic time standard, because rating differences are averaged out across many jobs and many operators. In short, no rating factor is required with these systems.

2. Distortions that arise because of observer bias and interaction between the observer and the worker can be controlled and removed from the synthetic times, which is not the case for time studies.

3. Time studies are normally based upon an established job. For all new jobs there is a learning period for the worker. During this period, observations are unreliable. The problem is bypassed through the use of predetermined time standards.

4. The cost of determining production standards is reduced.

5. The synthetic production standard is founded upon element times derived from very large samples of observations. This increased reliability of the standard time cannot be obtained with time studies, because it is out of the question to utilize such large samples for studying any one particular job.

6. The speed of preparing cost estimates, as well as their reliability for new jobs, new products, and so on, is greatly improved. Production schedules can be quickly determined and modified. Product-mix analyses can be expedited similarly.

INCREASED SCOPE OF PREDETERMINED TIME VALUES

In recent years, there have been important new developments in the Work-Factor system of elemental times. Hitherto unmeasurable work functions have yielded to operational work measurement. For example, the detailed Work-Factor system now includes time values and techniques for measuring *micro-miniature assembly operations* performed under high-powered microscopes, both with hand tweezers and micromanipulators. And a system called Mento-Factor has extended the use of predetermined time values to include mental functions involved in the performance of useful work by the human. Mento-Factor embodies some 450 fundamental mental process times, representing such functions as: proofreading, visual inspection, calculations, reading, problem solving with slide rule, tool design problems, and scanning blueprints. No synthetic time standards are applicable to human mental process functions in creative areas.

WORK SIMPLIFICATION

The notion that work patterns could be studied and improved was the core from which modern production management evolved. Taylor, Gantt, Gilbreth,[10]

---

[10] See pp. 428–30.

and others recognized that intuitive and judgmental methods of managing could be assisted by "scientific" analysis. The form that the analysis took was based on the premise that *if the parts were improved, then the whole must be better.* We now know that analysis can go just so far, and that, in fact, it can mislead us. We talk about the system, and wherever we use analysis we subsequently require synthesis. We reject efficiency without the simultaneous consideration of effectiveness.

None of this, however, reduces the *utility of work simplification when properly applied.* After all, efforts to improve efficiency represent investments. Like all investment alternatives, the burden of proof that an efficiency study is the best possible way to proceed falls upon those who would use it. But it must also be remembered that diminishing utility is likely to set in when what is already quite efficient is asked to be more so. The desire for efficiency and *perfection* is frequently more a matter of personal values than of systems rationality. When this is not the case, work simplification, job evaluation, value analysis see pp. 292–93, and methods analysis are legitimate and desirable investments for company funds.

It was from this basic urge to improve "things" that production management methodology began to search for new ways to look at the process. It was recognized that the process was composed of operations and that the operations could be further broken down, until such *micromotion units* as therbligs were created as sort of the ultimate in microcategorization. Thus, on the one hand, classification was a fundamental tool of the work simplification analyst. On the other hand, a means to organize and sequence these data was required. The fundamental method used was the visual representation of work flows. Such schematics typify the contributions of the early scientific management pioneers. Many of these charting techniques are still widely used because they are the best way presently available for coping with the level of complexities that characterize this problem area.

As in any method that relies heavily on categorization, an important decision is *how fine* or *how broad* to make the categories. The choice was made to develop analytic tools for each of the various levels that would be encountered. Thus, the *process chart* was relatively *macro* in its view of the system (see pp. 352–57). Essentially, it charted the space-sequence flow of materials through the various stages of the production transformation process. At the next level of detail came *operation charts.* In this case, observation was concentrated on a specific worker and his particular work station. Frequently, the level of analysis was in accord with the element interval requirements of time study methods. An example of this kind of schematic is shown in Figure 12.6. The *right and left hand movements* could be traced in terms of as fine a breakdown as the therblig classes, or with equal facility at grosser levels. Various symbols were developed to facilitate visual orientation and communication. There is nothing fixed or unalterable about these charts and the symbols used. Practice has produced the general form which can be regarded as a standard. Modifications should be made according to requirements. The charts are intended to be *data organizers* that permit *intelligent evaluation of the situation* so that reasonable alternative

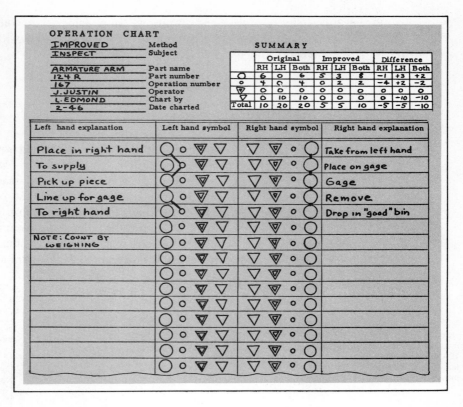

FIGURE 12-6 chart:

OPERATION CHART

	Field
IMPROVED	Method
INSPECT	Subject
ARMATURE ARM	Part name
124 R	Part number
167	Operation number
J. JUSTIN	Operator
L. EDMOND	Chart by
2-46	Date charted

SUMMARY

	Original			Improved			Difference		
	RH	LH	Both	RH	LH	Both	RH	LH	Both
◯	6	0	6	5	3	8	−1	+3	+2
○	4	0	4	0	2	2	−4	+2	−2
▽	0	0	0	0	0	0	0	0	0
▽	0	10	10	0	0	0	0	−10	−10
Total	10	20	20	5	5	10	−5	−5	−10

Left hand explanation	Left hand symbol	Right hand symbol	Right hand explanation
Place in right hand			Take from left hand
To supply			Place on gage
Pick up piece			Gage
Line up for gage			Remove
To right hand			Drop in "good" bin
NOTE: COUNT BY WEIGHING			

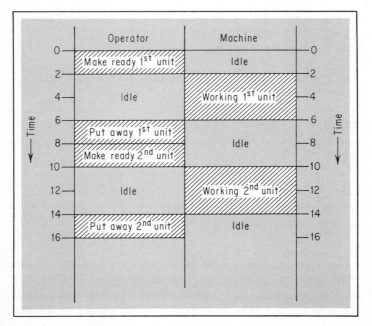

FIGURE 12-7 chart (Man-machine time chart):

Operator / Machine

Time	Operator	Machine
0–2	Make ready 1st unit	Idle
2–6	Idle	Working 1st unit
6–8	Put away 1st unit	Idle
8–10	Make ready 2nd unit	Idle
10–14	Idle	Working 2nd unit
14–16	Put away 2nd unit	Idle

401

arrangements of process and operations can be achieved. In common practice, a chart that portrays present conditions is compared readily with charts for one or more competing alternative plans.

MAN-MACHINE SYSTEMS

Another familiar work simplification chart is concerned with the operating characteristics of the *man-machine system*. This is the *man-machine time chart* which encourages visual analysis of the way in which man-machine operations are coordinated. In Figure 12.7 we observe that both the operator and his machine are idle 50 percent of the time. The problem seems to stem from the fact that the machine cannot be used during the *make ready* or the *put away* operations. In other words, the primary machine function must be interrupted, both to prepare and to remove successive parts. *If this were not true, then the*

FIGURE 12-8
Man-machine time
chart—Machine A is
modified to permit
100 percent utiliza-
tion of both man and
machine.

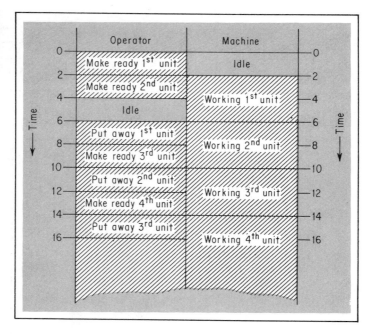

more efficient arrangement shown in Figure 12.8 could be used. Here, after the first cycle, both man and machine are 100 percent utilized.

Let us, now, assume that a different facility, machine *B*, can be used where make ready and put away idle the facility but can be simultaneously performed. Then, if a helper is supplied to the operator, the machine utilization can be increased from 1/2 to 2/3. Both the operator and the helper have only 1/3 utilization factors. This is shown in Figure 12.9.

We shall complete this discussion by assuming that the data below are descriptive of the situation:

Operator's wage = $3.00 per hour
Helper's wage = $1.50 per hour
Machine A's cost = $10.00 per hour
Machine B's cost = $14.50 per hour
Value of output = $2.00 per piece

FIGURE 12-9
Man-machine time
chart—Machine B,
Plan 2.

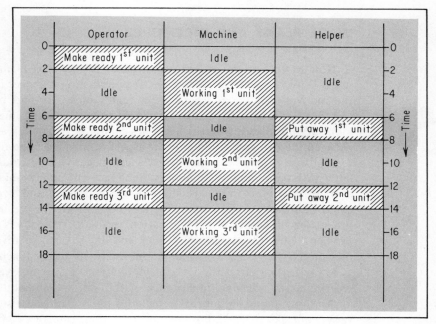

We can analyze the situation in the following way:

PLAN 1: Machine A is utilized 50 percent of the time. It takes four minutes to make a part, therefore, 7.5 parts are made per hour. These are valued at $15.00. From this we subtract the sum of machine A's hourly cost and the hourly wage of the operator, that is, $15.00 − $13.00 = $2.00, which is the measure of profit per hour for plan 1.

PLAN 2: Machine B is utilized $66\frac{2}{3}$ percent of the time. Therefore, 10 parts can be made per hour. These are valued at $20.00. We subtract machine B's hourly cost and the hourly wages of both the operator and his helper. This gives $20.00 − $19.00 = $1.00 of profit per hour. *Therefore, we prefer Plan 1.*

We can see how closely related work simplification is to time study analysis.

Before production standards are set, *jobs should be studied* and brought to a point where common sense and good judgment can no longer be readily used to improve the operations. Nervertheless, at a particular moment in time an individual may get a sudden insight as to how a well-studied job can be further improved. In recent years, there has been de-emphasis on work simplification in certain industries because: product life is getting shorter and line change-overs to new and modified output designs are becoming more frequent; high-level mechanization and automation require intense preplanning which obviates the need for on-going improvement of operations; and more elaborate method-ologies of operations research and management science have appeared which compete for investment study dollars with the older work simplification methods.

WAGE PLANS AND INCENTIVES

Now we turn to the second aspect of the two-part problem: fair output-fair wage. With respect to a "fair" wage, the production manager is concerned with the motivational forces which affect man's creativity and productivity. The fact that man's behavior can be influenced by various inducements (for example, monetary incentives) whereas machines cannot be, points up a major difference between the two and is still another aspect of man-machine relations.[11]

Motivation can be both positive and negative. We usually associate the latter with poor employee morale. On the face of it, one would suppose that an average level of morale existed from which positive and negative deviations could be measured Of course, there is no standard to use in this way. With discussions of incentives and motivation, the major difficulty is the measurement problem. Nevertheless, accepting the lack of precision involved, we recognize that motivation exists as a real causal factor in a man-machine system.

Many factors affect the level of motivation of an employee. These include *prestige*, *social standing*, importance of the job, and the ability to participate in decisions about the job. Also included are vacations, leisure time, and the variety of tasks assigned. For the most part, these categories represent intangible qualities that escape definition and measurement. Thus, we speak of leadership—knowing that an undefinable characteristic is involved. It is a characteristic that is intimately involved with the subject of motivation and incentive. We lack a yardstick by which to measure it. One of the few ways to set an objective standard for the control of incentives is through wage plans.

What is an equitable wage? Do we measure real wages in terms of the *cost of living*, or do we compare monetary wages as they are found in different parts of the country? Is it reasonable to compare, for a given industry, rural with

---

[11] A startling case history was obtained in the 1930's by a study group from Harvard at the Western Electric Company in Chicago. The original study concerned levels of illumination and their effect on productivity. It was discovered that whether the illumination was raised or lowered—productivity was improved. The key discovery was that employees responded positively to management's *interest and attention*. The response level overrode the functional effects of the illumination level. This complex behavior provides important differentiation between man and machine.

urban wages? There has been a continuing attempt to relate monetary wages to real wages. For this reason the minimum wage as fixed by law has been steadily increased over the years in order to keep pace with a rising cost of living.

From each company's point of view there is some level of wages that is optimal. High wages remove dollars that could otherwise be invested in expansion possibilities. Salary increases might cause dollars to be withheld from stockholders. This action produces unpredictable results on the stock market. It generally lowers the credit ratings that banks will offer. Low wages, on the other hand, discourage highly skilled and able personnel; produce negative motivation, increase turnover rates, and increase recruitment costs. From the company's point of view, therefore, neither high nor low wages are desirable. Rather, a wage rate that produces a balanced system of costs is desired. It is not our intention to discuss in detail questions involved with job evaluation and the determination of an equitable wage. However, the question of whether to design a job for a man or a machine is inescapably involved with those issues that underlie worker and machine performance.

There are many different but reasonable approaches to the problem of *job evaluation*. The first requires purely qualitative evaluations. A second possibility calls for the ranking of jobs. A third approach is based upon a point system. The purely qualitative approach is overly susceptible to personal bias. Because of this, it is disappearing from use. Ranking is certainly superior, but ranking does not indicate how much one job differs from another. Let us, therefore, consider the most elaborate of the named approaches, that is, the point system. A job is classified in terms of a number of factors, such as:

1. Intelligence required for the job;
2. Physical skill required for the job;
3. Physical effort required for the job;
4. Responsibility that must be assumed in order to accomplish the job;
5. Working conditions, including the environment and other human factors relevant to job accomplishment.

Any job can be described in terms of these variables. Each task requires a varying amount of each factor. By assigning point values to each factor it is possible to derive a total score for any job. The score is equivalent to a monetary wage rate. It is intended to reflect the requirements of the job in terms of the significant factors. Presumably, in this way an approach is made to the problem of determining true worth to the company. After all, the real issue in a rational, laissez-faire society is: What is a particular job, or set of operations, worth to the company? For machines, the costs are easily derived. For men, the problem has never been totally resolved.

To convert job point levels into appropriate wage rates, the key-job concept can be used. Certain key positions exist that are commonly found in the industry. These might include the position of secretary, foreman, and skilled tool and die-maker. The key jobs are carefully studied in terms of the kind of factors listed above. Then, a job rating is assigned. Based upon an industry-wide, geographical analysis of the going wage rates for key positions, a curve can be drawn such as is shown in Figure 12.10. We see that first the key jobs are located on this graph. Then, a curve is put through the key job points. It follows that all other jobs can be assigned appropriate wage rates by estimating their positions on the curve between the key job points.

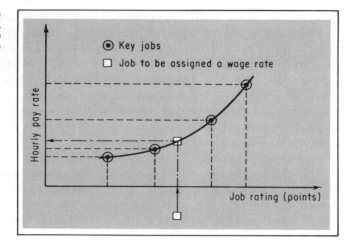

Although this is a relatively straightforward method for pricing jobs, many additional factors intervene. These include the use of incentive plans, merit rating systems, the importance of seniority, the effect of cost of living factors, the supply and demand both regionally and nationally for certain skills, and the notion of a guaranteed annual wage. We shall turn particular attention to the question of incentives.

Before proceeding further, let us recapitulate the steps required to establish a rate structure:

1. Develop relevant job factors;
2. Classify jobs in terms of the relevant factors;
3. Select key jobs and determine appropriate wage rates;
4. Assign wage rates to nonkey jobs by interpolation and extrapolation;
5. Take special factors into account such as seniority, merit ratings, and incentive plans.

Many jobs can only be assigned a wage according to the amount of *time* that the worker contributes. This is characteristic of executive and administrative positions. It is also true of creative and research jobs. Indirect labor, by definition, cannot be paid on the basis of production output. This applies to most clerical operations. Only those jobs that are directly associated with the volume of production can be paid for on the basis of physical output.

Various models that are suitable for the analysis of employee motivation have been developed.[12] They are concerned with the methods used to obtain maximum worker participation. They are designed, on the one hand, to provide equitable distinction between workers who expend different amounts of energy and contribute different benefits to the company. On the other hand, they are intended to provide a balanced system of wages for the company. Many different plans or models have been conceived. We shall mention only a few.

1. *Straight Piece-Work Model:*

$$W = HA\left(\frac{O_A}{O_S}\right)$$

where:

H = Hourly rate in dollars per hour.

A = Actual time worked in hours per week.

O_A = Actual output per hour in pieces per hour.

O_S = Standard output per hour in expected number of pieces per hour.

W = Weekly wage rate in dollars per week.

H/O_S is the rate in dollars per piece of completed work and is derived in terms of an output standard (from time studies) and a wage standard (from job evaluation). The worker, however, has no security with this fundamental wage plan. His weekly wage decreases proportionally as his actual work output falls.

2. *Piece-Work Model with a Guaranteed Base:*

for $O_A \leq O_S$ $\qquad W = HA$

for $O_A > O_S$ $\qquad W = HA\left(\frac{O_A}{O_S}\right)$

In this case, the worker is guaranteed at least a weekly wage rate of $W = HA$. As his actual output becomes greater than standard output he can take home additional money.

3. *General Incentive Model:*

for $O_A \leq O_S$ $\qquad W = HA$

for $O_A > O_S$ $\qquad W = HA\left[1 + k\left(\frac{O_A}{O_S} - 1\right)\right]$

Here again, the minimum is established at $W = HA$. Now, however, we observe that the incentive given is proportional to the size of the coefficient k. For O_A greater than O_S, some fraction of the value of the extra production of the worker is paid to him as both reward and incentive. The value of k depends upon the plan that is used. For example, there is the Halsey 50-50 plan where $k = \frac{1}{2}$. In the 100 percent bonus plan,[13] $k = 1$. In the Bedaux plan, $k = \frac{3}{4}$. Many other

[12] Historically, we find great interest in this subject regarding the development of incentive plans. Frederick W. Taylor, Henry Towne, Henri Fayol, and others were concerned with incentive, profit sharing, work definition, work division, authority and responsibility, and the question of satisfactory pay.

[13] This is equivalent to the piece-work model with a guaranteed base.

plans also have been tried. The history of these plans, their results, and the subsequent design of new and improved plans is an area of specialization in itself.

DESIGN OF THE JOB AND THE WORKPLACE

Man works in an environment; he changes that environment and he exercises control over it. A big step forward was made when the nature of interrelated systems was recognized. The relations and dependencies of parts of the system always play a significant role. The production system must be designed according to managerial objectives. Automation implies that controls will be designed and built into this system so that it can function *more* or *less* untended. The degree of control reflects the technology of the process. No matter what the characteristics of the input-output process model are, it is impossible to design adequate controls *for all eventualities that might occur.*

Even in fully automated systems a "red emergency light" or its equivalent must be included so that the attention of a human monitor can be attracted and directed to the serious malfunction that is signaled by this emergency procedure. The treatment of such malfunctions requires abilities that are uniquely human. The degree to which a system is automated—therefore, the degree to which man is removed from the process—must be a function of both an economic and a technological criterion. There are systems in which it is neither economically sensible nor technologically feasible to replace man. In other cases, a machine or a control mechanism can out-perform the most highly skilled workers and do this at a lower cost.

SAFETY

The safety of both the production worker and the user of a product or service is an overriding condition of all decisions made in the production management field. Acceptable levels of safety are difficult to discuss and even harder to specify. We know that the ideal situation is "perfect" safety, but it is an unobtainable state. So called "safety factors" are designed into bridges, ships, and planes. Sometimes, we speak about "fail-safe" systems. By this we mean that the system is immune to crucial accidents or disastrous, fortuitous events except where the probabilities of such occurrences are so small that they can be ignored.[14] To achieve this, high-level safety factors must be incorporated into the basic design of the system for all system vulnerabilities.

---

[14] According to Borel, these might be events associated with probabilities in the neighborhood of one in a million (0.000001).

Emile Borel, "Valeur Pratique et Philosophie des Probabilities," *Traite du Cacul des Probabilities et de ses Applications,* Tome IV, Fascicule 3, ed. by Emile Borel (Gautier-Villars, Paris, 1950).

Safety poses a curious problem. We cannot really evaluate the value of an arm, or a leg, or a life. If faced with the question, we would state unequivocally that a life is of infinite value; but we do not act as though this were so, nor could we if we tried. It would mean that each and every swimmer has his own personal retinue of lifeguards; that after each flight, a plane would be completely overhauled, and new parts installed for all the old ones. The fact that we do not behave in this manner does not lessen our concern for safety. If anything, our concern increases as a direct result of the fact that we cannot act in accord with our moral values, but rather, in terms of an obscure compromise between moral and economic values.

Bypassing the complicated philosophical and ethical problems involved in this subject, we can all readily agree that safety is a major consideration. Although we cannot find a behavioral model to determine the value of life and limb, we can attempt to minimize accident rates subject to a reasonable set of system constraints.[15] Thus, machine designs must assure a reasonable level of safety to machine operators. Here, the differences between people play a part. A satisfactory machine design for a male worker may not prove to be equally safe for a female operator.[16] (See the discussion of *human factors* which follows on pp. 413–20).

In certain cases, humans are susceptible to damage where the source of trouble lies beyond the capabilities of their own sensory protection. This is true, for example, where odorless toxic gases find their way into the air supply. Another case is where workers are inadvertently exposed to radioactive materials which cause radiation poisoning before detection is possible. Positive steps must be taken to prevent these conditions from arising, correcting them immediately if they occur. Processes that produce toxic gases must be isolated so that they cannot contaminate the air supply. Nontoxic impurities can be kept out of the air by utilizing exhaust hoods close to the source of such impurities. For this vacuum cleaner-type action to be effective, the through-put rate of the air intake must be regulated according to the weight of the contaminent particles. For radiation hazards, proper shielding is a necessity. Where this is not possible, machines are substituted and controlled at safe distances from the radioactive materials. Geiger counters and other protective devices are used to provide warning if some dangerous malfunction occurs. Radioactive substances are being used with increasing frequency. The irradiation of foods, plastics, and other materials is becoming relatively commonplace; similarly, medical uses have increased.

Similar examples of undetectable hazards can be given with respect to the designs of products and services. Thus, the manufacturer of a radio or television set must be certain that the metal chassis of the set is adequately grounded, so

---

[15] We maximize safety, but subject to economic constraints. In this way, we can soothe our consciences that all possible steps are being taken (although this is not so). The underlying procedure is the same as that used for profit maximization in enterprise decisions constrained by the status quo. The comparison raises some interesting philosophical points.

[16] During the Second World War, a famous movie actress started a fad for long hair that was worn partially over the face. Machine designers had not taken this possibility into account and a number of serious accidents occurred. Various government agencies requested the actress to change her hair style, which she did. This improved the situation.

that when it is touched by a small child standing on a wet tile floor no harm results. Food and drug manufacturers must be absolutely certain of the quality of all materials that are used in their products. Airlines must properly service and maintain the equipment they use. These are all examples of safety problems where the worker or the consumer proceeds on faith.

Many safety problems arise because of laziness or corner-cutting. In these cases, the danger is apparent to all concerned, but somewhere along the line adequate measures are not taken. It is not enough to supply goggles to workers where, either because of intense light or flying particles, eye impairment might result if they are not used. It is necessary to make *certain* that they are used.

Problems of safety also involve a *proneness* to accidents which seems to arise from psychological factors triggered by an initial chance occurrence. The problem of accident proneness has been studied, but the search for an antidote appears to require further research.

Safety problems for workers arise because of the complex equipment and processes found in the production area. It is production management's beholden obligation to insure worker safety. The model of man shows a hardy soul but a vulnerable body. Fundamentally, the best way to ensure safety is to design a total system of products, tools, facilities, and services that adequately considers the range of detrimental conditions that can occur. Safety models, therefore, constitute an area of total interaction between individuals and physical elements of the production system. Often, preventative measures may be more effective than remedial ones.

THE MAN-MACHINE INTERFACE

The industrial revolution was based on the fact that for certain kinds of operations a machine was superior to a man. Over a period of time there has been an increasing level of sophistication with respect to the design of mechanisms. This has led to many instances where the replacement of man by machine has been unequivocally warranted.

Initially, *repetitive physical jobs* were particularly susceptible to improvement by utilizing machines instead of workers. Now we find that mechanical and electronic control systems can be substituted for many mental activities formerly relegated exclusively to men. At the heart of this change is the *computer*. We should note that for the most complex activities, neither man nor machine is ideal for the job. Rather, some *combination* of man and machine, working as a well-*coordinated* team is usually desirable. We speak of the way in which *man and machine are intercoordinated as the man-machine interface*. For example, man's eyesight is considerably augmented by both microscopes and telescopes. Man's hearing is extended by dint of audio-amplification. On the other hand, no fully automatic recognition systems are available for either visual symbols or for spoken phonemes. Where seeing and hearing are requirements, the man in the system is essential. The lever and the pulley served to enlarge the feats of strength that man could perform. For pure muscle power, however, machines acting by themselves are capable of producing enormous forces. Man in the system—where the objectives are brute power—will seldom provide meaningful assistance. Most often, he will cut down on the system's capabilities.

On the cerebral side of the ledger—just as is the case with the sensory system—a coordinated effort is usually rewarding. Books, films, tapes, and records provide mechanical storage or memory. But man's memory is of a basically different form. The two types of memory can be combined to produce a superior, coordinated memory. But memory is only one aspect of the thinking process. No one knows how man thinks. But we have learned a great deal about the nature of thinking as a result of the computer. For some jobs, man is ideally suited. For others, the computer has definite advantages. The man-machine interface problem is to find the optimal pattern and utilization for both kinds of systems components. This is a major production management responsibility. It requires a knowledge of both behavioral models and machine models. Let us, therefore, make a brief comparison between man's abilities and the computer's abilities.

1. Human memory has approximately 10^{14} greater capacity than the largest available computing equipment. This difference is major. It will require a technological breakthrough in the design of computing equipment if this difference is to be reduced. There is no prospect in sight for such a breakthrough.

On the other hand, an important characteristic of man's memory is that it is highly selective; it rejects repetitious data, and it forgets easily. Man's memory appears to require associations between the elements that are to be stored away for future recall. Perhaps the most important liability of the human memory, aside from the forgetting characteristic, is the fact that it can so easily distort information *without realizing* that this transgression has taken place.

2. Perseverance is an area where man cannot compete with the computer. The brain fatigues rapidly when repetitive, routine operations are required. The computer, on the other hand, is indifferent to the number of repetitions that must be furnished. Meanwhile, the computer is literally incapable of handling situations where no prior pattern has been discovered and objectified. Some people take this to mean that the computer cannot be creative. The conclusion does not appear to be valid. If anything, we must say that we do not yet know how to make the computer behave creatively. The failing lies with man—the model builder and computer programmer—not with the machine.

3. In the same sense, man is able to devise intricate rules of logic. He can program these rules for use by the computer. He himself, however, is quite unable to consistently apply the logical rules that he has devised.

4. Speed of computation for routine operations definitely points with favor to the electronic computer. We must not lose sight of the fact, however, that a substantial amount of time can be required to preplan the procedures and steps that will be followed by the computer system. Whenever automated systems are under consideration, the preplanning time must be included if a relevant man-machine interface analysis is to be made.

5. Variability is the last factor that we will mention in this comparison. Man does not work at a constant rate. The distribution of times required by a human operator has substantially greater variance (variability) than would apply to

a computing mechanism. We can afford to sympathize with the fact that the human operator requires time off to refresh himself—be it a coffee break or a few moments of conversation with a fellow worker. Even if he tried to, man could not maintain the exact same rate of productivity. His time sense and motor controls would fail him.

Analysis of the interface (or boundary) across which men and machines communicate reveals that sensory models are related to the monitoring function in control systems. In some cases, physical devices are clearly preferred; for example, for tracking temperature we use thermometers and thermostats. A particular advantage of mechanical sensing equipment is that it can be designed to handle cross-talk situations. *Cross-talk* occurs when several sensory perceptors are simultaneously called upon to receive input data. Human perception can be improved if the inputs to the different senses reinforce each other. For example, a message is shown on the TV screen and read aloud at the same time. However, when the inputs are not related to each other, then conflict can occur, causing an inability to treat either input. Because machines can be designed to operate under such circumstances, a reasonable definition of how to draw the man-machine interface for a particular situation will depend upon the monitoring requirements for the system. When control devices are too expensive to warrant designing them to handle cross-talk, *sample-data designs* can be substituted for continuous ones. The essence of the sample-data system is the fact that it will open one sensory channel at a time. It samples what is going on at various places in the system. Man inherently acts as a sample-data system. He cannot continuously monitor the behavior of a system. Good systems design calls for proper scheduling of the sample periods, whether a man or a device is used. Because the human monitor can be ineffective when subjected to cross-talk situations, it is necessary to permit him access to only one of these inputs at a time.

Many other interface characteristics must be explored if the production manager is to properly assess the systems requirements and provide the proper process and control designs. Under certain circumstances, man has an ability to blank-out background noise, for example, the ticking of a clock. Machines can also be designed to do this (for example, low-pass and high-pass frequency filters). If it is not desirable to blank-out some of the inputs, then the cross-talk situation exists and our previous remarks apply. Man is subject to sensory illusions. Many examples can be found in psychological literature of physical relationships that are distorted by the human sensory mechanism. Machine sensing fallibility also occurs. Almost without exception, machines misinterpret different kinds of physical relations than do man's senses. Interface design must take this factor into account.

Another topic of great importance to production workplace design is the reliability of system components. For human machines, failures of physical and mental health are treated by the class of repairmen known as medical doctors and psychiatrists. Health is affected by various kinds of overloads. In addition, failings in one human component are frequently contagious. Thus, the common cold is readily communicable among a group of workers. Machine failures, on the other hand, are often independent of the condition of other mechanical units in the system. This is not always true, however. Figure 12.11 illustrates how the failure of one machine can result in the shutting down of other machines. The doctor in this case is the repairman. Interface design requires full consideration of such factors and must allow for the possibility of a speck of dust getting in the operator's eye, or a piece of grit getting into a gear train.

FIGURE 12-11
The failure of one mechanical component can produce the equivalence of failure in other mechanical components. There is only one mechanical unit in this diagram which when broken down will shut off the entire system.

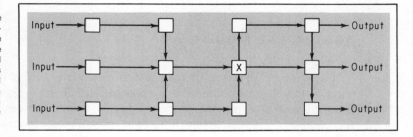

HUMAN FACTORS

Many fundamental considerations must be taken into account when determining the extent to which man should participate in the production process. The study of such problems has given rise to the development of behavioral models which are concerned with the way in which man fits his environment, the control he has over it, the design of the tools that he uses, and the design of the products and services that he requires. Such studies are called by a number of different names. We have used the label "human factors," but we could have called this subject "human engineering," "bio-mechanics," or a British term, "ergonomics." The behavioral models derived from the *human factors approach* interrelate with the production manager's function and are of particular interest to him.

The design of the plant and the working environment is a form of industrial architecture. In many ways, it represents the same kind of approaches and the same set of human factors objectives as those of industrial designers.

The human factors area treats both the physiological and psychological characteristics of people. It attempts to provide high levels of *safety* and comfort. It is concerned with "the appearances of things," and the way they affect efficiency. All the senses and the interrelationships of the senses to both motor and mental responses are part of the fabric of these factors which describe the interactions of the worker, the workplace, and the plant. Thus, not only sight, illumination, and color concern us; but also hearing, noise, taste, smell, the effects of temperature and temperature changes, body orientation, and all other factors that condition the performance and attitudes of the workers of a system. In addition, the social factors, the mental set, and attitude of the individual and the group play an overriding role in determining behavior. We shall examine briefly some of the generalizations that can be made about human participation in a system. But we must remember that each problem is unique. The most that we can succeed in doing in these sections is to convey the nature of existing models. We shall not catalog them because they are too many in number and too diversified in type. They fall properly in the domain of the specialist upon whom the production manager must rely when the occasion calls for him to do so.

ANATOMICAL MODELS

The physical structure of man affects workplace design in many obvious ways. What is not so immediately apparent is that the logic of an individual, using himself as a physical model, is hardly a sufficient design guide—either for consumer product design or employee workplace considerations. Many different physiological models have been derived by the researchers and practitioners of human engineering.

Because people come in different shapes and sizes, it is necessary to study their relevant statistical characteristics with respect to the objectives of the system's design. The analysis of physical differences between individuals has proven to be of great benefit in all areas where man operates on or interacts with his physical environment. For example, the design of a telephone handset poses many difficult human-factor problems. These include choosing the size and weight of such a unit that will be most convenient. Because of the differences that exist between people, this last statement will not be operationally meaningful. We want to know the answer to the question: Most convenient for whom? It is operational, therefore, to select a design that satisfies a statistical criterion relative to the distribution of pertinent human wants and needs.

Let us consider the design problem concerning the relational orientations of the ear and mouth piece of the telephone handset, and the distance between them. The requirements of a representative distribution of individuals can be determined. Presumably, a design based on this statistical knowledge regarding these dimensions would satisfy the minimum requirements for a majority of potential users. The basic idea is illustrated by Figure 12.12. We know that an ideal relationship for a small person could not, at the same time, be ideal for a large one. Counter design for a soda fountain presents similar opportunities. Design problems can be resolved only by determining the satisfaction of a representative cross-section of potential users. The final design cannot provide equal satisfaction for all people, but it can be *sufficiently* satisfactory for an appropriate number of users.

Another example can be derived in terms of a consumer product which has far reaching implications. Suppose that a shoe manufacturer wishes to reduce the variety of shoe sizes (that is, lengths, widths, and so on) that are traditionally required—but without losing sales. Or, this manufacturer might have a different

FIGURE 12-12
Summary of face dimensions used in design of telephone handset. The chart indicates the number of people for whom specific distances and orientations were found to be suitable. [From Ernest J. McCormick, *Human Engineering* (New York: McGraw-Hill, Inc., 1957), p. 446; based on the work of W. C. Jones and A. H. Inglis, "Development of a Handset for Telephone Stations," Bell System Technical Journal, Vol. XI, 1932, p. 262.]

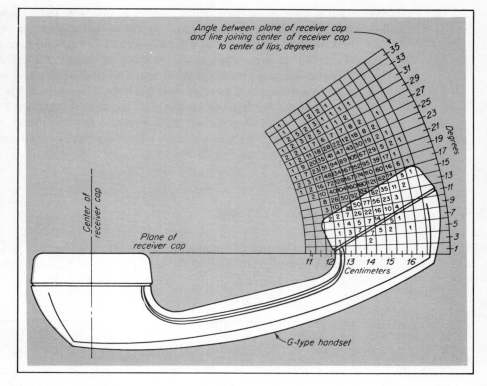

objective; namely to keep the same level of variety, but to alter the sizes and shapes of his shoes with the intention of improving the resultant level of comfort, thereby increasing his sales. To achieve this objective it is necessary to obtain statistical distributions of foot measurements. These would describe the various foot characteristics of the population of potential shoe users. The characteristics of feet chosen to be studied would be those that are relevant to the comfort of users. The appropriate set of dimensions have to be determined before an empirical study can be conducted. Once specified, the set of dimensions constitutes an anatomical model. Other dimensions must be irrelevant to be ignored by the model. Then, with a sufficiently large sample of people properly measured for the appropriate dimensions, a reasonable design decision can be made.

A concrete example of the way in which an anatomical model serves as a guide for the design of equipment is shown in Figure 12.13. This improved design for the foot pedal of a lift truck was developed by the industrial design firm of Henry Dreyfuss. In all cases, the determination of the relevant dimensions is the first model-building phase of the problem. Obtaining the actual measurements from a representative sample of the population is the second phase.

Consider still another example. Presume that our objective is to design a chair that would be standard equipment in an office. Many different body forms, heights and weights would have to be considered if we are to offer a reasonable level of comfort to the greatest number of potential users. Toward this end, we would measure a representative sample of users of these chairs. But again, first we must determine: of what measurable dimensions is comfort a function. We note that the sample would be quite different if the office is to be staffed with men only, or women only, or a combination of men and women. Chairs for a kindergarten would pose another problem. Generally, the larger the diversity among users, the less the satisfaction that can be obtained for any one user. Although this is an argument for uniqueness among designs, it must be counterbalanced against the added costs of providing greater satisfaction to a smaller number of users. (See pp. 465–71.)

SENSORY SYSTEMS

Another aspect of human-factor models concerns the sensory abilities of human beings. Here too, *differences between individuals* must be taken into

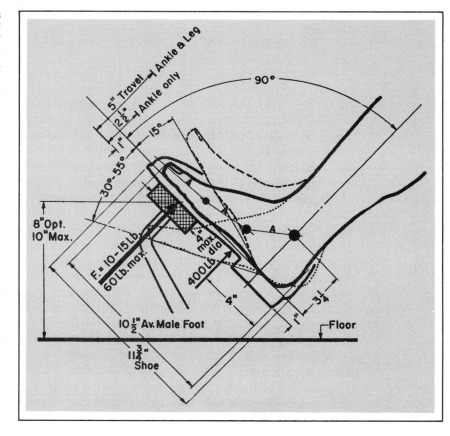

FIGURE 12-13
Detailed studies and drawings were made of the foot pedal to determine its final placement. The Henry Dreyfuss design group believes that the foot pedal should serve as an extension of the foot. Foot pressure studies were extremely important for the early development of Monotrol Control. [From William F. H. Purcell, A.S.I.D., *Designing for Heavy Duty* (Philadelphia: Chilton Company, 1962).]

account. For example, a certain combination of colors might produce higher attention levels for one type of viewer than for another. A practical problem would be the determination of what colors to use for a stop sign on the road. If color relates to worker productivity, then we might wish to know how to color the various parts of machines. Some other examples would be the optimal colors for a classroom, a library, a plant cafeteria, street pavement, or a blackboard. Color seems to affect the behavior of an individual in various ways, for example, the degree to which fatigue occurs, general alertness, and perhaps, even mood and attitude. Thus, the superiority of a certain color combination for a specific purpose must be predicated on the fact that differences exist among people. Design superiority is statistically determined—just as it was in the case of the anatomical models.

FIGURE 12-14
Combinations of brightness and target size required for discrimination of various contrasts. [From M. Luckiesh and F. K. Moss, *Transactions of the Illuminating Engineering Society,* Vol 25, 1930.]

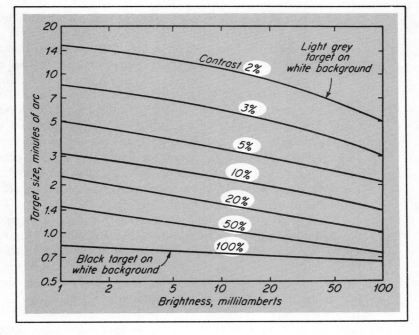

In addition to color, there are many other factors that affect the operation of the visual sensory system. For example, adequate light and contrast must be provided for accomplishing tasks of differing shapes and sizes. The chosen level of illumination will vary, depending upon the kind of task that is to be performed as well as in terms of individual preferences. Figure 12.14 illustrates the way in which illumination requirements can vary as a function of the type of job that must be done. But this is for some average individual. For proper design criteria, we must consider variance measures as well.

Individual preferences vary with respect to the amount of light that is both comfortable and satisfactory for accomplishing a given job. The range can be quite large as shown by the following distribution for the amount of light that is preferred for reading.[17]

FOOTCANDLES	0–50	50–100	100–150	150–200	200–250	250–300	300–350	350–400	400+
NUMBER OF PEOPLE	none	4	38	46	62	89	45	22	3

During the Second World War, many studies were undertaken to determine superior (if not optimal) designs for aircraft controls such as dials, gauges, tracking devices, gunsights, and the like. Since that time, a great deal more work has been done by various organizations and institutions. As a result, a large body of literature concerning the visual sensory system is now available. Certainly, much work remains to be done. The reader will find that the subject is treated under such headings as human factors, human engineering, and ergonomics.

The sense of hearing has been studied with almost equal fervor. Many production operations are very quiet but others produce extremely high noise levels, for example, a jet plane or a drop forge. Two questions arise with respect to this noise factor. First, how does it affect the workers' performance and second, to what extent can it damage hearing? The appropriate answers seem to be that within reasonable limits, noise does not decrease the performance of an individual; however, varying degrees of hearing loss are associated with exposure to a noisy environment.

Noise levels are measured in decibels. This is a logarithmic transformation of the ratio of a given sound level to a standard value.[18] Figure 12.15 presents a chart of some representative noise levels as they are generated by different sources. Because workers suffer a degree of hearing loss when repeatedly exposed to certain types of sound, it behooves the production system designer to provide adequate protection for all individuals who are exposed to such hazards. He can utilize appropriate materials and structures to achieve noise control or abatement when it appears that the process itself is not susceptible to design changes that will decrease the noise levels.

Another important issue concerns the nuisance effect of noise. If there is inherent, high-level noise associated with a particular production process, this fact should be taken into account when geographically locating the plant, for example, airport location, in the case of jet aircraft. Community goodwill can

[17] These results are reported by W. S. Fisher, General Electric Company, Large Lamp Department, Nela Park, Cleveland, Ohio, in November, 1963 in a private correspondence with Sylvester K. Guth, Manager, Radiant Energy Effects Laboratory, General Electric Company. The sample of 309 individuals were given the visual task of reading from the pages of a telephone book. See also: J. M. Ketch and W. S. Fisher, "Experience with High Level Office Lighting," *Illuminating Engineering*, Vol. 52, 1957, p. 529.
[18] The standard of just audible sound.

FIGURE 12-15
Noise level of typical
noises. This figure also
shows for various
decibel levels the ratio
of sound energies.
[From Ernest J.
McCormick, *Human
Engineering* (New
York: McGraw-Hill
Book Co., Inc., 1957),
p. 134.]

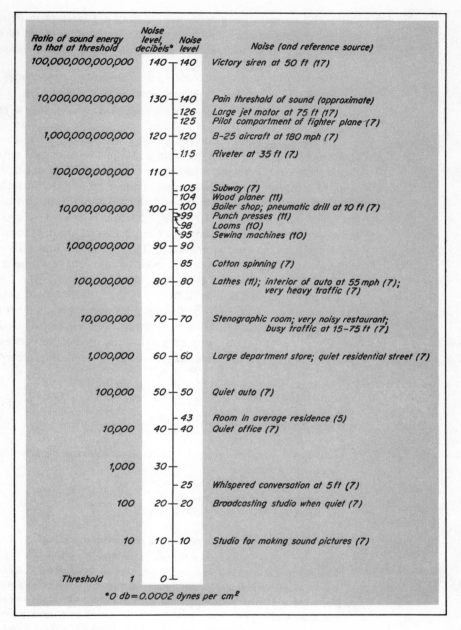

Ratio of sound energy to that at threshold	Noise level, decibels*	Noise level	Noise (and reference source)
100,000,000,000,000	140	140	Victory siren at 50 ft (17)
10,000,000,000,000	130	140	Pain threshold of sound (approximate)
		126	Large jet motor at 75 ft (17)
		125	Pilot compartment of fighter plane (7)
1,000,000,000,000	120	120	B-25 aircraft at 180 mph (7)
		115	Riveter at 35 ft (7)
100,000,000,000	110		
		105	Subway (7)
		104	Wood planer (11)
10,000,000,000	100	100	Boiler shop; pneumatic drill at 10 ft (7)
		99	Punch presses (11)
		98	Looms (10)
		95	Sewing machines (10)
1,000,000,000	90	90	
		85	Cotton spinning (7)
100,000,000	80	80	Lathes (11); interior of auto at 55 mph (7); very heavy traffic (7)
10,000,000	70	70	Stenographic room; very noisy restaurant; busy traffic at 15-75 ft (7)
1,000,000	60	60	Large department store; quiet residential street (7)
100,000	50	50	Quiet auto (7)
		43	Room in average residence (5)
10,000	40	40	Quiet office (7)
1,000	30		
		25	Whispered conversation at 5 ft (7)
100	20	20	Broadcasting studio when quiet (7)
10	10	10	Studio for making sound pictures (7)
Threshold	1	0	

*0 db=0.0002 dynes per cm²

be rapidly alienated, with many hardships ensuing, if this point is overlooked. Thus, the reduction of noise has been a critical objective with respect to design of the SST because the decibel levels that are generated by supersonic flight can be quite high. Engine design, airframe design and airport design have all been affected.

Noise abatement can be achieved in a number of different ways. This is the job of the acoustical engineer, and we shall not attempt to delve into the technology relevant to noise control. On the other hand, it might be useful to specifically distinguish between three major ways of coping with noise:

1. Eliminate or reduce it by introducing technological (design) change;
2. Isolate it by moving the source to a remote or protected location;
3. Dampen or absorb it by using specially designed materials such as fibre glass.

Human sensory systems have the ability to receive many other stimuli besides light and sound. Even as a beginning, we must include such sensations as smell, touch, taste; the perception of body orientation, temperature, humidity, vibration, and the sense of passing time. Pain is an additional factor produced by external conditions. Passing beyond the pain threshold can occur for each of the sense modalities. Human-factor models have been developed, and are being developed to measure such sensory characteristics not only for averages but also for differences between individuals. Thus, comfort and pain share the same dimensional continuum. What is comfort for one may be less comfort for another and perhaps painful for a third.

The key in all these considerations is the fact that most design, in the past, has proceeded on the basis of the designer's own personal set of sensory, anatomical, motor, and mental characteristics. Such egocentric design produces an amount of penalty that is proportional to the divergence between the designer's preferences and the statistical distribution of population preferences.

PROBLEMS

1 Prepare a human factor analysis, treating all variables that might be relevant with respect to the following situations:
   a. the design and manufacture of a belt;
   b. the redesign of an automobile;
   c. the design of an electric circuit fuse;
   d. the design of a hearing aid;
   e. the arrangement of high noise-level equipment in a plant.

2 There is a visual phenomenon known as the Purkinje effect:
   The fact that a great decrease in the intensity of illumination darkens red, orange, and yellow much more than blue and green, so that the point of maximum brilliance in the spectrum is shifted from the yellow into the green. A suggested explanation is that the rods which give vision in faint light are tuned to shorter wave lengths than the cones that dominate vision in bright light. (*Webster's New International Dictionary* Second Edition, unabridged.)
   Under what circumstances might this human factor be of importance?

3 How would you go about taking into consideration the percent and distributional characteristics of color blindness? When might this factor be significant?

4 Describe the characteristics of the man-machine interface with respect to the following:
   a. a pin-ball machine;
   b. a dictionary;

c. a pencil;

d. a computer programmed to prepare invoices;

e. a continuous conveyor;

f. a television set;

g. a 35 mm camera.

5 What factors would ordinarily be considered when a proposed plan calls for replacing a man with a machine? What criteria would apply to the decision?

6 The Ficus Company is a fig packer. The imported figs are weighed out in lots of one pound. There are 12 figs to the pound, on the average. The figs must be inserted in a jar to which a portion of fig syrup is added. Then the jar is sealed with a twist cap.

   a. Analyze the job. Develop what you consider to be a good sequence of work elements.

   b. Sketch the process flow and layout.

   c. Use an operation chart to detail the work involved.

   d. Prepare a time sheet.

   e. Assume that the time study has been taken and supply your own hypothetical data for these observations. Then determine the standard time for the job. (Use at least ten cycles.)

   f. Check to see if the sample size is sufficient. If it is, stop. If not, supply additional hypothetical data until an acceptable size is achieved.

7 The President of Ficus learns about predetermined time standards. He calls you in and asks for a report on the applicability of synthetic time methods to check the above times. Develop the appropriate report.

8 Assume that the man-machine situation in pp. 401–404 is now as follows: Both *make ready* and *put away* can only be accomplished when the machine is idle. These operations cannot be performed simultaneously. Two machines are used and are to be tended by a single operator. The element times are unchanged. Use a man-machine time chart to find the best way of handling this situation.

9 Develop a work sampling schedule where the objective is to determine how the personnel in a research laboratory spend their time.

references

ATTNEAVE, F., *Applications of Information Theory to Psychology.* New York: Holt, Rinehart & Winston, Inc., 1959.

BARNES, R. N., *Motion and Time Study*, 4th Ed. New York: John Wiley & Sons, Inc., 1958.

CHAPANIS, A., W. R. GARNER, and C. T. MORGAN, *Applied Experimental Psychology.* New York: John Wiley & Sons, Inc., 1949.

DALLA VALLE, J. M., *The Industrial Environment and Its Control.* New York: Pitman Publishing Corp., 1948.

FLETCHER, HARVEY, *Speech and Hearing.* Princeton, N.J.: D. Van Nostrand Co., Inc., 1950.

HANSEN, B. L., *Work Sampling: For Modern Management.* Englewood Cliffs, N.J.: Prentice-Hall, Inc., 1960.

KRICK, EDWARD V., *Methods Engineering.* New York: John Wiley & Sons, Inc., 1962.

MAYNARD, H. B., G. J. STEGEMERTEN, and J. L. SCHWAB, *Methods-Time Measurement.* New York: McGraw-Hill, Inc., 1948.

McCORMICK, E. J., *Human Engineering.* New York: McGraw-Hill, Inc., 1957.

MUNDEL, MARVIN E., *Motion and Time Study: Principles and Practice.* 4th ed. Englewood Cliffs, N. J.: Prentice-Hall, Inc., 1970.

QUICK, J. H., J. H. DUNCAN, and JAMES A. MALCOLM, *Work-Factor Time Standards.* New York: McGraw-Hill, Inc., 1962.

ROETHLISBERGER, F. J., and W. J. DICKSON, *Management and the Worker.* Cambridge, Mass.: Harvard University Press, 1939.

SAYLES, LEONARD R. and GEORGE STRAUSS, *Personnel: The Human Problems of Management*, 3rd ed. Englewood Cliffs, N. J.: Prentice-Hall, Inc., 1972.

SIMON, H. A., *Models of Man.* New York: John Wiley & Sons, Inc., 1957.

423
manpower
management

SPECIAL DEVICES CENTER, *Handbook of Human Engineering Data*, 2nd Ed. Office of Naval Research, Technical Report SDC 199–1–2, NavExos P-643, Project Designation NR-783–001, 1951.

TEEVAN, RICHARD C., and ROBERT C. BIRNEY (eds.), *Color Vision*. Princeton, N. J.: D. Van Nostrand Co., Inc., 1961.

part **SYNTHESIS**
three **OF**
SYSTEMS

chapter thirteen
some history of production management

Let us take a brief backward glance at the field of production management. By examining a little of the historical development we can achieve greater perspective about the present and future of this field.

Begin with the Renaissance period (14th-16th centuries) when a rebirth of vitality occurred in Europe that swept away the dark ages and fostered great accomplishments in the arts and sciences. Production activities centered around artisans, apprentices, and the craft guilds which were primarily organizations designed to protect and foster the interests of the artisans. By the 17th century, the effects of the European Renaissance were noticeably present in England.

The first signs of industrial *evolution* appeared in medieval Italy. It was hardly a revolution but signs of industry began to appear. Industry can be said to exist when factories and plants are developed. The individual no longer owns the specific fruits of his labors. He is employed and receives a wage for his time or output.

The rudiments of industrial activity then spread northward to Augsburg, Lyons, Bruges, Antwerp, Amsterdam and west to England during the 16th and

17th centuries. By the beginning of the 19th century, with the utilization of steam-driven machines, the *evolution* of industrialization in England became so rapid and dramatic that it could be described as an industrial revolution. Why did this occur in England? A complex of factors can help to explain this, including the presence of coal, a growing population with high unemployment, a limited agricultural output, the existence of investment capital, growth of trade with colonies, interest and belief in scientific methods, and the earlier acquisition of refugees from the Inquisition.

Technological invention was the keystone. Hand labor in every field began to be replaced by machinery. The effects of this industrial revolution trickled to the North American continent as the years went by. But a variety of factors impeded the growth of American industry. These included a fundamental dependency on agriculture and English hostility toward the industrialization of its colony. In 1798, however, American industry received an enormous impetus. Eli Whitney[1] developed and engineered the notion of interchangeable parts for the manufacture of guns. Within a short time, sewing machines, clocks, and other products were utilizing these same principles. There was no shortage of American inventiveness, and industry began to prosper. In the early 1900's, Henry Ford introduced the moving assembly line. Based on the high-level realization of Whitney's principle of *interchangeability*, Ford succeeded in achieving almost total *synchronization* of the production process flows.

Up to this point we have presented in capsule form the technological changes that brought the *production* management field into being.[2] Now let us consider the growth in the recognition and treatment of production *management* problems. Less than 100 years after Eli Whitney had obtained a United States government contract for "Ten Thousand Stand of Arms," Frederick Winslow Taylor[3] began a concerted attack on existent production management practices. He and his associates developed principles and practices that ultimately revolutionized the field of production management. His work was essentially *analytic* and stressed the development of standards and improved efficiency. (We should note that the concept of interchangeable parts is predicated on standards and repetitive patterns of operations. Whitney's contribution, with compelling logic, required the course of events that was to follow.)

Taylor's initial studies related to the cutting of metals. Many thousands of experiments were undertaken, and the results were recorded and analyzed. In order to carry out these experiments, Taylor and his group had to identify the *relevant variables* in the metal cutting process. Thus, Taylor laid the groundwork for an era of operations-oriented analyses. It should be noted that at about the same time, physical scientists were confidently extolling the virtues of scientific method and predicting an ultimate ability to explain the nature of the universe through analysis. Taylor's achievements paralleled those of the physical sciences. It is quite natural that they were *mechanistic* because in keeping with

---

[1] See p. 216 for another aspect of this development.
[2] See the bibliography (pp. 434–35) for a list of references to books that deal at length with the history of technology.
[3] 1856–1915.

the spirit of the times, they reflected a belief in the total perfection and determinism of all phenomena.

In line with this thinking, operations which included an operator could also be studied. The operator was fundamentally thought of as an extension of the machine. Thus, Taylor found that the repetitive task of moving iron castings from one place to another could be achieved at a lower cost by improving the way in which the job was done and by giving the operator an incentive for increasing his output. Taylor's philosophy with respect to workers, management, and organization was quite primitive. Nevertheless, as his work progressed he became more and more involved with these interrelationships. The time was ripe to be concerned about such incipient synthesis. But the available knowledge and methodology permitted little more than speculation. In France, Henri Fayol was attempting to develop theories of management. In the United States, at about the same time, Henry Towne, Harrington Emerson, George Shepard, and others were similarly tussling with new concepts for managing. The emphasis was on human labor. Questions concerning the role and utilization of manpower in the enterprise were beginning to form heavy storm clouds on the horizon. The analysis of employee operations accelerated that process. Taylor concentrated on the analysis of operations and operators. He labeled his efforts *scientific management*. He practiced it, talked about it, and wrote about it.

Henry L. Gantt[4] was an associate of Frederick Taylor. Gantt also was concerned with operators and operations in a basically analytic sense. But he added a new dimension. Gantt recognized the fact that a process was a combination of operations. He developed methods for sequencing operations which are still in use (the Gantt load chart and the Gantt layout chart)[5]. Taylor was a founder. Gantt followed, but with somewhat broader views. He also had his theories about organization and incentive plans. In many ways these come closer to presently held points of view than do Taylor's notions.

A large group of operation specialists developed. Foremost among these was the team of Frank and Lillian Gilbreth. Working together, they categorized operations in a way that permitted these categories to be independent of the specific job. For example, *search*, *grasp*, *release*, and so on, were work components that could be put together in different ways to create different operations. Thus, the Gilbreths recognized the interchangeability of finely categorized operations between jobs.[6] Unnecessary operations could be dropped and if superior sequences existed, the job could be suitably rearranged. In order to study each job and break it into its proper components, the Gilbreths began using motion picture records. They thereby advanced the cause of reliability and validity in the measurement of work. Later use of predetermined or synthetic time standards was based on these earlier efforts, see pp. 394–99.

Of particular interest is the fact that Lillian Gilbreth was a psychologist. Her training mitigated against a purely mechanical view of the operator-machine

[4] 1861–1919.

[5] See pp. 161–62.

[6] Gilbreth developed 17 such categories. They were called "Therbligs," which is almost Gilbreth spelled backwards.

team. In the Gilbreths' work we find the seeds for the eventual recognition of the psychological components of the system. Many other well-known names could be added to our list. It is not, however, our intention to present a detailed history of production management.[7] Rather, the purpose is to catch the highlights of the development. In that regard, eventually, operation specialists were called methods engineers—and more affectionately by the popular press— efficiency experts.

The application of exclusively operation-oriented analysis continued unabated for many years. But gradually, the emphasis shifted to the concept of a process that was composed of operations. Aside from Gantt's efforts at project planning there is little indication that much thought was given to long-term planning problems.[8] However, at both the operations and process levels of analysis several new dimensions were added. First came the realization that risk and uncertainty exist and that they play a part in planning. Statistics and probability had become recognized and reputable fields for study. Scientists no longer held to the notion of a mechanistically perfect universe. Physicists had accepted a nondeterministic description of basic phenomena. It behooved engineers and production managers to accept this change and to apply it to their own situations.

Undoubtedly the greatest impact from the viewpoint of production management resulted from Walter Shewhart's invention in the 1920's of statistical quality control (SQC).[9] At last, the economic implications of Whitney's contribution for the interchangeability of parts was resolvable. Tolerances and specifications required technological capabilities that could be analyzed in cost and profit terms. More than this, Shewhart's work demanded application of the *system's principle*. It was not immediately recognized that *the process in isolation* had been transcended. But, with the passing of time it became quite evident that product design, materials, equipment, labor skills, employee attitudes, work flow, and environmental factors interacted with consumer requirements of quality and price, and with financial considerations pertaining to the allocation of resources. Other statistical developments that affected the production management area included the use of sampling plans for inspecting materials,[10] work sampling,[11] and much later, queuing theory, inventory theory, and other operations research (OR) techniques.

Second, and also in the period of the 1920's and 1930's, psychological factors were understood to be a lot more complex than had been thought to be the case. F. J. Roethlisberger, reporting on the Hawthorne studies,[12] tells how the pro-

[7] For an interesting discussion of this history, see Smiddy, H. F. and L. Naum, Evaluation of a "Science of Managing" in America, *Management Science*, Vol. I, No. I, October, 1954, pp. 1–31.
[8] Martin K. Starr, "Product Planning from the Top (Variety and Diversity)" University of Illinois Bulletin, Vol. 65, No. 144, Proceedings, *Systems: Research and Applications for Marketing*, July 26, 1968, pp. 71–77. More generally, see Martin K. Starr, *Management: A Modern Approach* (New York: Harcourt Brace Jovanovich, Inc., 1971), pp. 300–420.
[9] See pp. 310–14.
[10] See pp. 303–306.
[11] See pp. 390–94.
[12] The studies were sponsored by Harvard University and began in 1924 at the Hawthorne Works of the Western Electric Company, in Chicago.

ductivity of workers increased, whether desirable or undesirable changes were made in their working environment (in this case the illumination of the work area). The result of the study, it was hypothesized, could be traced to the fact that the morale of workers increases when attention is paid to them. As morale increases, so does productivity. The original corps of scientific management people believed that they could intuit the responses of workers without having to study these behaviors. The field of industrial relations has grown to be an accepted contradiction to this idea. The strength of the labor movement helped to convince management that it did not live in an egocentric world where the premise that "papa knows best" could be consistently applied. Therefore, not only were employees recognized to be as complex as employers—they were also recognized as being people. Much of production management history and present-day effort is involved with these developments.

We now speak about man-machine systems wherein the behaviors and abilities of men are required to be integrated with the attributes of machines in some "best possible" way. The recognition of the individual's psychological and physiological make-up is of paramount importance when automation and computer-controlled systems are involved. Furthermore, the consumer is also recognized as a complex being to whom a product must be fitted in many different ways. The employee's relationship to the equipment that he uses and to the environment of the plant are also vital. The field of human factor analysis[13] considers such issues.

A third new force resulted from the growth in interest and knowledge of the field of economics. Governmental planning during the depression years triggered deep involvement—whether pro or con—with fundamental questions concerning the role of the government in welfare planning, and the responsibilities of the industrial community in this regard. Economics formed the base for the planning function. From this point on we recognize that the big drive for synthesis had begun. It is still underway. An important achievement occurred in the 1930's when Walter Rautenstrauch,[14] an industrial engineer, and professor at Columbia University, *invented* the planning device known as a break-even chart.[15] It was one of the first *synthetic* tools that became available to production managers. To a greater extent than ever before it permitted and, in fact, encouraged an integration or synthesis of the planning function. At the same time, managerial and engineering economics were recognized as fundamental to the production management field. Synthesis required the simultaneous consideration of all functional areas within the organization that were relevant to the planning problem. The divergence from accepted practice was great; boundaries were being crossed continually. As a result, managerial economics was treated as a special field of inquiry—a unique view in its own right. Only in this way could it cope with the systems problem. But it was also recognized as being totally relevant to production management. Modifications of the break-

---

[13] See pp. 413–20.
[14] W. Rautenstrauch and R. Villers, *The Economics of Industrial Management* (New York: Funk & Wagnalls Co., 1949).
[15] See pp. 28–35.

even chart that introduce risk make it an even more useful tool for the synthesis of the production management field.[16]

Fourth and last in our brief survey, we come to the development of operations research and management science. (Note: Taylor founded *scientific management*. The difference in word order is strictly adhered to by practitioners of management science.) OR was an offspring of the Second World War. Prior to 1940 the name OR did not exist. The concept began in Britain where it is still called operational research. Scientists from many fields were recruited by the United States and British governments to assist in the resolution of complex problems of logistics[17] and military strategy. These scientists were successful in spite of the fact that they had little training in military systems. The reason is that they were methodologists—willing and able to borrow knowledge and method from any and every field of scientific endeavor. Where no useful analogs existed, new ones were developed.

The pattern today remains essentially the same. Military organizations continue to support operations research groups. At the same time, industrial activity in this area has grown enormously. The name "operations research" may be quite suitable for military purposes where operations are conceived as being large scale processes such as Operation Alpine Violets[18] or Operation Dynamo.[19] In industry, operations analysis means quite another thing. It is work that Taylor, Gantt, and Gilbreth pioneered in at the beginning of the twentieth century. Consequently, operations research was neither a suitable nor a likeable label for industrial practitioners. This distaste resulted in coining still another new term, namely, "management science."

"What's in a name? That which we call a rose—By any other name would smell as sweet." So said the Bard of Avon, and these words still ring true.

What is important here is the *participation of methodologists in the production problem*. The goal of these methodologists is the *resolution of problems*. Pursuing this objective, they have called upon simulation techniques, systems analysis, decision theory, and mathematical methods such as linear programming, queuing theory, information theory, and control theory. The advent and improvement of computers has permitted the resolution of many problems, using methods that would otherwise be untenable because of the computational burden involved. Management science methods shifted the emphasis of study from *analysis to synthesis*. As a direct result, efficiency studies were relegated to a logical second place—effectiveness became a primary issue.

We must point out with emphasis the fact that methodologists do not manage. Neither technological specialists nor methodological specialists are managers. In studying the field of production management, we are concerned *with the use of these specialists* and with the use of their specialties. Just as an expert in a particular technological process can ultimately join the administrative team and become a production manager, so can a production methodologist join the ranks of management.

---

[16] See pp. 62–66.
[17] Problems concerned with transporting, sheltering, and supplying troops.
[18] The code name for the German plan to send reinforcements to Albania.
[19] The code name for the plan of the British Admiralty to evacuate Dunkirk.

Herein lies the answer to a fundamental question. What are the differences between an industrial engineer, a management scientist, and a production manager? For historical integrity it should not be left unanswered or shunted aside. It can be answered in terms of the logical and sensible interpretation of their historic courses of development. Both industrial engineering (IE) and management science (MS) are primarily methodological fields. That is their common area of specialization. Industrial engineers are further specialized in *production* methodology; management scientists in management, being uncommitted to a particular functional area. Management scientists will be found in production, marketing, finance, and more generally, *cutting across such boundaries.* Production managers are concerned with the way in which methodology is used. They actually manage, reach decisions, see to it that buttons are pushed and orders placed. They are responsible for doing something real and constructive about production problems. In order to properly manage the production complex, the production manager must understand the relevant technology and the relevant methodology, and he must know how to harmoniously administer these functions within the total organization framework and the society. He does not have to be an expert in either field (although it helps).

PROBLEMS

1   Describe the relationship of production management to technology for the following systems:

a.   agriculture

b.   a movie theater

c.   a television broadcasting station

d.   garbage removal

e.   the telephone company

f.   a local food manufacturer

g.   a paper manufacturer

Name some industries of your own choosing and indicate the way in which technology and production management interact.

2   Explain the relationship of production management and methodology.

3   Why was production management one of the first industrial areas to be studied rigorously?

4   In what way does the development of the computer affect future developments in the field of production management?

5   Name some new technological developments, and discuss how these might affect future developments in the production management field. For example, consider bionics.

6   Differentiate between industrial engineering and production management.

7   Does the historical development of the production management function appear to follow a consistent pattern? If so, how would you describe this pattern? Is it likely that there will be a logical successor; another step, after operations research?

references

ARNOLD, HORACE LUCIEN, and FAY LEONE FAUROTE, *Ford Methods and the Ford Shops.* New York: The Engineering Magazine Company, 1915.

BARNARD, CHESTER I., *The Functions of the Executive.* Cambridge, Mass.: Harvard University Press, 1938.

BEARD, MIRIAM, *A History of Business.* Ann Arbor: The University of Michigan Press, Vol. I, 1962, Vol. II, 1963.

BURLINGAME, ROGER, *March of the Iron Men.* New York: Grosset & Dunlap, Inc., 1938.

CROMBIE, A. C., *Scientific Change.* New York: Basic Books, Inc., 1963.

DRUCKER, PETER F., *The Practice of Management.* New York: Harper & Row, Publishers, 1954.

——, *The Age of Discontinuity.* New York: Harper & Row, Publisher, 1969.

HERTZ, DAVID B., *New Power for Management.* New York: McGraw-Hill Book Company, 1969.

MUMFORD, LEWIS, *Technics and Civilization.* New York: Harcourt, Brace & World, Inc., 1934.

——, *The Myth of the Machine.* New York: Harcourt Brace Jovanovich, Inc., 1970.

NEWMAN, WILLIAM H., *Administrative Action.* Englewood Cliffs, N. J.: Prentice-Hall, Inc., 1950.

——, and CHARLES E. SUMMER, *The Process of Management.* Englewood Cliffs, N. J.: Prentice-Hall, Inc., 1961.

PARKINSON, C. NORTHCOTE, *Parkinson's Law.* Boston: Houghton Mifflin Company, 1957.

435
some
history
of
production
management

SARTON, GEORGE, *A History of Science.* Cambridge, Mass.: Harvard University Press, 1959.

SINGER, CHARLES, E. J. Holmyard, and A. R. Hall (eds.), *A History of Technology,* 5 Vols. London: Oxford University Press, 1954–58.

SIU, R. G. H., *The Tao of Science.* New York: John Wiley & Sons, Inc., 1957.

STARR, MARTIN K., *Management: A Modern Approach,* New York: Harcourt Brace Jovanovich, Inc., 1971.

STRASSMAN, W. PAUL, *Risk and Technological Innovation.* Ithaca, New York: Cornell University Press, 1959.

USHER, A. P., *A History of Mechanical Inventions.* Boston: Beacon Press, Inc., 1959.

WALKER, CHARLES R., *Modern Technology and Civilization.* New York: McGraw-Hill, Inc., 1962.

WHYTE, WILLIAM H., JR., *The Organization Man.* New York: Simon and Schuster, Inc., 1956.

WILSON, MITCHELL, *American Science and Invention.* New York: Bonanza Books, 1960.

WOLF, A., *A History of Science, Technology, and Philosophy in the 16th and 17th Centuries,* Vols. I and II. New York: Harper & Row, Publishers, 1951.

——, *A History of Science, Technology, and Philosophy in the 18th Century,* Vols. I and II. New York: Harper & Row, Publishers, 1961.

chapter
fourteen
the financial context of production management decisions

BY REIN PETERSON
Faculty of Administrative Studies
York University, Toronto, Canada

INTRODUCTION

All decisions made within a business organization have a financial context. Some decisions involve the expenditure of money directly. Others have a less direct impact by consuming managerial or worker effort, stored up resources or time—all of which ultimately cost money. The conception of a company as a *system of cash flows* to and from, as well as within the firm, will be our focus in this discussion.

In most organizations the planning and control of cash transactions, over time, within such a "financial system" is primarily carried out by the financial officers. Through their cash-flow planning and control activities financial managers also become involved with broader issues such as the compilation of company budgets, policies, and plans. As a result, today in practice the finance function is highly centralized. Its officers have assumed over-all responsibility for guiding and controlling a firm's financial transactions in relation to policies

* In preparing this chapter I have benefited from several discussions with Professors Martin K. Starr and Ronald J. Huefner. Any errors that remain are, of course, my responsibility alone.

437
the
financial
context
of
production
management
decisions

and guidelines set out in the interest of the firm as a whole. This complete involvement of financial managers in the operations of the enterprise is, however, distinct from saying that any decision that involves the expenditure of money is the responsibility of financial management *alone*.

We will attempt to delineate some of the responsibilities of production and financial management within the financial system beginning with a brief overview of the financial function as it exists today. Then we will provide some historical perspective, describing the interaction of production and financial management decisions in the past. In particular, the effect of events external to the firm (in the economic system) on the behavior of financial officers will be emphasized. The last two sections will deal with the two main concerns of financial management: working capital management (the management of cash flows) and capital budgeting (the allocation of cash to investments).

THE FINANCIAL FUNCTION TODAY

Modern financial management adopts a rather broad role within the management of the firm.[1] As a guardian of the general financial affairs of the company, financial managers address the following issues:[2]

1. How large should the enterprise be?
2. What growth rate should the enterprise seek in terms of sales, assets, employees, and profits?
3. What degree of (financial) stability should the enterprise seek?
4. What kinds of (financial) instability should it seek to avoid?
5. What kinds of assets should the firm acquire and at what rate?

In addition to these broader issues financial managers continue to be involved with such traditional problems as:[3]

1. Should the terms of financing new debt be of short or long duration?
2. Should debt or equity financing[4] be used?
3. What impact will the newly acquired funds have on the profitability of the firm?
4. What impact will financial decisions have on risk, income and control of the firm?
5. What options should be offered to investors to change the form of their claims under certain economic conditions?

The making of effective decisions in all of the above areas and the subsequent control of financial transactions in relation to these decisions requires an extensive information system to keep track of the monies received, retained, and spent by all components of the organization. To fill this need, financial officers have developed accounting, a system for recording financial transactions. Two

---

[1] See J. F. Weston, *The Scope and Methodology of Finance* (Englewood Cliffs, N.J.: Prentice-Hall Inc., 1966).
[2] *Ibid.*, p. 96.
[3] *Ibid.*, p. 97.
[4] Debt includes all funds obtained through borrowing. These obligations must be repaid eventually. Equity refers to funds obtained by the firm in return for which the lender received the right to share in the profits of the company as a part owner.

types of records are kept. Financial or general accounting is concerned with the classification, the recording, and the interpreting of cash transactions so that periodically summary statements can be prepared. Such statements attempt to measure the financial condition of the firm at the end of a fiscal period via the "balance sheet." Results of past operations are also presented in the form of "profit and loss statements." These statements about the over-all financial condition of the firm provide general information and are of interest mostly to outsiders such as potential investors, the government tax agencies and stockholders.

To provide day-to-day control over the various parts of the business another set of accounts is kept. In order that financial management may know in detail whether or not various divisions are operating efficiently or whether specific products or services are profitable, several systems of cost accounting have been developed. Most of these cost accounting systems deal largely with internal transactions by accumulating the costs of materials, labor, and services that are spent on each of the products in inventory. Thereupon, when the products are delivered to the customers, the costs of selling and distribution are also recorded. These accumulated costs are then compared to planned expenditures (budgets). As a result, through cost accounting, financial managers become intimately involved with the daily problems of both production and marketing management by monitoring the costs of the actions taken by the latter two. We will describe the cash budget, an important means of monitoring the decisions made in the financial system by operating management on pp. 442–447.

In most large firms it has become impossible for a single "financial manager" to deal with all of these activities. Modern financial management is the only functional area that can have as many as four members in the top management group. These officers are usually referred to as: the treasurer (custodian of cash), the comptroller (manager of accounting systems), the corporate secretary (legal problems, issues new stocks and bonds) and the vicepresident of finance who coordinates the efforts of all three.

Large corporations usually also have a financial committee composed of members of the board of directors and senior officers from production, marketing, finance, research and development, and engineering. The finance committee is primarily responsible for the acquisition of additional funds, with the director-members often acting as contacts with financial institutions such as banks. Secondly, the finance committee is often called upon to make major decisions in the allocation of investment funds among the various departments in the company. We will consider the capital allocation problem in some detail on pp. 447–460.

A HISTORY OF THE FINANCE-PRODUCTION INTERACTION

We begin our history by describing the state of affairs in the early 1900's. Throughout the period described the major concerns of financial managers often

439
the
financial
context
of
production
management
decisions

changed rapidly in response to general economic conditions. But as financial management became more adept at their art and more confident in their understanding of economic matters, they increased their control over everyday operations. From approximately 1920 on, financial controls continued to impinge on the freedom of action of operating departments that were required to account for more and more of their decisions in terms of the firm's over-all strategy and objectives. As a result, production and marketing managers joined the financial officers in top-management decision making. The financial context of their decisions bound the three together.

At the turn of the century the economy of the United States was undergoing a period of consolidation. A merger movement was sweeping the country. Large corporations and trusts were being formed by bringing smaller firms under one management. National markets were emerging as a result of the completion of railroads that now traversed coast to coast. During this nascent period of modern financial management, financial managers were primarily concerned with the problems resulting from the consummation of mergers, the financing of new acquisitions and the determination of appropriate capital structure.[5] Previously, we labelled these problems as the traditional concerns of financial management.

Production management decisions during this period tended to be heavily weighted toward the engineering aspects of manufacturing. Managers who believed that production decisions had a financial context, found a lack of appropriate tools to carry out financial analysis in this manner. In the next decades, Shewhart (quality control), Rautenstrauch (break-even chart), Joel Dean (capital budgeting), and others began to meet this need.

When we look at the large firm of today it is difficult to believe that only 50 years ago most large organizations operated with comparatively meager financial controls and on incomplete information that was often out of date. This oversight on the part of financial management threatened, rather suddenly in the early 1920's, the existence of many large organizations.

At the close of the year 1920 the General Motors Company, for example, faced simultaneously an economic slump on the outside and a liquidity crisis[6] on the inside. The existing financial controls on the business had proven ineffective. The size of the automobile market had contracted considerably but the corporation as a whole was not reacting to this dramatic change in economic conditions. Alfred P. Sloan Jr., president and then chairman of the board of General Motors from 1923 to 1946, describes the situation in his book:[7]

> . . . uncontrolled purchases of raw and semifinished materials by the division managers had . . . by October of 1920 . . . (exceeded) the amount that could be used in the plants. . . .

---

[5] At any point in time, the total funds available to the firm can be classified according to their source (e.g., debt, equity, internally generated, etc.). Such a classification is called the company's capital structure.

[6] The concept of liquidity will be discussed later. For now it is sufficient to think of liquidity as a measure of the ability of a firm to rapidly convert some of its assets into cash which may be needed to pay for unexpected contingencies.

[7] Alfred P. Sloan Jr., *My Years With General Motors* (Garden City, N.Y.: Doubleday and Company, Inc., 1964), pp. 116–143.

Each division controlled its own cash, depositing all receipts in its own accounts . . . none of these cash receipts flowed directly to the corporation. . . .

. . . in the absence of a system for control of appropriations each manager got his maximum request satisfied. . . .

. . . (a) big gap in our information system at headquarters and in the division was at the retail level. We knew how many cars and trucks our divisions were selling to our dealers, but we did not know the current rate at which those vehicles were being resold to the public. . . . I (visited) the dealer's lots and saw the inventories parked in rows. . . . Everywhere (I went) the inventories were excessive.

Survival of the corporation was at stake. Mr. Sloan took drastic steps to revamp the existing financial controls. To reconcile available resources with appropriations requests from the divisions Mr. Sloan established in 1920 formal procedures and criteria for the evaluation of investment proposals. Following up on the above action, General Motors consolidated in 1922 its cash control system. Under the new system all incoming receipts were deposited in some one hundred banks in the United States to the credit of General Motors Corporation.

To curtail excessive inventories general managers were required to submit monthly budgets to the Inventories Committee (consisting of top management personnel). Finally, in response to adverse sales trends in 1924, Mr. Sloan developed an information system which would provide up-to-date monitoring of retail sales by requiring dealers to submit a progress report every ten days. Old forecasting procedures were overhauled so that the more accurate retail data could be used. But more importantly, the reaction time to a wrong forecast was shortened so that production rates would rapidly reflect changing retail sales rates as indicated in the dealer reports. This new aggregate scheduling and production control system was essentially complete by 1925. Since then most progress made in the area of financial controls has been largely one of refinement of the basic structure conceived during this period.

In sum, the 1920's resulted in the introduction of formal financial controls on the activities of the production managers at many companies. New methods of compiling aggregate schedules, appropriation requests, budgets, and other forms of financial control forced the production manager to devote an increasing amount of his time to nontechnical, nonengineering problems. Most of these new controls dealt with larger issues than the production manager had faced habitually in the past. But, as we will see, in later years financial controls continued to impinge on his freedom to operate primarily as an engineering innovator. At the same time, the financial manager also took a more balanced view of corporate problems by adding the concern about appropriate financial controls and the technology of manufacturing to his previous preoccupation with financial structure.

In the 1930's the newly instituted financial controls of all companies in the economy were severely tested. Weston describes the state of affairs rather vividly:[8]

---

[8] Weston, *The Scope and Methodology of Finance*, p. 25

441
the
financial
context
of
production
management
decisions

The recession which began in 1929 was unprecedented in its duration and severity. In the business field, it carried in its train a great wave of financial reorganization and bankruptcies. A scramble for liquidity took place. The public began to claim their deposits from the commercial banks. The banks in turn reduced their lines of credit outstanding; loans were not renewed and in some cases were called. Forced inventory liquidations ensued. Prices declined and the inventory liquidations did not provide sufficient funds to meet obligations. The importance of liquidity was demonstrated (once again). . . .

In response to these severe economic shocks, financial managers reverted back to their more traditional concerns which had occupied them during the early part of the century when the maintenance of financial liquidity in the face of rapid growth was a major problem. In a depressed economy it was difficult to find attractive markets. The efficient planning and control of production operations under such circumstances were of relatively less concern. Survival, once again, was at stake. The production manager was expected to cut all fixed costs and obligations sharply and operate with a minimum of overhead.

With the coming of World War II all industrial activity was geared to the war effort. Financial officers of companies were busily engaged in negotiating with the government the terms of contracts and financing for the specialized production needed by the war. For business firms as a whole, liquidity increased even though profit margins were controlled by the government in many cases. Toward the end of the war an increasing worry for many companies was the impending conversion of their plants back to peacetime operations. During the War, production management emphasized production quotas, quality standards, production methods and the training of new personnel brought into their plants by the emergency. Financial and cost controls were often of secondary concern. The production manager was called upon to be primarily technologically competent, to produce the needed output.

The suddenness of the end of the war made orderly transition to peacetime operations almost impossible. Most companies in the United States took the opportunity to reorganize their plants. Existing production facilities were rebalanced, new machines and equipment installed and some new plants built. All this was to be accomplished in a relatively short period of time, so that production could be started to reap the profits from the large stored up consumer demand, backlogged during the war. Again, financial controls requiring undue deliberation often tended to be ignored in such an onrush.

In the early 1950's labor costs began to rise. In order to meet the profit goals set for their companies, production managers were forced to make increased use of mechanized equipment. Cost controls imposed by financial management once again started to exert their constriction. To control day-to-day operations the production manager had to learn also to cope with and provide information for the increasingly more sophisticated cost accounting and budgetary systems. Where some fifty years ago he could afford some time to tinker personally with machine innovations, etc., a wall of paperbound systems was slowly descending upon him, making such indulgences more difficult.

The economy of the 1960's featured an increased pace of technological change. The production manager was faced with updating and readjusting his production processes. Bound by appropriation procedures and rules, capital budgeting and investment analyses became an important part of his job. As the economy continued to grow, large scale computers became available as a means of controlling financial operations. Given this new means of monitoring a company's operations, financial managers became even more demanding in their requests for information about the cost of daily production operations. Computerized inventory control and purchasing of materials along with periodic cost performance reports became commonplace. Operating data, more readily available to all, brought the production manager's decisions under closer scrutiny by other members of the top management team.

The systems approach to management advocated by most modern management thinkers promises to continue to break down the traditional compartmentalization of management functions such as production, finance, and marketing. To cope better in this new environment, the student of production systems management in the future needs a better grasp of some basic financial concepts, some of these will be outlined in the remaining sections. The techniques that will be discussed are aids often used by production management in quest of their traditional goal of cost minimization. But as we saw in this section, the historical emphasis on cost reduction has varied in intensity in response to economic conditions.

THE MANAGEMENT OF CASH FLOWS WITHIN THE FINANCIAL SYSTEM

An Overview. Because of accounting convention a firm's financial resources are generally divided into two categories: liquid and fixed.[9] For our purposes we will also talk of financial management decisions as being mainly of two types. First, the administration of the firm's liquid resources—cash (including marketable securities), receivables, and inventories, will be referred to as working capital management. The remaining group of decisions involving the acquisition or disposition of fixed resources will be called capital budgeting. As a result, according to our categorization, financial managers are primarily concerned with the planning of cash flows and the acquisition and disposition of fixed assets so as to control expenses effectively and influence revenues favorably.

In striving for this goal the financial manager is continually faced with a dilemma: how much of the corporation's cash should be invested and how much should be kept on hand to meet contingencies? The problem arises because the cash on hand is seemingly idle—not earning profits for the company. But in fact without some cash on hand it would be impossible to operate most large concerns. The question is, what is the appropriate amount of cash that should be kept on hand?

The more cash the financial manager has on hand, the more readily he can

---

[9] It is common practice to denote those resources which are normally converted into cash within a year as liquid and the remaining as fixed. But the year remains as an arbitrary standard, the concept of financial liquidity is more complex.

443
the
financial
context
of
production
management
decisions

meet the bills that accrue daily. With more cash he also has greater flexibility in handling unforeseen outflows of cash which otherwise might necessitate that he borrow money on short notice. With cash on hand he can take advantage of unexpected lucrative investment opportunities that may appear suddenly.

Diametrically opposed to his motives for holding cash (the financial manager's desire for liquidity) is his motive to earn profits. The more cash he can effectively put to work within the business, the greater will be his profits. What constitutes an appropriate amount of cash on hand for any particular firm is usually a hotly contested issue between the various financial officers, the production and the marketing managers. The former usually want more liquidity, the latter two almost always could use more cash to invest in projects that they believe will yield a high return to the firm. In practice, the amount of cash held by different firms varies between industries and among firms in the same industry.[10] The actual amount of cash available is probably, at least to a degree, a function of the personalities of the men holding the top managerial positions and their ability to convince each other of the relative advantages of their proposals.

The Flow of Cash Through a Business. For better appreciation of the above dilemma, it is often useful to present the situation in a diagram. The cash flows within a firm can be thought of as being analogous to the flow of water through a system of pipes and reservoirs. Figure 14.1 is such a simplified model of a hypothetical firm. The system presented focuses on the cash reservoir—the cash on hand. Into this reservoir flows cash received from outside sources and in turn some cash flows out of the reservoir as payment to outsiders.

Cash is also generated internally from sales and collections of accounts receivable (note the circular flow). Any cash realized immediately from the sales of inventory, flows directly into the cash reservoir. But usually most inventory is sold on credit—increasing accounts receivable—whereupon after a period of time cash is realized through collection of these accounts. Presumably, the cash realized from the sale of inventories, in most cases, is greater than the cash withdrawn from the reservoir to produce the inventories in the first place. The difference between these two flows represents profit before taxes.

Note that the reservoir labelled "inventories" is actually a complex system in itself. Had we chosen to draw Figure 14.1 in more detail, we would have included reservoirs for work-in-process, finished goods, and raw materials inventories, etc. In fact the inventories reservoir in Table I actually summarizes many of the responsibilities often assigned to production management.

Some cash is also withdrawn from the cash reservoir to purchase fixed assets. This latter flow represents the cash reinvested back into the firm via projects generated by the different departments of the company, including production. As these assets age and get used up, part of their original cost is recovered through depreciation charges.

---

[10] During the fourth quarter of 1969, as a percent of total assets, in the U. S. manufacturing industry, cash on hand ranged from 3 to 6.5 percent (4.4 percent, average). In the drug industry the range was 8 to 12 percent (10.6 percent, average). See the *Quarterly Financial Report,* U. S. Federal Trade-Securities and Exchange Commissions.

The outflow of cash, shown on the diagram at the bottom of the cash reservoir, represents a major concern of the financial managers. A failure to meet these external obligations would risk the very existence of the corporation. Similarily the financial manager must continually monitor the amount of cash needed by the inventory and fixed asset reservoirs so that the company can continue to increase its sales and profits, and grow in an orderly manner. Historically, many a firm has gone bankrupt by not being able to generate enough funds for the cash reservoir to pay outsiders or to provide funds for continued growth. Previously in this chapter, we referred to such a situation as a liquidity crisis. In most companies, through the use of budgets—notably the cash budget —the financial managers spend considerable time trying to route cash effectively in the system presented in Figure 14.1 so as to avoid such catastrophies.

FIGURE 14-1
The cash-flow system.

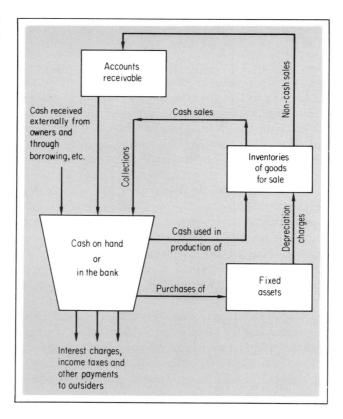

The Cash Budget. A budget is a written plan, expressing management's strategy for routing cash so as to meet forecasted sales over some future period. The plan may be expressed in dollars or in units of production. Since it deals with the future, many of the elements in the budget are estimates or forecasts which in fact will not materialize exactly in the way planned. But a good set of budgets

445
the
financial
context
of
production
management
decisions

help to focus the attention of all functional areas on a single set of documents which become an expression of how the group plans to coordinate their efforts, given the sales pattern predicted for the future. Thereafter, when the period for which the budget was presented has passed, the budget becomes a valuable yardstick for measuring actual performance against that which was expected.

In this section we will consider the preparation of the cash budget. Our example will be simplified and is intended only as a means of transmitting the concepts involved. Note that in terms of Figure 14.1 the cash budget is merely an attempt to predict the flows into and out of the cash reservoir during some future span of time. Suppose, for illustration purposes, that a financial manager wants to construct a cash budget for the next three months. Actually most budgets are prepared usually for longer periods of time—depending on their purpose and on the amount of lead time needed to implement the plans.

The preparation of the cash budget starts with a forecast of sales. To make our presentation simpler we will assume that only one product is sold by the hypothetical company for which the budget is being prepared.[11]

FORECASTS

Month 1	3,000 units
Month 2	6,000 units
Month 3	9,000 units

The next step involves the decision of how the forecasted units will be produced. Since the forecast predicts a rather rapid linear increase in sales, we could either level production and produce 6,000 units each month, match the production rate to the sales rate, or use some other strategy that meets the forecasted sales requirements. Suppose that a level production pattern is chosen:

TABLE 1 Production Budget (In Units)

		MONTH 1	MONTH 2	MONTH 3
1.	Beginning Inventory	5,000	8,000	8,000
2.	Production	6,000	6,000	6,000
3.	Total	11,000	14,000	14,000
4.	Sales	3,000	6,000	9,000
5.	Ending Inventory	8,000	8,000	5,000

As seen in Table 1, the forecast of sales and the decisions on monthly production automatically determine the monthly inventories of finished goods. Further-more, the production decisions made will have a pronounced effect on the tim-

---

[11] We will assume that each unit is sold for $20.00.

ing of raw materials purchases and on the size of the work force that will be needed each month. The financial manager must estimate the cash flows needed to meet all of these expenditures. Suppose that using the production budget presented above, along with other estimated ancillary cash flows, he prepares the following:

TABLE 2 Cash Budget

RECEIPTS	MONTH 1	MONTH 2	MONTH 3
1. Sales	$60,000	$120,000	$180,000
2. Collections*	12,000	72,000	132,000.

PAYMENTS	MONTH 1	MONTH 2	MONTH 3
3. Purchases	$50,000	$ 50,000	$ 50,000
4. Wages	20,000	20,000	20,000
5. Administrative Expenses	10,000	10,000	10,000
6. Capital Investments	20,000	—	—
7. Net Monthly Cash Gain (Loss)**	(88,000)	(8,000)	52,000
8. Cash Balance End of Month	(67,000)	(75,000)	(23,000)

FINANCIAL TRANSACTIONS	MONTH 1	MONTH 2	MONTH 3
9. Cash Balance Beginning of Month	$21,000	$ 7,000	$ 9,000
10. Borrowings (repayments)	74,000	10,000	(50,000)
11. Net Monthly Cash (from line 7)	(88,000)	(8,000)	52,000
12. Cash Balance End of Month	7,000	9,000	11,000
13. Cumulative Borrowings End of Month	74,000	84,000	34,000

* It is assumed that 20 percent of sales will be in cash, 80 percent will be collected one month later. For simplicity it is also assumed that no collections from previous years are due in Year 1.
** Total payments less collections

Based on Table 2, lines 8 and 7, the financial manager would conclude that he must borrow *at least* $67,000 in Month 1, $8,000 in Month 2, and in Month 3 he could repay *at most* $52,000 of the money borrowed. In addition he must borrow more funds to replenish some of the $21,000 originally in his cash reservoir at the beginning of Month 1 and thereby maintain the level of liquidity he wants to plan for. According to Line 10, he actually borrows $74,000 in Month 1, $10,000 in Month 2 and repays $10,000 in Month 3 to meet the production budgets presented to him. Note that the total amount of money that he owes at the end of each month is given by Line 13.

The Timing of Production Decisions. As can be seen from Table 2 the sales, production, inventory, and purchasing budgets form the basis of the cash budget. The two key inputs to the above budgetary process were the sales forecasts and the production budget. Note that any decision on the part of the production manager to change his production schedule would also alter the cash budget shown in Table 2.

447
the
financial
context
of
production
management
decisions

Most management-science models for scheduling aggregate production (Line 2 of Table 1) do not include the effect of production schedules on the cash flow of the firm. Clearly different production plans will engender different patterns of borrowing (given on Line 13 of Table 2)—resulting in potentially different costs of borrowing. Therefore, a truly optimal production schedule must take account of both costs of production scheduling *and* the cost of borrowing the money that may be needed to meet any production plan proposed.

Similarly almost all other production decisions affect the cash flows in a firm through their timing.[12] Given the present state of knowledge, theoretical formulations of production decisions (e.g. the aggregate scheduling decision) in the cash-flow context are not available. As a result, if a production manager is to behave in the interest of the company as a whole, he must make the ultimate trade-offs himself by using his own judgment (in concert with the financial managers) in determining the appropriate timing of production decisions. It is only through a skillful modification of the suboptimal decisions made by most "mathematical" decision models that over-all company objectives can be attained.

CAPITAL BUDGETING

Introduction. In this section on investment analysis we will concern ourselves primarily with the evaluation of alternative investment proposals from a financial standpoint. In practice, a successful investment program also depends heavily on the ability of operating managers to evaluate correctly the feasibility and engineering performance of competing proposals. Even more crucial to the success of an investment program in practice is the mechanism by which new investment opportunities are generated. But we will have little to say about either of the latter two parts of capital budgeting. Success in both of these activities seems to depend largely on the experience and the creativity of the operating management personnel involved. Comparatively speaking, little of a definitive nature has been discovered or written in this area. The converse is true of the financial analysis of investment proposals.

In many ways the investment decision is one of the most difficult faced by the production managers. The problem is not one of calculating a return on investment (ROI), *given* a set of assumptions about future events. The difficulty arises with the making of appropriate assumptions. Many estimates have to be made for any investment proposal: the amount of the initial investment, the revenue that will be received in each future period, the economic life of the project etc. Each of these estimates will in fact turn out to be wrong to some degree. To make a rational investment decision we also need an estimate of the

---

[12] Consider the effect of a change in inventory policy on the cash budget presented in Table 2. Suppose, for example, that top management decreed that the beginning inventory for any month cannot exceed 5,000 units ($100,000).

probable cumulative effect of these errors. That is, we need a measure of the risk[13] of making a wrong decision given the data at hand.

Armed with an estimated return and risk, we still face the problem of selecting a set of investments with the appropriate risk and return characteristics for the organization we represent. How one should make decisions in such an environment will be the topic of this section. Throughout we will attempt to focus on the role of the production manager in this important area. We will begin by defining some basic concepts. Most of the concepts discussed will be presented via an example investment problem which will be elaborated on from section to section.

The Determination of Relevant Cash Flows. From an economic point of view, it is clear what a relevant investment cost is. To a decision maker only costs and benefits which influence the decision to accept or reject the particular project under consideration are relevant. From this deceptively easy truism flow numerous definitions and concepts that in a specific situation can be difficult to apply. We will only consider some of the more important concepts.

A Relevant Cost is a cost that will be incurred in the *future* if a particular proposal is chosen. Alternatively it is a cost which can be escaped if a particular alternative course of action is not chosen. Therefore, for example, allocated general overhead is usually not a relevant cost. Over-all overhead cost is relevant if it increases or decreases because of an investment decision.

An Opportunity Cost is incurred if the selection of a particular alternative involves the commitment of a scarce resource. The opportunity cost of such an action is the profit that is foregone by not using the scarce resource for the next best alternative. Traditional accounting systems do not record opportunity costs.

Cash Flows are of two types: cash proceeds (a positive flow) and cash outlays (a negative flow). Cash flows for purposes of investment analysis are calculated after taxes.

Cash proceeds refer to all cash inflows generated by a particular alternative. It is usually assumed that all revenues are accompanied by an immediate generation of cash. Cash proceeds are *not* identical with accounting income. In estimating cash proceeds depreciation charges and other amortization of fixed assets are not subtracted from gross revenues because no cash expenditures are required.

Cash outlays are cash expenditures that result either directly or indirectly from the choice of a particular alternative. It is usually assumed that all cash outlays, except the initial investment, are charged to expense—i.e. none is charged to inventory—and that inventory is not reduced. Thus cash outlays are equivalent to expenses (excluding depreciation).

Sunk Costs are not cash flows because they do not require a utilization of

---

[13] Risk according to Webster's Dictionary (unabridged, second edition) is "The chance of injury, damage, or loss." Starting on p. 452 we will present a methodology for determining the probability distribution of return for any investment given the errors that are likely to occur in the estimates made. From such a probability distribution a decision maker can determine the *chance* of a lower return than any desired amount that he has in mind.

449
the
financial
context
of
production
management
decisions

current resources. These costs were usually incurred in the past and are not altered by any decisions we will make in the future. For the purposes of capital budgeting these costs are irrelevant.

A Fixed Cost is a cost that does not vary over a short period of time with production volume.

A Variable Cost is a cost that varies directly with production volume.

To illustrate the use of these cost concepts consider the following example. The problem presented is one that has been studied for many years in the production management literature: the make or buy decision.

THE FPM COMPANY

The production manager of the FPM Company is trying to decide whether he should manufacture or buy from an outside supplier a new product that FPM wishes to market. He estimates that if the company produced the product itself the following per unit costs would be incurred:

Direct Labor	$ 3.00
Indirect Labor	2.00
Variable Overhead	1.00
Allocated Overhead	4.00
	$10.00

The product could be manufactured on a machine that the company purchased 12 years ago for $50,000. The machine has been completely depreciated for tax purposes. The production manager estimates that the normal maintenance repairs amounting to approximately $10,000 per year will be required for the old machine. In addition an auxiliary machine costing $5,000 must be bought during the first year to bring the quality of the old machine up to par. The company could continue to operate under such a scheme for the next 2 years at the end of which the auxiliary machine and the old machine would be worthless. The financial manager informs him that for tax purposes the auxiliary machine may be depreciated on a straight line basis during the first two years.

Alternatively, the FPM Company could have an outside manufacturer produce the product. The following quotation, which is not subject to change during the next two years, has been received:

Fixed charge per year	$5,300
Unit Cost	$8.00

The company's income tax rate is 0.40. The marketing manager estimates that the company can charge a price of $10.00 per unit for its new product and forecasts sales of 3500 and 4000 units for the next two years, respectively. Should the company make or buy the product?

For the above example let us determine the relevant costs. We have listed in Table 3 and Table 4 the after-tax-cash flows involved. An explanation follows the tables.

TABLE 3   A. After-Tax-Cash Flows Generated If FPM Manufactures Product

ITEM	BEGINNING OF YEAR 1	END OF YEAR 1	END OF YEAR 2
1. Aux. Machine	−5,000		
2. Tax Saving (from depreciation charges)		+0.4(2,500)	+0.4(2,500)
3. Repairs Expense		−0.6(10,000)	−0.6(10,000)
4. Net Inflow		$(10 - 6) \times 3,500 \times 0.6$	$(10 - 6) \times 4,000 \times 0.6$
Totals	−5,000	3,400	4,600

TABLE 4   B. After Tax Cash Flows Generated If FPM Buys From Supplier

ITEM	BEGINNING OF YEAR 1	END OF YEAR 1	END OF YEAR 2
1. Fixed Charge		−0.6(5,300)	−0.6(5,300)
2. Net Inflow		$(10 - 8) \times 3,500 \times 0.6$	$(10 - 8) \times 4,000 \times 0.6$
Totals	0	1,020	1,620

In Table 3 we have included $5,000 as a cash flow—the amount we have to pay for the auxiliary machine at the start of Year 1. Subsequently at the end of the first and second years we charged one-half of the purchase price of this machine as depreciation and thereby saved 40 percent of $2,500 each year in taxes. Note that these tax savings are positive cash flows because without this "tax shield" we would have had to pay 0.40 × $2,500 a year more in taxes. Observe that no money for depreciation is actually paid in Years 1 or 2.

Item 3 in Table 3 is an expense that will be incurred in producing the product. Since expenses are deducted from revenues to determine the amount of taxable revenue, once again, 40 percent of this expense is saved through lower taxes. That is, only 60 percent of every dollar spent on expenses is an actual cash outflow (a negative flow). Turning to Table 4 we see that no cash flows occur at the beginning of Year 1. Thereafter, in each of the two years a fixed cost of $5,300 per year is incurred of which again only 60 percent is a negative cash flow.

The remaining cash flows in each table are labelled net inflow and represent the after tax amount per year that we expect to receive from selling our product. In calculating this figure we have subtracted from the price the variable cost of producing the unit and then multiplied the difference by the unit sales per year. Only 60 percent of this latter amount is received by the company, the remainder being paid out in taxes to the government. Since the $10.00 selling price does not change between the two alternatives, the revenue received could have been left out of the analysis without affecting the final decision. Note also that the manufacturing cost per unit (a variable cost) is $6.00 and not $10.00.

451
the
financial
context
of
production
management
decisions

The $4.00 of allocated overhead is an arbitrary allocation for accounting purposes and is not a relevant cash flow. Presumably the total amount of overhead that we have termed "allocated" will not be affected by our decision to make or buy. Furthermore, the $50,000 we paid for the old machine is past history (a sunk cost) and therefore irrelevant to our calculations. Since the old machine has been completely depreciated we cannot claim any tax savings from it as we have done above for the auxiliary machine. Having identified the relevant cash flows we face the task of striking a fair comparison between the two alternatives.

The Concept of Present Value. In comparing projects, such as the one we have just considered, a complication arises because of the different patterns of cash flows generated over time by competing investment alternatives. For example, one project may offer a series of cash proceeds that are equal for each period. Another project may promise greater cash proceeds during the early part of the proposal and lower cash proceeds later on. How can we put both of these series of cash flows on a comparable basis? Such cash flow patterns are usually compared on the basis of their net present values.

The present value concept is actually a formalization of the general belief that a dollar received today is worth more than a dollar promised to us some time in the future. For one thing, the dollar earned today could be put into a bank account to earn interest and would be worth more to us in the future.

For example, suppose that we put $10.00 into a bank account earning five percent interest.[14] A year from now our bank account would contain 10(0.05) or $10.50. Two years from now the bank account would contain 10(0.05)(0.05) or $11.03. Alternatively, if someone promised to pay us $11.03 for an item *two years from now* then the present value to us of such an offer is given by $11.03/(0.05)^2$ or $10.00. On the same basis, note that $10.00 two years from now has a present value of $10.00/(0.05)^2$ or $9.06. That is, $10.00 two years from now is worth less to us than $10.00 received today.

In this manner, the value of any stream of cash flows can be converted to net present value. Generally speaking, the net present value of any series of cash flows is given by:

$$\text{Net Present Value} = C_0 + \frac{C_1}{(1+i)} + \frac{C_2}{(1+i)^2} + \cdots + \frac{C_n}{(1+i)^n} = \sum_{k=0}^{n} \frac{C_k}{(1+i)^k}$$

Where i is the discount (interest) rate per period

C_k is the cash flow (positive or negative) generated in period k

Returning to the problem faced by the FPM Company we can now calculate the present values for the two alternatives make or buy:

$$\text{Net Present Value (Make)} = -5,000 + \frac{3,400}{(1+0.05)} + \frac{4,600}{(1+0.05)^2}$$
$$= -5,000 + 3,237 + 4,172 = \$2,409$$

---

[14] We are using the bank interest rate as a convenient example. If the investor has other better opportunities for investing his money he should avail himself of these investments. Presumably he would then earn more than 5 percent on his money.

$$\text{Net Present Value (Buy)} = 0 + \frac{1,020}{(1 + 0.05)} + \frac{1,620}{(1 + 0.05)^2}$$
$$= 0 + 971 + 1,469 = \$2,440$$

Therefore on the basis of net present value the two alternatives are almost equivalent with the alternative "buy" holding a slight edge ($2,440 − $2,409). But as we shall see, other factors, namely risk, can make one or the other of these alternatives look much more attractive. Buried also in the above illustration is our arbitrary choice of an "appropriate" discount rate of 5 percent. We shall discuss the choice of an appropriate discount rate on p. 456.

The Riskiness of An Investment. In the above example we assumed somewhat glibly that the cash flows in Years 0, 1, and 2 were known with certainty. In practice, benefits occurring in the future from investments made now cannot be forecast with such confidence. Many things may happen between now and the time when the forecast benefits are expected to accrue. Note our statement that Project A (in Table 3) will yield $3,400 in cash inflow during Year 1 is predicated on a number of assumptions. The forecast of sales for Years 1 and 2, for example, implicitly incorporates beliefs about both the state of the economy and the relative success of the firm between now and then. At the same time the unit production costs probably assume a certain volume of operation so that the productivity of labor reflected in the cost estimates can be achieved. As a result, the net inflow figures in Tables 3 and 4 are far from being known with certainty.

Similarly the repair expense per year incorporates assumptions made by the production manager as to how the machine will be used so that "normal" wear at the estimated rate will result. It is unlikely that major unexpected breakdowns (not an unlikely occurrence with an older machine) are allowed for in his normal yearly repair expense. Therefore the actual treatment accorded to the machine by production personnel is an important determinant of this particular cost and makes this estimate subject to error. Presumably the cost of the auxiliary machine is known exactly, although even this cost could differ from expectations. The cost of installation may vary. It is also possible that the final purchase price may be determined by the lowest bid submitted by competing machine manufacturers. Both of these factors can make the final cost uncertain.

Depending on the severity and the direction of the errors made, the preference ranking between the two alternatives could be changed. As an example, suppose sales for each of Years 1 and 2 turn out to be higher than predicted by 1,000 units. Then by using the present value methodology outlined on p. 451 we would calculate:

$$\text{Net Present Value (Make)} = -5,000 + \frac{5,800}{(1 + 0.05)} + \frac{7,000}{(1 + 0.05)^2} = \$6,871$$

$$\text{Net Present Value (Buy)} = 0 + \frac{2,220}{(1 + 0.05)} + \frac{2,820}{(1 + 0.05)^2} = \$4,671$$

Alternatively if the sales for each of the two years turn out to be lower than

453
the
financial
context
of
production
management
decisions

predicted by 1,000 units, then:

$$\text{Net Present Value (Make)} = -5,000 + \frac{1,000}{(1 + 0.05)} + \frac{2,200}{(1 + 0.05)^2} = -\$3,053$$

$$\text{Net Present Value (Buy)} = 0 - \frac{180}{(1 + 0.05)} + \frac{420}{(1 + 0.05)^2} = 210$$

Note that, based on net present value calculations alone, if sales turn out to be 1,000 units higher, then FPM should make the product itself. Alternatively if sales are lower than predicted by 1,000 units FPM should buy the product. Otherwise, if sales turn out as predicted then we are (given the accuracy of our estimates) almost indifferent. As a result, we can say that this decision of whether to make or buy the product is *sensitive* to an error of 1,000 units (plus or minus) from the forecasted sales.

Since we do not know ahead of time how much the actual sales will deviate from the forecast we *risk* making the wrong decision. In the next section we will expand on the above argument by describing a methodology for measuring other risks (not only in the forecasts) involved in investment alternatives.

Computer Simulation As a Means of Assessing Risk.[15] In the previous section we calculated the net present values that would result if actual sales turned out to be lower or higher by 1,000 units from the amounts forecast. There is no reason why we cannot continue to analyze the sensitivity of the net present value figure in this manner by considering other possible errors in the estimates. In this section we will describe how through the use of computer simulation such an extension can be carried out.

Suppose we asked the operating managers to estimate a *range* (instead of a single value) for all of the costs and revenues in the make or buy decision. In addition, suppose each manager was also asked to estimate the probability that each of the values within the range would actually occur.[16] Given these distributions for individual estimates, we face the task of estimating the probability distribution of the net present value of each of the projects under consideration. This task is well suited for computer simulation.

The logic outlined by the flow chart in Figure 14.2 is one way in which such a simulation of Project A (Make) could be carried out. Step 1 involves the estimation of the probability distributions by managers for each of the 5 estimates needed as discussed above. Thereupon one value from each of the 5 distributions is drawn randomly (with proper weight given to the relevant probabilities) in Steps 2 through 7. Using the random set of cash flows, in Step 8, a net present value is calculated in exactly the same manner as we did on p. 451. The net present value thus derived is then recorded in Step 9. Step 10 determines the number of times we want to repeat the simulation. Finally, in

[15] For an approach that is similar to ours see David B. Hertz, "Risk Analysis in Capital Investment," *Harvard Business Review*, Vol. 42, No. 1, January-February, 1964, pp. 95–102; David B. Hertz, "Investment Policies That Pay Off," *Harvard Business Review*, Vol. 46, No. 1 January-February, 1968, pp. 96–108.

[16] In fact most managers, in practice, prefer to deal with such ranges or, alternatively, estimates such as pessimistic, optimistic, etc., They can in this manner incorporate much more of their experience and opinions into the estimates that they are asked to give.

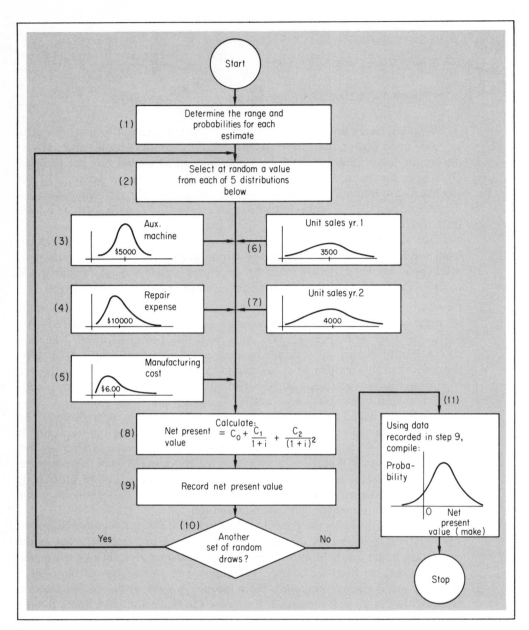

FIGURE 14-2
Flow chart for simulation of investment alternative *A* (make).

Step 11 the results of the simulation are summarized, using data collected in Step 9, in the form of such statistics as the mean net present value, the variance of the net present values and the probability (frequency) distribution of the resulting net present values. The probability distribution of net present values is a complete description of the risk that is inherent in the estimates made.

455
the
financial
context
of
production
management
decisions

Often the variance or standard deviation of this distribution is taken as a specific quantitative measure of risk.

Figure 14.3 presents the results of one set of such simulation runs for both alternative A (Make) and Alternative B (Buy). We will return to this figure later.

The Evaluation of Alternatives. It is generally agreed that projects that offer higher mean net-present values also tend to have a higher variance (risk) asso-

FIGURE 14-3

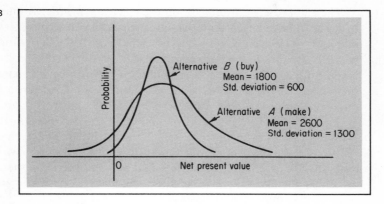

ciated with them. We can represent such a relationship by means of a graph as in Figure 14.4, where each of the points is derived by simulation as on p. 453. Suppose the firm can afford to select only one of these projects, which one should be chosen?

Most managers are adverse to accepting greater amounts of risk in their investment projects. But at the same time they do prefer the greater mean net present values available from riskier projects. Therefore a production manager faces two opposing desires. To make a decision he must trade off between the risk he believes appropriate and the mean net present value available to him at that level of risk.

FIGURE 14-4

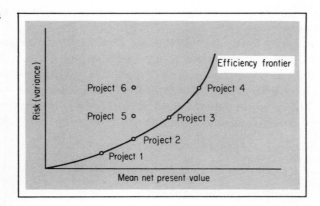

Some comparisons in Figure 14.4 are relatively easy to make in this way. For example, Projects 6, 5, and 2 all offer the same mean net present value in Figure 14.4. But Project 2 has the lowest risk associated with it. As a result a rational manager would rank these three projects: 2, 5, 6. Similarly Project 3 is preferred to Project 5 and Project 4 is preferred to Project 6. In the latter cases the manager would opt for the maximum available net present value at any level of risk under consideration. In fact, any project in Figure 14.3 to the left of the curve (often called the efficiency frontier) is an inferior choice to a project available on the curve.

The choice between projects on the efficiency frontier is much more difficult to make. It is here that the production manager must consult with the financial manager to determine what the best choice is from the point of view of the whole company. But before continuing it may be well to point out that there is some question about the validity of allowing production managers to impose their values on the selection of a firm's investments. There are a number of other interested parties whose value systems also qualify for consideration. For example, there are the president and management personnel who represent marketing production, finance, etc. They will often be affected by investment decisions made in other departments and should therefore have the right to also exercise their judgment. Aside from management there are the stockholders. As owners of the firm it is their right that the business be run in their interests. In practice it is impossible to satisfy the risk taking values of everyone in such a diverse group.

As a result, for smaller investments, production managers often must act as intermediaries—as interpreters of the degree of risk desirable for the company. For larger, more complex, investments it is usually the financial committee of the board of directors who exercise their collective judgment in trying to make decisions in the general interest. Admittedly everyone's interests will not always be served by such an operational approach. But dissatisfied stockholders always have the choice of selling their stocks and investing in another company.

A Risk-Premium Approach to Ranking Investments. In the discussion above we assumed that an appropriate discount rate was available to evaluate the cash flows through time. In the theoretical literature on capital budgeting the choice of the discount rate is one of the major controversies.[17] For our purposes, we will advocate the risk-free discount rate approach recommended by Bierman and Smidt.[18]

Bierman and Smidt suggest that we should retain the assumption that a reasonable person would prefer to have a dollar now rather than a dollar in the future. But unlike other economists[19] they believe that *we should allow for our time preference for money separately from our evaluation of the riskiness of a project.* That is, we should discount the cash flows through time using a "risk-free rate" to arrive at a net present value. Thereupon we should subtract a

[17] A good discussion of opposing points of view appears in Chapter 6, G. David Quirin, *The Capital Expenditure Decision* (Homewood, Ill.: Richard D. Irwin Inc., 1967).

[18] Harold Bierman Jr. and Seymour Smidt, *The Capital Budgeting Decision*, 2nd Edition (New York: The Macmillan Company, 1966), p. 326.

[19] Quirin, *The Capital Expenditure Decision*, Chapter 3.

457
the
financial
context
of
production
management
decisions

"risk premium" from the net present value to reflect our opinion about the relative riskiness of the project. We will discuss and illustrate both of these concepts below.

The *default-free discount rate* is defined as the interest rate at which the investor could lend money with no significant danger of default or alternatively the rate at which he could borrow if his creditor would feel that there was a negligible chance of default. As a practical means of arriving at such a rate, Bierman and Smidt suggest the interest rate on government bonds as a good approximation. In fact, very few companies can borrow at this rate. There is always at least a small risk that the company will be unable to meet its obligation on time. But the default-free discount rate is only intended as a means of evaluating our time preference for money.

The *risk premium* is a more difficult concept to pin down. Consider the following example. Suppose that an investor is willing to pay $150.00 for a share of stock of some company and that the current rate of interest on government bonds is 5 percent (an approximation of the default free rate). For illustrative purposes, assume also that the company promises to pay $10.00 in dividends per year in perpetuity (forever). What is the amount of the implied risk premium that the investor has subtracted from the value of the company's stock?

The present value of the series of cash inflows (dividends) can be calculated using the default-free rate of 5 percent.

$$\text{Present Value} = 10 + \frac{10}{(1.05)} + \frac{10}{(1.05)^2} + \frac{10}{(1.05)^3} + \cdots + \frac{10}{(1.05)^n} + \cdots + \frac{10}{(1.05)^{n \to \infty}}$$

$$= \frac{10}{0.05} = \$200.000$$

That is, if the investor considered the company's promise to be completely believable (riskless) then he would be willing to pay $200 for such a stock. But actually he is willing to pay only $150. The difference of $50 is then the risk premium that he has subtracted from the net present value of the investment to reflect his judgment about the riskiness of the promise made. Therefore, the *risk premium* can be defined as the difference between the net present value of the expected future cash flows discounted at the default-free rate and the actual perceived value of these cash flows as judged by the investor considering the project.

Admittedly, such an evaluation is far from cut and dry. But risk evaluation is basically a subjective process in any case. We can never really make such a process completely mechanical. In practice, the experience and knowledge of several managers is often pooled and a concensus judgment whether by the risk premium method, advocated here, or by some other method must always be made. If a consensus is to be arrived at, then it is important that all underlying assumptions and subjective trade-offs made by any group of managers be clearly stated and that the effect of these assumptions be apparent to all. The risk-premium method that we have presented here we believe to be the most appropriate from this standpoint—it separates the time value of money from risk evaluation.

The Portfolio of Investments. At any point in time a company has money invested in several projects. This group of investments owned by a firm is often referred to as a *portfolio*. In the discussions above we have ignored two important realities. First of all, in most firms there is not enough cash available to meet all promising looking investments. As a result, the available funds have to be rationed. Secondly, we should not consider projects by themselves. As we shall see below the financial manager must consider the effect of a proposed project on his portfolio if he is to act in the interest of the entire financial system. We will illustrate our point by example.

| | PROBABLE STATES OF ECONOMY | | | | STANDARD DEVIATION OF NEW PRESENT VALUE (RISK) |
PROJECT	POOR (0.3)	GOOD (0.6)	EXCEPTIONAL (0.1)	EXPECTED NET PRESENT VALUE	
A	300	500	1,000	490	196
B	300	600	800	530	153
C	700	500	0	510	192
D	400	400	400	400	0

In the example above the figures represent net present values. For example, for Project *A*, $300 is the net present value that will accrue if the state of the economy over the life of the project turns out to be poor, a probability of 0.30. Let us assume that the company's present portfolio is represented by Project *A* and that only one of the three other Projects *B*, *C*, or *D* could be invested in, given the available cash. Which of the three projects should be chosen? Project *C* would be eliminated because it has a lower expected net present value and a higher risk associated with it than Project *B*. We might prefer *D* to *B* since Project *D* has no risk associated with it even though it offers a lower expected net present value. That is, we may prefer the $400 guaranteed return to a $530 return that is less certain. But in fact, given that we look at the above problem as a portfolio, the best choice turns out to be Project *C* as can be seen from the example below:

| | PROBABLE STATES OF ECONOMY | | | | STANDARD DEVIATION OF NET PRESENT VALUE (RISK) |
POSSIBLE PORTFOLIOS	POOR (0.3)	GOOD (0.6)	EXCEPTIONAL (0.1)	EXPECTED NET PRESENT VALUE	
A + B	600	1,100	1,800	1,020	343
A + C	1,000	1,000	1,000	1,000	0
A + D	700	900	1,400	890	196

As a portfolio *A* + *C* is the best because it offers an expected net present value of $1,000 *with no risk*. The cash flows of *A* and *C* under the different states of

459
the
financial
context
of
production
management
decisions

the economy complement each other perfectly. The financial manager is, of course, always looking for similar projects that improve his portfolio as a whole.[20]

The Decision Faced by The FPM Company. Let us now return to the make or buy decision we last considered on p. 455. As we saw in Figure 14.3, Alternative *A* (Make) had a higher mean net present value and also a higher variance (risk). In particular, under Alternative *A* a considerable probability exists that the project will have a negative return. (Note that the left tail of the distribution extends below zero.) The production manager must determine with the help of the financial manager a risk premium that is appropriate for each alternative. Presumably the risk premium for *A* will be larger than that for *B*. In addition to a higher variance and a significant probability of a loss, Alternative *A* also involves a higher initial investment ($5,000).

Although it is clear that the risk premium for *A* should be larger than for *B*, a difficult evaluation remains: by how much? A seemingly precise figure (the risk premium) must be subtracted from the mean net present values of each alternative. In this the final step of analysis we can offer no further help. To this point we have laid out a comprehensive picture of the problem at hand. The production manager must now exercise his judgment, given the data in front of him and his experience with projects in the past that were similar. The better managers will make correct evaluations more often than not. Therefore, for the problem faced by the FPM Company we cannot give a definitive answer. Instead we ask the reader: which alternative would you choose?

Such an answer may be difficult to accept by those who like to make financial analysis a precise science. But capital budgeting in practice is far from cut and dry. A production manager engaging in investment analysis must recognize that what he is undertaking is really a mixture of well-defined theory and art. Often the acceptance of his project will depend on his ability to argue effectively and cogently about the merits of his proposal in front of a group such as the finance committee. In particular, he must always attempt to convince the committee that his evaluation of the riskiness and the suitability of a project is correct in relation to the over-all goals of the firm.

Given the discussion above, the production manager may find it sometimes difficult to agree with the decision by the financial committee to reject his project. Although his project may have been well conceived, with an acceptable expected net present value (even after it was adjusted for the risk premium) it may not be suitable given the current composition of the company's investment portfolio. This may at times be indeed a bitter pill to swallow, for the good of the company as a whole.

Some Concluding Comments. Undoubtedly the single most pervasive objective criterion used in production management is the minimization of cost. To reach this goal, production managers generate a continual stream of cost saving investment proposals and make production decisions that affect others within the financial system. As we pointed out before, financial officers are primarily con-

---

[20] For a good discussion of portfolio analysis see Harry Markowitz, "Portfolio Selection," *Journal of Finance,* March 1952, pp. 77–91.

cerned with the budgeting of cash flows so as to control expenses effectively and influence revenues favorably. Given the above, one could hastily conclude that groups labelled "finance" and "production" should find it easy to coordinate their efforts toward this common goal. But as we have seen, coordination of production and financial management efforts to this end is far from easy. Leaving aside the age-old rivalries between the two oldest members in the finance-production-marketing triumvirate, the conflicts that most often ensue can be traced to the difficulties encountered with identifying and estimating *relevant costs and benefits* in specific proposals. Disagreements can also occur regarding the relative ranking of the numerous project proposals generated by all departments (including production) within the company. Risk, over-all company policy, and available alternative opportunities must always be weighted subjectively in addition to monetary considerations. To further complicate matters some important theoretical issues on the evaluation of investments remain to be settled. As a result, effective investment analysis requires a considerable amount of subjective evaluation.

Finally, in pursuing their goal of cost minimization production managers must not forget that they share joint responsibilities with financial and marketing managers when operating within the financial system. If any one of these three ignores his part in this joint responsibility then the resulting decisions will be suboptimal from the point of view of the firm as a whole.

PROBLEMS

1   Suppose the financial officer in charge of a company's cash budget discovered at the end of the year that the company actually had used 25 percent more cash than he had estimated at the beginning of the year. Has the financial officer failed to exercise his responsibilities? How should his performance be evaluated?

2   Historically financial managers have tended to emphasize different aspects of financial control in response to the prevailing economic conditions. Is it reasonable to assume that they will continue to do so in the future? If not, why not? If so, what aspect of financial control is dominant in the minds of financial managers today?

3   An analyst estimates that an investment of $100,000 in new machinery will yield a positive cash inflow of $30,000 in the first year. Thereafter he expects that the yearly cash flow from the project will grow by 10 percent each year. What assumptions and simplifications is the analyst probably making? As the production manager, what additional information would you request? How readily available is the information that you request? Under what circumstances would you consider the proposed investment acceptable?

4   A popular investment criterion used in practice by the production manager is the "payback period":

$$\text{Payback Period} = \frac{\text{Total Initial Investment}}{\text{Net Yearly Cash Inflow}}$$

Under such an investment criterion all projects with a payback period of less than,

461
the
financial
context
of
production
management
decisions

say, three years would be considered acceptable. For example, in problem 3 above:

$$\text{Payback Period} < \frac{100,000}{30,000} = 3.33 \text{ years}$$

(Note that the Payback Period is less than 3.33 years because in subsequent years the cash inflow is expected to be greater than $30,000.) Under what circumstances would you use this simple criterion? When would the payback criterion lead to erroneous decisions?

5 Should a production manager accept an investment that requires an outlay of $10,000 if it could be a complete bust (no cash inflow) with a probability of 0.60 or if it could generate a cash inflow of $30,000 immediately with a probability of 0.40. Explain your reasoning in full.

6 Suppose that the purchase of a $20,000 machine guarantees certain cash inflows of $5,000 per year for the next two years and thereupon $10,000 per year for the next three years. After five years the machine must be scrapped and has no salvage value. The company has a policy requiring a two-year payback period on all equipment purchases and also requires a 10 percent return on money invested.
Should the machine be purchased?

7 The management of a company has determined that it is *worthwhile* to acquire the use of a complex piece of production equipment. The equipment can either be *rented or purchased*.
The rental fee would be $120,000 per year, payable at the beginning of each year. Included in the rental fee is the cost of maintenance which is to be done by the company from which the equipment is rented.
The purchase price of the equipment is $400,000. If purchased, a maintenance contract would be obtained at a cost of $12,000 per year, payable at the beginning of each year. The machine would be depreciated over a five year period on a straight line basis with a zero salvage value at the end of five years.
The income tax rate that is applicable to taxable income of the firm is 50 percent. The relevant opportunity cost, or cost of capital for the investment outlay is 8 percent per year which is applicable to dollar returns *after* taxes.
Should the machine be rented or purchased? Show your analysis.

references

BIERMAN, HAROLD and SEYMOUR SMIDT, *The Capital Budgeting Decision* (2nd ed.). New York: The Macmillan Company, 1966.

FRIEDLAND, SEYMOUR, *The Economics of Corporate Finance.* Englewood Cliffs, N.J.: Prentice-Hall, Inc., 1966.

HAMADA, R. S., "Portfolio Analysis, Market Equilibrium and Corporate Finance," *Journal of Finance*, (March, 1969), pp. 13–31.

HERTZ, DAVID B., "Risk Analysis in Capital Investment," *Harvard Business Review,* (January-February 1964), 95–106.

JOHNSON, ROBERT W., *Financial Management* (3rd Ed.). Boston, Mass.: Allyn and Bacon, 1966.

MAO, JAMES C. T. *Quantitative Analysis of Financial Decisions.* London, England: Macmillan & Co., Ltd., 1969.

MARKOWITZ, HARRY M., "Portfolio Selection," *Journal of Finance* (March 1952), 77–91.

QUIRIN, G. DAVID, *The Capital Expenditure Decision.* Homewood, Ill.: Richard D. Irwin, Inc., 1967.

SMITH, VERNON, *Investment and Production.* Cambridge, Mass.: Harvard University Press, 1966.

TERBORGH, GEORGE, *Business Equipment Policy.* Washington, D.C.: Machinery and Allied Products Institute, 1958.

VAN HORNE, JAMES C., *Financial Management and Policy.* Englewood Cliffs, N.J.: Prentice-Hall, Inc., 1971.

WEINGARTEN, MARTIN, *Mathematical Programming and the Analysis of Capital Budgeting Problems.* Englewood Cliffs, N.J.: Prentice-Hall, Inc., 1963.

WESTON, J.F., *The Scope and Methodology of Finance.* Englewood Cliffs, N.J.: Prentice-Hall, Inc., 1966.

chapter fifteen
marketing-production interaction

BY WILLIAM T. MORAN

The term *Industrial Revolution* designates that period when the wide use of machinery began to displace individual artisans. The initial cost of machinery and the tendency to replace labor with machinery within a single enterprise brought increasing need for capital financing to launch a production business. Thus, the dependency relationship between *production* and *finance* has a long history. Because a machine cannot be paid on a piece-rate basis the importance of full utilization of productive facilities quickly became apparent to the owners. For this reason, the Industrial Revolution brought a greatly intensified concern with large volume production. Unit costs of finished goods could be reduced and, thereby, profit to the producer increased. The importance of this relationship is in the forefront of every manufacturer's mind, even to this day.

As competing industrial manufacturers increased in number and efficiency, individual producers intensified their efforts to increase production volume in order to maintain competitive cost structures. These pressures inexorably led manufacturers to reach further and further to find market outlets for their production. In this manner, the dependence of *production* upon *distribution* increased.

As manufacturing enterprises became more complex, finance extended beyond capital formations and assumed the role of score-keeping controllership. The controllership function exists because of the convenient single dimensionality of the financial measuring stick—in the unit of currency. Until the most recent years, financial accounting has provided us with virtually our only criterion for measuring and controlling those many management decision functions which occur between the original act of capital formation and the scorekeeping act of striking the final balance.

The third and most recent member of the finance-production-distribution triumvirate eventually came to incorporate sales and promotion effort and all those activities which have been relabelled *marketing*. It is now accepted that dependencies exist between finance, marketing, and production. The exact nature of these interdependencies is not clearly understood, and, as a result, there is frequent disagreement concerning how each should behave in relation to the other. Our purpose is to explore and define the relationship between marketing and production.

THE VALUE OF PRODUCT MANAGEMENT

The interrelationship of marketing and production arises from their common goal—the welfare of the enterprise. Today, the principal objective of all entrepreneurship—both from a profit as well as from an ethical standpoint—is the production of *value*. This was not always the case. The fact that the production of value to the consumer is also the road to profit for the producer more than anything else explains what has happened to the Industrial Revolution since the time of Karl Marx. He, noting the direct price competition produced by manufacturing companies with identical product objectives, observed that "the battle of competition is fought by cheapening of commodities." The nature of this *change in the objectives of entrepreneurship from cost-cutting to value-building* and its consequences with respect to production management is the principal subject of this paper.

The Declining Importance of Efficiency. Until recently, marketing objectives and practices have reflected the production economics which grew out of the Industrial Revolution. The very success of the Industrial Revolution, however, in recent years has brought important changes in the nature of competition and in the sources of profit. Where once trade secrets and patentable production processes gave one manufacturer great profit advantage over another, broad development of the engineering sciences has spread the base of expertise to the point where production costs no longer are the overwhelming components of selling prices that once they were. *Thus, the profit leverage of production efficiencies has declined.*

Today, production cost *efficiency*, alone, is no guarantor of profit because competitors can enjoy equivalent efficiencies. More subtle factors—*seldom reflected* in the convenient categories of *cost accounting*—are the principal determinants of successful marketing and production practice. Since World

War II manufacturers have tended increasingly to design and market their products so as to appeal more sharply to some segment of the total marketplace rather than to attempt to appeal to everyone. In this manner, manufacturers who might appear to be competing directly with each other actually are subdividing the market. This same practice enables a single manufacturer to market more than one brand of a product—as is prominently the practice in the automobile, soap, and cigarette industries.

The practice of marketing goods designed to appeal differentially to various customer subgroups in the marketplace has the effect of checking the tendency for competition to concentrate output in a few, high-efficiency plants. *We observe here a force which runs directly counter to the classic source of production cost efficiency.* Today's economic environment places the emphasis upon the creative notion of *the production of value. The value of the production division, in turn, is in direct proportion to its ability to accomplish this end.* The profit effectiveness of the business enterprise is a function of the integrated effort of production and marketing.

Because production and marketing are most efficiently performed by different individuals who utilize different skills, it was convenient in large manufacturing organizations to institutionalize these two functions into separate organizational compartments. This separation inevitably led to individual traditions and planning procedures. As a result, the conflicts which arise between them usually are issues of divisional *efficiency* rather than those of combined company *effectiveness.* It is because of the importance of common goals and the need for coordinated approaches that committee superstructures arise in large organizations which have both a strong Production Division and a strong Marketing Division. Staff committees represent an effort to overcome the lack of organic coordination. The tendency to attend to strictly divisional objectives violates the *systems concept. The optimization of the behavior of the total enterprise frequently requires the suboptimization of its component divisions,* but it is always difficult to get divisions graciously to accept such restraints on their individual objectives.

Unfortunately, the perception and assessment of efficiency is much easier than the assessment of effectiveness. Part of the reason that we do not deal more directly with the more important issue of effectiveness is that the recent changes in the economic environment with which we lived for two centuries are still difficult to perceive and interpret.

The New Opportunity—Market Segmentation. Our domestic market is so large, so widely dispersed, and so financially capable of high consumption that the simple relationship—mass production plus mass distribution equals mass value—is greatly modified. Recent technological developments have reduced the size of the optimum production facility in a number of industries: Return on capital investment does not increase commensurately from the smallest to the largest production facility. Also, the distance between our geographic boundaries sharpens the significance of distribution cost. The increased precision of our inventory control methods in recent years enhances attention to the cost of extended delivery times and augments awareness of the cost of keeping goods in transit. *Also, the size and the heterogeneity of our populace makes it economi-*

cally possible to produce and market different goods *differently* designed for *different* segments within the populace. The availability of goods designed to appeal more closely to one's own needs and tastes *increases the actual value* of the fruits of production in the eyes of the individual customer.

This happy optimization of production efficiency and of production value, originating in the United States, has been an important economic phenomenon for approximately thirty years. Where once we recognized only a one-way dependency relationship between production and marketing we have become aware of a high order of synergistic interaction where each reinforces the other and the value of the whole is greater than the sum of the parts.

The key to this important development lies in the word *value*. As beauty is in the eye of the beholder, value is in the taste of the consumer. We have noted that the production of value is the principal objective of all entrepreneurship and, thereby, of production. *It is the continuing task of marketing to seek constantly to define value in all its manifestations in all segments°of the marketplace.* It is because of this role that marketing interacts with and affects production efficiency.

Utilitarian and Nonutilitarian Functions Cannot Be Categorized. High value, great utility, or high quality, used here as synonyms, is something about which each of us may speak with great authority—provided we refer only to our own value systems. A great presumption of some economists is that they can differentiate between good and bad utility. The untenable notion that goods or services can be classified as "utilitarian" or "nonutilitarian" presumes a universal and invariant value system. Such a set of uniform values certainly does not exist in our heterogeneous culture and very likely never did exist anywhere outside of theology.

We need another set of terms which will permit useful discussion of the value of individual attributes——one which permits recognition of the value systems of everyone in the marketplace. For purposes of convenience, individual attributes or qualities may be classified as *fundamental* or *arbitrary*. This categorization only reflects the *degree of variance* with which the marketplace identifies the most desirable state of the attribute for a particular product class. If the variance is slight, we decide that we have a *fundamental* quality standard and our measurement problem is, thereby, greatly simplified. We are further tempted to substitute the terms *functional* or *utilitarian* for those attributes whose standards are *fundamental*. If the variance is great, we declare that we have an *arbitrary* quality standard. Such dichotomization bears a kinship to John Locke's nonevaluative classification of object (product) qualities into *primary* and *secondary*. It was his notion that some attributes, such as substance and shape, were *intrinsic* to an object, whereas others, such as color and aroma, were secondary because they would not appear to exist within the product except for the sensory organs of the perceiving human being.

Those quality standards which are most common to our culture were the earliest targets of mass production because they offered the broadest markets. It is for this reason that product classes originally were defined and separated in accordance with their "functional" attributes. During the early years of the

Industrial Revolution when economies were relatively restricted this was a useful system for separating product classes. Today it is an anachronism and a source of costly errors in product design and testing.

Quality Standards Are Unevenly Distributed. The dichotomization into fundamental and arbitrary product qualities is itself an arbitrary categorization of the graduated spectrum of quality standards by which consumers judge value. There are some product qualities about which there is very uniform agreement within our culture; for example, there would be widespread agreement that food should be safe or that soap should clean. There are, of course, other qualities about whose standards there are many shades of opinion; perhaps the shape or even the speed of automobiles are such qualities. Other product qualities range across all degrees, from cultural uniformity to highly dispersed individuality. For these reasons it is preferable to use the terms *culture-wide* quality standards (near-uniformity—low variance standards—throughout the marketplace) and *subculture* quality standards (segmented—high variance—sets of standards).

There are several reasons for this preference. One is that the tradition of defining product classes by so-called functional attributes is virtually synonymous with definition by similarity of *ingredient* or *production process* rather than by similarity of *value* achieved. Such a rigid functional definition of a business led to the failure of locomotive manufacturers to realize that they were in the *transportation* business. They thought in terms of their production processes, such as iron-working, and the familiar ingredients including boilers and steam pistons. They rejected the opportunity to engage in a "different" business involving internal combusion engines, electric motors, and so on. They thus failed to meet the challenge of a changing marketplace and lost their markets to more value-oriented companies.

Another reason for preferring these terms, *cultures* and *subcultures*, is that the size and wealth of the American market has created potential for many affluent subculture segments. Because our production technology has developed and proliferated to such a remarkable extent, competing producers are equally able to deliver optimum satisfaction of those widely distributed, low variance culture values toward which their principal attention has been directed. The consequent reduction of competitive differentials has brought about the present shift in production and marketing attention toward unique products directed at subculture systems as a means of avoiding the unprofitable consequences of such direct competition.

The culture-wide values represent the most obvious market targets and, in the past, these have attracted the greatest amount of competitive attention. The products associated with these values are the price-competitive, commonplace products which, because of their similarity from manufacturer to manufacturer, are often dubbed "commodities" as opposed to "specialties." In fact it is the richly varied kaleidoscope of subculture values that forms a prolific hunting ground for new consumer product opportunities. There are countless unsatisfied human wants represented by the subculture segments of the populace and, frequently, little technological invention is required to produce a new product or brand especially for them. Thus, *subculture values often represent potential markets*. They pose a particular challenge to the flexibility of automated production techniques.

There Are No Universally Better Designs. This shift in business attention to subculture values has inevitable implications regarding our understanding of *utility* in production and marketing if we are to meet the challenge of our market place. The only definition of *acceptable utility* which will stand up is "any function which in our society is regarded as socially acceptable and beneficial." The concept of acceptable utility changes with time and varies from group to group and from person to person.

We are forced to recognize the *different* utilities offered by frozen foods and their canned counterparts, bakery cakes and home-mix cakes, small cars and large cars, Courrege and Givenchy clothing, Dove toilet soap and Lux, and by Bufferin and Anacin. Some people prefer one member of each pair, other people prefer the other. This is because their ideas of utility differ. They also change over time. For example, the perception of the positive value of baths and of toilet soap is of quite recent origin and already there are signs of recidivism in some subcultures in the land of the Puritans. In the business of producing value we cannot afford to be literal and unimaginative about human wants. Neither can we be dogmatic. *There is no such thing as a universally better design or function.*[1] *All wants are utilitarian to their possessors.*

PRODUCTS PERFORM SERVICES

The Value of Services Performed is Equivalent to the Value Received. All goods have their service counterparts which establish their intrinsic value. This relationship holds for even the most simple production outputs, such as food. The seed became the food through cultivation within the confines of the farm. Thus, food was easier to locate in quantity than it was when nomads depended upon encountering it in the natural state. Thus, the production process of farming replaced the service of foraging, and the value of farm food was determined by the amount of foraging which would otherwise have been required. This relationship becomes increasingly apparent when we consider more complex production outputs. It is for this reason that the *goods which represent intricate combinations of services which are difficult to obtain and utilize in proper porportion and with appropriate timing are those goods which command the highest marginal prices.*

The Interchangeability of Production and Service. Bottled boric acid solution differs from the crystals in that the mixing of this medicine has already been done for the customer. This is a service. Also, mint flavored cigarettes are a way of conveying a sensation of freshness along with smoking. The production process of mixing or blending ingredients performs services which otherwise

---

[1] There are no value standards which are absolutely universal. This extreme notion is no more outrageous to logic than the more socially acceptable notion that there are universal design objectives.

would have had to have been performed by customers. Thus, production is always the equivalent of some alternative service.

Information, too, can take the place of service in the same sense as production. The marketing man who suggested that Johnson & Johnson First Aid Cream could be sold, not only for cuts and burns, but for "detergent hands" as well, added a vast new area of service to the product just as clearly as if he had performed additional production processes. His act differed from the usual production process in that it neither modified the utility of the product with respect to its previous services[2] nor incurred additional production cost. Thereby, unlike physical modification of the usual production process, this addition to the combination of services within the product did not narrow the range of applications, but, on the contrary, opened a whole new market.

Production is the equivalent of service. Information is the equivalent of service. So, information and production must be different forms of the same thing. No wonder they interact!

Combining Services Enhances Value of Production. Few, if any, goods represent only a single value or service. The higher products of our technological civilization represent various combinations of services, and the greater the number in combination, the more that the ultimate range of applications of an individual product is restricted.

Processing Reduces Range of Use. Similarly, the greater the amount and complexity of the production processing that a good undergoes, generally the more restricted and specialized its potential applications become. Shaped wooden molding has a more restricted range of use than the plain planks from which it was formed. *Thus, production is the process of restricting use;* and in order for production to be economically worthwhile to the producer, the contemplated restriction must *increase value faster than it reduces the range of application.*

It follows that the fewer, less complex production processes a good undergoes the greater the need for additional services which must be performed at the time of consumption in order that the total value of the consumption situation be realized. The plain wooden planks require more carpentry at the scene of consumption in order to achieve equivalent value with the molding which was previously produced and stored. Thus, production processes, such as those performed to produce molding, are the equivalent of services. They are services which are built into the good.

It is these services, contained and stored in the good, which create its value. *The value is determined by the alternative services which would have to be purchased if the good were not produced.* Thus, the value of the molding is determined by the cost of the plain wooden plank *plus* the cost and inconvenience of the carpentering service required to convert the plank to molding and *minus* the value placed upon the lost opportunity (when buying preshaped molding) to have individually styled molding.

[2] That is to say that from a technical standpoint the utilities of the previous services were not affected. From the standpoint of an individual consumer, on the other hand, Johnson & Johnson First Aid Cream may well have lost or gained perceived value as a medicinal antiseptic as a result of the communication service.

Production Stores Services. The value represented by physical goods lies in the fact that goods are devices which store services. They store services in the sense that they preserve these services in time so that they may be stored for future use. *So physical production also is a process of storing services.*

Service Combinations and Product Proliferation. Inevitably, the greater the number of services stored in a good, the smaller the range of creative adaptations and applications possible by the consumer. Also the fewer the people to whom the particular stored combination will appeal, but the more uniquely and intensively it will appeal to those people.

Thus, in a society devoted to increasingly complex production processes, the only route to increased received value by all is through greater proliferation of models, types, styles and brands of goods. The alternative of a return to Nature, requiring the performance of a range of service functions by each individual, periodically attracts some sub-cultures such as the Amish, Shakers and communal "hippies". Some social planners, on the other hand, wishing to have a technological civilization without proliferation, prefer to prescribe standards of value for their neighbors.

A middle course lies in compatible component production[3] which will permit virtually limitless combinations from a sharply constrained set of alternative components at very little effort by the consumer. The automobile industry and the audio-visual entertainment equipment industry already have progressed well down this path. It has been said that in an entire year's production of Chrysler automobiles no two are produced which are exactly alike. The consumer virtually is handed a catalogue of alternative body styles, engines, radios, tape cassette players, heaters, brakes, interiors, etc., etc. from which to construct the car of his choice.

It is not coincidental that the component approach has first taken root in high-cost product categories. There also are service alternatives, however, of sufficient unimportance to some individuals, where the perceived financial or performance risk is so low, that it does not appear worth the effort, to those consumers, to process all the information necessary to study the choices and arrange the components. To these people for their purposes suboptimization of value and/or proliferation of brands are preferable alternatives. The package goods industry is a present example of an industry where most consumers feel the risks are so low as to warrant brand proliferation. Indeed, new brand introduction is the way of life and of profitable survival for package goods marketers.

Birth and Death: Product Life Expectations. The A. C. Nielsen Co., a major marketing research firm, studied the seasonally adjusted sales trends of 275 brands from 37 product classes handled in grocery outlets over a five year period beginning in 1961. These product categories fell in three large classes in about equal numbers: food products, household products, and health and beauty aids.

At the end of 1960 only 170 of these brands were in existence. From 1961

---

[3] Martin K. Starr, "Modular Production—A New Concept", *Harvard Business Review*, Cambridge, Mass., Vol. 43, No. 6, Nov.-Dec. 1965, pp. 131–142.

through 1966 105 new brands were introduced. Some of the original 170 brands were withdrawn; many suffered major declines in sales and will likely be withdrawn in following years.

When a to-be-successful brand is introduced, it goes through a period of sales growth. This initial cycle is considered terminated by the A. C. Nielsen Co. when its sales share of its product class recedes to below 80% of its peak introductory share of market. Using this arbitrary definition of termination of initial growth cycle, the average duration of the initial cycle dropped from about three years in 1961 and 1962 to eighteen months in 1964. (1965 and 1966 new brands could not be included because they had not all completed their initial cycles.) The length of time that a manufacturer can enjoy the fruits of a successful new product is growing short indeed. Virtually all brands undergo termination of the initial growth cycle and unless the product and/or its marketing is redesigned, will fall prey to the newer brand, the newer package or type, or the newer flavor. The end of the initial growth cycle will then be followed by continuing decline.

This same study established that 88 percent of brands which do not redesign show continuing losses in share of market. Of those which redesign, almost half show recovery and subsequent increases in share of market with an average duration of only twelve months. A substantial improvement but, nonetheless, the profitable period of the average new product has become very short. Investment planning should be conducted accordingly.

The implications for production are clear. A brand in such product categories must face the likely necessity of redesign every twelve to eighteen months. Because of lead-time requirements redesign planning must have begun by the time the present design is introduced to the market. Because redesign can only be accomplished with additional investment expense, the accumulated investment grows larger while the duration of favorable sales response grows shorter.

WHAT IS THE BOUNDARY OF A PRODUCT?

Product Attributes Cannot Be Categorized as Primary and Secondary. Where does the defining boundary of a product end and the marketing function begin? The product boundary ends where the description of all its services end. It is apparent that the boundary of a product is very difficult, if not impossible, to define. Does the aroma belong to the rose? Is the musical note intrinsic to the piano?

A Product's Attributes Are Its Utilities, Its Services. A radio would not be a radio without the sound which emerges from it; the package which contains the perfume contributes to the intended experience; the instructions for use and the design on a label help to establish the perceived value of the product; the price, the type of stores in which a product is distributed, and the images and implications conveyed by the advertising communication are all indistinguishable from the shape and styling of the product. All the above contribute to the total experience which establishes the perceived services and determines the value which a prospective customer places upon the product. *Every aspect of sensing and experiencing a product—the services which it performs—are just as centrally a part of the product as the material of which it's made.*

Thus, as in the illustration of the Johnson & Johnson First Aid Cream, every aspect of marketing is a part of the product. And it is primitive to think of product advertising as being something apart from the product itself. The product includes advertising in that bundle of service values purchased by the consumer. An illuminating example is that of toy advertising on television. The value and success of a toy is directly related to the richness of the fantasy life which the toy stimulates. Television advertising for toys provides the visual and dramatic context, the very fantasies themselves, for children who might never conceive such mental lives on their own. The intrinsic performance characteristics of the physical toy being sold are of relative inconsequence. The price of the toy serves only to pay for the cost of experiencing the commercial and to restimulate memory of the commercial fantasy. In a very real sense the commercial is the product and the toy is its advertising.

Because marketing operations produce value, because they limit and direct the utility of a product, and because these values frequently are storable along with the product, *marketing might be said to be a form of production and vice versa.*

A Service Economy Requires Changed Financial Concepts. One of the significant aspects of our advancing technology is that greater quantities of services are being fixed in goods without commensurate increases in the utilization of physical resources. This decline in the use of physical resources relative to total value underlies the decline in the relative importance and profitability of our so-called "basic industries," such as steel and transportation. *As the relative use of physical resources declines, production and marketing tend to merge and become indistinguishable; our economy becomes less object oriented and more service oriented.* A study of the composition of our Gross National Product shows great relative increases in the consumption of services over goods in recent years—despite the relatively crude nature of the "service industry" categorization.

As society evolves into a service dominated economy, the accounting practices by which we attempt to measure economic health, our notions regarding patents, depletion, and depreciation, and our investment principles must shift their emphasis *away* from fixed plant, equipment, and physical inventory *toward* the service basis of value and the productive value of service. *Or else, as our well being increases, our economic indices perversely will depict a declining economy.* Developing awareness of ecological and other "quality of life" considerations with their implicit value trade-offs and interactions indicates that these shifts are gathering momentum.

If we do not revise our accounting and investment practices to reflect the reality of the new economy, we might absurdly find that the most efficient means by which we will be able to maintain the appearance of an increasing Gross National Product will be by the deliberate destruction of natural resources, forced and artificial obsolescence and depreciation of goods or, perhaps, by an increase in the numbers of rockets which we disperse beyond the earth's gravity. The GNP is a measure of production, not of market value. Yet, it comes to be used as an index of the standard of living. This discrepancy has been of concern to marketing people because so much government and financial planning is predicated on GNP trends. Because of its necessary effect on production, the trend of the new economy also should be of concern to production and finance. The obverse of this condition—economic indices heralding a prospering society while its members sense an ebbing well being—creates feelings of frustration, dislocation and alienation because people believe the indices are describing a real world but one in which they do not participate. Thus, the misrepresentation of the *value economy* by irrelevant economic indices can lead to social unrest.

Recent efforts by Bauer and others to dramatize the need for a meaningful index of the quality of life[4] in our society appear to be bearing some fruit. The Executive Office of the United States Government has established a group at the White House, the National Goals Research Staff, to pursue actively the development and use of such an index. Behavioral science and marketing research technology have evolved to the point where it is quite feasible to produce the "quality of life" equivalent of the temperature-humidity index of comfort which appears in our daily newspapers during the warmer months.

We are becoming less and less a materialist society. Yet, some bills have been introduced to the Congress in recent years with the intent of reducing the variety of product forms, sizes, and qualities. The objectives of such bills have been to force our productive resources to revert to uniform concentration upon "fundamental" and "utilitarian"—materialistic—values, in order to bring about more direct price competition. These efforts are curiously anachronistic. The measure of GNP however, would not reflect the great loss in value which such efforts would bring about.

The necessity to face the equivalence of information with product, service and value has been forced upon the U. S. Patent Office by the computer age. The first crack in the eighteenth century wall of resistance to the patenting of information occurred in 1969 when the Patent Office was forced to give favorable consideration to the patentability of computer programs.

The basis for this historic acknowledgment of the "material" nature of language instructions was that a patent had previously been awarded the designer of a new type of computer which, as the result of its particular structure, could perform certain tasks which lesser computers, lacking the same physical components, could not. Then, later, a creative programmer devised a program of instructions, describing logic and computations which would permit those lesser computers to perform the same advanced tasks without the necessity of the patented material components.

Thus, either a service replaced a good or instructions constitute a storable, transferable service—the definition of a good.

4 The Institute for the Quality of Life, Inc. was formed in 1971 to pursue just such a development—blending descriptive forecasts by experts of technical and cultural developments and inter-actions with the measured value systems of our culture's and sub-cultures'. Their QOL Index tracks and forecasts the quality of life for government and industry planning and investment purposes. (QOL Index is the property of The Institute For the Quality of Life, Inc.)

This acknowledgment of the product equivalence of information comes at a time when it is increasingly important to increase value——the quality of life—— without continued depletion of physical resources and degradation of the environment. The nature of production will turn increasingly to the production of information to provide the values once obtainable only through physical products. Fritz Machlup noted as long ago as 1965 that the production and distribution of knowledge was the largest industry in the United States. Information under many disguises already is the principal area of consumer expenditure.

All these changes in the areas of production and consumption have inevitable consequences for the process of capital formation and other financial concepts which were generated in the era of commodity production. Capital formation will lose importance to perishable human talent—knowledge and creativity. Property will lose ground as the source and symbol of wealth. As we have seen a breach of fundamental patent theory perhaps next the Internal Revenue Service will acknowledge the varying depreciability of human talents and performance capabilities in different occupations as they do for other resources. Already we see athletes incorporating, being owned by syndicates, receiving enormous bonuses for their initial contracts, all in an effort to compensate for the risks and perishability of their occupations and talents. Why only athletes?

PROFIT AND COST ANALYSES

Market Segmentation Modifies the Relationship of Profits to Sales Volume. The notion that greater production volume means greater production efficiency and, coupled with equivalent sales volume, leads to greater profit has been widely accepted for a long time. Although this relationship has by no means been repealed, it has been greatly modified by the shift in marketing attention toward subculture values. As we move away from relatively exclusive concentration upon the marketing of highly competitive "commodities," we find that the straightforward relationship between sales volume and profit has sharply proscribed limits.

Promotion Costs Behave Differently from Other Costs. Also, as we move away from "commodity" products, the role of communication becomes increasingly important in order that the consuming public can find out what different service mixes, combinations of qualities, and values are represented by each of the differentiated products available. The role of communication is largely played by promotion, including advertising. It is because promotion cost behaves so differently from production and distribution cost that the simple "mass sales equals mass profits" relationship is modified. The simplified example shown in Figure 15.1 and supporting Table 1 will help clarify why promotion cost is such a modifying factor in subculture marketing as to *call for restricted sales objectives to maximize profits.*

In the example, we see that production and distribution costs typically decline on a unit basis with increasing volume. Promotion costs, on the contrary, dis-

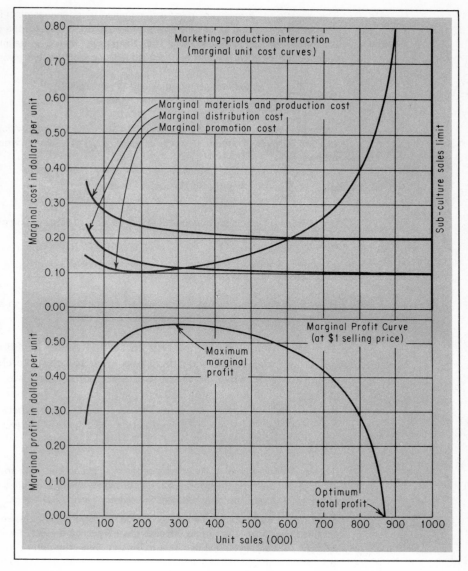

FIGURE 15-1
Economic interaction
in a firm for a single
product.

Marketing-production interaction
(marginal unit cost curves)

Marginal cost in dollars per unit

Marginal materials and production cost
Marginal distribution cost
Marginal promotion cost

Sub-culture sales limit

Marginal Profit Curve
(at $1 selling price)

Marginal profit in dollars per unit

Maximum
marginal
profit

Optimum
total profit

Unit sales (000)

play this behavior, if at all, only over the lower volume ranges and then rise asymptotically as some kind of a limit on achievable sales volume is approached. This limit frequently is called "the potential market."

The practical application of such marginal analysis of advertising costs has been reported by Friedman (see bibliography). A major consumer products company successfully applied the principles derived from the analysis to the setting of advertising budgets. Friedman says:

Common objectives in marketing problems include sales, profits, and market share. The objective in this study was the maximization of "long range" expected profits . . .

The advertising "Breakeven" point is determined when the marginal income in the sales caused by advertising equals the cost of the advertising. [This is the point of "Optimum total profit" shown in Figure 15.1] The "Breakeven" ratio B, is defined as the dollars of sales which must be caused for each advertising dollar spent in order to break even.

$$B = \frac{P}{P - C} \quad \left[\begin{array}{l}\text{where } P = \text{selling price and } C = \text{marginal} \\ \text{cost of producing the merchandise}\end{array}\right]$$

In the case where management wishes to put an equivalent profit value on sales, such as $50,000 for every $1,000,000 worth of sales, the "Breakeven" would be adjusted as follows

$$B = \frac{P}{1.05P - C}$$

In a company in which the marginal costs are 60 percent of the selling price, the Breakeven would be

$$B = \frac{1.00}{1.05 \times 1.00 - .60} = 2.22$$

Thus, the advertising budget would be set at that point where an additional dollar of advertising would produce no more than $2.22 sales.

The advertiser used this analysis to set individual advertising budgets for each TV sales area and to vary them over time according to changes in performance. The result, which persisted over a period of years, was approximately a 20 percent gain in advertising efficiency.

Friedman drew some conclusions from this practical experience which compare interestingly with our own *Implications of Economic Interaction For Product Planning and Evaluation* (Chart 15.1). Friedman writes:

If costs can be reduced, there is more profit in a sale and one can spend a little more to get it, thus increasing the optimal budget. Similarly, changes in price can affect the profit margin in a sale and raise or lower the optimal advertising budget . . .

It can easily be shown that if advertising becomes more efficient, more impressions being obtained per dollar, one should increase the advertising budget. Similarly, a decrease in efficiency should result in a decrease in budget. Since the optimal strategy is to operate at a "Breakeven", increasing impressions per dollar means more sales per dollar and hence a higher budget can be justified.

If production costs should increase without a corresponding increase in price, the marginal profit would decrease, the "Breakeven" ratio would increase, and the total advertising budget would be decreased. Similarly, if the total margin increases, total advertising would increase. Thus, the total advertising budget would become responsive to the general operations of the business, as it should be.

It is easy to see from these examples why, over short periods, advertising budgets necessarily are relatively small and subject to extreme variation from one time period to another in the case of expensive products where production and distribution costs are high and variable relative to the selling price. In such

CHART 15-1

IMPLICATIONS OF ECONOMIC INTERACTION FOR PRODUCT PLANNING AND EVALUATION

"Potential Market" is a sales limit imposed by product characteristics. This difficult-to-comprehend limit is determined by the size of the subculture to which the product has sufficient perceived value to obtain some probability of purchase. The size of this subculture is a function of the product's service mix: the particular design, production, and marketing characteristics used. The reason this subculture sales limit is difficult to establish is because it is defined in terms of a probability notion. There is no hard, clear limit. **The probability of additional purchases decreases relatively rapidly at volume levels beyond the point of maximum marginal profit.**

Lower production costs call for higher promotion expenditures. Further study of the functions in Figure 15.1 reveals that the lower the production and distribution costs are as a proportion of unit revenue, the closer will be the optimum sales level (that point at which total profit is maximized) to what would be the optimum sales level if promotion costs were the only costs. Therefore, given a fixed selling price, the lower the production and distribution costs, the closer the optimum sales level will be to the subculture sales limit, and the larger will be the gross profit. **It follows, then, that the lower the production and distribution costs, not only the larger the promotion costs *can* be, but, rather, the larger the promotion cost *should* be in order to maximize profit.**

Higher promotion efficiency reduces sales responsiveness. It can be deduced from these functions that changes in promotion *efficiency* also affect the sales point of maximum profit. Upon study of Figure 15.1 it can be seen that efficiency changes are reflected in changes in the *shape* of the promotion cost curve; the more efficient, the more concave or flat until the limit is reached. Thus, the point of maximum total profit moves toward the sales limit.

Greater promotion *efficiency* does not, however, alter the locus of the *limit:* Only a change in the perceived service mix can do that. It does reduce the rate at which the probability of an additional sale decreases despite large increments in promotion. Thus, a highly efficient promotional effort would be reflected in rapidly decreasing responsiveness of sales to promotion cost increments *at or near the optimum sales level.*

Another aspect of the promotion cost curve indicates that at any sales level between the point of maximum marginal profit and maximum total profit there is more to be lost by underspending for promotion than by overspending by the same amount. This relationship becomes increasingly true as the point of maximum total profit is approached. The magnitude of the particular case, of course, is dependent upon the profit margin.

Promotion expenditures are strongly related to changes in the subculture sales limit. Another deductive inference which follows from these functions is that attainable profits also are a function of changes in the subculture sales limit (potential market). This limit will vary in accordance with changes in product design, selling price, and the service implications of the other marketing components. These are changes in the service mix represented by the product. For a given product design it can be demonstrated that to determine the maximum profit point studies of promotional efficiency must be accompanied by studies to determine subculture sales limits, and that under normal operating conditions changes in the subculture sales limit will result in greater effects on profits than will changes in marketing efficiency. This phenomenon is difficult to observe empirically because of interaction between the subculture sales limit and marketing efficiency.

TABLE 1   Economic Interaction in a Firm for a Single Product

UNIT SALES (000)	MARGINAL COST OF MATERIALS AND PRODUCTION	MARGINAL COST OF DISTRIBUTION	MARGINAL COST OF PROMOTION	MARGINAL TOTAL COST	MARGINAL UNIT REVENUE	MARGINAL UNIT PROFIT
50	$2.080	$0.234	$0.145	$2.459	$1.000	−$1.459
100	1.090	0.164	0.115	1.369	1.000	−0.369
200	0.596	0.128	0.100	0.824	1.000	0.176
300	0.431	0.117	0.114	0.662	1.000	0.338
400	0.348	0.111	0.133	0.592	1.000	0.408
500	0.300	0.107	0.160	0.567	1.000	0.433
600	0.266	0.105	0.200	0.571	1.000	0.429
700	0.242	0.103	0.267	0.612	1.000	0.388
800	0.223	0.102	0.400	0.725	1.000	0.275
900	0.211	0.101	0.800	1.112	1.000	−0.112
1000	0.200	0.100	∞	∞	1.000	$-\infty$

cases an added dollar of advertising must produce an extremely large amount of added dollar sales to break even.[5]

The higher the marginal costs, the more efficient the advertising must be; and the higher the unit selling price, the more efficient the advertising must be—in order to justify any given total advertising budget. Thus, the less efficient the advertising, the greater the pressure on production to reduce costs, to use less costly materials and processes; and thus the more production is forced to demand fewer models and types and longer production runs before redesign—all of which increase the burden on the already inefficient advertising. Efficient advertising, on the other hand, permits production to maintain more costly ingredients and processes—affording the opportunity to maintain or increase current quality standards. Production and Marketing indeed interact with each other and with Finance.

Product Changes Alter the Potential Market and, Therefore, the Spectrum of Competing Products. Changes in the service mix represented by the product are reflected in the composition and size of the subculture to which the product appeals. Is it automatically desirable, then, to redesign the product, its marketing, or advertising in order to increase the subculture sales limit? Classic "mass production" economics would indicate in the affirmative. But we must keep in mind that we cannot change our target market without, at the same time, changing the composition and number of competitive products which provide services similar to ours.

Any increase in the competition which we face also will be reflected by a change in the efficiency of our promotion. We can see, therefore, that *the marginal promotion cost curve* in Figure 15.1 *also is a reflection of the perceived value of our product.* It depicts the inverse of the marginal value of the product to the next additional customer.

[5] This economic analysis omits consideration of the role of advertising in adding value and, thereby, supporting either a higher selling price or lower selling costs.

The Key Objective: Maximize Potential Market While Minimizing Competition.
Because an increase in the potential market frequently is accompanied by a
disproportionate increase in competition, we must *optimize* the value which our
product offers to consumers in order to maximize its profitability to us. *To
accomplish this end, we must seek constantly to maximize the potential market
size to which we appeal while at the same time minimizing the number of alternative products which are perceived by our target consumers to be in direct competition with ours.*[6] In this manner, the dynamics of our economic system
perform to avoid the value-cheapening battle of direct price (cost) competition,
which Karl Marx believed to be the unchangeable consequence of the Industrial
Revolution.

Both product design and marketing decisions—frequently between alternatives of equal cost—pose difficult problems for standard accounting practice, but
they are of towering importance to the profitability of the enterprise. A choice
between coloring the product blue or red, shaping it oval or elliptical, labeling it
with one design or another *not only can affect the attainable sales but can affect
sales costs* by moving the value mix closer to or further from competitive products.[7] *Thus, mass sales are not the direct equivalent of massive profits.*

Heavy Purchasers Are Not Necessarily the Most Profitable Customers. Additional
marketing factors bear importantly upon the relationship of sales to profit. In
the case of consumer package goods, in particular, an important part of total
sales volume comes from *repeat sales to* the same customers (the ultimate consumers). Because not all customers purchase the same amount or purchase
with the same frequency, it is axiomatic that some customers account for more
sales than do others. Customers can be classified by purchase volume. This
distribution frequently is such that the top one third of the customers for a
particular product usually accounts for two thirds or more of the total sales
volume.

But this 67 percent of sales is not necessarily the most profitable 67 percent,
for large volume purchasers frequently tend to be "price shoppers." This customer group does not tend to be the most stable of franchises—it often switches to
competitive products perhaps for reasons of satiation or boredom, or to take
advantage of a temporary price offer by another product. The promotional cost
of retaining high volume customers frequently reduces their profitability to the
enterpreneur below that of lower volume customers. But because it is difficult to
identify or control expenditures against these customers separately from all
customers, *the importance of restricting the appeal of a product can go unrecognized.*

The unit savings effected by greater production, thereby, can be offset both
by the immediate cost of incentives to high volume customers and by the high

[6] There is a substantial amount of uncertainty in such decisions, but dynamic competition can only exist in areas
of uncertainty.
[7] The recent development of non-parametric scaling and analytic techniques (such as MAPP under the auspices
of the Marketing Science Institute) has provided marketing research with a tool for estimating these effects on
the value mix.

rate of turnover of these customers. Also, such promotional efforts often disrupt regular production runs, lowering efficiency. A serious effort should be made to estimate the net effect on profit—including alternative uses of capital and production facilities—of seeking high volume customers. *Control by sales goals can easily affect profits adversely* while erroneously appearing to have the contrary effect because of fixed accounting relationships.

MARKETING OBJECTIVES AND MANAGEMENT CONTROL

In the mid-1940s business practice reflected growing awareness of the inadequacy of management control by sales volume. Control based upon the *hard data* of internal company figures gave way to the *softer*, less accurate estimates of *share of market*. Share of market data, though lacking in precision of measurement, clearly were more relevant to company success. Potential profitability, it was becoming apparent, reflected less the simple economies of production and marketing scale and more the *relative* advantage of market dominance *vs* competition.

Management control by share of market quickly became a "rule-of-thumb" symbol of enlightened management practice, advocated by the best business schools, employed by the growing legion of data-oriented marketers who sprung from the generation of post-World War II growth of consumer markets. Meanwhile, however, the very popularity of the principle began to blunt its competitive edge. New and better probabilistic estimation procedures were developed, and knowledge of market share, while becoming more precise, also became even more widely distributed between competitors sharing the same marketing research resources.

But, more important, the old market structures began to give way. Consumers no longer conformed to traditional product categories. They not only made choices of brands *within* categories but *across* categories as the categories had for so long been so conveniently defined by manufacturers. Suddenly, it seemed that the key question became: "Share of *what* market?" How a "market" is defined radically affects the determination of "share". Again, the danger lay not in accuracy of measurement but in relevance of specification.

Unless a marketer's definition of his "market" conformed to the consumers' definition, the most precise measurement of share and trend could lead to disastrously unprofitable decisions. In marketing as elsewhere, errors of relevance, i.e. of understanding of processes, produce more spectacular mistakes than the grossest errors of measurement. Rough approximations of relevant facts inevitably win over the most precise measurement of less relevant facts.

In the past few years, as a result, the profitable practitioners of marketing have sought information to enable control of operating decisions by, necessarily, even *softer* data than standard market classification share. Paralleling the evolution of science in other fields, marketing practice is moving to the employment of higher abstractions to gain higher perspective. The new edge lies in control by *parameters of profit*.

Estimating the Profit Effect of Design and Marketing Decisions. Recent marketing research developments have opened the door to new criteria for estimating the profit effects of alternative actions—prior to large-scale production and marketing commitments. One of these developments, which combines a market concentration index with a measure of brand substitutibility, enables rough estimates to be made of the effect of decisions both on market potential and on value exclusivity (change in competitive composition) along with the effect on price elasticity and profitability. Because these data are obtained through consumer survey techniques, they can be produced not only for one's own brand but for competing brands. For that matter, they permit study of the competitive situation in consumer product categories outside one's present line of business. The Hendry Corp. in the United States and The Eddington Group, Inc. outside the U. S. are leading consultant and service organizations in the application of marketing profit parameters from consumer research data.

How Should Marketing Decisions Be Made? A brief discussion of the more prominent problems affecting decision making in the marketing area will serve to illuminate the breadth of the interrelationship between marketing and production. *There is wide-spread confusion regarding who should make what decisions and on what grounds*, particularly with respect to new products.

New Products Are Important Because They Are Different.

Why is a company interested in developing new products? It is interested in new products, not because they are new, but because, being new, they are different. It is looking for different ways of performing familiar services or ways of performing different combinations of services which previously had to be performed separately. By being different or differentiated, as we have seen, the profitability of the enterprise is increased.

Around What Class of Characteristics Should New Product Ideas Originate?

In attempting to establish the point at which the decison sequence begins, we are faced with a paradox: One of the unsettling but inescapable facts of new product development is that, because of the interaction of design features, there is no logical starting point to the merry-go-round of design criteria. It is no more logical to begin with some physcial components than with some marketing idea or with consumer needs. Any effort to legislate an arbitrary precedence for the responsibility in new product development will seriously restrict the new product output.

The board of directors or the executive committee can (and should) define the boundaries of the business enterprise beyond which the new product development activity should not stray in order to focus attention where special management, technological or equipment resources can best be exploited. But this is the process of *exclusion. Creative* acts are performed by individuals. Yet, an individual is most likely to approach the initial development of new product ideas with the particular bias or set of his organizational unit. For this reason an effort to establish a fixed starting point within the organization, such as the Research and Development Laboratory for new product idea development and initial screening, inevitably will act to restrict the number of viable new product developments. It would seem logical, then, that there should be no invariable organizational starting point.

Decision Criteria.

From a marketing standpoint we find it helpful to redefine the traditional design criterion: "Form follows function." We have three criteria which we label *motivating power*, *differentiation*, and *consonance*.

1. By motivating power is meant the *size* of the subculture to which our product's service mix appeals and the *intensity* of that appeal.[8]
2. The differentiation criterion is concerned with the degree to which the service mix of design components being contemplated must share its market potential with similar, competitive products.
3. The consonance criterion reflects the extent to which all the physical and marketing design components support and interact with each other in order to convincingly convey the values which were contemplated for the product by the entrepreneur.

Consonance is particularly important because it spells the difference between a coherent, meaningful creation and a product which is an amalgam of unrelated components. Such amalgams are the familiar consequences of compromise decisions reached by committees. They also occur in cases where the responsibility shifts from division to division: as the package is added to the product, and the marketing is added to the package, and the advertising is added to the marketing. Consonance is the compatibility of the values which are imputed to the total product by the separate production and marketing characteristics. It is a measure, then, of the total output—the synthesis—rather than of the individual production activities taken individually out of the context of the whole.

Estimating the Market Potential.

The sales volume of a related product class frequently is utilized as an estimating source for prediction of the new product production needs. This is a most crude method and, in fact, really is irrelevant as it denies the very reason for our interest in new products—which is to create a *new* product class. The amount and timing of production needs is a function, among other things, of all three decision criteria, above.

A measure of *motivating power* supplies an estimate of the distribution and intensity of wants related to our contemplated product values. This implied potential market would then be restricted by the amount of *differentiation*—the degree to which our product's contemplated values are offered by competing products. A measure of *consonance* would supply us with an estimate of the degree to which our new product, taken as a whole, would be perceived as supplying those values which we have contemplated for it. The creditability with which the new product's attributes convey these values obviously further restricts the achievable market potential originally visualized. *It is apparent that the accuracy of potential market estimates is highly dependent upon the ability to anticipate the interaction of all the product design characteristics.*

[8] *Intensity* would be reflected in price elasticity and rate of consumption.

It would seem, then, that it is impossible to estimate the market potential until the entire risk and expense of development has been incurred. Because such a point of view would entail unreasonable financial risk, it is necessary to make crude volume and profit estimates prior to product development. It is important to realize, however, that *these estimates should be revised at each successive stage of development*. Comparative estimates of any two new product ideas which are at different stages of development should not be made, of course, without full account being taken of the fact that one estimate is necessarily more accurate than the other. The later the stage of development, the better the estimate. Because of the creative nature of new product development[9] it is an inescapable concomitant that errors of optimism will eventually be discovered by poor market performance, but that errors of pessimism will remain unknowable lost opportunities. Though it never appears on accounting ledgers, a heavy price is paid for lost opportunities.

It is for this reason that a *company with a very high* proportion *of successful new product developments is not realizing as much return on investment as another company which deliberately sets a lower risk criterion* and allows more product ideas to survive the screening process.

Actually there is no single screening process. Alternatives exist at each stage of the development process from early concept development through R & D and planning of the product, package, label, name, pricing, promotion and advertising, to pilot production and eventual full production, distribution and sales. At each step there is a screen—formal or informal—and the number of alternatives allowed to pass through each screen should be a function of the relative costs of carrying alternatives a step further, a step closer to realistic market appraisal of the interactions, the synergy of the different components of the product-to-be.

It is inescapable that the more alternative versions of a single product idea (as well as the more different product ideas) which can be brought to later stages of development, the more successful new products there will be. How many a company can afford to bring how far is a function of the cost of each stage. If the early stages are the most expensive, then very few will be brought very far; if the later stages are the most expensive, then more of them will be brought further.

The key to efficient management of new product (or brand) development programs swivels around the identification of the types and amounts of company resources expended or committed at each identifiable decision point in the development process. Other important elements include the length of time between decision points, the amount of new information about the product ideas which is developed by each decision point, and the degree to which this added information improves the ability to forecast financial outcomes.

It will help materially to speed products through the development pipeline merely to identify key decision points in the development stream. These are such points as the commitment of an R & D team, the assignment of a full marketing team to produce a marketing plan, product and package design, copy and label development, pilot plant, a decision to go to test market, etc.—

---

[9] Strictly imitative developments are excluded from this observation.

whenever new resources (financial, material, or human) are to be committed.

The purpose of all this is to insure that at each one of these decision points a new sales and profit forecast is made utilizing all the information made available since the last decision point. This *principle of successive forecasting* is critical to the optimum allocation of company resources among alternative new product ventures. In this way it is less likely that a product venture will either move along merely because it got started first or that a higher potential idea will languish for lack of available resources.

And—no small gain—it will force marketing research to translate its arcane measures into their meaning in terms of sales or profit implications. Marketing research should participate with each operating department to help get successive forecasts produced, to insist that they do get produced at each and every commitment point.

A new product development decision system for a single company would include periodic situation reports which contain information such as the number of new product ideas currently at each decision point, the current profit (ROI, cash flow, etc.) forecast for each one, the estimated error surrounding each forecast, the drain on resources by type of resource at each decision point, available resources, estimated elapsed time for each stage (Figure 15.2).

FIGURE 15-2

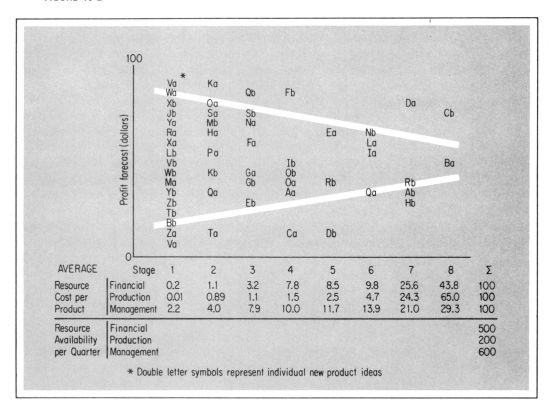

AVERAGE	Stage	1	2	3	4	5	6	7	8	Σ
Resource	Financial	0.2	1.1	3.2	7.8	8.5	9.8	25.6	43.8	100
Cost per	Production	0.01	0.89	1.1	1.5	2.5	4.7	24.3	65.0	100
Product	Management	2.2	4.0	7.9	10.0	11.7	13.9	21.0	29.3	100
Resource	Financial									500
Availability	Production									200
per Quarter	Management									600

* Double letter symbols represent individual new product ideas

The system illustrated is designed on the premise that there are more new product ideas at various stages of development than the company's resources can handle. The objective is to pick the ones with the greatest likelihood of future success, within policy constraints and resource limitations, and to advance them a stage—thus committing additional resources and moving closer to market.

Here we see a situation where a variety of new products (indicated by the double letter codes) is scattered across eight stages of development. As in this example the greatest number usually is at Stage 1, the written idea in the file. Gradually, through product and marketing development to Stage 8, national marketing, there is an attrition of new products as some fall by the wayside.

The system is designed around the principle of successive forecasting. That is, as a product idea completes each stage of development, a new sales, cash flow and ROI forecast is made. As a product proceeds through development stages, frequently it changes its character in some degree, it assumes a more visualizable form, and added consumer response information is acquired.

Based on these developments, a new forecast will be made which can be used to help determine which products should be pushed ahead in the next period.

Built into the decision system, moreover, is a provision to take into account the fact that forecasts in the earlier stages have greater error ranges than those in the later stages. This provision, symbolized in the chart by the converging lines, makes a probabilistic decision system part of the model. This financial probability *plus* a similar probabilistic notion regarding the estimated time required in each devlopment stage means that the system could be run as a computerized simulation model, providing management with an array of possible outcomes, each with a particular probability. This is just the way the real world works . . . nothing is ever certain. It will rain on some of the days with a forecasted 90 percent probability of fair weather.

The company has finite resources, and the demand on those resources—financial, research and development, pilot plant, production, management time—varies by stage. A new product at Stage 2, typically, will consume a great deal of the research and development resource and no production or marketing effort. By Stage 5 marketing resources are beginning to be consumed in increasingly significant amounts.

It is easy to see that if the flow of new products should move erratically, the company will face, alternately, a bottleneck situation and an underutilization of certain resources. A study of the rate of flow will enable the company to consider the alternative either of re-allocating the distribution of resources or else of adjusting the mesh of the screening system to alter the rate of new product flow.

This decision system can take into account a variety of policy constraints such as the mix of long and short-term development products, different classes of products, different risk levels, etc. The cost of stalling a product at an intermediate stage after some investment has been put in it can be considered. And, in addition to deciding among alternative products for advancement and investment, the system would provide forecasts of return on investment and cash flow for alternative policy decisions including the provision of additional capital and other resources.

Such a system is an aid to corporate planning, reaching far out from the narrow concerns of individual new products. But it must be remembered that all such systems concern only matters of efficiency—not effectiveness, not creativity, not vision. Successul new product development requires tolerance of and encouragement of risk enterprise. By their nature, committees and controllers can maintain but cannot give birth to an enterprise.

Division of Responsibility for Development Decisions.

We have advocated a dispersion of responsibility for new product idea development among all the divisions concerned and the avoidance of any fixed organizational starting point. But how should responsibility be allocated for the development of the specific product characteristics once the idea has been accepted for development? At the outset, we have very little to go on but *faith in the leader* whose idea it is. But further development requires additional resources and talent. The problem calls for an organizational principle which may be termed the "one starts, others follow" concept.

The responsibility for starting should deliberately be allocated to each functional division for some proportion of the new products. Under this conception the role of each division will *differ* from occasion to occasion, *depending* upon whether it is starting or following in the particular instance. A hypothetical example may serve to illustrate this point:

1. Let us say a laboratory scientist makes a basic research discovery: A device which can be incorporated into the body of a cigarette and which traps certain components of smoke, tars, and nicotine, while permitting the balance of the smoke to pass through. Once this happens, then the organizational units responsible for the measurement of human wants and of marketing should be directed to suggest ways in which this technological innovation could be developed profitably.[10] Perhaps this was the way the opportunity for filter cigarettes was identified.

2. Or, we can assume that it did not happen that way but that, rather, a marketing man initially conceived the possibility that a market could be created for a cigarette which differed from others in that the tars had been removed—on the theory that some people prefer smoke without tars. In this case, it becomes the task of the technologist, not to make a basic research discovery, but to perform commercial research to implement this specification: "Removal of tars from cigarette smoke." The consumer research activity is directed to establish how many and what kinds of people would be attracted to such a product and for what reasons.

3. Or, conceivably, the individuals responsible for consumer research may have initiated the idea. They may have recognized that light smokers tend to be people who emulate the class of people who are unusually concerned with cleanliness and healthfulness. In this instance, the marketing man is set to work on the specific problem: "Through what type of service might we satisfy these consumer wants?" He then may conceive the idea that the tars in cigarettes, if removed, would provide a basis for a cleaner, more

---

[10] For the purposes of this illustration, we should mentally place ourselves back in time before cigarette filters were developed and before the relationship between tars and lung cancer was common knowledge.

healthful brand which could be advertised in high prestige magazines and sold at a premium price. The technologist, in turn, is directed to try to find a way to remove tars from cigarette smoke, and he develops the cigarette filter.

The point of this hypothetical example is not just that the idea might have come from any one of these three organizational units, but that the *duties* of each organizational unit in the development process *differ* according to whether or not it initiated the idea. Thus, if the idea originates in marketing terms, the technological and consumer reserch units must direct their *efforts to implementing* that idea as closely as possible. Similarly, a marketing man performs different tasks if the idea originates in technological rather than in consumer research terms. His task, in that case, becomes one of following rather than leading.

The practical lesson here is that the role of leader should fall to the unit in whose terms the idea originally was expressed. The other units should be *obliged* to follow and to implement, making use of the design criteria: motivating power, differentiation, and especially, consonance. It is the demands of this third criterion which necessitate that the organizational units play "follow the leader" because *there must be some central product idea with which the rest of the design evolution shall be in harmony*.

The idea which led to filter cigarettes might easily have died aborning because each organizational unit is seldom obligated by ironclad administrative policy to work at implementing ideas initiated by other units. *Each unit should be formally required to devote some substantial portion of its facilities, time, and energy to the implementation of ideas specified by the other units, whether they think they are good ideas or not.*

Voluntary coordination is desirable, of course. But, as a practical matter, action cannot await committee unanimity or the certainty the future might bring. As in the military, there is a point beyond which further debate cannot be tolerated; the question no longer is, "Should we invade Normandy?" but "How can you best help make it a success?" In the case of established brands, events in the marketplace eventually force action upon even the most reluctant organizations. But in the contemplation of a new product, the process of reconsideration can go on forever, with the only cost being the invisible one of lost opportunities.

Packaging. This decision area deserves special mention because it most clearly bridges the traditional realms of production and marketing. Packages are used to perform "functional" services such as storage, protection, and dispensing. Also, through shape, texture, and the label symbols (which, as is frequently the case in cosmetics, may be physically indistinguishable from the body of the package), the package characterizes the product and communicates information *about* the contents. A package is a complex part of the product; *it should be evaluated both in functional and characterizational terms.*

Inventory and Distribution Lines. The production facility is protected from the shocks of fluctuating consumer sales by the buffering effect of inventories and distribution lines. This is not, of course, without cost to the manufacturer.

The carrying cost of low volume items often is instrumental in decisions to reduce the breadth of the product line. Some relationship such as "10 to 20 percent of the product line accounts for 60 to 80 percent of the sales, so the balance of the product line is a burden on profits" is cited in support of a recommendation to a manufacturer to drop low volume items. The sales force typically resists such recommendations on the grounds that many of these items are necessary to the total line appeal. When the consumer perceives value dependencies between the number and types of items in the line, the sensible course of action must be to maintain that product mix which maximizes the total profit to the enterprise. Thus, low volume items, despite unfavorable accounting reflection, might more profitably be kept in the line.

The further from the factory (that is, from the wholesaler to the retailer to the consumer), the longer the order lead-time. The longer and the more unpredictable the lead-time, the greater the feedback effect. Thus, the longer the distribution pipeline, the greater the likelihood of fluctuations which sometimes are erroneously interpreted as "seasonal effects" intrinsic to the marketplace.

Such misinterpretations frequently result in the reinforcenemt of marketing and production decisions calculated to "take advantage" of important buying periods. Such decisions reduce the efficiency of the production operation by enhancing uneven production flow. And because they frequently are accompanied by incentive price promotions to encourage distributors to take on larger quantities of stock, such practices reduce the average profit margin realized on the goods even more by reducing the unit return.

The ability of distribution lines to disguise the consumer sales pattern can be especially important during the introduction of a new product. Because of initial production limitations and a disinclination to take massive risks unnecessarily, the distribution of new products frequently begins in a relatively small geographic area and gradually fans out across the rest of the market. As a result, distribution pipelines are filled over a protracted period. The fanning-out process usually is designed to smooth the demands on the production facilities.

Although the smoothing process helps production efficiency, it can do great harm to the total management of the product by obscuring retail sales conditions. Severe sales fluctuations and out-of-stock conditions may exist in individual retail outlets, but the overlapping of these separate cycles will depict a smooth progression of the product introduction at the factory sales level. Package goods are dependent upon high repeat sales levels for their success. During the early months of a new product's life, however, the bulk of its sales is to first-time triers. The fanning-out process protracts this period, and an enthusiastic initial response may hide a very poor repeat sales prognosis until after national distribution has been obtained.

Because the ultimate consumers of package goods do not place orders and specifications directly with the manufacturer, because the consumer's order lead times are extremely short, and because there usually are reasonably acceptable alternatives to the preferred product available in the retail outlet—the interaction between distribution and sales is two-directional. "Expected" sales produce retail distribution and inventories, and retail distribution and inventories produce "unexpected" sales.

The interaction effect of inventories and sales is particularly sharp when the inventories are clearly visible to shoppers. Retailers long have noticed that displays of large quantities of a product, such as in bins or piles on counters or floors, will increase the rate of sales of that product. Manufacturers vie for advantage in number of shelf facings, number of packages abreast visible on the shelf, because of the very clear effect on sales. Retailers strive to develop optimum strategies for allocation of available shelf frontage between product categories and between brands to maximize the total dollar sales per foot of shelf space.

These relationships have been much studied by many types of retailers from department stores to drug stores to supermarkets. Because of the ever-changing array of products, types, sizes, brands and prices, optimal solutions are difficult to develop and are of transient accuracy. Also, the relationships are not rectilinear. The relationship of shelf-space allocation to resultant sales effect for a single supermarket brand is illustrated in Figure 15.3. A very small amount of space is underproductive and, eventually, a point is reached where the marginal return from additional space also is underproductive.

Only 17 percent of the 200,000 grocery stores in the United States do an individual sales volume of over $500,000 annually. These stores, however, *average* over $1,000,000 annual sales and do more business, in total, than two-thirds of all stores, which are classified as "small stores" and which gross under $150,000 sales in a year. This enormous disparity in store size accounts for many of the inequities of product availability and pricing throughout the distribution system. The availability of numerous alternative brands, types and sizes, as well as price and promotion competition is heavily concentrated in the larger stores which, in turn, are concentrated in and around metropolitan areas.

FIGURE 15-3

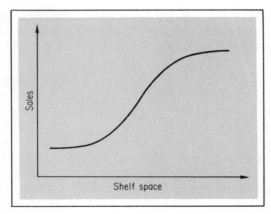

The cost of gaining distribution in the 150,000 small stores usually is so high relative to the potential sales that manufacturers' sales forces do not call on them. These stores place their orders with wholesalers and brokers, and the manufacturers reach them largely through communications media, much as they reach the ultimate consumer. As a result, new products gain distribution more slowly in these stores, and old products lose distribution more slowly. Without advertising, the cost of gaining distribution in these stores would be even higher, penalizing their customers even more.

For grocery store distributed brands there is a general relationship between breadth of distribution (i.e. number of stores carrying the brand, expressed as the percent of total grocery store sales volume in all commodities represented by those stores) and sales per point of distribution. The greater the sales per point of distribution, the greater the breadth of distribution the brand will achieve (Figure 15.4).

FIGURE 15-4

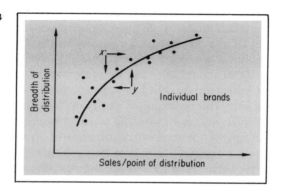

Although the curve in Figure 15.4 is a fitted curve with few brands falling exactly on it, the interesting characteristic is that *over time* the individual brands will tend to regress to the line either by changes in distribution *or* by changes in *rate* of sales. Brand X in Figure 15.4 has more distribution than is warranted by its sales rate. It may be an old, dying brand which is still hanging on in the small stores. If it doesn't regain its old sales rate, it will begin to lose distribution. Brand Y is outperforming its distribution. If the sales rate continues, its breadth of distribution inevitably will grow.

Because sales produce distribution, *and* distribution produces sales, a distribution change in either direction will *accelerate* whatever change has been occurring in total sales of the brand. The only way a brand can continue to maintain distribution above the regression line is by payment of a subsidy to the retailer for the use of his valuable shelf space. Because package goods net-profit margins are subject to the constant attrition of competition it is seldom possible for a brand to maintain distribution by subsidy for long unless it is a highly differentiated product—virtually a product class unto itself—with a consequently strong consumer franchise.

Pricing. It is a familiar notion that the art of pricing a product should reflect cost, quality of the product, delivery, availability, distribution, and value as perceived by both distributors and consumers. It should be kept in mind, however, that price plays an important characterizational role.

Customers perceive the value of products partly in terms of their price. There have been a number of instances of products which were suffering stagnant sales and which later sold at a brisk rate because the retailer raised the price. The earlier, lower price apparently served to destroy the credibility of the other values in the product. This phenomenon occurs most often among nonbranded, department store items where consumers have little besides retailer opinion on which to base their judgments of value.

Pricing strategy is the subject of careful analysis and a poker player's judgment in many industrial product and service lines. The same is true in department store soft goods, where experimental pricing frequently is practiced to test for the optimum level. Perhaps the aggressive use of pricing as a flexible marketing tool is easier where products are highly individualized.

In package goods, where product uniformity *within a brand* is a characteristic feature, pricing seldom is regarded as a strategic implement. Manufacturers' selling prices reflect great uniformity *within product classes*—seldom varying by more than 25 percent from each other on a unit basis. Yet, we have seen how greatly the optimum advertising budget is affected over the short term by the relation between the unit marginal cost and the average selling price.

The reference to *average* selling price is to distinguish from brief pricing changes as in "price promotions." Special price offers and disguised price incentives such as coupons and premiums, either directly to consumers or indirectly via incentives to the trade channels to gain distribution and stocking of inventories, illustrate the fine line of distinction between pricing and sales promotion.

The mechanics and economics of temporary price incentives differ greatly from average pricing strategy in that the basis for the promotional purchase by the consumer is necessarily different from the basis for any future purchases at the average or full price. Consequently, customers acquired by temporary incentives are less likely prospects for future sales than customers acquired at full price sales. Promotional pricing, therefore, is a short-term tool of limited value for frequent use unless the promotional price leaves a satisfactory profit margin.

Unlike other marketing tools promotional pricing, disguised or not, intrinsically exploits and detracts from the perceived value which painstakingly has been invested in the product under average pricing conditions by all the other product attributes.

The other marketing elements, principally the advertising, then must work harder at repairing the damage to the perceived value of the product, to the satisfaction it will afford in the future not only to those consumers who bought at the promotional price but to those consumers who were aware of it.

Advertising/Promotion. Advertising is a term which covers some similar appearing mechanics (communication) but which disguises an enormous variety of objectives and marketing/economic processes. The corporate advertisements in business magazines may be directed at influencing the investment support of the financial community or at potential stockholders so that management stock options will increase in value. The sponsorship of socially enlightening television programs may be justified in the hopes of fending off adverse legislative action. The manufacturer's magazine advertising for a particular product may largely be directed at enhancing the perceived value of the product while its radio advertising for the same product may principally be for the purpose of reminding and stimulating a decision to purchase on the weekend shopping trip. The retailer's advertisement for that same product in the Thursday night edition of the local newspaper may be to invite price comparison with other stores.

Some advertising is to offer things for sale while other advertising is by prospective purchasers looking for something to buy: a man looking for a used car, a summer house to rent, an employee to hire. Some advertising is merely to announce the availability and whereabouts of something someone is presumed already to desire, while other advertising seeks to focus a desire—suggesting a particular source of satisfaction.

Some advertising is employed as an alternative to sales promotion to perform the same function, other advertising is employed in conjunction with sales promotion to serve complementary ends: one to invest the product with value, the other to exploit that investment and trigger a purchase.

Some things people buy relatively seldom, such as automobiles and refrigerators. For these products the advertising investment in acquiring a new customer must come close to being returned on the price economics of a single sale. Other things people buy quite often, such as toothpaste and dessert topping. For these products the advertising investment in acquiring a new customer can exceed the value of a single sale and can be justified only if the probability of future sales to that customer then becomes greater than the brand's percentage share of market.

This distinction in large measure accounts for why some products display low advertising : sales ratios and others high ratios.

As a result, some product-selling advertising must produce sales near-term at today's prices to be economically justified, whereas other advertising finds economic justification in its ability to invest a product with added value and, thereby, to protect it in the future from value cheapening price competition. The criteria by which advertising and advertising budgets can properly be evaluated will vary by the mixture of purposes for which it is used. So will its interaction with production vary accordingly. There is no single thing called advertising.

The manufacturer with several low priced, high margin, frequently purchased products, then, can generate very large advertising and sales promotion budgets. The manufacturer with a number of higher priced or low margin or infrequently purchased products cannot generate marketing budgets nearly so large.

There are benefits which accrue to being able to promote individual products under individual identities to produce consumer franchises with high-repeat purchase rate characteristics However, it takes large advertising budgets to accomplish this highly profitable condition. The manufacturer whose products can support only low promotion to sales ratios has two choices—he can use sales promotion alone, or use advertising as a form of sales promotion, seeking only near-term payout; or he must group together a number of his products under a common promotional identity as a means of accumulating a larger promotional fund—at the possible expense of diluting the identity, the message and the consumer franchise if consonance is not achieved.

Choosing the Promotional Identity. For example, one of the earliest advertising promotion decisions which must be made is the identity or identities which will be treated as an entity.

Should a product be known to consumers by the corporate name, a divisional name, or by an individual brand name? Following is a typical case in point.

> The ABC Bolt Corporation, reasonably well-known to the trade and to consumers, has acquired a smaller company, the Alpha Corporation, which is a successful consumer goods business. ABC Bolt has under development a number of new products. Some of them are related to its present line, some are not.
>
> With an eye to maximizing promotional coverage and intensity through mutual support, the question arises as to whether all ABC Bolt products should be promoted under a single umbrella. Perhaps it would be advantageous to promote all lines as "another fine product of the ABC Bolt Corporation." Such a course would lend greater meaning to the ABC name which, in turn, would provide a launching platform for proposed new products.
>
> Another possibility would be to change the name of the ABC Bolt Corporation to a name more amenable to association with consumer goods, e.g. by dropping the word "Bolt." Similarly, the name of its subsidiary, the Alpha Corporation, could be adopted as the umbrella name.
>
> This latter option would be taking advantage of a name with highly developed consumer goods associations. However, it is anticipated that some of the new products might not be appropriate for association with the rest of the Alpha line. Many successful consumer products, for that matter, are promoted solely under individual brand names without reference to the parent company, and this would be another alternative.

What is the logical business rationale that could be applied to this dilemma? How much help is an umbrella?

How important to marketing success is it to limit associations to psychologically appropriate products?

When is single brand marketing best?

Study of marketing practices in a number of industries reveals a complete range of practices, all the way from the sole use of the corporate umbrella to the use of several divisional umbrellas within a company, to the promotion of individual product brands. Some companies employ all three approaches, depending upon the product and its market (see Table 2). Study also reveals that the choices made by these companies have been neither random nor whimsical.

A look at current business practices suggests that there is a strong underlying decision pattern:

> The lower the dollar ratio of advertising to sales in an industry (A/S ratio) the more likely that the corporate umbrella will be used by a company; the higher the A/S ratio, the more the brands are promoted singly. The use of divisional umbrellas is the middle course for the middle A/S ratios.

This relationship of promotional identity to A/S ratio is a very significant and revealing correlation. It is not, itself, an explanatory reason, but it is a symptom, a reflection of some important realities of marketing economics.

As we have seen, a key source of profitability in business is to offer a product or service which is differentiated—for which no equally satisfactory alternative is available. By so doing, the producer does not need to engage in as heavy promotion—merchandising, price competition—in order to retain his consumer franchise. This lower promotional support means greater unit profit.

In some cases this differentiation is maintained by control of basic patents, raw materials or distribution lines. In other cases the high capital investment required discourages the entry of competitors. But in most consumer goods lines, *it is the job of marketing and advertising to maintain a differentiation in the minds of consumers* so that they do not consider other brands to be equal alternatives. Greater need for points of differentiation brings with it the need for increasingly specific promotional identity—unique identity, which is not interchangeable with other products.

TABLE 2 Types of Promotional Identities

	PRODUCTS		
CORPORATE PARENT	CORPORATE	DIVISIONAL	BRAND
American Home Products	Industrial Products	American Home Foods, Chef Boy-ar-dee, Whitehall Laboratories	Plastic Wood, 3-in-1 Oil Anacin
General Electric	All Products		
General Foods	Industrial Products	Jell-O Products	Tang
General Mills	Bakery Products	Betty Crocker	Wheaties
General Motors	Trucks	Chevrolet Buick	Nova Le Sabre
Johnson & Johnson	Surgical Products	J & J Personal Products	Micrin
Lever Brothers	Industrial Products	Glamorene	Wisk, "all," Lifebuoy, Pepsodent
Procter & Gamble	Industrial Products	Duncan Hines	Tide, Cheer, Camay, Safeguard

In some industries the points of differentiation exist on obvious technological levels. Purchases are made by trained purchasing agents who buy on detailed specifications. In consumer goods there are products which, due to the great expense or other risk involved, are subjected to much more careful scrutiny by consumers than are other products. In all these instances the purchaser will take the time necessary to study the differences between products through careful examination. *Where high risk to the purchaser is involved and quality cannot be entirely ascertained, broad acquaintance with the sponsoring company is a source of assurance.*

Other products and services for which purchase is commonplace; consumer risk low; and points of differentiation are submerged, subtle, or complex; find themselves in the midst of aggressive, competitive, marketing practices and high A/S ratios. Unless, through distinctive marketing and advertising action, these products can create keen consumer awareness of their differentiated identities, their profit margins will be dissipated in merchandising and price competition.

The job of the promotional identity, and the key job of advertising, is to strengthen and stabilize the consumer franchise by creating a sharp and meaningful differentiation. By so doing, the risk to the consumer is reduced and, thereby, the needed amount of total promotional expense is reduced. By this means profitability is increased.

Some products, however, do not generate sufficient sales volume to support widespread promotion of their identities. And in this event, they must share a promotional identity with other products. The objective here is to tie together as many products as is necessary to generate sufficient promotional support, while *being careful not to dissipate the specific identity to such an extent that the profit-protective differentiation is severely reduced.*

It is in an effort to maximize both these contradictory objectives that divisional groupings are utilized, banding together products with common characteristics, e.g , dessert items, proprietary pharmaceuticals, fashion items, or even more sharply characterized groups such as high fashion, sportswear fashion, youthful fashion, etc. Grouping *across* traditional product lines—pulling together items which are complementary rather than supplementary and which can be combined to express a particular life-style, the *boutique* notion—is a rapidly growing means of creating new competitive dimensions and of rapid associative characterization of the individual brands. Such opportunities to restructure familiar markets increasingly will be used as lowcost means of entry for smaller brands.

Also, the *boutique* approach admits of much greater variety and more frequent product change without added consumer confusion. Proliferation without kaleidoscopic confusion is possible in this way because the variety is given larger perceptual frames. The larger frames, which bound the particular *boutique* themes, rather than the several separate products, are able to organize and structure more variety. Consumers will "join" that *boutique* grouping which best *fits* his or her life-style of the time. *Boutique* groupings will prove increasingly useful to advertisers whose markets, in functional attribute terms, have become too fractioned by multiple competitive brand entries to be profitable.

It is in the interests of a multi-product company to assay its present and prospective lines of products with respect to a number of decision criteria which bear on the promotional identity problem. The characteristics of these products in conjunction with the available identities (corporate name, divisional names, brand names) will provide a basis for determining the most potentially profitable course.

Conceivably, the situation may be resolved by grouping some products together under a corporate umbrella, others into one or more divisional groups, and others marketed individually. Once this decision is reached, it is then possible to investigate the desirability of refashioning or changing the corporate identity to best support the particular products under its umbrella.

Table 3 lists a number of criteria which will aid the basic decision. These criteria apply to considerations of *consumer* marketing success. Different solutions are frequently desirable for maximizing the company's success with industrial customers, suppliers, distributors and the financial community. For these groups the corporate identity frequently is of great importance. Fortunately, it is both possible and convenient to apply separate promotional solutions to these separate target groups.

Holding and Switching Strategies. Because packaged goods represent the largest users of advertising and because the economics of their use of this business tool is the most difficult to comprehend, let us put ourselves in the place of the advertiser of a typical grocery or drug store distributed brand. Unlike the case for most industrial products or even of consumer hard goods, our advertising to sales dollar ratio is so high that by the time a prospect switches and makes a purchase of our brand she has absorbed very many exposures of our advertising. The accumulated cost to us of gaining those exposures is so great that we have a substantial net loss on that new customer. Usually, we have invested many times the full selling price in gaining a new customer.

In order for us to make a profit on that new customer our loss has to be amortized across future full-price sales to that person before we can begin to creep out of the red. The proportion of her future product purchases that is

TABLE 3   Type of Promotional Identity

PRODUCT DECISION CRITERIA	CORPORATE◄——►DIVISIONAL◄——►BRAND		
A/S Ratio	Low		High
Market Volatility (consumer switching)	High		Low
Price elasticity	High		Low
Risk to Consumer	High	◄————————————►	Low
Purchase Cycle	Long		Short
Sales Volume	Low		High
Source of Differentiation	Patent—) Technical) Visible)		(Marketing (Advertising

devoted to our brand determines how long it will be, if ever, when we get our investment back.

Meanwhile, competitive inducements abound, and if we lose her again, even for a while, she is absorbing even more of our advertising money before we get her back—and our investment in her has become even greater, stretching out the payout period even more.

That is the way a sales force accounts the value of making missionary calls on customer prospects. We don't account advertising that way because we cannot identify the individuals who received the advertising. But that is the only way we can accurately account advertising costs.

A brand with a 10 percent share averages only one sale for every ten purchases made in the product class by the average customer. It must be that we believe that, once converted, a new customer will, indeed, give us much more than 10 percent of her future purchases. Otherwise, it cannot pay to advertise.

Getting new triers, in fact, would appear not to be much of a problem for most brands. In the most typical situation there is a constant and high rotation of customers in and out of the brand franchise. A brand in a monthly purchase category with a share of 10 percent of households in a purchase period will have been tried by about 25 percent of all households over the course of a year—or 250 percent of its share of market. More than enough to become enormously successful—if only so many weren't leaving.

So, how do we do with the new triers? Who is doing the leaving?

Studies of purchase behavior in numerous established product classes indicate the situation looks pretty much like this (Figure 15-5): Start with the people buying the average brand in any given purchase period. Those customers

FIGURE 15-5

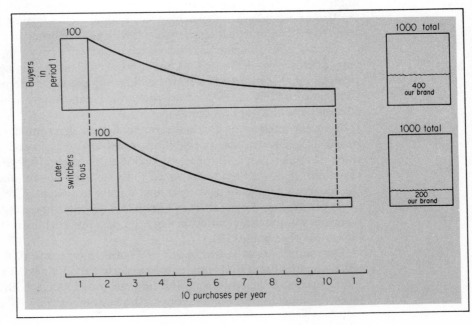

give that brand over 40 percent of their product class business over their next ten purchases. Thus, to every one hundred customers in period one we sell four hundred units over the next ten periods.

Of people not buying that brand in the given month, some later are switched and buy that brand. These new triers then give only about 20 percent of their product class business to that brand over their next ten purchases. Thus, to every one hundred new customers we sell only two hundred units over their next ten periods.

Thus, a new trier is worth only half as much as a current customer. It not only costs a lot in accumulated advertising absorption to switch them, but then new triers are not held as well.

The trick of profitability in packaged goods marketing is to stem the outflow. That is a major and, for most brands, the principal job of national advertising— to conserve the energy which has been expended in getting a customer to switch to our brand. In fact, it is only by acknowledging this role of national advertising that it is possible to reconcile the financial accounting of packaged goods advertising with the observable fact that advertised brands do make profits.

It should be acknowledged that the task of stemming the outflow does not accrue to advertising, alone. Perhaps first and foremost it is the job of product and package design. Maintenance of distribution by size and type, shelf frontage and display are critical to holding customers. But these functions have been well understood. That is why marketers have become more concerned with the intensity and internal consistency of appeal than with breadth of over-all appeal in product testing research.

Product and package design decision alternatives don't come up as frequently as advertising-copy decisions. And the distribution and display decision is automatic (it is just a problem of performance). As a result, the question of the strategic emphasis on switching vs. holding tactics is most frequently there to be faced as a practical concern of advertising management.

Assuming for the moment that we have a way of comparing two advertising copy alternatives—learning that one is more efficient at gaining new triers and that the other is more efficient at holding our present customers—which one should we run? What is the most profitable balance of switching and holding efficiency? Will it vary by brand?

A recent analysis of this issue began with a description of the switching matrix of gain and loss probabilities necessary for a brand to maintain its share of market from one purchase period to the next. This general expression of stabilization was then transformed to economic terms in order to investigate the economic implications of spending dollars to switch *vs.* to hold.

As pictured on the pie chart in Figure 15.6, for most brands (A) the consumer world in any purchase period is made up of a few customers and many more buyers of other brands (B).

The switching matrix on the left of Figure 15.6 depicts all the possible purchase combinations from one purchase period to the next. In the upper left quadrant are all the customers who buy our brand (A) in both periods. In the lower right quadrant are all the people who buy other brands (B) in both periods.

FIGURE 15-6

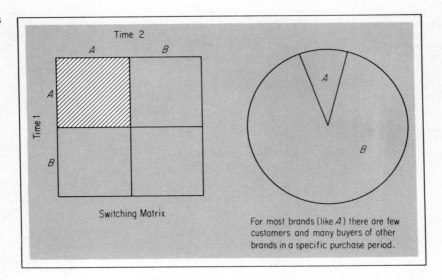

Time 2

Switching Matrix

For most brands (like *A*) there are few customers and many buyers of other brands in a specific purchase period.

The remaining two quadrants contain the people who switched from one period to the next—either from A to B (upper right) or from B to A (lower left).

Our concern, as Brand A advertisers, is to increase (or at least to stabilize) the number of people in the two left-hand quadrants—i.e. to try to get most period #1 A buyers to buy A again (holding) and to try to switch as many period #1 B buyers as possible to A in period #2 (switching).

In pursuing the analysis further it turns out that, for a given brand at a given time, there is a single proportion of the marketing/advertising dollar which should be spent on holding *vs.* switching to obtain optimal brand share. This optimum proportion, however, will be a function of the total marketing/advertising dollar expenditure as well as of the relative efficiency the brand enjoys in holding and in switching customers.

Figure 15.7 depicts the equilibrium results for various brand shares and different proportions of holding *vs.* switching expenditures. Each curve corresponds to a fixed total budget. This chart depicts a situation in which the holding and switching parameters reflect equal holding and switching efficiency. The implication is that a dollar spent to get a Period #1 Brand A buyer to buy A in Period #2 is no more likely to produce the desired result than if the dollar were spent, instead, trying to get a Period #1 Brand B buyer to switch to A in Period #2. The same implication applies to the use of the dollar to reduce the purchase price of Brand A. This case, then, is the equivalent of pure price competition. Fortunately, it is seldom faced outside the pages of economic texts or else we would see confirmation of Marx's characterization of price competition: that it would lead to the degradation of product quality.[11]

Under the hypothetical conditions shown in Figure 15.7 it can be seen that for brands with about 30% market shares or less, the entire marketing dollar

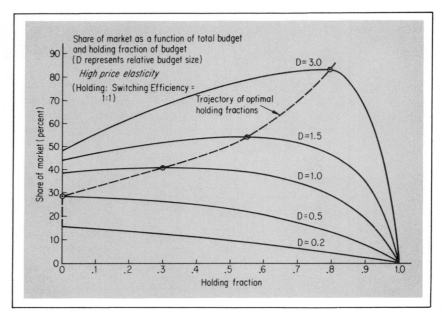

FIGURE 15-7
Equilibrium market
shares curves (equal
holding and switch-
ing efficiency).

should be spent on new customer acquisition to optimize the use of marketing budget expenditure. The added implication is that any other holding: switching strategy for such brands will result in a lower market share equilibrium point. Above the 30% share point, however, it can be seen from the dashed trajectory of optimum points that higher market shares (and bigger budgets) call for increasing proportions to be spent on holding.

In contrast to the previous example under conditions of pure price competition Figure 15.8 depicts the case for brands which have developed high probabilities of repeat purchase as reflected in the holding : switching efficiency parameters. At this other extreme (a 50 : 1 ratio) two cents spent on holding will be as effective in producing a Period #2 sale as will a dollar spent on switching. This situation reflects brands which have developed strong consumer franchises (irrespective of their size) through previous marketing investment in the creation and communication of meaningful and satisfying (to their consumer segment, at least) differentiation *via* product design, distribution, advertising, etc.

Here we see a substantial difference. Even for brands with market shares as low as about 10% the optimal condition is to spend seventy cents of the market-ing dollar on holding. Thus, the more holding efficient a brand, the greater

---

[11] The slightest shift to a situation where the brand is more switching efficient than holding efficient would reflect a condition where a recent user of the brand is less likely to buy it again than someone who had not bought it. Such a situation characterizes an unsatisfactory or "fad" product (or a mis-defined product class— e.g. when someone who had chicken on one day is less likely to order it the next day than someone who had not).

proportion of its marketing dollar should be spent on holding to maintain share. Again, of course, the higher the market share or (in related terms) the bigger the marketing budget, the higher the proportion which should be spent on holding.

Under these conditions of high holding efficiency it is apparent that a painful price might be paid in lower market share equilibrium points for deviations from the optimal holding proportion. Non-optimal allocation will in time (the actual time is a function of the length of average purchase cycle and competitive volatility of the product class) result either in a loss in share of market or else a compensating increase in marketing expense to maintain the prior equilibrium point.

A comparison of Figure 15.8 with Figure 15.7 reveals not only that the optimal holding proportion differs substantially—especially over smaller market

FIGURE 15-8
Equilibrium market
share curves (high-
holding—low switch-
ing efficiency.)

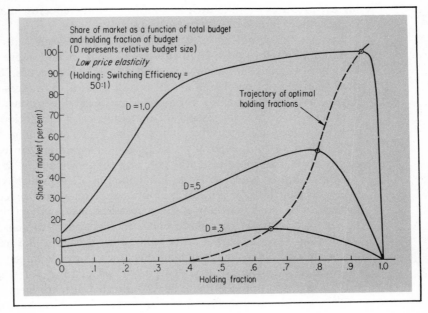

shares—but that the same marketing budget size will support widely different size brands. Significantly, these analyses show us that a small brand must pursue competition more aggressively than a larger brand if it is to be a growing brand. But if a brand can make itself less easily substituted for (i.e. develop a stable consumer franchise, become holding efficient and price inelastic), then it should spend more of its marketing dollar holding, and the same budget will support a bigger brand. In other words, as a brand becomes holding efficient, it can grow faster *and* more economically, but it must keep shifting its holding : switching ratio as it grows. Package goods largely fall between the conditions depicted in the two illustrations. Doubtless the more successful companies are closer to the situation in 15.8 than in 15.7.

These findings indicate one reason why it proves to be so difficult to learn marketing by experience. Lessons learned in one product class or even on one brand in the same product class can fail us on another.

There are numerous derivative implications of this analysis. Industrial products companies, for example, are in a relatively favored position to know how much of their marketing effort is expended against holding or switching and to measure the incremental productivity of a dollar on each. They have fairly close control over salesmen's calls on old customers *vs.* prospects. Package goods brands as well as other products can see that they would be spending more efficiently if they adjusted their holding: switching ratios and total marketing expenditures by sales area to conform to differences in market share and to differences in price elasticity/substitutibility.

Because this is not an issue which has attracted a great deal of systematic attention heretofore there is no substantial body of knowledge on the relative holding : switching efficiency of various marketing tactics. So, empirically clear rules of implementation are lacking at present. As suggested above, sales force activity is fairly easily controllable on these dimensions. Most forms of sales promotion activity (especially sampling, price promotion and disguised price incentives) are more efficient at switching than at holding. Maintenance of visible distribution in depth (by size, type, etc.) would appear logically to more greatly affect continuity of repeat purchase than switching efficiency.

Advertising, as noted earlier in this chapter, is a term which covers a remarkable variety of things. Forms of promotional or retail and direct mail advertising tend to be more switching efficient. National media advertising for branded package goods performs a more balanced function. National advertising for branded hard goods, on the other hand, must act more like retail advertising or promotion because the switching investment must be largely written off on a single sale." Institutional or "corporate" advertising, for whatever type of product is proportionately more heavily directed at investment in holding.

The big problem at this point in time—when the subject has not been studied and when there are no rules for how to plan the holding: switching balance of the whole marketing program—is how to tell after-the-fact, at least, how each tool is working. This question is most relevant to advertising testing. Some pertinent data are available for media allocation planning. Advertising copy assessment is more difficult. What is required is measures of changes in brand substitutability among present brand customers as well as measures among non-customers. Measures such as the gain in total persons moving from an "unaware" status to an "aware" status necessarily deal only with effect on non-customers. Measures such as the gain in total persons moving from an "unaware" status to an "aware" status necessarily deal only with effect on non-customers. Even measures of shift in degree of "favorable attitude" heavily emphasize non-customers. Advertising decisions based upon such criteria increasingly push the brand's advertising copy to become maximally switching-efficient.

If everyone in the market buys all the brands for the identical reason, perhaps "switching efficient" is the same as "holding efficient". But, then, we are describing a market characterized by pure price competition. No brand seeking profitable growth would wish deliberately to create such a market.

Patterns of Production Scheduling. The nature of the promotional effort can have important effects on the production pattern. A common example is the special promotion which produces an "artificial seasonal" effect. Because these sales fluctuations frequently are viewed as natural market forces, they tend to become self-reinforcing. Each year a greater and greater promotional effort is mounted to "take advantage of" the peak buying season.

Such promotional efforts not only affect current production but borrow sales from the future, causing cycles. Some promotional incentives, such as the offer of a larger quantity at a reduced price, attract present users of the product who tend to stock up against their future requirements. Such activity represents lost sales later at the regular price. Other types of promotional activities are more attractive to noncustomers, and the effect on sales and production, consequently is entirely different.

During the introduction of a new product, the effect of promotion (and advertising) on production scheduling is especially apparent. The interaction of the nature of the market with the particular marketing promotion tactics can produce an apparently erratic sales curve where, in fact, considerable market stability exists. The example in Figure 15.9 illustrates how the use of promotion in the introduction of a new product can effectively disguise the orderly nature of the underlying market forces, and significantly affect the demands placed upon production:

The Stated Conditions. In this example we are given a new product which has a potential consumer market consisting of 35 percent of the families in the country. Preliminary market research studies have indicated that the product will have an average purchase cycle of 4 months and an exponentially distributed repeat purchase rate.[12] The net effect of the advertising and other promotion is to

---

[12] As packaged goods brands mature in their market development, the effect of advertising and other promotion on the repeat rate becomes an increasingly important aspect of the promotion activity. As the acquisition of new triers slows down, the sales rate becomes increasingly dependent upon repeat purchases. The objective of the promotional effort alters accordingly. The importance of this promotion function is not as great in the case of high-priced durable goods, because the length of time between purchases is so great that the next sale is similar to the initial sale.

Changes in the repeat purchase rate are reflected as changes in the average purchase cycle. From the standpoint of our brand, a customer who switches to another brand for the next purchase has simply not returned to our brand in the expected time period. This customer's behavior alters the length of time between purchases for our median customer.

FIGURE 15-9
Effect of promotion
strategies on produc-
tion and inventory
requirements.

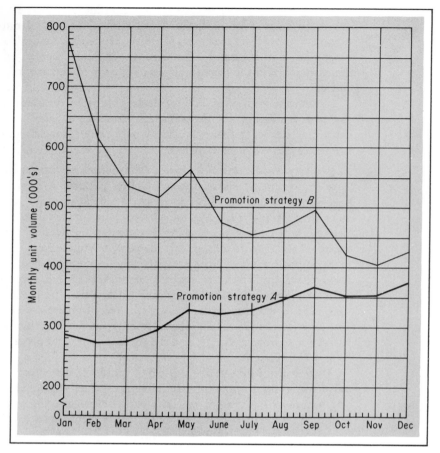

obtain 3 percent of the population as new purchasers for the first $100,000 of promotion.[13]

Given these conditions, Figure 15.9 demonstrates how two different promotion strategies would affect the resulting sales curve. Strategy A calls for the expenditure of $100,000 per month for the first year; strategy B calls for the expenditure of $300,000 per month for the first year.

Production Demands Differ Widely.

The result of strategy A would be to obtain trial (initial purchase) by 21 percent of the families in the first year. The twelve month sales would be 3,793,500 units at a promotion cost of $0.316 per unit. Strategy B, on the other hand, results in trial by 29 percent of the families and twelve month sales of 6,136,000 units at a promotion cost of $0.588 per unit.

Regardless of which promotion strategy is used, however, the second-year sales will stabilize at about 400,000 units per month. Under these conditions,

[13] Additional increments of $100,000 produce an effect at a diminishing rate.

the promotion strategy for the second year would be no more than $100,000 per month.

Perhaps of greatest importance in the eyes of the production man is the enormous difference in sales levels achieved by the two promotion strategies. During the first six months under strategy *B*, sales would average more than twice as much as under strategy *A*.

Choice of Strategy.

Whether *A* or *B* is the better strategy depends on a number of things. Because of its higher promotion cost per unit sold, the choice of strategy *B* will depend importantly upon the profit margin before promotion expense. It may be that such considerations as the need to begin marketing by a certain date or the unavailability of production equipment may render strategy *B* unfeasible from the standpoint of production efficiency. The availability of operating capital, the degree of risk entailed in the new venture, and the anticipated timing of other new product entries[14] by the company or competitors are among the many considerations which govern the choice of promotion strategy.

Prediction of Effects Possible.

Package size changes, line extensions, price changes, and promotion activities all affect either the rate of entry of new customers or the purchase cycle. As a result, the timing of these activities can have important effects on store inventories and on production scheduling.

For example, in Figure 15.9 the introduction of a larger package size in the June—July period would create a change in consumer home inventories, resulting in a lengthened purchase cycle.[15] This change in the marketing pattern would appear in Figure 15.9 as a deepening of the November trough and would result in a delay in the December recovery. Such consequences, although actually having no long term effect on total sales, might be interpreted by retailers as a discouraging trend for the new product. They, in turn, might react by reducing

---

[14] Strategy *A* is more efficient than strategy *B* from a production standpoint, and there is less immediate risk. However, unless the company enjoys a monopolistic command of its industry through sheer size, resources, or patents it cannot count on maintaining technological leadership all the time. Competitors might either share in the new market which is being developed or, worse, given the greater time provided by strategy *A*, they might come out with a development which out-flanks our product before we have recovered our investment. Thus, under the usual competitive conditions, careful planning of the timing of new product entries must be sacrificed to the goal of maximizing cash flow from new product Number 1 to provide the capital for the introduction of new product Number 2 as soon as competitive pressures and/or the maximum utilization of capital resources dictate.

New product developments which replace present products in the company's line should be timed more deliberately than products which are supplementary. The timing of replacement products requires consideration of the change over time of the rate of return on investment for a representative product, the rate of capital formation, the predictability of successful introduction, and so on. Unless these things are well-known—and they seldom are outside tightly controlled technical industries—timing is not significantly controllable, and the best rule of survival is "the sooner, the better."

Such a policy, as we can see in our example, works a hardship on production efficiency. Because faster exploitation means shorter product life, it raises questions on appropriate depreciation policies, the utility of elaborate inventory studies on the specific product, and so on.

[15] The task of Quality Control is to reduce variability in the values offered by the product. Changes in consumer behavior in relation to the product, such as larger home inventories, which produce increased aging of consumed products can alter the necessary quality control standards. Uniformity must exist in the product as *consumed*.

their inventories and product displays, thereby, turning an *apparent* market weakness into a real one.[16]

CONCLUSION

We are doing business in a dynamic economy. Its distinguishing feature is *value*—value for the individual. The forces of economic law and of technological advancement have combined to thrust us beyond the early thumb-rules of mass production. The chief concern of the entrepreneur has shifted from cost-cutting to value-adding.

Marketing is the nervous system of the production process. As the sensory organ, it seeks and describes value in all its manifestations. It is the unbiased judge of what services have value for various subcultures—those services which are widely valued, and those which are intensely though, perhaps, less widely valued.

The task of Production, then, is to take basic materials with relatively limitless service applications, select a specific set of these services, shape them, limit them, fix them, and store them away for future selection and use. This great array of service possibilities provides the new opportunities for profitable production. The greater the number of such opportunities, the smaller the optimum volume of production; production volume and profit no longer move as one.

Marketing not only is the sensory receptor of Production but the transmitter, as well. In its receptor role it seeks to find an imperfect resolution of the paradox: maximize the size of the potential market; minimize the competitive alternatives. As the transmitter, it adds to production-based values. But it does so at increasing increments of unit cost until, eventually, the law of diminishing total returns is felt.

Thereby, marketing is impelled to seek ways to increase value by choosing among alternative courses of action for the product design, packaging, pricing, distribution, and promotion. This must be done within the framework of cost efficiency. Through interpretation of the countless currents in the marketplace, through planning and selection of optimal strategies, and through the completion and transmission of these values to the subculture target, Marketing modifies the objectives and performance of Production.

The optimization of value-adding across services and goods, across wants and needs, across subcultures and planning horizons is the optimization of the *quality of life*—the integration of the marketing and production objectives of society.

---

[16] Computerized models, such as Lever Brothers' NEWLEVER and Young & Rubicam's Natural Sales Projection Model, of the functions represented in Figure 15.9 permit the study of possible sales effect of promotional and other contemplated marketing changes on sales volume. Further developments of this kind can be anticipated to control many of the factors which have been discussed in this chapter.

PROBLEMS

1 What are some major factors which limit the utility of "economy of scale" considerations for manufacturers?

2 Does production require manufacturing?

3 How should subculture quality standards be set for production quality control purposes?

4 In what way are information and production synonymous?

5 Why is advertising part of the product design?

6 Should the selling price determine the available advertising budget or *vice versa*?

7 In what ways does the purpose of advertising differ from that of price promotion?

8 Will increased production per man hour and full employment increase our standard of living?

references

ALDERSON, WROE, *Marketing Behavior and Executive Action.* Homewood, Ill.: Richard D. Irwin, Inc., 1957.

AMSTUTZ, A. E., *Computer Simulation of Competitive Market Response.* Cambridge, Mass.: The M.I.T. Press, 1967.

EINSTEIN, ALBERT, *Essays in Science.* New York: Philosophical Library, Inc., 1934.

FORRESTER, JAY, *Industrial Dynamics.* Cambridge: MIT Press, 1961.

FRIEDMAN, LAWRENCE, *A Variable Budgeting System For Consumer Advertising,* Cambridge, Mass.: A Working Paper of the Marketing Science Institute, 1970.

GERHOLD, PAUL, *Predicted Advertising Yield: ARF Proposes an Outline of How Advertising Works.* New York: Advertising Research Foundation, 1969.

GHISELIN, BREWSTER, *The Creative Process.* New York: The New American Library of World Literature, Inc., 1960.

GORDON, W. J. J., *Synectics.* New York: Harper & Row, 1961.

GREEN, PAUL E. and FRANK J. CARMONE, *Multidimensional Scaling, and Related Techniques in Marketing Analysis.* Boston: Allyn and Bacon, 1970.

GREEN, P. E. and D. S. TULL, *Research for Marketing Decisions,* 2nd ed. Englewood Cliffs, N.J.: Prentice-Hall, Inc., 1970.

LOCKE, JOHN, "Essay Concerning Human Understanding," 1690. Citations appearing in Edwin G. Boring, *A History of Experimental Psychology.* New York: Appleton-Century-Crofts, Inc., 1929.

LONGMAN, K. A., *Advertising.* New York: Harcourt Brace Jovanovich, Inc., 1971.

LUCE, R. DUNCAN, *Individual Choice Behavior.* New York: John Wiley & Sons, Inc., 1959.

MACHLUP, FRITZ, *The Production and Distribution of Knowledge in the United States,* Princeton, New Jersey: Princeton University Press, 1962.

MAYER, MARTIN, *Madison Avenue U.S.A.* New York: Harper & Row, Publishers, 1958.

MILLER, DAVID W. and MARTIN K. STARR, *Executive Decisions and Operations Research* (*2nd* ed.), Englewood Cliffs, N.J.: Prentice-Hall, Inc., 1969.

MONTGOMERY, D. B. and G. L. URBAN, *Applications of Management Science in Marketing.* Englewood Cliffs, N.J.: Prentice-Hall, Inc., 1969.

————, *Management Science in Marketing.* Englewood Cliffs, N.J.: Prentice-Hall, Inc., 1969.

MORAN, W. T., "Practical Media Decisions and the Computer," *Journal of Marketing,* July 1963.

REISS, SAMUEL, *The Universe of Meaning.* New York: Philosophical Library, Inc., 1953.

SHELDON, ELEANOR BERNETT and HOWARD E. FREEMAN, "Notes on Social Indicators: Promises and Potential," *Policy Sciences,* Vol. 1, No. 1, Spring 1970.

SHUBIK, MARTIN, *Strategy and Market Structure: Competition, Oligopoly, and the Theory of Games.* New York: John Wiley & Sons, Inc., 1959.

STARR, MARTIN K., *Product Design and Decision Theory.* Englewood Cliffs, N. J.: Prentice-Hall, Inc., 1963.

————, "Modular Production—A New Concept," Cambridge, Mass., *Harvard Business Review,* Vol. 43, No. 6, pp. 131–142, Nov.—Dec. 1965.

STEFFLRE, VOLNEY, "Simulation of People's Behavior Towards New Objectives and Events," *The American Behavioral Scientist,* May 1965.

APPENDIX I

TABLE OF THE NORMAL DISTRIBUTION

AREAS UNDER THE NORMAL CURVE FROM K_α TO ∞

$$\int_{K_\alpha}^{\infty} \frac{1}{\sqrt{2\pi}} e^{-x^2/2}\, dx = \alpha$$

K_α	.00	.01	.02	.03	.04	.05	.06	.07	.08	.09
0.0	.5000	.4960	.4920	.4880	.4840	.4801	.4761	.4721	.4681	.4641
0.1	.4602	.4562	.4522	.4483	.4443	.4404	.4364	.4325	.4286	.4247
0.2	.4207	.4168	.4129	.4090	.4052	.4013	.3974	.3936	.3897	.3859
0.3	.3821	.3783	.3745	.3707	.3669	.3632	.3594	.3557	.3520	.3483
0.4	.3446	.3409	.3372	.3336	.3300	.3264	.3228	.3192	.3156	.3121
0.5	.3085	.3050	.3015	.2981	.2946	.2912	.2877	.2843	.2810	.2776
0.6	.2743	.2709	.2676	.2643	.2611	.2578	.2546	.2514	.2483	.2451
0.7	.2420	.2389	.2358	.2327	.2296	.2266	.2236	.2206	.2177	.2148
0.8	.2119	.2090	.2061	.2033	.2005	.1977	.1949	.1922	.1894	.1867
0.9	.1841	.1814	.1788	.1762	.1736	.1711	.1685	.1660	.1635	.1611
1.0	.1587	.1562	.1539	.1515	.1492	.1469	.1446	.1423	.1401	.1379
1.1	.1357	.1335	.1314	.1292	.1271	.1251	.1230	.1210	.1190	.1170
1.2	.1151	.1131	.1112	.1093	.1075	.1056	.1038	.1020	.1003	.0985
1.3	.0968	.0951	.0934	.0918	.0901	.0885	.0869	.0853	.0838	.0823
1.4	.0808	.0793	.0778	.0764	.0749	.0735	.0721	.0708	.0694	.0681
1.5	.0668	.0655	.0643	.0630	.0618	.0606	.0594	.0582	.0571	.0559
1.6	.0548	.0537	.0526	.0516	.0505	.0495	.0485	.0475	.0465	.0455
1.7	.0446	.0436	.0427	.0418	.0409	.0401	.0392	.0384	.0375	.0367
1.8	.0359	.0351	.0344	.0336	.0329	.0322	.0314	.0307	.0301	.0294
1.9	.0287	.0281	.0274	.0268	.0262	.0256	.0250	.0244	.0239	.0233
2.0	.0228	.0222	.0217	.0212	.0207	.0202	.0197	.0192	.0188	.0183
2.1	.0179	.0174	.0170	.0166	.0162	.0158	.0154	.0150	.0146	.0143
2.2	.0139	.0136	.0132	.0129	.0125	.0122	.0119	.0116	.0113	.0110
2.3	.0107	.0104	.0102	.00990	.00964	.00939	.00914	.00889	.00866	.00842
2.4	.00820	.00798	.00776	.00755	.00734	.00714	.00695	.00676	.00657	.00639
2.5	.00621	.00604	.00587	.00570	.00554	.00539	.00523	.00508	.00494	.00480
2.6	.00466	.00453	.00440	.00427	.00415	.00402	.00391	.00379	.00368	.00357
2.7	.00347	.00336	.00326	.00317	.00307	.00298	.00289	.00280	.00272	.00264
2.8	.00256	.00248	.00240	.00233	.00226	.00219	.00212	.00205	.00199	.00193
2.9	.00187	.00181	.00175	.00169	.00164	.00159	.00154	.00149	.00144	.00139

K_α	.0	.1	.2	.3	.4	.5	.6	.7	.8	.9
3	.00135	$.0^3968$	$.0^3687$	$.0^3483$	$.0^3337$	$.0^3233$	$.0^3159$	$.0^3108$	$.0^4723$	$.0^4481$
4	$.0^4317$	$.0^4207$	$.0^4133$	$.0^5854$	$.0^5541$	$.0^5340$	$.0^5211$	$.0^5130$	$.0^6793$	$.0^6479$
5	$.0^6287$	$.0^6170$	$.0^7996$	$.0^7579$	$.0^7333$	$.0^7190$	$.0^7107$	$.0^8599$	$.0^8332$	$.0^8182$
6	$.0^9987$	$.0^9530$	$.0^9282$	$.0^9149$	$.0^{10}777$	$.0^{10}402$	$.0^{10}206$	$.0^{10}104$	$.0^{11}523$	$.0^{11}260$

APPENDIX II

TABLE OF LOGARITHMS

N	0	1	2	3	4	5	6	7	8	9
10	0000	0043	0086	0128	0170	0212	0253	0294	0334	0374
11	0414	0453	0492	0531	0569	0607	0645	0682	0719	0755
12	0792	0828	0864	0899	0934	0969	1004	1038	1072	1106
13	1139	1173	1206	1239	1271	1303	1335	1367	1399	1430
14	1461	1492	1523	1553	1584	1614	1644	1673	1703	1732
15	1761	1790	1818	1847	1875	1903	1931	1959	1987	2014
16	2041	2068	2095	2122	2148	2175	2201	2227	2253	2279
17	2304	2330	2355	2380	2405	2430	2455	2480	2504	2529
18	2553	2577	2601	2625	2648	2672	2695	2718	2742	2765
19	2788	2810	2833	2856	2878	2900	2923	2945	2967	2989
20	3010	3032	3054	3075	3096	3118	3139	3160	3181	3201
21	3222	3243	3263	3284	3304	3324	3345	3365	3385	3404
22	3424	3444	3464	3483	3502	3522	3541	3560	3579	3598
23	3617	3636	3655	3674	3692	3711	3729	3747	3766	3784
24	3802	3820	3838	3856	3874	3892	3909	3927	3945	3962
25	3979	3997	4014	4031	4048	4065	4082	4099	4116	4133
26	4150	4166	4183	4200	4216	4232	4249	4265	4281	4298
27	4314	4330	4346	4362	4378	4393	4409	4425	4440	4456
28	4472	4487	4502	4518	4533	4548	4564	4579	4594	4609
29	4624	4639	4654	4669	4683	4698	4713	4728	4742	4757
30	4771	4786	4800	4814	4829	4843	4857	4871	4886	4900
31	4914	4928	4942	4955	4969	4983	4997	5011	5024	5038
32	5051	5065	5079	5092	5105	5119	5132	5145	5159	5172
33	5185	5198	5211	5224	5237	5250	5263	5276	5289	5302
34	5315	5328	5340	5353	5366	5378	5391	5403	5416	5428
35	5441	5453	5465	5478	5490	5502	5514	5527	5539	5551
36	5563	5575	5587	5599	5611	5623	5635	5647	5658	5670
37	5682	5694	5705	5717	5729	5740	5752	5763	5775	5786
38	5798	5809	5821	5832	5843	5855	5866	5877	5888	5899
39	5911	5922	5933	5944	5955	5966	5977	5988	5999	6010
40	6021	6031	6042	6053	6064	6075	6085	6096	6107	6117
41	6128	6138	6149	6160	6170	6180	6191	6201	6212	6222
42	6232	6243	6253	6263	6274	6284	6294	6304	6314	6325
43	6335	6345	6355	6365	6375	6385	6395	6405	6415	6425
44	6435	6444	6454	6464	6474	6484	6493	6503	6513	6522
45	6532	6542	6551	6561	6571	6580	6590	6599	6609	6618
46	6628	6637	6646	6656	6665	6675	6684	6693	6702	6712
47	6721	6730	6739	6749	6758	6767	6776	6785	6794	6803
48	6812	6821	6830	6839	6848	6857	6866	6875	6884	6893
49	6902	6911	6920	6928	6937	6946	6955	6964	6972	6981
50	6990	6998	7007	7016	7024	7033	7042	7050	7059	7067
51	7076	7084	7093	7101	7110	7118	7126	7135	7143	7152
52	7160	7168	7177	7185	7193	7202	7210	7218	7226	7235
53	7243	7251	7259	7267	7275	7284	7292	7300	7308	7316
54	7324	7332	7340	7348	7356	7364	7372	7380	7388	7396

APPENDIX II (CONTINUED)

N	0	1	2	3	4	5	6	7	8	9
55	7404	7412	7419	7427	7435	7443	7451	7459	7466	7474
56	7482	7490	7497	7505	7513	7520	7528	7536	7543	7551
57	7559	7566	7574	7582	7589	7597	7604	7612	7619	7627
58	7634	7642	7649	7657	7664	7672	7679	7686	7694	7701
59	7709	7716	7723	7731	7738	7745	7752	7760	7767	7774
60	7782	7789	7796	7803	7810	7818	7825	7832	7839	7846
61	7853	7860	7868	7875	7882	7889	7896	7903	7910	7917
62	7924	7931	7938	7945	7952	7959	7966	7973	7980	7987
63	7993	8000	8007	8014	8021	8028	8035	8041	8048	8055
64	8062	8069	8075	8082	8089	8096	8102	8109	8116	8122
65	8129	8136	8142	8149	8156	8162	8169	8176	8182	8189
66	8195	8202	8209	8215	8222	8228	8235	8241	8248	8254
67	8261	8267	8274	8280	8287	8293	8299	8306	8312	8319
68	8325	8331	8338	8344	8351	8357	8363	8370	8376	8382
69	8388	8395	8401	8407	8414	8420	8426	8432	8439	8445
70	8451	8457	8463	8470	8476	8482	8488	8494	8500	8506
71	8513	8519	8525	8531	8537	8543	8549	8555	8561	8567
72	8573	8579	8585	8591	8597	8603	8609	8615	8621	8627
73	8633	8639	8645	8651	8657	8663	8669	8675	8681	8686
74	8692	8698	8704	8710	8716	8722	8727	8733	8739	8745
75	8751	8756	8762	8768	8774	8779	8785	8791	8797	8802
76	8808	8814	8820	8825	8831	8837	8842	8848	8854	8859
77	8865	8871	8876	8882	8887	8893	8899	8904	8910	8915
78	8921	8927	8932	8938	8943	8949	8954	8960	8965	8971
79	8976	8982	8987	8993	8998	9004	9009	9015	9020	9025
80	9031	9036	9042	9047	9053	9058	9063	9069	9074	9079
81	9085	9090	9096	9101	9106	9112	9117	9122	9128	9133
82	9138	9143	9149	9154	9159	9165	9170	9175	9180	9186
83	9191	9196	9201	9206	9212	9217	9222	9227	9232	9238
84	9243	9248	9253	9258	9263	9269	9274	9279	9284	9289
85	9294	9299	9304	9309	9315	9320	9325	9330	9335	9340
86	9345	9350	9355	9360	9365	9370	9375	9380	9385	9390
87	9395	9400	9405	9410	9415	9420	9425	9430	9435	9440
88	9445	9450	9455	9460	9465	9469	9474	9479	9484	9489
89	9494	9499	9504	9509	9513	9518	9523	9528	9533	9538
90	9542	9547	9552	9557	9562	9566	9571	9576	9581	9586
91	9590	9595	9600	9605	9609	9614	9619	9624	9628	9633
92	9638	9643	9647	9652	9657	9661	9666	9671	9675	9680
93	9685	9689	9694	9699	9703	9708	9713	9717	9722	9727
94	9731	9736	9741	9745	9750	9754	9759	9763	9768	9773
95	9777	9782	9786	9791	9795	9800	9805	9809	9814	9818
96	9823	9827	9832	9836	9841	9845	9850	9854	9859	9863
97	9868	9872	9877	9881	9886	9890	9894	9899	9903	9908
98	9912	9917	9921	9926	9930	9934	9939	9943	9948	9952
99	9956	9961	9965	9969	9974	9978	9983	9987	9991	9996

TABLE OF RANDOM NUMBERS

96268	11860	83699	38631	90045	69696	48572	05917	51905	10052
03550	59144	59468	37984	77892	89766	86489	46619	50263	91136
22188	81205	99699	84260	19693	36701	43233	62719	53117	71153
63759	61429	14043	49095	84746	22018	19014	76781	61086	90216
55006	17765	15013	77707	54317	48862	53823	52905	70754	68212
81972	45644	12600	01951	72166	52682	97598	11955	73018	23528
06344	50136	33122	31794	86423	58037	36065	32190	31367	96007
92363	99784	94169	03652	80824	33407	40837	97749	18364	72666
96083	16943	89916	55159	62184	86208	09764	20244	88388	98675
92993	10747	08985	44999	36785	65035	65933	77378	92339	96454
95083	70292	50394	61044	65591	09774	16216	63561	59751	78771
77308	60721	96057	86031	83148	34970	30892	53489	44999	18021
11913	49624	28510	27311	61586	28576	43092	69971	44220	80410
70648	47484	05095	92335	55299	27161	64486	71307	85883	69610
92771	99203	37786	81142	44271	36433	31726	74879	89348	76886
78816	20975	13043	55921	82774	62745	48338	88348	61211	88074
79934	35392	56097	87613	94627	63622	08110	16611	88599	02890
64698	83376	87524	36897	17215	74339	69856	43622	22567	11518
44212	12995	03581	37618	94851	63020	65348	55857	91742	79508
82292	00204	00579	70630	37136	50922	83387	15014	51838	81760
08692	87237	87879	01629	72184	33853	95144	67943	19345	03469
67927	76855	50702	78555	97442	78809	40575	79714	06201	34576
62167	94213	52971	85974	68067	78814	40103	70759	92129	46716
45828	45441	74220	84157	23241	49332	23646	09390	13032	51569
01164	35307	26526	80335	58090	85871	07205	31749	40571	51755
29283	31581	04359	45538	41435	61103	32428	94042	39971	63678
19868	49978	81699	84904	50163	22625	07845	71308	00859	87984
14294	93587	55960	23149	07370	65065	06580	46285	07884	83928
77410	52195	29459	23032	83242	89938	40510	27252	55565	64714
36580	06921	35675	81645	60479	71035	99380	59759	42161	93440
07780	18093	31258	78156	07871	20369	53947	08534	39433	57216
07548	08454	36674	46255	80541	42903	37366	21164	97516	66181
22023	60448	69344	44260	90570	01632	21002	24413	04671	05665
20827	37210	57797	34660	32510	71558	78228	42304	77197	79168
47802	79270	48805	59480	88092	11441	96016	76091	51823	94442
76730	86591	18978	25479	77684	88439	35112	26052	57112	91653
26439	02903	20935	76297	15290	84688	74002	09467	41111	19194
32927	83426	07848	59327	44422	53372	27823	25417	27150	21750
51484	05286	77103	47284	05578	88774	15293	50740	07932	87633
45142	96804	92834	26886	70002	96643	36008	02239	93563	66429
12760	96106	89348	76127	17058	37181	74001	43869	28377	80923
15564	38648	02147	03894	97787	35234	44302	41672	12408	90168
71051	34941	55384	70709	11646	30269	60154	28276	48153	23122
42742	08817	82579	19505	26344	94116	86230	49139	32644	36545
59474	97752	77124	79579	65448	87700	54002	81411	57988	57437
12581	18211	61713	73962	87212	55624	85675	33961	63272	17587
00278	75089	20673	37438	92361	47941	62056	94104	45502	79159
59317	31861	62559	30925	23055	70922	47195	29827	68065	95409
59220	42448	70881	33687	53575	54599	69525	76424	98778	10459
00670	32157	15877	87120	13857	23979	38922	62421	03043	19602

index